Every story
is over
before it begins

———

TELLING STORIES

TELLING STORIES

Postmodernism and the Invalidation of Traditional Narrative

MICHAEL ROEMER

ROWMAN & LITTLEFIELD PUBLISHERS, INC.

ROWMAN & LITTLEFIELD PUBLISHERS, INC.

Published in the United States of America
by Rowman & Littlefield Publishers, Inc.
4720 Boston Way, Lanham, Maryland 20706

3 Henrietta Street
London WC2E 8LU, England

British Cataloging in Publication Information Available

Library of Congress Cataloging-in-Publication Data

Roemer, Michael
Telling stories : postmodernism and the invalidation of
traditional narrative / Michael Roemer.
p. cm.
Includes bibliographical references and index.
1. Postmodernism (Literature) 2. Narration (Technique)
3. Storytelling. I. Title.
PN56.P53R64 1995 801'.95—dc20 95-1677 CIP

ISBN 0–8476–8041–X (cloth : alk. paper)
ISBN 0–8476–8042–8 (pbk. : alk. paper)

Printed in the United States of America

♻™ The paper used in this publication meets the minimum requirements of
American National Standard for Information Sciences—Permanence of
Paper for Printed Library Materials, ANSI Z39.48–1964.

for
Barbara

Contents

Acknowledgments

Among the many without whom this book could not have been written, I would particularly like to thank Edward Edinger, Ronald Grant, Stimson Bullitt, Robert Young, Frank Auerbach, Albert Cook, Carol Cook, Edwin Dolin, Alice Ettinger, Solomon Ettinger, Leon Kossoff, Frank Lewin, Terry Lewis, Charles Mandelstam, Wilhelm Marckwald, Giuliano Pedretti, Stanley Plotnick, Franz Rath, Paula Roemer, Marianne Shoopak, Margaret Strauss, Frederick Wiseman, Irwin Young, and my colleagues at Yale College and the Yale School of Art. I am indebted to Fred Rush, Jeffrey Bub and Sam Levin for reading the manuscript and making helpful suggestions. Barbara Lassonde provided invaluable assistance in preparing both the footnotes and the index, and Rebecca Pocock patiently typed and retyped the text.

PART ONE

Traditional Stories

CHAPTER

1

———

The Preclusive Form
of Narrative

ALL STORIES ARE PRECLUDED

Every story is over before it begins. The novel lies bound in my hands, the actors know all their lines before the curtain rises, and the finished film has been threaded onto the projector when the houselights dim.

Stories appear to move into an open, uncertain future that the figures try to influence, but in fact report a completed past they cannot alter. Their journey into the future—to which we gladly lend ourselves—is an illusion.

We think we see differences between myth, in which fate and the gods determine the outcome, and the stories of today, in which people appear to be shaping their own lives. But all stories are over before they begin.

Story derives from the Latin *historia*, which is related to the Greek *histór*, "one who knows."[1] The Assyrians knew that Gilgamesh would fail in his quest for immortality, and the Greeks that Daphnis would be united with Chloe. Shakespeare's audiences knew that Shylock would not get his pound of flesh, just as we know that Bonnie and Clyde are doomed. *The Tragical History of Doctor Faustus* cannot end happily and the title of Bresson's *A Condemned Man Has Escaped* assures us he will not be executed, though we watch anxiously as he makes his getaway.

It is clear to us from the start how tragedies, fairy tales, and Westerns will end. We watch the figures from fate's elbow, knowing full well the one thing they cannot know: their future. Yet, despite our knowledge, we lend ourselves to their adventures, worry about Snow White, and hope against hope that Romeo and Juliet will escape their fate. Perhaps we are caught

3

up in their stories because we sense that with respect to our own future, we are as blind as they. Our vantage point would seem to be ironically detached but since we find ourselves deeply engaged, perhaps we suspect that our own apparently open future is as foreclosed as theirs, though we cannot acknowledge it in daily life.

All stories, including history and biography, are past and therefore precluded. When we watch a documentary film years after it was shot, we know the outcome that the figures on screen are trying to bring about or prevent. They have all aged or died, and what was present or future to them has become past.

We make distinctions between fiction and drama, but in their essential form all stories are alike. We might call tragedy an exacerbated story, for it makes us most vividly aware of the discrepancy between the intentions of the figures and what we know to be the outcome. *Oedipus Rex* is emblematic of all stories.[2] We know absolutely what will become of him, for it has already happened. His fate was announced before he was born and accomplished before the play begins. All *he* can do is find out about it. Like his parents, he thinks he has options, but we in the audience are without illusions. The preclusive structure of his story is softened by no palliatives.

THE FICTIVE FIGURE HAS NO FREEDOM

The figures in story are no freer than those in a painting. Their destiny is set out on a scroll that the storyteller unrolls before us in time, but it exists like a painting in space. All narrative is synchronic, though those who figure in it and we who are watching experience it diachronically.

No one would claim that the figures in paintings are endowed with free will. Yet, when a story unfolds, we are easily caught up in the illusion that what the figures do or fail to do will determine the outcome. We go so far as to praise or blame them, as if their actions were freely elected; we forget that what they intend is already done and what they are trying to change has already happened.

Stories in a Positivist culture—our movies, for instance—suggest that the hero's will is effective by letting him achieve what he sets out do do. But story's preclusive structure invalidates such a claim, and Positivist stories undermine themselves in the telling. Sherlock Holmes is no freer than Oedipus, and Rambo no more effective than Woyzeck.*

---

*When Positivism is capitalized in the text, reference is to the school of thought associated with Comte. In a later chapter, I endeavor to show that in a more general sense positivism is as old as consciousness and critical to our survival; it constitutes a necessary attempt to combat our sense of helplessness and to potentiate us vis-à-vis the gods, necessity or nature.

In traditional story, the manifest narrative is often in harmony with the preclusive plot: the events themselves suggest that our will is of no avail. What happens in comedy as in tragedy, in Brecht as in Sophocles, is seldom what the hero intends. He has an effect on the action but the results are not often those he has worked for, and when the outcome *does* reflect his intentions, it is not simply as a consequence of his own efforts. The hero of myth succeeds in his undertaking with the help of nonhuman forces: Perseus slays the Medusa because Athena has come to his aid; his own strength and courage are not adequate to the task. Fairy tales often center on a passive figure who survives and wins because the supernatural is on his or her side, while the villain—with his active, plotting will—is thwarted. In Shakespeare, the only figure to command the outcome of a play is Prospero, a magician who is no longer altogether human.

THE CENTRAL FIGURE IS OBLIGED TO ACT

We may think the hero *chooses* to be active, but when we look at traditional story we find that his actions are almost invariably imposed. He does not assume his task or mission voluntarily. *Task* is derived from the Latin *taxo*, "to tax," and *mission* means "a sending." The labors of Hercules, Jason's quest for the Golden Fleece, Parsifal's for the Grail, and the search undertaken by Oedipus are all obligations that *must* be assumed. Hansel and Gretel do not go into the forest of their own accord; they are abandoned by their parents. Hamlet may wish for the cup to pass from his lips, but he is heir to the throne and forced to act by an oath exacted by his father's ghost. Lear appears to give away his kingdom voluntarily, but the irrationality of his act suggests a compelling unconscious need. Raskolnicov attempts to prove his freedom by killing an old woman, yet proves the opposite, and though Captain Ahab seems to have an option when the *Rachel* asks for his help, he chooses the inevitable.

The central figure in traditional story is often double bound. Agamemnon must sacrifice his daughter or prevent the Greek fleet from sailing; Orestes and Electra must kill their mother or leave their father unavenged. The structure of Racine's *Andromaque* is a web of no-win situations, and *Godfather Death*—one of the few Grimm fairy tales that centers on an active figure—forces the main character to choose between losing his wife or dying himself. The situation of the double-bound figure is untenable. Either course of action has grave consequences, yet he must choose one: to do nothing is not permitted him. It has been said that the tragic figure is incapable of compromise, but he might be delighted to compromise if it were an option.

Hegel points out that the classical tragic figure is never divided against himself—that Oedipus, Orestes, and Antigone are wholly committed to their course of action, whereas the modern tragic hero is often vacillating and self-divided.[3] But perhaps what he observed is a shift from an external double bind to one experienced *internally*. In the *Oresteia* and *Antigone*, the double bind is manifest in the *situation* of the figures, whereas Hamlet—who could attribute his dilemma to the suspected complicity of his mother—finds its source in his own make-up instead. A situational double-bind has been internalized as self-division.[4]

We think of heroes as eager to act but only a few, like Don Quixote and Emma Bovary, *seek* great deeds or adventure. Most of them do not go looking for trouble but do what they must to return life to an equilibrium. Odysseus, like Hansel and Gretel, is simply trying to get home. In comedy as in tragedy, action is *thrust* upon the figures. A crisis is upon them and they cannot afford to let time and process resolve their situation. Even Emma Bovary is doomed to act. She is not just a bored housewife led astray by romantic notions, who should be at home with husband and child. Though she is foolish, vain, and egotistical, she is also helplessly enthralled. The story places her in an implicit double bind: to do nothing would suffocate an essential part of herself, however shallow and vulgar its manifestations, while obeying it leads to disaster.

In religious stories, the heroes or heroines are obliged to act, but act in a different spirit. They are not blind to the forces that impel them, but know and trust them. They do not suffer the illusion of being free or self-started and are not in conflict with themselves or their situation; they accept their fate modestly instead of trying to change it 'arrogantly.'[5] Their story is seldom dramatic, for they are consciously and gladly God's servants. They start out with the very attitude that comes to most heroes and heroines at the close of their adventure, if at all.

Religious heroes are not often engaged in an active pursuit, like slaying dragons. It is their task, instead, to prove their absolute trust in God. Abraham is prepared to sacrifice his only son without questioning Yahweh's command: he is neither in conflict nor double-bound. Since the outcome of his story was familiar to those who heard it, an implicit no-win situation is resolved even as it is set up. His acceptance of God's will and his unquestioning obedience permit him to act with confidence—to walk hand in hand with his fate, instead of struggling against it. For Abraham, Yahweh's authority is absolute; there is no quandary. But Agamemnon is caught between two human imperatives: family and community, his obligations as father and as leader. Though the gods, like Yahweh, demand the sacrifice of his child, they are remote and of no help in resolving his dilemma. Double-bound, he is forced to act against his own family, and must suffer both a father's anguish and the killer's fate.

EVERY ACTION IS A REACTION

Traditional story sees action as far from desirable. We who are watching may find it satisfying and even pleasurable, but to those who are trapped in it, comically or tragically, it is painful and frightening. Only fools and villains are eager to act, for they are more deluded than everyone else. In story, all action is unmistakably a *re*action: it originates not in the doer but in something within or beyond him over which he has no control. Even the evil that seems to erupt out of motiveless malignancy is the response to a wound. There *is* no *acte gratuit*. The actor is always an agent, and what he is and does has its origin in events that lie beyond the scope of his own story.

In daily life, our actions seem to constitute freedom and a potential mastery over events. But story tells us otherwise, for the figures are trapped into an *enchaînement* of causes and consequences. While our own small acts appear to be freely chosen and often produce the desired results, the actions in story have compelling causes and lead to immediate, equally compelled reactions. The figures are neither free to choose what they do nor can they predict or control the results. The crime at the heart of many stories is emblematic of all action. It cannot be undone: it commits him who commits it, and makes graphically clear the web of connections that constrain all of the figures.

Revenge, which is as central to television drama as it is to myth, illuminates vividly the reactive nature of action. In myth, the Trojan war begins as an act of vengeance. The *Oresteia, Medea, Phèdre*, much of the Elizabethan and Jacobean drama, *Moby Dick*, and a whole range of popular fictions from *The Count of Monte Christo* to *film noir* are fueled by revenge. So are many comedies. Even *The Tempest* is a revenge play, albeit one in which revenge is averted.

The wrong that sets off a story is often a vengeful deed by one who has himself been gravely wounded. We call him a villain because his wound was struck in the past and his hurt has turned into malice, whereas the injuries he inflicts on others are done before our eyes and so arouse our consternation. But he, too, is reacting and in turn detonates an interlocking series of reactions that come to a halt only when the evil has been extirpated and equilibrium is briefly restored.

The villain deludes himself into thinking he is in charge, just as the hero believes he has a measure of freedom. But neither is free and our own interest is focused on the figure under the greatest, most immediate constraint. In *Macbeth* and *Crime and Punishment* it happens to be a murderer. As Hitchcock points out, if a movie begins with a thief ransacking a house and we see the owner drive up, we find ourselves rooting for the thief. Perhaps we identify with the person under greatest pressure because we, too, often feel up against it and vulnerable, though we cannot afford to admit it.

THE CENTRAL FIGURE MUST ACT ALONE

Communal action is rarely story's domain. The wrong in most narratives cannot be righted by the community. Instead, the task falls to an individual—Hamlet or a rogue cop—who, for a variety of reasons, cannot go to the authorities and must act alone. Story centers on the very action society restricts: that of the loner. But whereas the villain acts entirely in his own interest, the hero acts on behalf of the group even when he appears to oppose it, and even when the meaning of his actions is not apparent to him. The community, in turn, does not always appreciate what he is doing. The Chorus turns away from Oedipus at the end of the play without a word of gratitude, and the lynch mob howls at the sheriff who saves the prisoner from its fury. In comedy and Positivist story—which includes most popular fiction today—the hero survives, whereas in tragedy he dies, but in most stories he is obliged to take upon himself a task the community cannot carry out.

TO ACT IS TO SUBMIT

Traditional story suggests that though our actions are ineffective, they are necessary and inevitable. The figures *must* attempt to change what cannot be changed—and in acting, they *submit*, though they are seldom aware of it. Pascal says all our troubles spring from the fact that we cannot sit in a room and do nothing.[6] Locke speaks of our "restlessness"[7] and Hegel of our *Unruhe*—our disquiet.[8] Perhaps we are not free to do nothing—to be accepting and at peace—because consciousness, which is neither willed nor freely chosen but mandated by our very existence, obliges us to act. Unlike other creatures, we are aware of our situation and cannot help trying to do something about it.

Stories Connect Us

STORY CONNECTS AND FRAMES US

The central figure sees himself as acting alone but is, in fact, everywhere connected. Like all structures, story integrates and relates. The narrative relates all of its parts to each other and is, in turn, "related" by a narrator to the audience. "Narration" derives from the Latin *narrare*, "to relate," which is in turn rooted in the Greek *gno*, "to know." To know *is* to connect.[1]

In narrative, no one is an island, however isolated or free he may believe himself to be. Some stories, like *Bleak House*, establish a web of explicit relationships: all of the figures and incidents are interconnected. But even when the relationships are not explicit, whatever is included is thereby connected. In a narrative of the absurd, deliberate disconnections *are* the connection, just as an *absence* of feeling can constitute the emotional tenor of a work. However disjointed and fragmented the elements, their very inclusion links them.

Text comes from the Latin *textus*, "that which has been woven or intertwined." The *context* of a story is always present to the audience, though we may on occasion become so deeply involved that we forget what we know. Positivist stories delude us into seeing the central figures free of their context, while in traditional story we tend to remain aware of the social, economic, or historical situation and almost never forget the absolute context constituted by story's preclusive form.

A visual narrative like film keeps the *physical* circumstances before us, whereas a novel can leave us freer to disregard them. Figures on the screen move through streets and crowds that establish scale and the relationship between human beings and their physical surroundings. In film, as in painting, the image is surrounded by an edge or frame that clearly limits it. We could think of the frame as an analogue of context and of context as a kind of frame. Our context imposes limits; it 'frames' us by setting us up for the roles we are expected to play.

IN LIFE, WE THINK WE ARE FREE OF CONTEXT

As we move through daily life, we are not generally aware of the frame that limits us. We tend to see ourselves as free individuals, albeit with a role to play in our community. Ideally, we perceive ourselves as at once independent *and* connected. Perhaps our sense of freedom derives in part from the fact that we do not actually *see* ourselves. We can hear our voices and feel our bodies, but whereas others see us, we catch only an occasional glimpse of ourselves. As we look out into the world, we are our own blind spot. We certainly have no sense of being inextricably framed by our context. We experience ourselves as separate or apart, and are more likely to attribute what happens to us to our own failings and accomplishments than to circumstance.

To see is often to know. So we say "I see" when we mean we understand.[2] In the theater—from the Greek *theaomai*, "to see"—we see or know that the figures are clearly bound, while they think of themselves as free and with a measure of influence over the outcome. *We* see and *they* don't—a discrepancy as evident in documentary film as in tragedy. In *Happy Mother's Day*, the mayor of a small town is no less convinced than King Oedipus that what he does is up to him, and of the greatest consequence in the scheme of things.[3]

STORY IS BUILT ON SITUATION

Traditional narrative renders the context that frames the figures by establishing their situation. No story begins at the beginning. There is always a given, something the figures did *not* make. "Situation" derives from *situ*, "a site." The site, place, or scene—from *skena*, "a covered place"—exists before the figures appear in it. We were the land's before the land was ours.

At the beginning, King Lear seems to be making his own situation, but his story has a long prehistory. What he does, moreover, is in large part done unconsciously and therefore not freely chosen. A *free* person is of no interest to story: he or she would float in a vacuum and fail to reflect the reality of our own situation—a reality we sense even if we cannot afford to acknowledge it. As Henry James says:

> (Characters) are interesting . . . as subjects of fate, the figures around whom a situation closes, in proportion, as sharing their existence, we feel where fate comes in and just how it gets at them. In the void they are not interesting.[4]

Indeed, if they *were* in a void, or free, there would *be* no story.

It is often said that men like Napoleon are made by their situation. But the same is true of Hamlet. He too is crystallized by his circumstances and exists as a response to them. At Wittenberg, he might well be indistinguishable from other students and of little interest to us. It is in his encounter with the situation at Elsinore that we come to know him and recognize ourselves in him—just as the ordinary fellow in the *The Thirty-Nine Steps* becomes interesting once his life is in danger. The situation, whether it be existential or entertaining, *creates* the figures for us. We understand and identify with them because we can see ourselves in their *place*. Chaplin said that a comic situation must always be familiar to the audience, no doubt because it is their situation and not their character or feelings that gives us access to the figures.[5] It forces them to act—to commit and so to show themselves.

Fairy tales often establish their situation in the very first sentence: "Once there lived a king and queen who said every day: 'If only we had a child!' " "Once upon a time there were three brothers who became ever poorer till they had nothing left to eat." The situation in *Rumpelstiltskin* is as clear as it is in myth: the princess will lose her only child if she cannot discover Rumpelstiltskin's name—just as Admetos must die unless he can find someone to die in his stead. In the novel, situations emerge more slowly and may not attain the stark clarity of earlier narrative forms, but they are as central to Kafka, Hemingway, and Proust as in *Oedipus Rex*.

We can call situation an attenuated crisis and crisis an exacerbated situation. In myth, fairy tale, and both comic and tragic drama the figures are transfixed by a crisis. Even documentaries seek out those who are pushed to extremes: the man on death row or the mother of quintuplets. At the beginning of *Chronicle of a Summer*, Jean Rouch confronts people on a Paris street with the question: "Are you happy?" His camera provokes a mini-crisis that makes them vulnerable and reveals them.

The situation may originate *within* the figures rather than outside them. Lear's crisis is triggered by an inner imperative: he rashly divests himself of power, promises the largest share of his kingdom to the daughter who loves him most, and disinherits and exiles Cordelia, who is devoted to him. We can, of course, see his inner situation as a product of events in the world: he was for years an autocratic ruler and his long-neglected feelings assert themselves with a vengeance. Often, there is no clear dividing line between inner and outer realm. Events constitute us and we, in turn, constitute them. The two realms are a fluid continuum—which we must attempt to separate in order to achieve a measure, or necessary illusion, of freedom and control.

THE STORY IS ALWAYS PAST

Every situation is a product of the past. Though in Greek mythology memory, Mnemosyne, is the mother of *all* the muses, story is more clearly linked to the past than the other arts. By the time it is told every story is over, as if to suggest that, given our limitations, we cannot know an event of any complexity until we look back at it. *All* knowing is predicated on observation and experience, and therefore linked to the past.

A story not only *is* past but *has* one. Every narrative has a prehistory, and many start in *medias res*. Nothing can come from nothing. Even creation myths begin with a deity who makes the world. An *event*—from the Latin *e*, "out," and *venire*, "to come"—is an *outcome*, which implies that something preceded it.

If we are persuaded that the past is irrelevant to the present, we cannot tell stories, for they accrue their own past. Every action and incident *becomes* past for all that follows. Story's form makes it difficult if not impossible to sever the link between events, and every attempt to elicit a narrative out of nonrelationships quickly exhausts itself. The preclusive plot suggests that the past is always present and may, indeed, be our destiny.

In *Oedipus Rex*, the present is simply the arena in which the past asserts its primacy. The future of Oedipus lies behind him. Revenge stories are fueled by the past, and so are all ghost and many horror stories. The haunted house is the scene of past crimes, and the subhuman monster that roams our horror movies is a creature of primeval urges. As Freud suggests, the terrifying is often something we think we have overcome that suddenly reasserts itself—something we have buried in the unconscious that re-emerges into consciousness.[6] We used to speak of "rehearsing" stories—a word related to "hearse" and derived from the French *herser*, to "harrow." To rehearse a story is to uncover something that has been covered.

MOST STORIES ARE FAMILY-CENTERED

In childhood, the family is the arena in which we encounter both situation and past. It is our first 'given,' the structure into which we are born and which at once holds and constrains us. Most stories, from myth to situation comedy, are family centered. *Oedipus Rex* begins with an issue of the greatest public concern but turns into a family tragedy; the survival of Thebes becomes so irrelevant that the play ends without a single mention of the plague, of which Oedipus has presumably freed the city. Since the family is the building block of most communities, what happens within it is, of course, of immediate public concern.

We do not choose our families any more than we do our bodies or innate capacities. We are enthralled to them during our most helpless and unconscious years; they constitute a first and often indelible encounter with necessity. Family experiences and relationships imprint or inform our lives. Just as Oedipus escapes the family of his origin only to reconstitute it in Thebes, so we too tend to reconstellate our original family in every deep and lasting relationship. It is easy to understand why, in other times, family was perceived as fate, for we neither choose nor altogether escape it.

Our relationship to family is necessarily complex and contradictory. We are at once determined by it and determined to free ourselves of it. It shelters and bonds us but must also cast us out. It has the power to nurture *and* undermine, to wound *and* heal, to sustain *and* strangle. Not infrequently, it does both. Those who are closest to us are the most dangerous; those who love us can also destroy us. As the critical interface between the community and the individual, the family gives rise to paradox after paradox, and holds us helplessly double bound. It socializes us and yet, throughout life, is our access route to the powerful and often disruptive energies of the unconscious. In story as in life, it serves as an intimate yet public stage, on which the critical issues of our existence are rehearsed and enacted.

IN STORY, CHARACTER IS GIVEN

"Character," says Heraclitus, "is fate for a man."[7] A Positivist reading might suggest that fate is *subject* to character—that we can influence what happens to us by changing who we are.[8] This coincides with the needs of society, for no community can sustain itself without the belief that we are in some measure responsible for what we are and do. Yet *character* originally meant "a distinctive mark made by cutting," and implies that the cutting was done by forces not under our command. Character might thus be defined, in keeping with depth psychology, as a response system generated either without or within us, over which we have little control. Perhaps it constitutes fate because, like family, it is a crystallization of the past and therefore not subject to our will.

15

Character plays almost no part in myth or fairy tale, and though comedy and melodrama *do* have characters, they are locked into their roles from the start and hardly ever change. The villain is always and unambiguously evil, the heroine virtuous and incapable of deceit. Louie in *Taxi* is always nasty Louie, and if he surprises us with an act of apparent generosity, it turns out, most of the time, to be motivated by malice or greed.

Aristotle assigns character no primary role in tragedy.[9] Though there have been persistent attempts to salvage a measure of freedom for Oedipus Rex—and ourselves—by making his character in some way responsible for his fate, his situation was clearly determined before he was born and cannot be altered by what he is or does. Even if he took no pride in his responsibilities and past accomplishments, he would hardly be free to disregard the oracle of Apollo, turn away his subjects, and live on in blissful ignorance. His persistence in the face of repeated warnings is not simply the product of *hubris*: he has no viable alternative. The commonly held view that he is in some measure responsible for his own fate endows him with a freedom that both his situation and story's preclusive form deny him.

For Barthes, "there are no characters in the Racinian theater . . . only situations."[10] Schopenhauer says that tragedy never exhibits real "character development," only "character revelation"—the revelation of something "previously latent as disposition."[11] This is as true of documentary film. The figures do not change, even when they are observed over a period of time, but are simply *revealed* to us through the action. As Hebbel puts it: *Was einer werden kann, das ist er schon*; we already are whatever we can become.[12]

It is often said that Shakespearean tragedy is a tragedy of character, as against Greek tragedy of circumstance. But here, again, "character" is deemed to be separate from and free of situation, rather than its embodiment. Though *King Lear* and *Hamlet* have more "character development" than *Antigone*, they are as deeply rooted in circumstance as *Oedipus Rex*.

Given its larger time frame, the novel engages us most seductively with characters, which proliferate and flower and can easily become the focus of our interest. They effectively divert us from the main form and thrust of the narrative. They may even seem to originate the action, and so mask the grave doubt about our freedom that all story raises. Yet the figures in a novel do not choose or command their own characters any more than those in a play or fairy tale. Don Quixote and Captain Ahab are no freer than Medea or Phèdre.

WE NO LONGER BELIEVE IN CHARACTER

In our own day, the concept of character has become obsolete. Colloquially, a 'character' is now someone who is unintentionally funny. He is too clearly defined and sticks out, albeit inoffensively. In a rapidly changing context like our own, we survive by continuous adaptation, and the Greek saying: "You are what each day makes you" is appropriate to us. In a fluid, often unpredictable world, to 'have character' in the traditional sense—to be predictable and therefore rigid—can spell trouble, if not disaster.

We have, moreover, lost all confidence that our once seemingly impregnable character can withstand real pressure. Traditionally, in both life and fiction, character or self derived from and served a stable context, though it also preserved our integrity when the context crumbled. But in an age of concentration camps, when so many have been crushed psychologically and not just physically, we have been forced to recognize that what we are and do is largely beholden to circumstance.

This can be true even of heroes. On a construction detail at Buchenwald, two Jews whose strength was failing drew the angry attention of an SS sergeant. He pushed them into a ditch and commanded a Polish prisoner to bury them alive. When the Pole refused, the sergeant, instead of shooting him at once, pushed *him* into the ditch and ordered the Jews to bury him:

> In terror of their lives and in the hope of escaping the ghastly fate themselves, (they obeyed). When only the head of the Pole was still uncovered, the SS man called a halt and had the man dug out.

Once again he commanded the Jews into the ditch and again ordered the Pole to bury them. This time he did.

> Slowly the ditch was filled with soil. When the work was done, the Detail Leader personally trampled down the soil over his two victims.[13]

17

Fictive Figures Must Think They Are Free

THE FICTIVE FIGURE IS A VICTIM

In the *formal* sense, all fictive figures are imprisoned and victimized by their stories. René Girard has shown that in myth and tragedy their victimization is borne out by the narrative events themselves.[1] "The doer must suffer."[2] Lear, Antony, Othello, and Macbeth are men of action whom circumstance or proclivity has reduced to a state of near-helplessness. They bear an unexpected resemblance to Büchner's Woyzeck and Lenz's Hofmeister. There is no substantive difference between the royal hero as victim and the ordinary victim as hero—between King Oedipus and Kafka's K. Even villains are victimized in the end. Iago's plot goes awry and—in the view of some interpreters—leaves him on the verge of discovering that just as he gulled Othello into killing Desdemona so he has, himself, unwittingly destroyed the person he loves.

The hero of story is a victim who does not see himself as one. His blindness protects him. He does not know that his situation is hopeless. We who watch or listen are aware of the inevitable outcome, but he struggles blindly on. In his *own* eyes, even Woyzeck is not totally helpless. The figures do not see themselves as victims because they are blind, and we do not see them as victims because they refuse to quit. Sheer endurance, or the effort to understand what is happening to them, constitutes an action in the face of the inevitable.

If the figures *knew* the truth, they might, like the religious hero, become wholly accepting or surrender to utter passivity. Prometheus, in the *Pro-*

metheus Bound, is an exception, for though he knows he is immobilized, he keeps on fighting. But he is immortal and has a chance of outmaneuvering Zeus himself.[3] Our own, very different situation is rendered by mortal figures. Since they are obliged to act, they cannot *afford* to know the truth. Their ignorance of the outcome, and the illusion that it is open-ended, permit them to think they can do something about it. Their blindness keeps them going.

THE HERO MUST NOT KNOW

In life, we acquire knowledge to achieve some control over our fate, and try to understand the workings of necessity in the hope of arresting it. If we knew with certainty what lies ahead, we would be, *ipso facto*, incapable of preventing it. The Latin *certus* means "fixed, determined." Whatever is certain or ascertained is inevitable. Our knowledge of the future would, in most instances, permit us only one option: to act in accordance with it—whereas uncertainty gives rise to hope and the illusion of freedom.

If we could be sure of a positive outcome, foreknowledge would serve as a source of powerful, enabling energies. Religious movements potentiate their believers by predicting a happy outcome for them. Conversely, to know we are doomed is utterly disabling. Though we are aware we must die, there is a distinct change in our situation when, like a man facing execution, we know the hour of our death. It may potentiate us spiritually but is unlikely to engender the will to do anything about it. Few of us, given the option, would choose to know it.

"True knowledge," says Nietzsche, "kills action; to act one must be enveiled by illusion."[4] If we are to carry out the tasks assigned to us, we cannot afford a fatalistic attitude and must believe that what we do will make a difference. Our blindness, or 'enveilment,' is of critical consequence to the community and may well be fostered by it. It is, moreover, necessary to our survival as individuals, for it gives us the 'right' and strength to fight on our own behalf despite the claims of others, as though we were of primary importance. Our limited awareness protects us against a knowledge that would cripple us. As Yeats says:

The knowledge of reality is always a secret knowledge. It is a kind of death.[5]

The blindness of the fictive figures, which at first seems a mere limitation, turns out to be necessary. The conviction that they can *change* their destiny is a crucial element *of* their destiny—and of story's design.[6]

20

Some figures are blind not just about their situation but about themselves. Othello, Don Quixote, and M. Jourdain are self-deceived. Though Iago masters the actions and reactions of others, he fails to uncover the motive for his own malice, and Hamlet, despite his awareness and insight, cannot penetrate to the source of his own malaise. Baudelaire says: "One of the most distinctive marks of the *absolute* comic is that it remains unaware of itself,"[7] and Bergson adds:

> The comic person is unconscious. As though wearing the ring of Gyges with reverse effect, he becomes invisible to himself while remaining visible to all the world.[8]

The blindness of the fictive figures can on occasion extend to those enacting them on stage. As school children, we once performed a Chinese folkplay, to which we lent ourselves wholeheartedly. When the curtain fell on the first act, we noticed that many adults in the audience were weeping, which greatly astonished us, since we were having a jolly time and saw nothing poignant in our doings. Like the figures in the play, we perceived the story from *within* our own roles, or parts. The connection between the parts and the meaning of the whole were not apparent to us.

HUBRIS

It is often said that an extreme form of blindness, *hubris*, causes the fall of the mythic or tragic hero. His *hubris* may have its origin in his obscure parentage—his illegitimacy, for instance—which leaves him without a clearly defined place or role in the community, and obliges him to establish himself by excelling. His status as an outsider engenders his immodesty: since he is different from others, he thinks the rules do not apply to him. The community may actually *foster* his alienation and blindness, so that he can be induced to undertake a difficult, dangerous task—like an encounter with monsters or the unconscious. By enhancing his sense of self-importance and distinction, he is persuaded to risk what most of us hold precious—safety, comfort, even life itself—in the hope that his actions will safeguard the community or extend our knowledge of the unknown. His reward is fame and a place in story or history.

Though the Shakespearean hero does not display *hubris* in its Greek form, he too sees himself as a figure of central importance. He talks at great length, explores and gives vent to his feelings, complains about his lot, and bemoans his suffering. Even the actor playing him may need an exaggerated sense of his own importance, for he too is at risk, albeit only in front of the audience.

In daily life, we do not take kindly to those with an inflated sense of themselves. Yet *hubris* may be nothing more than an extreme form of a common and *necessary* condition. We, too, as we go about our work, whether it be raising children or piloting an airplane, need an enhanced sense of our own significance. A measure of *hubris* is essential to the community, especially in an industrial society where even ordinary activities, like driving a car, involve the safety of others, to whom we have no actual relationship and feel only an abstract connection.

The limited and often distorted perspective of the fictive figures is glaringly apparent to us, yet we are just like them. We see further than they while we are watching, but as soon as the house lights go up, we pull in our horizons and re-enter the realm of our own narrow concerns. By disconnecting from the whole—by separating from the context, of which we, like the figures, are clearly a part—we can once again delude ourselves into thinking we are independent and free. This is not a matter of choice, but comes as first and second nature to us: it is rooted in biology *and* in our heritage as socialized beings.

Like the hero's *hubris*, our often intensive preoccupation with our own concerns is both necessary and dangerous to the community. It prompts us to meet our obligations but may tempt us to think we *are* more important than others. In just this way, all specialization of labor, with its urgent and exclusive concentration on a single task, endangers the community it benefits. The threat is gravest when it involves a heroic leader. Because he must take risks and make sacrifices, he may urge them on the entire community without regard for its welfare. Society is rightfully suspicious of the heroes it breeds. Since they are not given a place at birth but must earn it through unusual accomplishments, since their role—from *rotulus*, "wheel"—is to *have* no recurring, predictable role, and because their very function requires that they go beyond the bounds and control of the community, they cannot be trusted.

Story both fosters the importance of the hero by focusing on him and his actions *and* renders him as inflated and self-deluded. The central figures in comedy and tragedy believe they are special cases. Gilgamesh sets out to attain immortality, and M. Jourdain is deceived into thinking he is a Mamamouchi whose daughter is marrying the Great Turk. Stories build up their central figures only to shatter or shrink them, while the modest nobodies in fairy tales end up as kings and queens. Even a sympathetic figure like Hamlet is 'reduced' by the play. After a great deal of frantic activity, several killings, and a suicide, he comes to the realization that revenge and the righting of wrongs are beyond the scope of his will. He accepts, consciously, what fate has in store for him: "Let be."

Some figures never realize that they have been stripped of their power or pretensions. Don Quixote and Malvolio remain deluded to the end. But even their extreme, impenetrable *hubris* may touch a chord in us, for we know that a measure of stubborn blindness is necessary to our own survival. The whole truth, if we could attain it, would implode all but a few.

The mythic hero could not become a *theomachos*, or god-fighter, without the restricted consciousness that engenders his inflated state. But while he may be aware of the risk that his task entails, he hardly expects to be sacrificed if he succeeds. Yet this is often what happens, albeit in camouflaged form. The community—in order to distance itself from the trespasses he has committed on its behalf and to keep him from bringing home his dangerously enlarged sense of himself—may disown him. His death, if it should occur while he carries out his task, is not altogether unwelcome. It appeases the offended gods and permits the community to honor and mourn him at a safe distance.

Not only in myth and tragedy but in many stories the central figure is offered up as a sacrifice. At the very least, his restricted consciousness serves to enhance ours: he is blind on our behalf; if he were knowing, there would be nothing for *us* to know. He fails to see precisely what we *do* see—in *his* situation and, by inference, in our own. He seems different from us, but we are like him, for we too, when we become conscious, lose our 'natural' place, our 'natural' right to be, and must earn it back by slaying dragons—those *within* us. What we regain is not, of course, our place in the *natural* scheme of things, for it is lost irrevocably, but a surrogate place in the community.

THE AUDIENCE IS BOTH ABSENT AND ENGAGED

Between our knowing and the ignorance of the fictive figure lies an ironic gap on which traditional story is founded—a discrepancy that is always present, even when it is so narrow as to pass unnoticed. In comedy, it is unmistakable. The figures are so obsessed by their greed, lechery, ambition, vanity, or cowardice that they become mindless of everyone and everything—leaving us at a comfortable distance. We may recognize ourselves in them but their very attachment detaches us and makes it possible for us to laugh instead of identifying with them. Within the coordinates of the story, what they do and feel makes perfect sense to them, but we, who are privileged to watch from a safe distance, see it as exaggerated and laughable—though our own behavior is often no less absurd.

The top balcony in the nineteenth-century theater was called the *Gods*, but the audience has only the *knowledge* of gods and not their power. We owe our privileged perspective to our physical absence from the scenes on stage. In life, though we may be psychologically detached from an event, we remain bodily present and so potentially involved. But we cannot be drawn, physically, into a staged imitation of events that occurred in the past. There is nothing we can do to affect them and they, in turn, pose no physical threat to us.

Baudelaire suggests that comedy engenders a feeling of satanic superiority in the viewer.[9] But while we see the figures from the perspective of gods, we do not feel simply superior to them. We may laugh at the clown but our *impulse* to behave as he does, and our secret knowledge that we often do, bring him uncomfortably close. His behavior, like his ridiculous dress, is so extreme as to be unreal, yet his needs and impulses are utterly real and familiar to us. The tension between our presumed detachment and our unexpected identification explodes into laughter—especially when the laughter of others in the theater assures us that we are not the only shameful culprits. Consciously, we assume we are different, but our laughter reveals we are not.

Whenever we are truly superior and safe, a story holds no interest. The easy hindsight of historical re-creations that flatter the audience by displaying the limitations or prejudices of an earlier time—upper-class antisemitism in *Chariots of Fire,* for instance—is fatuous, for it fails to touch our own vulnerability. It is our *kinship* with the figures that makes them persuasive or 'real,' for it allows us to endow them with our own experiences and feelings. Indeed, the gap our awareness or knowing opens between them and us, the insight it affords us into their motives and conflicts, and the contradictions it reveals within their natures, do not distance us but bring us closer.

OUR DOUBLE EXPERIENCE OF STORY

Most of us don't go to the movies or read a novel to remain godlike outsiders but to participate. Historical and sociological accounts render *situations* clearly, but do not allow us to share the experiences, hopes, and fears of the figures; they don't engage us on a personal level. Lévi-Strauss assumes that when primitive peoples listened to their myths they did not become empathetically involved in the action but responded to the pattern or structure of the whole. Personhood as we know it was not a factor in tribal life, and while there was surely a form of audience participation, it was no doubt different from ours. Myth, says Lévi-Strauss, was perceived in space—synchronically—rather than experienced in time: the figure was always seen in context or as part of the ground. A similar observation was made by Worringer in 1908, when he explored the preeminence of pattern or design in "primitive" art.[10]

In Western culture, however, story both contextualizes *and* decontextualizes. It allows us to remain detached and *yet* to become engaged—to know *and* feel. We are involved in a double experience, at once observers and participants—whereas in daily life we are apt to occupy one position or the other. Though comedy, as Chaplin says, happens in long shots, we are pulled into his movies by our kinetic, tactile, and emotional participation; though we know that Oedipus has no chance of extricating himself, we nonetheless share his hope and feelings. We are familiar with the plot, the general line of the action, and its outcome, yet participate in the action from moment to moment. There is a gap not only between the figure and us, but *within ourselves.*

Our double experience may be equivalent to Worringer's abstraction and empathy. In his view, visual art began with abstraction or design—which is impersonal, objective, and repetitive—and developed toward empathy: personal, subjective, and involving. In Western art, the two polarities coexist and an individual work will often oscillate between them, just as the audience in the theater oscillates between detachment and engagement. The divergent elements do not undermine but complement each other. Perhaps even the synchronic structure of Lévi-Strauss's oral myth produced a participatory response in the listener. Surely a Greek or Norse myth—in its unadorned, or summary, form pure pattern—inspired feelings of awe and communal participation when it was told by a gifted storyteller. Though listeners were aware of its synchronic structure, they may nonetheless have *experienced it in time.*

Our own double response is most apparent in the theater: we lend ourselves to the figures as if they could actually achieve their goals, though the preclusive context is clear. But prose narratives, too, are marked by the discrepancy between a completed past and an apparently open-ended 'now.' They are usually told in the past tense, yet prompt us to transpose moments of action and dialogue into the *present*, for the storyteller makes them as immediate and vivid as possible. The scenes in a novel are clearly completed, but occur for us in the same 'now' as the scenes in a play and engage us as persuasively.

25

SURPRISE

Our knowledge or sense of what is about to happen allows us to anticipate it, and anticipation is a form of participation; we look forward to the expected moment, be it comic or tragic. The tension it arouses in us is pleasurable because, while the figures are up against it, we ourselves are safe. Storytellers often forewarn the audience or reader of an unexpected turn of events. By letting us in on something that will come as a shock or surprise to the characters, they enhance our involvement and pleasure.

When our expectations are upset, the story appears to lose its precluded form and to take on a spontaneous life of its own. Chaplin was asked how he would film a man slipping on a banana peel—whether he would show us the banana or keep it from us till the man slips. He said he would let us see it, then have the man himself notice it and step carefully over it—into an open manhole. He engages us through anticipation *and* surprise: we enjoy what we *think* is going to happen and laugh when our expectations are violated.

Surprise is as important to story as the known. A live performer is often of greater interest to us than the piece he is playing, for—unlike the author—he is at risk before our eyes, hazarding a fate we all dread: public failure and rejection. He may, moreover, do the unexpected even in a part we know well, and so generates uncertainty, unpredictability, and a kind of freedom in a familiar, predetermined text.

When surprise and tension in a narrative derive entirely from our ignorance of a *fact*—the identity of the killer, for instance—they barely affect us the second time around. But if we are engaged on a deeper level and move along with the action from moment to moment, the way we hum along internally with a familiar piece of music, surprises continue to work even though we anticipate them.

Once we have grasped a thought or *idea*, it ceases to be of narrative interest and doesn't bear repetition. But our senses and feelings respond to a stimulus even when it is familiar and repeated. Cold water will always shock the skin. Though sight and hearing are not as primary as touch and taste, the processes of story are akin to sensory experience. Keaton's action and movement continue to delight us even if we have seen the movie many times, just as a kettle drum will startle us though we know exactly at what point in the score it occurs. Familiarity and anticipation may, indeed, heighten the sensation. By engaging our sensory and emotional participation, story permits us to become 'innocent' despite our knowing, and gives us a direct experience of the very blindness—the envelope of sensation—that limits the fictive figure.

POINT OF VIEW

Though we know more than the hero or heroine, we tend to adopt their perspective even when it isn't explicitly rendered. Most narratives imply a point of view.[11] Even myths and epics are focused on an individual or small group, and by reporting only those events that are crucial to them, what happens to the other characters becomes less important. A central perspective is established and we, who watch and listen, adopt it almost unconsciously since it approximates our own experience. For better *and* worse, we are at the center of our own stories.

Our identification with a point of view is further enhanced in narratives that permit us to know the central figure more completely than we know our relatives, friends, and indeed ourselves. Hamlet keeps only those secrets from us that he also keeps from himself. Knowing him intimately and sharing his perspective intensifies our participation in the play. We quite literally take his part, which is of course our own as well. We become insiders even as we remain observers.

STORY ENCOURAGES US TO FORGET WHAT WE KNOW

The hero sees himself as at least partially free, and since we make the same assumption about ourselves, we tend to ignore his actual situation. In story—as in daily life—we gladly move from moment to moment, preoccupied with his actions and reactions as we are with our own. Story continually tempts us to forget what we know and to endow the figures with the very freedom it denies them. Of course their freedom exists entirely in our minds, much as the figures in a movie *move* only in the eye of the beholder. But just as there is no movie without the illusion of movement, so there is no story without the illusion of freedom. It is as critical to story as our—often dim—awareness that it *is* an illusion.

Some fictive figures seem free because they are powerful, important, or rich. Kings and gangsters play by different rules or make up their own, and so appear to have more options than the rest of us. They are active and have a clear effect on the lives of others; they make and implement decisions, and are more likely than most of us to get what they want. Options, decisions, and action suggest freedom, though—according to story—they do not actually constitute it.

When *we*, today, watch *Oedipus Rex*, it seems utterly precluded and hopeless. But to the Athenians, the figures may have appeared no more helpless than those in our movies seem to us. Perhaps the presentation of the familiar myth in a new, dramatic form provided an experience that was so different and surprising that even the doomed figure of Oedipus appeared to enjoy a measure of freedom and choice.

It is generally assumed that before the inception of tragic drama, the dithyrambic singers at the festival of Dionysus sang about gods and heroes in events that were clearly past. But when first one and then several singers stepped out of the Chorus and took an independent role, the action was seemingly transposed into the present and the Chorus, instead of looking back at the events in omniscience, became just another participant—one who had no advance knowledge of the outcome. In the eyes of the audience this surely opened up the familiar and precluded story to human intervention, particularly since the playwright added characters and variations even as he preserved the basic 'facts' and outcome of the myth.[12]

Aeschylus presented some of his plays in linked trilogies like the *Oresteia*, and so maintained a sense of the connectedness or *enchaînement* found in the epic. But Sophocles wrote only one linked tragedy and clearly preferred the single play. With the shift from epic to linked trilogy and then to the single play, narrative became increasingly discontinuous. Aeschylus referred to his tragedies as "*slices* from the great banquets of Homer."[13] The German word for play is *Stück* or piece—in French, *pièce*—making explicit its fragmentary form. By separating the events on stage from all that has gone before, a dramatic presentation endows its figures with the appearance of greater freedom.

Though the epic is effectively centered on individuals, it keeps them connected to their temporal and spatial context. But the dramatic figure is isolated or decontextualized, and becomes the absolute focus of our attention. We remain knowing spectators but no longer see the events from the vantage point of Olympians, as we often do in the *Iliad*. Our perspective has become engaged, subjective, and limited. While the *Oresteia* continues to invoke the web of the whole, the link between the murder of Agamemnon and the events leading up to it has become partly internal or psychological: it cannot be verified 'objectively.' The audience is no longer just dealing with familiar 'facts' but with an inner or subjective reality as well.[14] Connections that were once concrete and unequivocal have become personal and ambiguous—endowing the figures with a semblance of freedom and individual responsibility.

TRAGEDY AND THE UNIQUE INDIVIDUAL

In its mythic form, the story of Oedipus is also the story of Laius and Jocasta. But in the theater, Oedipus occupies center stage. He appears as

28

the prime mover and we pay special attention to what he does, says, thinks, and feels. He has become unique: the gods have marked him; his is a special fate, and only *he* can save the city. A remote figure has been brought close. The myth is personalized.

The *Oresteia* has an atragic ending, for the life and death of the individual are set within a larger whole. But when the figures become unique and irreplaceable, their death or downfall ends a world and their story becomes tragic. Of course, even as drama appears to make the figures unique by liberating them from their natural and social context, it sets them more clearly within story's preclusive form—a context from which there is no escape and one in which the hero is unmistakably like the rest of us.

We have noted that while the action in comedy is often communal, in Western myth and tragedy collaborative effort is of little interest. The focus is on an individual acting alone, without the customary delays and safe-guards, and often without the benefit of communal sanction. Because he is on his own, he seems solely responsible for what he does and is therefore praise- or blameworthy. Aristotle appears to support this view, for he assigns a central role in tragedy to *hamartia*, the mistake or blindness that leads to the hero's downfall. But one cannot help wondering how a figure so clearly determined by both fate and story's form could make a 'mistake' of any consequence. A modern tribunal would surely find him innocent of wrongdoing. His *hamartia*, like the pride of Oedipus, may simply be a means of persuading us of his freedom.

THE ILLUSION OF FREEDOM IN RENAISSANCE DRAMA

One suspects that Elizabethan audiences would have been as unwilling to sit through *Oedipus Rex* as most of us are today. They might well have rejected it as fixed, lifeless, and without relevance to their own world. But when Renaissance playwrights violated the classical unities of action, time, and place, the dramatic figure gained a semblance of liberty and stories could be told in which a venturesome people, living in a period of rapidly expanding horizons, could recognize their own experience.

Since the action in Greek tragedy has a single strand, fate seems more clearly in command than in Shakespeare's plays, where the double action obscures the working of the plot. His stories evolve along several convoluted lines, and whether they parallel each other as in *King Lear* or diverge as in *Antony and Cleopatra*, they obscure the underlying thrust of the narrative and make it seem less purposeful and prescribed. Greek tragedy is unified in time and place, focused on a few figures, and easily summarized; but on the Elizabethan stage the action is complex, involves a great many people, extends over longer periods, and shifts freely from place to place. While the Athenian actors apparently moved little and most of the physical action occurred offstage, the Elizabethan figures were highly mobile and active; they fought and killed right in front of the audience.

In daily life, our physical activities—even those without substantive consequences, like gardening and shopping—can allay our sense of passivity and impotence without endangering anyone. We are apt to feel we are free and in charge of our lives because we can drive to the mall, where a wide choice of products awaits us. In much the same way, the activity and movement on the Elizabethan stage may lend the figures a persuasive if unsubstantiated appearance of freedom. As Conrad says:

> In our activity alone do we find the sustaining illusion of an independent existence as against the whole scheme of things of which we form a helpless part.[15]

Elizabethan and Jacobean drama is powered by the intrigues of villains or hero-villains, like Macbeth; even Hamlet is forever scheming and counterscheming. Their ceaseless plotting, and the action attendant upon it, create an illusion of the human will at work though almost none of the plots work out as they are intended. Hegel notes that in classical tragedy there are no figures of evil,[16] but the plays of Marlowe, Shakespeare, and Webster *depend* on them. In Greek myth and tragedy, the destructive element is nonhuman, while Shakespeare's audiences—and we—see evil largely as a product of the will. We don't think of Lady Macbeth, Edmund, or Goneril as helplessly enthralled, and assume that Claudius *chose* to murder his brother, usurp the throne, and marry the queen. The evil they do—their deceptions, betrayals, murders, and rapes—contribute to the apparent freedom of the Renaissance figure.

Yet, in the final analysis, the stories of Shakespeare and his contemporaries are as precluded as *Oedipus Rex*. Movement and sensory pleasure are precious to us, for they separate us from the inanimate and the dead, but they do not constitute freedom. If Hamlet's fate seems less foreclosed than Agamemnon's, it is only because we *discover* the design of his story as it unfolds, instead of knowing it from the start. The difference lies in the way we *learn* about it.

Auden suggests that "Christian tragedy is the tragedy of possibility—of hope,"[17] but Oedipus is no less hopeful than Romeo. The Shakespearean figures and their audiences just get a longer run for their money. The plays begin at an earlier point in the action than *Oedipus Rex*, but something *has* happened before the beginning that turns out to be as binding. Hamlet's father was murdered, Antony is enthralled to Cleopatra, and the Capulets have been feuding with the Montagues for years. The power of the plays derives in large part from the gap between the very vitality and confidence of the figures and the foreclosed structure of their lives.

STORIES ARE AT ONCE NEW AND OLD

In the novel, the preclusive form of story is camouflaged even more effectively than in Renaissance drama. Its length and scope permit the multiplication of major and minor figures, extended digressions, shifts from objective to subjective reporting, and the inclusion of material no earlier narrative could accommodate. The action can extend over days or decades, proceed at a leisurely or accelerated pace, swing forward and backward in time, and render a world at war or the minutiae of domestic life. For several centuries, it presented readers with what appeared to be an accurate and complete record of their experience.

As its name implies, the novel claims to be new. But this is itself traditional, for story's province has ever been the new. From *Gilgamesh* to the movies, story is a journey of discovery, an encounter with the strange, abnormal, and frightening. Though the assumptions and coordinate systems of earlier cultures changed far more slowly than our own, their narratives, too, explored the unknown. Yet even as it ventures into the strange, story discovers the familiar. What Delacroix says about painting—that "the new is always the old"—is true for story as well.[18] As Brecht puts it:

> Nothing comes from nothing; the new comes from the old, but that is why it is new.[19]

In part, this is reassuring: our assumptions are confirmed, the alien becomes familiar, *terra incognita* turns into home ground. But it can also be seen as a form of colonization: the other is reshaped into the known, into the same, into oneself. It could be called a severe limitation, for if nothing is really and fundamentally new, the possibilities for change are very limited.[20]

To those who see traditional narrative as a defense of the status quo and a tool of the established power structure, story's presentation of the old in the guise of the new is self-deceptive or corrupt. Consciously or unconsciously, the storyteller engages in a manipulation of familiar narrative elements to persuade his audience that there is nothing new under the sun,

31

that nothing new is needed or possible. In the view of the Russian formalists, what the storyteller does is defamiliarize familiar material by reassembling a known chronological sequence into one that seems unfamiliar; he serves old wine in new bottles and so revitalizes and confirms the assumptions of his culture.

The formalist approach—which is clearly valid for genre narratives like the Western—has been adopted and extended by an influential sector of the critical establishment. Most theorists today hold that *all* narratives are entirely conditioned by their culture and therefore subject to genre formularization. Tragedy is deemed to confirm the coordinate system that produced it no less than *film noir*. But even if we define genre very broadly—as an "internalized probability system"[21] or "a set of fore-understandings exterior to a text which enable us to understand that text"[22]—the genre approach seems limited. For the preclusive structure of story makes *all* stories—in every age and every culture—fundamentally alike, and what is deemed to be a historically conditioned form may be subject to an *ahistorical* structural principle—one as old as humankind.

NOT ALL STORIES CONFIRM
CULTURAL ASSUMPTIONS

Storytellers, like most of us, are apt to be prisoners of their perceptions—which, in turn, are almost entirely conditioned by society. But there have long been narratives that undermine rather than confirm our assumptions. Some storytellers seem to resemble the alienated, placeless individuals, or 'heroes,' who carry out tasks the community cannot accomplish or risk. They stand outside the coordinate system, less blinkered by its limitations, and may, indeed, have an interest in *invalidating* the very structures that excluded them. As outsiders, their experiences are often unprocessed, anomalous, and inexplicable—encounters with the unknown or unconscious that have not yet been filtered through the cultural sieve. If they succeed in assimilating their anomalous experience into the familiar context—if their stories familiarize the unfamiliar—they are welcomed as a useful extension of the coordinate system. If, however—like the scientist who observes and reports phenomena that undermine established theory—they render experiences that invalidate our basic assumptions, their work is often ignored or rejected as a threat. Their stories do not function as an endorsement of accepted wisdom and the status quo, but report encounters that are difficult if not impossible to assimilate.

It is nonetheless true that even unorthodox storytellers cannot escape story's preclusive form. They must report the new and anomalous within a foreclosed structure—a structure that may stand for an inescapable fact of our existence, or perhaps merely confirms that the new can be reported only in the context of the old. Art, like science, must investigate the unknown with instruments predicated on the known, and in art, as in science,

Anomaly appears only against the background provided by the paradigm.[23]

Stravinsky says we need traditional order so that we can cope with the new.[24] But one can understand the mistrust and impatience of those who see story as an instrument of institutions that inhibit our freedom and deny the possibility of change in order to safeguard their own power.

THE STORYTELLER RESISTS STORY'S PRECLUSIVE FORM

The storyteller himself is caught in the contradiction between the freedom of his figures and story's preclusive order. We don't know whether Sophocles, in the composition of *Oedipus Rex*, struggled against the external skeleton that both the myth and story's form imposed on him. Perhaps he accepted the limitations from the start and composed his play within them.[25] But modern writers, unless they are working within an established genre, resist the possibility that the story is over before they begin telling it—even if they sense that, like Michelangelo's sculpture, it 'pre-exists' in the stone and that their task is simply one of hewing it out.

Flaubert struggled against the inevitable in *Madame Bovary* and did what he could to arrest it. In the course of composing it, he wrote to Louise Colet:

What I should like to write, is a book about nothing, a book dependent on nothing external, which would be held together by the strength of its style, just as the earth, suspended in the void, depends on nothing external for its support; a book which would have almost no subject, or at least in which the subject would be almost invisible, if such a thing is possible. The finest works are those that contain the least matter. . . . I believe that the future of Art lies in this direction. I see it, as it has developed its beginnings, growing progressively more ethereal. . . . Form, as it is mastered, becomes attenuated; it becomes dissociated from any liturgy, rule, yardstick . . . as free as the will of its creator.[26]

In another letter, he reports with satisfaction on "fifty uninterrupted pages in a row without a single event."[27] Indeed, the entire novel—encrusted with metaphor—seems intended to dam up all movement and flow. Flaubert called his scenes *tableaux*—motionless pictorial renderings—as though time had passed by Yonville and Tostes and all those who live there. Yet a contrary force is clearly at work. As Victor Brombert points out:

> Though he claimed he hated plans and outlines, Flaubert was an inveterate planner and plotter.[28]

He composed "a staggering number of outlines," and elaborated them with great care and patience, just as Beethoven ceaselessly reworked the melodic line, or 'plot,' of his compositions. Sainte-Beuve observes that nothing in *Madame Bovary* is left to chance.[29] *L'enchaînement* is Flaubert's own word for the inexorable sequence of cause and effect that moves Emma and everyone else along their paths.[30] He must have become aware that *Madame Bovary* was *not* a book "about nothing at all," without a subject and with an attenuated form, abandoning all liturgy and rule, "as free as the will of its creator." In a necessary and deeply meaningful contradiction, his left hand undermined the work of his right: his concrete, visual style seems to *arrest* time, while the plot carries the figures inexorably forward. Despite "fifty uninterrupted pages in which there is not a single event," the novel is a chain of linked events from which no escape is possible. Just as the earth *cannot* hold itself "unsupported in the air," so Emma is held and determined by forces beyond her control. *Madame Bovary* in no way controverts story's traditional form: Emma's life is utterly foreclosed.

When we look back at *Oedipus Rex*, the figures are so clearly bound that the play may seem pointless and irrelevant to us, whereas the figures in our own stories breathe *our* air, hold our assumptions, know what we know, see what we see, do what we do, make our discoveries, and are surprised when we are. We recognize ourselves in them, and since we must believe in our own freedom, we believe in theirs. *Willen wird hineinempfunden*, says Nietzsche;[31] because we think *we* have a will, so must they. When we declare, with unconscious irony, that we are 'determined' to do something, we think we are saying that we *will* it. As Trotsky puts it:

> If a thistledown, whisked this way or that by each passing breeze, were endowed with consciousness, it would consider itself the freest thing in the world.[32]

34

FILM ENGENDERS THE ILLUSION OF FREEDOM

Though novels seemed realistic to readers for centuries, they no longer persuade us; we are too aware that the game is fixed. Perhaps movies have become our preferred way of telling stories because they still permit us to become so deeply engaged that we forget what we know. They appear to render us and the immediacy of our experience so faithfully that, from moment to moment, we can ignore their foreclosed, predictable form.

We live in a Positivist culture and most of our movies are predicated on the assumption that human beings make significant choices and can work effectively to implement them. While secondary characters are often help-less victims, the central figures seem free and triumph over adversity by dint of applied effort. There are exceptions, like *Citizen Kane* and the com-edies of Chaplin and Keaton, but even our documentaries—those shown on commercial television—tend to be Positivist. *Sixty Minutes* makes clear distinctions between right and wrong, good guys and bad. It usually tells us where the problem lies and what can be done about it. Like all Positivist narratives, it avoids situations that are ambiguous and cannot be resolved. In this sense, it subscribes to the philosophy of Ernst Mach, who said that if a problem *has* no solution, it isn't a problem—at least not one we need think about.[33]

POSITIVISM AND TRADITIONAL NARRATIVE

As we have noted, story's form undermines Positivist assumptions. In a precluded context, there is no way the figures can make significant choices or use their will effectively. While the hero of traditional story, acting on the assumption that he can predict the consequences of his actions, turns out to be wrong, the hero in Positivist fiction operates on the same assump-tion and turns out to be 'right.' But predicting a future that is completed and therefore fixed is Monday-morning quarterbacking. There is no way that narrative, with its preclusive form, can validate a Positivist coordinate system. If we need to believe absolutely that our will is free and that our actions lead to predictable results, we had best not tell or hear stories.

In the recent past, the critical establishment has made a concerted attempt to undermine narrative's claim to reality. The basic issue may well be the depotentiation of humankind inherent in story's structure. Positivism in all its forms was, like the Enlightenment before it, a potentiating force. Not illegitimately, it perceived itself as delivering us from physical, metaphysical, philosophical, and political bondage. But traditional story turns *all* of us into victims and so could be said to inhibit action and change. By blurring differences between those who rule and the rest of us, it appears to serve the status quo and the prevailing power structure. If the rich and powerful are impotent, what the rest of us lack in freedom and possessions may not be worth having; we are all in the same leaky boat.

The contemporary *political* view of story maintains that there is a relationship, albeit one that is often distorted, between narrative and reality. A subtler, more complex challenge—with less obvious political implications—dismisses the link altogether and sees story as pure artifice, which could not render reality even if there *were* such a thing. It is a game played entirely by its own rules, a wholly independent formal arrangement. Though it may *use* elements we call "realistic," it in no way derives its form or 'meaning' from our existence.

Yet stories are at least as old as recorded time, and perhaps audiences believed in them and passed them on because they sensed that they, too, were caught in contradictions—that they, like the fictive figure, had to proceed as if they were free though they were bound. Traditional story is clearly predicated on human limitations. "Death," says Benjamin, "is the sanction of everything the storyteller can tell."[34] Perhaps facing our limits need not simply make us docile and mindful of our place. Tragedy thrived during periods of heady outward expansion and progress, even though it reminds the audience that we are neither free nor powerful, and one cannot help wondering why the Elizabethans, who believed in their freedom no less than we do, enjoyed such a forbidding view of human existence.

STORY AS A SAFE ARENA

Perhaps it has ever been a function of narrative to serve as a separate and safe arena in which we can confront what we cannot afford to face in daily life. Nietzsche's

We have art so that we need not perish of the truth[35]

could imply that in art we can *encounter* the truth without perishing of it. Perhaps traditional story tells us what we already know but must forget or deny. Though we may sense that, like the fictive figure, we are absolutely connected and therefore helpless, we can acknowledge it only in the safe arena of art or religious ritual. Even here we must draw a clear line of demarcation: I may recognize myself in the hero-victim on stage, but must remain fully responsible for my own actions in the theater. Though what is true for the hero is true for me, I cannot live in accordance with it.

We could consider story a compensatory realm—not because it fulfills our wishes or consoles us with visions of a better world, but because it counterbalances our daily existence. From time to time, for our own sake and the community's, we need to be released from the often intense involvement that family and communal life impose on us. A preclusive form, which limits the figures and by implication the rest of us, frees us briefly from our attachments. It liberates us, as well, from the sense of isolation and displacement that is the lot of many, and connects us to a larger whole.

In story, we are free to become vulnerable—to lend ourselves to the figures and their situation without risk. They make no claim on us and we are not responsible for what happens; nothing we think or feel will make any difference. While story appears to be a process of depotentiation, the helplessness of the hero does not render us impotent. His very effort to change what cannot be changed frees us briefly of the burden of willing, and permits us to acknowledge that we are not our own masters—that the consequences of our actions are not finally under our control. For a little while we are absolved of responsibility and guilt. If Oedipus is innocent, so are all of us.[36] Paradoxically, his very lack of freedom sets us free.

Yet once we leave the theater, we must forget what we know. According to an old Jewish legend, when the soul is about to be reborn, it remembers what it has suffered in past lives and begs to be spared, whereupon an angel touches it with forgetfulness.[37] We too, when we leave the safe arena of story, must forget what we know, become blind, and once again assume the illusion of our liberty, so that we can go forward into the future—which, in story, is also the past.

37

CHAPTER

4
_____

Plot

CONTEMPORARY AND TRADITIONAL DEFINITIONS

In common usage, "plot" suggests a plan or scheme devised by human beings to achieve their own ends, often with unfortunate consequences for others. We tend to think of it as an intrigue or conspiracy. Significantly, the word has a similar connotation in contemporary criticism: the plot of a narrative is devised or constructed to manipulate, entertain, move, and surprise the audience. The Russian word for plot, *sjuzet*, is used by the formalists to describe the "*arrangement*" that an author makes of the original events, and it is this arrangement which they—and most analysts of narrative today—consider the important element, while the events themselves—the *fabula*, or "story"—are, in Shklovsky's words, "only material for plot formulation."[1]

Traditional storytellers had a very different perception. For them, the plot *is* the story, and many stories consisted of little *but* plot. Plot was not their handiwork; it was the component they inherited and passed on. When the events were well-known, as in myth, they might be rendered in a new or contemporary manner, with altered details and added characters, but the plot itself remained unchanged. In presenting his version of the Oedipus story, Sophocles preserved the basic structure of the myth. His "arrangement" of the events was a way of *serving* the myth and keeping it alive, but the events themselves and not his version of them constituted the telling element. In the *Poetics*, Aristotle defines plot as "the arrangement of things done in the story"—which seems to support the formalist definition.[2] But the word he uses for plot is *mythos*, and myth clearly preexists the storyteller and any arrangement *he* may make of it.[3]

39

Dostoevski says: "Never invent stories or plots."[4] Nineteenth-century storytellers often drew their narratives from historical or newspaper accounts—sources that were deemed 'objective.'[5] The events of *Crime and Punishment* and *Madame Bovary* are the central, form-giving force and hard to dismiss as "only material for plot formulation." The formalist distinction between story and plot—between the original events and the author's arrangement of them—is a radical departure from traditional storytelling, in which plot and story are one: the author knows or discovers it but—like his figures—he is not free to manipulate it at his will or pleasure.

PLOT IS SPATIAL

Plot derives from the Anglo-Saxon *plot*, "a spot of ground." It is related to the Gothic *plats*, "a patch," and the German *Platz*, "place." We still use the word in its spatial meaning as the site for a building, small garden, or grave. Synonyms for *plot*—"plan," "scheme," and "design"—originate in words with a spatial connotation. So do *theme* and *thesis*, which serve as the structuring principle, or 'plot,' of nonfiction. Several terms related to storytelling—"situation," "circumstance," and "background"—are *spatial* concepts that have acquired a *temporal* meaning. *Scene* originally referred to the covered place where the action occurs, but has come to mean the event itself; a spatial term has been redefined as an action. Conversely, we say that an event "takes place."

The original meaning of plot as "a spot of ground" suggests that it is perceived synchronously, like a plan or design. We might say that we see it from above. The word *synopsis*—the summary of a story or plot—means "a seeing together." The plot, which *we* see or know and the figures don't, exists in place before they discover it in time, and gives absolute expression to the fact that the story is over before it begins. They merely discover what already is.

LIKE THE FICTIVE FIGURE, WE EXPERIENCE OUR LIVES IN TIME

In life, our perception and awareness are so severely limited that we, like the fictive figure, are fated to perceive one thing *after* another, moment by moment, despite our effort to be aware of as much as possible. It was once thought that if we *could* perceive the world synchronously, like an Olympian, we might see the plot of our own lives as we see the hero's. If all

40

connections were apparent to us, perhaps we could read our own future as we read his—with the road clearly laid out for us though we have not traveled it yet.[6] But given our limitations, we too must experience our lives by burrowing through what a god might see as space in a tunnel we call time.

The concept that time and space are really one, or aspects of the same entity, is older than modern physics. In many religions, time is perceived as a limitation of mortal existence; to the vision of an immortal, it appears *as* space. Victor Hugo says: "Nothing sequential is applicable to God,"[7] and the parish priest of Combray tells us that from the top of the steeple "one encompasses at once things he can habitually see only one by one."[8] Our own intense and continuous preoccupation with causality is entirely time-bound. In a realm without time, cause and effect have no meaning. When we look at a painting, we see that everything is clearly connected and belongs together, but since no one thing *follows* another—since they coexist—we don't think of the connections as causal.

WE KNOW THE PLOT BUT EXPERIENCE THE ACTION

Inasmuch as we know the plot, it is synchronically present to us like a painting, yet we *experience* it in time. We rediscover the familiar plot alongside the figures, sensuously as it were. Our double experience at once attaches *and* detaches us. We become involved in the action, yet remain aware of the plot as the field of force that bounds and determines whatever happens. Though the action catches us up and surprises us, the plot stands in an ironic relationship to it. The action renders the immediacy of our experience, while the plot removes us from it. The action individuates or particularizes the figures, while the plot conjugates the particular to the universal.

THE PLOT MANIFESTS *AS* ACTION

Since the action consists of a willed effort on the part of the figures to change or thwart the plot, plot and action may appear to be opposites. Yet Aristotle equates them:

It is the action . . . i.e., its fable or plot that is the end or purpose of tragedy.[9]

We can think of the action as the means by which the plot reveals or manifests itself. Just as Laius, Jocasta, and Oedipus bring about the very fate

41

they are trying to avoid, so the action in every story serves the plot: the figures are its agents and their will is its instrument. The action isn't plot's opposite—it *is* the plot. The figures are focused on the action while *we* see both action and plot. But in truth there is *only* plot—which is the inexorable, form-giving force of story.

E. M. Forster says, optimistically:

> There are in the novel two forces: human beings and a bundle of things not human beings.[10]

In his view, it is "the novelist's business to adjust these two forces and conciliate their claims."[11] But there may be just *one* force—the plot—with the action as a necessary illusion that catches up the storyteller, as it does the rest of us. If he is to tell the story, he cannot just observe it from a timeless, Olympian perspective, but must burrow through time in at least partial blindness, alongside his figures and focused on their action—just as we must immerse ourselves in our own limited concerns if the community is to function and children are to be born and raised. We are confined to our own small domain, yet it is out of the narrow strands of individual concerns that the broad pattern, or plot, of life and story is woven.

STORY'S PRIMARY CAUSE IS BEYOND OUR UNDERSTANDING

When Aristotle speaks of "the things from outside" that complicate the tragic story, he means those that lie outside the time frame of the narrative.[12] But we can think of the plot itself as an element "from outside"—a manifestation of 'forces' that are beyond the reach of the figures. The story begins when something goes wrong, when the social order is disturbed. In myth, this disruption is often caused by a supernatural force or figure, like the plague or sphinx. But even when the source of the trouble is human, it tends to come from a realm beyond our control. This is as true of the mad-dog killer in a Clint Eastwood movie as in *Medea*. Often the action begins with an eruption of the irrational or unconscious, which may well be a modern-day version of the supernatural.

The outcome of story is known but its origin is shrouded in mist. No story begins at the beginning. The roots of the action extend back into uncertainty, and the known is determined by the unknown and unknowable. Most narratives are presented as skeins of connections that reflect and depend on the cause-and-effect relationships which appear to govern human life. But though they may unfold in an *enchaînement* of social, economic, and psychological links that are clear and plausible, the *primary cause*—the origin of the plot—remains beyond our understanding. Traditional story tells us *what* happens and *how*, but not, finally, *why*. We know the fate of Laius, Jocasta, and Oedipus, but are never told why it befalls them. Even *Genesis*, which places us close to the primary source, leaves shrouded why Yahweh permits—or wills—the fall of man.

At its edge, all story shades into darkness. The plot connects the action to a past that neither the storyteller nor we can penetrate. In myth even the gods, who seem all-powerful, are not the ultimate cause. Zeus himself appears in an ambiguous relationship to the three Fates, and beyond them stands a more mysterious figure still: Ananke, Necessity. In Norse mythology, the gods are powerless to prevent the end of the world and their own doom. The myth that traces the origin of the Trojan war back to the Judgment of Paris suggests that ultimate causes are beyond our reach and understanding. Paris is commanded by Zeus to award a golden apple to the fairest of three quarreling goddesses. Confronted with a no-win situation, he offers to cut it into three parts, but this is not acceptable and he is forced to make a choice—offending two of the goddesses, as he knew he would. By tracing the cause of a great war back to a hapless mortal, the myth suggests—as Tolstoy does of Napoleon's Russian campaign—that in the end "nothing is the cause":

> So all these causes—myriads of causes—coincided to bring it about. And so there was no one cause for that occurrence, but it had to occur because it had to.[13]

As Henry James says:

> Really, universally, relations stop nowhere, and the exquisite problem of the artist is eternally to draw, by a geometry of his own, a circle in which they *appear* to do so.[14]

STORY DOES NOT MAKE ORDER OUT OF CHAOS

Contemporary aesthetics claim that story creates order out of chaos, or makes sense of a welter of confusing experiences and impressions.[15] In this spirit, Peter Brooks calls the plot the "embracing concept for the design and intention of the narrative"[16] and Paul Ricoeur defines it as "the intelligible whole that governs a succession of events in a story."[17] He reads

Aristotle's *plot* as "emplotment," and calls it "the ordering of events"[18] or "the triumph of concordance over discordance."[19] For him, "the narrativists have successfully demonstrated that to narrate is already to explain,"[20] and "a narrative that fails to explain is less than a narrative."[21]

These definitions seem, however, to be hostage to an unacknowledged Positivism—one that takes the optimism of the Enlightenment to extremes. The plot of a traditional story is not really "intelligible." In human terms, it often makes no sense whatsoever. The events follow each other in a plausible causal sequence but allow for no clear meaning or explanation. This is most evident in myth. Agamemnon must sacrifice his daughter and is murdered by his wife, who is, in turn, killed by their son. In some versions of the story, moreover, Iphigenia is not actually dead but has been spirited to safety by Artemis. The "succession of events" is ultimately inexplicable and, in this sense, meaningless. Therein, of course, may *lie* its meaning:[22] the plot seems to render the unaccountability of the gods in their relationship to humankind; they are as unpredictable in their cruelty as in their kindness and may affect our lives no differently than chance.

Even the plot of religious story is not intelligible, despite its deceptively simple appearance. All rational understanding of it founders on the problem of evil. Since the narrative is predicated on an all-knowing, all-powerful, and just God, the evil that sets off the action contradicts the story's very premise. It can only be accepted on faith—as a mysterious dimension of the sacred. The existence of evil in a world created and ruled by a just deity is no more accessible to human reason than the sequence of events in the *Oresteia*. Neither 'makes sense;' neither is 'meaningful'—unless we take its meaning to be its inaccessibility. The plot of traditional story is rooted in an enigma, a word derived from the Greek *ainissomai*, "to speak darkly"— which, in turn, derives from *ainos*, "a tale or story."

Lévi-Strauss may be closer to the truth of narrative than contemporary narrativists:

> (Myth) gives man . . . the illusion that he can understand the universe and that he *does* understand the universe. It is, of course, only an illusion.[23]

Yet myths—and the plot that effectively reincarnates them—don't really give us this illusion. When we listen to story, we may well sense that it cannot be understood. It suggests, rather, that if there is an order in the universe, it plays havoc with our order, with the life of the individual and, indeed, with entire communities.

TRADITIONAL STORY AND SCIENCE

Rooted in uncertainty and the unknowable, traditional story is unlike most science, which is Positivist in spirit and approach. Yet some of the foundation theories of modern science penetrate no further into first causes than myth. They too elicit a causal sequence without accounting for its origin. The theory of evolution tells us by what means the species evolved but makes no attempt to explain what powered them with the 'will' or energy to propagate and survive. Many physicists believe that though we will come to understand everything that *followed* the creation of the universe, there is a point beyond which we may not be able to penetrate. Heisenberg says:

> Causality can only explain later events by earlier events, but it can never explain the beginning.[24]

In a similar vein, Heidegger speaks of "astonishment" at being—echoing Leibniz's question why there is "something" rather than nothing.[25] As in myth and story, we can only conclude that it occurred because it occurred. Very likely, we shall never know whether the universe, or life on earth, began by accident or 'design,' just as we may never know with certainty what, if anything, awaits us after death.

OEDIPUS REX EXPLAINS NOTHING

Since its primary cause is inaccessible, traditional story cannot tell us how the outcome could have been prevented. We don't find out how we can avoid the fate of Oedipus; like the Chorus, we can only be grateful it has not befallen us. While a cycle of myths or stories may contain cautionary motifs, they often contradict each other, just as proverbs do.[26] Actions that are life-preserving in one tale spell disaster in another. The only consistent cautionary motif in the fairy tales of central Europe appears to be that anyone who mistreats an animal is in for trouble.[27] The tales are exemplary but endorse contrary ways of being: Hansel and Gretel are saved by self-reliance, resourcefulness, and a capacity for deceit; Snow White by innocence, trust and kindness.

Though Grimm's fairy tales consistently reward virtue and punish wickedness, virtue and vice in them are intrinsic or innate qualities. Only a few of the figures have—or appear to have—a choice between good and evil. Most are what they are from the start, just like wicked witches and good fairies. Moreover, since their lives are clearly determined by supernatural forces, any cautionary or exemplary meaning is countermanded. The word *fairy* ultimately derives from the Latin *fatum*, "fate." A fairy tale is a fate tale.[28]

THE INJUSTICE OF STORY

Snow White and Cinderella don't deserve what happens to them any more than do Oedipus or Othello. All are more sinned against than sinning. Though we, today, may assume that Lear contributed to the monstrous behavior of his daughters, he is justified in raising his anguished voice to the gods, for myth and tragedy are full of grave, inexplicable injustice. Not only individuals but entire families and communities are made to suffer for reasons we cannot fathom. Even in comedy, the figures—fixed in their tracks from the start—do not bring about their own fortunes or misfortunes. Charlie's poverty isn't his fault, and Malvolio's blindness is as involuntary as M. Jourdain's. In a preclusive context, no one can be held responsible or deserving of their fate. The lucky survive and the unfortunate perish. Justice has little to do with it.[29]

There is, however, one exception. Though traditional story—like religion—fails to explain why bad things happen to good people, it carefully avoids situations, common enough in life, when good things happen to the wicked. The guilty in story are always punished. Murderers and tyrants never die of old age and the villain reaps his just rewards. Though the evildoer is finally as unfree and helpless as everyone else, his punishment appears to be the one concession that story makes to our deep need to see justice, or order, wrought out of chaos.[30] In all other respects, the plot is profoundly indifferent to our merits and faults. The sun shines on the good and wicked alike. As Heraclitus says:

> To god *all* things are beautiful and good and just, but men have supposed some things unjust, others just.[31]

UNLIKE OTHER STRUCTURES, PLOT DOES NOT SHELTER US

Most communal structures serve to shelter us from the known and unknown. The law, by establishing and guaranteeing cause-and-effect relationships, enables our will and gives us a measure of freedom, responsibility, and control. Within its context, our actions have—or are meant to have—predictable consequences: we can tell true from false and right from wrong, justice can be done, and order is created out of chaos.[32]

But though plot, too, is a structure, it appears to serve a different purpose. It embodies and confronts us with the very forces against which our institutions try to protect us, and so exposes the daily order of our lives to chaos. Communal structures are of no avail to a hero who is alone and face to face with forces he cannot control or comprehend. While our institutions may become more precious to us when we see what lies beyond them,[33] the plot renders them as frail and inadequate.

Yet facing the unknown within the safe arena of story does not frighten us. It may indeed be liberating. For though we prefer not to think about it, we are perfectly aware that our communal and religious structures are limited and often fail us. We are reminded every day that human justice is imperfect, that our judgment is often flawed, that good can come from evil and evil from good. We know our control is tenuous at best and that, despite all progress, we remain beholden for our very existence to processes and occurrences we cannot command. Much of the time we don't even know what is going on, or growing, in our own bodies. We are well aware that both good and bad fortune befalls us undeservedly, that our most carefully executed plans are often counterproductive, and that our lives continue to be determined by "Acts of God," though we no longer believe in Him.

IN STORY, EVERYONE IS INNOCENT

The law must affix responsibility and blame for everything that goes wrong. It draws a circle in which relations *do* stop. Yet the policemen who brutalize a black motorist are inextricably tied into a system that appoints them to a task the rest of us fear or disdain, and exposes them, day after day, to corruption and violence that desensitize them to suffering. If society is to function, our courts must try them as individuals responsible for their own actions, even though their brutality is an expression of *our* racism, and though it is we who pay them to protect us against the disadvantaged. Unlike the law, however, the storyteller is free to see his figures as helplessly constrained by what Balzac calls "the concatenation of causes,"[34] and in the safe arena of story we can face the possibility that "relations stop nowhere," that no one is free, and that the assignment of blame is likely to be an error.

TRADITIONAL STORY OFFERS NO SOLUTIONS

Our institutions must insist that problems have solutions. They cannot admit to uncertainty but must, instead, provide answers and explanations. We expect them to determine how an undesirable outcome could, and therefore should, be prevented. But traditional story renders events that cannot be averted and problems that can't be solved. Indeed, if there *is* a solution or explanation, there isn't much of a story. Emma Bovary brings about her downfall by violating the structures of her community but her nature—and so the causes of her actions—are a given, and she cannot escape them. Though, at times, Flaubert himself seems critical of her, he knew she could not avoid her fate. Story is focused on exactly those problems that the positivist Ernst Mach refused to acknowledge *as* problems because they cannot be solved.[35]

In farce, there often appears to be a simple solution to the predicament. Individual scenes and, indeed, the entire play may hinge on a missing piece of information—like a telephone call that could clear up the whole sorry mess. But while the solution is obvious to *us*, it utterly eludes the figures. They are frantic marionettes, as ineffective and helpless as Oedipus, jerked about by outside forces. No less graphically than tragedy, farce renders events that cannot be prevented or managed by those who are caught up in them.

Traditional story does not explain what determines our lives or how we might control them. Any explanation would, moreover, be countermanded by the plot, which demonstrates that we cannot for long harness cause and effect to our own purposes. In narrative all solutions are temporary. Even the harmony at the end—a wedding in comedy and death in tragedy—is but a brief respite before a new eruption or conflict sets off a new story. A true and lasting solution would constitute the end of narrative. It is no closer than utopia and would become possible only if we were to accept the dictates of the forces "from outside"—or brought them under our control. Until such a time, we shall continue to be out of harmony with the often incomprehensible whole of which we are a part—trying at once to accommodate to it and to find ways of bending it to our purpose.

It is often assumed that story endorses our social structures, and it is true that those in fiction who stand outside the community pay a price for violating its rules: communal laws are broken only to be reaffirmed when the perpetrator comes to a sorry end. But the relationship of traditional story to our structures is complex and contradictory. Though it seems to endorse them, and though the hero often protects the community against an intrusion of chaos—like the sphinx or plague—the plot is *itself* an analogue of the very forces that play havoc with our lives.[36]

STORY IS AN ENCOUNTER WITH THE INCOMPREHENSIBLE

The chaos rendered by the plot is not simply a means of frightening us back into the bounds of our structures, but an encounter with the nonhuman, the incomprehensible, the 'meaningless.' Since the unknown cannot be rendered without becoming known and so losing its reality, story can only evidence it *indirectly*—in the effect of the plot on the figures, its shrouded origin, and its indeterminate meaning. It may seem as though the known outcome of story transforms the fearful and uncertain into the familiar. But knowing that Snow White will survive and marry a prince does not 'familiarize' or tame the supernatural powers without which she would perish, nor account for the evil in her stepmother. The assurance of a happy ending fails to dissipate the sense of human helplessness and marginality that pervades the tale, though it may make it easier for us to face them.

Traditional story is paradoxical and so is its effect on us. Confronting our fears can free us of them and facing the unknown can be liberating. For the unknown is less confining than the known, and we—like the figures themselves—may take hope from a situation that shades into ambiguity and uncertainty. Despite its precluded ending, traditional story is never deterministic, since its origin is indeterminate. We may, moreover, find comfort in our limitations, for if we *could* control our existence some people would surely get their hands on the levers and work them to their advantage. The knowledge that we are at the mercy of forces no one can long command is—like death itself—not simply devastating but also reassuring.

49

Plot and Necessity

PLOT AS ENERGY AND PROCESS

We can think of plot as an embodiment of the energy that created and fuels the universe and governs life through the forces and laws of nature. We too are governed by it, but evolution has endowed us with what appears to be a margin of freedom. We have learned to protect ourselves against nature's destructive element, know how to harness its energy, and how to exercise control over the natural forces within us—our instincts—by repressing and transforming them. We therefore find it hard to accept that the energy we use and transform may ultimately 'use' and transform *us*—just as the plot uses and transforms the fictive figure.

Plot embodies process—a "moving forward" that changes those who are caught up in it. Though in story the community and its structures remain intact, the fictive figures are often subject to transformation. They don't *choose* it but have it thrust upon them; they cannot escape it any more than we can escape growing older. Lear is transformed by a process he appears to initiate but neither intends nor controls. In story, crises and confrontations accelerate changes that, in life, occur gradually and almost imperceptibly, and so make the impact of process on our existence visible.[1]

Communities and their institutions change far more slowly than individuals and only under pressure—in an effort to remain in balance and as close to stasis as possible. They are designed both to resist change *and* to make it possible by providing a basis of continuity. But today communities that were once largely isolated are exposed to constant contact with others, whose structures may be altogether different and so pose a radical threat to them. Change has accelerated everywhere. While earlier cultures thought they could minimize and even arrest it, we can either fight or embrace it, but we have no way of escaping it. As Heisenberg says:

> The process (of scientific and technological progress) has fundamentally changed the conditions of life on our earth; and whether one approves of it or not, whether one calls it progress or danger, one must realize that it has gone far beyond any control through human forces. One may consider it as a biological process on the largest scale.[2]

In our day, even processes we *initiate* involve so many factors that they often envelop those who are nominally in charge, and take on a life of their own. Some of the scientists who built the atomic bomb believe it was dropped on Japan in part because the machinery for dropping it was in place and had developed its own momentum. Like the sorcerer's apprentice, we often find that we are unable to contain the changes we make or the energies we tap. The vaster they are, the less we are in command of the outcome. The greater our power, the more we are enthralled to it. Our awareness that rapid change has become inevitable and relentless may explain why we worship it and, indeed, see it as our road to salvation. For we have always worshiped the inevitable or necessary, and so try to transform a relationship that holds us helpless into one that seems to promise a measure of influence, if not control.

The accelerating transformation of our communities and institutions would appear to make traditional story obsolete. But story has never held our structures sacrosanct. Though the end of *Hamlet* suggests that a stable order will prevail, it is a mere stay against chaos. Trouble—and with it a new story—is sure to emerge, for the nonhuman forces embodied by the plot are as indifferent to our institutions as they are to individuals. They continually undermine the structures we erect to keep them at bay.

PLOT AS AN EMBODIMENT OF TIME

The flow of time may be central to narrative because the 'discovery' and recording of time—as in counting, astrological observations, and calendars—were critical to the evolution of consciousness.[3] Before we could tell time we didn't 'exist,' for consciousness derives from a process of continuous *re*cognition—of knowing that I, today, am the I of yesterday. Before we could tell time, we had no way of taking action, no way of intervening in natural events—of knowing when to sow and reap. Telling time and telling stories are deeply connected, for both make us continuous.[4]

52

Biological time, which limits human existence, also gives it meaning and value. It sets priorities both in life and story: it determines what should be included and what may be left out. Though the figures in a novel are under less pressure than in drama, they too are governed by time. Indeed, narrative forms that are not *action*-centered let time emerge more clearly as the force that carries the story forward and gives it shape. Time *is* the plot of *Remembrance of Things Past*, the basis of its "vigorous though veiled construction."[5] On the surface, Proust's elaboration of every moment, feeling, and sensation seems to silt time's flow to a standstill, but under the encrustation of detail the current moves ceaselessly on and carries the figures with it. It erodes them yet, in the end, gives them their continuity and identity— just as story both records change *and* stays it by recording it.

PLOT EMBODIES THE PAST

Since plot preexists the action, we can think of it as embodying the past. Like time and process, the past constitutes necessity, for we can neither escape nor undo it. We *are* the past. Not only our families and communal structures, but our perceptions and experiences subject us to it; whatever we know, think, and feel is conditioned by it. Our bodies, our genetic disposition, and our psychology link us inexorably to those who gave us birth and to *their* ancestors. As Faulkner says: "The past is never dead. It's not even past." It is at once our mainstay and an often crippling limitation. To be related to it, to derive continuity and stability from it without being imprisoned within it, is of critical importance to the individual and the community. In story, the plot *is* the past and our attempt to escape it is the action. Paradoxically, though the figures cannot escape it, their effort to do so is mandated *by* the past.

In tragedy, from *Oedipus Rex* to *The Death of a Salesman*, the lives of the figures are determined by events that preceded the story's beginning, or by communal structures that are themselves deposits of time past. Once the action gets under way, moreover, every moment *accrues* to the past and further confirms the inevitable outcome. The mortgaging of present to past is most evident in revenge tragedies. Here the figures, compelled to avenge an old wrong, are clearly puppets of the past, even though—at story's end—the present gains a breathing spell.

In comedy, the past plays almost no part. Indeed, it often turns out not to have happened: the parent, child, or sibling who was presumed dead is found alive, and the family—destroyed in tragedy—is reconstituted. In fairy tales, the past can actually be undone: the frog becomes a prince again and those who were turned to stone by a magician's spell are restored to movement and life. The figures we laugh *with*—Punch, Pierrot, and Charlie—are neither burdened by events that preceded the story nor inhibited by laws and institutions. They are, instead, in close contact with our instinctual or generic core—which assures our survival by alerting us to the dangers and opportunities of the present.

While figures of ridicule cling rigidly to their habits and preconceptions, the comic hero lives *now*. He has a short memory and a shorter fuse. He does not long bear grudges, his wounds don't fester, and he carries out his revenges instantly, as with a slapstick. The great clown often improvises or appears to improvise. Though the comedian himself may suffer old and deep wounds—"I only laugh when it hurts," says Woody Allen—the past does not haunt or cloud his work. When it does, as in Shakespeare's late comedies, it is apt to spoil present laughter.

Within the safe arena of art, comedy can celebrate the triumph of the present over the past *without* invoking the grave threat that our ancient instincts pose to communal life. Indeed, the survival of the comic hero is assured by his *proximity* to our generic past—the unconscious drives that at once perpetuate life and threaten the fabric of society. He thrives on the very energies that doom a tragic figure like Medea or Phèdre. He liberates us briefly from our structures and puts us in touch with the very forces they are designed to contain.

THE GENERIC AS AN ASPECT OF NECESSITY

Our generic past determines much of what we are and do, including our effort to repress and countermand it. Our attitude to it is necessarily ambivalent, for it is at once the source of positive, or life-preserving, and of negative energies; it makes our existence and communities possible *and* threatens them with destruction. The plot resembles it, for it gives birth both to monsters and to those who slay them. Because we must divide the energy within us—which is neutral—into 'good' and 'evil,' or helpful and harmful, we are ourselves deeply divided: we prefer to be good but need access to our evil to survive. Since our dividedness makes us vulnerable and our negative qualities are not appreciated by others, we hide them or project them onto the monsters and villains we send the hero to slay. When he succeeds, he frees us briefly of our own evil and of the self-division that is our lot. We should, however, note that the hero, too, is often a monster, for it takes one to kill one—just as we need the evil in ourselves to defend against the evil around us.

Our communities and their structures are often more concerned with combating the natural forces within us than with those that threaten us from outside; they constitute a graver, more abiding danger. But while the generic must be held in check, we remain beholden to it and depend, from moment to moment, on the unconscious operations of the body, laid down in our cells millions of years ago. There is no way we can *consciously* manage our heartbeat, breathing, reflexes, and all the other functions that sustain life and are controlled by the part of the nervous system we call "autonomous." Moreover, it is nature itself, both within and without us, that generates society and civilization, even as it threatens them with extinction. It engenders the very structures that inhibit it—to the advantage of our species. We might say that culture is nature turned against itself, and therefore self-divided like us.

Under the influence of Positivism, with its emphasis on scientific and technological progress, we slipped rather easily into an arrogant, adversarial relationship to the natural realm. We assumed we could control it, both within and without, and so perfect our lives and ourselves. To an age that deemed itself on the verge of mastering necessity, Freud's statement that "we are lived by unknown and uncontrollable forces" came as shocking news.[6] But what seemed shocking at the end of the nineteenth century had been perfectly plain to humankind ever since the dawn of consciousness, and the "unknown and uncontrollable"—or sacred—forces that were dismissed by Positivism continued to be respected by ordinary folk long after the privileged and educated became convinced that we can control our own destiny.

PLOT EMBODIES THE UNCONSCIOUS

Traditional story has always insisted that we are not masters in our own house, that the 'must' within us is a manifestation of fate—just like the oracle of Apollo and the witches of *Macbeth*. In comedy as in tragedy, the figures are often possessed by something within that they can neither control nor understand. The external forces that determine the action in Homer, Aeschylus, and Sophocles are internalized by Euripides and appear in the form of passions and obsessions. In his plays, the gods have already become diseases, as Jung was to say of our own age.[7] Medea has no more control over her jealousy and her need for vengeance than Oedipus has over his destiny. The unconscious is as inexorable as the Fates and as little subject to our will.

The plot can assert itself within or without. The line that separates them

55

is in any case arbitrary: the generic and unconscious are clearly continuous with the natural world, and the psyche—which may be largely a product of outer events—can in turn generate events in the physical realm. While society must keep them apart and insist that we are responsible for what is within us, story can safely fuse or reconcile them. It allows us to recognize—as on occasion the law does also—that to be subject to our psychic 'constellations' is no different than being determined by gods or the stars.[8] The fate the witches predict for Macbeth is at one with his inner proclivities,[9] and in the family feud that dooms Romeo and Juliet we may also see the genesis of their passion. Perhaps the onslaught and overwhelming intensity of their feelings is rooted in an unconscious need to heal the very hate and violence that doom their relationship, and their death may be an unintended sacrifice to heal the wounds of the past.

In daily life, we are not usually conscious of the 'plot' spun by the unconscious, though we are never truly free of it. Along with culture, economics, history, biology, and grammar it informs whatever we do, think, and feel. The very relationships that appear to meet our most personal needs are determined by unconscious factors. We assume today that marriage, once arranged by the family, is subject to our free choice. Yet when we *fall* in love, the 'decision' has merely shifted from the family to the unconscious. We are no freer when our mates are 'chosen' for us by forces *within* us than we were when we submitted to arrangements made by our parents. Many relationships that were at one time determined by social and economic factors are now subject to psychological needs. Yet need constitutes a form of necessity, and unless it is met and mediated within our communal structures, it may assert itself in the very obsessions and passions that fuel fiction.

The unconscious rules in comedy as it does in tragedy. The figures of Molière and Dickens are as driven as those of Racine and Dostoevski, the characters in *Volpone* as helplessly enthralled to greed as Raskolnicov is to his compulsions. If M. Jourdain were not stopped, he would ruin his family as surely as Captain Ahab takes down the crew of the *Pequod*. Low comedy, from the satyr play to Harpo Marx, is a defeat of the ego or consciousness;[10] it asserts the primacy of instinct—a word derived from the Latin *instinguo*, "to impel."

Just as in life unconscious forces mandate the conscious, so the plot of story mandates the action. We could indeed define plot as Lacan defines the unconscious: as "the discourse of the Other." In story, that "Other" is necessity, the sacred, fate, nature, process, time, the past, the generic, and the unconscious—all those "things from outside" that govern our lives.

Plot and the Sacred

TRADITIONAL STORY SERVES THE SACRED

Rudolf Otto calls the sacred "the wholly other."[1] It is beyond our reach—within or without—and we cannot know or predict it with certainty. Like necessity, with which it may be identical, it changes its face from age to age. Though we make inroads on it and so extend our reach, true control must forever elude us, and we exceed our boundaries only to find that we are up against new limits. The sacred, uncertain or necessary recedes as we advance toward it and appears to us in ever new form.[2]

Like most art, story was once in the immediate service of the sacred. East and West, it was called upon to incarnate religious truth as palpable human experience. Myth reported the physical encounter between the human and the divine, just as Scripture made the sacred actual and accessible to us. European drama had its origin in the liturgy: the mass was given dramatic form, with several voices separating from the choir, to give worshippers a religious experience of greater immediacy.[3]

Though our own stories no longer serve religion, they remain linked to the sacred, or necessity, for the plot continues to determine the lives of the figures. The words that end *The Women of Trachis*—"There is nothing here which is not Zeus"—are true for narrative still: whatever happens in it is subject to its preclusive form.

Jung has suggested that in earlier ages—when members of a community were less specialized and more alike—the psychic 'constellations' that, in his view, shape religious faith were projected onto a set of 'universal' symbols, which could be recognized and acknowledged by everyone.[4] But when communities increased in size and were fragmented by specialization, a single set of symbols could no longer serve.[5] In just this way, the central myths of our culture had to splinter into a great variety of stories, serving different classes and groups. But while they vary widely on the surface, their underlying structure has remained unchanged and makes all variants fundamentally alike.

POSITIVIST STORIES UNDERMINE THEMSELVES

We think of ourselves as no longer having a relationship to the sacred, but since we continue telling stories, we seem to remain mindful of forces that were once deemed aspects of the divine. The major difference between narratives with an explicit religious perspective and our own is that our plots are camouflaged and, at least superficially, more surprising. Whereas the folk tale was told and retold for generations, we, who are subject to constant change, require ever new versions of our basic myths to accommodate changes in the external world and in our continually shifting image of ourselves. In *our* stories we know, generally, *what* will happen but not *how.* We are, moreover, encouraged to become so deeply involved with the feelings and point of view of the central figures that when the inevitable, or sacred, asserts itself, we are surprised—though we knew it was bound to happen. Positivist fictions even manage to persuade us that though the outcome is fixed from the start, the figures bring it about themselves. Our narratives are no less precluded than a Greek myth but the audience is allowed—by a kind of legerdemain involving its own feelings and expectations—to subscribe to the freedom of the figures. Ironically, our Positivist belief system appears to be confirmed by a structure that, in fact, undermines it. A Marxist critic might say that the audience is deceived into believing itself free even as it is manipulated, though Marxist narratives are, of course, caught in the same contradiction; they too lay claim to human freedom, yet are utterly precluded.

Whenever stories are told, we are close to myth. Their preclusive form has us beholden and helpless. The kinship we feel with the figures, and the sense of foreboding or anticipation we have about their fate, are linked to the pity and fear induced by classical tragedy: a pity—from the Latin *pietas,* "piety"—for both the figures and ourselves, and a fear that is basic to our existence and to all religious feeling. Though we are no longer nakedly exposed to the physical forces that determine us, Artaud reminds us that:

> We are not free. And the sky can still fall on our heads. And the theatre has been created to show us that first of all.[6]

Even if we are not aware of it, when we tell stories or listen to them we become kin to those who, millennia ago, gathered at their fires, with the unknown palpable in the darkness all around, to give voice to their awe and fear in the tales they told.

PLOT AS AN ANALOGUE OF FATE

Fate, like plot, is preclusive. *Fatum* means "that which has been spoken," and the plot of traditional story is an analogue of fate. There is little difference between the oracle in the Oedipus myth and the chancery suit in *Bleak House*, which constitutes fate in an urban, mercantile setting: people are enmeshed in it at birth and can neither escape nor comprehend it. Schopenhauer says:

> The dramatic or epic poet must know that he constitutes fate and thus be impervious to human pleading.[7]

Racine, raised as a Jansenist, wrote a prose treatment of every scene in *Phèdre*. When the outline was done and he knew how fate was manifest in the action, he said: *Ma tragédie est faite.* Balzac—who kept a statue of that seemingly self-made man, Napoleon, in his study and announced that what the Emperor had conquered with the sword *he* would conquer with the pen—nonetheless believed that:

> Everything in human life, like everything in the life of our planet, is predestined—including the slightest and most trivial accidents . . . As soon as one admits the truth of predestination—that is to say the concatenation of causes—judiciary astrology resumes its ancient role as a mighty science.[8]

In our culture, fate has entirely negative connotations: *fatal* means "deadly" and we call events that befall us "from the stars" *disasters*. As positivists, we tend to take credit for our good fortune and are suspicious of everything beyond our control. Yet in story, ill fortune is not all that befalls. In comedy and fairy tale, the rule of fate is clearly benign. At the last moment a twist in the narrative, a miraculous *cognitio*, an unexpected reprieve or the intervention of a royal personage resolves all problems—just as events in tragedy conspire *against* the figures and seal their doom: virtue and innocence are protected and preserved by the very forces that, in tragedy, bring about their destruction.

Bergson says that in comedy society or the "social will" asserts itself—

that laughter is a corrective that represses separatist tendencies, converts rigidity into plasticity, and readapts the isolated individual to the community.[9] But the "social will" is surely an aspect of nature or necessity—of Schopenhauer's "objective will" and Bergson's own *élan vital*—just as the community is nature's most effective means of preserving and propagating the species. Though high comedy is directed at the misfit outsider—and privileges society, family, order, reason, and the golden mean—low comedy favors anarchy, the irrational, and the instinctual. It sides with outsiders like Punch and Charlie against a community that is itself mechanical and badly in need of correction. Bergson says:

> Any individual is comic who automatically goes his own way without troubling himself about getting in touch with the rest of his fellow beings.[10]

Yet in Fields and the Marx Brothers we *celebrate* that very individual. The laughter Bergson defines as a corrective, Baudelaire legitimately calls "satanic," for comedy springs from the rebellious and instinctual as often as from the social.[11] The two are not, of course, antithetical: Punch with his 'natural' or antisocial behavior serves the community, just as the community is ultimately in the service of nature.

In farce, the figures are clearly puppets governed by fate. Eric Bentley says:

> What do the coincidences of farce amount to: Not surely to a sense of fate, and yet certainly to a sense of something that *might* be called fate if only the word had less melancholy associations.[12]

In his view, farce and melodrama derive from "paranoid fantasies." But these "fantasies" may be an intensified form of the anxiety that is a by-product of consciousness. Farce is haunted by the awareness that we are not separate, free, or in charge. If a comedy like *Twelfth Night, or What You Will*, appears to attach less importance to its plot than *Volpone*—since its structure is open and fate manifests in a loose, lighthearted way—it may simply be that it stands in the sign of eros, while *Volpone*—with its tight structure, adherence to the unities, and severely restricted action—is governed by greed. The will of the comic figure—be he fool or knave—is of no more consequence than the hero's or villain's in tragedy. *The Tempest*, in which the outcome coincides absolutely with the intentions of the central figure, is a rare exception. Prospero is himself the story's benign fate; supernatural forces obey his command and the events on his otherworldly island resolve into an enchanted, all-forgiving dream.

IN *OUR* STORIES, FATE APPEARS IN HUMAN FORM

While the sacred in myth takes the shape of gods, giants, and monsters, in our fictions it appears in human form. For us, fate is most often other people. We tend to think of the personal and interpersonal as subject to our will, but they stand in the sign of the transpersonal or communal. The *agon* or contest in drama seems to be between two people, two groups, two opposing wills: on the surface, *King Lear* is a deadly conflict among members of the same family. Yet Lear rightfully raises his voice against the gods, for the parents, children, and marriage partners who wound or kill each other in tragedy are subject to all-powerful, impersonal forces.

PLOT AS AN ANALOGUE OF UNCERTAINTY

Before the plot, as before fate, we are all equal. Like death, it recognizes no differences between us. Like the archaic gods, it is neither on the side of the weak nor the strong but on *all* sides or none. Whether plainly visible as in myth, or camouflaged as in our stories, the known plot is an analogue of the unknown and unknowable. *We* know that the figures can't know the plot of their lives just as we can't know the plot of our own. Paradoxically, at the core of the known story is our knowledge that we *cannot* know it. Story may, like history, be an inquiry into why things happen—but it ends in a question.[13]

Story renders the imprint of the nonhuman on the human without rationalizing or justifying the ways of the sacred. Its meaning, like its origin, is indeterminate, and any system—be it psychological or economic—that claims perfect understanding of why things happen is inimical to story, as story is inimical to it. The sacred remains unknown even if we believe it has a covenant with us. The gods do not reveal themselves clearly. In Hegel, God or Being is indeterminate—the equivalent of Nothing.[14] Though *Exodus* says that Moses was given the ten commandments by Yahweh, the *Zohar* tells us he received a mere jumble of letters, which he had to assemble into the Law himself. The truth, says Melville, is always incoherent.

STORY AND CHANCE

The inscrutability of the sacred is vividly rendered in story by the role of chance. Hegel points to the profusion of accidents in *Hamlet*[15]—a comment that applies to other Shakespearean tragedies as well. The accidents, moreover, are crucial to the structure of the plays. The immediate cause of the double suicide that ends *Romeo and Juliet* is chance, and Cordelia dies because the messenger sent to stop her execution arrives too late. In comedy, it is often a set of "curious chances" that both engenders and resolves the narrative.

We call chance 'blind' and luck 'dumb,' for they do not 'see' or 'mean' us. The words *chance* and *accident* derive from the Latin *cado*, "to fall," and we use them when we can find no causal connection between events—when an occurrence 'befalls' that makes no sense. But if the accidents that determine so many stories were truly meaningless, we would reject them; perhaps we accept them because they confirm what we have sensed all along. Their meaning, which we grasp intuitively, may lie in their very absence of meaning: they are the inscrutable manifestations of "the things from outside"—our version of the *deus ex machina*.[16]

The Positivist in us has no use for chance, since we cannot control it; only when we find a law governing the accidental can we guard against it. We are intensely uncomfortable with uncertainty and seek shelter in the reassuring predictabilities of our structures. Like Einstein, we prefer to think that the eternal mystery of the universe is its comprehensibility. What Oppenheimer says of him is as true for us also:

> He did not like (quantum) theory. He did not like the elements of indeterminacy. He did not like the abandonment of continuity or of causality.[17]

He maintained until the end of his life that wherever science saw chance, it had simply not found the causal connection yet: "God did not play dice with the universe."[18]

All human communities have surely been based—at least in part—on principles we might call rationalist or even 'positivist.' No doubt we have always *had* to believe that there was something we could do about our situation, even if it was only prayer and sacrifice. But while all civilized life is predicated on some form of causality, ancient and primitive societies were far more comfortable than we with the role of chance in human affairs. Perhaps they had no alternative, since they encountered it wherever they turned; they often institutionalized it and gave it a voice in their decisions. In Athens, those magistrates who were not specialists, like generals, were selected by lot, which was deemed more egalitarian than elections,[19] and at the *Dionysia*, the prize awarded the best playwright was in part determined by chance: ten judges, who were themselves chosen by lot from a pool of suitable candidates, placed their votes in a jar, and five were drawn to determine the winner. Thus a playwright with only two votes might win first prize over a competitor who had five votes or more. Since the plays with their mythic plots were themselves rooted in the incomprehensible, giving chance a role in determining the winner seems altogether appropriate. In some 'primitive' societies, even justice was decided by lot. Chance was perceived as a manifestation of the sacred and the loser was deemed guilty.

Though chance has never, of course, been absent from our awareness, we live in an age and culture in which Positivist assumptions govern our view of reality. Until recently, science supported and shared these assumptions. While Darwin assigned a major role in evolution to the accidental, it was only with quantum theory and the uncertainty principle that chance emerged as an integral component of scientific thought:[20]

> While with Laplace chance was nothing but the name of ignorance, it now forms a fundamental and irreducible element in any description of nature.[21]

> The uncertainty principle marks the final break with the past. It does not merely state that though there may be causal laws governing atomic events, they are at present unknown: it flatly denies the existence of such laws. This is the Copenhagen interpretation (Bohr and Heisenberg), accepted today by the great majority of physicists.[22]

Of course events within the atom have no direct bearing on our conduct and we continue, quite properly, to act as though our lives were governed by causality. Societies depend on causal relationships, and we expect our structures and institutions to guarantee them. Even so, the findings of modern physics may parallel certain aspects of contemporary experience. In the quantum realm, the possible results of a measurement occur "with probabilities that can be predicted exactly," and it is only "the outcome of any *one* such measurement . . . that cannot be predicted."[23] This is not unlike our situation as individuals: I myself may be subject to chance—or what appears to be chance—even when the outcome for the group can be predicted statistically.

Quantum indeterminism can undermine our faith in a predictable, determinist universe. Like the plot, it casts doubt on our notion of control through planning and will. But even *within* the community—which we might call a *determinist* system—predictions have become hazardous. We are uncomfortably aware that in a great many situations not only the individual will but the will of the community no longer produces predictable results. With the ever-accelerating complexity and interconnectedness of events, our lives are subject to "collateral chains of causation which in principle can never be completely comprehended."[24] This is the burden of chaos theory. It suggests that even in a determinist system, measurements are not always sufficiently accurate to allow reliable forecasts. Though unpredictability is not the equivalent of chance, its effect on us is the same, prompting Karl Popper to say that an unstable or chaotic system is effectively nondeterministic.[25]

Despite our Positivist assumptions, our sense of human existence may once again be close to traditional narrative. In story, the unknown and unpredictable—known and predictable only to those who watch or listen—are of central importance. "A god is hidden in *Tristram Shandy*," says E. M. Forster:

> His name is Muddle . . . Muddle is almost incarnate . . . (It) is the deity that lurks behind this masterpiece—the army of unalterable muddle, the universe as a hot chestnut.[26]

For Muddle we can read chance or the unaccountability of the gods. Yet nothing in fiction or art can ever be *truly* subject to chance, for whatever is included thereby ceases to be accidental and becomes meaningful. It *connects*, even if the connection lies in the disconnection. The accidents that the painter Francis Bacon staged on his canvases were inevitably integrated into his paintings. We may, in fact, be unable to *create* something accidental; even random numbers spewed out by a computer are properly called "pseudo-random," since the same sequence is produced when the computer is run a second time.

Though story cannot actually *render* the accidental, the plot approximates the *impact* of chance on our existence. It seems kindly in comedy and cruel in tragedy, but when the two are combined into a single picture, the sacred appears as a contradictory force that seems indifferent to us, like the gods of old. Through the plot, the accidental is integrated into narrative structure.

Myth and traditional story render a view of human existence that may be closer to our own than we are ready to admit. Chance or indeterminacy have reentered our experience. It may be a manifestation of necessity and so subject to laws we shall one day understand, or simply the way in which we, as individuals, experience the larger patterns of which we are a part. While it would seem that story's preclusive form can report only a determinist and not an indeterminist universe, as far as *we* are concerned, there is little difference. We no longer have the confidence—or illusion—that our predictions are accurate and feel, much of the time, that we are not in command of our lives. We have to accept the possibility that even if Laplace and Einstein turn out to be correct and the universe at large is not only comprehensible but—given sufficient knowledge—predictable, our lives as individuals may be subject to chance.

ACCIDENT AND COINCIDENCE

In our Positivist context, "accident" and "coincidence" are used interchangeably. Both are unwilled and 'befall' us. But in traditional story, coincidence is different from accident. It is a "falling together" that suggests pattern and even design. Statisticians define it as "a surprising concurrence of events, perceived as meaningfully related, with no apparent causal connection."[27] The crossroads encounter between Laius and Oedipus is a coincidence, not an accident—part of a larger design that exists outside time and is not subject to cause-and-effect relationships as we understand them.

We can't always *tell* coincidence from accident. No doubt Laius and Oedipus thought their meeting accidental, while *we* perceive it as a meaningful coincidence. Conversely, some people are apt to misread every chance occurrence in their lives as the work of Providence. An event, moreover, may constitute an accident in one life and a coincidence in another. If a drunk driver runs down a pedestrian, it is part of a significant pattern in *his* life—and, in this sense, predictable—but very likely a meaningless accident in the life of his victim.

Since Positivism dismisses the sacred, it has no use for coincidence and lumps it together with accident as meaningless. Yet it is central to traditional story—comedy and tragedy alike—and no narrative would work without it. Romeo meets Juliet, and Hansel and Gretel the witch; Myshkin and Rogoshin encounter each other in a railway compartment on the first pages of *The Idiot*. Coincidence, scorned by Positivist aesthetics for its "long arm," is at the very heart of traditional story. When we look back and see how the events fit together, what at first seems irrelevant becomes consonant and meaningful. Hebbel notes that "the whole secret of dramatic style is to present the necessary in the form of the accidental,"[28] and Dickens, in whose stories every incident turns out to be part of a significant pattern, writes to a friend:

These are the ways of Providence, of which ways art is but a little imitation.[29]

If we were not confident that the events in a narrative will cohere, we would not bother to sit through them. The meaning may be postponed—as in riddle, which story so deeply resembles—but we feel sure it is there, and if it isn't, then *that* is its meaning. The forces that determine the action in

Kafka seem utterly indifferent to the figures and may well 'mean' nothing. Yet these stories bespeak "the wholly other," or sacred, no less vividly than the novels of Dickens. Only when the accidents and coincidences of fiction become subject to the storyteller's wishes and manipulations—when, in other words, the human will becomes master of the plot—does storytelling cease to be traditional.

Despite our Positivist orientation, many of us continue to lend ourselves to traditional stories—perhaps because we know that our lives are part of large, impersonal patterns, even if we no longer have faith in their providential design. We continue to see the coincidences of the plot as an analogue of such patterns, and accept the encounter between Oedipus and Laius as 'fated'—though we may attribute it to the unconscious rather than the divine. Freud's view that in the psyche nothing is accidental permits us to read narrative coincidence as an analogue of intrapsychic events and relationships—which, in turn, often have a direct bearing on occurrences in the real world. What is 'willed' by the unconscious has a way of happening, just as the will of the gods is done in myth. Othello is sure to meet his Iago and Hansel and Gretel the witch; story just takes the liberty of bringing about sooner rather than later an encounter it deems inevitable. As Dickens says:

> We shall meet those people who are coming to meet *us*, from many strange places and by many strange roads . . . and what it is set to them to do to us, will all be done.[30]

OUR VIEW OF THE SACRED IS CLOSE TO THE ARCHAIC

Those who continue to believe in traditional story may appear captive to superstition—to notions of God and fate they should have discarded. But after millennia of believing in a covenant between God and humankind—and, more recently, between God and the individual—our own sense of the sacred may be closer to those ancient myths in which the gods are utterly indifferent to us. *We* encounter the sacred in the form of impersonal patterns that do not 'mean' us and may not 'mean' anything. Heidegger describes the human condition as *Geworfenheit*, and Jung suggests that God is unconscious—that the forces that determine us do not know us. His answer to Einstein's "What interests me is whether God had any choice in the making of the universe" would be that an unconscious god *has* no choice. Jung nonetheless insists on the reality of the sacred and its central role in our lives:

> To this day God is the name by which I designate all things which cross my willful path violently and recklessly, all things which upset my subjective views, plans and intentions and change the course of my life for better or worse.[31]

He reconciles the religious and the scientific, to the discomfort of both. In his view, consciousness is the task that nature or the sacred has—unconsciously—imposed on us. We are in the strange position of knowing, or studying, the forces that determine us, though *they* know neither us nor themselves. As Nietzsche says:

> We are the figures in the dream of a god who understand how he dreams.[32]

There is a significant coincidence here with quantum theory, which suggests that "through man nature observes itself"—a possibility classical physics could not envision.[33] It coincides, as well, with those stories in which the nonhuman forces of the plot are as unconscious as the central figures. Moby Dick and Ahab are *both* blind, and only we, who stand apart and cannot change the outcome, are knowing. Perhaps a sustained belief in traditional story is not, after all, rooted in superstition but in a willingness to countenance the sacred as it manifests in our time.

The Desacralization of Story

THE FORMALIST DECONSTRUCTION
OF NARRATIVE

While for the devout the sacred is a source of strength and security, nonbe-lievers have long perceived it as a depotentiation of humankind. This view is deeply embedded in rationalism and flourished during the Enlighten-ment. With the emergence of nineteenth-century Positivism, which dis-missed the fearful aspect of our existence, the sacred was widely identified as the enemy of progress and liberty—a bulwark of reaction. If humankind was to become truly entitled, it would have to discard its faith in the divine, the spiritual, "the wholly other." Bakunin says:

If God exists man is a slave. If man is free, God does not exist.[1]

Yet even in the heyday of nineteenth-century Positivism, traditional nar-rative continued to thrive, and not until our own century did critics suggest that the image of our helplessness purveyed by story is inimical to our emancipation. The Russian formalists were consequential materialists who, in an effort to make the study of literature into a rigorous Positivist science, initiated the process of demystifying and desacralizing narrative that has continued to be a central endeavor of criticism.[2] Though they did not say so explicitly, they seemed to sense that plot is the element in story that holds us captive.

The formalists broke with the aesthetic tradition in which the *events* are the heart of narrative and inform every other element. For them, plot is no longer synonymous with story and becomes, instead, the handiwork of an individual author.[3] The *events*—or *fabula*—are relegated to relative unim-

69

portance, and the central interest is deemed to lie in the *arrangement*—or *sjuzet*—that the storyteller makes of them. The plot thus ceases to stand for the sacred and is subject to human control. Though Tomashevsky continued to assign a measure of importance to the basic story, he distinguished between "bound" motifs—which are essential to the narrative and refer to a reality *outside* the text—and "free" motifs, which are inessential and do not refer to reality. In his view, only the free motifs are of real interest.[4] The center of story is thus displaced: it resides in the freedom of the author and no longer in the 'authority' of the known plot.

In the formalist enterprise of divorcing literature from reality, Shklovsky's concept of defamiliarization plays a critical role. Presenting the familiar in an unfamiliar way is, of course, central to art. The very process of 'rendering'—as in caricature, for example—defamiliarizes an object that we nonetheless recognize: we are surprised or struck anew by the known. But to Shklovsky, defamiliarization is primarily of interest because it suggests that art is not a rendering of life, but a play on previous aesthetic forms.[5] In his view, the storyteller's arrangement of the events inverts their chronological sequence in order to defamiliarize a *defunct narrative convention*. This neglects, though it does not altogether exclude, the possibility that defamiliarization springs from an artist's urgent need to carve closer to his own experience, which is often at painful variance with the aesthetic conventions of his time. Moreover, the conventions themselves may simply reflect that process of 'normalization,' or de-individualization, to which every society must subject individual experience in order to make communication and community possible.

LIMITATIONS OF THE FORMALIST VIEW

Though Shklovsky's views are a helpful commentary on the way Sophocles revitalized the Oedipus myth, the inversion of chronology in *Oedipus Rex* is surely more than a variation on an aesthetic convention. It seems aligned, as well, with a new experience or 'reality'—one which the myth, with its bird's-eye view of events, could not approximate. Centering the story on Oedipus may have reflected a new life situation—in which the individual, or hero, could no longer subscribe to a communal belief system but was obliged to stand alone. Perhaps *Oedipus Rex* unfolds in a nonchronological sequence because Oedipus—and by inference the spectator—is no longer able to accept an 'objective' and predictive view of his situation and must, instead, find his way through the action on his own—blindly, as it were, and taking nothing for granted.

The arrangement Sophocles made of the familiar events reflects an experience not unlike our own. We, too, are unwilling to accept predictive patterns. Like Oedipus in the play, we too tend to read reality backward: effects draw our attention before we begin looking into their causes, and our search for continuity—or story—often begins with a present situation or problem, which urges us back into the past, and then shuttles to and fro between past and present, like the search of Oedipus for the killer of Laius.

In his discussion of *Tristram Shandy*, Shklovsky makes much of the fact that Sterne "gives the results before . . . the causes."[6] But perhaps this reversal is not—as he suggests—just a literary device that plays off narrative conventions current at the time. It may also be a more accurate reflection of our perceptive and experiential processes than can be rendered in a straightforward, chronological account. Unlike the presentations of science, history, philosophy, and literary theory, our encounters with reality don't often take an orderly, sequential form, even though they are largely coded by convention. There are invariably inversions, gaps, and anomalies.

Shklovsky's suggestion that plot is an *arbitrarily* inverted, nonmimetic arrangement of events may be based on the assumption that our perception and experience are—or ought to be—rational and orderly. Yet story tends to focus on exactly those tragic or comic occurrences when we disrupt the rational, civilized order, violate communal structures, and act without thought or inhibition. An inverted, 'disorderly' narrative may, moreover, reflect not our actions but our ever-present if largely unconscious *impulses*, which we repress precisely because they *are* irrational and disruptive. Like the action in many stories, the unconscious can only be read backward, after we see its manifestations—after the damage is done. E. M. Forster tells of a woman who never knew what she thought until she heard what she said. The same is often true of our actions, though with graver consequences.

POSTMODERNISM MUST DIVORCE STORY FROM REALITY

Divorcing narrative from reality is central to the desacralization of story for, in aesthetics, "reality"—with its basis in *res*, "thing"—is the materialist term for what was once called "truth." If story, though it is of our making, can render the *effect* on us of an 'objective' reality or truth—if there *is* an unchanging, ahistorical, necessary, or essential component in the human situation, an awareness of which can be passed on from generation to generation—the sacred is reconstituted.

71

Traditionally, artists have believed in reality or truth, though they know it cannot be accurately rendered. They are Platonists; Schopenhauer calls the Platonic *idea* the "objective of art."[7] The events on the stage, page, or canvas are abstractions, a pale reflection of something we cannot know—but the *existence* of that 'something' was not until recently in doubt. The artwork can, of course, render only the subjective, psychological dimension of reality—or give visible expression to inner, invisible states. While we are not often in *physical* danger, hardly a day passes when we do not feel psychologically vulnerable, and so the physical adventures of Theseus or Charlie seem palpably real and immediate to us. Even circus jugglers and tightrope walkers could be said to give concrete expression to the pressure we are under to maintain our often precarious psychological balance.[8]

At first the formalists did not think of art as hermetically locked up in art, since, by making us *see* instead of merely "recognize," it serves a useful social function. But they soon came to insist that art is a wholly separate entity, one in no way derived from or contingent upon reality. In Shklovsky's formulation, "art is a way of experiencing the artfulness of an object: the object is not important"; and "the forms of art are explainable by the laws of art; they are not justified by their realism."[9]

The formalist enterprise of separating narrative from reality has been intensively carried forward by others. Saussure's linguistic theory, which suggests that there is no direct link between words and their referents in the real world, has been used—not always legitimately—to demonstrate the lack of connection between literature and reality.[10] Structuralism and semiotics provide evidence that reality does not determine our structures and language but is, instead, determined or defined *by* them; and poststructuralism asserts that there *is* no reality—only text.[11] Since everything is structured and coded by man, the one thing we can study with any hope of accuracy is language or the text itself: reality is a chimera, and all claims by story to render it are a delusion—one with grave consequences.

REALITY AS IDEOLOGY

Contemporary Marxist critics continue to *link* literature to reality, but define reality as an ideological construct that keeps the actual facts out of sight. In what may be the aesthetic equivalent of Marx standing Hegel "right side up," they identify what was once deemed the sacred source of story as the product of a political system intent on perpetuating itself. Consciously or unconsciously, the artist promotes the value system of his own time and society. All art is effectively *genre*, conditioned by a particular time and place—by history. Put more crudely, art is ideology, propaganda, a kind of party line. To achieve its objective, ideology must conceal itself by having its vehicle—story, for instance—appear as a mere medium for transmitting the 'truth.' Its hidden agenda is camouflaged by its apparent transparency: it claims to be nothing more than a means of giving us access to 'reality.' The critic must therefore unmask what we *deem* to be real by making the techniques for reporting it explicit or visible, so that the spectator will cease to be an unconscious captive of story's hidden agenda. We should note, however, that it has always been the *promise* of being story's captive that has drawn us to it.

Barthes, who often fuses Marxist, structuralist, and poststructuralist perspectives, identifies myth as an unconscious attempt to make what is culturally and historically conditioned appear natural, essential, and immutable:

> The end of myths is to immobilize the world; they must suggest and mimic a universal order that has fixated once and for all the hierarchy of possessions. . . . Myths are nothing but this ceaseless, untiring solicitation, this insidious and inflexible demand that all men recognize themselves in this image, eternal yet bearing a date, which was built of them one day as if for all time. For the Nature, in which they are locked up under the pretext of being eternalized, is nothing but a Usage. And it is this Usage, however lofty, that they must take in hand and transform.[12]

Barthes is addressing "bourgeois myths," but his strictures apply to ancient myths as well. In his view, myth—and by inference plot—is "on the right," a bulwark of the old order. Its preclusive form postulates human helplessness, or, as he puts it, "the irresponsibility of man."[13]

FEMINIST CRITICISM AND TRADITIONAL NARRATIVE

Feminist critics see traditional story as a tool of the patriarchy. Positivists like most of us, they are intent on demystifying narrative, so that it may serve to potentiate women instead of keeping them enslaved. Since so-called 'essential,' 'natural' or noncultural sexual differences have long been used to keep women subservient, feminists understandably cast doubt on 'objective,' ahistorical reality. In this spirit, a feminist critic defines narrative as:

> An ideological construct reflecting an epistemology based upon a linear logic, the assumption of a comprehensible, expressible, and exclusive "reality."[14]

While this is a valid description of Positivist narrative, it hardly defines traditional story, with its ambiguous, indeterminate meaning. *Gilgamesh, King Lear,* and *Woyzeck* are no linear constructs, nor do they assume "a comprehensible, expressible, and exclusive 'reality.' " Though socio-economic systems have promoted sexual differences and gender roles that clearly disadvantage women, plot would seem to disregard such distinctions. It grants no freedom or control to anyone: the male figure is no more capable of determining the outcome than the female. This may, of course, be interpreted as an insidious attempt to reconcile women, and all others without power, to their lot. But even if story, like religion, can obscure the fact that power and wealth are the preserve of a particular group or sex, its preclusive form is not necessarily an invalid rendering of the human condition.

The women's movement is concerned with creating options, and the plot of traditional story seems to offer none. The recognition by an audience that Oedipus and Lear—no less than Antigone and Phèdre—are victims, hardly serves the cause of the oppressed, for they are helpless in a larger existential context constituted by the plot. Only by invalidating this apparently timeless structure and making explicit its historical origin can the seemingly conservative thrust of story be blunted. A helpless hero or heroine will not potentiate the spectator. A victimized figure arouses our pity—for him or her, as well as ourselves—and so weakens our will to change and make changes. Feminists, like all who want art to potentiate us, are determined to invalidate the element in story that promotes "the irresponsibility of man"—its preclusive form or plot. Sensing the enforced passivity of the fictive figure, Laura Mulvey concludes that it is *"sadism"* that demands a story.[15] The plot is perceived as a symptom of a perverse and cruel patriarchal psychology, with no connection to any reality outside the system.

ART AS GAME

Those contemporary critics who are without explicit social and political commitments—or lack the hope of furthering them by aesthetic means—are no less determined to rid art of its sacred component. If fiction is a form obeying only its own rules, its claim to obeying and reporting the 'real' can be dismissed. "We have realized," says Barthes, "that art is a game;"[16] Nabokov describes his Cornell lectures as an attempt to reveal "the mechanism of these wonderful toys—literary masterpieces";[17] and Northrop Frye

74

speaks for many when he asserts that the storyteller is entirely in command of the story:

(Myth), like the folktale, is an abstract story-pattern. The characters can do what they like, which means what the storyteller likes: there is no need to be plausible or logical in motivation. The things that happen in myth are things that happen only in stories; they are in a self-contained literary world. Hence myth would naturally have the same kind of appeal for the fiction writer that folktales have. It presents him with a ready-made framework, hoary with antiquity, and allows him to devote all his energies to elaborating its design.[18]

The view of art as game finds support in that narrative game *par excellence*: the detective story. Here the author is unquestionably in charge of the plot, confirming a Positivist view of reality. A puzzling event that may, at first, appear as a manifestation of the incomprehensible or sacred, turns out to be the work of man—just like the plot itself. Hitchcock's work has been useful to contemporary theory, for *his* plots are explicit manipulations by an *auteur*-director, who even appears personally on screen, as if to remind us of his presence *behind* it. Since we are subject to nothing more than the manipulations of an author, we can enjoy the very sense of helplessness that is at issue in traditional story. Though Hitchcock may have been *compelled* to tell his stories, as far as the audience is concerned, he remains in charge and is applauded by critics for ringing changes on a narrative form that openly identifies itself as artifice. Of course he may have himself insisted on the artifice or unreality of his movies in order to be freer of the compulsions that *drove* him to make them.

BARTHES ON NARRATIVE

Though Barthes shifted from structuralism and semiotics to a poststructuralist position, he maintains a consistently skeptical view of traditional narratives and their authors. For him, myths—and by inference all stories—once read as a "factual system," are merely semiological ones.[19] Authors who claim to render reality have no freedom; they are effectively "dead," and only the author who recognizes that art is a game and "plays with signs as with a conscious decoy—whose fascination he savors and wants to make us savor and understand," is truly free.[20]

Up to a point, traditional storytellers would have shared Barthes's view of their situation. They did not see themselves as free agents;[21] they took the validity of story's preclusive form for granted and served it without question. Even in the heyday of nineteenth-century Positivism, when authors like Flaubert and Dostoevski were forced by their own doubt to *revalidate* story's ancient form for themselves, they often found that narrative 'decisions' were not subject to their will. Freedom was claimed only by those authors who were wholly imbued with Positivist principles.

Ironically, Barthes may himself be captive to an unacknowledged Positivism, which prompts him to salvage for the critic and reader the very freedom he denies the traditional author: "In the text, no one speaks but the reader."[22] Since there is no objective reality and therefore no central meaning, the reader is free to "structurate" the text, which he can enter at any point. The given structure or plot is irrelevant and may be disregarded. In other words, what *happens* in the story does not matter and has no authority. In Barthes's view, the classic 'realist' text has a severely limited range of meanings and is merely *lisible*, while a modern work like *Finnegan's Wake* affords us a multiplicity of options: it is *scriptible*.[23] As we have noted, however, the basic indeterminacy of myth and traditional story—the uncertain relationship of the human to the sacred, of the action to the plot—opens them to multiple and ever-shifting interpretations, and so effectively *makes* them *scriptible*. Since Barthes perceives the sacred or real to be an ideological construct that *immobilizes* us, he can hardly see it as a possible source of the reader's freedom. Positivism has little tolerance for a *non*playful ambiguity—which Marxists tend to identify with bourgeois ambivalence and equivocation. Yet it may well be the uncertain relationship between the human and the sacred, fiction and reality, text and unknowable truth, that leaves traditional narrative open to continuous reinterpretation, even if it holds out no promise of actual freedom.

Like all of us, Barthes wants to have his cake and eat it, too. The author is dead, but the critic is very much alive. Man is dead, long live man!

> Here I am, before the sea; it is true that it bears no message. But on the beach, what material for semiology! Flags, slogans, signals, signboards, clothes, suntan, even, which are so many messages to me.[24]

He may not have *wanted* to hear the "message" of the sea, since it might cast his blend of Positivism and humanism—his insistence on human freedom—into grave doubt. Meanwhile, the sea continues to convey meaning to most of us.

Three years before his death, Barthes acknowledged both the 'real' and the author's inevitable belief in it:

> From ancient times to the effort of our avant-garde, literature has been concerned to represent something. What? I will put it crudely: the real. The real

is not representable, and it is because men ceaselessly try to represent it by words that there is a history of literature. That the real is not representable, but only demonstrable, can be said in several ways: either we can define it, with Lacan, as the *impossible*, that which is unattainable and escapes discourse, or in topological terms we observe that a pluri-dimensional order (the real) cannot be made to coincide with a uni-dimensional order (language). Now, it is precisely this topological impossibility that literature rejects and to which it never submits.[25]

With good reason. For the paradoxical and ambiguous structure of narrative *approximates* our "pluri-dimensional" reality.

ALL ART IS INTERTEXTUAL

The assumption that story can reflect only the manmade is a predicate of contemporary criticism. All those who do not share it—which, by virtue of their calling, includes a great many storytellers—are deemed not truly aware of what they are doing. In contemporary theory, art begets art and literature is entirely intertextual. As Robert Scholes puts it:

> The artist writes and paints not from nature but from his or her predecessors' way of textualizing nature.[26]

Woelfflin's statement that "a great picture owes more to other pictures than to the painter's observation of nature" has been carried to extremes.[27]

In its insistence on intertextuality, postmodern theory creates a system of interlocking mirrors that nothing from 'outside' can penetrate. What we commonly think of as our 'actual' experience cannot assert itself, for there *is* no individual and, in this sense, no experience. Thus one way in which 'reality' or the sacred has survived into our era is eliminated.

A totalizing intertextuality may be the source of Bloom's anxiety of influence. In his view, individual talent has, since the late Renaissance, been bound to the work of a predecessor and struggled, often with limited success, to assert the validity of its own identity.[28] Bloom confines himself to poetry, and one wonders why painters—no less bound to the past than poets and just as obliged to break with their progenitors by changes in the world around us, as well as by our continually shifting and shrinking sense of ourselves—have had enough confidence to shoulder the burden of influence without feeling overwhelmed or "belated." Toulouse-Lautrec's relationship to Degas was marked by the deepest respect and so, no doubt, contained an element of anxiety. Yet Degas was clearly the *good* father, who made possible Lautrec's existence by enabling his work. It was he who asked to be introduced to the young painter at his first show and said to him: "I am glad to see you are one of us."[29] The artist must assert himself against his progenitors, but works to be accepted into their company—a spiritual community that makes up for his own isolation:

> And I may dine at journey's end
> With Landor and with Donne.[30]

His precursors are ancestry, family. They may make him anxious, but they also save his life. When Vlaminck said: *J'aime Van Gogh plus que mon père,* it was surely because Van Gogh made it possible for him to *be.*[31]

The modern tradition enabled the artist to discover and assert the validity of his own as yet nameless experience. It fostered individual talent. Semiotics to the contrary, it held that not all experience is coded or integrated into an existing structure, and that in art, as in science, "discovery commences with the awareness of anomaly."[32] On this critical point, artists themselves seem to recognize no sharp dividing line between modernism and postmodernism. For Warhol no less than Lautrec, experience is out of phase with the code. We are subject to continuous change and those who live on the edge of the uncoded can demonstrate their existence by conducting raids on the inarticulate—the 'real' or "impossible" in its contemporary manifestation. Warhol's violation of traditional aesthetics renders his own, anomalous experience and establishes his identity. His very 'nothing' becomes a something, at least for fifteen minutes and possibly for longer.

POSTMODERN THEORY IS ANTINARRATIVE

In its valid and necessary drive to change society by casting doubt on essence and reality, we can hardly expect contemporary critical theory to include its own opposite—traditional story, with its burden of the essential and necessary. Postmodern thought is inherently antinarrative.[33] Despite its strong objection to every form of totalization, it *fuses* art and the 'real'— either by reducing 'reality' to text or by reading both art and 'reality' as a form of ideology. This may, in part, spring from an ancient need to reestablish the human realm as *whole,* for when either the human or the sacred—the text or the 'real' beyond it—are denied, a painful burden of our existence—traditionally at once *apart from* and *part of* the whole—is lifted from us. Yet it is the very tension and dialogue between the text and the 'real,' the human and the sacred, culture and nature, the individual and the group, that make society possible—even if the sacred or 'real' has often been used to exploit us, and even if it must, like the self, remain a forever unprovable assumption. Traditionally, the dualities were deemed to be the foundation of our existence. As Borges says:

The world, alas, is real, and I, alas, am Borges.[34]

In his view, we cannot be whole. Our duality is essential to us and certain to last as long as we do.

MARX AND FREUD AS REALISTS AND ESSENTIALISTS

Marx and Freud, whose work and methodology are basic to contemporary criticism, deemed themselves realists and essentialists. While they agreed that the truth, or reality, is heavily camouflaged, both were convinced they had uncovered it. For Marx, the ultimate reality was economic, for Freud instinct and the unconscious. Though Marx stressed change and Freud the unchanging, both saw their work as resting on foundations that were objectively true. Freud says: "We possess the truth. I am sure of it,"[35] and the realist component in his aesthetic is clearly borne out by his theory of wit and joking. Our laughter erupts from an unexpected link between the joke—or text—and *objective* psychic components that have been repressed;[36] we laugh when a surprising connection is made between the conscious and the unconscious—which Freud described in terms we could call Platonist:

The unconscious is the true psychical reality; in its innermost nature it is as much unknown to us as the reality of the external world, and it is as incompletely represented by the data of consciousness as is the external world by the communications of our sense organs.[37]

The positions of Marx and Freud are akin to that of traditional story. For Marx, history is the inexorable plot, which unfolds without regard for those who enact it. Base and superstructure are equivalents of plot and action: the base determines the superstructure just as the plot determines the action.[38] In Freud, the plot is constituted by instinct, or drive, and the action by civilization and consciousness. Here, as in story, the plot determines the action, and we—like Oedipus—are free only to the extent that we can sometimes choose consciousness over remaining unconscious.

Neither Marx nor Freud believed in human freedom. According to Marx, history and change are not subject to our control, even if they can be accelerated by a philosophy or theory that makes for greater awareness among the masses. As Engels says:

> The historical event . . . may . . . itself be viewed as the product of a process that works as a whole unconsciously and without volition.[39]

He writes in a letter to Bloch that "what each individual wills is obstructed by everyone else, and what emerges is something that noone willed."[40] This is story's perception also. As A. S. Cook says of Balzac's fiction:

> The force of each will is deflected by all the other wills, and the deflection, unperceived by the characters, is the "comedy" of La Comédie Humaine.[41]

It is of course no accident that Freud's foundation theory is attached to that Greek myth which most clearly denies human freedom. His dictum "We do not live, but are lived" might well have been phrased by Marx as "We do not act, but are acted."

THE ESSENTIALISM OF LÉVI-STRAUSS

The structuralism of Lévi-Strauss leaves no greater room for free will:

> Starting from ethnographic experience, I have always aimed at drawing up an inventory of mental patterns, to reduce apparently arbitrary data to some kind of order, and to attain a level at which a kind of necessity becomes apparent, underlying the illusion of liberty.[42]

As langue speaks parole and plot action so myths speak men, not men myths:

> I therefore claim to show not how men think in myths but how myths operate in men's minds without their being aware of it.[43]

Lévi-Strauss calls Sartre's existentialism, with its assertion of a heroic human role and its differentiation between actor and agent, a defense of humanism and "the last embodiment of metaphysics in the grand style."[44] In structuralism, as in story, actor is agent.

Like Marx and Freud, Lévi-Strauss is resolutely unsympathetic to the sacred and our need for it. In his studies of primitive communities, he finds little evidence of the dread or "primal numinous awe" that Rudolf Otto calls the source of religious feeling.[45] Instead, he attributes to them the pragmatic, rationalist approach that is his own. But despite his belief that "the poverty of religious thought can never be underestimated,"[46] his work is resolutely essentialist—a "quest for the invariant, or for the invariant element among superficial differences."[47]

It is this essentialist premise that deconstruction means to undermine, for the sacred is reconstituted wherever there is the assumption of an invariant—whether it be Lévi-Strauss's "order of orders," his binary structure of the mind, Marx's view of economics and of man's social being, or Freud's unconscious. Even the Marxist view of history as continuous change could be said to reconstitute the sacred as a basic force that keeps changing its appearance. Seen from sufficient distance, Marx, Freud, and Lévi-Strauss are in the tradition of 'religious' or Platonist thinkers, who claim to have discovered, under the superstructure of appearances, an all-determining reality. Even Nietzsche—who wonders whether "all our so-called consciousness" isn't "a more or less fantastic commentary on an unknown, perhaps unknowable, but felt text"—implies the existence of a reality independent of *our* text.[48]

For Durkheim—as for Marx and Lévi-Strauss—the community is the basis and essence of human existence. But though he does not believe in the objective reality of the sacred, he, like Feuerbach, sees it as a necessary predicate of all social structure. It alone can guarantee our relationships to each other and so make society possible. We need an order beyond our own to infuse our structures with authority and meaning, and since no such order exists, we must invent it. Man creates God, not God man; the community does not serve to mediate our relationship to the sacred, but the sacred is called into being to sacralize the community. In earlier times, the divine or natural was powerfully present to us and could thus serve as the force that gave coherence to our existence. But we, who have mastered nature and isolated ourselves from physical necessity, must endow man-made constructs like the law with attributes of the sacred. As Hegel says:

> It is absolutely essential that the constitution *should not be regarded as something made*, even though it has come into being in time. It must be treated rather as something simply existent in and by itself, as divine therefore and constant, and so exalted above the sphere of things that are made.[49]

It is surely no accident that in the United States courts of law, like the government buildings of the Third Reich, borrowed their architecture from sacred buildings of antiquity.

81

THE REALIST AND ESSENTIALIST POSITION
OF MOST SCIENCE

The concept of an objective and essential reality, independent of our own existence, has been as critical to science as it is to society and its institutions. Classical science assumed that its signs stood for real forces or "facts." Newton claims to have *discovered* gravity; it never occurred to him that he might have "created" or invented it. In the seventeenth century, most scientists saw no conflict between their work and the existence of God. As Robert Boyle says:

> Whatever God himself has been pleased to think worthy of making, its fellow creature Man should not think unworthy of knowing.[50]

While eighteenth- and nineteenth-century science substituted physical forces and nature for the realm of God, it continued to see itself as nature's subject. So Thomas Huxley could say:

> Science seems to me to teach us in the highest and strongest manner the great truth which is embodied in the Christian conception of entire surrender to the will of God.

Today quantum theory, and specifically the Copenhagen interpretation, have undermined the realist stance of classical physics in the atomic range. Yet most science could not proceed without assuming a realist position:

> Every scientist who does research work feels that he is looking for something that is objectively true. His statements are not meant to depend upon the conditions under which they can be verified. Especially in physics the fact that we can explain nature by simple mathematical laws tells us that here we have met some genuine feature of reality, not something that we have—in any meaning of the word—invented ourselves. This is the situation which Einstein had in mind when he took dogmatic realism as the basis for natural science.[51]

Einstein's adherence to "naive" or "dogmatic realism" is well-known:

> I cannot prove that scientific truth must be conceived as a truth that is valid independent of reality, but I believe it firmly. I believe, for instance, that the Pythagorean theorem in geometry states something that is approximately true, independent of the existence of man. . . . Our natural point of view in regard to the existence of truth apart from humanity cannot be explained or proved. But it is a belief which nobody can lack—not primitive beings even. We

82

attribute to truth superhuman objectivity; it is indispensable for us, this reality which is independent of our existence and our experience and our mind—though we cannot say what it means.[52]

Einstein's objections to quantum theory have continued to be the subject of intense debate among physicists. Bohr and others thought they had answered them conclusively decades ago, but, in recent years, there have been renewed efforts to establish quantum mechanics within a realist and largely deterministic context. While some, like the mathematician John von Neumann, argue that "quantum mechanical systems are inherently probabilistic and cannot be embedded in deterministic systems," the issue appears to remain open.[53] As Arthur Burks says:

While the non-deterministic character of current quantum theory is a strong argument against determinism, it is not at present decisive.[54]

Like our lives, the work of most scientists continues to be predicated on realist—though not necessarily determinist—assumptions. Even quantum theory can be interpreted realistically:

Some draw the conclusion from (quantum mechanics) that "the universe does not exist 'out there' independent of all acts of observation," and that reality is created by the observer. But that view is not shared by the overwhelming majority of physicists.

The standard ontology of (quantum mechanics) is a realist position. It accepts a qualitative difference between the quantum world and the classical world. The world of electrons, protons, and all the rest does exist out there even if we do not observe it, and it behaves exactly as QM tells us it does. . . . The quantum world (is) no less real than the classical world.

The change brought about in the physical system due to the interaction with the measuring apparatus should not be interpreted to mean that "reality is *created* by the measurement." Just as two dice are real before they hit the table, and not only after they show snake eyes, so does a quantum mechanical system exist in a real state (specified by a wave function) before the interaction with the apparatus sets in. Reality is not created by the observation. The system is present all the time.[55]

In the view of physicists who take a realist position—no longer, today, a minority—quantum theory accepts energy or universal matter as an objective reality, even if the same entity "appear(s) both as matter and as force," as particle stream and wave.[56] We may not know with certainty what is outside the cave, but there *is* something outside it. Moreover, quantum measurements can, in the aggregate, be predicted with an accuracy that approaches certainty, and "it is only the outcome of any one such measurement . . . that cannot be predicted."[57] Bohr's own correspondence principle posits that "where large numbers of quanta are involved, quantum laws lead to classical laws as statistical averages."[58] While Einstein's confidence that whenever we encounter uncertainty we have simply failed to penetrate to the truth has had to give way to the realization that in the atomic realm there are elements of the causeless and unpredictable, they are not only in the mind of the observer but an aspect of reality.[59]

THE REALIST POSITION OF TRADITIONAL STORY

Like quantum theory, traditional story acknowledges that we cannot observe the 'real' accurately or directly. Plot is a record or metaphor of our uncertain, unpredictable relationship to the sacred or 'real,' which may—or may not—indicate an unpredictable, acausal element in the sacred itself. Plot renders the one thing about the sacred we know with certainty: its unknowability. Stories, like most physicists, take a realist position. They acknowledge that what is 'out there' cannot be known, but their very form commits them to its existence.

"DEATH IS THE SANCTION OF EVERYTHING THE STORYTELLER CAN TELL"

In life, the most immediate evidence we have for the 'real' or sacred is death, which constitutes our most persuasive encounter with necessity. Death limits and therefore determines us—a word derived from *terminus*, "boundary, limit." Though we don't generally know how or when it will occur, it can be foretold with certitude. Alone among creatures, we know we must die, and this knowledge could be said to govern us. If the propagation and survival of the species is biologically programmed into all creatures, the awareness of our mortality—which dawns in early childhood—must play a central role in establishing our priorities. Death gives meaning and order to the life of the individual and to the community. It is a predicate of our existence that links the thinking of common folk to the investigations of philosophers, and informs our shared understanding of the human condition. It sanctions story as it does relationships and morality, and may indeed constitute a link—at the deepest level—between ethics and aesthetics.

Though the evidence of death is all around us, the positivist in us tends to turn away from it, unless we are actively engaged in trying to 'defeat' it. Even those who see themselves and their death as part of a larger continuum are apt to be fearful of it. Since life's design has it that we should think of our bodies as our own, we render them up with the greatest reluctance. Our fear of death, which is both exacerbated and assuaged by consciousness, is an inevitable consequence of our will to live. Though we know that in the larger context our death is a minor matter, our entire being strains against it.[60]

In the face of death, humankind has for millennia turned to the sacred, and the altar has ever been found near the grave. As Edward Edinger says:

> The earliest forms of religious expression . . . seem to be associated with burial rites. The outstanding example of death as the genesis of religion and consciousness is the elaborate mortuary symbolism of ancient Egypt.[61]

Even for those without religious faith, death constellates necessity and human helplessness. "In our dreams," says Marie-Louise von Franz, "death and . . . God's image are *de facto* indistinguishable."[62] In her relationship to death, Emily Dickinson reencounters God. It constitutes an essential, objective reality that confronts us with the limits of our power. However fully we may be engaged in living, we never altogether forget that our survival depends on the tiniest blood vessel in our brain. As Yeats says: "At stroke of midnight, God shall win."[63] But while the knowledge of our mortality makes us fearful, it can also induce the concern and tenderness—not just for those close to us, but for all others—that are a distinguishing mark of our species. Mortality makes us alike: it makes us kin and can make us kind.

Death is at once certain and unknown. We may feel confident that when we're dead we're dead, but we have no conclusive evidence. We assume that we are closer to the truth than earlier ages, but death, like the sacred, remains beyond our knowledge. While those who say there is nothing to know or think about may be correct, they are begging a question that will continue to haunt us, since we shall never answer it with finality.

Just as death limits and governs our existence, so it governs traditional story. We know how the story—like our lives—will end, but not, generally, how the figures will get there. Death is, indeed, the source of story's authority, "the sanction of everything the storyteller can tell."[64] In myth and tragedy, death is present on stage, while in *The Decameron* and *The Arabian Nights* it waits in the wings. "Pull up your chair to the edge of the precipice," says Fitzgerald, "and I'll tell you a story." The limitations that death or biological time imposes on individuals, communities and the species itself are intrinsic to story. All narrative is time-factored, though it both renders *and* stops time—invokes death and, like Sheherezade, keeps it at bay in the telling.

THE SAFE ARENA

Traditional art reflects human reality but is clearly separate from it. In the safe arena of story, we can afford to face our vulnerability and helplessness; it offers us a nonparalyzing look into the abyss and serves to remind us of the essential facts which, though they govern our existence, must be kept well out of sight. We cannot *live* in the presence of the gods. 'Light' fiction entertains precisely because it keeps at bay the existential issues that might turn us to stone; it obeys no rules except its own, and gives pleasure because it allows us to dismiss the plot as a confection that in no way renders the impact of outside agencies on our lives. But traditional story *invokes* the 'real,' the unpredictable, the terrifying, and so—like ritual—must be confined to a clearly circumscribed arena:

> The work of art still has something in common with enchantment: it posits its own, self-enclosed area, which is withdrawn from the context of profane existence, and in which special laws apply. Just as in the ceremony the magician first of all marked out the limits of the area where the sacred powers were to come into play, so every work of art describes its own circumference which closes it off from actuality.[65]

The frame that encloses the story, play or painting not only defines the area within which the simulated event can become 'real' or credible, but *quarantines the sacred* or unconscious 'powers' it has invoked, lest they invade and destroy the participants.[66] A confusion of realms is dangerous not only to the spectator but—especially—to artists, since they often authenticate their work by becoming, however briefly, the thing they render. The history of our time is studded with those who—in a compelled attempt to give their work actuality—blurred the line that separates art from reality and suffered death or madness.

Because art is quarantined within a frame, we can submit or lend ourselves to it—willing to be surprised, shocked, overwhelmed, passive, defenseless, and depotentiated.[67] In the theater, we surrender even the freedom to choose what we see and hear: we can neither stop the performance nor easily walk away from it. But though we *can* put down the novel and move from painting to painting, all art involves a voluntary loss of control.[68] Knowing we are safe, we consciously render up a part of our consciousness. Even the joke, as Freud points out, is a temporary defeat of the ego, both for the figure we laugh at and ourselves;[69] we can neither command nor repress our response. Laughter, as Girard says, is a loss of autonomy: it shakes us.[70]

For Freud, art—like the dream—is in part wish-fulfillment. It constitutes a separate realm, though one contingent upon reality. In his view, story is an arena in which we are briefly liberated from adult responsibility and awareness, from separation and guilt; in our identification with a figure who is neither free nor responsible, we are ourselves returned to a state of innocence and connectedness that resembles childhood.[71] For Jung, however, art is akin to ritual and—like the dream in *his* psychology—stands in a compensatory rather than wish-fulfilling relationship to life. It reflects reality inversely and stresses what we neglect or repress. It serves, as well, as a safe point of contact between the human and the sacred, and gives us access to the energies of the unconscious without exposing us to a direct encounter with the "living god."[72] Although the views of Freud and Jung seem mutually exclusive, with respect to narrative they may well be complementary.

STORY FREES US OF GUILT

We noted that the preclusive plot lifts the burden of responsibility from all of the figures. Even stories that appear to *accuse* equivocate: Cain, like Oedipus, is protected against human retribution by divine edict. His guilt is directly linked to our own, for when Yahweh endowed us with consciousness, he made it impossible for us to accept life as given—to sit in a room doing nothing. Like Cain, we must violate the creation by trying to change our situation. Schopenhauer's view of tragic guilt holds true for all traditional narratives:

> The true meaning of tragedy is the deeper insight that the hero atones not for his own particular sins but for the . . . very crime of being.[73]

Aristotle's *hamartia* makes sense only if we see it as an *unavoidable* mistake, akin to original sin. A figure whose every move is compelled is clearly not free to make a mistake. Napoleon was right to speak of the "fatality which makes a criminal of Oedipus without his being guilty."[74]

Hegel says there is no evil in Greek tragedy.[75] But there is no evil—in the sense of a freely willed rather than compelled action—in *any* story. The preclusive form absolves everyone. Though our attention is focused on the individual figure, there is finally no difference between the individual and his context, between figure and ground. By virtue of its preclusive form, a story set in Auschwitz would make even the SS helpless—despite the seemingly absolute power they exercised over their prisoners. Understandably, an aesthetic that subordinates the relationship between master and slave, between sadist and victim, to an unspecified 'force' holding both captive, is regarded with the utmost suspicion. It will almost inevitably appear to be an instrument of repression.

STORY AND RITUAL

Oedipus and Othello believe they are at least in part responsible for their own fate, for no society can survive unless its members think they have a measure of freedom and control, and are therefore accountable for what they do. But freedom and responsibility—predicated as they are on our separate existence—set us apart from others, and so contribute to the fragmentation of the very community they are meant to preserve. Story *allays* our sense of isolation by fusing us into an undifferentiated group. In our identification with a tragic hero who is neither free nor responsible, we too lose our freedom—and with it our sense of separateness. By laughing together at the comic figure, we acknowledge that his failings and limitations are ours also; we shed our differences, and become alike. A view of story as an integrative force may help to explain its omnipresence in our society, for the more persuaded we are of our freedom, the greater our isolation, the deeper our sense of guilt and anxiety, and the more urgent our need to be absolved of the 'sin' of separateness. In story, as in ritual, we atone for existing or standing out; we become *"at one."*

In Girard's view, tragedy liberates us from the impulse to strike back at those who have injured us, an impulse society must inhibit if it is to survive.[76] Tragedy purges the community of vengeful violence by carrying out a symbolic revenge not only against the villain but against the hero, who becomes a sacrificial victim or *pharmakos*. Once we recognize or sense his utter helplessness—which is, of course, our own as well—we briefly cease to discriminate, judge, and assign responsibility or blame. Significantly, we forgive not only others but ourselves. Like ritual, story releases us from the often harsh judgement we must level at our own actions and reactions in order to remain good citizens, husbands, wives, and parents. By freeing us of freedom and confronting us with our helplessness, it permits us to abandon the vigilance urged upon us by our presumed liberty. In purging us of guilt and difference and by releasing us from vindictive anger, it makes us whole and joins us to the group.

The connection between story, or myth, and ritual has long been noted and debated.[77] Ritual too constitutes a safe arena in which we can encounter the sacred or 'real,' acknowledge our helplessness and limitations, abandon our weapons and defenses, surrender control, forgive others, and be ourselves forgiven. Both ritual and plot conjugate the particular to the universal. Moreover, in ritual as in comedy and tragedy it is largely our fear, weakness, and failure—the very secrets that keep us apart in daily life—that bring us together. Thus art and ritual both compensate for positions and attitudes we are obliged to take as conscious, responsible members of the community. Stories are linked as well to rites of passage, for the central figures are often loners: they exist in a liminal state and the narrative "holds" them by connecting them to a larger, sacred whole: they may not be part of the community but they are an integral part of the plot.

SEPARATING ART FROM RITUAL

In order to invalidate the sacred while preserving the value of the artwork, which serves as the critic's subject and livelihood, criticism has had to sever the ancient link between art and ritual. Since ritual, like the gods and myth, appears to be "on the right,"[78] components of the aesthetic experience that invoke it—the submission of the spectator to the work, empathy, identification, catharsis, and the suspension of disbelief—must be declared invalid. Though Benjamin's aesthetic is happily inconsistent, his statement on the need to free art of its "aura" of metaphysics is frequently cited:

> For the first time in world history, mechanical reproduction emancipates the work of art from its parasitical dependence on ritual. . . . Instead of ritual it begins to be based on another practice: politics.[79]

Contemporary critical theory rejects the concept of art as a separate, safe arena. Literature, says Barthes emphatically, "*is no longer protected.*"[80] The dualism that permitted the coexistence of the sacred and profane, deeming both real, has been discredited.[81] Everything is profane or, some would say, political. A kind of absolutism rules, inspired by reason. Reality can no longer accommodate both subject and object, but is totalized as one or the other.

The need to eliminate dualism has made it difficult for many critics to conceive of art and ritual as *partial* truth—as *also* true. Yet most of us continue to see them from a traditional perspective—as at once reflecting reality *and* separate from it. We know we cannot translate the truth of story into daily life without grave risk, just as we have always known that if life is to go on we cannot follow the radical example of the saints. But while we don't often obey the precept of turning the other cheek and cannot love our neighbor as we do ourselves, we recognize them as truths that complement or compensate for the baser inclinations that must, perforce, govern much of our conduct.

Perhaps only the rationalist, convinced that we can attain a perfect or totalized understanding of reality, is threatened by traditional story. Postmodern theory claims to oppose totalization and stresses contradiction and undecidedness, yet is unwilling to entertain the duality of text *and* reality. Though deconstruction is often charged with endorsing irrationality, it is committed to reason and, with respect to the 'real,' obeys the precept of classical logic that:

> Either the statement or the negation of the statement must be correct. *"Tertium non datur,"* a third possibility does not exist.[82]

Perhaps, as we noted, postmodern theory cannot accommodate the 'real' because it threatens to reconstitute the sacred. Most of us, however, haven't the intellectual rigor to be consistent rationalists. We accept the contradictions of our existence by ignoring them. For us, traditional story—though it is not *the* truth—is *also* true. It neither interferes with nor directly influences our lives, but acts to compensate or balance them out. Here, as elsewhere, we see no need to face an 'either/or.' We accept the 'either' *and* 'or' implicit in the contradictions of story, as we accept them in the community and in ourselves.

Story and Consciousness

STORY NEGATES *AND* AFFIRMS THE INDIVIDUAL

Worringer calls form or design in art the negation of the individual.[1] Plot is clearly such a design. It denies that any of us are special cases. And yet the action in story centers on the very figure the plot invalidates, and it is the action, not the plot, that holds our attention. Even epics like *Gilgamesh* and the *Odyssey* are focused on an individual, whose singular adventures define the parameter of the narrative. Though the figures in mythology and the Old Testament are placed in a large context, some are of far greater interest to the storyteller than others. The New Testament renders the life of Jesus as altogether distinct from all who came before Him; He is unique. In Greek and Shakespearean tragedy only the central figure really concerns us: Ophelia's death is but a moment along the way, and significant only because it affects Hamlet. But once the hero himself dies, there is nothing more to tell. We may know that the tragic hero *isn't* unique and that what happens to him could happen to anyone, but he nonetheless becomes special to us, and his death, by ending the story, confirms his singularity.[2] The plot itself is reported substantially as it impinges on him, though its indifference to his fate is in no way mitigated. Reinhardt's comment that "tragedy delights in affirming the very person . . . it negates" is true for most traditional narratives.[3]

Ritual has no hero and is deeply conservative: it urges immersion, acceptance, and reconciliation. But story is centered on an isolated, often rebellious figure, who cannot remain passive or 'obedient.' The plot demands that he *countermand* the plot. Though the central figures in religious legends and fairy tales accept what happens without complaining, most stories avoid situations that engender a sense of utter helplessness and impotence. Neither Greek nor Renaissance tragedy renders those events we call 'tragic' in daily life: a child's death, a fatal accident, or natural disasters. Almost no one dies of illness, though it was surely a more common cause of death than warfare, murder, suicide, or an encounter with dragons. Even Lear is endowed with robust good health. He may go mad, but he doesn't get sick. Few heroes die a 'natural' and therefore inevitable death, and illness, significantly, did not become a central element in story until the advent of modern medicine gave us an effective means of fighting it. Myth and story may, as Barthes suggests, "immobilize" man, but they place considerable emphasis on human action:

> The meaning of the *Oedipus* is not to be seen in the unalterability of the hero's past once uncovered, but rather in (his) struggle to defend against great threat . . . the apparent or "seeming" order of his life. Such a struggle is imposed by the hero's very humanity.[4]

We might amend this to say that the meaning of the play resides both in the "unalterability" of the plot *and* in the hero's struggle against it.

WE ARE OBLIGED TO OPPOSE THE GODS

Our humanity is inextricably rooted in a rebellion against the gods or nature. We have evolved an order that is separate from and set against theirs, and cannot live by their 'rules.' However reluctant we may be to admit it, the sacred or natural has always been in some sense our 'enemy,' and the human community is engaged in a continuous, often unconscious process of desacralization. We must oppose, transform or repress nature not only around us but—more critically—within ourselves. Our violation of the sacred is a necessary transgression. In Greek mythology, mortals often offend the gods by what they *are*, not just by what they do. They cannot help giving offense; their very being is the source of trouble. Original sin is "the crime of existence itself."[5]

In *Genesis*, the story of humankind begins with the violation of a divine prohibition. Like every story, it has its inception in a wrongdoing. Without transgression, or—in religious narrative—the *possibility* of one, there *is* no story. Melody, says Schopenhauer, is always a departure from the *Grundton*, the basic tone or harmony,[6] just as drama began when the first actor separated from the chorus.[7] In myth and complex narratives, the hero himself is often the 'evil-doer,' marking the fact that all human action, however well-intentioned, is a violation.

92

The Greek God-fighter or *theomachos* must—like Siegfried in Norse mythology—kill an aspect of the sacred on behalf of the community, and pay with his life. The monsters that Perseus and Oedipus slay are creatures of a sacred order—embodiments of its destructive element, which cannot be tamed or domesticated. Since they are immortal, they must be killed over and over, in myth after myth. Only if the primal energy in us were exhausted would they become extinct—along with us.

Since the Renaissance, most narratives have embodied the destructive element of the sacred in human rather than bestial form. Yet the pattern remains the same: evil must be vanquished in story after story and, since it is part of the sacred, a price must be paid. In traditional story, only the comic hero—who outwits rather than confronts the monster or villain— survives without a scratch. However, once the Enlightenment and Positivism *dismissed* the sacred, the hero could kill the villain and live happily ever after. When evil is no longer deemed integral to the creation or nature— and so to *us*—he who destroys it need suffer no harm.

HUMAN IDENTITY DERIVES FROM OUR REBELLION AGAINST THE SACRED

The hero of myth and tragedy violates divine command *on* divine command. God is on both sides. The struggle of the action against the plot is mandated by the plot. In traditional aesthetics, this illuminates an essential aspect of our existence: *because* the hero tries to assert his will, we discover the limitations of the will. Necessity is clearly revealed to us by his struggle against it:

> Only by overstepping the limits of civilization and suffering the consequences can the hero fulfill his role in the cosmic order. His task is the paradoxical one of enacting the necessity of that order by negating it.[8]

The hero's challenge to the gods reveals the sacred *and* establishes our identity. Perhaps the human can only prove or define itself in an interface with necessity. Durkheim suggests that communities and individuals establish themselves by what they are *not*, by the deviant other—by difference.[9] In just this way, we may need the sacred to define the human and once we dismiss it, we, too, are apt to lose our identity. Humankind and the sacred are interdependent.[10] Hegel says that God without man is no more than man without God.[11] Or, as Jung puts it:

93

The destruction of the god-image is followed by the annulment of the human personality.[12]

CONSCIOUSNESS IS NOT FREELY CHOSEN

Our separation from nature, engendered by and embodied in consciousness, is itself an expression of nature's 'will.' It is a given of our situation and integral to human evolution. Hegel says that consciousness is an internal necessity.[13] For him, as Marx observes critically, the *essence* of man is self-awareness.[14] Freud calls it a "a fact without parallel, which defies all explanation or description,"[15] and Neumann perceives it as "veritable instinct compelling man in this direction."[16] In our first story, Adam and Eve do not *ask* to choose between good and evil; it is clearly Yahweh's idea. They are *obliged* to become conscious, to discriminate between the permitted and the forbidden, to recognize the difference between male and female—to cease being 'one' with each other and the creation. As Nietzsche says:

> It was God himself who, at the end of the great work, coiled up in the form of a serpent at the foot of the tree of knowledge.[17]

MASCULINE AND FEMININE CONSCIOUSNESS

According to *Genesis*, human existence has its origin in a prohibition, a 'shalt not' that established differences where there had been none. And indeed, consciousness—at least in the West—is both derived from and largely focused on difference:

> The motto of all consciousness is *determinatio est negatio*. As against the tendency of the unconscious to combine and melt down . . . consciousness strikes back with the reply "I am not that."[18]

We must, however, add that difference is the element stressed most emphatically in *masculine* consciousness. Mead, Dinnerstein, Chodorow, and others have pointed out that feminine identity and consciousness are largely focused on relationship and connection.[19] In most societies, young children are raised by their mothers:

> A boy, in his attempt to gain an elusive masculine identification, often comes to define this masculinity largely in negative terms, as that which is not femi-

94

nine or involved with women. . . . Internally, the boy tries to reject his mother and deny his attachment to her and the strong dependence upon her that he still feels. He also tries to deny the deep personal identification with her that has developed during the early years. He does this by repressing whatever he takes to be feminine inside himself, and . . . by denigrating and devaluing whatever he considers to be feminine in the outside world.[20]

A girl's development, unlike the boy's, stresses relationship and likeness:

> Femininity and female role activities are immediately apprehensible in the world of her daily life. Her final role identification is with her mother and women . . . with the person or people with whom she also has her earliest relationship of infantile dependence. The development of her gender identity does not involve a rejection of this early identification. . . . Because her mother is around, and she has had a genuine relationship to her as a person, a girl's gender and gender role identification . . . depend on real affective relations.[21]

A number of studies have demonstrated that, as a result, women have "more flexible ego boundaries" or "less insistent self-other distinctions." But even feminine consciousness is, of course, partly derived from difference, just as masculine consciousness serves to connect and relate—albeit on an abstract or object-centered rather than interpersonal level. Men have historically had to perform more specialized tasks, which require their separation from others, nature, and themselves. Today, these gender roles—which have contributed to the association of women with nature and the unconscious,[22] and have often led to their murderous repression—are no longer warranted, and we are beginning to see changes in the consciousness of both sexes.

STORY EMBODIES MASCULINE *AND* FEMININE CONSCIOUSNESS

Perhaps one reason why tasks involving specialization and difference have been accorded greater importance is that 'importance,' or fame and honors, compensate the striving individual for the psychological danger of being isolated from the community. In daily life, the 'unimportant' tasks, like raising children or caring for the old and sick, are *more* essential to the community than the 'important' ones. They are under-rewarded because, in theory, 'anyone' can do them.

We have noted that myth and tragedy single out the highly differentiated individual—who exemplifies masculine consciousness and identity—only

95

to reduce and sacrifice him. Story clearly *straddles* masculine and feminine modes of awareness: like the community, it fosters both difference *and* sameness, separation *and* connectedness. We recognize the singularity of the hero *and* see him as part of the whole. It is nonetheless true that even when the central figure is a woman—Antigone, Emma Bovary, or Hedda Gabler—she, like the hero, is rendered as isolated and different. Story may therefore appear to focus on masculine awareness.

CONSCIOUSNESS SEPARATES US FROM THE SACRED

When Saussure says that "in language there are only differences"[23] and suggests that all meaning is differential, he is describing the operations of consciousness as well. Like language—with which it may be identical—consciousness, most emphatically in its masculine form, is a system of contrasts or opposites, a network of eternally negative differences.[24] It constitutes a process we do not control; we cannot help differentiating or discriminating, for our identity and existence derive from it. Camus says: "To breathe is to judge."[25] Or, as Lacan puts it: " 'I am' means: 'I am that which I am not.' "[26]

Since *all* consciousness—feminine no less than masculine—separates us to some extent from nature or the sacred, as well as from each other and ourselves, it is perceived as a transgression against the whole, or the holy.[27] Like Satan or Mephistopheles, it is *der Geist der stets verneint*—the spirit that forever negates. Edward Edinger says:

> The (Eden) myth depicts the birth of consciousness as a crime which alienates man from God and from his original preconscious wholeness. The fruit is clearly symbolical of consciousness. It is the fruit of the tree of the knowledge of good and evil, which means that it brings awareness of the opposites, the specific feature of consciousness. Thus, according to this myth and the theological doctrines that rest on it, consciousness is the original sin, the original *hybris*, and the root cause of all evil in human nature.[28]

Traditionally, evil—like consciousness—*derives* from difference: Satan insisted on being different; he rebelled against God.

Consciousness can lead to an *exacerbated* state of differentiation, or alienation.[29] While Marx and his followers see it as the product of a historical situation—one that can be remedied—a less extreme form of alienation is intrinsic to our existence. We haven't always been as painfully aware of it as we are today because our institutions could compensate for it. Yet inasmuch as it is our destiny to *exist*, or "stand out," we were never completely 'at home' in the creation. The Kabbalah calls it "the Breaking of the Vessels," a damage done to the deity.[30] In Nietzsche, it appears as *die ewige Wunde des Daseins*, the eternal wound of being.[31] Adorno holds that life's essence is estrangement,[32] and Heidegger says:

> *Unheimlichkeit* is the basis of Being-in-the-world, even though in an everyday way it has been covered up.[33]

OUR SEPARATENESS BONDS US

Paradoxically, our alienation may be the very 'absence' or 'negativity' that makes human relationships and community possible.[34] If we were not separate and in exile, we might well lack the urge that brings and keeps us together. We seek to be connected with others as a substitute for the connectedness that marked our preconscious state, and it is our individual existence—with its burden of *incompleteness*—that bonds the community.

Traditional story renders consciousness as a curse-blessing that at once exiles us and makes human society possible. The story of Oedipus, like the Fall of Man, is a consciousness myth. Thebes is dying of the plague. The crimes of Oedipus have, as Girard points out, abolished fundamental differences and so threaten the community—which depends on difference as much as it does on sameness—with extinction.[35] Just as he *had* to commit his crimes, so Oedipus is now forced to become conscious of them; the plague makes clear that remaining unconscious is not an alternative. By establishing the truth—at tragic cost to Jocasta and himself—he re-establishes differences and saves the city.

CONSCIOUSNESS AND ACTION

Consciousness is deeply linked to action. As conscious beings, we are not free to do nothing, for we are aware of the threats to our existence and, in the face of them, find it impossible to remain passive.[36] *Aware* derives from the Anglo-Saxon *gewaer*, "wary, cautious," and consciousness could be called a refined form of fear. We are compelled to act—not just to fend off immediate threats but to guard against those we see looming ahead. Human action is thus mandated by nature itself, just as in story the action is mandated by the plot.

As long as Adam and Eve were in paradise, at one with the creation and

97

each other, there was nothing for them to 'do.' But once they ate of the tree of knowledge, life no longer seemed whole or perfect and they *had* to do something about it. The work they did by the sweat of their brow wrought changes in the creation. Their son Abel was a peaceful keeper of sheep and died without offspring, but his murderous brother Cain—a tiller of the ground—became the progenitor of all those who have been making inroads on the sacred ever since.[37] He was rejected by Yahweh and yet, as we have noted, *protected* by Him against human retribution. His story even suggests that our existence is, in some measure, fueled by anger and resentment of the sacred. Cain is openly resentful of Yahweh, who both curses *and* spares him. Like Oedipus—and like all of us—he has been chosen for a special, contradictory fate.

NATURE PROMPTS US TO VIOLATE IT

Though nature or the sacred gives us birth and sustenance, it is also indifferent to us. Since it protects us and strikes us down with no apparent pattern or reason, our will to survive urges us to intervene in natural process to the best of our ability. Before science and technology, we had prayer, ritual, sacrifice, and magic. Even the devout hope, in an unacknowledged corner of their minds, to influence the divine, and ritual—despite its stance of submission and obedience—clearly involve an effort to get on the right side of the gods, to make a useful relationship to them.

'Primitive' peoples were well aware that much of what we do is a violation of the sacred, and we, too, used to acknowledge it when we said of certain actions—not only of ceremonies, but of executions, operations, autopsies, and the sex act—that we 'performed' them, as if an unseen audience were watching. We clearly perceived them as an interface with the gods.

The demarcation line between the sacred and the human is forever shifting. It recedes as we advance toward it. But abolishing it altogether may have graver consequences than the Enlightenment and Positivism anticipated, and the human community, despite the siren song of reason, seems to redraw and reaffirm it whenever it has been blurred, invalidated, or crossed.

As long as the sacred was set apart—as long as the 'reality' of ritual and art was separate from daily life—a confrontation with our helplessness in story did not immobilize us. The attempt by contemporary aesthetics—or the thought systems that underpin it—to totalize our existence within the profane in order to stop the sacred from being used by an exploitative ideology, may carry with it almost as many dangers as it averts. Perhaps it is little different from the attempt, by religious systems, to totalize our existence within the sacred.

AN ENCOUNTER WITH NECESSITY CAN LIBERATE US

We have noted that an encounter with the sacred, even in its most forbidding aspect, need not immobilize us. Facing our limitations may well be a necessary first step in extending our scope. The discovery of natural laws forms the basis for circumventing or counteracting them, just as the work of Marx and Freud can be seen as an effort to escape the very determinism they uncovered and described. As Binswanger says:

> Freud succeeds in demonstrating mechanism at work in what was apparently the freest reaches of the human mind, thereby creating the possibility of mechanically 'repairing' the mind.[38]

Through psychoanalysis, Freud attempts to subvert his own conclusion that "we are lived by unknown and uncontrollable force": if the past is destiny, analysis gives us a way of liberating ourselves from it.

Any admission on our part that we are *not* free becomes, almost inevitably, a charged effort to regain our freedom. So a study of contexts is an attempt to liberate us from them. As I write this, I have a subtle sense that I am freer for having written it. All theories, however foreclosed, offer a margin of separateness, or freedom, to their authors, if not to the rest of us. As Hegel says:

> Every system is at once a system of freedom and of necessity.[39]

Thus the work of Lévi-Strauss is both a denial of the individual and a highly effective demonstration of his own individuality. In Derrida, the process of writing and his astounding proliferation of texts may serve to establish his identity, continuity, and originality.[40] Since writing is less public than speech, less attached to those who produce it, and therefore less subject to external or unconscious influences, it is vested with greater independence. When we write, moreover, a visible trace of us remains, whereas our spoken words 'disappear' into others. The written text enhances the very individual—the critic, for instance—whom the process of writing appears to undermine by placing him in a context of "reproduction" and intertextuality. Though, as Foucault says:

99

The researches of psychoanalysis, of linguistics, of anthropology have "decentered" the subject in relation to the laws of its desire; the forms of its language, the rules of its actions, or the play of its mythical and imaginative discourse,

it may *take* a subject to decenter one.

Like the theorist, the storyteller attains a measure of freedom, separateness, and identity in the *telling*. He serves the plot just as his figures do, but is more conscious and less victimized than they. Even when myths, like divine laws, were believed by everyone, he may have been engaged in staking out new realms of action—as Sophocles did in *Oedipus Rex* when he centered the play on the hero's *knowing*: he asserted the human 'against' the very myth he served. In the modern era—with myth no longer viable and with human beings apparently free to choose among many options even though our very existence has been put in doubt—it may have become the storyteller's task to *rediscover* necessity. For by telling a persuasive story about necessity, he too becomes necessary—and so, by implication, do we.

STORY IS PARADOXICAL

Plots used to originate over long periods of time—in the telling and retelling of many who would, on occasion, add or subtract something. The known plot was not simply taken for granted but required confirmation and re-proving. If what it tells us could have been transmitted and made credible in a simple declarative statement or 'message,' there would have been no need to embody it in story. Perhaps, indeed, it seemed valid and persuasive *because* its 'message' was contradicted or put in doubt even as it was sent. Traditional story does not, as both the formalists and their heirs have it, create an uncertainty in the telling only to affirm a familiar, reassuring meaning at the end. Its very structure is paradoxical, with plot and action countermanding each other throughout. It cannot be pinned down or defined; it can only be rendered *as an uncertainty.* Surely audiences have always sensed the contradiction in story's form, even if they were not fully aware of it. The discrepancy is too fundamental to be ignored, and may continue to seem valid to most of us because it reflects the basic paradoxes of our existence.

Uncertainty and instability are plainly evident in modern storytelling. Our fictions are seldom precluded for those who tell them. Hemingway said that if he knew the answer, he would not have to tell the story.[41] The task of the contemporary storyteller is not unlike that of the scientist. "My method," says Niels Bohr, "is to try and say what I cannot say, since I do not understand it."[42] Though the plot, like natural law, could be said to exist from the start, the storyteller isn't sure of it and must ascertain it by working his way through the action. Even if he *does* know it, he is apt to doubt it and must re-prove it to his own satisfaction. That, indeed, is why he is compelled to tell it. Flaubert says of *Madame Bovary*:

> The poetry of the adulterous wife is only true to the extent that she is at liberty in the midst of fatality.[43]

When he set out to tell her story, Flaubert—like Emma herself—may have thought she was free, but his work led him to the inevitable discovery that she was not. When Dostoevski started *Crime and Punishment*, the story must have seemed open and undecided to him; he could hardly have told it without the sense of hope or uncertainty that Raskolnicov himself maintains almost to the end. Even when the outcome is apparent to the story-teller, he may 'forget' it in the telling. Shakespeare, who transformed and elaborated existing plots, often surrendered the action to forces he could neither predict nor control. The ending was known to him, but the process by which his figures arrive at it must, at least on occasion, have come as a surprise: Iago dominates *Othello*, Shylock takes over *The Merchant of Venice*, and, until her virtual disappearance at the end of Act III, Lady Macbeth threatens to become the main focus of our interest.

Free of the author's will, the fictive figures are subject to the forces of necessity, which may not be known to the storyteller until they manifest in the action. By substantiating the action, he *re-proves* the plot—or, as Jung says, dreams the myth on and gives it a modern dress.[44] Conversely, the attempt by modern writers to use a myth or story that has only *metaphoric* reality for them is unlikely to charge their work with energy and cohesion. However helpful the *Odyssey* was to Joyce, *Ulysses* draws its organic structure and force from sources that have little to do with Homer or the original myth. Mythology cannot be *used* by the storyteller. It can only be served, and then—perhaps unwittingly—countermanded in the telling. For the same reason, a deliberate use of genre—with the author fully cognizant of its conventions and styling—is apt to produce a work without lasting tension and interest.

THE STORY FREES THE STORYTELLER

"The particular plot," says Elizabeth Bowen, "is something a novelist is driven to."[45] Yet the storyteller can *speak* the plot whereas her figures must *enact* it. As it carries or 'drives' her along, she becomes aware of its direction and shape. Unlike her figures, who may never learn what has them in its grip, she ceases to be blind and passive, begins to 'rehearse' or repeat and revise the story, and so becomes a conscious participant in the process. She is no longer truly helpless in her helplessness. By telling the story, she controverts her own victimization. Her very proving of the plot could be said to *disprove* it.

Traditionally, art embodies the tension between helplessness and control, passivity and action, constraint and freedom. The storyteller is at first enacted by the myth but learns, through a disciplined devotion to his craft, *how* to enact it. By reporting the effect of superior forces, he is no longer entirely at their mercy. Chaplin and Keaton, like Kafka and Beckett, *tell* the very stories that appear to victimize them. They are at once the hero-victims and chroniclers of their own adventures. They subject themselves to situations dictated by their experience—or the unconscious—yet survive in the telling. As the speaker in Lévi-Strauss is spoken by the text so the storyteller is told by the story. But he also *tells* it. He rides the wave that carries him. It is as though *parole* were mandated to speak back to and seek independence from *langue*. The very act of telling constitutes a measure of freedom—as do our own listening and knowing.

If the plot were controlled by the storyteller—as the formalists and their heirs have it—his control, and story's form, would be of little interest. If a story did not invoke the very forces that threaten to destroy it *and* us, telling it would hold no more challenge than would skiing down a mountainside that we can modify as we descend it. "I love the danger," says Emily Dickinson. Turning art into a game, toy or text with no connection to anything beyond it avoids all danger. Once the safe arena becomes a playing field without binding rules and limitations—one on which death and the gods have no dominion—the game becomes irrelevant, however well it is played. That, of course, is precisely the intention of the contemporary aesthetic, even if it is not acknowledged.[46]

STORY AS AN ANALOGUE OF CONSCIOUSNESS

In life, when we cannot change what is happening, consciousness may offer us a measure of relief by distancing us. In situations that hold us passive and helpless, our awareness can even constitute a form of action. The storyteller often starts out wholly identified with his story. As Matthew Arnold says:

—such a price
The Gods exact for song:
To become what we sing.[47]

Most of us trust the singer because he *is*—or was—the song, and the story-teller because he has lived the story. Yet in the course of telling it, both he and we who listen become freer, or more detached. Perhaps only those who must live their story *without* knowing or telling it are utterly helpless.

WORDS INSTEAD OF DEEDS

Traditionally, stories serve as an alternative to action: we need not commit the act because we can speak it. In the beginning was the *deed*, not the word. We ate, mated, fought, and killed before we became conscious of doing so. Nature, or the sacred, precedes our awareness of it—a sequence culture has ever tried to invert by putting the word *ahead* of the deed, substituting the word *for* the deed, and qualifying the deed *through* the word. Implicit in traditional story is the assumption that culture itself is a response to something beyond it, something we cannot know, which is nonetheless very much with us. In story, the word enacts the deed it means to displace: it conjures up, in mediated form, the horror of the unmediated deed, so that we who are watching may be spared having to enact it. Myth does indeed, as Barthes puts it, "immobilize" us. Like most of our social structures, it tries to inhibit our dangerous proclivity for instinct-impelled action.

The traditional primacy of act over word is, of course, overturned if the text is the sole reality—if everything, as Derrida says, begins with "repro-duction."[48] The implication of postmodernism seems to be that the deed—like our perception and experience—is structured by culture. Whatever input there is from instinct and primal fear is processed, or conditioned, by society to the point where it has no separate life or reality, and constitutes no danger. Would it were so! For if the world were truly and exclusively text—if it had *begun* with the word and if there had been no creation until we 'spoke'—the inchoate act would constitute no threat, our instincts and unconscious would require no inhibition, and humankind could look for-ward to a progressively more civilized existence.[49]

Rousseau, like other Enlightenment thinkers, dismisses original sin. In a reaction to Hobbes, he inverts the traditional view of humankind as frail and prone to evil, and of nature as a force to be contained by religion and culture. He is therefore widely interpreted as asserting that humankind and

103

nature are good, and that *society* is the corrupting force. The opening line of *The Social Contract*—"Man was born free and is everywhere in chains"—is often applied to our enslavement by *all* structures and institutions. But as Peter Gay points out:

> Rousseau, who shocked and delighted thousands of readers with his reiterated claims for man's essential goodness, regarded that goodness as a mere collection of possibilities, an absence of original corruption, and a mere hope—a rather slim hope—that in the right circumstances, with the right education and the right society, man might become a decent citizen.[50]

Rousseau's positions are complex and contradictory yet have often been used to support a positivist view of the human condition. Contemporary thought continues to be deeply influenced by them. Perhaps even the concept that the text is all we have is predicated on the assumption—or hope—that human nature is fundamentally harmless, that the word is not needed to modify the deed.

No doubt there is truth in saying that in daily life the word *does* precede the deed—that for most of us, most of the time, there is nothing outside the text. All communal 'knowing'—which forms the basis of our structures and society—is clearly instilled or conditioned in us.[51] It is a given derived from the experience of generations and leaves us in no position to challenge it. Since it constitutes the very premise of our existence and identity, and informs all our perceptions, we find it next to impossible to step outside it. It is equivalent to what Marxists call ideology, though it does not operate in us merely to preserve an unjust system, but because *no* system—unjust *or* just—can maintain itself by depending on our individual, spur-of-the-moment responses. The community cannot survive by relying on our *conscious* decisions any more than we could survive if we had to carry out consciously all of the functions maintained by our autonomous nervous system. Society's approach to us—though it continually invokes our freedom and responsibility—is necessarily 'behaviorist.' It must condition our responses and reactions, for consciousness—like philosophy in Hegel—always arrives upon the scene too late.[52] Unlike the 'text' that has been instilled in us, it cannot be counted on to preserve order.

Our communal 'knowing,' like the institutions that depend on it, is profoundly restrictive and conservative: it tries to exclude the other, the unfamiliar, the anomalous. Yet our structures—to maintain their validity in an ever-changing context—must *include* the new and coopt, to the extent that this is possible, whatever threatens or contradicts them: they must relate themselves to the unknown and forbidden. If, as is generally believed, new consciousness can arise only in individuals, the community will stand in an ambivalent relationship to those who at once threaten *and* help to preserve the existing order by venturing beyond the known and sanctioned.[53] Perhaps it is this ambivalence that is reflected in story's contradictory relationship to its central figure—the individual it raises up only to dash down, and dashes down only to raise up.

Story As Paradox

HUMAN DUALITY

Hegel says:

> (Contradiction) is the root of all movement and life. Only insofar as something contains a contradiction does it move, or have drive and activity.[1]

But whereas in Hegel the contradictions are essential and inescapable, Marx sees them as a time-bound phenomenon, like alienation, and links them to what he calls the dictatorship of the bourgeoisie. His rejection of the antinomies would appear to spring from an ancient dream of wholeness. For him,

> (Communism) is the *definitive* resolution of the antagonism between man and nature, and between man and man. It is the true solution of the conflict between existence and essence, between objectification and self-affirmation, between freedom and necessity, between individual and species. It is the solution of the riddle of history and knows itself to be this solution.[2]

Lukács follows Marx in attributing the antinomies that have dominated Western thought at least since the Renaissance—the pervasive dualism of subject and object, for instance—to the bourgeois mode of production and the commodity structure of capitalism. The object has been split from the subject just as the reified or fetishized product is divorced from those who produce it. Even the best efforts of Western philosophy will not overcome the polarities—and the contradictions they have engendered—until they are resolved in social and economic reality.[3] Derrida—for whom the "violent hierarchy" of binary oppositions is rooted in Western thought—appears directly linked to this tradition.

Conversely, structuralism holds an essentialist view of the opposites and sees them as central not only to our own culture but to human life everywhere. They are inextricably linked to thought itself. For Saussure, language is a binary relationship between identity and difference, and Henri Wallon says:

> At the origin of thought we can note the existence only of paired elements. The elementary unit of thought is this binary structure, not the terms that constitute it. Duality precedes unity. The pair exists before the isolated element. Any term that is identifiable by thought—that is "thinkable"—requires a complementary term from which it may be differentiated and to which it may be contrasted. . . . Without this initial relationship of the pair, the building of further relationships would be impossible.[4]

For Lévi-Strauss, the opposites are so central that, as a consequential materialist, he attributes them to a binary chemical structure of the human brain. As we have noted, it is this essentialist core of structuralism that Derrida rejects.[5] For him, the polarities are a limitation of Western philosophy, which exist in the *text* only and need not be granted an independent or primary reality. Though he insists that his positions are part of a discursive process that questions rather than asserts, his view of the opposites, like his claim that there is nothing outside the text, would appear to be basic to deconstruction. Without it, an essence—and so a form of the sacred—is reconstituted.

CONSCIOUSNESS AS A SOURCE OF OUR DUALITY

For Jung, as for Lévi-Strauss, contradictions are integral to the human situation.[6] But he and Neumann locate their origin in consciousness, which separates us from the rest of creation and—by establishing differences between what we are and are not—may be the source of the dualism that pervades and informs our existence.[7] The real "trauma of birth" does not occur when we come into the world physically but when we begin to be conscious and realize that we are separate, alone, and self-divided.[8] Animals suffer no birth trauma, but we do—retroactively, as it were—when being cast out into the world becomes a metaphor for consciousness. Unlike the creature, we need our parents for an extended time—to cushion our fall into conscious existence and to integrate us into the human community that substitutes for the natural whole from which we have been exiled.[9]

Though consciousness brings with it a host of problems, it has what Darwin calls "survival value."[10] More accurately than our instincts, it discriminates between elements in nature that foster and those that threaten us. If Darwin is correct and we are programmed to preserve and propagate the species—an essentialist premise, to be sure—our continuous effort to differentiate, discriminate, and judge may derive from a biological imperative. Since the creation is at once life-giving and death-dealing, we must separate from and protect ourselves against it.[11] Jung makes the same point with reference to the unconscious, which belongs largely to the realm of nature or the sacred:

> If, as many are fain to believe, the unconscious were only nefarious, only evil, then the situation would be simple and the path clear: to do good and to eschew evil. . . . (But) the unconscious is not just evil by nature; it is also the source of the highest good: not only dark but also light, not only bestial, semi-human, and demonic, but superhuman, spiritual, and, in the classical sense of the word, "divine." . . . Since this is so, all hope of a simple solution is abolished.[12]

THE INDIVIDUAL AS A SOURCE OF THE OPPOSITES

Perhaps consciousness sees or generates the opposites everywhere because it is itself separate and therefore 'opposite.' As Nietzsche says: *Einz wird zwei*—"one becomes two."[13] Our propensity for dualism may be rooted as well in certain biological patterns—the division of creature life into 'opposite' sexes, for instance, each with specific physical functions that appear to serve the species more effectively than would a single sex. But the *primary* source of our duality is the individual, for though he is an integral member of the group, he must stand in some measure apart from it.[14] All societies, including theocracies and police states, depend on his 'separate' existence, even if his 'free' will is needed only to subordinate him to the community. Hegel says that the history of the Christian world is the history of individuality.[15] But in fact *every* community depends on individual members who must assume they are free to choose between 'right' and 'wrong'—even if, as Fromm suggests, all they actually contribute is a *"wanting to act as they have to act."* [16] Social structures continually reinforce and refine our ability to discriminate and choose, beginning with the games of childhood.

THE COMMUNITY AND THE INDIVIDUAL

Though the word *individuum* means "undivided, indivisible," the individual *must* be divided against himself, for he is the point of contact with our generic energy, which is at once essential to us and constitutes a grave threat to the community. The individual being, in whom generic forces find their expression, is the juncture at which they are most effectively channeled and curbed. Even in shame societies, antisocial behavior—those biological impulses that disregard the well-being and rights of others—has always been in part curbed by each member individually. If, as Freud suggests, the motto of civilization reads: "Where id was there shall ego be," the individual is clearly crucial and must be self-divided in order to serve. He must maintain *access* to 'his' generic energies, yet be their 'master' and know how to inhibit them. He is the critical interface between the generic or instinctual and the community. *We* may consider Oedipus unfree and innocent but *he* must assume he is guilty. He blinds himself in atonement for his crimes because, without the assumption of individual freedom and responsibility, his kingdom could not survive.

Though both Marx and Durkheim believed that the group is "the order of orders,"[17] it never occurred to them that society could function *without* the individual, or self:

Society . . . cannot do without individuals any more than these can do without society.[18]

Nothing collective can be produced if individual consciousness is not assumed.[19]

As Ernst Bloch says, Marx recognized that "private interest" is ultimately the strongest of drives[20] —no doubt because "private interest" is *itself* a form of impersonal or generic energy. The group *uses* this "drive" and manages, much of the time, to suggest to its members that they are serving their own purposes though they are, in fact, serving the community. We say 'my land,' 'my children,' and 'my work' though they do not belong to us, but if we did not *think* of them as ours, 'our' energy would not as readily flow into them and so serve the purposes of the group. In much the same way, nature lets us take pleasure in those activities that further *its* purposes. Schopenhauer points out that in the sexual act the individual—particularly the male—suffers the delusion that he is meeting his own need, whereas he is fulfilling the aim of the species.[21]

Since society needs the individual just as it does the sacred, it has to invent him if he does not exist. It can build on the plain fact that, physically, we are separate beings with discrete organic systems: when we bleed or die, we do so alone and without threatening the survival of others. The community at once affirms our separateness *and* reinforces our sense of kinship with the group. It sends us double messages: we are to be both independent of the community and an integral part of it, whole *and* deeply divided, so that we may effectively police ourselves. Nature, too, would seem to contribute significantly to our self-division, for our collaboration with others is often in conflict with our needs as individual creatures, yet both are clearly in the service of the species and part of nature's design. The self is double bound and often painfully divided by conflicting altruistic and egoistic impulses—though *both* are engendered by nature and serve it, just as they do the community.[22] Moreover, individual and community often operate at cross purposes, with consequences that can be tragic, even though both are obedient to a common 'purpose.'[23]

Traditionally, our sense of dividedness—of self from other and of self from self—has been perceived as an intrinsic element of the human condition. It would appear to be inculcated in the infant at the earliest stages of development. As Winnicott and others have observed—albeit only in a Western context—the separation of 'me' from 'not me' is based on the infant's recognition of the mother, or mother substitute, as an "objectively perceived environmental feature." "The precursor of the mirror is the mother's face," for she is the first to give proof of the infant's separate existence.[24] The establishment of self and world as distinct entities is commonly held to be the factor that makes society possible, even as it threatens to undermine it. It serves as the basis of consciousness and may well be the original source of the dualism that pervades our lives. It appears to parallel the binary relationship between difference and sameness that Saussure posits as the predicate of language.

We have noted that postmodern theory refuses to accept dualism and the opposites as an intrinsic part of human existence and attributes them, instead, to historical conditions specific to Western culture.[25] Descartes is almost invariably cited as the villain. Cartesianism, with its predicate of *Cogito ergo sum* and the separation of "thinking" from "extended" substances, clearly contributed to the ever-widening separation of self from non-self and so to the accretion of the individual.[26] No doubt it met urgent historical needs. When a community becomes highly specialized and finds itself subject to rapid change, it requires the services of a large number of individuals whose presence, in turn, leads to further fragmentation and change. If—as Horkheimer and Adorno suggest—the separation of subject from object is rooted in the division of labor and in our attempt to gain control over nature,[27] it clearly antedates capitalism, Descartes, and the Renaissance.[28] The fact that Cartesianism greatly enhanced our capacity for domination and exploitation, both of nature and each other, does not justify the contemporary dismissal of dualism and the antinomies, even though it is politically helpful. Nietzsche takes a traditional position when he speaks of *Urwiderspurch und Urschmerz*,[29] and Phillip Rieff points out that:

> Freud's . . . attitude to a variety of historical dualisms, including Christianity, was always respectful, for he considered that they were but versions of a more fundamental dualism in the nature of man and in the cosmos. For this reason he never seriously entertained any utopian aspirations.[30]

Adorno, despite his Marxist orientation, acknowledged that life's "very essence" is estrangement[31] and saw our existence as a force-field of opposites that may be held in balance but cannot be reconciled. Like Rousseau, he had no confidence that we can recover an original wholeness:

> The picture of a temporal or extratemporal state of happy identity between subject and object is romantic . . .—a wishful project at times, but today no more than a lie. The undifferentiated state before the subject's formation was the dread of the blind web of nature, of myth; it was in protest against it that the great religions had their truth content.[32]

The findings of modern physics may appear to support the postmodern position. Heisenberg says:

> The common division of the world into subject and object, inner and outer world, body and soul, is no longer adequate.[33]

As we have noted, this is also the basic premise of story—in which figure and ground are ultimately inseparable: "There is nothing here which is not Zeus." But what may be true in the *absolute*—both in physics and in the safe arena of story—does not apply in the realm of daily life, where the separation of self from other, inner from outer, and body from psyche are mandated by both consciousness and the community. We are obliged to live in two realms: the 'real' world outside us and the one within—which is, of course, just as 'real'—and though the inner world may be a mere extension of the outer, our failure to distinguish between them will land us in prison or the asylum.

Few scientists today defend Descartes's dualism of body and mind. On the most fundamental level, mind and 'soul' are, as Jung says, "simply carbon."[34] Yet life within us seems to divide 'against' itself, and there are moments when our consciousness, though material in origin and very likely chemical in substance, seems to exist 'separately' from the body, and to exercise a kind of influence over it; it can play a part in making us sick or keeping us well. The point at which our thoughts and attitudes, affected by events in the world, retranslate into *physical* events within us has not been mapped. But even if the process is entirely rooted in matter, consciousness seems to serve a dividing or separating function. Perhaps we can think of it as life separating from life for the sake of life.

DECONSTRUCTION AND THE OPPOSITES

If the source of our duality lies in the "fissured structure" of human existence rather than in Western culture and philosophy, it would seem to be irredeemable. While Derrida, in his discussion of writing, recognizes that self-alienation is inherent in the human situation, he, like Lukács, sees binary oppositions and the contradictions they engender as historically and locally conditioned:

> He associates contradiction with the fissured structure of Western philosophy.[35]

Postmodernists perceive the split between subject and object as central to all idealism and see those who continue to *hold* a dualistic view of human nature as misguided. Though Derrida himself remains politically uncommitted, and calls his work a method and not a system, his vantage point does lend itself to "utopian aspirations."[36] So feminists have used it to attribute binary oppositions exclusively to the patriarchy, just as in the academy today human duality is often associated with an exploitative power structure.[37]

In *Positions*, Derrida differentiates between the "violent hierarchy" of opposites we encounter in the West and their "peaceful coexistence."[38] Traditional thinkers would no doubt agree that the polarities, if they are to serve as an effective balancing mechanism, must coexist as peacefully as possible. But as communitites increase in size and complexity—both in the West and elsewhere—the tension between opposites becomes increasingly difficult to balance and reconcile.

Ideally the antinomies, instead of leading to a "totalizing dialectic," and so constituting a grave danger to both the individual and the community, become the gateway to the irreducible and generative multiplicity envisioned by Derrida. In story, the binary opposition of plot and action—which we might call "peaceful," since one is mandated by the other and, indeed, *is* the other—generates story's multiplicity and "undecidability." But in life, individuals as well as groups find it difficult to maintain a relationship to two opposites at once; it threatens confusion and paralysis, and prompts us to polarize ourselves—especially when we are under pressure to act. We are far more comfortable with an either/or than with an either *and* or. Since the identity of groups and individuals derives from difference, there is, moreover, an almost inevitable tendency to *insist* on an either/or.

Perhaps the pluridimensional reality envisioned by postmodern thought is one in which a wide *spectrum* of dualities can coexist, so that one set of opposites need not exclude another. Given our limitations, this seems more realistic than trying to eliminate duality altogether.

HOMOGENEOUS SOCIETIES WERE FRAGMENTED

In Western society, specialization has been a major force contributing to the fragmentation of the community and to our emphasis on the individual. But while members of a nonspecialized, homogeneous, and 'cold' culture no doubt found themselves outside or 'opposite' the group far less often than we do, there is clear evidence that even here—in periods of crisis and change—individuals were thrust into positions of specialization and leadership that separated them from the group.[39] We know that a warrior caste emerged whenever a community was under or on the attack. Moreover, even cultures that appear homogeneous in hindsight surely depended on the individual, whose identity is derived from difference. They too may have been less cohesive than we assume.

As societies increased in size and complexity, the individual became ever more important and differentiated. In the words of Victor Turner, he effectively replaced "the group as the crucial ethical unit":

> As societies diversify economically and socially and as particularistic multiplex ties of locality and kinship yield place to a wide range of single interest relationships between members of functional groups over ever wider geographical areas, individual option and voluntarism thrive at the expense of predetermined corporate obligations.[40]

This process of diversification and the increase in "individual option" or freedom require a counterforce to the threatened atomization of the group. Philip Rieff points out that:

> (The) rise of psychological man parallels the rise of the modern state, which has centralized all power. Thus Hobbes, the first absolutist political philosopher, is also the first philosopher of the private man.[41]

The emergence of 'free,' specialized, and increasingly private individuals called into existence the central authority of the modern state.

Members of our complex contemporary communities often experience themselves as outsiders even when they are *not* specialists. In an intricately interdependent society like our own, we find ourselves in the paradoxical situation of being at once totally replaceable cogs in industry, technology, or the bureaucracy—and therefore of dubious value as individuals—yet often playing a critical role, for the failure of one can jeopardize the well-being of many.

THE SPECIALIZED INDIVIDUAL IS SENT A DOUBLE MESSAGE

Just as specialized functioning confers a biological advantage, the division of labor and a high degree of specialization have, in the past, benefited the community. It is a process over which we have, in any case, little control. But while it benefits the community, it also threatens it with continuous change,[42] fragmentation, and the creation of an elite.[43] Highly skilled and distinct individuals are unlikely to have much in common with each other or with the rest of society, and so the community must reintegrate them even as it stresses and exploits their differences. The specialist, like the rest of us, is sent a double message. He is urged to develop his capacities to the fullest extent *and* made to feel anxious or guilty about them. His 'guilt'—as in *noblesse oblige*—serves both as a source of his energy and keeps him tied to the group. In order to reap the greatest benefit from his gifts and skills, the community must both protect his 'rights' and reconcile them with the interests of the group. Hegel, optimistically, sees the modern state as a resolution of the tension between these contraries: a union of the universal with the full freedom of the particular or individual.[44]

WE MUST ALL BE DIFFERENT AND THE SAME

Even members of a community who are without specialized roles must become separate or different in order to join, for only when we are separate or 'independent' do we become full-fledged, dependable members of the community. We must *all* be both different and alike, separate but part of the whole. Rousseau says Emile is to be educated *outside* society, for only when he is set apart can he be educated *for* society.[45] Hegel speaks of "The I that is a we and the we that is an I"[46]—a variant of Luther's

A Christian is a perfectly free lord of all, subject to none; a Christian is a perfectly dutiful servant to all, subject to all.[47]

In an effort to escape the contradictions that face us, we may try to derive our identity from difference/separateness *or* sameness/connectedness. Thus Kierkegaard and Marx offer us opposite resolutions of the problem, and we may call ourselves followers of one or the other. But our identity cannot long derive from an either/or; it must be based on either *and* or, and is therefore self-contradictory. Though self-division has no doubt been exacerbated in the West, it is as old as the human community, for only when we are different can we be truly the same, and only when we are separate are we truly connected.

Foucault, whose work, like Derrida's, lends itself to "utopian aspirations,"[48] appears to attribute our radically contradictory or double-bound situation to the state:

> Since the sixteenth century, a new political form of power has been continuously developing. This new political structure . . . is the state. But most of the time the state is envisioned as . . . a political power which ignores individuals, looking only at the interests of the totality, or, I should say, of a class or a group among the citizens. That's quite true. But I'd like to underline the fact that the state's power (and that's one of the reasons for its strength) is both an individualizing and a totalizing form of power. Never, I think, in the history of human societies—even in the old Chinese society—has there been such a tricky combination in the same political structures of individualization techniques, and of totalization procedures.[49]

Every society has surely had to subject its members to the same "tricky combination"—albeit in less extreme form. Since the unfolding of the individual is both necessary to the community and threatens to undermine it, he must be kept moving back and forth between the polarities of separation and connectedness. Only by mediating between them can we, and the community at large, remain in balance. We shift continually—though for the most part unconsciously—between structure and chaos, rigidity and openness, certainty and fear, security and freedom. As Jung says:

> Life is a continuous balancing of opposites. . . . The abolition of opposites would be equivalent to death. . . . The yogi attains the state of *nirdvandha* (freedom from opposites) in the rigid lotus position of non-conscious, non-acting *samadhi*. But the ordinary man stands between the opposites and knows he can never abolish them.[50]

THE PARADOXES OF OUR EXISTENCE ARE MEDIATED BY OUR STRUCTURES

Even if the ordinary individual is not fully aware of being suspended between opposites, he surely senses it. He must act in concert with the group, yet assume he is not merely its agent but an independent actor who can be called to account. He is *obliged* to believe in his freedom.[51] Since being fully conscious of our contradictory state would be painful, and naked exposure to irreconcilable conflict might paralyze us or tear us apart, the contradictions of our existence are mediated by our institutions—which give us clear, unambiguous directives and enable us to act in situations that would otherwise leave us confused and helpless. Our structures could be said to substitute for the unconflicted instincts that guided—or impelled—us before we became conscious beings. They lift us out of the state of self-contradiction that few can tolerate for long, and help us make the unequivocal distinctions between true and false, good and evil, right and wrong, that society requires of us.

THE OPPOSITES KEEP US IN BALANCE

Though, as Hegel says, the polarities are a potent source of movement and change, their primary function may be to keep us balanced in a context that is forever changing.[52] The spectrum of paired opposites, with their contrary pull, constitutes a 'system' of checks and balances that engages us in an uninterrupted process of equilibration. Our physical and psychological well-being demands that we stay away from either polarity and, instead, move—often without being aware of it—to and fro between them. As Rabbi Moshe Loeb says:

> The path through this world is like the cutting edge of a knife. On this side is the underworld and on that side as well; the path of life leads through them.[53]

Our tension and anxiety—Hegel's *Unruhe* or disquiet—are inevitable by-products of being poised on the edge.

The opposites are neither 'good' nor 'bad' but keep changing their value. A 'positive' polarity can become 'negative' when our balance requires that we move away from it, and a 'negative' polarity becomes 'positive' when we need to be drawn toward it. Much of the time, the adjustments we make are gradual and subtle, and only a crisis will fling us back and forth between extremes. At such a time, total identification with one polarity or

117

the other may promise relief and wholeness, but any extended polarization spells disaster. The attempt to do away with the contradictions in *life*—rather than within the safe arena of ritual or art—brings with it far graver dangers than the discomfort of living suspended between the polarities.

The community, too, maintains its balance through the opposites. Their contrary pull serves as a homeodynamic 'system' that shifts the entire organism back and forth between order and chaos, structure and openness, security and freedom, the rights of the individual and communal imperative. Indeed, some individuals help the group maintain its equilibrium by means of their own polarization. Thus saint and evildoer, hero and coward, rebel and reactionary, celebrity and skid-row failure all serve as exemplary alternatives that keep the group in balance. Since they often perish in the process, identifying with one or the other of the opposites is clearly dangerous.

Polarization is as threatening to the community as it is to the individual. Lévi-Strauss says:

> Native institutions, though borne along on the flux of time, manage to steer a course between the contingencies of history and the immutability of design and remain, as it were, within the stream of intelligibility. They are always at a safe distance from the Scylla and Charybdis of diachrony and synchrony, event and structure, the aesthetic and the logical, and those who have tried to define them in terms of only one or the other aspect have therefore necessarily failed to understand their nature.[54]

History is witness to the dangers besetting a society—and its neighbors—when it becomes wholly identified with one opposite or the other.

THE COMMUNITY AND NATURE

The community's relationship to nature, or the sacred, parallels the individual's to the community. Just as the individual must be both part of and independent from the group, so the community must accommodate to nature, yet remain separate. Since we depend on natural process but must protect ourselves against it, our structures both respect *and* subvert it. Religious institutions acknowledge the superior powers of the gods without submitting to them entirely: they at once make human action possible and keep it within bounds. They recognize and accept the contradictory relationship of the human to the creation.

The equilibrium of nature, which seems superior to our own, is not one we can adopt. Nature mandates individual creatures yet is utterly indifferent

118

to them, while the human community—which depends on them—must foster and protect them. But society, too, is perfectly ready to sacrifice us. Indeed, unless forcefully corrected, it tends to neglect and sacrifice entire groups that are not immediately useful to it and lack power. Like nature—of which, as "the order of orders," it is an integral part—the community is wasteful and often unconscious.

LASTING STRUCTURES AND INSTITUTIONS CONTRADICT THEMSELVES

Since societies owe their capacity for survival to the polarities, our lasting structures invariably contradict themselves, though the contradictions are—for our comfort and safety—kept out of sight. So criminal law mediates between a necessary insistence that we are fully responsible for what we do, and an awareness that we are often helpless. Liberty, Equality, and Fraternity are invoked together and deemed to constellate a harmonious whole, yet Liberty clearly contradicts Equality and Fraternity, and Mario Vargas Llosa is right to call them "harsh antagonists."[55] Even national character is necessarily contradictory:

> It is commonplace to state that whatever one may come to consider a truly American trait can be shown to have its equally characteristic opposite. This, one suspects, is true of all "national characters" . . . so true, in fact, that one may begin rather than end with the proposition that a nation's identity is derived from the ways in which history has, as it were, counterpointed certain opposite potentialities; the ways in which it lifts this counterpoint to a unique style of civilization, or lets it disintegrate into a mere contradiction.[56]

On occasion, religious teaching will admit its paradoxical foundation. Rabbi Bunam tells his disciples:

> Each of you must have two pockets, so that you may reach into one or the other, as it becomes necessary. In the right pocket lies the word: "For my sake the world was created," and in the left: "I am ashes and dust."[57]

Underneath a deceptive but necessary surface harmony, our complex structures make no attempt to reconcile the polarities. They simply accommodate them and let them stand. "The Constitution," says Justice Potter Stewart, ". . . establishes the contest, not its resolution."[58] Institutions truly committed to one polarity or the other are totalitarian in spirit. Even Puri-

tan New England, with its rigid and one-sided view of human reality, accommodated the opposites:

> According to the Puritan reading of the Bible . . . there were only two classes
> of people on earth—those who had been elected to everlasting life and those
> who had been consigned forever to hell. These decisions, of course, had been
> made before the people affected by them were born, and nothing they did in
> the course of their lives would have any influence on the outcome. . . .
>
> Now this was fatalism of a most exaggerated kind, but like so many tenets
> of Puritan theology it was seldom taken literally. It was necessary for the Puri-
> tans to feel that every movement of the universe was supervised directly by
> God, but it was also necessary for them to feel that people who infringe the
> rules of society were both morally and legally responsible for their own devi-
> ancies; and soon the Puritans developed the kind of legalistic solution for
> which their minds were so superbly trained. God, so the reasoning went,
> arranges every moment of human history in advance and regulates the affairs
> of men down to the smallest detail. Every act of man, then, whether it be a
> saintly deed or a frightful crime, has been fully preordained. Yet at the same
> time God demands that each person *consent* to the future which has been
> chosen for him, so that he is always acting on the basis of his own volition in
> the very process of carrying out God's will.[59]

In our rationalist context, it is often assumed that contradictions *undermine* a system. Logic persuades us that a thing and its opposite cannot both
be true. Thus Marx and Marxists point to the contradictions in capitalism
as a symptom of its inevitable demise. Yet the opposites—which imply
contradiction even when they don't openly express it—insure the *survival*
of the system; they endow it with tensile strength and the capacity for
change and renewal. The checks and balances so often identified with
bourgeois society are actually found in all complex, lasting structures, and
the dialectical process Hegel sees at work everywhere preserves their equilibrium.

Contradictions sustain not only our political, social, and religious institutions but our thought structures or theories as well. The work of a major
theorist like Marx is rife with paradox. If his 'system' were truly consistent,
it would have long lost its relevance to our situation. "His words are like
bats," says Pareto. "We can see in them both birds and mice."[60] Though
Marx claims that humankind is not helpless, he insists that history makes
men and not men history:

> Men make their own history, but they do not make it just as they please;
> they do not make it under circumstances chosen by themselves, but under
> circumstances directly encountered, given and transmitted from the past.[61]

Like Christianity, he promises us the inevitable triumph of the good, whatever we do or don't do—yet assigns a critical role to the human will. The individual can make a substantive contribution and difference, but all he does is accelerate or delay the inevitable. Like Nietzsche, Marx exhorts us to push down what is already falling: *Was faellt, das soll man auch noch stossen!*[62] In an attempt to give the individual a meaningful role in an inexorable historical process, he claims that

(Historical) accidents . . . fall naturally into the general course of development and are compensated for, again, by other accident. But acceleration and delay are very dependent upon such "accidents", which include the "accident" of the character of those who at first stand at the head of the movement.[63]

Though he is a committed materialist, Marx must assign a significant role to the nonmaterial—to theory and consciousness—or his own work would be irrelevant. History carries us inexorably toward an already visible terminus, yet philosophy—which has been confined to interpreting the world—can *change* it. Theory in Marx, unlike philosophy in Hegel, no longer arrives upon the scene *after* the fact, too late to make any difference:

Material force can only be overthrown by material force, but theory itself becomes a material force when it has seized the masses.[64]

As Marcuse puts it:

According to Historical Materialism, *the revolution remains an act of freedom*—in spite of all material determination. Historical Materialism has recognized this freedom in the important role of the revolutionary consciousness.[65]

The validity and impact of Marx's own work is in large part derived from its capacity for contradiction, yet he wrote scathingly of all those who seem to undermine themselves and their effectiveness by shilly-shallying between the opposites:

Proudhon naturally inclined towards dialectic. But since he never understood the really scientific type of dialectic, he only succeeded in producing sophistry. In practise this was in keeping with his petty-bourgeois point of view. The petty-bourgeois is . . . made up of "on the one hand" and "on the other hand." This is so in his economic interests, and *therefore* also in his politics, in his religious, scientific and aesthetic opinions. So it is in his morality, in everything. He is a living contradiction.[66]

Critics who have applied Marx's theory to literature and art tend to overlook the contradictions in his own work. In their rationalist endeavor, and focused on his disdain for those who shift back and forth between "on the one hand" and "on the other," they either dismiss the profound contradictions in art or attribute them to the bourgeoisie.[67] In part, Walter Benjamin's continuing relevance lies in his willingness to let the contradictions in Marxism stand instead of trying to rationalize or reconcile them. He refers to the Janus face of his own work, in which materialism exists side by side with a deep interest in Jewish mysticism. As a Marxist, he—like Brecht—could assign no theoretical importance to the individual or the particular, yet his concern with the central significance of experience in art focuses on precisely the individual and the particular—on *das Kleinste*. As Ernst Bloch says:

> Benjamin had something, which Lukács so frightfully lacked; he had an extraordinary eye . . . for the unusual and unschematic, the disruptive, individual being (*Einzelsein*) which doesn't fit into the mold.[68]

When Marx was working for the bourgeois press, he indulged what he deemed to be its pitiful penchant for the empathetic and particular, but for Benjamin and Brecht *all* valid aesthetic work is specific and concrete. As Adorno says:

> Almost the entire effort of (Benjamin's) philosophy can be defined as an effort to rescue the particular.[69]

Like Adorno—and, indeed, like Marx himself—Benjamin was unwilling to sacrifice either the individual or the group.

Brecht inscribed the motto "The truth is concrete" on a board in his Danish study. He knew that while a figure rendered in its particularity and concreteness is "different" and separate from others, only an individualized character truly represents us. Every great 'type' is unique, perhaps because his or her qualities have been pushed to extremes. Yet without this unique quality we will not recognize ourselves in the figure, for the community demands of us that we, too, be separate and 'unique.' A generalized, non-specific fictive figure is lifeless and nonrepresentative, whereas Mother Courage is both singular *and* emblematic. Brecht renders her, moreover, in a classical antinomy: despite his own declared disdain for empathy, she is seen from without *and* within; we identify her as the blind 'killer' of her own children even as we share her anguished effort to save them from destruction. The power of her situation derives from its contradictions—

from her indomitable but misguided will to continue in the very enterprise that both provides for her family *and* destroys it.

EVERY STORY CONTRADICTS ITSELF

Like all complex structures, stories contradict themselves—not only in the West but wherever they are told, and not just since the Renaissance but long before the emergence of the middle class. Myth acknowledges the absolute power of the sacred without abdicating the role of the human, just as our own stories confirm the commanding power of the community without invalidating the individual. The contradictions are left to stand. Though at story's end the opposites are briefly reconciled, we know that as soon as another story gets under way—and there is *always* another story—the gap between them is sure to reopen. Stories, like history, will not come to an end until *we* do—until the contradictions of being human are permanently *aufgehoben*. Those who proclaim that narrative is the vestige of an irrelevant past are very likely believers in a utopian future; in their understandable eagerness to advance the millennium, they claim for art what is not yet—and very likely never will be—possible in reality.

Story decides for neither plot nor action, the sacred or the human, but lets both stand. It suspends decision or, as Derrida would say, practices the *hymen*.[70] If it saw the truth on one side *or* the other, it would be untrue to our self-contradictory situation. The plot says we don't exist, the action says we do. Plot—like death—denies differences, while the action affirms them. Plot represents divine rule or natural process, yet the action, too— though foreclosed and 'hopeless'—constitutes a natural force and bubbles forth, unconscious of its own limitations.

The plot of story is known and certain, while the action keeps puzzling and surprising us. Plot is an abstraction that detaches us, while the action is concrete and engages us empathetically. As Worringer says:

> We (find) the need for empathy and the need for abstraction to be the two poles of . . . artistic experience . . . They are attributes which, in principle, are mutually exclusive. In actual fact, however, the history of art represents a ceaseless disputation between the two tendencies.[71]

The "disputation" is inherent in story's very form. We can think of plot as an abstract or formal constraint, a frame that—like all formal constraints in art—engenders the tension that *makes* the work: the hot, 'anarchic,' turbu-

123

lent material of the action is forged into shape by the 'cold' limitations imposed by the preclusive form of the plot.

Plot contradicts not only the action but itself. It is at once man-made, yet denies the human will. It renders us as mere creatures but—since *we* are the ones who render it—asserts the very thing it denies.[72] Though plot is an imitation of divine or natural process—of a reality we experience as overwhelming—it is, as well, an attempt to master that reality; for mimesis, *despite* its respect for the object it imitates, is also an attempt at mastery. Plot is a structure or design, yet embodies the very elements against which we *erect* our structures: unpredictability and unaccountability. It is a riddle to which we know the answer, but the answer spells our ignorance; for the one thing story permits us to know with certainty is our uncertainty.

Barthelme says: "Writing is a process of dealing with not-knowing," but it *leaves* us not-knowing. In an often cited letter to Suvorin, Chekhov says:

> You are confusing two concepts: *the solution of a problem* and *the correct posing of a question*. Only the second is obligatory for an artist. Not a single problem is solved in *Anna Karenina* and *Eugene Onegin*, but you find these works quite satisfactory because all the questions in them are correctly posed.[73]

Perhaps the correctly posed question satisfies us while the solution does not, because we know that *all* solutions are temporary.

Whenever one polarity or the other is neglected, story loses its interest and energy. Determinist fiction is flawed by an absence of tension between plot and action, perhaps because the author endows his figures with his sense of helplessness but not with the energy that drove him to tell their story. We are unpersuaded by figures who believe there is nothing they can do, for biology does not encourage resignation and most of us do not quit. Narrative theories that devalue individual effort are apt to turn story into case history, while those that try to *dismiss* determinism turn art into a game. Neither reflects the reality of our experience.

Lukács wrote, critically:

> Every modern drama carries within itself (the) duality of its origin—the simultaneous emergence and cancellation of individuality in bourgeois society—this dialectic of modern life.

But what he calls the "dialectic of modern life"—on the assumption that since it has an historical origin it can be resolved by history—is characteristic of all story, beginning with *Gilgamesh*. As Baudelaire says:

The duality of art is one fatal consequence of the duality of man.[74]

Story is an expression of this duality. It makes no difference whether the artist begins with the subject (himself) and moves toward the object—qualifying and limiting the subject in the process—or whether, through a determined rendering of the *object*, he 'proves' the existence of the subject (himself). The relationship of one to the other *makes* both, and *without both* neither exists.

Traditionally, as we have noted, art is an arena in which we can confront the opposites that would paralyze us in life. By claiming to be an artifact or 'untruth,' it permits us to face the very contradictions, ambiguities, uncertainties, anomalies, and surprises which the community renders harmless and conforms to the certain and familiar. In a setting in which we are not required to *act*, we may actually enjoy what would, in life, produce confusion and conflict. Even in life there are, of course, situations in which it is safe—at least for our *senses*—to delight in 'conflict' and contraries: sweet and sour, hot and cold, hard and soft, gentle and rough, action and passivity. Each polarity brings out the other *and* is reconciled to it.

Like ritual, art affords us an opportunity to cease discriminating and separating—to fuse contraries, subject with object, self with other. It permits us to abandon the very boundaries of the self that the community obliges us to maintain, or to expand them to include others and the world. As Baudelaire says:

> What is pure art according to the modern idea? It is the creation of an evocative magic, containing at once the object and the subject, the world external to the artist and the artist himself.[75]

Story at once integrates and diffuses us. It frees our congealed identity by permitting us to be briefly the other, to identify with the other—who, it turns out, is also us. The storyteller himself is at once distinct from *and* an integral part of the community: by telling his story, he—the outsider—becomes like everyone else.

> An artist is only an artist on condition that he is a double man and that there is not one single phenomenon of his double nature of which he is ignorant.[76]

All story is rife with contradiction. In comedy, sense makes *no* sense and nonsense sense. The jester's motley embodies the polarities. *Joculare* meant not only "to joke" but "to juggle"—to be poised on the edge of the knife. The clown is a moron-genius, a world-renowned nobody like Chaplin, or a millionaire-nebbish like Woody Allen:

Since laughter is essentially human, it is in fact, essentially contradictory . . . a token of an infinite grandeur and an infinite misery.

Laughter is the expression of a double, or contradictory, feeling; and that is the reason why a convulsion occurs.[77]

The ambiguity of tragedy is well-established:

The minute it becomes impossible to read (tragedy) equally well in two different senses . . . the formula loses its enigmatic character, its ambiguity, and the tragic consciousness is gone. For there to be tragedy it must be possible for the text simultaneously to imply two things. . . .

For our mentality today (and even to a large extent, already for Aristotle's) the two interpretations are mutually exclusive. But the logic of tragedy consists of "operating on two planes," in shifting from one meaning to the other, always—to be sure—conscious of the opposition between them but never rejecting either.[78]

Since tragedy is most intensively focused on the individual, it is also the narrative form in which the individual is most graphically in the grip of forces that invalidate the very concept of the individual. The murder Raskolnicov commits in order to prove that he exists proves that he *does not*. The answer to the question posed by his alter ego, Svidrigailov, "Am I a monster or am I myself a victim?", is that he is both. A living contradiction, he is at once a monster to his victims and a helpless victim of the plot.

THE FICTIVE FIGURE IS CAUGHT IN THE CRUX OF THE OPPOSITES

The hero of myth and tragedy is almost invariably self-contradictory. By going forward, he uncovers the past. By using his will, he reveals necessity. By acting, he discovers—or permits us to discover—that he is merely an agent. The double bind in which he finds himself is surely an analogue of our own contradictory situation. Though he is unaware of it, he is exposed to the full force of the opposites, and crucified by them. Often he is himself both hero *and* transgressor—embodying not just the 'positive' but the 'negative' qualities that simpler stories project onto the unambiguous figure of the villain. While we, in the audience, see clearly that he is connected and bound, the hero experiences himself as free and alone. The facts as *we* know them and his own perception of them countermand each other. Objectively, he is powerless, but *subjectively*—and here the poetic language of tragedy forcefully contradicts the plot—he projects both power and free-dom. Stage and film render him as at once puny and huge: Lear, small and vulnerable, fills the theater with his voice, just as the camera can shift from a long shot of an actor to a close-up filling the entire screen with his face. We are both tragic and ridiculous.

Some heroes move from one polarity to its opposite: Lear's prideful self-confidence gives way to an abject recognition of his mortal limitations. Others remain fixed at one polarity throughout—with consequences that are essentially comic in *Don Quixote* and tragic for Mark Antony, a military leader who has fallen into helpless identification with passion and feeling. We can think of the hero as an embodiment of *specialization*. Whether slaying dragons or intensively focused on his own experience and feelings, he is 'unique.' The warrior-heroes of myth were surely among the first to develop a high degree of skill that set them apart from others; explicitly trained for battle, they had to abandon the bonds of civilized society, un-cage their rage, and disconnect from everything but the killing task at hand.

The warrior is specialized in action, and action—unlike contemplation—excludes. *All* specialization requires a degree of polarization and blindness. Nothing else can be allowed equal importance, for if the warrior or special-ist were to see things in proportion, as the rest of us presumably do, he might be unwilling to carry out his task. The blind obsession or 'flaw' of so many tragic and comic figures may be the mark of the specialist.[79] An-tigone, Don Quixote, Antony, Romeo and Juliet, Captain Ahab, Emma Bovary, and Raskolnicov sacrifice their balance and any semblance of wholeness, though without being aware of it. In their excess or polariza-tion, they at once serve the community and endanger it. Like the warrior returning from battle, they can easily rupture the fabric of communal life, and our attitude to them is an ambivalence of fascination and fear, admira-tion and disdain, respect and pity, envy that we are not like them *and* gratitude that we don't have to be. In life, we stay at a safe distance from them; only those who wish to emulate them seek their company.

WE ARE ALL LIVING CONTRADICTIONS

The heroic figure in life is as contradictory as his fictive counterpart. Victor Turner says of Thomas Becket:

(He became) a powerful, "numinous" symbol precisely because, like all domi-nant or focal symbols, he represented a coincidence of opposites, a semantic structure in tension between opposite poles of meaning. Becket was at once lion and lamb, proud and meek. The drama of his pride gives drama and pathos to his self-chosen role of lamb. . . . The intriguing feature of Becket's end was that formally it was a lamb's fate, psychologically it was a lion's.[80]

Charismatic figures in any field tend to constellate the opposites. Napoleon was the self-made man *pàr excellence*, yet clearly determined by a confluence of historical forces:

What I am, I owe to strength of will, character, application and daring.[81]

The greater one is, the less will he must have. He depends on events and circumstances.[82]

I sense that I am driven toward a goal I do not know. As soon as I have reached it, as soon as I am no longer necessary, an atom will be enough to destroy me. Until then, all human power is impotent against me.[83]

Jesus stressed individuality *and* and leveled all differences. It was the leveling of differences—not in ritual, but in life itself—that made him politically dangerous, and prompted Dostoevski's Grand Inquisitor to say that were He to return, the Church would have to burn Him. Every figure who embodies the polarities, or is wholly identified with one or the other, is apt to become 'numinous.' Nietzsche's life and work oscillated between opposites: Dionysus and Apollo, art and science, nihilism and positivism, a tragic sense of life and faith in reason. He served as an interface between irreconcilable polarities and, like many an artist in our time, was torn apart by them.

In fact and fiction, the hero is an outsider for whom the opposites are not mediated by our structures. He must face them alone, often at great cost to himself and those close to him. Yet if he were altogether exceptional and unlike us, his story would have no hold on us. Since we are all obliged to be individuals, we too see ourselves as outsiders and 'special cases'— divided from each other, the community, and ourselves. We identify with the hero and not with the chorus, because we too feel ourselves to be different, 'abnormal,' isolated, and guilty. Though the polarities may not tear us apart, we too are deeply divided—selfish and altruistic, brave and fearful, generous and envious, kind and ruthless, proud and abject, assertive and helpless, hopeful and despairing, certain and insecure, believers and skeptics. We too are living contradictions.

Story Affirms What It Denies

THE IRRELEVANT INDIVIDUAL

Marxist, structuralist, and postmodernist aesthetics appear to agree that the individual is no longer relevant. Nineteenth-century efforts by Marx, Durkheim, and others to reintegrate the subject into a larger whole have given way to the conviction that individual existence and experience are a fiction.[1] Lévi-Strauss says: "The self is not only hateful: there is no place for it between ourselves and nothing";[2] postmodernists call for the deconstruction of the "unitary subject"; and Jameson suggests that:

> The most crucial need of literary theory today is for the development of conceptual instruments capable of doing justice to a post-individualistic experience of the subject in contemporary life itself as well as in the texts.[3]

The dismissal of individual existence in contemporary aesthetics may reflect a widely shared experience of personal impotence, which is a matter of the greatest *public* concern. No doubt the conscious undermining of the self responds, as well, to the excessive emphasis on self that has haunted our recent history. But while individuals like Hitler affected the lives of millions, and though his death before 1939 would have changed the course of our time,[4] his power may have been partly rooted in the very *invalidation* of individual identity—his own and that of the German people—that "the death of man" seems to urge on us. Perhaps it was their gravely threatened sense of themselves—both as a nation and as individuals: the two cannot be separated—that made the Germans identify with a seemingly all-powerful figure, who fused their own sense of helplessness into a national will— subject to *his*—and reestablished their identity by excluding and vitiating the existence of those he deemed subhuman.[5] It was surely no accident that in the camps fascism visited upon its victims the very annihilation of identity that had fed its own origins. A threat to individual existence can lead to its brutal reassertion.

In academic aesthetics, the dismissal of the subject may derive in part from the painful realization by members of a cultural elite that the selfhood to which they aspire is no longer attainable. Perhaps the sense of melancholy belatedness that afflicts some critics springs from the assumption that the self was, at one time, secure and of great significance. Yet individual identity has always been uncertain and ambiguous, for it is simultaneously fostered and undermined by both nature and the community.

No doubt there was a time when communal structures sustained the individual more effectively than today. They gave him a place or role at birth that was his for life and could be passed on to his offspring. They relieved him of contradictions and when he was threatened by liminality, reintegrated him through rites of passage. As long as change was minimal, the individual was secure in his role or station. He could be given his identity—from the Latin *idem*, "the same"—by a set of external coordinates that remained constant for a generation or longer. Moreover, in a 'homogeneous' community members of the group readily confirmed each other. But once specialization required ever greater degrees of differentiation, stable hierarchic structures crumbled and the relationship among individuals became fluid and tenuous. Public institutions, invalidated by the accelerating rate of change, could no longer shore up the individual—who became more disconnected from others as his differences with them were emphasized. New, more specialized structures were required: God was transformed from a public to a personal, or private, deity, whom each of us could address individually: He heard us when no one else listened; He saw and acknowledged us when others ceased to recognize or respect us. The nuclear family emerged to shelter and foster us, and love and friendship became necessary to us as an affirmation of our existence. Instead of being assigned a lasting *public* place, we became special or unique to a few—to 'our' God, our family, our lovers, and our friends.

HEGEL'S CONCEPT OF RECOGNITION

Hegel, in Kojève's interpretation, points to the process by which our existence is sustained. We exist as selves when we are recognized or acknowledged by others:

The human *reality* is nothing but the fact of the *recognition* of one man by *another*.[6]

Every man . . . would like, on the one hand, to be different from all others . . . "the only one of his kind in the world." But on the other hand, he would like to be recognized, in his unique particularity itself, as a positive value, and he would like this to be done by the greatest number, if possible by all. And this is to say, in Hegel's terminology, that the truly human Man, radically different from an animal, always searches for Recognition, and realizes himself only as actually recognized.[7]

Althusser rephrases this in terms of ideology:

You and I are always *already subjects*, and as such constantly practise the rituals of ideological recognition, which guarantees for us that we are indeed concrete, individual, distinguishable and (naturally) irreplaceable subjects.[8]

To be recognized is at once to be confirmed as a separate being *and* reintegrated into the community. When I am known as a discrete individual, I become part of the whole.

OUR IDENTITY CAN NO LONGER BE SUSTAINED

The relationships we make, the web of human connections that hold us, confirm that we are. They are the means by which most of us are acknowledged. When an old man loses his wife, there is often no one left who knows or 'recognizes' him, and he too is threatened with nonexistence. Today, many of us are no longer acknowledged by others. We are at best recognized intermittently and so become intermittent ourselves. Subject to constant change, most relationships are no longer dependable. The nuclear family, which took over from the community the role of affirming and integrating the individual, is in disarray. Since we are no longer known— not even, on occasion, to ourselves—we barely exist. Moreover, in our own highly diversified, heterogeneous society, differences among us extend to every area of our lives—heritage, race, religion, economic class, vocation—and further undermine our identity. We are not at all alike. If *you* are okay, there must be something wrong with me. Since we live in perpetual social and economic flux, we find it hard to maintain our 'sameness.' The modes of production—which require a pool of interchangeable workers, flexible and ready to move from one place and job to another—make it difficult to sustain a sense of our continuity. Even gender differences can no longer be counted on to support our identity.

131

Many of us are permanently marginalized. We have no role or place. "Homelessness," as Heidegger says, "is coming to be the destiny of the world"—whereas, in time past, it was the experience of just a few.[9] Perhaps the postmodern assertion that man is dead and the self a delusion is an attempt to make a virtue of our painful reality. It issues, however, from a small group of intellectuals who have shored up their own identity in the process, and is most loudly proclaimed in France, a country that has, among its intellectuals and artists, a deeply entrenched tradition of individualism. They can well afford such a doctrine and may indeed need it to offset their own isolation. As to its general validity, the words of Marcuse continue to apply:

> The rejection of the invidual as a "bourgeois" concept recalls and presages fascist undertakings.[10]

"THE 'I' MUST ALWAYS BE MAINTAINED"

Ironically, "the death of man" was announced at the very moment when many people saw, for the first time in recent history, the possibility of establishing an identity and a measure of individuality for themselves. The self may be an illusion, but it is worth every sacrifice to them. It may, indeed, be tragically related to the reemergence of nationalism and ethnocentricity—to the retribalization of the earth—for individual and communal identity are inextricably linked.

No society can afford the death of man. The more our existence as individuals is in doubt, the more urgently the community must affirm it. The value of the subject has to be demonstrated continually because the modes of production and our weapons of destruction make it ever more irrelevant. While thousands perish in our slums, ignored, anonymous and unmourned, the entire nation watches spellbound as no effort and expense are spared to save the life of a single child trapped in a well-shaft. The self is stressed wherever possible and asserts itself whenever and however it can. Our physical survival is clearly primary, but since we cannot survive outside society and since society depends on our identity, the self is as essential to us as our physical being. A young woman who was dying of leukemia told me: "If I could go on living by being someone else, I'd still choose to be me and die."

Today the individual, faced with his own irrelevance, must grasp at straws to shore up his 'unique' identity. As Adorno says:

The weaker he becomes, from a societal perspective, the less can he become calmly aware of his own impotence. He has to puff himself up into selfness.[11]

Power, wealth, publicity, the envy of others, physical sensations, even obsessions, illness, and anxiety can serve—however inadequately—to give us a sense of identity. Our belongings substitute for the place to which we once belonged. Since we have no sense of self, we become narcissists. We take photographs because they permit us to see ourselves and so appear to *be*. A friend told me that when he was diagnosed as having cancer, one thought that came to him was: "Now I *am* someone; now I have something of consequence." When our structures fail to validate us, we try to do so on our own—often by asserting ourselves over or against others.[12] Violence, crime, cruelty, and suicide will get us a response. If I have an effect on you, or if you read and talk about me, I exist. The celebrity is known for being known. Fame and notoriety, always an incentive, have become an end in themselves. The young man who killed John Lennon told the police:

"I was an acute nobody. I had to usurp someone else's importance, someone else's success. I was 'Mr. Nobody' until I killed the biggest Somebody on earth."

Lee Harvey Oswald may have been driven by the same need.

Our anomie and homelessness, despite the burden they impose on us, are not without use to society. They make us conveniently interchangeable *and* fuel competition and achievement. Our sense of inadequacy and incompleteness prompts us to 'distinguish' ourselves. By getting ahead of others—by 'winning'—we make a place for ourselves and do the work the community needs to get done. We are urged to establish our identity as specialists—to become 'special' to the community through persistent and rigorous effort.

If we are truly interested in modifying the abrasive, destructive nature of our relationships, what may be called for is not the extinction of the self but its restoration, albeit in altered and more inclusive form. As Bloch says: We must "let Kant burn through Hegel: the 'I' must always be maintained."[13] Our present situation is surely nothing but the painful uncertainty from which new structures and a new conception of the individual will emerge.

OUR IDENTITY HAS ALWAYS BEEN TENUOUS

We have noted that human identity has ever been in doubt. Most groups have had to reconfirm themselves over and over. Like has clung to like and fought, often to the death, with those who are *unlike*—who both threaten our identity *and* confirm it by being different. Want and greed alone cannot account for the ferocity of our wars and conflicts, in which the need for asserting our doubtful existence has clearly played a part.

Though the subject was at one time sheltered by the group, it has always been marginal—or, as the postmodernist says, "in crisis." The individual has never been in charge of his own destiny. He cannot decide his birth or heritage, his physical and intellectual endowment, or his gender. He comes into the world helpless and beholden, and needs years to acquire what is at most a narrow margin of independence, will, and self. Moreover, once the community has proclaimed his independent or 'free' existence—his coming of age—it must place him in a double bind: he is at once expected to *be* and *not* to be. He must be flexible yet steadfast, fragmented but continuous, integrated yet open to change. His situation is profoundly ambiguous. As Jung puts it:

> One is oneself the biggest of all one's assumptions, and the one with the gravest consequences.[14]

Of course not just the individual but humankind itself is marginal and in doubt. Consciousness—the knowledge that we *are*—brings with it an awareness that we are *not*. And so each individual, like the hero, serves not only his community but the species by proclaiming his brave "I am" and "I can."

STORY AS AN AFFIRMATION OF IDENTITY

If the self had not always been in doubt, there would be no stories. Just as historical accounts confirm the identity of a group or nation, so story clearly serves the continuity of the individual. All stories are centered on the survival of the subject, which is embodied in the hero or heroine of myth, epic, tragedy, comedy, fairy tale, novel, and movie. We have noted that the comic figure is *immune* to change. He remains Punch, Charlie, and Malvolio—'eternal' stuff, whether it be Punch's aggressive instincts, Charlie's will to survive, or Malvolio's delusional system. Even the deceptions, disguises, and mistaken identities that fuel the action in comedy are evidence of its concern with a continuous, invulnerable self. The figures may deceive each other, but their essential nature is evident to us from the start.

Tragedy values the self so highly that its survival is purchased with the hero's life. What is at stake for Antigone is more important to her, and to us, than her physical existence. She dies, but she is not annihilated. We would lose all interest in *Moby Dick* if Ahab gave in to the entreaties of the *Rachel* and turned away from his doomed pursuit, for he would cease to be Ahab.[15] Like Oedipus, Macbeth, and Antony, he must persist and in persisting, affirm his identity. In story, common sense, decency, and a concern for others have no dominion. Disaster is acceptable to us, but abandoning the self is not. Significantly, in their relationship to *us*, all tragic figures are 'authentic.' They may dissemble in front of the others on stage, but they reveal themselves to the audience. In daily life, our own 'inauthenticity' is not, of course simply deceitful; it is part of the necessary process of compromise—of qualifying our responses, feelings, thoughts, and needs—that makes relationship and community possible. But in the safe arena of fiction, this 'inauthenticity'—and the sense of discontinuity and marginality it engenders—is compensated by the 'authenticity' of the central figures and their actions.

Story is almost invariably focused on the personal. The public aspect of the action is of little interest, and major events are rendered largely in their impact on the private realm. Though the hero of *Gilgamesh* is a king, the epic deals entirely with his own experience. The *Iliad* personalizes even war. Work is invariably shortchanged in fiction: rulers spend little time ruling, and it is their ambitions, passions, and relationships to their families, lovers, and friends that occupy us. Stories are rarely concerned with the administration of law and justice, while *private* vengeance is a common source of comic and tragic action.

Revenge is inextricably linked to consciousness, and so to our existence. No animal is vindictive. Only a conscious being, who sees himself as separate and continuous with his own past, can be held accountable for an injury, and only a conscious being can exact retribution. Because revenge is rooted in the very core of our social being—in our accountability—it is a central concern. For while we must be held personally responsible for our actions, we cannot be allowed to exact personal retribution from those who have injured us, or our accountability would undo the very order it is meant to preserve.

Artists and storytellers have always been guardians of the self. They may have been specialists almost as long as the warrior and the priest. With the Renaissance, when the place of the individual was undermined by accelerating processes of specialization and fragmentation, the artist himself became a 'hero.' As one who very likely suffered from an *exacerbated* form of the "homelessness" that is our shared destiny, he became both liminal and famous. His place and identity were put in grave doubt and needed to be constantly reaffirmed by his work. Very likely his search for public recognition springs from a need for communal approval of his lonely, asocial task. Like the hero, he must risk himself to gain his place. Cézanne says: "With every brushstroke I risk my life." But with every brushstroke he also *saves* his life, and perhaps ours as well. In being true to his own experience, and by appearing to reject his commonality with others, he renders an aspect of our own existence to which we have no ready access. He serves the community by *not* being part of it. It is his social function to specialize in himself, to bear witness to his own singularity and so to ours. As Rilke says:

> *Once*
> each but *once. Once* and no more. And we too,
> *once.* Never again. But
> to have been here *once,* even if only *once,*
> to have been on earth *once* would seem irrevocable.[16]

Art confirms the self by intensifying our experience: we become important and, indeed, invaluable. In the poem—though only in the poem—every death diminishes us, for every death is our own.

Poulet has traced the pervasive experience of our personal discontinuity that prompted storytelling in the modern era and may—in my view—have informed it from the start:[17]

> If I could have the assurance of duration, I would be perfectly content with my lot.
>
> Constant[18]

> Every minute of my life seems cut off at a stroke from every other by an abyss; between yesterday and today there is an eternity that appals me.[19]

> Something undefined separates you from your own person and rivets you to nonbeing.
>
> Flaubert[20]

> One is no longer a person.[21]

> The disintegration of the self is a continuous death. . . . The natural stability which we assume to exist in others is as unreal as our own.
>
> Proust[22]

Proust knows he has much in common with Sheherezade. By telling his story—in sentences and paragraphs that resist their period as long as possible—he postpones and finally escapes altogether the threatened extinction of his own identity. No other storyteller has so persistently used every available scrap of his own experience, weaving apparently random and disconnected bits into a continuous whole. His inquiries into the clothes friends had worn on a particular evening years earlier were not, of course, made in the service of verisimilitude, but in an effort to substantiate the reality of his own existence. The search for and recovery of lost time is the search for and recovery of the lost self.[23] What is perhaps the longest story in world literature is ultimately an effort to shore up humanity's smallest unit—the individual.

> When the bell tinkled, I was already in existence and, since that night, for me to have been able to hear the sound again, there must have been no break of continuity, not a moment of rest for me, no cessation of existence, of thought, of consciousness of myself, since this distant moment still clung to me and I could recapture it, go back to it, merely by descending more deeply within myself. It was this conception of time as incarnate, of past years as still close held within us, which I now determined to bring out into such close relief in my book. . . .
>
> There came over me a feeling of profound fatigue at the realization that all this long stretch of time not only had been uninterruptedly lived, thought, secreted by me, that it was my life, my very self, but also that I must, every minute of my life, keep it closely by me, that it upheld me, that I was perched on its dizzying summit, that I could not move without carrying it about with me.[24]

As Kierkegaard says: recollection banishes anxiety and continuity is "the first sign of salvation."[25]

THE MODERN WORK AFFIRMS
THE THREATENED SELF

The artist's permeable identity places him on a threshold between being and not being. Like the hero, he is a coincidence of opposites and riven by contradictions. His parentage, like the hero's, is often obscure or in doubt. Psychologically, he *has* no parents. He is not sure who he is or whether he is at all. *Car JE est un autre*, says Rimbaud, echoing Rousseau's "the me is another."[26] "I don't know who I am or who I was," says Giacometti. "I know it less than ever. I do and don't identify myself with myself."[27] Van Gogh, who painted hundreds of pictures called "Vincent," was the second son in his family to be called Vincent—after an older brother who died—an acceptable custom as long as our identity was guaranteed by the community at large, but surely a heavy burden for anyone whose existence must be validated by the nuclear family. "Above all," says Nietzsche, "do not mistake me for another."[28]

The modern artist secures his identity by being deeply different. His concern with the tradition is, in part, an effort to establish his lineage, and his preoccupation with posterity and the continuing value of his work is a concern for a lasting identity.[29] His work, in turn, is often patronized and collected by aristocrats and captains of industry—outsiders for whom an independent and highly differentiated individuality is of critical importance.

Since style is the individual man, each artist—even today—is expected to discover and develop a style of his own. You can learn from Cézanne but you must not paint like him, for to do so is to vitiate the very thing he and his predecessors have passed on to us. Style is forged by experience and experience is always in some sense personal, even when it is shared, for our sensory and nervous systems are discrete from other people's. Traditionally, art stresses the anomalies of individual experience; it particularizes. Even in myth and fairy tale the action is sensory, concrete, and specific; it is focused on the personal, the immediate, the 'different.' "Is not style," Synge said to Yeats, "born out of the shock of new material?"[30] Benjamin opposes the "shock experience"[31] of the artwork to "the increasing atrophy of experience,"[32] and Shklovsky's defamiliarization renders the object as *seen*, not as *recognized*, as "perceived," not as "known."[33] Individual experience has been at the heart of Western art at least since the Renaissance, and the focus of story for much longer. El Greco, in subsuming the visible world with his brushstroke, asserts the same self that James tries to shore up by telling his stories from a single point of view. As Benjamin says:

> It is not the object of the story to convey a happening *per se*, which is the purpose of information; rather, it embeds it in the life of the storyteller in order to pass it on as experience to those listening. It thus bears the mark of the potter's hand.
>
> Proust's eight-volume work conveys an idea of the effort it took to restore the figure of the storyteller to the present generation.[34]

The "figure" or identity of the storyteller Proust restores to us is, of course, our own.[35]

POSTMODERNISM AFFIRMS THE SELF

Despite its declared intentions, postmodern art continues to affirm the self. Warhol doubts his existence; he was "obsessed with the idea of looking in

138

the mirror and seeing no one, nothing."[36] And yet he proves what he doubts in the very act of doubting it. He establishes his name and place by disclaiming them: I know I am not; therefore I am. Even if we no longer believe in our separate being, we cannot escape the effort to exist or "stand out," for society demands it of us.

Deconstruction, too, may affirm what it undermines. As we have noted, writing—carried out in solitude, and far less open than the spoken word to the immediate influence of others—confirms our identity. As I write, I become continuous. My concentration and effort, the flow of the pen and the sentence, prove I exist in time, however marginally.[37] Postmodernism's 'attack' on the "unitary subject" may be an inverted attempt to shore it up. Surely it is no accident that America's foremost deconstructionists were once students of Romanticism, with its determined struggle to save the self. Their elaborate linguistic play and the sophisticated reasoning they bring to bear on Western logocentrism establish a peer group of the select, who confirm each other as individuals. Though it has been said on behalf of their work that a sophisticated attack is needed to penetrate the defenses of the self, the annihilation of the subject can be achieved, as the death camps demonstrate, with far less intellectual effort.

THE EXPECTATIONS OF MOST AUDIENCES REMAIN TRADITIONAL

Even as postmodern theory appears to affirm the existence of the critic, it undermines the individuality of everyone else and challenges the concept of the self that has, traditionally, been the focus of narrative. Since most of us, however, do not suffer the critic's existential anxiety—so close to the artist's own—and lack his intellectual gifts, we retain a traditional view of art and story, and continue, perhaps naively, to seek in them a confirmation of our own identity. We expect fiction to involve us with a central figure, to engage us in a process of discovery, and to provide an uninterrupted flow of experience—most often tense or intense—so that we may ourselves become continuous as we watch or listen. Some stories wholly occupy our feelings and thoughts, while others, like horror movies, do little more than bombard us with sensations. Either way, our reactions make us continuous in time. Even the *dis*continuity and absence of feeling in contemporary fiction can make for a continuous experience on our part, for they mirror our own and so confirm us. The basic expectation we bring to story from childhood on—that we be allowed to believe it—suggests its existential function: if it is credible, 'real,' or 'true' to our experience, it confirms that

139

we ourselves are 'real' and exist. Music, too, can give us a continuous sense of ourselves. Perhaps Muzak is piped into public places in part to countermand the fragmentation to which we are subjected; it is a reassuring *continuo*.[38] If the piece is familiar—as Muzak always is—it hearkens back to an earlier occasion, like the tinkling bell in Proust. Memory is the mother of all the muses.

SOCIETY MUST GENERALIZE OUR EXPERIENCE

It is well understood that our experience is, and must be, prestructured— that we could not perceive anything if it were not already known and comprehensible. There nonetheless remains a trace of the new or shocking. Indeed, what we encounter in the contemporary world is often so unfamiliar, disconcerting, or brutal that we shut off our responses and perceive or feel nothing in order to get through the day.

Even if perception did not depend on a known *Gestalt* that creates 'order' out of the welter of stimuli bombarding our senses, the community can function only because our experiences are generalized, or homogenized, to resemble the experience of others. We must come as close as possible to experiencing 'reality' as others do, so that we may all understand and mean the same thing. Potentially glaring differences between your experience and mine are reduced to a common denominator. Much of what we might *actually* perceive and feel is thus devalued or repressed—especially in a diverse and heterogeneous society like our own. In the process, our sense of self is likely to become intermittent.

Story serves to make us briefly continuous by *stressing* the very differences we must disregard in life. We connect with the central figure of myth and tragedy *in* his difference, and recognize ourselves in his anomalous situation. We are like him because he is *unlike* the others. Surely stories about an elite figure, a king or leader, were meaningful to commoners because his 'difference' and special status confirmed their own separate, 'unique' being. Even popular movies—which assimilate individual experience to a broadly inclusive norm—focus on an outsider, who has trouble fitting in. He is usually 'right,' while the community is blind and in error. Moreover, both popular and unpopular stories enhance our sense of continuity by giving us access to the very impulses—fear, aggression, lust, envy—we must repress or hide in life. They integrate what is vulnerable, weak, shameful, and unconscious in us. They make us whole and continuous by including our secret, 'authentic' selves.

140

OUR CONTINUITY IN TIME MAKES UP
FOR OUR LOSS OF PLACE

We have noted that our identity is largely determined and guaranteed by our place in the community. Indeed, we can think of identity as a *form* of place. Before we were conscious, we—like other creatures—were presumably linked to a group and its territory. But once we became conscious, we were no longer wholly continuous with the rest of creation. We lost our unconscious or natural place, and had to be integrated into the scheme of things by our communal structures and institutions—a word derived from the Latin *in* and *statuere*, "to place or set." When these structures fail us, we are set adrift and disintegrate, for place is meaning and to lose one's place is to lose one's reason for being. As Gerhardt Adler says: "Meaning resides in the experience that the individual personality is included in a suprapersonal totality," that he has a place in the scheme of things.[39] Our search for meaning is a search for place or connection—for an order of which we are a part.

We might call identity "a moveable territory."[40] For millennia, our link to an actual place on earth helped to anchor us. Many of our gods were gods of place and most family names derived from locality—with work, or our social role, as the next most common source.[41] As long as we felt connected to an actual place, we belonged and existed. But as we became increasingly mobile and our ties to a specific territory grew ever more tenuous, we had to locate ourselves in *time*. We acquired a temporal continuity—a history and an identity that permitted us to play our role and kept us linked to the group even when we were on our own. The footloose and differentiated individual needed a past and a future, so that he would know who he was. The scouts and 'heroes' who were dispatched on distant journeys were surely among the first to depend on their continuity in time. Anyone who was called upon to separate or distinguish himself from others, and so lost his connection with them, required an identity.

WE ARE NO LONGER NECESSARY

Until recently, our lives were governed by necessity, which was immediately present to us. It placed us, assigned us our roles, formed the predicate of all our structures, and forged clear, inescapable connections among us. Even today most of us derive our sense of being, our 'right' to be, from being needed or necessary—if only to one other person. When we are needed, we have meaning and value; we know who we are and what we must do. When necessity asserts itself—when our survival is threatened, for instance—it sets clear priorities and informs our perceptions and actions. It orients and harmonizes us, and concentrates our being wonderfully; we know why we are alive. Conversely, when we lose touch with necessity, we become aimless, scattered, and marginal.

Yet humankind has always endeavored to *escape* necessity, and in the modern era some of us have actually succeeded in distancing ourselves from immediate physical need and danger. In the process, we too have become unnecessary. Our newly gained power has made us superfluous. We are no longer needed to provide our own food and shelter. When we were short-lived and vulnerable to nature, we were in short supply and each one of us was precious to the community. But by the nineteenth century, Hebbel could say: "The tree has more leaves than it needs, and the world more people."[42] With necessity at bay, established priorities lost their claim and the structures that depended on them crumbled. It is surely no accident that once we began to think we had vanquished necessity, both God and the self died. For God *is* necessity, and with necessity no longer constraining and connecting us, individual existence, too, has lost its meaning and 'reality.'

Since necessity limits us, it confers value and meaning, for we treasure whatever is scarce and subject to loss. Our communities, institutions, relationships, and commitments were engendered by our biological limitations. Life was both limited and sacralized by death. Mortality informed morality, and aesthetics, too, was informed by limitation and scarcity. Less was more. Matisse reduced the figure to a single line, and Chaplin derived maximum use from every object and situation. Economy and density were not a matter of choice but dictated by a world view governed by necessity. Stravinsky says:

> Limitations are precisely what I need and am looking for above all in everything I compose. The limits generate the form.[43]

For him, as for Hebbel: "Form is the expression of necessity."[44]

PLEASURE HAS BECOME NECESSARY

Today, for those who live in plenty, what was once scarce and precious is precious no longer. Even *time*—once fully taken up with meeting our needs—is not scarce or essential any more. We have more time than we need: we have leisure. Since we live longer and healthier lives, death is no longer a constant presence; we have managed to push it into the margin of our awareness, and our aesthetic has changed accordingly. Less is less now and pleasure—so Barthes and others tell us—is the *sole* purpose of art.[45] We can even afford the 'free-play' of deconstruction. Indeed, with the essential no longer pressing in upon us, we seem, like Oscar Wilde, to *need* the unnecessary or superfluous.[46] Pleasure itself may have become essential to us,[47] for we must fill our vacant, leisure time or come face to face with nothingness. Art only *appears* to serve itself—to be art for art's sake. It remains essential or necessary, since it fills the void and fosters a sense of community. No 'primitive' audience could have been more addicted to story than we are to the distractions of film and television.

Our new freedom leaves us anxious, for we sense that even as we seem to have escaped the grip of necessity, we have lost our place, role, and identity. Our concern with the present, possible only because we no longer need worry about the immediate future, has left us without continuity and purpose, just as our escape from the constraining structures of the past has left us disoriented and marginal. We have lost our hold on *time* just as, earlier, we lost our hold on place.

STORY AFFIRMS US BY AFFIRMING NECESSITY

Our escape from necessity is, of course, an illusion. It governs us still, whatever we may tell ourselves and whatever our Positivist tradition proposes. Most of us sense that we can't escape it, even if we cannot acknowledge it. We continue telling stories because they remain valid—because they remind us that we are not free and so countermand our liminality. We may deem homelessness to be our special fate but it has always been with us, and story shelters us against it.

As we have noted, plot is place. It is an analogue of necessity or destiny—from the Latin *destinare*, "to place down, to make secure." The dramatic crisis—from the Greek *krinein*, "to separate"—divides the essential from the inessential. It establishes priorities and commits the hero to a course of action. Once he is committed, he knows who he is and what he must do. His situation—from the Latin *situ*, "a site"—integrates him into the larger scheme of things. He may see himself as alone and isolated but is, in fact, everywhere connected. The plot holds him as firmly as the design of ancient Peking held its citizens, assigning to each a place in the universe. The very element in story that seems to *in*validate the hero—the "immobilization of man"—validates his existence. It places him in both time and space, which are, in story, one. He is part of necessity and therefore necessary.

143

More explicitly than the heroes of old, Captain Ahab sets out to reestablish his place in the universe. He seeks vengeance—for only if Moby Dick has injured him malevolently does he himself have a place and meaning. Though he is unaware of it, he is looking for a plot to hold him—a plot *against* himself. He hunts down the whale until, at last, it turns on him and destroys him. He dies—at the end of the Christian era, and in an inversion of the life and death of Christ—to prove that God *hates* him, for hate is preferable to indifference. His shipmates are sure that the whale is unconscious and utterly indifferent to him:

> "Oh! Ah," cried Starbuck, "not too late it is, even now, the third day, to desist. See! Moby Dick seeks thee not. It is thou, thou, that madly seekest him."[48]

Melville himself seems less certain. In the final battle, he describes the whale's "predestinating head":

> Retaliation, swift vengeance, eternal malice were in his whole aspect.[49]

But even if Moby Dick is indifferent and without memory or malice, and even if Ahab's life has no 'meaning' in the universe at large, the novel—like a memorial stele—*gives* him his place. The quest itself becomes meaningful and the hero survives in the *telling*. If the white whale is unique, so surely is Ahab. There is a secret link between him and his lowliest shipmate: both are displaced and homeless. "Call me Ishmael."

WE EXPECT STORY TO PLACE US

We come to story in large part to be placed. For just as it reintegrates the central figure into the whole, so it joins us who are watching or listening into a community. It compensates for the sense of isolation, dread, and guilt that is, in some measure, the lot of all. Our conscious existence—the 'freedom' that society must impose on us—makes us anxious. "Dread," says Kierkegaard, "is the possibility of freedom."[50] To be separate from the group—from our place and matrix—is frightening and dangerous, and story countermands it by placing, connecting, and 'immobilizing' us. In rites of passage, the sacred serves as a catchment for those who have become liminal, and in just this way, the plot—as an analogue of necessity or the sacred—integrates and places us. Schopenhauer's definition of tragedy as a shattering of the *principium individuationis* is true of all story.[51] We identify with the helpless fictive figure and with his effort to change what cannot be changed and, by recognizing ourselves in him, become alike. Through our shared identification with a hero who is like us in his very otherness, we are joined to all those who are watching with us. If the comic hero were truly different from us, we would not laugh at him. Our response is a public confession of our likeness and purges us, briefly, of difference. The very shame that attaches to our otherness in life *bonds* the audience. As in the sociology of Durkheim, the outsider or deviant *creates* the community, though in story we are ourselves the outsiders. One could liken the audience to a therapeutic community, brought together by a secret, shared vulnerability in a context that allows us to admit to it without risk.

STORY AND *COMMUNITAS*

Not only the young, who must separate from their families and suffer a pervasive sense of liminality, flock to the movies. Adults, too, spend hours each day watching television, which offers them membership in the community at large. We may even choose the most popular programs or read best sellers because they link us to the greatest number of others.

Story, like ritual, engenders a state Victor Turner calls *communitas*,[52] which complements and compensates social structure. It is egalitarian, undifferentiated, and nonlogical, whereas our structures are hierarchic, differentiated, and emphatically ordered. It offers us relief from the conflicts, competition, and tension that are a byproduct of communal life:

> Exposure to or immersion in *communitas* seems to be an indispensable human social requirement.[53]

> Paradoxically, the ritual reduction of structure to *communitas*. . .has the effect of regenerating the principles of classification and ordering on which social structure rests.[54]

Communitas is an equivalent of the temporary merging of the self with the rest of creation, of subject with object, which has always been central to the processes of ritual and art.[55] It compensates for the differences that make civilized life possible—differences that must and will reemerge. As Lévi-Strauss says:

> We can easily now conceive of a time when there will be only one culture and one civilization on the entire surface of the earth. I don't believe this will happen, because there are contradictory tendencies always at work—on the

one hand towards homogenization and on the other towards new distinctions. The more a civilization becomes homogenized, the more internal lines of separation become apparent; and what is gained on one level is immediately lost on another. This is a personal feeling, in that I have no clear proof of the operation of this dialectic.[56]

Turner is less tentative. He claims that "no society can function without this dialectic."[57]

STORY AT ONCE CONFIRMS AND SUBSUMES DIFFERENCE

We have noted that the community can permit the elimination of differences only within clearly defined limits. Ritual is carefully circumscribed both in time and place, and story constitutes a safe arena—an as-if situation we can believe and disbelieve at the same time. In story, moreover, *communitas* is created in a contradictory process: our difference or identity is at once subsumed *and* confirmed. We surrender our selves, but surrender them to the hero—or self—at the center of the action. We are recrystallized even as we are diffused or dissolved. In story, we can become "the I that is a we and the we that is an I."[58] It achieves what Hegel asks of philosophy: "The union of union and non-union,"[59] and attains to "spirit"—which he defines as "pure self-recognition in absolute otherness."[60] Opposites are at once *aufgehoben* and maintained—a utopian state we may strive for in life but can achieve only for brief moments.

STORY'S CONTRADICTIONS CONFIRM US

Though the plot seems to undermine us, both as a species and as individuals, the self-contradictory situation of the hero confirms our very being, our identity. Like him, we obey necessity by rebelling against it, serve the community by 'opposing' it, and join it by remaining 'outsiders.' Like him, we must heed the double message both nature and the community send us. The very contradictions that threaten to tear the hero apart mirror and so confirm our own condition. Like him, we exist at the edge of nonbeing. Like him, we are an interface with the sacred.

Our *experience* of story is contradictory—most vividly in the theater. We remain who we are even as we merge with the rest of the audience. We at once observe the events *and* participate in them, lend ourselves empathetically to the action though we know the outcome in advance, and find ourselves tense and hopeful despite our foreknowledge. In story, we are surprised by what we already know. The very fact that we don't register these contradictions but accept them without question may suggest that they are analagous to our life situation. Contradictions are basic to human existence and may, as we have noted, be the very element that makes story persuasive or 'real' to us. The tension between opposites that sustains narrative is the very tension that sustains *us*.

Our experience of story is paradoxical at the deepest level. We look to it for reassurance, seeking its familiar pattern, like the child who asks for the same bedtime story night after night. Propp has established that what he calls the thirty-one "functions" of the folk tale occur in ordered sets or sequences,[61] and Forster speaks of the novel as "repetition with variations."[62] But the familiar and expected pattern in story is not altogether reassuring. The certainties that the plot offers us and the place it assigns us put our existence in doubt, for they are linked to our *non*being, to a loss of separateness. They are linked, indeed, to that other 'plot' awaiting us: the grave—in which the figure literally merges with the ground. We do and *don't* want to be placed. We both *want* to know what story tells us and *don't*. Our need to be part of the whole may find expression not only in eros but in *thanatos*—the "death instinct" that Freud opposes to *eros*.[63] Though a "death instinct" is hard to demonstrate, our need for wholeness or fusion is evident everywhere. Freud was fond of an old saying: *Alle Liebe ist Heimweh*—"all love is homesickness"—and perhaps *thanatos*, like *eros*, is a response to the state of homelessness that consciousness has imposed on us.

The truth we seek in story is a truth we already know. We want to evade it even as we are drawn to it. If we did not already know it, we would not be looking for it.[64] If we were not terrified of it, we would not need to find it in story—which countermands it even as it asserts it. We dare face it only in an as-if situation, one we can leave behind at story's end—knowing all the while that it is our deepest reality. As Heidegger says:

> The most difficult learning is to come to know actually and to the very foundations what we already know.[65]

We must both know *and* forget it, for to live in its presence would constitute a kind of death. Yet a life without it is a life without meaning. Story arouses that "strange state of mind" Freud describes, "in which one knows and does not know a thing at the same time."[66]

STORY LETS THE CONTRADICTIONS STAND

Coleridge sees art as a reconciliation of opposites.[67] He follows Schelling in suggesting that it begins with "the feeling of a seemingly insoluble contradiction," which is completely resolved at the end.[68] But though this may apply to story on the surface, it is patently untrue of its contradictory structure. Lévi-Strauss proposes that

> The purpose of myth is to provide a logical model capable of overcoming a contradiction (an impossible achievement if, as it happens, the contradiction is real).[69]

Since story's form, which governs American Indian myths as it does all narrative, is *itself* contradictory and 'illogical,' it cannot possibly overcome contradictions 'logically.' Instead of attempting to resolve them, story lets them stand. Plot and action cannot be reconciled any more than we can reconcile the contradictions of our existence. Like Cleopatra, we can solve the paradox of our being—"this knot intrinsicate of life"—only at the moment of death. If she were to go on living, she would once again become subject to the contrary pull of the opposites.

We cannot pin story down. If we find its meaning in the plot, we fail to account for the action. If we stress the human, we neglect the sacred. Story's meaning is inherently unstable, shifting continually between polarities. Because it permits us to slide in either direction, it has often been read to justify one position or the other, but its form refuses all final solutions and undermines all authoritative interpretations. It gives us no directives. It is not open to the effort of traditional criticism, which, as Derrida says, tries "to determine a meaning through a text, to pronounce a decision upon it, to decide that this or that *is* a meaning."[70] What de Man says of the poem is true of story as well:

> The poem doesn't simply (have) two meanings that exist side by side. The two readings have to engage each other in direct confrontation, since the one reading is precisely the error denounced by the other and has to be undone by it. Nor can we in any way make a valid decision as to which of the readings can be given priority over the other; none can exist in the other's absence.[71]

Story's contradictions effectively approximate the "pluridimensional order" of reality that Barthes says cannot be rendered. Its polarities provide a seemingly endless source of *Unbestimmtheitsstellen*—points of indeterminacy.[72] Every reader, and certainly every generation of readers, is 'free' to fasten on a different point in the range of possibilities that is open between them. The polarities make the text *scriptible*. They give us access to the work and leave us with a measure of freedom that allows us to interpret it *in accordance with our own experience.*

THE JANUS FACE OF ART

Like religion, story is Janus-faced—at once radical and conservative. We can read it as advocating submission *or* rebellion; it serves as a source of pacification *and* resistance. Thus comedy is both subversive and a safety valve. Since reason, however, is uncomfortable with ambiguity, aesthetic theories, too, tend to take an either/or position. They call art either radical *or* conservative. As Girard says:

> The fundamental duality of tragedy led to the opposing formulations of Aristotle and Plato. . . . In (Aristotle's) view the art of tragedy affirms, consolidates, and preserves everything that deserves to be affirmed, consolidated and preserved.
> Plato, by contrast, is closer in spirit and time to the crisis. It is not the stately affirmation of great cultural rites that he discerns in *Oedipus The King*, but rather the differences.[73]

The either/or view of art is maintained in contemporary aesthetics. Barthes sees myth—and, by implication, traditional narrative—as immobilizing and scorns its ambiguity as a justification for doing and changing nothing. For him, myth is "on the right."[74] Conversely, Adorno—though fully aware of the Janus face of art[75]—tries to integrate the traditional work into a contemporary political context, and to reconcile it with a Marxist perspective:

> A successful artwork . . . is not one which resolves objective contradictions in a spurious harmony, but one which expresses the idea of harmony negatively by embodying the contradictions, pure and uncompromised, in its innermost structure.[76]

In Adorno's view, great art is "negative" and "critical." His aesthetic was an "attempt to see the new in the old instead of simply the old in the new."[77] For Marcuse, too,

> Art has its magic power only as the power of negation. It can speak its own language only as long as the images are alive which refuse and refute the established order.[78]

But art is on *both* sides and, like religion, has always been used by both. It isn't for *or* against anything. It at once gives new life to old structures and invalidates *all* structures. It creates order and vitiates it. It takes no positions and thereby remains inclusive, for every position inevitably excludes. We could say it is deconstructive and postmodern—and *has* been from the very beginning—for it erases what it tells us and reconstructs, in the telling, the very thing it denies. It is a strong rendering of a frail figure, a far from helpless narrative of human helplessness, a controlled picture of an uncontrolled state, a successful account of human failure. Indeed, the advantage art enjoys over all linear or logical descriptions of our reality is that it can sustain two opposites at the same time without invalidating itself. Beckett says:

> I take no sides. . . . There is a wonderful sentence in Augustine: "Do not despair; one of the thieves was saved. Do not presume; one of the thieves was damned."[79]

And Kundera notes that

> The novel is, by definition, the ironic art: its "truth" is concealed, undeclared, undeclarable. . . . It denies us our certainties by unmasking the world as an ambiguity. . . . It is futile to make a novel "difficult" through stylistic affectation; any novel worth the name, however limpid it may be, is difficult enough by its consubstantiated irony.[80]

The 'consubstantial' tension between the opposites in narrative may resemble Bohr's principle of complementarity:

> The quantum theoretical dualism of waves and particles makes the same entity appear both as matter and as force.[81]

> Bohr advocated the use of both pictures, which he called "complementary" to each other. The two pictures are of course mutually exclusive, because a certain thing cannot at the same time be a particle (i.e., substance confined to a very small volume) and a wave (i.e., a field spread out over a large space) but the two complement each other. By playing with both pictures, by going from the one picture to the other and back again, we finally get the right impression of the strange kind of reality behind our atomic experiments.[82]

Art, like quantum-theoretical dualism, reflects our *own* "strange kind of reality," and must exist on the edge of uncertainty or meaninglessness:

Like ice on a hot stove the poem must ride on its own melting.

Frost[83]

Today the poem sustains itself on its own edge: in order to exist it must forever retrieve itself from Not-anymore into Yes-still.

Celan[84]

The artist plays across a line that separates the meaningful and the meaningless, being and not being. Charlie is helpless, but Chaplin is in control; Charlie is commanded by fate, but fate is in turn commanded by Chaplin. Or is it? "I don't get satisfaction from my work, I get relief."[85] The storyteller is driven to and *by* his plot, and his confrontation with the sacred, like his reenactment of childhood, is not a task he *chooses* to undertake.

STORY IS COMMITTED TO A REALITY BEYOND THE TEXT

Though our view of story may seem to coincide with the postmodern aesthetic, there are fundamental differences. For we see story's preclusive form as predicated on human limitations—which we deem objectively 'real,' or *de hors-texte*. In our view, the contradictions and ambiguities at the heart of narrative are ahistorical in origin, and may well have persuaded us for millennia because they suggest a truth *beyond* story, albeit not one we can pin down and label. Story's binary structure of plot and action creates the instability that has been a constant of narrative from *Gilgamesh* to the present—an instability, uncertainty, or doubt that appears to be an absolute of story everywhere and at all times. In postmodern theory, uncertainty is a *liberating* element that undermines the power structures of Western society. One can, however, see it as an analogue of our existence and experience, for doubt is not only a constant of the text but the predicate of everything human. Our uncertainty may be the one absolute we can count on with certainty.

As we have noted, deconstruction cannot permit the text a parallel in 'reality.' Even uncertainty must be read as a linguistic or aesthetic operation, for if it *were* to reflect a reality beyond the text, the sacred in its many and varied guises would be reconstituted. In our view, however, story's instability and subversion of all authoritative interpretations derive from its structure, which denies the possibility of a stable and therefore knowable relationship between the human and the forces that determine us. Story sees us as forever beholden to something that will not reveal itself—something we can neither control nor put under contract. Unlike theology,

151

it does not comfort us with the presence of an all-knowing, all-powerful deity—who, very likely, is fashioned out of our own needs and who, in turn, often serves as a model for domination and control. Story insists on the utter alterity of the 'other'—an alterity that makes all of *us* alike while we are in its presence. Though story harmonizes and connects, it does *not* reduce otherness to sameness. The forces that move the plot, and which the plot analogizes, cannot be known by us or transformed into our likeness. "Every concept (*Begriff*)," says Nietzsche, "derives from making the unlike alike."[86] Story is no *Begriff*.[87]

Though it cannot tell us what the sacred or 'other' is, story is unequivocally committed to its existence. It implies something beyond us that determines us—very possibly without being conscious of us. While the aesthetics of Schelling, Hegel, and even of Heidegger propose that art gives us access to 'truth' in some form,[88] story suggests that the only truth we can attain to is uncertainty. Yet the knowledge that we *cannot* know may be essential to us. We can build on it. Our uncertainty, though we must countermand it in a ceaseless effort to establish certainties, remains a necessary predicate of our existence and can serve, like the limitations mortality imposes, as a dependable and 'realistic' premise for our undertakings.

STORY AS AN ANALOGUE OF CONSCIOUSNESS

Criticism, like most human activities, is 'positivist' in spirit. It is predicated on the assumption that we can do something about our situation. As Wittgenstein points out, even skeptics assume that there is a certainty to be ascertained.[89] But story is neither critical nor skeptical; it does not discriminate, judge, accuse, defend, find guilty, explain, or offer solutions. It serves an altogether different 'purpose' than those linear processes of which criticism—even postmodern criticism—is representative. It engenders our awareness of the narrow margin between being and nonbeing, separateness and belonging, exile and home, that constitutes our existence.

By reflecting human marginality, story substantiates that ephemeral yet central node of our existence: the self. The self is indeterminate, decentered, and protean. It changes from one period to another, and—today— from one hour or situation to the next.[90] There is no way we can 'prove' it. Like Frost's poem, it rides on its own melting. It is an interface between inner and outer forces, malleable yet constant, both a response *and* an assertion—perhaps asserting itself most effectively in its capacity *for* response.

Like story, the self may be nothing more than a narow margin of consciousness, and our being—both as individuals and as a species—may be little more than our knowing. Story supports the view that the long-range effect of our actions is beyond our control and that the one freedom we may have in the context of necessity is the still-point of our awareness.[91] In *Genesis*, as in *Oedipus Rex*, even our knowing is not freely chosen but imposed. It is necessary to us. It *constitutes* us. As Emily Dickinson says:

Consciousness is the only home we *now* know. That sunny adverb had been enough, were it not foreclosed.[92]

Like story, consciousness is deeply contradictory—at once disabling and enabling. Even as it makes us aware of our limitations, it gives us the means and the hope of exceeding them. It hovers on the edge of the unknown, a part of it but apart from it. It separates us from nature, others, and ourselves, yet also serves as the means of reconnecting us. It is at once the source of our guilt and of forgiveness.[93] It creates difference and reestablishes sameness. It gives rise to the polarities and helps us balance between them. It both makes and undermines community. While it limits us by placing us within the context of necessity, it also sets us free. For, as Kafka says, we are free only when we are bound,[94] a point on which he and Hegel agree.[95] Until recently, the 'truth' or the 'facts', even when they were forbidding or "immobilizing," were thought to liberate us. Perhaps we cannot hope to attain even a margin of freedom until we realize our beholden condition—just as the addict cannot begin to free himself until he acknowledges that he is captive to his addiction.

Story may liberate us by asserting our limits. Myth and tragedy, in which the preclusive form of narrative emerges most clearly, render and record our naked encounter with the powers that determine us. Though we are fated to struggle against them, we must live in accord with them if our lives are not to become excessive and destructive. Perhaps what we find in the safe arena of story is not only a margin of freedom engendered by our knowing, but the relationship to necessity that Nietzsche celebrates:

My definition of human grandeur is *amor fati*: not wanting things to be otherwise—not in the future, not in the past, not in all eternity.[96]

Though we cannot submit to *amor fati* hour by hour and day after day, we are, in story, briefly free to accept and perhaps even to love our fate. Here we can connect with and submit to the forces that both give us life and threaten to destroy us. As Rilke says: *Das Schöne*—all that which harmonizes us and makes us one with the creation, with others and ourselves—is but the onset of the terrifying.[97] It is a merging or immersion we

153

can risk nowhere but in the safe arena of ritual and art. Yet when we emerge at story's or ritual's end, we may be freer of the terrifying. For the gods are present—acknowledged or unacknowledged—and perhaps we are better off facing them in a context in which their presence will not turn us to stone than trying, in vain, to deny their existence.

PART TWO

Postmodernism
and
Traditional Narrative

We Have Always Been 'Positivists'

CONSCIOUSNESS ADMITS WHAT IT CAN USE

"I am an optimist," says Churchill, "because there's not much point in anything else." Optimism may be less realistic than fear and trembling, but we cannot live without it. We focus on whatever helps us survive and turn away from everything that undermines our confidence. With regard to the 'truth' or 'reality,' we have always been pragmatists, and Goethe's "What is fruitful alone is true"[1] has no doubt been our criterion all along. We deem 'true' or 'real' whatever secures our existence and ignore, whenever we can, those things about which we can do nothing. We know that a sense of impotence will undermine us and may actually make us ill, whereas a positive outlook often serves as a self-fulfilling prophesy.

Though consciousness clearly has survival value, it is a two-edged sword that can harm as well as help us. The 'truth' or 'reality' may set us free, but since it can also destroy us—as Oedipus and Jocasta discover—our awareness is, and must be, severely restricted. It excludes far more than it admits and functions, like the immune system, to keep out whatever might impair or paralyze us.[2] Just as the fictive figure is blind to his own situation and struggles confidently against what we know to be hopeless odds, so we too close our eyes and ignore the frame that both holds and limits us. Instead of seeing ourselves as helpless and beholden, we insist we can influence and indeed master the course of our stories. Marx says:

Mankind always takes up only such problems as it can solve[3] and Merleau-Ponty speaks of the "radical intentionality" of our awareness.

If a rat, trapped in a water maze, is periodically lifted out so that its situation seems less hopeless, it swims on twice as long. And we too, as long as we believe we have a measure of control, can face even grave situations without despairing. *Genesis* tells us that from the start we assumed responsibility for our own condition by transforming the "wound" of human existence into sin. By accepting *blame* for our own suffering and mortality, we ceased to be mere victims and became empowered. By claiming to have *caused* and, indeed, deserved our afflictions, we acquired a measure of control over them.[4] We clearly prefer feeling guilty to feeling helpless—though some of us manage to feel both guilty *and* helpless.

PREDICTABILITY

Our need for power and control springs from our will to survive. Nature has fostered an awareness in us that enables us to protect ourselves *against* nature. Consciousness has always found it hard to *trust* the sacred and its uncertain relationship to us. As long as we had no other recourse, we tried to influence it through worship and sacrifice. More recently we have made every effort to transform the unknown into the known and predictable.

Predictability is the premise of all deliberate action. We find it hard to make a decision without some assurance of its outcome. Long before Francis Bacon, knowledge was deemed a kind of power; the verbs *can, ken,* and *know* derive from the same root. Though, at different times, our knowledge has taken different forms, we surely subscribed, for as long as we have been conscious, to Comte's *savoir pour prévoir et prévoir pour pouvoir.* Nietzsche suggests that our attempt to know originates in fear:

> Knowing is the will to discover in everything strange, unusual, or questionable, something which no longer disquiets us. Is it not possible that it should be the *instinct of fear* which enjoins upon us to know? Is it not possible that the rejoicing of the discerner should be just his rejoicing in the regained feeling of security?[5]

The attempt to potentiate ourselves, which we have called 'positivist', is a form of Nietzsche's will to power, a biological response to consciousness itself—to its potentially devastating assessment of our situation—and so a manifestation of the energy that is the source and substance of all life.

In order to exercise our will and feel potentiated rather than helpless, we must believe in causality. We may be aware of the complex nature of reality, but our ability to *act* depends on our faith in relatively simple, linear sequences of cause and effect. Causality gives us the confidence—or necessary illusion—that we can influence events by intervening at one or several critical junctures, and our reason is largely employed in establishing causal relationships. Indeed, the word *reason* describes both our capacity for analytic thought and the cause of an event.

The causeless terrifies us, for there is nothing we can do about it except pray. When the unexpected happens, we try to establish a sequence of events that led up to it. Causes reassure us, and we perform autopsies on everything that transpires without a known reason. From Leucippus, who said five centuries before Christ:

Nothing happens without a cause, but everything with a cause and by necessity[6]

to Descartes's principle of Universal Causation, Leibniz's "There is nothing without a reason, or no effect without a cause,"[7] and Laplace's conviction that a perfect knowledge of the present would guarantee a perfect knowledge of the future,[8] cause and effect have reassured and potentiated us.

Today, however, we have come to realize that causal relationships are in many instances neither direct nor linear, and that some events have so many causes, they may never be subject to our knowing intervention. Yet we continue to believe that we can influence their outcome, and causality—more than two centuries after Hume questioned its existence—remains the predicate of our lives. Despite occurrences in the subatomic realm that *have* no cause, and though, as Nietzsche says, cause and effect are not a "truth but a hypothesis—one we use to humanize the world"[9]—we are committed to the

Unshakable delusion that thinking, guided by the thread of causality, can reach into the darkest abyss of being and that it is capable not only of knowing but indeed of correcting existence.[10]

Already in the heyday of nineteenth-century Positivism there were those—like Durkheim—who denied that events are linked in time or that we can predict the future. But while much of our planning may be nothing more than the "the substitution of error for chance," plan we will and must. However radically causality oversimplifies, it is the premise of every lasting human relationship and of all communal life. Our institutions—the law, for instance—attempt to create and guarantee an order in which our actions will lead to predictable consequences. We must generate—within a complexity we cannot hope to command—a reality so structured that it is accessible to our understanding and, through it, to our will. Cause and effect remain the most important means we have of coping with our existence, and as soon as they are undermined we effectively reestablish them. When we cannot determine a cause—or when, indeed, there *is* none—we use statistics to ascertain a pattern that holds out some sense of control. So quantum events are subjected to statistical analyses that leave but the narrowest possible margin to the unknowable or chance. Chaos theory—the "butterfly effect," for example, in which a tiny and random change in the atmosphere can queer predictions for an entire weather system—is countermanded by computer studies that attempt to reestablish a predictable pattern. Like our ancestors, we are engaged in taming the gods—in creating certainty out of uncertainty.

FAITH POTENTIATES

We noted that Enlightenment 'positivism' perceived the sacred as depotentiating. But while the religious person stands in awe of the deity—our dismissive word "superstition" *means* "a standing in awe of"—the sacred also potentiates. The children of Israel believed they had a special covenant with an all-knowing, all-powerful God. They were His chosen instrument and as long as they kept their end of the bargain, their undertakings were sure to succeed and they could proceed with the greatest confidence. Christianity proposed an even more positive view of our existence: it promised us life everlasting and so allayed our deepest fear. Aeschylus has Prometheus say:

> The thought of death obsessed mankind until . . . I gave them the illusion that they weren't doomed.[11]

This very "illusion" became the cornerstone of Christian faith. The conviction that by committing oneself to God one might gain eternal life gave humankind a new, far more hopeful outlook, and no doubt helped to foster Christianity's rapid spread. As Marie-Louise von Franz says:

> The early Christians felt more alive, they had greater vitality, new enthusiasms, and a hopeful attitude . . . whereas the heathen were disillusioned and their spirit was worn out. . . . People watch for signs of vitality and join the movement that will make them feel better and be better.[12]

160

As a response to the exhausted materialism of Rome, Christian asceticism and spirituality no doubt served as a source of energy. If one believes, as we once did, that suffering is an inevitable component of human existence, even Christianity's focus on suffering—at a time when we had few means of alleviating it—may well have been 'positive.' For if it is part of God's design, it has meaning and can be more easily endured.

Every religion, though rooted in awe and fear, has a 'positivist' component. 'Primitive' peoples, with little apparent confidence in their ability to know and understand, nonetheless believed that the gods were approachable and subject to human influence through ritual, prayer, and sacrifice. All new religious movements and every deep religious commitment can serve as a source of empowerment. Medieval cathedrals, raised to the greater glory of God, were also· monuments to human skill and ability, and the Reformation not only repotentiated Christianity but contributed directly to the Peasant Revolt—an empowerment Luther resolutely rejected. Though the alliance between organized religion and worldly power has, throughout history, kept entire populations docile or enslaved, religious institutions maintain their hold in large part because faith potentiates: the devout draw strength and certitude from their very submission. They are sure of their place and purpose. They know who they are and what they must do.

Islam, which means "submission," may seem fatalistic or fanatical to us. In 1951, the king of Jordan traveled to Jerusalem despite warnings that he might be assassinated; when cautioned not to enter the Al Aksa mosque, he replied with an Arab proverb:

> Until my day comes, no one can harm me.
> When my day comes, no one can guard me.

He entered the mosque and was killed. Though we see little but blind faith and 'defeatism' in his attitude, it relieves those who hold it of the anxiety that haunts the West—an anxiety that springs from being 'free' and 'responsible,' from having to know and understand, from our commitment to doubt and our need to *do*.[13]

Most of us cannot conceive of a God who would ask us, as Yahweh did Abraham, to sacrifice our only child to demonstrate our faith and trust in Him. Yet Abraham's unquestioning obedience must have been a decisive break with the past, for *his* God, unlike the heathen deities, *could* be trusted. Our own concept of God has been further modified by centuries of rationalism; we expect Him to be comprehensible and just. Zeus would never have justified himself to Job as Yahweh did. The relationship of the Greek gods to humankind—at least as the myths have it—is profoundly ambiguous: no hero has all of them on his side, and to be loved by one is often to be hated by another. They rule by impulse or whim and they are not accountable—in part, perhaps, because they are themselves subject to higher powers, the Fates and Necessity, whereas the Judeo-Christian God is all-powerful and all-knowing we might say: He *is* necessity.[14]

Today we would call the gods of Greece unconscious. "As a brute has no vice or virtue," says Aristotle, "neither has a god." Even Yahweh is an angry and vengeful deity, who causes the flood and destroys cities. But the Christian God is a model of virtues to which we can all aspire—conscious, responsible, caring, and, in the deepest sense, 'civilized.' Satan has been cast out of heaven; God no longer contains the negative, and His relationship to us is *unambiguous*: He loves us and sent his only son to die for our sins. He is a God of hope, to whom we have access, whom we can influence by our actions and faith. He is not only just but merciful and forgiving; the true believer has Him on his side, always and forever.

WE HAVE BECOME GOD'S EQUALS

Ironically, the Judeo-Christian tradition, with its emphasis on a dependable relationship between God and humankind, may have prepared the ground for the death of God. During the Middle Ages, Maimonides rationalized Judaism and Aquinas Christianity, though both reserved a place for pure, unquestioning faith. But neither religion remained truly hospitable to mysticism—to the view that God is ultimately inaccessible to reason: the Gnostics were suppressed, Meister Eckhart was excommunicated, and the Inquisition came close to executing St. John of the Cross. Perhaps the very foundation of the Judeo-Christian tradition—the premise that God is reasonable, just, all-knowing, and all-powerful—led to the eventual elimination of the deity. For as we perceive God, so we perceive ourselves. Once God became self-determined, we too could begin to see ourselves as free and fully responsible for our fate. We ceased being God's children and began to father or create ourselves. *Sors de l'enfance, ami,* says Rousseau, *réveille-toi!* "Leave childhood, my friend. Wake up!"[15]

With the Enlightenment, and more explicitly with the advent of Positivism, we began to think of our own powers as potentially unlimited. Democracy, in its deconstruction of all higher authority, contributed by suggesting—however indirectly—that human beings might be God's near-equals or partners, and once we were His partners, we were well on our way to dismissing Him. Nineteenth-century Positivists instituted a "Religion of Humanity," with man replacing God as the supreme being and the proper object of worship.[16] Marx saw humankind as creating itself through labor and read Hegel's *Phenomenology of the Spirit* as "the self-creation of man." He transformed Christianity's faith in an eternal life into the conviction that life *on* earth would become truly harmonious, and discovered in history an impersonal but predictable force that would move us inexorably toward the resolution of human suffering. Until recently, the committed Marxist was a confident, potentiated figure.

While, at a shallow level, our 'positivist' impulses can degenerate into a narrow if 'efficient' belief in power as the only reality—a reductive, cynical position that did not, of course, originate in the modern era—it has, in less virulent form, been an essential, perhaps *the* essential, ingredient of being human. In Eden, at the beginning of our 'history,' we see a clear shift from a passive or obedient to an active, disobedient attitude to God—to things as we find them in nature. Our 'story' began when we *dis*obeyed. Though we don't know whether early communities had any notion of progress, improving their condition and the thought that with time and effort it could be done, must have been with them in some form.[17] It seems likely that consciousness itself impels us to make changes, to turn things to use, to organize and neaten up the world into a safer, less fearful place, and to master natural process wherever possible. All culture and society are *built* on what we might call a 'positivist' foundation.

THE COMMUNITY AND EVIL

In order to potentiate ourselves, we need to separate right from wrong. Science may strive for *Wertfreiheit*, but no community can function without dividing the permitted from the forbidden. It must draw a clear line between the binary opposites of right and wrong, or good and evil, for when they are defined ambiguously, relationships and action become difficult, if not impossible. Human cooperation depends on attributions of responsibility or blame. We must, moreover, be able to blame the *living*, for when the causes of a wrong are traced back into the past, we embark on an infinite regression: everyone has to be forgiven; we cease to be accountable for our own actions, and so effectively cease to *be*. Society cannot afford the possibility that evil is diffused and undefinable, that good and evil are finally one, and that we are all equally guilty or innocent—a notion so threatening that it can be entertained only in the safe arena of ritual and art.

A clear definition of evil preserves our structures and enables us to act. It is a source of energy, for if the evil isn't in us, it can be extirpated: we know who we are and what to do. Marxism potentiated its believers, in part, by providing a set of villains.[18] Perhaps all political movements with an active agenda need enemies who have an effective and preferably malevolent will—so that we can model *our* will on theirs and fuel it with outrage and anger. We have noted that feminist theory is uncomfortable with the possibility that men might themselves be helpless.

Since we establish who we are by what we are *not*, the evil other helps create the community. As Durkheim says:

> Crime brings together upright consciences and concentrates them. We have only to notice what happens, particularly in a small town, when some moral scandal has just been committed. They stop each other on the street, they visit each other, they seek to come together to talk of the event and to wax indignant in common. From all the similar impressions which are exchanged . . . there emerges a unique temper . . . which is everybody's without being anybody's in particular. That is the public temper.[19]

Of course our tendency to define ourselves by the evil other has a distinctly negative dimension. As Neumann says:

> Not only is the evil experienced as alien but . . . the alien is, in his turn, experienced as evil.[20]

By serving as a scapegoat, a convenient vehicle for all that is negative and destructive in ourselves and in those to whom we are close, the evil other frees us of guilt and self-division. Significantly, Marxism not only targets capitalism and the bourgeoisie as enemies but rejects the traditional view that our self-division is a permanent condition.

EVIL IS ENERGY AND CENTRAL TO BEING HUMAN

Understandably, we call those among the gods and our fellow-beings evil who cause suffering and destroy life. But evil is a category we have had to *split* from the energy that both gives us life and takes it away. Evil is clearly linked to energy and energy to evil. Blake, who called energy "Eternal Delight," also says: "Evil is the active springing from Energy";[21] and fire, stolen from the gods and brought to us by Prometheus, is the devil's element. Our separation from evil is necessary but we would not be human without it, for it stops us from being passive and accepting. In the Judeo-Christian tradition, evil and consciousness are inextricably linked. Evil has

164

a 'positivist' component, and our 'positivism'—in its rejection of life as it is given or decreed—comes close to constituting a traditional definition of evil. Like Satan, we refuse to accept God's will and creation.

Rabbi Nachman of Bratzlav recognizes that what we call good and evil spring from the same central source:

> To break with evil is not truly to overcome it; rather, one must transform the entire force of passion that powers the evil into the good.[22]

In Nietzsche,

> All virtue is the transformation of something wicked. Every god has a devil for a father.[23]

And Binswanger notes that Freud "saw in evil the prerequisite for the existence of good":

> Concerning the positive value of evil, evil considered as an active ontological force, Freud stood in strict opposition to Augustine and Fichte, who see in evil only that which is limiting and negative. . . . Experience shows "that the pre-existence of powerful 'bad' impulses in infancy is often the actual condition toward 'good' in the adult."[24]

The Catholic concept of original sin may attempt to reconcile a complex, ontological view of evil with our need to distance ourselves from it. The church rigorously separates good from evil, yet recognizes sin as a predicate of our existence. Humankind is seen both 'negatively'—for we cannot escape our heritage—and 'positively': we are free to choose virtue.

EVIL AND FREEDOM

Our view of evil as at once harmful and necessary resembles the contradictory view of human freedom that informs our structures and institutions. Just as we must shun evil though it is integral to us, so we must be both free and part of the whole. Indeed, the concept of evil is directly linked to our concept of freedom. Since communal life depends on our ability to choose between right and wrong, evil and freedom are necessary to us— even if we have to split them from the totality of our existence by main force.

No community can function effectively if its members feel helpless and unfree. Yet when we are actually left to our own devices, we are quite apt to choose evil over good. Since the vices tempting us may—like our virtues—be in the unconscious service of the 'natural' or sacred, our responses must be carefully conditioned. For the most part, we are 'free' to act only as we *have* to act, though the community must persuade each of us that we have a choice and can exercise our will. Institutions at once confirm and undermine our freedom—a contradiction that cannot become explicit, or we would cease to believe that we are self-determined. Thus our structures often seem enabling or 'positivist' at the surface, while at their core they are restrictive or 'conservative.'

LEADERSHIP IS 'POSITIVIST'

We will not follow someone—be he a general or a teacher—who fails to empower us. Since we cannot be led in two directions at once, those who lead cannot be self-divided and ambivalent, or take a view of reality so complex that we are paralyzed into inaction. We expect them to be prudent but decisive, and accept their arrogance and self-importance more easily than vacillation or uncertainty. Oedipus is a prototypical 'positivist': logical, clear, and resolute. The successful leader is often a happy warrior, who allays our fears—"we have nothing to fear but fear itself"—and inspires us with the confidence that there is always something we can *do*.[25] While spiritual leaders may invoke fear or uncertainty, even here the ultimate prospect must be affirming or enabling. The closer we get to the realm of action, the less room there is for complexity and contradiction. Political leadership must carry the conviction that our will, supported by planning, is an effective instrument for achieving our ends. Hitler's appeal to the Germans rested in large part on his repotentiation of their will, and Herzl said to the Jewish people, who had been condemned to political passivity for two thousand years: "If you want it, it is no dream."

Napoleon appeared to the nineteenth century as an incarnation of human power, the very embodiment of 'positivist' principles. "His aim," says Valéry, "was to remake the world in the space of ten years." While he believed in his "star" and, on occasion, admitted that he could affect events only when he was working *with* the press of circumstance, he nonetheless trusted nothing but his will, his intuition, his superb analytical intelligence, and his extraordinary powers of concentration. Combining a profoundly cynical, reductive, and materialist view of humankind with a mystical faith in power and a need to leave his mark on every European institution, he held the nineteenth century spellbound.[26] He was perceived as a man who had truly created himself and his own destiny. Like Paganini, he did the seemingly impossible; he performed miracles without the help of the supernatural. *Voilà un homme!* His mother, raised in an older tradition, was given to saying: *Pourvu que ça dure!* "Provided it lasts."

Lincoln, alone among successful political leaders, appears to have given voice to self-doubt and self-division in a time of crisis. His proclivity for undermining himself—expressed in his often rueful and self-deprecatory humor no less than in his tragic perception of our need to act—was surely engendered by the divided state of the nation. In a country at war with itself, no simple perspective could serve, since every battle pitched men of the same heritage and sometimes of the same family against each other. The foe could not become hateful if, as the war intended, he was to rejoin the body politic. Lincoln's tragic awareness of the task facing him and the nation, which resonates in his public and private utterances and makes them unique in the annals of political leadership, was necessary to the moment: there was no other way to lead in a civil war.

Even so, *our* view of Lincoln—which tends to stress the complexity of his perspective and responses—is largely derived from our knowledge of the *private* man. He did not go public with his qualms or moments of self-doubt, and certainly would not have broadcast them on television. Nor was he in any way immobilized by the situations facing him: once he determined that a position was justified by the values to which he was committed, he held to it without wavering, and effectively forged public awareness of the issues that made the war necessary and worth winning. We know that he relished the exercise of power as much as he felt burdened by the responsibility. At a cabinet meeting early in his presidency, when he was outvoted eight to one, he noted: "Eight noes against my aye—the ayes have it."

EVEN STORY HAS A 'POSITIVIST' COMPONENT

Though story is predicated on the precluded nature of our actions and the inadequacy of our will, its effect is not disabling. As Nietzsche says:

> The representation of the terrifying and confounding is in itself a sign (*Instinkt*) of power and grandeur on the part of the artist: he is not afraid of them. . . . There is no pessimistic art.[27]

Freud observes that when a child turns a painful experience into play, it no longer overwhelms him:

At the outset he was in a *passive* situation . . . but by repeating it, unpleasurable though it was, as a game, he took an *active* part.[28]

Like the child at play, the storyteller—and we who are his audience—can transform our relationship to the sacred into a game or play, and cease to be overwhelmed by it. What Bernard Meyer says of Houdini—

He sought to master his fear by recreating it under his own authorship.[29]

—is true of the storyteller. He, too, briefly masters his fear and fate by reenacting them under what appears to be his own authority.

The connection between art and power is ancient. The artist transforms reality. Like a magician, he gives substance to shadows and, like a god, seems to breathe life and movement into the inanimate. He can turn one thing into another and create altogether new shapes. He stuns his audience into wonder and amazement, holds them spellbound, terrified, delighted, angry, tearful. "What a thing it is to have power," Dickens noted after one of his readings[30]—a power that readily accrues to the spectator's own sense of worth, just as the athlete can potentiate those who watch him.

Some critics maintain that story lulls us into passivity—that, by giving us the *illusion* of action or movement, it 'abreacts' our own need to act, and so serves as a safety valve for the status quo. But if confronting the realities of our existence ventilates our fear of them and lifts from us briefly the burden of responsibility for what we are and do, story may leave us *freer* to act. Few of us, in any case, confuse the safe arena of art with daily life. Though we may recognize that the fictive figure cannot determine his own fate, we are not likely to conclude that *we* should give up acting on our own behalf; *biology* prevents it. Moreover, the very uncertainty on which stories are predicated can enable us. We may as well *try* to change our situation in the hope that we are working *with* rather than against the tide of events. Even tragedy does not teach us resignation.[31]

THEORY ENABLES US TO ACT

Art is not disabling, though, by accommodating the opposites, it undermines all simple, clear-cut directives. But intellectual theories *intend* to enable us. This is true even of those theories that deem us unfree. Behaviorism takes a wholly deterministic view of our existence, yet Skinner suggests that humankind can gain control of its destiny by changing those factors that will determine the life of future generations. His vision of an "engineered utopia" is Positivist through and through. In the human sciences most theory is, as Sartre says of existentialism, *une doctrine d'action*.[32] It does not intend to remain theoretical but proposes a truth about our reality that means, explicitly or by implication, to serve as a guide to action. Unlike art, it tends to take an either/or position; it rests on the assumption that its own opposite is false.

There is a notable difference between Sartre's definition of human existence—"To be is to act, and to cease to act is to cease to be"[33]—and Conrad's far more forbidding: "In our activity alone do we find the illusion of an independent existence."[34] One speaks of "action," the other of "activity." One is a theorist, the other a storyteller.

POSITIVISM AND PRAGMATISM

Richard Rorty draws a sharp line between positivism and Pragmatism[35]—from the Greek *pragma*, "a deed"—yet the two appear linked not just in our own culture but historically.[36] The positivism of the Enlightenment was deeply committed to the premise that experience must shape theory and that theory must, in turn, be actualized in practice. Our own leading pragmatists, James and Dewey, were intent, as Rorty himself says, on "making our future different from our past," and Dewey was firmly convinced that we are free to *make* ourselves.

> James (and) Dewey . . . shared a common skepticism of absolutes, wholes, certainties, and finalities and a common faith in the efficacy of the will, in the compatibility of science and democracy, and in the sufficiency of experience as the source of knowledge of the good and the true.[37]

Men of action—'positivists' by nature—are usually pragmatists. They subscribe to "the theory of non-theory."[38] Oliver Cromwell says:

> No one goes so far as he who knows not whither he is going,

and Napoleon's course of action was largely determined by his pragmatism:

> I had few really definite ideas, and the reason for that was that, instead of obstinately seeking to control circumstance, I obeyed them, and they forced me to change my mind all the time. Thus it happened that most of the time, to tell the truth, I had no definite plans but only projects.[39]

169

Though he uses the term pejoratively, Heidegger seems justified in speaking of "pragmatic-positivistic" thinking.

SCIENCE IS 'POSITIVIST'

All acquisition of knowledge—from reading the entrails of animals to observing events in the atom—is 'positivist' in spirit. All science is intent on understanding the forces that govern our existence and the workings of the universe. "The scientist," says Einstein, "is possessed by the sense of universal causation," confident, even today, that the laws determining our lives can be understood—that "the eternal mystery of the universe is its comprehensibility."[40] If he *ceased* to believe that nature and the universe can be understood he would abandon his inquiries, since they are predicated on reason.

The primary concern of science has always been with those forces—at once the most powerful and least accessible—we used to call sacred. Kolakowski observes that though neither Descartes nor Leibniz were Positivists,

> Both shared the positivist conviction that interpretation of the world by unseen faculties or forces, inaccessible to empirical investigation, is absurd. We must not leave room for the operation of inexplicable forces in the ordinary course of nature. . . . Science should divest the world of mystery, should fill the gaps in our cognition with real knowledge, not mask our ignorance with purely verbal formulas.[41]

Heisenberg says of Newton:

> (His mechanics) and all the other parts of classical physics constructed after its model started from the assumption that one can describe the world without speaking about God and ourselves. This possibility soon seemed almost a necessary condition for natural science in general.[42]

Like the artist, the pure scientist may be little concerned with the *practical* application of his work, since he meets his own need for 'action' and control in his investigations. But to most of us, the importance of science lies in the greater control it offers us over our lives. Descartes says his theories were intended as

> (A) practical philosophy by means of which, knowing the force and the action of fire, water, air, the stars, heavens and all other bodies that environ us . . .

170

we can employ them in all those uses to which they are adapted, and thus render ourselves the masters and possessors of nature.[43]

For Claude Bernard:

> The whole natural philosophy is summed up in a single phrase: to discover the laws that govern phenomena. Even the most elaborate experiment comes down to predicting and controlling phenomena.[44]

Helmholtz says that:

> The final aim of all natural science is to resolve itself into mechanics.[45]

And Heisenberg suggests that, as a consequence of the mechanical and causative concepts proposed by classical physics,

> The human attitude toward nature changed from a contemplative one to a pragmatic one. One was not so much interested in nature as it is; one rather asked what one could do with it. Therefore, natural science turned into technical science; every advancement of knowledge was connected with the question as to what practical use could be derived from it.[46]

Though on the subatomic level physics has now added the element of chance to cause and effect, most science remains committed to the laws of causality. As Planck himself says:

> (The law of causality is a) heuristic principle, a signpost and in my opinion the most valuable signpost we possess, to guide us through the motley disorder of events and to indicate the direction in which scientific inquiry must proceed in order to attain fruitful results.[47]

In response to quantum mechanics, random events in the atom have been subjected to statistical analysis, permitting Bronowski to claim that:

> (Though) the laws of chance seem at first glance to be lawless . . . they can be formulated with as much rigor as the laws of cause.[48]

And the physicist Victor Weiskopf confidently refers to science as:

> A search for meaning (which demonstrates) that universal laws exist, that the universe is not run by magic, that we are not at the mercy of a capricious universe, that the structure of matter is largely known, that life has developed

slowly from inorganic matter by evolution in a period of several thousand million years, and that this evolution is a unique experiment of nature here on Earth, which leaves us humans with a responsibility not to spoil it.[49]

Our effort to control our destiny continues at an ever accelerating pace. Until recently it appeared that the process of natural selection, occurring over millions of years, would remain impervious to human intervention. Yet recently a molecular biologist announced that within a hundred years the human race may be able to "design" itself genetically.[50] We won't, of course, be designing ourselves but our children and grandchildren—who may not always be happy with choices they themselves were not free to make. In the brave new world of genetic engineering nothing would seem to remain essential or necessary, though one might guess that we will be no more successful at predicting the eventual consequences of our actions than Laius, Jocasta, and Oedipus.

THE ENLIGHTENMENT AND NINETEENTH-CENTURY POSITIVISM

A form of 'positivism' was a central component of the Enlightenment, with its commitment to human freedom and the construction of a science of society that would "do for the human world what Newton had done for the natural world."[51] Kolakowski says:

> The positivism of the Enlightenment was an attempt to view mankind in its natural, this-wordly, physical and social environment, an attempt to minimize differences among men by a sensationalist theory of knowledge (every human being comes into the world a *tabula rasa*. . .), an attempt to project a life in time freed of chimerical "wrestling with God," designed to improve the concrete conditions of human existence through co-operation, to speed up the accumulation of knowledge, to do away with prejudice and barren speculation.[52]

A. J. Ayer points out that an excellent statement of the Positivist position on metaphysics is already found in Hume:

> If we take in our hand any volume; of divinity or school metaphysics, for instance; let us ask, *Does it contain any abstract reasoning concerning quantity or number?* No. *Does it contain any experimental reasoning concerning matter of fact and existence?* No. Commit it then to the flames: for it can contain nothing but sophistry and illusion.[53]

And Marcuse notes that:

> The philosophies of the French Enlightenment and their revolutionary succes-
> sors all posited reason as an objective historical force which, once freed from
> the fetters of despotism, would make the world a place of progress and happi-
> ness.[54]

Yet despite their fundamental optimism and faith in progress, eighteenth-
century thinkers, from Hume to Diderot and Rousseau, preserved a sense
of human limitations. They dismissed original sin but continued to believe
in the unchanging nature of Old Adam, and were haunted by "the limits
of rational inquiry into ultimate mysteries, the impotence of reason before
passions."[55] Not until the advent of nineteenth-century Positivism were
Enlightenment principles transformed into an uncontradicted, totalizing
faith, which—in its determination to free and empower us—dismissed the
uncertain, unpredictable, and irrational altogether. Satan's promise to
Eve—"You shall be as gods"—was finally to be fulfilled.

Comte intended the system he called Positivism to be a corrective to the
critical philosophy of Hegel; he dismissed the negative polarity that plays
an essential role in Hegel's dialectical process. However, by the nineteenth
century, Enlightenment assumptions were so widely adopted and radicalized that—from *our* vantage point—the positions of a "negative" thinker
like Marx are often indistinguishable from Comte's. Both take for granted
the material foundations of human existence and the inevitability of progress—though Marx insists that change will come only with the violent
overthrow of the old order, while Comte and Saint-Simon believed that
the system would transform itself peacefully.[56] The role Marx assigned to
history—with its progression toward a rational, harmonious society—
parallels Saint-Simon's conviction that men are "mere instruments" of a
progressive force they can neither alter nor arrest, just as history, in the
"negative" philosophy of Hegel constitutes an inevitable "advance to
something better, more perfect:"[57]

> The history of the world is the progress of the consciousness of freedom—a
> progression we must recognize as inevitable.[58]

Marx, like Comte, was determined to destroy every vestige of the sacred:

> The abolition of religion as the illusory happiness of the people is a demand
> for their real happiness.[59]

In his youth, Hegel had taken a similar position:

> Religion and politics have played the same game. The former has taught what despotism wanted to teach, contempt for humanity and the incapacity of man to achieve the good and to fulfill his essence through his own efforts.[60]

POSITIVISM TODAY

In our own day, a form of positivism informs the assumptions of capitalist democracies and socialist societies alike. It is the very air we breathe. Even nonindustrial societies may commit themselves to it once they can meet the material expectations it awakens. Just as Enlightenment positivism helped to shape the American Bill of Rights, the Declaration of Independence, and the Constitution, so American attitudes—one might even say our national character: our optimism; our faith in science and progress, in the human will and in work; our belief in the potentiation of the individual; our commitment to happiness; our often uneasy relationship to the sacred; our pervasive if somewhat shallow materialism; and our conviction that enlightened self-interest is both the driving force and the glue of society—bear the mark of Enlightenment thought, albeit often in oversimplified form.[61]

While we emphatically stress our differences with Marxism, we share a common heritage. We too are committed to creating a 'paradise' on earth; we too believe in the potentiation and liberation of the oppressed; and we too have little use for abstractions and ideals that cannot be actualized. Like Lenin, we are primarily concerned with *What Is To Be Done*.[62] Our pragmatic idealism, as given expression by John Dewey, seems close to Marx's insistence that philosophy must go beyond understanding the world to changing it:[63]

> The chief function of philosophy is not to find out what difference ready-made formulae make, if *true*, but to arrive at and to clarify their *meaning as programs of behavior for modifying the existing world*.[64]

The American republic became a major force in the world not simply because of its vast resources but because it exported "a formidable commodity—the program of Enlightenment *in practice*."[65]

OUR POSITIVISM IS COUNTERMANDED

The positivist orientation of American culture does not, however, go uncontradicted. Since societies maintain their balance by shifting back and

174

forth between opposites, our positivism is at once fostered *and* held in check by our institutions. As Peter Gay points out, *The Federalist* takes a dialectical position—combining "a pessimistic though wholly secular appraisal of human nature . . . with an optimistic confidence in institutional arrangements."[66] It trusts us, yet treats our efforts—*including* those we make to govern ourselves—with deep skepticism. The positivist thrust of our society is hedged by our institutions: action, change, and progress are moderated, and indeed inhibited, by a system of checks and balances—just as individual rights and freedom are countermanded by laws safeguarding the public weal. Though positivism and faith in progress imbue every aspect of our lives, they constitute a *polarity*, not the totality. In principle—if not in daily practice—our system is open and nonexclusive: it accommodates, as Marcuse observes ruefully, even "reaction and regress";[67] it tolerates even intolerance. Its most radical—and sanest—attribute may well be its rejection of all radical, totalizing solutions.

Science, too, though it has been the principal means of our potentiation, countermands its own positivist thrust. It is predicated on general laws governing the universe and life on earth, and—like classical philosophy—has always been concerned with eliciting truths that are presumed to be independent of us. Its positivism is tempered by an awareness that our place in the scheme of things is marginal and that our understanding far exceeds our physical reach. What Bertrand Russell says of classical philosophy is true of science also:

> The concept of "truth" as something dependent upon facts largely outside human control has been one of the ways in which philosophy has inculcated the necessary element of humility. When the check upon pride is removed, a further step is taken on the road towards a certain madness—the intoxication of power—which invaded philosophy with Fichte, and to which modern men, whether philosophers or not, are prone.[68]

We Don't and Do Believe in Stories

FACTS ARE OUR FICTION

American culture has long mistrusted fiction. Thomas Jefferson thought that novels "infect the mind with a poison that destroys one's natural respect for 'reason and fact, plain and unadorned.' "[1] Emerson called facts "the true poetry, and the most beautiful of fables," and Tony Tanner observes that

> Since the time of the Puritans, there has been a strong tendency for Americans to regard the fictional as the false.[2]

Yet the factual stories we *do* trust—history, biography, and documentary— may well meet the same existential and emotional needs that myth, legend, fairy tales, and fiction once did. As Lévi-Strauss says:

> I am not far from believing that, in our own societies, history has replaced mythology and fulfils the same function.[3]

The events reported by historical texts are—by the time we hear of them—as precluded as tragedy. The figures in an account of the Civil War have no more freedom than Othello or Snow White; they, too, are unable to predict or influence what happens with any assurance of the outcome. We lend our feelings to factual stories because we *believe* them, and read biographies because they present, as fiction once did, the continuous and coherent life of an individual in credible form—and so make *us* credible.

Even the news may serve fictive purposes. An executive producer of NBC News instructed his staff that:

> Every news story should, without any sacrifice of probity or responsibility, display the attributes of fiction, of drama. It should have structure and conflict, problem and dénouement, rising action and falling action, a beginning, a middle and an end.[4]

Though *myth*, today, is a synonym for the untrue, most of us have encountered or read about situations that vividly recall the extremes of ancient, seemingly irrelevant stories. Instead of watching them enacted on stage, like audiences in fifth-century Athens, we watch and participate intensively in criminal trials and events like the Hill-Thomas hearings—where, as in the theater, our secrets are revealed, the intimate becomes public, and we ourselves are ultimately on trial. Facts, reported or broadcast, serve as our fictions. In the murder of Nicole Simpson or the attempted murder by Amy Fisher, an archetypal deed is enacted—one that is *not* as closely linked to social and economic causes as most crimes, and so permits us to see our own darkest compulsions, or the gods, at work.

WE BELIEVE STORIES WE DON'T BELIEVE

We recognize that all stories are partial or limited in perspective, and say: "That's *your* story!" when it doesn't jibe with our own version of the 'facts.' Journalists often call their reports "pieces"—fragments of the whole truth. But like every other society, we remain confident that there *is* a whole and true story—one that exists independently of us.

If art is compensatory, it is not surprising that a culture as committed to objectivity as our own proliferates fictions that cater shamelessly to our feelings and offer us wish-fulfilling fantasies instead of facts. Most of our stories have little more than a veneer of reality. Marianne Moore says that poetry renders "imaginary gardens with real toads in them," but in our bestsellers and movies only the *gardens* are real, while the toads are largely imaginary.

We are of course aware, even as we consume them, that our fictions are mostly market products, reporting what we wish or need to hear. Though they may on occasion tell us an unfamiliar fact or truth, we put little credence in them and treat them as pure pastime—an escape from our routines and problems. They may please and reassure us but hardly reflect our reality. Yet one wonders whether our craving for narrative—with television a

178

seamless, interminable tale of Sheherezade available at any time of day or night—doesn't suggest more than a need for escape and wish-fulfillment. Even commercial fiction may confirm an aspect of our lives that we cannot dismiss—for what we believe consciously is not all we believe, and what we are taught is not all we have learned. Perhaps stories continue to be persuasive and necessary to us because they render—in a Positivist guise—a pervasive sense of human helplessness that Positivism can neither override nor acknowledge.

Most audiences tire quickly of narratives without a *plot*, suggesting that they *come* to story for its preclusive form. While the plot offers us certain guarantees—the wicked will be punished and justice will prevail—stories are not finally reassuring. We identify with the hero but can hardly fail to notice that in the course of most narratives innocent bystanders like ourselves are savaged, and end up as wet spots along the road. Though, on the surface, story would seem to assure us that our coordinate system is dependable, in its preclusive form even the shallowest, most sentimental tale reflects the limitations of human knowledge and power, and the unaccountability of the gods. Despite the guarantees that story, both fictive and factual, appears to offer, what happens is at once uncertain *and* fated—uncertain before it occurs and precluded in hindsight. It is hardly a reassuring prospect and suggests that even escapist fictions are not simply escapist. They may confirm a 'reality' we continue to encounter even if we no longer have a way of accommodating it.

PLOT AS A SOURCE OF EMBARRASSMENT

In educated circles, the demise of fiction has long been taken for granted. Benjamin notes that "the art of telling stories is coming to an end," and Robbe-Grillet says that "telling stories has become strictly impossible."[5] Sophisticated storytellers no longer believe in plot—the very element that keeps most audiences engaged in and persuaded by story. Donald Barthelme has no faith in connecting structures: "Fragments are the only form I trust";[6] and Andy Warhol told his scriptwriters: "Get rid of plot."[7] Yet without a plot there *is* no story, for the fundamental conflict—which *appears* to be between the figures—is actually between the figures and the plot. Once the plot 'wins,' as it always does, the story is over.

Today, sophisticated authors and their readers are drawn to fictions in which plot is relegated to unimportance. E. M. Forster is clearly embarrassed by narrative structure:

179

Yes—oh, dear, yes—the novel tells a story. That is the fundamental aspect without which it could not exist. That is the highest factor common to all novels, and I wish that it was not so, that it could be something different: melody, or perception of the truth, not this low atavistic form.[8]

Most contemporary critics disdain plot. Northrop Frye says:

When we read Smollett or Jane Austen or Dickens, we read them for the sake of the texture of characterization, and tend to think of the plot, when we think of it at all, as a conventional, mechanical, or even (as occasionally in Dickens) absurd contrivance included only to satisfy the demands of the literary market.[9]

Frye does not ask himself why "the literary market," or most readers, *demand* a plot. Even Shakespeare's plots are treated with condescension—an attitude already apparent in Coleridge:

The (Shakespearean) plot interests us on account of the characters, not vice versa—it is the canvas only.[10]

Walter Kerr comes to the same conclusion:

Shall we agree that audiences don't go to Shakespeare for the plots? In the first place, they know the plots, most of them all too well. . . . In addition, there isn't a plot that's not structurally troubled. . . . And those that aren't troubled are either casual or downright cavalier, as Shakespeare himself genially indicated when he subtitled one of his comedies "What You Will." A snap of the fingers for the plots. Shakespeare borrowed his plots, mixed up his plots, dismissed his plots.[11]

To the contemporary critic, plot is a primitive holdover, required, for reasons he does not respect or understand, by the unsophisticated. T. S. Eliot remarks that plot is the piece of meat the thief throws to the dog in order to distract him. Peter Brooks says:

Whereas plot continues in our time to be a dominant element in popular narrative fictions of many sorts and to proceed on principles little changed from the nineteenth century, in those works that claim to challenge their readers, that are in various ways experimental, plot is often something of an embarrassment.[12]

Umberto Eco, who turned from semiotics to storytelling, notes that "serious" writing has recently taken over narrative techniques from popular literature. In his own fiction, he borrows from the detective story, but with what he calls "non-innocent" and "ironic" eyes. For him, what has happened to story

> is similar to what happened in painting. The avant-garde painters went on destroying the human image, and they arrived at abstract painting, then action painting, then the blank canvas. At one point it became impossible to go forward and you had to rediscover the image. This is what writers have done who are coming back to plot. They exploit popular narrative forms, but they do it with an ironic, tongue-in-cheek kind of attitude.[13]

He injects his own novels with the unconvinced and unconvincing structures he deems appropriate to narrative.

Some storytellers, instead of using plot condescendingly, try to *exclude* it altogether. "I rarely use plot," says Neil Simon, "I use character development." Yet the characters in his plays are "developed" by *situation*, which is the building block of traditional plot. Like many writers and critics today, he considers stories predicated on "character development" a higher form, surely on the assumption that character is subject to our will. In our culture, situation is often dismissed—as in the widespread disdain for "situation comedy"—though traditional comedy, like tragedy, was primarily situational. Among our critics, and indeed our storytellers, plot is seldom allowed a relationship to human reality. "I'm not a plot writer," Steve Tesich tells us: "Plots don't move people's lives."[14] And the screenwriter Frank Pierson says:

> I don't think that plot is worth a damn. I hate movies with a plot. The only thing that's important is the story, and the story arises from the conflict between the characters.[15]

PLOT AS A RATIONALIZATION OF REALITY

When popular storytellers in the nineteenth century began manufacturing their plots instead of inheriting or finding them, they undermined the credibility of narrative. Serious authors today dismiss plot precisely *because* it has come to be a product of craft and craftiness, a mere device or convention, while critics dismiss it as a wishful, invalid rationalization of reality. Lévi-Strauss sees myth, which is *all* plot, as a nonorganic, rationalizing construct different from all other art forms:

The creative act which gives rise to myths is in fact exactly the reverse of that which gives rise to works of art. In the case of works of art, the starting point is a set of one or more objects and one or more events which aesthetic creation unifies by revealing a common structure. Myths travel the same road but start from the other end. They use a structure to produce what is in itself an object consisting of a set of events (for all myths tell a story). Art thus proceeds from a set (object + event) to the discovery of its structure. Myth starts from a structure by means of which it *constructs* a set (of object + event).[16]

Irving Howe says:

> When a writer works out a plot, he tacitly assumes that there is a rational structure in human conduct, that the structure can be ascertained and that (by) doing so he is enabled to provide his work with a sequence of order.[17]

It would seem, from these comments, that storytelling has become "impossible" because we have ceased to believe in an ordered universe and in our ability to make sense of the human situation:

> The stories we used to make up to explain ourselves do not make sense any more, and we have run out of new stories for the moment.[18]

Warhol's scriptwriter, Ronald Tavel, observes:

> As best as I can articulate about the average Warhol film, the way you work was for no meaning. Which is pretty calculated: you work at something so that it means nothing.[19]

No doubt Warhol felt that plot and story have become irrelevant or meaningless, along with the order they represent. Yet the perception of plot as 'order' is, as we have noted, a half-truth. Perhaps we think that because the 'stories' we tell to ourselves and each other about our *own* lives are largely rationalizations, those that are passed down from generation to generation are rationalizations also—that they impose an order that reassures and satisfies us. But the forces that govern traditional story remain incomprehensible and inaccessible to us. Even the 'order' that governs fairy tales is unfathomable, and the plot of many stories, far from supporting the structures of their society, makes a hash of them.

If traditional plot and story *fail* to constitute a meaningful order, storytelling cannot have become "impossible" because we have lost faith in such an order. On the contrary, we should find traditional narrative *relevant* to our situation and experience. And indeed, the stories of Kafka seem credible and pertinent to us because their universe, like our own, is at variance with a rational, Positivist model. Perhaps we believe the stories told by Chaplin and Keaton because they are full of chance occurrences, and the plays of Beckett because they are determined by forces we call "absurd"— from *ab* and *surdus*, "deaf or insensible," since they don't hear or notice us.

We may dismiss traditional plot not because it has *lost* its relevance, but because it seems painfully familiar and all too relevant.

Postmodern Theory and Traditional Art

ART AND PHILOSOPHY

Though philosophers know more about art than artists know about philosophy, the two endeavors have little in common. As Schlegel says:

> In what is called the philosophy of art, one or the other is usually missing: either philosophy or art.[1]

Philosophy is always finally prescriptive: "Authentic philosophers . . . say: thus it shall be!"[2] As we have noted, this is not the way of art.[3] Moreover, philosophy—"the science of reason"[4]—seldom has a sensory or explicitly subjective dimension. Its greatest strength lies in abstraction. The texts of Heidegger, despite his gift for poetic phrasing, are finally *denkend*, not *dichtend*. Our access to them is contingent on our understanding, whereas we can approach the 'philosophical' poems of Hölderlin and Rilke through our senses—without understanding them intellectually. Valéry says of the traditional artwork:

> We recognize (it) by the fact that no idea it inspires in us, no mode of behavior that it suggests we adopt could exhaust it or dispose of it. We may inhale the smell of a flower whose fragrance is agreeable to us for as long as we like; it is impossible for us to rid ourselves of the fragrance by which our senses have been aroused, and no recollection, no thought, no mode of behavior can obliterate its effect or release us from the hold it has on us. He who has set himself the task of creating a work of art aims at the same effect.[5]

Deconstruction, though intent on complicating our responses to a text, is concerned with shedding light and, like all philosophical enterprises, deems itself relevant to our institutions and conduct. It stresses uncertainty, ambiguity, contradiction, and discontinuity in order to undermine all power structures, which almost invariably derive their authority from the certainties they appear to offer us. Ironically, even uncertainty can thus become a tool for achieving practical, political ends.

Unlike classical philosophy, which seldom has more than a secondary interest in art and literature, postmodern theory is focused on the text and centered in aesthetics. But while its critical approach to our social-political structures is often persuasive, the deconstruction of narrative seems redundant, for narrative is and always has been the *realm* of the uncertain. Since uncertainty is the fundamental reality to which story refers itself, one could say that narrative has always been 'postmodern,' ambiguous, contradictory, and riddling.

Postmodernism may spell the end of classical philosophy with its predicate of reason and consistency, and undermine the assumptions on which our structures rest. But discovering an undecidable relationship between art and 'reality,' or fundamental contradictions in the text itself, is news only in an emphatically Positivist context. Not art but our simplistic, univocal misreadings—a product of the effort to turn the study of literature into a *Wissenschaft*—call for deconstruction. Though postmodern criticism is a necessary antidote to what were once deemed standard interpretations, the deconstruction of art is, as Hillis Miller says, an act which "has already been performed by the text on itself."[6]

TRADITIONAL ART AND REALITY

Traditional aesthetics confined itself to art. It assumed a relationship between art and reality, but did not perceive its own role—or that of the artwork—as a prescription for change. Art pleases; it is cathartic; it may be metaphysical; but its bearing on our lives is indirect.

Postmodern theory, however, is predicated on the assumption that there is just *one* realm—that art, like everything else, is also political, and that every aesthetic ultimately addresses public issues. As we have noted, while Marxists maintain that art is no longer separate or 'privileged,' non-Marxists undermine the relationship between the text and everything beyond it. For them, too, art is no longer separate, but instead of seeing it as a product of economic and social reality, they see reality itself as text. Their totalization occurs at the opposite end of the spectrum.

What appears to be a contradiction may be reconciled if both positions are traced to the Enlightenment[7] and Positivism.[8] For both are equally committed to changing the world—with Marxists urging us toward socialism and deconstructionists toward a more perfect democracy. Once art is no longer privileged, it is open to the same deconstructive analysis as all our structures and can itself become an instrument of change. Conversely, if reality is a text, it loses some of its power to limit and depotentiate us.

Like classical philosophy and science, traditional art—which includes the modern—refers to a reality that is presumed to exist independently of it. Kafka told Janouch that "genuine art is document, testimony";[9] Brecht believed that "all great poems have the authority (*Wert*) of documents"; Rilke wrote to a friend: "I have been all my life concerned with words that can be believed"; and Wallace Stevens says in *Opus Posthumus*: "The real is only the base, but it is the base . . . The ultimate value is reality."[10] As Robbe-Grillet notes:

All writers think they are realistic . . . One must conclude they are right.[11]

But while traditional art sees itself as serving the truth or reality, it is hardly "realistic" in the art-historical sense of the word. Flaubert objected to the realist label that was attached to *Madame Bovary*, and Dostoevski said he was "a realist in the higher sense of the word. . . . I depict all the depths of the soul."[12] The 'reality' to which their work makes reference, one to which both artist and audience are deemed to have access, is not for the most part physical. Since we are bodily *absent* from a story, it can only be 'real' to us psychologically or subjectively. Ancient tales of heroes may have reported actual adventures, but if they remain persuasive it is because we recognize the alien regions we traverse and the monsters we encounter as *inner* realities—inner landscapes and events. The journey out is always a journey in.

Most art has a mimetic component, which can range from an exact transcription of surfaces to the rendering of a few salient features, as in caricature. But the likeness we fasten on when we 'believe' an image or story—be it tragedy or farce—is not apt to be physical. We recognize and believe what is happening to the central figure because it has happened to us also—albeit subjectively or 'psychologically.' We too go from crisis to crisis; we too are often up against it, though we cannot afford to express ourselves in big, emotional scenes. Even animated cartoons may seem 'real' to us because we recognize, in the physical shattering and reconstitution of Road Runner, the continuous disintegration and reintegration of our own identity. We too keep having to 'fall apart' in order to accommodate new information—to change and survive.

Edith Wharton says:

> Modern fiction began when the "action" was transferred from the street to the soul.[13]

But in story, painting, and poetry, the "street," or external reality, has always been the soul. Mimesis facilitates our recognition of the inner realm by giving it physical expression. In this sense all art is 'expressionist.' Though no one we know moves or acts like Chaplin, what he does is plausible because we recognize his *impulses*, often those of the child we once were and may still be under the veneer of adult behavior. We give credence to his actions because they give substance to inclinations we have ourselves repressed or hidden.

In the world around us, color is not salient: we generally recognize objects by their shape and not their hue. Yet the fact that in painting color is often the most immediate and striking element seems neither strange nor unreal to us, for it gives expression to the subjective reality that is an immediate and integral part of our experience. The distorted, flamelike figures of El Greco, set in a landscape of like shapes, do not strike us as abstractions because we recognize them as manifestations of the inner realm.

The artwork exists 'materially' but requires our psychological and subjective collaboration. As Schopenhauer says:

> All art can function only through the medium of the imagination.[14]

A play or painting is completed by and within us. Violence in the Athenian theater was surely kept offstage to make it *more* persuasive, whereas the literal and complete rendering of brutality in our movies may shock us but makes us comfortably aware that we are watching "special effects." We enjoy the violence because it *isn't* happening: the very attempt at physical 'realism' undermines itself—no doubt intentionally. Conversely, Carl Dreyer planned to film the crucifixion of Jesus—which he did *not* intend for our simple enjoyment—by showing the nails splinter through the wood at the back of the cross.[15]

THE IMMEDIACY OF OUR SENSES

We are well aware that no two people mean the same thing when they use a word. But the sound of clashing cymbals or the sight of a severed head

188

are likely to affect us in similar ways. Art has traditionally had recourse to our senses and often works for the most direct, least mediated impact. Sensations and actions are far less ambiguous than words. Aggression, violence, tenderness, greed, cruelty, lust, and pain are something of a *lingua franca*, and when they are enacted in a story or movie, we recognize them. They refer to something we understand and share with others, since our bodies and senses are sufficiently alike.

Art engages us in experiences that are less processed, or less civilized, than those we have in daily life. We recognize what we see and hear in the artwork, yet it seems new—for it arouses impulses and feelings in us that have, for good reason, been inhibited since childhood. Baudelaire calls artistic genius "nothing more than *childhood recovered* at will,"[16] though the senses that art employs to elicit our 'uncivilized,' childlike responses are the safe and 'distant' ones of sight and hearing, which involve no physical contact or danger.[17]

ART MAKES VISIBLE

Worringer tells us that in 'primitive' cultures, design renders the unchanging in nonrepresentational form: it disregards the ever-shifting surface. But Western art has always been partly mimetic or representational, and keeps changing even in periods and communities that appear static—both to reflect *actual* change and to enhance its own impact. Even in Western art, however, there are underlying forms—the preclusive structure of narrative, for example—that remain as constant as 'primitive' design. *Like* design, they embody the unchanging beneath an ever-shifting surface.

The artwork that once served religion by making the spiritual realm palpable to our senses, has continued to give immanence and actuality to an invisible, inner reality. This makes it suspect to the aesthetic, for the psyche is but the most recent refuge of the sacred, and art endows it—and the intangibles that form the basis of so many of our assumptions—with a palpable sensory presence. It incarnates and substantiates them. It makes them credible.

Klee says:

Art does not reproduce the visible, but makes visible.[18]

It attends to what we neglect, recovers what we discard or reject, and gives value to what we deem worthless. Nietzsche—perhaps the philosopher who was closest to art—wrote to Georges Brandes:

I have asked myself what humanity has most hated, feared and despised—from just that have I made my gold.[19]

The invisible need not be remote or spiritual. As Kafka says:

The secret does not sit hidden in the background. On the contrary, it stands naked right in front of our eyes. It is the self-understood. That's why we don't see it.[20]

The Impressionists shocked their contemporaries by making nature, painted outdoors, the focus of their work, and when Van Gogh filled an entire canvas with brushstrokes that rendered blades of grass, he raised what we step on with our feet to the level of our eyes: he made it visible or conscious. In traditional art, as in religious renewal, the ordinary takes on significance and value. Stones, trees, and even we ourselves become numinous. What we desacralize in life in order to survive is resacralized. Reality in art has always been "magical": the familiar becomes strange and the strange familiar.

In this respect, modern art is entirely traditional. Matisse "retain(s) only what cannot be seen":

There is an inherent truth which must be disengaged from the outward appearance of the object to be represented. This is the only truth that matters.[21]

Underlying (the) succession of moments which constitutes the superficial existence of beings and things . . . one can search for a truer, more essential character.[22]

Modernists continue to 'speak' what pragmatists and Logical Positivists discarded as a meaningless topic of discourse. In their concern with the invisible and essential, they remain what the poets were to Plato: interpreters of the gods. Even some postmodern work may not constitute a radical break with the past. By focusing on the *inessential* and *random*, it simply shifts to the center of our attention what traditional art ignored. While, for Klee, art was "the essence behind the fortuitous," in *our* experience the fortuitous and random have become central and essential. When Warhol works for "no meaning," he approximates our reality.

Since all art is an abstraction and cannot escape metaphor, its very existence implies—or indeed, proves—a nonmaterial dimension. Perhaps the postmodern interest in conceptual work springs from an effort to make the *a*physical premise of art accessible and acceptable to reason. For concepts and ideas—though no more tangible than the psyche or the sacred—are subject to discourse, and thus serve the cause of enlightenment and progress.

FREUD AND THE UNREALITY OF ART

Postmodern theory favors Freud's view of art as wish-fulfillment, perhaps because it seems to confirm the unreality of the artwork. Freud suggests that we suspend our disbelief because art gives us pleasure, grants us the exercise of repressed wishes, provides us with reassuring evidence of a rational and just order, and gives us a sense of control.[23] Yet what is actualized in the artwork is not simply our wishes but our fears and forbidden impulses, which constitute an inner reality so immediate, persuasive, and frightening that we can face them only in the ostensibly unreal context of art. Picasso says painting "isn't an aesthetic operation":

> It's a form of magic designed as a mediation between this strange hostile world and us, a way of seizing power by giving form to our terrors as well as our desires.[24]

Freud often equates art and story with "daydreams." He stresses "the unreality of [the] poetical work of the imagination" and claims that

> The writer does the same as the child at play; he creates a world of phantasy which he takes very seriously.[25]

But Freud was, of course, primarily concerned with the welfare of his patients, in whose life the inner world wrought havoc. Since neurotics are inclined to "(equate) phantasy and reality," he had to separate them unequivocally.[26] Yet he was fully aware that while art lets us *escape* life, it also permits us to confront it. "The poetical work of the imagination" often reveals a hidden truth: the myth of Oedipus is clearly more than a "phantasy." Like the taboo, it points to a powerful and utterly 'real' impulse we cannot afford to actualize. Art may compensate or balance out reality but does so with the truth as often as with daydreams. Freud himself called it "a combination of the principle of pleasure and the principle of reality."[27] In *Jokes and their Relation to the Unconscious*, he clearly supports the view that fiction and art, in the guise of the imaginary, give expression to what we 'really' are or feel but must hide.

In comedy—particularly 'low' comedy—there would seem to be a demonstrable link between the text and a 'reality,' or signified, beyond it.

While variations on a familiar routine—which are a staple of comedy and the predicate of genre theory—elicit a knowing smile, belly laughter springs from a nether region. Pleasure at the sight of physical aggression or unlicensed sexuality, and our childlike glee at the overthrow of civilized order and sense, burst out of us *involuntarily*. Freud suggests that a short circuit is set up between the text and a forbidden or frightening element in the unconscious, and that the energy we must use to repress it in life is released as laughter. While the postmodern aesthetic sees art as an exchange between a text and the audience requiring no *'actual'* or *'objective'* element, our laughter implies the existence of just such an element. But since the unconscious is an equivalent of the sacred, constellates a remote, impersonal past, and suggests both depth and essence, the aesthetic pays it no heed.

WE NEVER FORGET THAT ART IS UNREAL

In life, we often confuse what is happening within and without. Need and subjectivity can play havoc with our perception of the world around us. But while we may lend ourselves intensively and subjectively to story, we always remember it is just a story. The slightest physical discomfort relegates the fictive event to secondary importance: a scratch on my finger is more real to me than the fall of the house of Atreus. We *choose* to suspend our disbelief and collaborate with the storyteller consciously. Huizinga says that even 'primitive' audiences are fully aware that ritual is a performance.[28] Though postmodern philosophy is justified in calling reality a text, we— quite appropriately—distinguish between text and reality. A text does not engage us physically; it does not put us at physical risk, and it cannot meet our physical needs.

Perhaps we believe in the 'reality' of art just as we 'believe' in games. They too are played in a marked-off field that separates them from life without making them irrelevant. Some are existential; the card player pits himself against the hand he has been dealt and uses his skill to make the most of it, while games of *pure* chance like bingo—which is often played in church basements—invoke our uncertain relationship to the sacred. Many of us, in keeping with our Positivist orientation, prefer *athletic* games, in which the role of chance is minimized. The tennis court is leveled to reduce the uncertainty of the ball's bounce, and the outcome is largely determined by the skill and will of the players—by the control they are able to exercise. Athletic games are clearly related to human reality: the players must balance individual achievement and cooperation with the group, and marshal their strength, energy, and aggression within strictly defined limits.

Freud observes that the games of children are directly relevant to their experience.[29] In *Peek-A-Boo*, a version of *fort und da*, the infant is threatened with nonexistence by an adult who keeps disappearing and can thus no longer acknowledge him. At first the child is bewildered and on the verge of tears, but when the adult reappears and the game is repeated, the frightening becomes fun. Yet the fear invoked is real. *Without* it, there would *be* no relief, fun, or laughter. Of course the game gives expression not only to the fears of the child but to the repressed aggression and ambivalence of the adult. Antoinette Baker suggests that the games we play with infants

> are often uncomfortably like the ones the cat plays with the mouse, with the admittedly crucial difference that the human variation does not end with the death and the swallowing-up of the infant. . . . They play with the very existence of the child, with the threat of death, whether this is in a direct bodily form through a physical attack or through falling, or on a psychic level.[30]

Stories, too, are reality-inspired games or 'plays' that permit us to abreact our feelings and experience. In the puppet theater, Punch and the devil pop up from below stage just as things pop out of 'nowhere' into the awareness of the child. The games Chaplin plays in *The Gold Rush* invoke our fear of abandonment, starvation, and being eaten alive; we lend ourselves to them only because we are physically safe. In the theater, the curtain, set, costumes, music, verse, and the presence of well-known actors all assure us that the unspeakable acts committed on stage are only make-believe—though we know perfectly well that they do, in fact, happen. The more unspeakable the truth, the more it must be camouflaged by artifice. Since comedy cuts closest to the bone and renders us in our most shameful aspect, it is also the most exaggerated and least 'credible' form of narrative.

WE EXPECT THE WORK TO PERSUADE US

We lend ourselves to story *because* it is unreal, but nonetheless expect it to persuade us. Within the context of the unreal we want it to be as 'real' as possible. The horror movie fails if it does not frighten us—if, in some part of ourselves, we don't recognize it as 'true.' We derive little use or pleasure from aesthetic *un*reality unless it harbors the threat of the 'real.' Art isn't like stage magic. When the magician saws a lady in half, we *know* he is deceiving us, whereas the traditional artist tries to avoid deception and tricks. Keaton not only insisted on doing his own stunts, incurring serious injury on several occasions,[31] but staged them in uncut long shots whenever possible, so that the audience could see no 'movie magic' was employed. For the same reason Astaire shot his dance numbers in uninterrupted takes; he and Rogers claim a spontaneous, effortless harmony that was, of course, the product of painstaking rehearsal. Their harmony *is*, in fact, achieved, and we delight in its actuality.

Unlike the magician, the artist does what he claims to do. He substantiates his work with his life, sometimes with tragic consequences. As Charlie Parker said: "If you don't live it, it don't come out of your horn." He may be at risk physically, like Keaton and many circus artists, or psychologically. Either way, he attempts to accrue to an insubstantial, aphysical work a reality so dense and persuasive that it can exorcise and bless us.[32]

Deconstruction Liberates
and Enables

Uncertainty—a cornerstone of postmodernism—has traditionally been a 'manifestation' or 'refuge' of the sacred. Positivists and orthodox Marxists had no use for it, and a critic like Lukács tries to demystify it wherever he encounters it. He is highly suspicious of the realistic details in Kafka, which he describes—accurately—as "cryptic symbols of an unfathomable transcendence." He notes that instead of constituting "nodal points of individual or social life"—as they do in the work of Thomas Mann—they render "an allegory of Nothingness."[1] Deconstructionists have no more use for the sacred than Lukács but are untroubled by Kafka's "unfathomable transcendence," for they grant it no existence outside the text. Their readings ultimately arrive at an *aporia*—an impasse, uncertainty, or contradiction[2]— whereas Marxists continue to believe they can lay bare a hidden truth beyond the text. But both are determined to undermine traditional certainties and the uses to which they have been put. Both mean to liberate and potentiate us.

Postmodern philosophy is intent on destroying the assumption that art renders anything beyond itself, whether it be an inner or outer 'reality.' Art is deemed a sign system, in which the signs reflect no signified. This has led some to the radical formulation that there *is* no signified, only signifiers. It would indeed seem that unless Derrida's *Il n'y a pas de hors-texte* is taken *literally*—and not simply as a restatement of the position, taken by Logical Positivism, that what cannot be demonstrated or proved is not worth discussing—the sacred retains its ancient place as a realm beyond our knowledge and reach.

In a 1984 interview, Derrida explicitly denies that *Il n'y a pas des hors-texte* is to be taken literally:

> To distance oneself from the habitual structure of reference, to challenge or complicate our common assumptions about it, does not amount to saying that there is *nothing* beyond language.[3]

Yet Derrida leaves no doubt that he means to do away with anything that might constitute an "ultimate referent,"[4] and if there *is* something beyond the text—however undefinable—how wrong is the Platonist?

Contemporary Marxists have their own reason for invalidating the relationship between art and reality. They continue to believe in an economic, social, political, and material realm beyond the text but have no use for 'inner truth.' Unlike Lukács, they see "realism" in art as a deceptive and self-deceptive product of middle-class society. As Barthes puts it: "Bourgeois society and the mass culture issuing from it" are reluctant to declare their codes and demand "signs that do not look like signs."[5] By associating the 'realist' component in art with the middle class, they ignore—as Nietzsche did not—that artists have always thought of their work *as* 'realistic.'[6] With the possible exception of late Mannerism,[7] traditional art has seldom declared its own codes or deliberately chosen a style. 'Code' may, in fact, be a contemporary word *for* style. At their inception, most styles were perceived as an accurate rendering of 'reality' or experience. They were not identified *as* style until a later time.

DERRIDA

Derrida's successful campaign to complicate our responses to philosophy and literature—his focus on uncertainty, ambiguity, and contradiction—constitute a critique of Western structures. As he says, deconstruction offers the basis for a non-Marxist reading of all ideology.[8] Since his enterprise is primarily philosophical, it seems appropriate to associate it with a 'political' agenda.[9] Like Foucault, he is engaged in exposing and undermining the way in which power is propagated and perpetuated. In *The Ends of Man*, he draws a parallel between the linguistic relationship that the West has established to the rest of the world and its "ethnological, economic, political, and military relationships."[10] As he sees it,

> (Deconstruction) is . . . at the very least a way of taking a position, in its work of analysis, concerning the political and institutional structures that make

possible and govern our practices, our competencies, our performances. Precisely because it is never concerned only with signified content, deconstruction should not be separable from this politico-institutional problematic and should seek a new investigation of responsibility, an investigation which questions the codes inherited from ethics and politics.[11]

He both agrees with and differs from Adorno, for whom

No authentic work of art and no true philosophy . . . has ever exhausted itself in itself alone, in its being-in-itself. They have always stood in relation to the actual life-processes of society from which they distinguish themselves.[12]

Derrida's emphasis on writing continues, in the realm of philosophy, the process of undermining the relationship between the text and 'reality' initiated by formalism. If the spoken word no longer has priority over the written—if there *is* no earlier, more 'authentic' text that takes precedence over the written one, in which it comes down to us—its authority can be subjected to a rational, deconstructive analysis. By discrediting the authentic or 'present'—from which traditional philosophy and metaphysics have, like ritual and art, derived their authority—he furthers Benjamin's enterprise of shifting the basis of life from ritual to politics.

Deconstruction responds to the forbidding aspects of structuralism. It would seem to agree with Sartre that Lévi-Strauss and his faith in objective reality permitted "God" to reappear. Conversely, its own radical skepticism constitutes a subtle reassertion of human freedom.[13] Since we find it hard to conceive of freedom without some kind of mastery or control, the concept of intertextuality—of world *as* text—may well harbor the hope that we can *change* that text or world. Deconstructive readings, far from being interpretations for interpretation's sake, are the predicate for a critical examination of the way we live. We might even call them a 'truth,' though truth as process and not as product—an approach that our pragmatic society finds comfortable and familiar.[14]

Derrida can be read as empowering. By demonstrating that classical philosophy deems the written word the "sign of a sign," and by insisting, conversely, that

From the moment . . . there is meaning there are nothing but signs. We *think only in signs*.[15]

he contributes to a central endeavor of rationalism: our liberation from a transcendent signified. His critique of Western phonocentrism and logocentrism discredits all ahistorical truth. The spoken, face-to-face encounter between Yahweh and Moses has no greater authenticity than the written Tablets of the Law, just as the Laws of Nature and Nature's God have, in his view, no greater authority than the Declaration of Independence, which claims to derive its legitimacy from them. Deconstruction is opposed to all metaphysical readings.[16]

In his effort to invalidate the authentic, primary or real—to reduce everything to "interpretation"—Derrida aligns Freud's dream theory with his own approach. He adopts a playful freedom in interpreting Freud that Freud himself indulged only in speculations that were not central to his work with patients or to his theory. He acknowledges that Freud is an essentialist but reads him as the interpreter *par excellence*. Megill says that the Freud of the postmodernist "teaches us not how to live but how to read."[17] As Derrida has it, Freud's readings are not "rabbinical"—not an attempt to decipher a truth—but interpretation as "self-justifying play."[18] While the meaning of dreams cannot be pinned down absolutely, Freud nonetheless sees them as subject to an entity beyond themselves, which speaks *through* them, however ambiguously and indeterminately. Derrida's observation that "everything begins with reproduction" does not—in Freud—mean that "there is no text present elsewhere as an unconscious one to be transposed."[19] In his work, as in Jung's, the dream derives from an unknowable and indeterminate 'other,' of which it is an analogue. The unconscious, like the gods, remains hidden, or 'obscures' itself—a process altogether different from the one in which Derrida deliberately and playfully obscures his *own* text. In deconstruction—as in all formalist-inspired aesthetics—the author takes over the role of the sacred or real. He lacks—and prides himself on lacking—the humility Freud brought to his work.

Feminist critics, who are always and for good reason politically engaged, find support in Derrida's observation that logocentrism and phallocentrism are "one and the same system." They believe, with Foucault, that "theory does not express, translate, or serve to apply practice: it *is* practice."[20] Theirs, too, is a liberation aesthetic:

> Feminist criticism is a political act whose aim is not simply to interpret the world but to change it by changing the consciousness of those who read and their relationship to what they read.[21]

The impact of Derrida on the American academy has been personal as well as political. Deconstruction overturns the hierarchical relationship between literature and the critic, so that one no longer dominates or 'enslaves' the other. De Man says that the difference between them is "delusional,"[22] Barthes calls on the essay to "avow itself almost a novel,"[23] and

Hartman implies that deconstruction cured him of an "inferiority complex vis-à-vis art."[24] Derrida's "play"—his "joyous affirmation of the play of a world of signs without fault, without truth and without origin, which is offered to an active interpretation"[25]—holds out the promise of freedom from the strictures of the text. The critic is liberated from the "ethical coercion" and rage for order and control that de Man found rampant in New Criticism. Uncertainty and ambiguity are perceived as an opportunity—a spur to an active, creative instead of a passive, obedient response to the artwork.[26]

Though Derrida's work is widely read as a means of undermining Western power structures, privileging the spoken text, with its reference to an elusive "transcendent," is common to *all* cultures, and the "violent" binary oppositions he identifies as attributes of Western philosophy are found in a great many societies. No doubt the stress on the individual in Western thought has exacerbated our self-division and produced a heightened emphasis on the 'other,' who defines us. Our *own* sense of otherness—and the pervasive isolation and anxiety it produces—may, in turn, oblige us to attempt that reduction of otherness to sameness that Adorno and Levinas call characteristic of Western thought. As Adorno says:

> Great philosophy was accompanied by a paranoid zeal to tolerate nothing else and to pursue everything else. . . . The slightest remnant of non-identity sufficed to deny an identity conceived as total.[27]

Yet identity everywhere has always been both *defined* by difference and *threatened* by it, and differences have been tolerated only within strict limits. Derrida observes that in Western philosophy

> We have not a peaceful coexisting of facing terms but a violent hierarchy. One of the terms dominates the other . . . (and) occupies the commanding position.[28]

He defines his deconstructive strategy as a reversal of these hierarchies. In order to free us, he sends whatever is—"at a particular moment"—on top to the bottom.[29] But while Western philosophy indeed promotes violent hierarchies, our communities and their structures—like those elsewhere—attempt to hold the opposites in balance. They promote neither union nor nonunion, sameness *nor* difference, but try to maintain our access to both. Like communities and structures everywhere, they rest on a series of contradictions that, ideally, open up a wide range of possibilities—perhaps the very "irreducible and generative multiplicity" called for by Derrida. In practice, of course, the community—like the individual—is often polarized or totalized, and thus committed to the violent hierarchies Derrida deplores. His call for multiplicity rightfully questions the confrontational stance that the opposites—in the East and Middle East no less than in the West—have often prompted. His position is akin to Adorno's:

> Peace is the state of distinctness without domination, with the distinct participating in each other.[30]

It seems appropriate to consider his work—which sends the transcendent signified to the bottom after its long ascendancy—part of a continuing dialectical process.[31]

The deconstruction of violent hierarchies and logocentric assumptions endeavors to create a single, level field on which everything may coexist, and so affords us new options. But whether, as many insist, it actually eliminates the transcendent signified is doubtful. For surely there is such a thing as 'nature,' even if we cannot know it, even though our perception of it qualifies it beyond recognition, and even if our very existence *derives* from the process of qualifying it.

Moreover, Western structures do not rest entirely on power relations. They are in some measure predicated on 'natural' law and order, and refer to nature or the sacred not merely to authenticate and authorize themselves but because we deny it at our peril. Just as those who build shelters and ships cannot ignore the weather or the sea, so our social and metaphysical structures must accommodate, as best they can, to those forces they cannot control.

Since we can't live in a simple accord with nature, we must at once acknowledge *and* inhibit it. Human law both integrates and supersedes natural law. We try to prevent the devouring of the weak by the strong, but accommodate to the 'survival instinct' by recognizing our 'inherent' right to self-defense and the defense of our communities. While we ceaselessly qualify and reinterpret nature—in part, no doubt, to serve the power structure—dismissing it altogether seems pointless. As C. S. Peirce says:

> Let us not pretend to doubt in philosophy what we do not doubt in our hearts.

Postmodern theory sees the uncertainty and instability of the text from a Positivist perspective—as an element that potentiates us personally and politically. So Barthes says:

> Literature . . . by refusing to assign a "secret", an ultimate meaning, to the text (and to the world as text), liberates what may be called an antitheological

activity, an activity that is truly revolutionary since to refuse to fix meaning is, in the end, to refuse God and his hypostases—reason, science, law.[32]

But uncertainty, far from "refusing" God, is the very core and origin of the sacred, and theology, reason, science, and law are simply our attempt to understand it, to make it acceptable and useful to us. They may claim its authority as their own and persuade us, much of the time, that they are valid interpretations of God's or nature's 'intentions.' But at their core they, too, must acknowledge our fundamental uncertainty. Even the contradictions that deconstruction elicits from the text or artwork could be seen as evidence of the sacred, for the sacred *is* contradictory—both life and death, creation and destruction. Uncertainty may indeed *be* our transcendent signified.

There is, moreover, a point of uncertainty and contradiction—an *aporia*—in Derrida's statements about the transcendent. On the one hand, he denies it—as in *Il n'y a pas de hors-texte*, the principle of "play," and the affirmation of "a world of signs without fault, without truth and without origin." But his very stress on uncertainty or undecidability suggests a reality beyond the text. For if the uncertainty is in *us*—in our inability to decide—we cannot be sure that there is nothing beyond it. If, on the other hand, uncertainty resides in the *object*—in an electron, for instance, that is both particle and wave—we are back with a traditional view. By putting reality in doubt—or into 'play'—Derrida may be affirming as well as undermining it.

Uncertainty plays a similar role in the work of Stendhal. What he calls *le divin imprévu* is at once a liberating force *and* a reassertion of the sacred.[33] Julien Sorel has no idea why he tries to kill Mme. de Rênal. It comes as an utter surprise to him. He does not see that fate, or the unconscious, has asserted itself and made a hash of his plans and ambitions.[34] Whereas, in a classical story, we would know all along what is to befall him, in *The Red and the Black we* are as surprised as he. Yet his actual situation is no different from that of Oedipus. Both are overtaken—"surprised" *means* "seized" or "overtaken"—by events, and it is only our own lack of knowledge that lends Julien a semblance of freedom. Perhaps Stendhal cherished *le divin imprévu* because—by opening his narratives to the unforeseen—it made anything and everything possible, even as it reaffirmed the ancient power of the sacred. It at once freed *and* placed him. It enabled him to tell stories.

15

Invalidating Traditional Aesthetics

ART AS INTENTIONAL

Though *poesis* means "a making" and suggests 'creation,' the traditional artist sees himself as 'discovering' or 'uncovering' as much as 'creating.' He subscribes to the principle of *ars inveniendi* that Bacon and Leibniz urged on science and philosophy. To *invent*, from the Latin *invenire*, originally meant "to come upon," and *imagination* is rooted in the Latin *imitari*, "to imitate." The truly imaginary—if there *is* such a thing—is of little interest to traditional art. It is likely to be unsubstantiated effect. Until recently, aesthetics might well have agreed with the physicist Richard Feynmann:

> Our imagination is stretched to the utmost not . . . to imagine things which are not really there, but just to comprehend those things which *are.* . . .[1]

Baudelaire speaks of Ingres's and Courbet's "war against the imagination"—a faculty which, in its most useful form, may be the artist's ability to conjure up an event or object not actually before him. Heidegger points out that the German word for "creating"—*schöpfen*—also means "to draw water from a well or body of water." Creation is *re*creation. The traditional artist deems himself an observer and not, in our sense of the word, an originator. "To originate," says Poe, "is carefully, patiently, and understandingly to combine." The artist serves the work, which inheres in the world, though it is *his* effort that makes it visible. Cézanne's

The landscape thinks itself in me. I am its consciousness.[2]

recalls Nietzsche's

We are the figures in the dream of a god who understand how he dreams.[3]

The storyteller is necessary to the story, yet beholden to it. He stands under it and serves it; he is its secretary—willing, open, available, and in many ways passive. On this point, there is little difference between Balzac—who inscribed his walking stick with the legend: "I break all obstacles"—and Kafka, who said: "All obstacles break me."

By undermining the relationship between text and 'reality,' the postmodern aesthetic invalidates the observational or devotional role of the artist.* To the contemporary critic, the painter who serves the landscape and the storyteller who obeys the plot constellate a master-slave relationship. The audience, too, is invidiously if unconsciously trapped into subservience to whatever claims to speak through the artwork. If we are to be truly free, the artist must be in charge of the work—its master, not its servant. When he is in control and we identify with *him* and not with the fictive figure, the story enhances our self-esteem. Nabokov says:

> The good, the admirable reader identifies himself not with the boy or girl in the book, but with the mind that conceived and composed that book . . . the individual genius who imagined and created it.[4]

We are to admire his inventiveness, his skill at manipulating us, and his ability to make us believe something that *isn't* true. The traditional view of God or nature as the ultimate author has given way to a view of the author as god.[5]

Of course even the traditional artist or storyteller is often possessed by a sense of his own power. In a society that expects him to shore up individual existence, and in light of his own threatened identity, he can easily slip into thinking of himself as the sole creator of the work. On occasion, Flaubert saw his task as godlike: *faire et se taire*—"to do and be silent". Yet every sentence he forged, godlike, to countermand the 'nothing' of his own existence ultimately serves Emma's story or fate. Throughout the composition of *Madame Bovary* he remained a painstaking 'scientific' observer, who sometimes went out to sketch a physical setting before writing the scene

---

*Though postmodern theory is in no sense monolithic, it rests on interrelated and widely shared assumptions that would seem to justify our calling its approach to art an aesthetic.

that takes place in it. Not until the twentieth century would artists rebel openly against observing and serving. So Clyfford Still says:

> I made it clear that a single stroke of paint, backed by work and a mind that understood its potency and implications, would restore to man the freedom lost in 20 centuries of apology and devices for subjugation.

We are on our way to postmodernism—to the conviction that there is no 'reality,' no given, that must be obeyed. John Cage observes:

> The thing that always annoyed me about harmony was that it was governed by laws. But . . . those laws need not be taken seriously.[6]

In this as in so much else, the contemporary aesthetic is heir to Enlightenment principles. As early as 1773, Mercier called for the liberation of art [7] and Kant—though he acknowledged that "in all the free arts something compulsory is still necessary"—defined the artwork as the product of "a will which makes reason the basis of its actions."[8]

The traditional storyteller was less certain of his freedom, his will, or the efficacy of reason. He at once identified with the hero—who thinks himself free—yet believed the plot, which tells us otherwise. It was not his task to make order out of chaos, but simply to *report* what he found—order or chaos—just as it did not occur to the scientist that he might be doing anything more than discovering the laws of nature and the universe. It is the humanists—even those who no longer believe in humanism—who have insisted that man is the *creator* of an 'order' rather than part of one, and it is they who, by implication, return us to a central place in creation. The Russian formalists insisted on the will and intention of the author, and excluded whatever might determine—or subordinate—us from 'outside.' Roman Jakobson said:

> If literary history wishes to become a science, it needs to find its hero.[9]

It found its hero in the "device." In formalist discussions of fiction, plot—at one time an analogue of necessity—became a device for "retardation,"[10] which postpones the pleasure of the ending—the restoration of order that is, in the view of many, a primary function of narrative.

The author's will and intention, with their clear implication of freedom and choice, remain central to the contemporary aesthetic. De Man attributes the failure of American formalist criticism to produce "works of major magnitude" to "its lack of awareness of the intentional structure of literary form":[11]

A truly systematic study of the main formalist critics in the English language during the last thirty years would always reveal the more or less deliberate rejection of the principle of intentionality.[12]

Since the New Critics believed that though "the poet knows exactly what he is doing,"[13] he is beholden to something outside the text, the structure of his work is not truly intentional. De Man's own insistence on intentionality—with its implied dismissal of all that is involuntary, passive and 'helpless'—coincides with his description of the artwork as "a perfectly closed and autonomous structure":

When a hunter takes aim at a rabbit, we may presume his intention is to eat or sell the rabbit and, in that case the act of taking aim is subordinated to another intention that exists beyond the act itself. But when he takes aim at an artificial target, his act has no other intention than aim-taking for its own sake and constitutes a perfectly closed and autonomous structure. The act reflects back on itself and remains circumscribed within the range of its own intent. This is indeed a proper way of distinguishing between different intentional objects such as the tool (the gun that takes aim at the rabbit) and the toy (the gun that takes aim at a clay pipe). The aesthetic entity definitely belongs to the same class as the toy, as Kant and Schiller knew well before Huizinga.[14]

Schiller indeed stressed freedom in art to the exclusion of necessity. He was, like Kant, deeply committed to the Enlightenment—just as de Man's insistence on intentionality seems beholden to the link that Sartre established between intentionality and the "free act."[15]

While de Man's manufacturer of a toy or 'device' has it under his absolute control, the traditional artist is at once in control *and* beholden—free *and* bound. Traditional plot evolved slowly—accruing over generations and indebted to the communal past, or emerging 'organically' from a process within the individual storyteller and so beholden to *his* past. Chaplin said that *The Gold Rush* grew "like a tree." Traditional art emerged from a mix of will and willingness, action and passivity. Rodin insisted on the equal importance of patience and work,[16] and Stravinsky notes:

I can wait, like an insect. I'm always waiting.[17]

To contemporary critics—who often speak of a writer's *strategy*, from the Greek *strategos*, "a general"—waiting, patience, willingness, passivity, and organic form are anathema, for they imply that the artist is not truly in charge, that he is dependent and reacts, rather than acts.

206

ART AS MANIPULATION

In late-nineteenth-century criticism, the word "intrigue," with its conno-tation of human scheming, was often substituted for plot, and today plot is almost universally spoken of as an artifact, a construct, a feat of engineering. T. S. Eliot calls *Bleak House* Dickens's "finest piece of construction," as if it were a piece of furniture, though he did not think of poetry in quite the same way.[18]

The author's command of the plot is nowhere more apparent than in detective stories and thrillers. While traditional story is a riddle the story-teller did not design and cannot 'solve,' detective stories are ingenious puz-zles with satisfactory solutions. They are put together entirely for our pleasure and permit us to enjoy violence, brutality, and a loss of control on the part of the figures while we are safely in the author's hands. We delight in being manipulated by his tricks and stratagems, since a human being and not an impersonal force is in charge.

Surprises in traditional story—the last-minute appearance of the hunter in *Little Red Riding Hood* or the death of Cordelia—often come from 'out-side'. They are intrusions from the realm of uncertainty and chance. But surprises in a detective story are *tricks*—evidence of the author's skill, of his ability to manipulate his material and us. They confirm our own sense of mastery.

There is a marked coincidence between the contemporary aesthetic and the premises of commercial entertainment.[19] If 'manipulation' is the pri-mary objective and 'technique' of every artwork, there is little difference between 'high' and 'low' art, or even between art and advertising. All are manipulative and the more overtly the manipulation is carried out, the better. Pop art sees itself as a frankly manipulative enterprise, while John Cage goes to the opposite extreme and proclaims that his work is "uninten-tion." He resolves the self-contradiction of will and willingness, of rebel-lion and obedience, that structures traditional art by subordinating his work to chance.

A double standard prevails in the critical community, for the critic does not generally permit himself the same manipulation of evidence he allows the artist. He holds himself to rigorous 'scientific' standards, and would not respect a critical approach that deliberately or naively attempts to deceive and manipulate the reader. Though Barthes, like Robbe-Grillet, claims that narrative is centered in deception, he does not himself intentionally falsify or withhold information. There may be a trace of condescension in his attitude. Art, unlike critical work, is a toy, and since it isn't altogether 'serious,' need not obey the same rules as science, philosophy, history, or criticism.

With critics and many storytellers in accord that fiction is a deception, Todorov defines three narrative perspectives: "The view from behind," in which both the storyteller and the audience know *more* than the characters; "the view from within," in which they know *as much* as the characters; and "the view from outside," when both know *less* than the characters.[20] "The view from behind" is an accurate description of traditional story, but "the view from within" and "the view from outside" are clearly manipulations. The storyteller may *pretend* he knows only as much as or less than the characters, but he in fact *always* knows more. Traditional storytelling invariably renders "the view from behind," in which both author and audience know *more* than the characters.

TRADITIONAL STORY PLAYS WITH AN OPEN HAND

Traditional story makes little effort to trick or deceive us; it plays with an open hand. The fairy tale not only identifies the evildoer but lets us know exactly what he or she has in mind. Macbeth, Richard III, and Iago tell us what they want and how they plan to achieve it. Though neither we nor Hamlet can be sure that Claudius is guilty until the Mousetrap is sprung, we are inclined to believe the Ghost, for there are no other suspects; and while Gertrude's complicity remains in doubt, the issue is unresolved not just in Hamlet's mind but in Shakespeare's own. The author doesn't deliberately keep us in the dark.

A genuine surprise derives from complexities and contradictions in the material and is far more difficult to achieve than one built on withheld information. The first audience of *Hamlet,* unlike the audience of *Oedipus Rex,* may not have known the basic story, but Shakespeare plants no false leads. While the *future* of the figures is hidden from us, the *present* is revealed—at least to the extent the storyteller himself knows it.

Detective stories, however, depend entirely on withheld information. The villain is hidden from view and the essential facts are only revealed at the end, when we may, if we choose, go back and see that everything has fallen into place. Reading a detective fiction is like watching *Othello* without knowing that Iago has contrived the disasters that befall the Moor and Desdemona. Our traditional relationship to the fictive event is reversed: we know *less* than the great detective, not more. He is ahead of us in solving the puzzle. Though *Oedipus Rex* has been called a detective story, we know from the start who the murderer is and only the royal detective himself remains in the dark until the end. Sherlock Holmes reassures us that human action is effective, whereas Oedipus—guilty and blind—affirms the opposite.

In *Bleak House*, Dickens—though he sometimes hints at a secret at the end of one installment to tempt his readers into buying the next—plays with an open hand. We always know what Tulkinghorn is up to. The facts are available to us though not, of course, to the other figures. But in a single scene near the end—significantly involving a detective—there is a lapse in our double perspective. For the first and only time, essential facts are kept from us: we don't understand what Detective Bucket is up to. The games he plays, both with the other figures and with us, serve no purpose but to demonstrate his—and the author's—ingenuity. The story, which has until now been wholly determined by forces beyond the reach of the figures, briefly appears to be subject to Bucket's manipulation—though he does not, of course, change the outcome. He merely turns the plot into a "retardation device" by putting a twist into our expectations.

A similar shift occurs near the end of *The Adventures of Huckleberry Finn*, when Twain—who announced in the preamble that anyone attempting to find a plot in his novel would be shot—lets Tom Sawyer, a Positivist with a literary streak, commandeer the action and scheme the liberation of Jim. Jim's escape is not enough of a challenge for him and so he complicates it with the conventions of escape literature. Significantly, the 'plotless' part of the novel is *not* without plot—one constituted by chance, the river, and historical circumstance—but when the story is subjected to Tom's *intrigue*, it loses its shape and force.

TRADITIONAL STORYTELLERS DON'T CLAIM PERFECT KNOWLEDGE

In the context of Positivism and nineteenth-century Realism, it was often said that the writer of fiction must know everything about his characters. Yet nothing could be more limiting and unpersuasive. On the assumption that knowledge is power, the writer deludes himself—and the reader—into thinking that we are in charge.

The traditional storyteller never claimed perfect knowledge. Though Shakespeare was intimately familiar with his major figures, they kept surprising him. One wonders when—or, indeed, *whether*—he learned why Iago hates the Moor, though he may have begun to sense it in the last moments of the play. The unresolved riddle of Iago—which puzzles Iago and Shakespeare as much as it does us—comes close to turning *Othello* into a play that should have been called *Iago*.

When Hamlet lies mortally wounded, he says to Horatio and those nearby:

> You that look pale and tremble at this chance,
> That are but mutes or audience to this act,
> Had I but time—as this fell sergeant, death,
> Is strict in his arrest—O! I could tell you—
> But let it be. Horatio, I am dead.

"O! I could tell you—." Why *doesn't* he? The author could surely have delayed his death long enough for Hamlet to tell us what he knows. But perhaps Shakespeare himself didn't know. He has followed him closely through five acts but now Hamlet slips beyond his reach. At this point, he may know what Shakespeare—still in mid-life and at some distance from the great divide—cannot know. In a gesture that seems at once truthful and poignant, he reveals the limits of his own experience. "O! I could tell you—." But not now. Not yet.

To a critic today, such a gesture might appear naive or manipulative. In an aesthetic that conceives of narrative as pure artifice and of plot as a "device," 'truthfulness' is irrelevant and, indeed, the height of deception. But the consequences for the serious storyteller are devastating, for he can neither subscribe to traditional plot—which is out of keeping with our Positivist coordinate system—nor employ a manipulated, manipulative form that belies his own experience. As we have noted, many choose to reject plot altogether.

THERE *ARE* NO PLOTLESS STORIES

Since, in a Positivist context, it is difficult to accept the relevance of plot to the human condition, some storytellers—aware that no narrative will stand up *without* a plot—have adopted a loose episodic form, which puts less emphasis on a central figure and cloaks its preclusive exigencies in a seemingly shapeless, nonrestrictive mantle. They opt for what appears to be an 'open' rather than 'closed' structure. Alan Friedman says:

> The impulse toward an open flux of conscience in the unfolding and finishing of a story cannot be considered an aberration peculiar to the temperament of particular novelists or to the meaning of a particular novel. It is a literary current which made itself felt in sporadic eddies before Hardy and has contin-

ued with force after Lawrence. The design of life in that open form is presented as an endlessly expanding process, a design in which protagonists are forced by the organization of events to attempt to resolve experiences which cannot finally be resolved.[21]

Yet the novels of Hardy, Conrad, Lawrence, and Forster that Friedman discusses are no more open than *The Idiot* or *Madame Bovary*. They are just open in a different way. *Tess of the D'Urbervilles* and *A Passage to India* are structurally as foreclosed as *Oedipus Rex*—which, like all traditional stories, is 'open' by virtue of its ambiguities and contradictions. Friedman says that the end of the modern novel "turns out to be only another opening."[22] But so does the end of traditional story. Even the legends of the saints, which conclude with their martyrdom, were deemed, at the time of their first telling, to end in a new beginning. All attempts to draw a defining line between contemporary stories and those of old are qualified by their fundamental likeness.

There *is* no story without a plot. *Remembrance of Things Past* has often been considered plotless, though Proust himself rightfully insisted on its rigorous structure: the role of fate or the gods is assumed by time and emerges gradually rather than suddenly or brutally—as it does in our own lives if we are fortunate.[23] The early stories of Hemingway were called nonstories, just as Satie was told that his meticulously formal compositions were without shape. Audiences at the Cannes festival booed Antonioni's *L'Avventura* for its lack of plot, while sophisticated critics hailed it as a milestone of non-narrative cinema. Both assumed that because a central figure vanishes early in the film and is never accounted for, Antonioni had broken with the conventions of narrative. Yet Anna's disappearance is the crux or nodal point of the story; it not only defines and determines what happens afterward, but expresses absolutely what has happened before. Her disappearance has almost no emotional impact on her circle of friends and seems irrelevant to their bored, leisured lives—which *is*, of course, its relevance. Moreover, this unexplained event is crucial to a story governed by indeterminacy. The very moment in the film that was deemed to violate narrative convention—a convention grounded in Positivism—effectively returns us to the archaic sources of storytelling: ambiguity and uncertainty.

DEMYSTIFYING THE SACRED

It is often said that interpretation resembles detective work, ferreting out a hidden truth through the painstaking examination of clues. But while traditional interpretation celebrates the buried material it raises, the postmodern critic is engaged in invalidating the 'truth' he brings to light. He aims to rob it of the power it exercised in the dark, just as the detective makes the criminal harmless by unmasking him.

Since art, as Nietzsche says, "raises its head where the religions fade,"[24] an aesthetic committed to potentiating us is obliged to undermine the very object it studies. Instead of serving literature, the academy today is bent on demystifying it—a form of Weber's *Entzauberung der Welt*. It means to *actualize* Hegel's observation that "art is and remains for us . . . something past."[25] For art is not yet truly 'past,' and stories—despite Barthes's proclamation of the *anéantissement de l'anecdote*—continue to grip and persuade a great many people.

Contemporary criticism is well aware that the sacred will not be abolished until narrative has been permanently reduced to illusion and entertainment, for what happens to fictive figures *befalls* them—just as disasters, accidents, and chance befall us. Until recently, the Soviet media made no mention of disasters and accidents, surely because—like miracles—they have a 'religious' connotation: they are intrusions by forces beyond the control of the will *or* the state. For similar reasons, our aesthetic refuses to recognize chance and disaster as legitimate plot elements. Sophisticated storytellers disdain 'the long arm' of coincidence and accident, while popular stories continue to hinge on them.[26]

When a storyteller abandons the controlled, manipulative plot and opens himself and his figures to whatever they might do and have done to them, he readmits uncertainty, chance, or the sacred. The painter Francis Bacon attempted, by creating accidents on the canvas, to undermine his own, highly accomplished control. He was clearly aware that an unchallenged order holds no interest, that only a work hovering on the edge of 'disaster' can render the tensions of being human. Picasso notes that he pushed his own paintings as close to chaos as possible, while staying just this side of it.

The elimination of chance is central to a Positivist aesthetic. De Man's definition of an artwork as "a perfectly closed and autonomous structure" and his insistence on its "intentionality" exclude chance as rigorously as A. C. Bradley, who said in the first decade of our century:

> Any *large* admission of chance into the tragic sequence would certainly weaken, and might destroy, the sense of the causal connection of character, deed, and catastrophe. And Shakespeare really uses it very sparingly. We seldom find ourselves exclaiming, "What an unlucky accident!" I believe most readers would have to search painfully for instances.[27]

As we have noted, a quick and painless search reveals that the endings of *Hamlet, King Lear, Romeo and Juliet,* and *Antony and Cleopatra* are *determined* by chance. Bradley continues:

> Some things which look like accidents have really a connection with character, and are therefore not in the full sense accidents. . . . I believe it will be found that almost all the prominent accidents occur when the action is well advanced and the impression of the causal sequence is too firmly fixed to be impaired.[28]

It seems more likely that we accept the role of accident at the end of the plays because we have sensed from the start that the figures are not in command of their own lives—that the "causal connection of character, deed, and catastrophe" is an illusion. In our identification with the figures, we may at first believe that their will determines the action, but as the story draws to its close, an incomprehensible fate, in the form of accident or chance, appears as nakedly on stage as the *deus ex machina* in the Athenian theater. Perhaps even a reader as thoughtful as Bradley misses the role of accident in Shakespeare because it countermands his own coordinate system, though he *does* recognize that in comedy "the tricks played by chance often form a principal part of the . . . action."[29] We should note that Aristotle takes a view of chance or the "irrational" that prefigures our own:

> The tragic plot must not be composed of irrational parts. Everything irrational should, if possible, be excluded.[30]

This seems hard to reconcile with the ultimately incomprehensible or "irrational" myths on which Greek tragedy is founded.

All enlightened criticism has sought to eliminate the sacred, whether constituted by chance, providence, or fate. Forster approvingly paraphrases the French critic Alain:

> History, with its emphasis on external causes, is dominated by the notion of fatality, whereas there is no fatality in the novel; there, everything is founded on human nature, and the dominating feeling is of an existence where everything is intentional, even passions and crimes, even misery.[31]

As a *storyteller,* however, Forster is less certain that "there is no fatality in the novel." *A Passage to India* is not only implicitly precluded by its structure, but explicitly:

> The horses didn't want it—they swerved apart; the earth didn't want it, sending up rocks through which riders must pass single file; the temples, the tank,

the jail, the palace, the birds, the carrion, the Guest House, that came into view as they issued from the gap . . . didn't want it, they said in their hundred voices, "No, not yet," and the sky said "No, not there."[32]

Unlike the storyteller, the critic can express his convictions without contradicting them in his own narratives. Peter Brooks locates the origin of modern fiction in *Madame Bovary*, a novel that is, in his view, free of "occulted meaning."[33] But as we have noted, every traditional plot constellates the "occult"—from *occulo*, "to conceal"—and *Madame Bovary* is no exception. Flaubert may be committed to Emma's freedom—as he is to his own in composing sentence after sentence—but he also knows she is fated and without recourse.

Brooks calls Kafka a "decentered" novelist, but the absence of center in *The Trial is* its center. The forces that determine K's fate are incomprehensible to him and to us, and his relationship to them is uncertain in the extreme. Their 'meaning' is that they make no sense. What K and we experience as an absence of center is, in fact, the very 'nothing' or emptiness that returns us to an archaic experience of the sacred. The "occult" is vividly, concretely present in its very absence. The gods are concealed, as they were before we claimed to know and understand them.

Bakhtin's focus on carnival as a 'prototype' of the novel is surely an attempt to place the sacred that is at the core of fiction in a social and historical context. Carnival, too, constitutes a safe and separate arena where differences are eliminated, barriers and boundaries are breached, and identity is diffused. Here "opposites meet, look at one another, are reflected in one another, know and understand one another." "Carnival time is divorced from historical time". We are in the presence of a god. Carnival is nonhierarchical, structureless, dionysian—akin, as Bakhtin observes, to Dostoevski's eternity, where "all is simultaneous, everything coexists."[34]

THE CRITIC INSISTS ON OUR FREEDOM

No doubt literary theory, which became a full-fledged discipline during the heyday of Positivism, is—like all of us—committed to shoring up human freedom. Even Aristotle's *hamartia*—the mistake, misunderstanding, or blindness that brings about the hero's downfall—has a positivist tinge: it implies that the outcome might have been different. The nineteenth-century concept of the "tragic flaw" was an attempt to pinpoint the origin of the disasters that befall the figures and to suggest, by locating them in the hero's character, that we can influence them.

The critic's reluctance to concede that tragedy undermines our free-dom—though only *myth* denies it more explicitly and with fewer diver-sions—is evident in most discussions of *Oedipus Rex*. Even writers with a sophisticated contemporary perspective go to great length to maintain the freedom of a man whose parents were correctly told what he would do before he was born:

> In the drama in which he is the victim, it is Oedipus and only Oedipus who pulls the strings. Except for his own obstinate determination to unmask the guilty party, the lofty idea he had of his duty, his capacities, his judgement . . . and his passionate desire to learn the truth at all costs, there is nothing to oblige him to pursue the enquiry to its end.[35]

Determined to put Oedipus in charge of his own destiny, Vernant and Vidal-Naquet ignore the plague that Apollo has visited on Thebes, which would clearly "oblige him to pursue the enquiry to its end" even if he were *not* "obstinate" and proud.

> It is this *hubris* characteristic of a tyrant—to use the chorus' name for him—that causes Oedipus' downfall and is one of the mainsprings of the tragedy.[36]

But his downfall isn't *caused* by his pride—which simply brings him to the realization that he 'fell' a long time ago—and his *hubris*, as we have noted, also leads to his self-awareness, suffering, and atonement. In order to evade the inexorable judgement that the play pronounces on our freedom, the critic must ignore the facts as both Sophocles and the myth present them:

> Whatever (Oedipus) does is prompted entirely by his own will, although the outcome is outside his control.[37]

There is, of course, no evidence in the play—nor can there be in any story—that what Oedipus does is "prompted entirely by his own will." His crimes are involuntary and unconscious, and no jury, today, would convict him of parricide or incest. He can be found guilty only of original sin.

Every aesthetic theory imbued, consciously or unconsciously, with En-lightenment ideals must reject the spectacle of the fictive figure as victim. This may account for the many awkward attempts to discriminate between figures who are properly 'tragic' and the rest of us, who are deemed merely 'pathetic.' Bradley says:

> If Lear were really mad when he divided his kingdom, if Hamlet were really mad at any time in the story, they would cease to be tragic characters.[38]

215

In this widely shared view, only the free individual can be tragic. Though contemporary criticism is less naive—or evades the problem by rejecting both individual and tragedy—an insistence on the free will of the fictive figure is with us still. John Updike says:

> Without the possibility of a mistake there can be nothing to repent of, and no tragedy.
> Lives that offer those who live them no alternatives . . . pass as sheer glossy spectacles, like the existence of animals.[39]

Büchner knew better. *Woyzeck* may be the first modern narrative in which not only the underlying structure but the manifest situation allows the hero *no* alternative whatever.

J. Hillis Miller, in his thoughtful reading of *Bleak House*, blames the figures themselves for what befalls them:

> The effect of (their) universal abnegation of responsibility is that many of the characters feel themselves to be caught up in a vast mechanical system of which they are the helpless victims.[40]

In Miller's view, they feel helpless because they have abnegated their responsibilities. But it seems more likely that they feel helpless because they, in fact, *are*. Miller says:

> The disintegrative process in which so many of the characters are caught is not necessary, but the result of the absence of moral relationships.[41]

Dickens saw it differently: "The disintegrative process" is clearly beyond the control of his characters; they have no way of escaping it, and "the absence of moral relationships" is a *consequence*, not a cause, of their situation. Miller's own assumptions are quite explicit:

> The world . . . is in man's hands. If its decomposition is his fault, it is possible that he might be able to reverse this decay and put the world back together.[42]

> (God) has left the human world, and the objective world to human beings. It is their responsibility.[43]

Even fairy tales have recently been given a Positivist interpretation— surprisingly by a psychoanalyst:

> The message that fairytales get across . . . (is) that struggle . . . is an intrinsic part of human experience—but that if one does not shy away but steadfastly

216

meets unexpected and often unjust hardships, one masters all the obstacles and at the end emerges victorious.[44]

This may be the manifest content of *some* fairy tales, but figures like Snow White don't "struggle" and "master all the obstacles," nor could she be said to "emerge victorious" at the end. She survives because a kindly fate comes to her rescue in the guise of a hunter, seven dwarfs, and a prince, whose men stumble fortuitously with her coffin and dislodge the poisoned apple from her throat. Not struggle and action but innocence and passive endurance are rewarded in many fairy- or fate-tales.

ART AND PASSIVITY

An aesthetic committed to our liberation must abjure passivity. Yet art has always been in part passive, and Nietzsche's view of it as the highest manifestation of "the will to power" is only half the story. The artist, like everyone else, begins life with an experience of helplessness, which—in his case—is often so intense or extended as to become a fundamental component of his being. Kafka notes in his journal: *Nichts als ein Erwarten, ewige Hilflosighkeit*—"Nothing but waiting, eternal helplessness."[45] The threat of being overwhelmed may be a major source of the artist's energy, as it indeed is in much of what we do. Passivity is a precondition of creativity, just as nonwilling is, for Heidegger, a predicate of thought. Schopenhauer defines genius as the ability to *abandon* one's own purposes, one's will and personality, and to become "will-less knowing, pure contemplation."[46] Keats's "negative capability" is in large measure a passive state—permitting one to be "in uncertainties, mysteries, doubts without any irritable reaching after fact and reason."[47] In art, as in meditation, the will is often engaged in *suspending* the will—in an act of submission. Rilke referred to himself as a secretary, Baudelaire and Proust thought that the task of the writer is that of a translator, and Stravinsky said: "I am the vessel through which *Le Sacre* passed." The artist plays across the line of doing and not doing, as he plays across the line of being in and out of control. He may not be "fearlessly passive," to use Adorno's phrase, but he is willing to *risk* passivity.

Marxism has always rejected passivity as a paralyzing poison. Engels and Lukács abhor Naturalism, which renders the human being as helpless, and Trotsky praised Futurism because

(It) is against mysticism, against the passive deification of nature, against . . . aristocratic and every other form of laziness, against dreaminess, and against lachrymosity—and stands for technique, for scientific organization, for the machine . . . for will power, for courage, for speed, for precision, and for the new man who is armed with all these things.[48]

Adorno—whose aesthetic, like Brecht's and Benjamin's, was forged in the context of fascism—insists that both artist and audience must maintain an active, critical relationship to the work. His call for "non-identity" is an equivalent of his political motto: *Nicht mitmachen,* "no joining in." Identification urges us to merge with the object, to immerse ourselves, to cease to exist, whereas "non-identity" insists we remain apart. He is critical of Hoffmannsthal, who "eliminated the role of the critical subject," tried to "save himself by throwing himself away," and became "the mouthpiece of things."[49] "The poet of modernity lets himself be overwhelmed by the power of things like an outsider by a cartel."[50] Yet art traditionally *served* as a "mouthpiece" and risked being "overwhelmed."

Postmodernists may be less confident than Marxists that art and theory can affect the world directly, but they too demand a free, active, and critical relationship of author and audience to the work. Barthes's *écrivain* produces an *écriture* or "Text" that is *scriptible* by the reader. In his view, the "logic" of narrative has "an emancipatory value":

> The function of narrative is not to "represent," it is to constitute a spectacle still very enigmatic for us but in any case not a mimetic order. The "reality" of a sequence lies not in the "natural" succession of the actions composing it but in the logic there exposed, risked and satisfied. Putting it another way, one could say that the origin of a sequence is not the observation of reality, but the need to vary and transcend the first *form* given man, namely repetition: a sequence is essentially whole in which nothing is repeated. Logic has here an emancipatory value—and with it the entire narrative. It may be that men ceaselessly reinject into narrative what they have known, what they have experienced; but if they do, at least it is in a form which has vanquished repetition and instituted a process of becoming.[51]

Yet traditional narrative *is,* in fact, repetitive, cyclical, or spiral in form, and Barthes's description of it may be skewed by his need to transform the redemptive 'function' of art—which Benjamin rightly associates with a cyclical, repetitive form—into a progressive one.[52] Kierkegaard took a different view. For him, repetition is happiness—"an untearable garment . . . a beloved spouse of whom one never tires":

> He who does not recognize that life is repetition, and that therein lies its beauty, has condemned himself . . . and will perish.[53]

Feminist criticism is understandably suspicious of repetition and abhors passivity, the mode that most societies have prescribed for women. So Laura Mulvey invalidates "the voyeuristic active/passive mechanisms" of film, and calls for a relationship to the artwork that is freed "into dialectics, passionate detachment."[54] Empathy is suspect, since it invokes the 'passive' role of living in and through others—which may, in life, originate in the relationship between mother and infant. Our traditional response to art—in which identification and closeness coexist with abstraction, detachment, distance, and irony—is deemed invalid. To avoid being sucked into a simple feeling reaction, we are urged into "passionate detachment."

We have noted that in traditional story not just women but the patriarchal figure himself is forced into a passive or 'feminine' relationship to the plot. Though he does not know it, the phallocentric image he projects is undermined by the narrative structure. There is little difference between the passion of Racine's Phèdre and the passion—from the Latin *patio*, "to suffer"—of Othello or Antony. Though they are generals, both are at the mercy of their feelings. Even Macbeth is—for much of the play—a weak, almost passive figure beside an active, unfeeling Lady Macbeth: from the first to the last scene he is "unmanned" by his wife or by prophesy. Men in Shakespeare's tragedies—and in the comedies as well—are often enthralled to feeling and, in this sense, passive or reactive. Even Iago is at the mercy of his hatred and jealousy.

Yet neither Shakespeare nor traditional story urge passivity on *us*. The complexity and contradictions of the events and figures encourage the viewer, if not to "structurate" the text, to respond on the basis of his or her own experience. The paradoxes and ambiguities inherent in narrative structure make traditional story *scriptible*—though Barthes could hardly agree since, in his view, these very qualities "immobilize" us with their double message. He fails to consider that freedom and choice *depend* on hearing two messages at once—that all freedom, like consciousness, is purchased at the risk of self-division and immobilization.

Story activates us when our feelings and hopes run counter to our knowledge; when we are uncertain and trying to puzzle out what is going on, and why;[55] when the figures are so complex that we don't fully understand them and they keep surprising us; and when several things are happening at once and we must decide which to privilege with our attention. The very specificity of the artwork engenders an active response. We become passive only when it is fashioned into a *device* for manipulating our responses—when its purpose is to create effect rather than to give density, substance, and sensory reality to an abstraction, to an absence—to the unspoken and unsayable.

Traditional Story Is
"On the Right"

STORY IS ESSENTIALIST

Like all art, story excludes. It abstracts or 'renders'—separating the 'necessary' from mere fat. Its preclusive form suggests an essential or timeless element, which makes it anathema to postmodernism, for essences clearly limit us and have been used—from Aristotle's concept of "natural slavery" to all theories of racial inferiority—to justify exploitation and inhibit change. They are associated, as Marcuse points out, with counter-revolutionary theory and rhetoric, particularly when the human being is defined as fundamentally irrational. Cyclical theories of history are essentialist and derive "from the idea of the basic unchangeability of human nature."[1] Thus the reactionary de Maistre charges that "the principle of the French revolution is in headlong conflict with the eternal laws of nature,"[2] whereas Sartre, on the left, tries to liberate us from the prison house of essentialism:

> What is meant . . . by saying that existence precedes essence? It means that, first of all, man exists, turns up, appears on the scene, and, only afterwards, defines himself. If man, as the existentialist conceives of him, is indefinable, it is because he is nothing. Only afterwards will he be something, and *he will have made what he will be.*[3]

Since every essentialist or organicist position is ahistorical, it is inimical to Marxism. Yet for Marx himself the concept of essence, though contravened in his attacks on idealism, remains a crucial polarity. Here as elsewhere, his writings maintain a relationship to the opposites. He frequently speaks of man's "essential powers" and "man's essential being."[4] In his view, as in Rousseau's, the *genus* man has been constrained into unnatural forms by society, and our true humanity, or essence, will be actualized when history comes to an end.[5]

Essences also run counter to American pragmatism. The truth, in James's view, is what is better for us to believe.[6]

> The truth of an idea is not a stagnant property inherent in it. Truth *happens* to an idea. It *becomes* true, is *made* true by events. Its verity *is* in fact an event, a process: the process namely of verifying itself, its verification.[7]

Kolakowski says that in the philosophy of Charles Peirce:

> Reality is not the "manifestation" of any other, "deeper," more enigmatic and so more authentic reality. The world contains no mystery, merely problems to be solved.[8]

Essences violate our democratic, egalitarian ethos. Like necessity, they create priorities and hierarchies, generate differences, and make some activities—and therefore some people—more important than others. Of course essence and necessity also render us all *alike* and equal, which may well be their 'function' in narrative. But postmodernism—like positivism—has fastened on their nondemocratic, order-preserving attributes. In its commitment to change, it insists that all differences can be minimized if not eliminated—that we are structured and determined by culture, not nature. On occasion, even Adorno dismisses essence:

> What is unchangeable in nature can take care of itself. Our task is to change it.[9]

Science, from Galileo to the present, has been a search for general law. It may recognize the provisional character of its structures, but is inevitably essentialist. It seems fitting that Foucault should present his writings as "antisciences," since his primary objective is "to participate in the formation of a political will"—to illuminate the many ways in which power manifests, is disseminated, and perpetuates itself. Science, with its "hierarchical order of power," is one such way.[10] In Foucault's view, all structures mask power relations and the will to dominate, and every system of knowledge or theory is "linked in a circular relation with systems of power which produce and sustain it."[11] He acknowledges, however, that there is no single identifiable villain: power is diffused and present everywhere. While this might lead some of us to see it as an essence or, indeed, as a version of the sacred, Foucault is resolutely anti-essentialist. As Megill says:

> Interpretation does not illuminate some "thing" that passively allows itself to be interpreted, but rather seizes upon an interpretation already in place, which (according to Foucault) it must "upset, overturn, shatter with hammerblows." . . . In consequence, depth itself, now reconstituted as "an absolutely superficial secret," is shown to be a deception, and the task of interpretation, which would otherwise have ended in the discovery of a foundation, becomes an infinite task of self-reflection.[12]

Barthes, for whom essences and balances are "like the zodiacal signs of the bourgeois universe," takes a similar position with respect to literature and art. As Susan Sontag notes:

> (He) is constantly making an argument against depth, against the idea that the most real is latent, submerged. . . . The aesthetic position not only regards the notion of depths, of hiddenness, as a mystification, a lie, but opposes the very idea of antitheses. . . . The idea that depths are obfuscation, demagogic, that no human essence stirs at the bottom of things, and that freedom lies in staying at the surface, the large glass on which desire circulates—this is the central argument of the modern aesthetic position, in the various exemplary forms it has taken over the last hundred years.[13]

It would seem that even mortality is no longer 'essential,' for Sontag calls Barthes "a denier of death"—perhaps on the assumption that since there is nothing we can do about the inevitable, we may as well deny it. But while the dismissal of essentials is politically and socially useful, the radical anti-essentialism of the postmodern perspective—its reluctance to countenance biological heritage, instinct, fear, and the unconscious—can lead to aesthetic blindness.

We should note that the emphasis our culture has placed on essence, depth, and authenticity may be of rather recent origin, and connected with changes in our socioeconomic circumstances. As long as communities were small and people knew each other well, they had few secrets and inauthenticity had limited use. As Thomas Wertenbaker says of seventeenth-century New England:

> The people of the community knew each other's virtues, weaknesses, habits. Every woman in town could tell just how many gowns Goodwife Collins had in her chest, just how many dishes in her kitchen, how many feather beds she inherited from her father, and shook her head when word went around that she had lost her temper when the cow kicked over the milk.[14]

223

Until recently, most people *had* no private life and little they did was hidden from public view. Essences, and the discrepancy between depth and surface, were for the most part a concern of theologians and philosophers, and seem to have focused on the sacred and its relationship to humankind. Today, however, many of us must interact with people we barely know, and the perception that the 'real' or essential is hidden is part of our everyday experience.

FEMINIST THEORY AND ESSENCES

The anti-essentialism of contemporary thought is crucial to feminist theory, which insists—for the best of political reasons—that one isn't born a woman but becomes one: "Woman as such does not exist."

To feminism, *nature* is suspect, since it has often been used to establish unchangeable sexual differences. Anne Fausto-Sterling attacks E. O. Wilson's "sociobiology"[15] as a "theory of essences,"[16] for though Wilson concedes that the preponderance of what we are and do is determined by culture, he claims that "the accumulated evidence for a large hereditary component (in) human behavior (is) decisive."[17] He carefully qualifies his departure from the concept of the newborn as a *tabula rasa*,[18] but is nonetheless engaged in the search for a "human biogram,"[19] which could be used to "biologicize" the social sciences by implying that some components of our being are not under our control. Fausto-Sterling, herself a biologist, is determined to place science in a social context:

> I do not argue for a program of behavioral research that ignores biology. Instead I put forth a plea to release biology from its sacrosanct status as First Cause and give it a more appropriate place in the network of disciplines that constitute the proper study of humankind.[20]

> The more we know about the brain, the less we will see it as a printed circuit and the more we will conceptualize it as plastic, constantly molded by the organism's interactions with its environment. Only by leaving behind fixed, linear models of the brain and behavior and progressing to complex, plastic, networked approaches will we get somewhere. What we will lose is a false sense of security. What we will gain is dynamic and contextual understanding and with it the knowledge that the social acceptance of sexual difference is ground to be gained through the body politic, not the body biological.[21]

GENRE THEORY AND ESSENCES

By placing every artwork in its historical context, genre theory undermines the concept of essence in art and literature. Originally genre was a term for

224

drawings and paintings depicting scenes of everyday life in a specific moment or place. Today, however, every artwork is deemed to be genre and contingent upon the historical situation that produced it. Genre itself is the only constant, and historical context is the one essential or 'timeless' element in every work of art. Bakhtin says:

> A literary genre by its very nature reflects the most stable, "eternal" tendencies in the development of literature. The undying elements of the *archaic* are always preserved in the genre. True, these archaic elements are preserved in the genre only thanks to their constant *renewal* and, so to speak, contemporarization. Genre is always the same and not the same, always old and new simultaneously. A genre is reborn and renewed at every stage in the development of literature and in every individual work of the given genre. This gives the genre life. Therefore the archaic elements preserved in the genre are not dead, but eternally living, i.e. capable of renewal. A genre lives in the present, but it always *remembers* its past, its beginnings. Genre is the representative of the creative memory in the process of literary development. Precisely for this reason it is genre which is capable of providing *unity* and *continuity* in this development.[22]

Though often cited in postmodern, anti-essentialist texts, this passage seems to suggest that there are, at the core or base of genre, certain "archaic," "eternally living" elements. When Bakhtin says that genre "remembers its beginnings," he may—or may not—imply that something antedates it: something that *hasn't* changed, that we continue to recognize—in short, something essential. Since, however, he at one point puts "eternal" into quotation marks, he may, like his fellow formalists, believe it is genre itself—and not the "archaic" elements it "contemporarizes"—that is "undying."

As genre theory has it, 'truth' in art is a *formula*, which is given presence and immediacy by variations in its presentation. Yet the artist has traditionally acted on the assumption that he can actually confront the truth anew, and his very willingness to court danger and destruction may spring from a need to break through the thick crust of conventionalized experience in order to connect with a 'reality' that is more intense and immediate.

The work of most American filmmakers confirms the genre view of narrative. John Ford knew that his Westerns bore little resemblance to historical fact. As he himself said, he "(printed) the legend," varying it skillfully from picture to picture. Whatever conviction his movies carry springs from his own urgent need to believe the legend, but in themselves they are mostly charades in which every scene, action, face, performance, and musical effect is designed to indicate or illustrate its intended meaning. Con-

225

versely, a work like *Madame Bovary* does not permit us to separate meaning and text. The details do not 'illustrate,' 'indicate,' or 'signify' but substantiate. Inner and outer reality are one: the word has, as it were, become flesh. The only 'legend' Flaubert prints is that of the preclusive plot—*l'enchaînement*—a 'legend' in which he believed utterly. His novel bears out the modernist motto that the work should not 'mean' but 'be'—whereas the films of Ford invert it: they make no claim to being, but their meaning is always evident. Of course their very failure to 'incarnate' makes them attractive to contemporary film theory: they are politically harmless, since their conservative ideology is always in plain view.

Genre theory disregards the way in which certain situations—a feud between two families, or between members of the same family—recur in stories of every culture and age. Perhaps they are basic to narrative not because they are reassuring conventions, but because they reflect our existence. If, moreover, we are correct in thinking that the preclusive plot is characteristic of *all* narrative, it cannot be identified as an attribute of genre. Whenever and wherever stories were told, the storyteller and his audience assumed that we are not finally in charge—an assumption that hasn't changed since the beginning of recorded time and is found the world over. It might therefore be called the *essence* of narrative. Every plot undermines the action and reflects the uncertainty of the future, and since the polarities of plot and action—of the knowing audience and the unknowing fictive figure—are the same everywhere, they can hardly be termed conventions of Western culture or expressions of a given moment in history.[23]

IN STORY, THE PAST IS ALWAYS PRESENT

We can speak of progress in science, but there is no progress in art. While defunct scientific theories are studied by no one but scholars, we continue to tell stories that were composed long ago, though their physical circumstances are not at all like our own. Science continually revises its assumptions and laws, while story's preclusive form has remained constant and suggests that a truth familiar to past generations still appears valid to us today. It is hardly surprising that an enlightened aesthetic finds story problematical. As Peter Gay says:

> The Enlightenment's concentration on the future as a realm of unrealized possibilities invited a corresponding depreciation of the past. The philosophes did not repudiate history; they found it amusing, instructive, and intensely interesting. But they could not take it as an authoritative guide. The past—

226

especially the classic past—was a storehouse of glorious, unsurpassable achieve-
ments, especially in literature and morals, and a museum of appealing figures.
But the past was also, and for the most part, a tragic pile in error and crime, to
be studied for mistakes to avoid and injustices to repair, not for models to
imitate. Of all arguments in behalf of an idea or an act, the argument from
tradition struck the philosophes as the most treacherous and least cogent: "At
best," Locke had laid it down, "an argument from what has been, to what
should of right be, has no great force," and the philosophes agreed with him.[24]

The French revolution radicalized Enlightenment attitudes: it attempted
to escape history by beginning the calendar anew. Nineteenth-century an-
archists anticipated a process of perpetual flux and renewal, a permanent
revolution that would allow no structure to congeal—at once a utopian
vision and a return to the boundless state of early childhood. Marx spoke
for many when he said:

> The tradition of all the dead generations weighs like a nightmare on the brain
> of the living.[25]

The American ethos, too, devalues the past. Our version of permanent
revolution is continuous change. We believe that all assumptions and structures are provisional and agree with Mach, of whom Kolakowski says:

> An important part in his philosophical reflection was played by his radical anti-
> dogmatism, his conviction of the harm caused to science and to life in general
> by stubborn adherence to inherited formulas.[26]

From a practical point of view, the past, today, is often of little use. It
gets in our way. Not tradition and usage but change is central to our lives,
and continuous adaptation critical to our survival. We are process oriented
and don't trust yesterday's product—neither refrigerators nor artworks;
rapid change seems to make them irrelevant. Our focus is on the future—on the child, not the 'wise' old woman or man—and we must doubt
an aesthetic tradition which claims that the old is valid still, that "the new
is always the old."[27]

Henry Ford II—whose grandfather called history "bunk"—told an inter-
viewer: "I don't believe in reading stuff you can't do much about." There
is nothing we can do about stories. They are over before they begin and
would seem to have little bearing on the issues that face us. Yet *much* of
what we perceive and experience is, in fact, 'over' before we become aware
of it: strictly speaking, once we *become* conscious of anything, it is, at least
in part, already past. Instead of the present moment, in which we are free

227

to act, there may be nothing *but* past.[28] Since this is the burden of story—threatening our confidence in action and planned change—we have, traditionally, confined it to a safe and separate realm.

STORY IS CENTERED ON INDIVIDUALS

Contemporary criticism rejects traditional story because it is focused on individuals. A strong anti-individualist current has always been evident in rationalism: like science, it questions the concept of a differentiated self. Descartes's "innate ideas" and Leibniz's "innate harmony" assert that God gave all of us the same 'rules' for comprehending the world and, in this sense, made us alike.[29] Marcuse points out that "the individual plays almost no part in Comte's sociology; he is entirely absorbed by society";[30] and Marx undermined our existence as individuals by undermining individual consciousness:

> It is not the consciousness of men that determines their existence, but on the contrary, their social existence (that) determines their consciousness.[31]

As Adorno and Horkheimer observe, reason—which originated as a tool for the control of nature—eventually turned "against the thinking subject himself."[32] For Durkheim, "the social being is richer, more complex and more permanent than the individual being";[33] and Lévi-Strauss endorses Rousseau as "the great innovator of unconditional objectivity," seeing in his work a "total repudiation of the *cogito* of Descartes":

> (He) frequently speaks of himself distantly as *he*, and eventually breaks down the *he* into the famous formula "the me is another."[34]

If Hegel is correct in saying that the free individual is inextricably linked to private property rights[35] —though we may, in fact, need the things we own to substantiate our doubtful existence *as* 'free' individuals—those who see private property as a major source of evil will seek to invalidate our separate being. The individual, moreover, has given rise to the concept of inner man and inner freedom—delusions that are deemed to keep us or others in servitude.

INVALIDATING THE INNER REALM

In rudimentary form, the concept of an inner realm must have evolved with consciousness itself, and was surely of critical importance to anyone who stood apart from the group as leader or scout. But while the prophets of the Old Testament bear witness to it, and though it constitutes a central component of Christianity, the inner realm did not become important to the community at large until we could no longer be guaranteed our place and identity from without, *by* the community.

With urbanization, and more rapidly still with industrialization, we became interchangeable and anonymous. The loss of our relationship to place, group, role, and craft threatened us with a loss of identity that the community had to remedy by granting us a new self, predicated on an inner realm. We were persuaded that though we were interchangeable on the outside, our *inner* life individuated us; it made us special and distinct. The inner realm, moreover, became the means by which an industrial society could keep us in line. As long as we were granted our identity from without—by the group—we could be largely controlled through shame. But once we ceased to have a permanent place and role and became anonymous transients, shame had to be reinforced by an inner 'mechanism': guilt.

Luther, who asserted that we have an independent, personal relationship to God, made it possible for us to live in an urban, industrial society. Henceforth our place and meaning would derive from *within*, from faith, and not from our effect on the world around us. As Marx said of him, critically:

> He freed man from external religiosity by making religiosity the innermost essence of man.[36]

In Marx's view, the inner realm accommodates us to an exploitative economic and social reality—our own or that of others; it compensates us for unacceptable conditions and drains away energy that should go into changing them. Sartre scornfully rejects the "internal liberty" Stoic philosophy and Christianity hold out to us—a liberty we think we "can preserve in any situation," but which "is nothing but idealistic mystification."[37]

Postmodern aesthetics, like the philosophies on which it is based, rejects the dichotomies separating inner from outer, spirit from matter, subject from object, *res cogitans* from *res extensa*. Since it has no use for Descartes's *cogito*, it is obliged to undermine the very object of its study. For art, at least since the Renaissance, has served to shore up individual existence, and the artist was assigned the solitary, seemingly self-indulgent but often lacerating task of focusing on his own development and continuity. He gave substance to the 'myth' of the self by his indifference to the scorn and neglect of the community, and until recently helped to prove that we exist by pursuing his work in secrecy, exile, and cunning.

Postmodernism puts an end to this by declaring that the self has lost validity. If the inner realm is nothing more than an interface between forces we don't control, it can hardly prove individual existence. There is, moreover, no longer a need for most of us to model ourselves on a solitary, inner-directed, task-oriented figure. The economy no longer requires independent enterprise and even science has shifted away from solitary effort to teamwork. Moreover, with so much impinging on us from without, it has become difficult to maintain even a semblance of inner continuity. We must be outer-directed in order to survive. In the community at large, the image of the hero has been replaced by that of the celebrity, who gives vivid if somewhat shallow expression to our need for confirmation from without.

Contemporary aesthetics has abandoned the intensive concern with the individual—both as the originator and subject of the work—that has prevailed since the Renaissance. Barbara Rose points out that in *Nouveau Roman* as in minimal art there is a "rejection of the personal, the subjective, the tragic and the narrative." Even psychoanalysis, once focused on issues facing the differentiated self, has—in the work of many—shifted from Freud's ego and drive model to a relational one. W. R. D. Fairbairn says:

> It is not the libidinal attitude which determines the object-relationship, but the object-relationship which determines the libidinal attitude.[38]

In a process that originated with Alfred Adler and was given impetus by Harry Stack Sullivan, psychology today perceives the individual almost entirely as a forcefield of biological, familial, and social forces.

To the aesthetic, even the family—which, in traditional story, justifies every hardship *and* often engenders the crisis—no longer seems a valid focus of concern. Marx saw modern families and marriage as

> the practical basis on which the bourgeoisie has erected its domination . . . (In) their bourgeois form they are conditions which make the bourgeois a bourgeois.[39]

For Marxists, the modern family is the guardian of private property. It is a reactionary force that promotes "the dependence of the woman on the man and of the children on their parents,"[40] and corrodes the community by nurturing the individual and fostering the illusion that each of us is unique.

Yet most of us continue—in our personal relationships as well as in ritual and art—to seek confirmation of the very self postmodernism has invalidated. Perhaps the pragmatist in us knows that we continue to depend on the inner realm, since society has yet to find alternative ways of validating and sustaining us through the ceaseless physical, social, and economic changes to which we are subject. We know, moreover, that we can be caught in circumstances about which we can do very little, when our only freedom would seem to lie in changing our orientation or attitude—when the only 'action' open to us *is* within. Though acceptance and resignation—our willingness to go along with the inevitable—have often been exploited by power structures, they are at times our only recourse.

We try to recognize the difference between things we can change and those we must accept. There are, moreover, clearly occasions when our refusal to submit to the seemingly inevitable can reverse it. It has traditionally been the task of the hero to attempt the impossible, and perhaps one reason we continue to need stories is that, despite their preclusive form, they encourage us to pit ourselves against necessity. They constitute that element in us—it used to be called the spirit—that survives and fights back even when we seem beaten. They continue to speak the inner realm—the subject or self—yet do so without dividing us from others. For though we are not Hercules or Chaplin's waif, *within* we *are* like them—and like all others in the audience, since they respond as we do. It is nonetheless true that by stressing the inner realm, or spirit, story can create a false sense of equality and paper over critical differences—in status, wealth, and power—that separate us from those above and below us.

The postmodern rejection of the inner realm may be directly related to the invalidation of the link between art and 'reality.' For if the inner realm—the only reality to which art can lay claim—does not exist, the artwork is indeed unrelated to anything beyond it.

CHAPTER

17

Invalidating the
Privileged Realm

We lend ourselves to traditional story willingly, for within the safe arena we can afford to abandon conscious control. We may indeed *come* to story largely to surrender our guard, to be overwhelmed. Schopenhauer says that "will-lessness" and the abandoning of individuality are central to the aesthetic experience.[1] We *cease* to be, in the personal sense, but regain our existence by becoming part of something larger. Whereas in life we require a physical *and* psychological immune system to reject 'foreign bodies,' in fiction we can be safely invaded by others. So the movie camera often follows rather than leads the action, making it easier for us to lend ourselves to the event. Like the artist, we play across the line of being and not being—though *we* are safe, while the artist may be in jeopardy.[2]

The temporary surrender of the ego in art is a conscious escape from the divisive aspect of consciousness. Within the formal, highly civilized artwork we can be open to the unconscious—to chaos and uncertainty—without imploding, and may actually *enjoy* the very experiences that would devastate us in life. Aggression, lust, jealousy, greed, violence, revenge, as well as our urge to act them out, are allowed vicarious expression and—in traditional aesthetics—purged. Here it is safe to feel intensely—to indulge emotions the community must embargo, since they may turn into action.[3] Art liberates the energy we need to inhibit them. It permits us to live out not only our negative but our positive impulses: we can be genuine, truthful, trusting, and show our deepest feelings without imposing them on others or being manipulated by them. Here private sorrow can become public event: in the guise of feeling sympathy for the fictive figure, we can

233

feel unashamedly sorry for ourselves. Free to focus entirely on our own responses, we become continuous, undivided, unambiguous, unfragmented, and conflict-free. As Kant says, we can recover the original unity of subject and object—become one with others, with the world around us, and with ourselves.

The community requires of us that we be constant. If we did not remain the same—or *idem*, as in "identity"—from one day to the next, our structures and relationships could not survive. To avoid confusion and chaos, we must conform reality—what we *might* perceive and experience, as well as what we are—to dependable, prefigured constants. Yet, in an age of rapid, radical change, constancy is dangerous, and the circumstances of contemporary life make it imperative that we not become rigid. We must be the same, yet accommodate to change—which is so much with us that many can keep from fragmenting only by *not* responding. Too much happens to and around us for us to react to the ceaseless flow of impressions and sensations; in order to preserve a semblance of continuity, we turn off, withdraw, become alienated.

In the safe arena of fiction, however, we can afford to become *discontinuous*, and permit our perceptions to undergo a process of continuous qualification without risk.[4] Movies are persuasive because they not only render the surfaces of our reality but integrate the jigsaw puzzle—or "montage"—of our fragmented experience into a continuum. A film is composed of hundreds of fragments of time and place, yet fuses the *Zerrissenheit* of our existence into a continuous whole. We should note, however, that the plays of Shakespeare render the fragmentation of our experience as effectively through the open, associative form of his verse. Human discontinuity is by no means a recent phenomenon.

Traditionally society, like the individual, needed the safe arena of art—or ritual—to remain whole. Even today, stories can create a temporary community through our shared responses, no matter whether we are laughing or crying. Our movies, like nineteenth-century melodrama, pursue a single reaction—Robert Heilman calls it "monopathic"[5]—so that we may all feel the same thing at the same time. Most films use music to underscore every moment and so make unequivocal what we are to feel, while more complex narratives allow members of the audience to make their own relationship to the events and figures—perhaps because some of us can lend ourselves to *communitas* only when a measure of our difference is preserved.

THERE IS NO SAFE ARENA

Postmodern and Marxist aesthetics must invalidate art as a separate realm, for—like the inner world and ritual—it constitutes a domain in which the unreal becomes real, the invisible visible, and the sacred manifest: it is a sanctuary.

"Literature," says Barthes, "is no longer protected."[6] It is deemed ideological or political, and therefore subject to a skeptical analysis. The core of traditional aesthetics is declared invalid: catharsis shores up the status quo; empathy and the suspension of disbelief are bourgeois fallacies rather than age-old audience responses; and the universal need for wholeness will be met when our true humanity is actualized in *society*, not—in illusory form—by art and ritual.

We should, however, recognize that Benjamin's attack on art *as* ritual was, like Brecht's critique of empathy and catharsis, in part a response to fascism.[7] The Nazis, though they had no use for religion, understood the universal need for ritual and exploited it. Their rallies were quasi-religious occasions, which fused the audience into an undifferentiated whole—one that, with the help of radio and film, could include the entire nation.[8] They too believed in a single realm and since for them—as for those on the left—everything was political, they consciously used ritual to serve the state. In this context, Benjamin's attempt to liberate art from ritual makes perfect sense. His position is akin to Plato's. As Girard says:

> The most striking parallel to the (contemporary) expulsion of ritual comes in *The Republic*. . . . To Plato, most poetry—and mythology—is a mimetic loss of differentiation and the concomitant production of undifferentiated monsters. All art is closely related to the undifferentiation of orgiastic ritual. . . . Plato, like Lévi-Strauss, wants to make his perfect city safe for differentiation.[9]

So did Benjamin, and for the best of reasons.

The contemporary expulsion of ritual seems to rest on the assumption that the irrational or sacred should and *can* be laid permanently to rest. Yet, as a folk-saying Freud was fond of quoting has it: When nature is tossed out the door it returns through the window. Ritual may be quite as hardy as nature, since most of us, when threatened by the uncertainties of nature, *flee* into some form of ritual with its reassuring repetitions. If ritual indeed reappears—in nature's wake—whenever it is repressed, we may be better off confining it to a circumscribed arena, where it is less likely to contaminate our reason and political processes.

HEIDEGGER'S TOTALIZATION FROM THE RIGHT

Like the postmodern and Marxist aesthetic, Heidegger rejects the traditional separation of art and ritual from life, albeit for the opposite reason.

His form of totalization calls for the *re*sacralization of our existence—for a return to *being*. He is deeply critical of the modern world—of our Positivism, which he calls nihilism:

> What has long menaced man with death, even with the death of his essence, is the absolute of pure willing, in the sense of the conscious imposition of man's will upon everything.[10]

In his view, we have become "so impoverished . . . we can no longer recognize the absence of God as an absence."[11] What we need is a return to "the beginning," which is "the strongest and the mightiest," to our "essence," our "abode in the truth of being," to *das Heile*, or wholeness.[12] We must find our way back to an archaic past, to an authentic relationship between the human and *Sein*.

Postmodern philosophy and criticism are in part predicated on Heidegger's perception of language,[13] which has led some to the conclusion that we 'create' the world, that there was nothing before we became conscious, that "everything begins with reproduction." But whereas Heidegger's philosophy—in *Sein und Zeit*—undermines traditional philosophy and metaphysics, his aesthetic is in many ways traditional. In his view, art links us to an archaic and presumably prerational state in which we were whole and truly immersed in *being*, rather than "homeless." Art speaks *being*, is a "workshop" of *being*—is, indeed *being's* "preeminent form." Like language, it is "the primordial sounding of the truth of a world."[14] Though he insists that *being* is not God, he calls it "the holy," "the ever beginning . . . and ever abiding," "older than the ages," and a *mysterium tremendum* that is "unapproachable" and dangerous, for it connotes "the violent concussion of chaos which offers no foothold."[15] In his *Letter on Humanism,* he asks: "What is *being*?" and answers: "It is It itself,"[16] which seems akin to Yahweh's "I am what I am." Though *being* is not God, it appears to have all the characteristics of the sacred as it manifests in our time.

We may doubt whether our relationship to *Sein* was ever authentic and whole—whether we were not from the start also suspicious, anxious, and skeptical. What Heidegger calls our "homelessness"—our alienation from *Sein* and ourselves—has also created science, modern medicine, decent homes, and an adequate food supply. Our falling away from *being*, like our self-dividedness, is surely an inevitable consequence of consciousness. Yet Heidegger urges us to reverse it by an "immersion" in *Sein*—not within the safe arena of ritual and art but in lived reality. He believes that what has been sundered can be rejoined. Like the Marxists, he calls for an actualization of wholeness. But while they totalize from the left, he is widely accused—after *Sein und Zeit*—of totalizing from the right, and criticized

> as an example of the crisis of bourgeois society in the period of late Capitalism. (He) represents . . . a flight out of time into *being* or into an irrational intuition, a neglecting of modern logic.[17]

Heidegger sees the philosopher's role as akin to the poet's, a view that may be rooted in German romanticism. Indeed, Nietzsche suggests that

> All of German philosophy—Leibniz, Kant, Hegel and Schopenhauer, to mention but the great—is the most thorough kind of romanticism and nostalgia.[18]

Like all of us, Heidegger wishes to be whole, to recover Eden. But his striving for wholeness employs not just the means of traditional philosophy: rational discourse and organization. It embraces, as well, a mythopoetic mode of thought. His *dichtendes Denken* conflates thought and *poesis*, and makes *one* what has traditionally been two.[19] His texts often attempt the 'function' of poetry: they fuse rather than separate. Hölderlin and Rilke are major influences, though Hölderlin spent thirty-seven years in madness and Rilke remained consciously self-divided—with his poems invoking the very alienation they briefly stay.

Heidegger's conflation of poetry and philosophy, and his implied rejection of self-division as an inescapable element of the human condition, surely made him susceptible to fascism, which, too, claimed a single realm and an actualized wholeness. The "immersion" he seems to call for in life, and which the Nazis promoted in their politics, is of course far more dangerous than traditional immersion experiences in ritual and art.[20] Political ritual does not permit a *conscious* or willing suspension of disbelief: since we are physically present and directly involved, we are *trapped* into believing; there is no aesthetic distance, no "as if," no mimesis, no empathy with another. We are beguiled into a state of wholeness that appears to extend beyond the ritual event; it is apt to infantilize us and may even prompt us into physical action. Not only must we ourselves pay a steep price for our 'wholeness,' but so must all those whose 'otherness' sustains it. For there *is* no *Volk,* no *Reich,* and very likely no *Führer* without the Jew or his equivalent. It is surely no accident that Nietzsche—another philosopher who on occasion conflates philosophy and poetry—served as an inspiration to fascism, though his own life and mode of thought were profoundly self-divided. Postmodernism has, of course, focused on the far more significant element in his work that undermines all forms of totalization.

DERRIDA AND WHOLENESS

Inasmuch as Heidegger claims a relationship to a truth outside time, even if he arrives at it by infusing philosophy with the intuited truth of poetry, he remains within the tradition of Western thought. Derrida, too, conflates philosophy and literature, but with the opposite intention. He believes, like Merleau-Ponty, that "the tasks of literature and philosophy can no longer be separated,"[21] and questions the privileged, timeless truth of philosophy by reading it as a literary text. If philosophy *is* literature, it can no longer make confident reference to a truth outside history, for literature is, of course, deemed to be historically—and rationally—conditioned even when it deals with the irrational. Derrida stands against the very totalization Heidegger invokes. Though his own style is literary, it is marked by wordplay and wit, which suggest detachment; his language is unpoetic, and makes no attempt to incarnate.

Derrida's approach to writing and speech could be seen as an affirmation of consciousness. The spoken word has, in his view, no more authenticity or authority than the written one, for it too implies separateness, absence and difference. The very term *différance* invokes consciousness—both in the sense of difference and deferral. His discourse on Rousseau and writing[22] asserts that no return to a natural state of wholeness is possible. If the spoken word is as "different" as the written one, we cannot go back to a prelapsarian oneness. He takes issue with Rousseau's vision, which has influenced not only Positivism but may even echo in Heidegger's return to *Sein*. In this respect, Derrida's view of language seems to confirm a nonpositivist—and, indeed, traditional—perception of the human being as self-divided and alienated. Like *Genesis*, he is convinced we cannot regain paradise. Reason and language—or consciousness—must and will prevent it. We cannot even *conceive* of an original state of wholeness without employing the "divisive" means of language—without "absence, dissimulation, detour, writing."[23]

LACAN

Lacan, too, maintains that we cannot recover our original or 'authentic' state. In his application of *metonymy* to psychoanalytic theory we observe, as Christopher Norris says:

> The endless substitution of signifiers, none of which restores the lost object of desire in its impossible, pristine reality.[24]

"Desire" in Lacan is a fundamental, incurable lack or absence—a "fall" that was, traditionally, thought to be the basis of human existence. "Desire" attempts to reverse our irreversible separateness; in it, the sexual urge commingles with our longing for a preconscious state of wholeness. It has often been noted that the language of love and worship are similar, for both speak to our need for oneness. Some—like the figures in Proust—elaborate "desire" endlessly; as long as it remains unsatisfied, it can continue to hold out the promise of wholeness; once it is met, however—and we become 'one' with the person we love—we must again confront our separateness. Of course relationships, especially today, are as powerfully determined by our fear of *not* being separate—of fusing with and disappearing into the other—as they are by our desire for oneness.

CONSCIOUSNESS AND RITUAL

Given the choice, we might have preferred to remain 'one.' But we *had* to become 'two'—or conscious and self-divided—so that the human community could be established on a higher, more complex level than the preconscious tribe or herd. The flaming sword of the angels prevents our return to Eden. Freud and Jung suggest that the incest taboo is found everywhere because it is the source and propagating force of consciousness. By establishing unequivocal differences, it evicts the child from paradise: the son may not do as the father does, nor may the daughter take her mother's place. It separates us from those who are closest to us and forces us into exile—into existence as both separate *and* social beings.[25]

Yet for life to continue, the channels to the unconscious—or *Sein*—must remain open, and from the beginning of human time ritual and art have permitted us to eliminate difference and to fuse safely with our nonhuman origins. Traditional art could be called "recursive,"[26] for here figure and ground are not clearly separated. In story, the plot—or ground—includes the figure, and the figure may be read as an integral part of the ground. This fusion with the unconscious—of the dancer with the dance[27]—is safe only in a separate arena, with limits clearly defined by consciousness; in life, reason and consciousness must—or should—prevail. Conflating the two realms leads either to the suppression of the irrational or to the invalidation of reason. The first, inspired by Western rationalism, can produce desiccation and sterility; the second, destruction and death. It is one thing for Artaud to advocate the overthrow of reason in his Theatre of Cruelty, quite another to have it promoted by philosophy or put into practice by a political movement.

239

There have clearly been times and cultures when the sacred and the community were 'one'—when art and ritual confirmed a living community instead of substituting the illusion of *communitas* where there is none. Perhaps those times are forever past, but to conceive, as the aesthetic does, of ritual and the sacred—and of art, when it invokes them—as bulwarks of reaction is surely an oversimplification. It rests on a belief in reason and progress that seems unwarranted.

Just as in rites of passage the sacred once 'held' those who were liminal, so art, at least since the Renaissance, has made it possible for those in exile to attain some sense of belonging. It cannot replace a genuine sense of community, but just as some medications help by relieving physical pain without addressing the underlying cause, there is no need to dismiss consolation. It may even help us survive.

Postmodernism—by assuming that nature and necessity, or the sacred, were created by the community and have no independent reality—appears to empower us. But it closes off some of the avenues along which we have tried to find our way back to a larger whole. What we are left with is our reason, and it remains to be seen whether it can—unaided—reconcile the conflicts and contradictions of being human.

The Rejection of Empathy

EMPATHY

Blake says:

> The Nature of my Work is Visionary and Imaginative; it is an Endeavour to
> Restore what the Ancients call'd the Golden Age.

In the safe arena of traditional art we can return consciously to a preconscious state, immerse ourselves, and risk the loss of difference. Not only
consonant but dissonant elements 'belong' and harmonize. Poetry joins as
rhyme-fellows things that appear to have no connection, just as wit and
jokes discover similarities among dissimilars. In some measure, all art shares
the animistic impulse of Van Gogh, in whose paintings everything swirls
with the same energy—not only trees and flowers but houses, chairs, and
shoes. Inanimate objects become expressive and 'speak,' like the trees and
stones in fairy tales and animated cartoons.

The barriers are down both within the work and between the work and
us. We expect to have access to it, to participate and become part of it. The
space in Renaissance painting extends not only away from us to a vanishing
point but out *toward* us: it includes the viewer and encourages us to enter
it. We don't want to be mere spectators, true outsiders, just as people at a
sports event expect to care who wins, and will often "hype" their participation by betting on the outcome. *Unless* we can share in the experience, we
are at two removes from the action, since we are physically absent.

Music involves us most immediately, for it makes few references to the
'real' world and requires no conscious 'understanding.' The song of the
sirens and not the sight of them penetrated the sailor's heart. Though the

'language' of music appears to be entirely subjective, *within* a culture it is so widely and immediately accessible that it seems to derive from a source as objective as physical action. We can, moreover, be totally open to it, for it affects only our feelings, our mood. Though as late as World War I music was played for troops marching into battle, it engenders no activity but the swaying of our bodies and the tapping of our feet.

In story, we become involved by identifying with one or more of the characters, sharing their experience empathetically. Empathy—like sympathy—may be a vestige of our original, preconscious oneness with creation. It permits us to recognize the like in the unlike, to identify with King Lear, Snow White, and Raskolnicov—to discover that *within* we too are kings, beggars, and murderers: kind, brutal, angelic, and monstrous. Derived from *em*, "in," and *pathos*, "suffering," the word suggests that we respond most directly to a figure who is suffering or under pressure—just as in life our bodies react kinetically when we see someone injured or in pain. The vulnerability of the fictive figures—their wound or weakness—gives us immediate access to their feelings and permits us to share them.

Empathy may be a form of Aristotle's *pity*, though "pity," as we use the word, implies we are in some way superior to those who arouse it. We don't feel "pity" for Oedipus, Cleopatra, or Raskolnicov. In its original meaning, "pity"—from the Latin *pietas*, "piety"—suggests human kinship and, like Aristotle's terror, invokes forces more powerful than we, which determine us just as they do the tragic figure.

In life, pity and empathy must be carefully hedged. Men, in particular, cannot afford to 'bleed' for others. They guard against their tender feelings and lend them to just a trusted few, for feelings interfere with the tasks society has assigned them. Unlike women—whose social roles are not, traditionally, object-centered—men experience empathy and pity as disabling. Even guards in the concentration camp were apparently not always invulnerable:

> The Germans couldn't stand it when people cried during the massacres. Whenever someone cried, they were clubbed to death, and we kept hearing: *Nicht weinen!*—"no weeping."[1]

In every society known to us, male children are turned over to women for a number of years, in part to 'breed' feeling and empathy into them by prolonging and fostering the original sense of oneness with their mothers. Our extended period of dependence and immaturity may be the foundation of our socialization—our mature sense of connectedness with others—though the child must, of course, also be taught to separate, to recognize the boundaries between self and other. Baudelaire speaks of "the existence of a permanent dualism in the human being—the capacity for being oneself and someone else at the same time."[2]

As adults we are only permitted to immerse ourselves in—or merge with—others in a carefully controlled, circumscribed situation. The risk as well as the opportunity is greatest at home, where one person can easily dominate another, and keep him or her from becoming a separate being. Away from home we cannot often afford to become empathetically involved—especially today, when we don't know most of the people we meet. Were we to lend our feelings to them, we might well become vulnerable to their manipulations or subject them to ours. In a large, heterogeneous society, moreover, responding to everyone would leave us totally drained. Finding an appropriate balance between knowing and feeling, detachment and empathy, has become difficult if not impossible.

TRADITIONAL ART COUNTERMANDS EMPATHY

In traditional art, immersion and empathy are *countermanded* by irony, distance, and abstraction. Even here we are only free to immerse ourselves because we are physically absent. Conversely, our physical absence—which enables us to see clearly—is meaningful only as long as our feelings are engaged.

The artist, like the audience, has traditionally stood in a double relationship to his subject—though for him seeing and feeling tend to *alternate*, instead of ocurring simultaneously. In commenting on his work, he may stress either immersion *or* detachment, empathy *or* abstraction, to compensate for whichever 'function' is weaker. But both are essential. The paintings of Matisse are cool and detached, not emotional, visceral, or tactile. Yet, when discussing them, he stresses feeling and identification:

> When I paint or draw, I feel the need for close communication with the object that inspires me, whatever it may be. I identify with it and this is what creates the feeling that is the basis of my art.
>
> I do not reason when I draw. The Chinese painters say that when you draw a tree, you must feel that you are growing with it. That's what I do. But one must not say as one draws: "I am growing with it," "I am growing with it," and try to work things out rationally. When I do something, I don't look for reasons. I simply give myself wholly to it.[3]

SENTIMENTAL STORY

Storytelling may have become "impossible" once 'objective reality' and the plot that was its analogue were declared invalid—when we ceased to believe in a shared body of knowledge, the common pool of experience that was the basis of dramatic irony and one polarity of traditional narrative.

Without the detachment that a shared knowledge engenders, story runs the risk of eliciting a *purely* empathetic response. Robbed of irony, narrative becomes monopolar and sentimental. Indeed, we may *owe* sentimental story to our Positivist orientation. For once the essential and necessary are deemed subject to our will—once the individual author is in charge of the story, as we are presumed to be of our fate—there is no reason why he shouldn't subject it to his own wishes and emotional needs, which, in the market place, are in turn apt to cater to *ours*. There is nothing to stop him—just as, presumably, there is nothing to stop us from making life over to suit our needs and preferences.

The postmodern aesthetic is severely critical of empathetic, sentimental story. It expects the author to manipulate the narrative but *not* the feelings of the audience, and fails to recognize that the invalidation of necessity and essence is very likely the *source* of a monopolar art that depends entirely on feeling.[4]

Since the aesthetic does not believe in necessity or plot—which, in traditional story, countermands the most powerful passions, puts them in their 'place,' and qualifies our own immersion—it must mistrust *all* feeling: the more powerful, the more dangerous. Once art is no longer a separate realm, lending our feelings to the artwork—responding empathetically to a suffering fictive figure, for instance—suggests entrapment or a master-slave relationship.

No doubt the loss of distance characteristic of sentimental art has been exploited politically and economically. Just as a loss of boundaries within the family inhibits the emergence of 'free-standing' individuals, so authoritarian governments can, by encouraging processes of uncritical immersion, link one to all and all to an authority figure. The aesthetic has reason to be on guard. And yet its refusal to see art and ritual as separate realms contributes directly to the very threat identification poses. For it tempts us to try and fuse in life and politics what can be safely joined only within a "privileged" arena.

In an industrial, specialized, and heterogeneous society, sentimental story affords us an opportunity of connecting emotionally with all those from whom we have been alienated by social and economic circumstance. As long as our relationships were dependable, and rested on 'objective' rather than subjective factors, feelings and empathy were less important—both in our relationship to others and in art. But with urbanization and industrialization, they became central, for they promised to replace what had once been *substantive* connections. Yet today, as we move beyond a small circle of family and friends and 'connect' with a great many others, our feelings are clearly inadequate. Stalin's comment that a single death is a tragedy while a million are a statistic, testifies, brutally, to the limits of our emotional reach. The only way we *can* connect with a great many others—the only way we have today for making the world 'one' and ourselves 'one' with it—is conceptual and rational, which may account for the stress on concept and intellect in contemporary art.

THE REJECTION OF SUFFERING

The rejection of empathy may be linked to our rejection of suffering as an inescapable part of human existence. Many of us are convinced, with John Stuart Mill, "that the basic sources of suffering—poverty, sickness, failure—can be completely controlled."[5] We share Lenin's "burning faith that suffering (is) not an essential and unavoidable fact of life, but an abomination that people ought to and could sweep away."[6] Like Adorno, we dismiss the old "jargon" that "suffering, evil, and death are to be accepted . . . not changed."[7]

The aesthetic suspects that the emphasis on suffering in Christianity—and in tragedy—is an attempt to justify the hardships that a privileged few impose on a great many, an effort to persuade them to accept their lot passively. As we have noted, tragedy—with its focus on failure, death, and the individual—is no longer deemed aesthetically viable.

Very likely, the denial of suffering is also linked to the undermining of the "unitary subject." For suffering, if it *is* inescapable, reaffirms the individual—isolated from others by a self-contained nervous system. Whereas most of our experience is preformed, physical pain is immediate, direct, primary, and 'authentic.' It may be exacerbated or mitigated by social, cultural, and psychological factors, but can hardly be classified as "text." It appears to be wholly our own.

Postmodern theory is deeply indebted to Nietzsche, yet chooses to ignore that he experienced self-division and uncertainty *am eigenen Leibe*. He *suffered* them; they made him ill. He did not observe the death of God dispassionately but was devastated by it. We might say that for him it was a numinous experience. He contradicted himself out of the depth of his own being and was quite unable to confine the tensions and conflict that beset him to an intellectual realm. He wrote that his sketch for the *Umwertung Aller Werte* was:

> The longest torture I have ever suffered, a real sickness . . . Grim hours, entire days and nights when I no longer knew how to go on living, and when a black despair, unlike any I have known, took hold of me.[8]

The elements of his philosophy that postmodern theory employs in rational discourse—where they can liberate and potentiate us, and may even be enjoyed 'playfully'—burst out of his unconscious and threatened to destroy him. He was the very figure postmodernism invalidates: a tragic individual.

Traditional art is, at least in part, a response to suffering—confronting it directly in tragedy and indirectly in music, poetry, and the visual arts, where dissonance and its resolution into harmony are presented *simultaneously* rather than sequentially, as in story. When Nietzsche said:

We have art so that we need not perish of reality[9]

he was surely thinking of the transmutation and not just of the *evasion* of suffering.

Though our culture at large holds that suffering can be eliminated, most of us continue to recognize and accept it as an inevitable aspect of being human. We pay a steep price for its desacralization, for once suffering is deemed unnecessary it becomes meaningless. If illness is not also a metaphor, we must be stoics in order not to be shattered by it. Surely aging and the eventual failure of body and mind are borne more patiently and gracefully if we accept them, like our self-division, as part of the human condition.[10] Yet today even death has been robbed of its meaning since, at least in theory, it is no longer inevitable—no longer part of the sacred.

In order to empower us and give us the means of alleviating physical ills and deprivation, materialism had to deny the validity of spiritual or psychological suffering. Yet in ever-growing numbers we are subject to severe 'emotional' distress, for which we can find no remedy. Chemistry, with its prescribed or addictive drugs, cannot cure our self-division, our uncertain connection to others and the community, or our ambiguous relationship to the sacred. Since we will never be altogether at home in either the natural or the civilized realm, a degree of psychological or spiritual pain may be inevitable. Its source and meaning are to be found at the core of our existence, and when we deny the legitimacy—and inevitability—of our distress, we may be denying existence itself, and so exacerbate our condition.

Traditionally, story permitted us to acknowledge a sense of victimization. Fairy tales are full of suffering, though it is rendered objectively—as fact and action, without a subjective or individual voice. Today, however—in popular novels, movies, and soap operas—suffering is merely indicated or 'illustrated,' rather than given palpable presence. Story has become a diversion and must deny the painful aspect of our existence. It can no longer console us, for consolation would *acknowledge* our distress. Though American lives *do* have second and even third acts, we don't want to hear about them, for they might drain our energy and confidence. The refusal to acknowledge suffering has contributed directly to the invalidation of narrative, for it can no longer report what we *know* to be true, and must instead purvey illusions few of us believe.

VERFREMDUNG

Postmodernism is committed to open horizons and rejects the existence of a known plot, which binds and limits the figures. Yet it promotes its own version of traditional irony by insisting that art produce a rational, critical response in us. Critics frequently cite Brecht and his *Verfremdungs* or "alienation" effect, though, in his own work, *Verfremdung* is but *one* polarity of the aesthetic experience, and meaningless without its opposite—*Einfühlung*, or empathy. In discussing scene of a woman weeping, he says:

> Should we lend ourselves to her pain entirely? Or not at all? We must be both able to lend ourselves to her pain and remain uninvolved. Our true involvement *(Bewegung)* will result from our recognition and feeling-experience of this two-forked process.[11]

Surely Brecht's "two-forked process" is an equivalent of Worringer's abstraction and empathy. *Verfremdung*, like irony in traditional story, is relevant only in a context of strong involvement. If we are truly detached, we are left with a mere case history—a *Lehrstück*—which makes its 'point' but does not prove it experientially. 'Alienating' us by means of songs and slogans makes sense only when the performance and physical detail are as persuasive as they were in the productions of the *Berliner Ensemble*. Brecht's work effectively recovers the traditional relationship between audience and fictive event, and many of his plays, set in the past, are explicitly precluded—so that the figures can arouse our feelings *without* becoming objects of sentimental identification, projection, or wish-fulfillment.

Ironically, the postmodern insistence on *Verfremdung* may camouflage a need, on the part of critics and others, for the very *attachment* it appears to reject. *Not* feeling *is* a feeling and may be the only way some of us can connect with the work of art. Alienation is a fundamental experience of our time, and perhaps we need to see it rendered *by* the work—and in our relationship to it—in order to become *involved*. In much the same way, we may need artworks that are superfluous rather than necessary, for that is how we perceive ourselves.

Artists often engage in what Brecht calls *plumpes Denken*: "thick" or "coarse" thinking—thinking with the body. But postmodern theory, like all philosophical endeavors, privileges clear, highly refined reasoning; it neglects the body and our senses. Though rationality is the necessary counterforce to the irrational, unconscious, or sacred, it has, in contemporary aesthetics, ceased to be a polarity and become the whole show. This parallels the devaluation of feeling and sensation in industrial and postindustrial economies. They are no longer useful to the modes of production or communication, and get in the way of 'effective' social functioning.

While philosophy has always attempted "to explore the irrational and integrate it into an expanded reason," the Enlightenment enthroned reason as a god.[12] The irrational was no longer to be accommodated in our communal structures, and society as a whole—not just its philosophers and scientists—could look to reason for the solution to all problems. The temple in which the French revolution worshipped it remains, even today, a fitting metaphor for the faith of the educated and specialized. Reason is deemed to hold the answer to our social, economic, and political difficulties, and constitutes, as Horkheimer says, the basis of all progressive social theory.[13] Many of us continue to be sustained by Thomas Mann's conviction that

Human reason need only will more strongly than fate and it *is* fate.

Postmodern theory is often called nihilist and irrational but in fact privileges the intellect—the critic's strongest suit. Derrida challenges Lévi-Strauss's definition of "mind" as a natural, biological entity, and predicates his own discourse entirely on reason. Foucault may claim to dethrone rationality—and, indeed, to speak for 'madness'—but, as Derrida points out, his investigations are inescapably bound to reason.[14] His work, like Derrida's, is clearly within the Enlightenment tradition: it attempts to liberate and potentiate us, even if it claims to liberate us from the repressive aspects of reason itself.

The Invalidation of Experience

TRADITIONAL ART AND EXPERIENCE

Art, at least since the Renaissance, has persuaded us of its 'truth' by approximating our experience. But even when we suspend our disbelief, we are well aware that art is only art. It may stress sensory and tactile values but it remains an abstraction, for every art form must transpose our experience into its own limited medium. Thus film transposes reality into a two-dimensional projection that is most effective when it renders movement, which it does so persuasively that our muscles may actually tense up in a mimetic response. Since all art is necessarily abstract, indirect, and 'absent,' artists have tried, traditionally, to make it as direct and palpable as possible—not only because the audience demands to be persuaded, but because they themselves believed in the 'reality' of their rendering.

Even the abstract and absent quality in art could be called 'realistic' or mimetic, for it mimics our consciousness that, in most situations, keeps us at some distance and allows us to remain alert to our own safety and interests. *Verfremdung*, as Brecht says, is an integral part of daily life, just as abstraction is the predicate of our perceptual processes. Though we see the world around us in color, black-and-white film seems perfectly real to us, for—like perception itself—it reports not what the eye takes in *physically* but what the *mind attends*. Like the mind's eye, the camera abstracts the salient features, and many elements of film that may seem merely 'technical,' formal, and specific to the medium are, in fact, mimetic of the way we perceive. My eyes 'report' the entire room but I *see* only you, and so make the equivalent of a close-up. In both film and painting, the frame around the image is a 'realistic' approximation of our partial, limited, and excluding vision—just as the apparently arbitrary mix of abstraction and specificity in the artwork constitutes an accurate rendering of our perceptual process. We read details for their general, or abstract, significance, and use them as clues to get our bearings.

In life, though consciousness creates a measure of detachment, we are always physically present. Whatever happens in our proximity concerns us, since it may affect our well-being. An artwork that fails to engage us, that *leaves us out*, will not correspond to our experience—which may be why every story, from *Gilgamesh* on, is told from a point of view, a perspective that gives us access by approximating the way we perceive the world. In *It's a Gift*, W. C. Fields is the only credible figure; the others are mere cutouts. Yet the film appears 'real' to us, for in life, too, other people seem less complex and more schematic than we are to ourselves. The exaggerated, predictable behavior of the Fields family is a realistic rendering of his point of view, with which we can identify even though it is radically biased and absurd.

Some viewers require an *actual* rather than an aesthetic event to be persuaded; mimetic renderings are inadequate and only physical facts engage them. The Roman circus with its brutal contests and executions, automobile races, bullfights, and boxing matches are nonaesthetic cathartic spectacles, in which the performance is authenticated by the physical risk, injury or death of the performers. Tertullian and Martial refer to a Roman practice of executing condemned criminals in the course of a play—no doubt to give greater reality to the performance. The death of an actor in our "snuff" movies—even if only rumored—caters to the same craving for literal, physical truth. It may be primitive, but what is at stake for the audience is the same experiential participation that others find in Shakespeare and Proust. Only the means of access differ.

To the postmodern aesthetic, the attempt to approximate our sensory or psychological experience is suspect, since it pulls us into the work, subjects us to it, and urges us to accept it as a rendering of the 'real.' The undermining of aesthetic experience is no doubt linked to the invalidation of experience itself. While it was once a predicate of our knowledge and belief systems, continuous change has robbed it of value. What was true yesterday is no longer true today and is apt to keep us from responding appropriately to the present. We have learned, moreover, that even our *physical* experience, the information we get from our senses, is often invalid—as philosophy and science have been telling us for centuries; we must, says Descartes, trust "the dictates of mature reason" rather than the senses, which he equates with "the inconsistent judgement of childhood."[1] We have become painfully aware that our eyes and ears, and even our aches and pains, are apt to deceive us; our perception of our own bodies is no longer trustworthy: technology does a better job. The very concept of the experiencing self has been put in doubt, for individuality and what we once deemed our 'inalienable' experience are interdependent. If one is invalid, so is the other. Derrida would like to dismiss perception.[2] His assertion that there *is* no 'primary' experience—that everything begins with reproduction—restates, in philosophical terms, *Gestalt* psychology's finding that all perception depends on learned structures; without them we have no way of apprehending what our senses transmit.

We noted that individual perception and experience have always been countermanded by society, and programmed to be as similar to the perception and experience of others as possible. In the course of maturing into socialized adults, our native sensory awareness and responsiveness—the basis of Descartes's "inconsistent judgement of childhood"—must be curtailed. We learn to disregard them—significantly, a "sensation" has come to mean something out of the ordinary—for to remain truly sentient would tempt us into trouble and disrupt the community. When sensate responses *assert* themselves, they are often improperly socialized.

Within the safe arena of art, however, we have been permitted and, indeed, encouraged to exercise our senses. Traditionally the artwork is a texture of details—*le bon Dieu est dans le détail*—that arouse a sensory response. In their original form, poems and paintings have a 'physical' texture and 'corporeal' presence that translations or reproductions cannot match. There is, in the original, a fusion of 'idea' and detailed substance that science—like most theory—disregards, since it is primarily interested in the transmission of ideas. As Kuhn says:

> Until the very last stages in the education of a scientist, textbooks are systematically substituted for the creative scientific literature that made them possible. . . . Why, after all, should the student of physics . . . read the works of Newton, Faraday, Einstein, or Schroedinger, when everything he needs to know about these works is recapitulated in a far briefer, more precise, and more systematic form in a number of up-to-date textbooks? [3]

But while a plot outline of *War and Peace* may help us pass an exam, the "recapitulation" of an artwork is useless. Unlike theory, art is not interested in generalizations but first and foremost in particulars. It would seem to agree with Adorno that *das Ganze ist das Unwahre*—"the whole is the untrue."[4] In the documentary film *The Times of Harvey Milk*, the shrouded body of a murdered man is wheeled onto an elevator. In order to fit it in, the attendant has to stand it upright and suddenly the body—no longer in its expected prone position—ceases to be an abstract object. But though the detail elicits a specific—one might say sensory—response from each of us, it also joins us to the community of others, for my response is apt to be similar to yours. The sensory detail confirms both Adorno's *das Ganze ist das Unwahre* and Hegel's *das Wahre ist das Ganze*—"the truth is the whole."[5] It substantiates the individual or particular *and* reestablishes its relationship to a totality.[6]

The difficulties we have with story today are clearly linked to the invalidation of what Jameson calls "individual or existential experience."[7] Benjamin says:

> Less and less frequently do we encounter people with the ability to tell a tale properly. . . . It is as if something that seemed inalienable to us, the securest among our possessions, were taken from us: the ability to exchange experiences.[8]

In Benjamin's view, *Erlebnis*—the isolated experiential moment—has displaced *Erfahrung*, a connected and coherent *sequence* of such moments.[9] Yet *Erlebnis* has always been as precious to storytelling as *Erfahrung*. For it is *Erlebnis* and not *Erfahrung* that is necessarily shortchanged in daily life— blurred, rushed through, repressed, not given its due. Adorno observed that

> It was Benjamin's intention to renounce all clear explanation and to let meaning emerge entirely through a shock-like montage of the material. Philosophy was not only to catch up with surrealism but to become surrealistic itself.[10]

Here the emphasis is clearly on reproducing disjointed *Erlebnis*, rather than coherent *Erfahrung*.

Shklovsky, in some of his comments on defamiliarization, seems intent on salvaging experience and sensation:

> The technique of art is to make objects "unfamiliar," to make forms difficult, to increase the length and difficulty of perception, because the process of perception is an aesthetic end in itself and must be prolonged.[11]

In this formulation, defamiliarization reflects on our perceptual processes. In order to get through the day, we must assume that our world is familiar and safe, though much of what we encounter is, in fact, anomalous and surprising. We deal with the unfamiliar by ignoring it, or conform it to the familiar. "Novelty," as Kuhn points out, "emerges only with difficulty":[12]

> In a psychological experiment . . . Bruner and Postman asked experimental subjects to identify on short and controlled exposure a series of playing cards.

Many of the cards were normal, but some were made anomalous, e.g., a red six of spades and a black four of hearts. . . .

Even on the shortest exposures many subjects identified most of the cards, and after a small increase all the subjects identified them all. For the normal cards these identifications were usually correct, but the anomalous cards were almost always identified, without apparent hesitation or puzzlement, as normal. The black four of hearts might, for example, be identified as the four of either spades or hearts. Without any awareness of trouble, it was immediately fitted to one of the conceptual categories prepared by prior experience.[13]

Though we manage, most of the time, to reduce the unfamiliar to the familiar, we sense that we are strangers in a strange land and, in fiction, identify with those who *don't* know and are trying to find out. Oedipus, Little Red Riding Hood, King Lear, Emma Bovary and Huckleberry Finn are all on a journey of discovery, just as we are ourselves. In the safe arena of art, we *expect* to be surprised and shocked. Here we *pay* to have an as-if encounter with the very calamities against which we take out insurance policies in life. In art, the known often becomes strange and the safe dangerous.[14] Defamiliarization infuses the artwork with the confusing and unexpected; it is a rendering of our half-conscious experience of the incomprehensible. Indeed, defamiliarization derives from *and* confirms the very link between art and reality that formalism tried to sever. We should note, moreover, that the invalidation of experience in postmodern aesthetics overlooks that for many of us life *is* continually and uncomfortably surprising. The assumption that we see nothing with "new eyes" is a half-truth, for little today is as advertised. In life we would much prefer to avoid Benjamin's shock effect—the impact of violence and disasters, for example—but we don't always succeed.

Though some postmodern works, with their *lack* of physical texture and sensory detail, would seem to break with traditional art, they may, in fact, mimic our own impoverished experience. Warhol's soup can has *less* sensory impact than an actual can of soup, and our response to it is largely cerebral. As in advertising, we see—or rather, recognize—a label or sign. But perhaps the very *absence* of experience, sensation, and involvement *is* the experience, just as its lack of 'originality' is, in the context of Western art, an original gesture. We might even call it a traditional work, inasmuch as our response to it both mimics and intensifies the *non*response we bring to most situations today.

Hegel suggested that humankind may some day outgrow its need for sensory expression—that art as he knew it would be replaced by symbols of *Vernunft*, or reason.[15] Perhaps something like this has come to pass,

253

though not because art has been replaced by philosophy. We are today bombarded by so many stimuli that, just as we have had to turn off emotionally, our senses too suffer an overload and shut down. Perhaps traditional art is deemed invalid because we no longer live in a world of real things, experienced sensorily, but in a world of mental symbols or signs.

INTENSITY

Traditionally, the artwork doesn't just mimic our experience but enriches and intensifies it. In life, most experiences are necessarily unintense, for intensity, unless carefully circumscribed, disrupts the calm that is a predicate of stable relationships and community. Hegel defines *Zufriedenheit*—a state of "satisfaction" or of "being at peace" that may constitute the opposite of our "disquiet"—as a "lasting, tranquil sense of accord without intensity."[16] Though intense moments between individuals and in the community can melt differences and engender *communitas*, they must be carefully hedged and subordinated to the flow of 'ordinary,' unintense existence. Yet specialization feeds on and breeds intensity. Strong "intent," as the word implies, makes us intensive, and most specialists—scientists no less than artists—are engaged in intensive pursuits. A physicist observes:

> In physics, I am opposite to what I am in life. In physics, I like extreme situations. I don't like intermediate steps. I am attracted to the extremes: the highest-pressure places, the highest-temperature places, the greatest speeds, the greatest densities.[17]

Even for nonspecialized members of a community, Hegel's "tranquil sense of accord without intensity" is viable only as long as we have a clear sense of identity and belonging. Once our continuity is threatened, we tend to seek out intense situations and experiences, for they bond us *within* as well as to *others*; they make us whole. "Peak" experiences prove to us, albeit briefly, that we exist; intense relationships confirm and hold us in place; and intense pleasure can compensate the individual for his isolation and the anxiety it induces.[18] But intensity also isolates us. Intense relationships are exclusive and frequently possessive, they establish hierarchies of 'significant' and less 'significant' others. The family—which once included not only relatives but retainers—has become a nucleus of exclusive, often intense relationships that nurture individuals, albeit in the context and service of the community. Conversely, nineteenth-century utopians like the Shakers rejected all intense emotions and connections. The Oneida Community was committed to a "We spirit" and replaced the "special attachments" of romantic love with the practice of "complex marriage." Oneida "perfectionists" discouraged dyadic relationships and all withdrawal into realms of intense personal experience. Males were expected to practice nonclimactic sexuality, and "amative" encounters were limited to a single night between two people; only "propagative" ones could be repeated until the woman became pregnant. Male sexuality was to be subordinated to reason and control—a premise that, like their preoccupation with eugenics, coincided with the tenets of Positivism, even though it may have been rooted in the pathology of the community's founders.

In human relationships, intensity and extensity are hard to reconcile, and in art, too, one often excludes the other. But there are works—the *Iliad*, Shakespeare, Dostoevski, and Proust come to mind—that balance the intensive with the extensive. They focus on the individual without neglecting the community.

Postmodern art may reject emotional intensity because, like nineteenth-century utopians, it is committed to an all-inclusive democratic society. The traditional Western work is condensed, enriched, intensified.[19] It claims to have a reality apart from the artist and his audience, and serves to reflect and confirm the existence of each individual viewer. But while postmodern art makes *no* attempt to be 'real,' its very *un*reality may prove us as individuals. For we, like Warhol's soup can, may be mere concepts or signs—two-dimensional, marginal, with markings imprinted from outside—yet an awareness and rendering of our nonexistence can establish that we exist.

Perhaps the postmodern work does not deny us but simply redefines us. Minimalism reflects our marginal, fractional selves and *not* a minimal world. Donald Barthelme's fictions, which he calls collages, and Rauschenberg's huge, fragmented canvases render our decentered awareness, which nevertheless *is* an awareness—a point of view. Postmodern discontinuity may be *our* form of continuity, and fragments may be the only form we trust because they are the only way we can survive. Our fragmentation and alienation are very likely a necessary adaption to urban life and contemporary modes of production. The fragmentation of our attention span and our tendency to notice and, indeed, do several things at once—instead of one after another—are our response to changes in the environment. Today a great deal impinges on us simultaneously or in rapid succession and we must be 'sketchy,' like a Rauschenberg canvas, if we are to survive. Surely no society would tolerate the disintegration of individual identity, the breakup of the family, and the destruction of our heritage were it not committed—in a blind, sleepwalking way—to the emergence of a new, more inclusive community, predicated on the erosion of old connections and purchased at great cost to our sense of security.

SEMIOTICS AND POSTMODERNISM

Our awareness that in an industrial and postindustrial society we have no permanent place or role, but exist as interchangeable 'signs,' may help to account for the influence of semiotics in the postmodern aesthetic.

It has been said that everything is a sign, or that we turn everything into signs in order to make sense of the welter of perceptions and impressions that impinge on us. Society has to evolve a system of signals, without which no communication or community is possible, and in today's complex, confusing world they must be absolutely clear, so that they can be read quickly and understood by everyone. If the traffic light were to say both Stop and Go, or if every traffic light used a different code, intersections would be disaster areas. Yet in many human situations we face signs that *are* ambiguous and open to subjective interpretation. Even when we do our best to communicate, signals are apt to be misunderstood—especially in a dynamic, heterogeneous society that lacks cohesion and a shared vocabulary. But while signs in a stable, homogeneous community were no doubt clearer, there too *some* 'signs'—those from the sacred, for instance—were ambiguous and self-contradictory. Despite all claims to the contrary, our structures have never been able to provide readings that do more than establish a workable code of behavior within the community and a reasonably reassuring picture of what lies beyond it. They cannot—and never could—resolve all ambiguity or allay all our uncertainties.

If art can be said to traffic in signs—and the term may well be inappropriate—it would seem to deal in exactly those ambiguous, contradictory ones that signal difficulty and conflict. In story, one sign often countermands another, and important signs, when read in conjunction with each other, cancel each other out. The action may say "Go" and the plot "Stop," or the plot says "Go" while the figures cry "Stop." Signs in story—unlike those that regulate traffic or try to facilitate relationships with a minimum of conflict—render experiences that are fraught with complexity and ambiguity.

Even the detective story, despite its Positivist orientation, trades on the ambiguity of its signs—though once the crime is solved their meaning emerges unequivocally and we are freed of uncertainty. While genre narratives are composed of signs with clear meanings, they often derive their interest from unexpected ambiguities: the vice squad detective in a thriller may find himself drawn to the very vice he prosecutes. The ambiguities are always resolved, and the signs end up confirming the coordinate system that has taught us how to read them, but only the simplest of genre fictions—the 'yarn,' for instance—traffics in signs that are totally unambiguous. Here our uncertainty is confined to wondering what will happen next.

For good reason, our fragmented and deeply divided society is preoccupied with "communication." We don't know or understand each other and keep having to explain ourselves. We meet in encounter groups to learn about others and tell about ourselves—to bridge differences. Our popular fiction, too, is largely concerned with getting across messages that are familiar and confirm us in the community. We need to be brought together, to be related to each other and reassured that our reading of reality is like that of most others in the audience. The last thing we want is further exposure to the divisions, ambiguities, and complexities we face all day.

Perhaps one could speak of "normal" art or story—an equivalent of Kuhn's "normal" science.[20] It is clearly coded and immediately recognizable. Its task is to address problems within the established paradigm system, which it invariably confirms. But as Kuhn points out, there are limitations to "normal" science, for "its object is to solve a puzzle for whose very existence the validity of the paradigm must be assumed."[21] "Normal" or popular art, like "normal" science, often attempts to force our experience "into the preformed and relatively inflexible box that the paradigm supplies."[22]

'High' or 'elitist' art operates *outside* the paradigm—in an interface between the known and the unknown or incomprehensible. It challenges rather than affirms the coordinate system by including exactly what the system *excludes*: people with a different perspective; experiences and responses that don't 'fit'; and aspects of the natural, sacred, or unconscious that fail to confirm the community and its structures. Since the unconscious is neglected or dismissed in our culture, a work that explores it and brings it into consciousness makes audiences uncomfortable and is apt to be rejected.

While 'high' art depends in some measure on signs, it exists at their edge. It cannot trust them, for it tries to render what we *could* experience and not the overlay of our assumptions. As Hemingway says, the artist's task and difficulty lie in discovering what we *do* feel, not what we are supposed to feel. Signs offer us an agreed-upon common denominator, and are notoriously slow to pick up on discrepancies that separate what actually happens from what we *think* happens.

Traditionally, the artist is engaged in a struggle *against* the sign, and only an almost illegible one, or a sign with a co-sign that undermines it and so makes it difficult to interpret, is of interest. In painting, legible signs are called 'illustrations'; in the theater, 'indication' or 'signification.' An actor indicates when he 'communicates' anger by crossing his arms and turning his back—signals that derive from our behavior but are so familiar that they address our pre-programmed understanding, and not our experience or senses. As the painter Francis Bacon says:

> An illustrational form tells you through the intelligence immediately what the form is about, whereas a non-illustrational form works first upon sensation.[23]

The 'signification' of anger on stage does not render what we *experience* when we are in the throes of rage—either our own or someone else's. It merely tells us that the character is angry. It *informs*, which—in an age preoccupied with and dependent upon the rapid processing of information—reflects our conscious daily experience. An 'illustration,' unlike traditional art, makes no attempt to intensify, enrich, or deepen what happens to us. It may, nonetheless, mimic the divorcement from feeling and sensation that marks contemporary experience, as well as our willingness to accept whatever meaning lies at the surface. One recalls Susan Sontag's comment that "the notion of depths, of hiddenness, (is) a mystification, a lie."

Though the community depends on coded and shared experiences, the artist—at least since the Renaissance and very likely for longer—has lived on the edge of a new, uncoded reality. As a scout who conducts raids on the inarticulate, he cannot use the sign with its familiar meaning. A writer once told me that what he did in his work was to "discover and bury."[24]

All writing, says Derrida, is intertextual and entirely intertextual: writing—and only writing—leads to more writing. But is there *nothing* outside the text? The artist, though he would not deny the impact of prior texts, lays claim to something that has not been—indeed, *cannot* have been—said before. He is confident that his own experience of our ever-changing world adds something new and unfamiliar to the known text, even if the words he finds for the new are inevitably conditioned by the old. He believes, moreover, that nothing he says is remotely adequate to reality. Like the Holocaust survivor, he is convinced that

> Everything I'm telling you is like a grain of sand by the sea—absolutely nothing compared to what happened.

All the artist can do is testify, as accurately as possible, to his own severely limited experience. But he often finds, in the overlooked or discarded, new ways of saying the as yet unsayable.

Though postmodern art appears to undermine individual or existential experience by using explicit and familiar signs, it also countermands them. The flags of Jasper Johns do not resemble mass-produced items; they are textured and detailed like traditional painting. Even Warhol's *untextured* signs have the effect of countersigns—at least in a culture that still expects art to confirm our existence as individuals. By startling or puzzling us, they mimic the 'shock effect' of experience, and so confirm what they seem to deny.

The impact of both modern and postmodern art is often described as "the shock of the new." But *Oedipus Rex* and the Jacobean theater may have shocked their contemporaries no less than the French Impressionists—who broke with the solid surfaces of academic painting and rendered, instead, the fragmented, discontinuous texture of their own experience.[25] All style, as Synge said to Yeats, is "born out of the shock of new material."[26] Even jokes depend on a shock effect.

But perhaps the shocking did not always shock. It may have been what we *expected* until we started to believe that we can absolutely understand the world and ourselves. As long as our view of reality *accommodated* the incomprehensible or sacred, popular or "normal" narratives—myths and fairy tales, for instance—could include the disturbing and ambiguous, which our own frail sense of identity has had to repress. As long as uncertainty was a given of our existence, both popular stories and those addressing an elite could render the incomprehensible and the terrifying without undermining communal structures. Indeed, the incomprehensible *confirmed* them. But once our culture fell under the domination of reason, popular and 'high' art moved in opposite directions. Popular art confirmed the community and its coordinate system, while 'high' art *appeared* to undermine them—though, in fact, it helped to preserve them by expanding their frontiers.

The current revaluation of popular art is entirely justified. The elitist, individual-centered tradition of 'high' art—with its emphasis on scouting, isolation, and risk—needs to be demystified. But the differences between them remain even if, in our heterogeneous and rapidly changing society, there is a necessary emphasis on evolving a shared language. A popular, commercial medium like the movie will inevitably employ signs that are accessible to a large majority. The focus is not on rendering an experience for which there is as yet no vocabulary, but on touching a common chord. Film, moreover, has to reach its audience in a rapidly changing context and must be produced and distributed quickly enough to capitalize on recognition factors of the moment. Both commerce and the community foster a predictable audience response that can be triggered by manipulative signals from the film maker or performer. The story is told not so much because the storyteller believes in it, but in order to elicit a preordained and widely shared reaction. Writing for movies tends to consist of "writing the *audience*" rather than the story.[27] There is often little more on the screen than a succession of wholly accessible signs, with an occasional surprise thrown in to foster the illusion of new, anomalous experience.

Warhol's work, like popular movies, traffics in signs but addresses a highly specialized, sophisticated viewer. Just as he validates our marginal existence and experience by denying them, so he employs the universally recognizable signs of mass culture to affirm the difference and identity of his own work. The modernist said: 'I exist whether I am recognized or not, for I make an object, which will be recognized sooner or later.' Warhol is less confident and less inward; he needs to be recognized right away, by as many as possible. Yet he made his objects out of the same anxiety that haunted the modernist.[28]

INVALIDATING MIMESIS

The rejection of experience by postmodern theory—which is at variance with the practice of many contemporary artists—is linked to its rejection of mimesis. Unlike the sign, which keeps us at a safe distance and intellectualizes our responses, mimesis pulls us into the work, holds out the promise of sensory and emotional participation, and creates the illusion of a reality beyond the text. The 'illusionist' element in art involves a partial submission of both artist and audience to the imitated event. Moreover, there is a reciprocal relationship between mimesis and identification: the mimetic encourages us to empathize or identify, and since we are apt to believe whatever happens to *us*, our identification in turn enhances the reality of the work. Paul Ricoeur defines mimesis as "poesis . . . fabrication, construction, creation,"[29] perhaps because his aesthetic cannot tolerate it as a reflection of anything outside the "perfectly closed and autonomous structure" of the artwork.

Excluding the mimetic from art is, however, possible only in theory, for in practice most renderings are linked to a process of imitation and identification. The very word *image* is related to the Latin *imitari*, "to imitate." Aristotle says:

> Poetry in general can be seen to owe its existence to two causes, and these are rooted in nature. First, there is man's natural propensity, from childhood onwards, to engage in mimetic activity (and this distinguishes man from other

creatures, that he is thoroughly mimetic and through mimesis takes his first steps in understanding). Second, there is the pleasure which all men take in mimetic objects.

An indication of the latter can be observed in practice: for we take pleasure in contemplating the most precise images of things whose sight itself causes us pain.[30]

Matisse told his students to "assume the pose of the model,"[31] and the images of Warhol are clearly mimetic of his experience. While Adorno and Horkheimer share the postmodern view of mimesis as a passive yielding, they know that without it there *is* no art:

The tendency to let oneself go and sink back into nature, Freud called it the death instinct, Caillois *le mimétisme* . . . underlies everything which runs counter to bold progress, from the crime which is a shortcut avoiding the normal forms of activity, to the sublime work of art. A yielding attitude to things, *without which art cannot exist*, is not so very remote from the violence of the criminal.[32]

All verbal art seems linked to the mimetic, for even if language originated as a wholly formal system, it has become contingent on the 'real' world. Unlike shapes, colors, and musical sounds, we associate most words with objects and actions, and though poetry reaches us first through rhythm and sound, we could not say of a page of verse or prose what Maurice Denis said of painting:

A painting—before being a battle horse, a nude woman, or some anecdote—is essentially a flat surface covered with colors assembled in a certain order.[33]

Denis's comment may, of course, be read as a rejection of nineteenth-century academic realism, and *not* as an invalidation of 'reality' in painting. In the work of many modernists, moreover, "a flat surface covered with colors assembled in a certain order" is a quasi-mimetic transcription of a subjective, nonmaterial state. Though the first "abstract" artists used pure color, shape, line, and texture rather than objective, recognizable correlatives, Kandinsky always insisted that his work was "concrete," not "abstract"—the incarnation of an inner or spiritual 'reality.'

There is a sense in which even music is mimetic. When we respond to a composition on first hearing it, it may remind us of one we have heard before. But when we are moved by a piece that seems altogether new and different, it may well render or evoke a subjective state that has never been phrased for us before, though we 'recognize' it as soon as we hear it. We respond to correspondences, to "like" is to recognize a likeness.[34] Just as we like those who are like us, so we respond to an artwork that renders or touches something familiar, which may be *within* us. One task of the artist—particularly of the storyteller—is to extend the range of our recognition, or likeness, so that we may recognize, and come to like, what seems, at first, utterly *un*like us.

In movies, only experimental work is openly anti-mimetic. Most films render what we, today, deem to be an accurate representation of the way our world looks and sounds to us. Though film is a recent medium, it is deeply traditional, for it preserves a direct relationship between the image and what we believe to be our experience of reality. In painting, subject matter has become irrelevant: a crucifixion holds no greater interest than a basket of fruit. But in film the subject still matters. Most of us are more immediately engaged by a scene involving human beings than by a photographic description of a garden, however seductively the camera renders it. Movies are our preferred medium for telling stories because they remain persuasively and, indeed, inescapably mimetic of our experience—just as novels and paintings once were. We can still enter and 'lose' ourselves in the world on the screen. Scratches or tears in the print, poor sound, faded color, and subtitles fail to interfere seriously with our involvement; we see right past them. Even when we insert a videocassette into the VCR and are empowered to interrupt the narrative at any point, we become engaged in the action and anxious about the outcome.

In commercial movies, mimesis is focused on surface likeness. While *inner* reality is sketchy and conforms to the way we would like—or hate—to be, a great deal of attention is paid to physical accuracy. The parallel with nineteenth-century academic painting is striking. But in 'high' art—as in movies that challenge rather than confirm our assumptions—surface likeness is not of primary interest. In this sense, most artists are anti-mimetic. "In no case an eye-deceiving job," Van Gogh writes to Emile Bernard,[35] and Matisse happily quotes Lautrec's "At last I don't know how to draw!"[36] Yet fidelity to the object—whether it be inner or outer—has always been of central importance. Artists are all too aware that their work is subjective, 'unreal,' abstract, and in large part derived from other art. Attention to the object serves as a corrective. It roots the work in sensation, anchors it in 'fact,' and countermands the inevitable abstraction with an *incarnated* rendering. Rilke obliged himself to render *das Ding*—the object—in order to countermand his own subjectivity; Rodin said he could do nothing without the live model; and Matisse moved ceaselessly back and forth between abstraction and representation. As Pierre Schneider emphasizes, he was all of his life bound to the model or object: "It is the source of my energy."[37]

Mimesis in art, even though focused on inner rather than surface reality, is clearly rooted in biological process. In the animal kingdom, camouflage is a form of mimicry that enables the creature to eat and avoid being eaten; the flounder mimics the ocean floor and the jaguar's fur a mottled pattern of leaves. Mimetic movement is both a way of parrying aggression and of attracting the opposite sex. Even in human life it often appears to be biological or involuntary. When someone walks toward me on the sidewalk, I am apt to mirror his moves in the very attempt to avoid him. Most of us respond kindly to kindness and belligerently to aggression—mimetically, without hesitation or thought, as if prompted by instinct.

Mimesis is essential to life and to the community, for it permits us to adapt to our environment and to the group. All learning is, as Aristotle says, in large part imitation. We imitate our role models: the child imitates the parent[38] and Christians imitate Christ. Many artists start out by imitating other artists. The young Count Basie imitated Fats Waller—submitting to his influence without anxiety:

> I sat on the floor watching his feet and using my hands to imitate him. I was a daily customer, hanging onto every note, sitting behind him all the time.

Though the postmodern aesthetic conceives of mimesis as slavish submission, in Aristotle's view it frees us of terror. The play of children may well give them a sense of control, and the storyteller who imitates the workings of natural or supernatural forces could be said to master what, in life, has him in its power. Freud points out that mimicry is "itself a fertile source of comic pleasure."[39] The mimic has mastered the object he imitates, even though his mastery begins with *submission* to the object.

In art, mimesis often permits us to see both the object imitated *and* the imitation. In *The Gold Rush*, Chaplin mimics a ballet dancer with an accuracy that delights us, though—or rather, *because*—her legs are forks, her feet two dinner rolls, and her face is Charlie's own. In art, mimesis can be a transformative magic that plays across the line of being and *not* being what it claims to be. It fuses with the object it imitates, yet remains itself— submits yet remains in control.

The rejection of mimesis by postmodern theory is not persuasive. Deconstructive readings are themselves based on complex contradictions and ambiguities in the text that no author could have invented or even deliberately inserted into the work. Surely the "warring forces of signification"[40] that deconstruction teases out of the text exist elsewhere as well—in the psyche, for instance. One might conclude that they refer to or 'mimic' the contradictions and ambiguities of our existence.

REFLEXIVITY

Since mimesis confirms a link between art and reality, the aesthetic countermands it by calling for, and giving a new meaning to, reflexivity. It expects the artwork to undermine its claim to reality by pointing to its own artifice. But traditionally, reflexivity served the opposite purpose: it enhanced the "illusionist" element in the work. Most people need no reminder that what they are watching is only a play or movie; their greatest difficulty is *forgetting* it. Even those devices in the artwork that seem 'alienating' to us may, originally, have given it greater verisimilitude. Very likely Athenian actors wore masks to make the human beings within them—some of them, perhaps, neighbors—more credible as gods and heroes, and male actors more persuasive as women. When Elizabethan dramatists acknowledged the noisy, clearly visible crowd on three sides of the stage by speaking to it directly, they surely intended to enhance rather than undermine the reality of the events on stage. The grocer, his wife, and their apprentice who climb into the action in *The Knight of the Burning Pestle* and—prefiguring Pirandello—appear to violate the written text, confirm the reality of the performance and engage the audience more immediately, just as the eighteenth-century novelist who addresses his readers directly, or makes reference to himself, is acknowledging facts—one that the reader, holding the book in his hand, could hardly forget.

Most stories work with the assumption that the viewer or reader is invisible to those engaged in the action, just as the figures in a painting are not usually 'conscious' of being watched unless they are sitting for their portrait. When the young woman in Vermeer's *Girl at Her Music* peers at the painter with a startled expression, or one of the figures in Van der Goes's *The Death of the Virgin* looks directly at us while the others are intent on Mary, our acknowledged presence draws us into the event and validates it. Reminding us that the painting is a painting or the play a play—which we have not for one moment forgotten—can undermine the *artifice* of the work, and not the work. The figures in an artwork who refer to *our* existence may be said to confirm their own—for our reality confirms theirs.

In traditional art, attention to the medium was minimized, no doubt to facilitate our participation in the aesthetic event. The artist made his work as transparent as possible, and his particular way of rendering was, as we have noted, seldom recognized *as* 'style' during his own day. Perhaps even 'primitive' art, which appears highly stylized to us, was in its time and place a persuasive, 'realistic' rendering.

Whereas in paintings, novels, and plays we are, today, almost always aware of the work as abstraction and artifice, film maintains the traditional relationship between audience and story. The camera claims to be invisible to the performers and does, in fact, represent an audience that is absent.[41] We watch the events well after they were recorded, and are ourselves shrouded in a darkness that hides all reminders of our own daily existence. We are free to lose ourselves, or, as the old word has it, to be "transported."

In film, reflexivity, when it isn't the postmodern gesture of a Godard, serves the 'reality' rendered by the camera. The male film makers of the documentary *Grey Gardens* include several shots of themselves, since the movie is about two women who constantly refer to them, compete for their attention, and perform for them. The *subjects* of the film and not the film makers motivate a reflexive use of the medium. In *Annie Hall*, Woody Allen in the role of a stand-up comedian addresses the camera directly. Alvy Singer is almost indistinguishable from Allen himself, just as the romance between Alvy and Annie draws on our knowledge of Allen's own relationship to Diane Keaton. His confessional, reflexive use of the medium *enhances* rather than undermines the fictive reality.

Though the frame that surrounds the movie, play and painting could be said to define the work as an artifact, it has traditionally served—like the shaman's circle—to make the incredible credible and to mark off an area we can enter without risk. It *facilitates* rather than countermands our immersion. We have noted that as a formal expression of the limits that bind and determine the figures, the frame renders the confines of our lives. It links us to the fictive figures even as it appears to separate us from them, for though we may not know it consciously, we are *all* framed.

In traditional art, the frame is often obscured by the creation of a second, inner frame *within* the first or outer one. When the actors in Pirandello drop their assigned roles and engage in ostensibly personal interactions, they create a *second* performance that seems more authentic than the first. At the beginning of Welles's *The War of the Worlds*, a musical feed from the Park Plaza Hotel sets up a second frame within the broadcast. It worked so effectively that many listeners accepted the "special bulletin" that interrupted the music as *fact* rather than performance. In painting, photography, and film, an inner frame can obscure the actual frame that bounds the image. Splitting or decentering the composition, crowding it with so much information that we are obliged to focus on *one* area, or creating—as the wide screen does—something akin to peripheral vision, all serve to *obscure* the frame and permit us to lend ourselves to the events within it.

Perhaps the aesthetic perceives the frame as limiting the *work*, rather than the figures *within* it, because it rejects the traditional view of human limitations. But it may also disdain transparency and insist on reflexivity because the contemporary self is too frail to lend itself to the artwork, which is expected to stress its own unreality so that we are spared the danger of being overwhelmed, inundated, or 'enslaved' by it. We may no longer be distinct or secure enough to lend ourselves to events in a fiction—or in life—without running the risk of losing ourselves entirely. Perhaps reflexivity and the rejection of the mimetic are a guarantee that we will remain safe within our ill-defined boundaries. Our fear of empathy and passivity may spring from a lack of autonomy which was, at one time, limited to the years of early childhood but now extends—for many of us—into adult life. We are not sufficiently secure to run the risk of being open and our sense of helplessness may be so overpowering—so 'real' to us—that we cannot face it even in art. The safe arena is no longer safe.

It also seems possible that those who reject mimesis unknowningly expect art to mimic their own experience. Perhaps the reflexive work renders the anxious, doubting view we hold of ourselves: its very unreality reflects the 'unreality' of the person who made it and so, by implication, of those who behold it—paradoxically *confirming* their existence. The stress on reflexivity, on the medium and on a frame that appears to *separate* us from the work may actually permit us to enter it, and so serves the very engagement and 'reality' it purports to countermand. We are not always conscious of the needs we expect art to meet.

Moreover, a postmodern insistence on reflexivity represents less of a break with the past than the aesthetic assumes. When myth, legend, and fairy tale—with their anonymous authorship—gave way to stories by named, often celebrated authors, narrative in fact *became* 'reflexive': it drew attention to its own immediate origin and 'manufacture.' Very likely the emphasis on individual authorship and consciousness mirrored the individuals who constituted the audience—a situation not unlike our own. The postmodern work—reflecting on itself—may render our 'narcissistic' need to *see* ourselves, for we have become invisible or, at best, intermittently visible to others. Seeing our experience reflected in a self-reflexive art may make us feel a little more substantial.

Art has long comprised the narcissistic and voyeuristic, which are but two sides of the same coin. Like the young child, we watch others in part to see ourselves. Those who watch Madonna, who herself appears to *be* only because she is watched continually—by the camera, her entourage, the crowd, and the bodyguard at her side—may be doing something akin to looking at postmodern art. Alone in a crowd that does not see us, we watch a celebrity who exists—as most of us do—because she is *seen*. She is 'created' by the camera, which is also the source of her wealth and power. When we watch her being watched—or spy on others in factual or fictive accounts—perhaps we too feel seen. The reflexive, voyeuristic, and narcissistic element, both in 'high' and popular culture, is very likely part of our effort to establish our presence, just as video recorders and Polaroid cameras confirm, instantaneously, that we *are*.

In the context of our situation, the postmodern aesthetic may be an attempt to achieve the very 'objective' of traditional art it regards as invalid. Despite its political and social agenda, it would appear to be rooted in anxiety and despair.

PART THREE

Storytellers—New and Old

20

Popular Stories

MELODRAMA

At one time, popular stories—myth, legend, and fairy tale—carried the same implication as *King Lear* and *Madame Bovary*. They suggested that our ability to predict and influence our lives is largely an illusion.

In the recent past, popular stories have often assumed the form of melodrama—a genre that evolved during the industrial revolution, when large numbers of people moved from rural communities to the city. Since they were illiterate and their oral tradition could not survive in an urban environment, they turned to the stage. Everyone went to the theater: men and women, young and old, parents with their children and nursing mothers with infants. London theatres in the 1860s could accommodate over 150,000 people on a single night.[1] The stories enacted in them clearly served an important purpose and, like television, ran much of the day. Peter Brooks says that in Paris

> (Audiences) absorbed their theatre going in massive doses: an evening's entertainment would consist of various curtain raisers and afterpieces, as well as one and sometimes two full-length plays, and would last five hours or more.[2]

Melodrama is related to the folk tales and fairy tales the audience brought with them from the countryside. In Paris, it evolved alongside the *féeriques*, musical pantomimes that survived until late in the nineteenth century and retained, as the name implies, a strong element of the supernatural. The world rendered by melodrama is a dark and dangerous realm, which we survive with the help of nonhuman forces. An innocent hero and heroine are subjected to calamity after calamity: abduction, imprisonment, torture,

271

and the continuous threat of rape and death. The soap operas of our day—though the 'action' in them is emotional rather than physical—belong to the same tradition. So do "disaster movies," in which an airplane is not only about to crash but carries a murderer and a cargo of deadly germs that threatens to spill whenever the plane lurches. A concatenation of catastrophes can, of course, be found in traditional story as well: Oedipus kills his father and marries his mother; Odysseus and his crew run a gauntlet of mortal threats; and our laughter in many a comedy derives from an uninterrupted series of disasters that the figures escape by the skin of their teeth.

The sense of helplessness and enforced passivity that pervades melodrama is expressed physically: the hero or heroine is confined to a dungeon and bound to the rack or some other instrument of torture. But despite the apparent hopelessness of their situation, they remain steadfast and uncomplaining, confident—like Snow White and unlike King Lear—that Providence is on their side, as it indeed is. The dark journey of melodrama has a happy ending. A kindly fate reunites lovers who have been kept apart by wicked enemies and returns long-lost children to their parents; villains are punished and virtue is rewarded. The nature of the adventure varies from era to era but the basic pattern of the fairy tale shines through:

> Infants stolen from parents, sold to gypsies, or abandoned on the Cathedral steps are . . . endowed with strawberry birthmarks . . . by which they are identified twenty years later as the long-lost heirs of vast domains. Lost children adopted by wealthy foster parents can be easily located by singing their favorite carols in the snowy streets below.[3]

We have noted that in traditional story the 'long arm of coincidence' is a manifestation of the sacred, and Peter Brooks observes that in melodrama, too,

> We do not live in a world completely drained of transcendence and significance.
> Melodrama daily makes the abyss yield some of its content, makes us feel we inhabit amid (larger) forces, and they amidst us.
> A form for secularized times, it offers the nearest *approach* to sacred and cosmic values in a world where they no longer have any certain ontology or epistomology.[4]

Significantly, though the dialogue and acting in the popular theater were highly stylized, storms, blizzards, shipwrecks, avalanches, waterfalls, and volcanoes were presented with awe-inspiring verisimilitude. Realism—historically associated with materialism and Positivism—was employed by melodrama to incarnate the *non*human or sacred. It rendered spectacular phenomena of the natural world in persuasive *coups de théâtre*, which both astonished *and* reassured the audience, since they evoked the numinous.

Even melodrama's relentless focus on death and disaster may be seen as an affirmation of the sacred, just as the virginity of the heroine—under constant attack but always finally preserved—may have constituted an incarnation of the divine in human form. It is easier to understand the central role of death and virginity in nineteenth-century narrative if we assume that, at a time when traditional religious forms were no longer persuasive, they represented aspects of the sacred—just as the middle-class home, ruled by a virgin-mother, constituted a sanctified realm that the crude world of commerce and industry could not sully.[5]

Throughout the heyday of Positivism, melodrama in various forms purveyed a deeply traditional, conservative view of the human situation. The supernatural or unconscious is as vividly present in the Gothic tale as saints and devils were in medieval legends. *Frankenstein* retells the story of the sorcerer's apprentice, though the forces over which he loses control appear, at first, to be of his own making. Despite radical changes in the environment, the burden of popular story remained unchanged: we may think we are in charge but we are not.[6]

Positivist values were promoted only in narratives addressed to the middle class, like the well-made play. Here social problems were confronted and resolved. The interactions on stage no longer invoke the natural or sacred but occur entirely within the human realm—in comfortably furnished homes, among people who know each other and are caught in situations that were familiar to the audience, rather than remote and exotic. The playhouse was small and intimate, and the action, dialogue, performances, sets, costumes, and props were meticulously attentive to detail. The narrative was governed by a self-assured materialism; instead of realistic avalanches, the stage featured working fireplaces and the smell of onions. Since the inner, subjective realm was deemed as irrelevant as the gods, the actors spoke prose and not verse.

Melodrama itself, however, remained untainted by Positivism, even in the United States—where, as Gilbert Cross points out:

> (It) called not for a new social order, but nostalgically for the restoration of the old order in which master and peasant had lived together on the land, their interest bound by mutual obligation.[7]

Not until the twentieth century—in Russia—was an attempt made to use melodrama for Positivist purposes:

Anatoli Lunacharsky and Maxim Gorky—two of the most influential voices for the revolution—engaged in a prolonged campaign to promote romantic and heroic melodrama as the desirable route for Soviet drama to follow. . . . (They) considered the theatre to be an effective tool of education and regarded melodrama as an entertaining means for promoting ideas.[8]

Gorky proclaimed that:

The drama of man . . . as a passive spectator of the tragedy of life—this drama should die out.[9]

He was not aware that the strong plot of melodrama inevitably turns the figures into its agents. Lillian Hellman made the same mistake:

If you believe, as the Greeks did, that man is at the mercy of the gods, then you write tragedy. The end is inevitable from the beginning. But if you believe that man can solve his own problems and is at nobody's mercy, then you will probably write melodrama.

Though she often cast her own plays in the form of melodrama, its true nature escaped her. Nor was she alone in thinking that narrative can and must promote the potentiation and betterment of humankind. John Steinbeck spoke for many when, on accepting the Nobel prize, he said:

A writer who does not personally believe in the perfectibility of man has no dedication nor any membership in literature.[10]

MOVIES AND POSITIVISM

Since popular story has, in the past, confirmed the world view of its audience, we might expect our own narratives to support *our* assumptions. But in popular story today, as in the nineteenth century, the intentions of the Positivist storyteller and the can-do attitude of the characters are countermanded by a strong plot.

The contradiction is most apparent in our movies, which replaced theater and vaudeville as the most popular form of storytelling and entertainment. Silent film grew directly out of melodrama, from which it borrowed both its plots and style. The broad, often acrobatic performances, accompanied and underscored by music, were familiar to audiences, and even the absence of speech was linked to the tradition of pantomime and *mimodrame*. The new medium was, of course, far more adept at rendering physical action and danger than the stage: the performers or their doubles could be *actually* cast into torrents, or tied to railroad tracks with a train hurtling toward them. Spectacles of nature were no longer just a climactic *coup de théâtre* but served as settings for the entire action.

The Western—which had established its popularity in printed form—became a favorite subject of early American cinema. From 1910 to 1960 one-fourth of our films were set on the frontier. Westerns employed standard melodramatic ingredients but enhanced their credibility by placing them in an American context and substituting American values and attitudes for those of nineteenth-century Europe. The hero's active will and skill, rather than the passive virtues of endurance and faith, carry the day. He can outride and outshoot the villain, and overcomes the obstacles nature places in his path on his own. Providence and fate no longer play a critical role and while he may, on occasion, profess his faith in God, he expects no help from the supernatural.

The Western hero often saves an entire community. He guides wagon trains through Indian territory, knows how to ford raging rivers, and protects women, children, and the infirm. But while he is the leader, he remains a 'common,' democratic man, and his actions, unlike those of King Lear or Julien Sorel, meet with the approval of the audience. If he opposes his fellow townsmen to prevent the lynching of an innocent prisoner, the community will eventually see the light. Conflicts and problems are invariably solved by courage and reason, and there is no need for suffering or self-division.

Though the Western was set outdoors, nature soon ceased to be a genuine force and became little more than a picturesque backdrop for the clash between hero and villain; human beings are clearly seen in command of their own fate. Conversely, a comedy like *The Gold Rush* is determined by storms, avalanches, bears, hunger, and a greed for gold engendered by poverty. Here the villain isn't killed by the hero but by an icy ledge that casts him into the abyss, and a blizzard produces the happy ending by blowing Charlie and Big Jim to their lost goldmine.

The reduction of nature to inconsequence in most of our movies is no doubt linked to its 'conquest' by man; it is an analogue of our relationship to the sacred. Indeed, the camera itself is clearly a device that has built into it the *materialist* assumptions of those who designed it. "Every tool," as Heisenberg says, "carries with it the spirit by which it has been created."[11] The camera reports the *physical* realm, which, in the context of nineteenth-century materialism, was synonymous with reality; it serves as a self-fulfilling prophesy by rendering what its designers deemed relevant or 'real.' Yet if medieval audiences could have seen a photograph or movie, they might well have found them unpersuasive, since the camera cannot report the light or halo emanating from the spiritual realm.

We have noted that even though 'high' art does not serve the sacred directly, it has continued to lend a nonmaterial dimension to the physical realm. But in our popular movies, with the exception of horror films, the nonmaterial no longer plays an explicit and credible role. *The Wizard of Oz* is a demystified fairy tale that permits us, for the duration of Dorothy's dream, to believe in the Land of Oz, only to return us safely to the familiar and reassuring reality of Kansas and home. Even *within* the dream, the supernatural suffers a debunking when the Wizard himself turns out to be a fraud.

In Disney's work—except for the wicked stepmother in *Snow White and the Seven Dwarfs*—the supernatural and magical are cute rather than awe-inspiring or frightening. His films are fairy tales for Positivists. Though Mickey Mouse as the sorcerer's apprentice in *Fantasia* cannot reverse the spell he has cast, his magic is unmistakably controlled by the storyteller; it exists by virtue of the animator's skill. Of course this has always been true of the puppet theater, and insofar as the storyteller maintains a measure of control, it could be said of all fiction. But traditional stories and their audiences *believed* in the sacred, while Disney only flirts with it. His faith is clearly in the mechanical and industrial genius of humankind, exemplified by his own extraordinary work and the amusement parks that bear his name. Not surprisingly, he arranged to have his body frozen after death, anticipating the day—sure to come—when we will have the power to reawaken the dead by curing retroactively whatever killed them. The mechanized figure of Lincoln in Disneyland may, unintentionally, present his vision of the future, not just of the past.

The success of Steven Spielberg can be in part attributed to his evocation of the otherworldly: voyagers from the far reaches of the universe; kindly extraterrestrial creatures; and monsters of the deep. But *his* myths, unlike those of traditional cultures, reconcile opposites: they see no conflict between Positivism and the sacred; they speak to and 'satisfy' our metaphysical yearnings without questioning our worldly orientation. *Jaws* can be 'read' as a Positivist retelling of *Moby Dick*: the evil here is entirely in the monster, and the valiant captain saves his community without having to sacrifice himself. Of course it could well be that if a malevolent beast *were* to appear on our shores, the sea would be littered with gung-ho Americans in their pleasure craft, eager to do battle. At least superficially, the hero of *Jaws* may be a more accurate rendering of our national psyche than the crew of the Pequod, who would rather sail home than pursue a white whale.

In *Apocalypse Now*, Coppola tries to combine Positivism with tragedy—an impossible mix. He set out to adapt Conrad's *Heart of Darkness*, but since our movies cannot accommodate a passive point of view, he turned the bystander Marlowe into an active figure, whose encounter with Kurtz has him emerge a better man—the moral of many a Positivist tale. Though Coppola was clearly influenced by Herzog's *Aguirre*, he approached his material very differently. *Aguirre* may be as close to tragedy as the medium can come: the central figure is a deranged monster and his crew, like Ahab's shipmates, are trapped on a raft—at the mercy of the river, the jungle, and a madman who thinks he is God. We know their journey is pointless and doomed, and watch them die one after the other, executed, drowned, or shot by Indian arrows. Even Aguirre is finally doomed to passivity, drifting downstream with a tribe of chattering monkeys. But Coppola, like most of our commercial film makers, was unwilling to tell a story that is explicitly foreclosed—one, moreover, in which the darkness is at the heart rather than comfortably on the periphery of the narrative.

Though our Positivist ethos may not inspire persuasive or lasting tales, it is, of course, central to the making of America and Americans. It engenders our confidence and optimism, plays a critical role in the processes of democracy, enables immigrants and minorities, and helps to power free enterprise. It accounts in large part for the international appeal of American culture—especially of our movies. Rambo, Dirty Harry, and the Terminator 'prove' we can change the world or at least rid it of evil. They purvey a fantasy of power that suggests a profoundly depotentiated audience, and very likely sell tickets because they compensate for a widespread sense of helplessness. The action, moreover, briefly permits men and boys to reestablish their gender identity as the active, powerful sex.

We are all perfectly aware that movies manipulate us for our money, but since the profit motive is a premise of our society, we don't mind being sold rather than simply told our stories. We expect a display of them in multiplex theaters, on television, and at the video store, and purchase the ones we need—those that make us feel good and confirm our assumptions.

Popular movies, like melodrama, simplify. We are seldom asked to feel two things at once, or even to split our attention and *notice* two things at the same time. Though comedy and tragedy, too, might be called monopathic—comedy excludes death and suffering, while few tragedies permit us to laugh—our relationship to the narrative and the central figure is complex. But in popular stories we are free of the ambiguities and contradictions we face in daily life. We know what to feel and think. The distinctions between right and wrong or good and evil are unequivocal. A crisis—from *crino*, "to judge"—is central to many stories, but whereas in tragedy it clarifies or illuminates the double bind of human existence, in melodrama it relieves us of conflict and doubt. In 1919, the Soviet Commissar of Education wrote:

> The playwright who dares undertake melodrama, in our view the sole possible form of tragedy for the new age, should clearly take sides for and against. For the melodramatist, the world should be polarized. At least while he writes he should cast off all skepticism and doubt.[12]

The rejection of ambiguity in popular story is not altogether unrealistic. There *are* cruel bosses, grubby landlords, sadistic policemen, vicious pimps, steadfast lovers, heroic young men, and self-sacrificing parents. Self-contradiction and indeterminacy—the subtle back and forth between generosity and greed, honesty and deceit, altruism and egotism—are marks of a privileged life and feasible only when we are not subject to dire necessity. Since, in the middle class, the private and public realms are separate, people can be greedy and ruthless at work, yet kind and generous within the charmed circle of family and friends. But among the poor, who live communally and are subordinate to others at work, there is no division between public and private; the kind are apt to be kind and the brutal brutal. All are up against it and there is little room for self-division, complexity, or contradiction.

POSITIVIST STORY AND THE PAST

Some Positivist stories—like the Western—are set in a bygone day. But the story itself is seldom concerned with the effect of past on present. A past event—the murder of the hero's wife or partner—may precipitate the action but won't structure or texture the events, as it does in Ibsen, Strindberg, Chekhov, Williams, and Miller. A personal past is characteristic of middle-class life; it engenders differences and is, in this sense, 'undemocratic.' Middle-class audiences become a 'community' by identifying with a figure who is individuated, or different, whereas the heroes of popular story are the way most of us would *like* to be—brave, generous, principled, and without complications or dark secrets.

To free themselves of the past, Americans used to go West—in fact as in fiction. But today, with the frontier closed and the myth of the West no longer viable, popular fiction has often gone into space and the future, where, too, the past can be left behind and everyone starts from scratch.

Since space is the new frontier, science fiction shares the Positivism of the Western. The physicist Leon Lederman says of Isaac Asimov:

> Intrinsic to his writing was the notion that there isn't anything we can't master. His world view was that we can solve all the problems of the world.[13]

Our Positivist culture prefers stories about the young, for their lives seem less mortgaged to the past as constituted by family and ethnic or economic group. Since their destiny is not yet manifest, they appear to be free whereas their elders are clearly situated, committed, fixed. The etched faces of older folk fit them to be 'characters'—from *charatto*, "to cut, engrave"—rather than central figures.

Among Hollywood movies, *Citizen Kane* is an anomaly. No less precluded than *Oedipus Rex*, it begins with Kane's death and becomes most compelling when he grows old. His life is explicitly dominated by the past, and its emotional high point, the destruction of Susan Alexander's room, takes us directly back to his childhood. Conversely, *Bonnie and Clyde*—whose alienation and brutality are surely rooted in their past—makes no mention of it, except for a maudlin evocation of Bonnie's mother, who is quite literally seen through a fog of sentiment.

And yet our movies, like all popular stories, are structured by a strong plot—which *constitutes* the past. Their relationship to the past is thus deeply ambiguous. The Positivist orientation of the figures—and, to all appearances, of the narrative itself—camouflages and so permits us to subscribe to a deeply traditional perspective. The preclusive plot confirms that the structures and assumptions of our community are valid, while the action assures us that we are free to change or escape them. One could, of course, say that we are allowed to eat our cake and have it, too.

POSITIVIST STORY AND EVIL

Before the Renaissance, evil belonged to the realm of the sacred. Sin was inevitable, and we could not attain perfection or regain paradise on earth. But once we desacralized and humanized evil, it ceased to be essential. As a man of the Enlightenment, Jefferson was confident we could free ourselves of it:

> Barbarism has . . . been receding before the steady step of amelioration and will in time, I trust, disappear from the earth.

279

Taine's "Vice and virtue are products like sugar and vitriol"[14] was widely quoted, and William James said that "evil is a disease." The next step was to eradicate the "disease" or control the "product" by changing the factors that *produced* it.[15]

Gershom Scholem points out that philosophy has always tried to give a rational account of evil. Philosophers refuse to accept it as an incomprehensible presence of which we cannot free ourselves. But the Kabbalists—who were, in Scholem's view, "the seal-bearers of the world of myth" or story—

> have a strong sense of the reality of evil and of the dark horror that is about everything living. They do not, like the philosophers, seek to evade its existence with the aid of a convenient formula; rather do they try to penetrate into its depth.[16]

In Greek mythology, too, there is no escape from 'sin,' at least for the hero. He almost inevitably offends a deity and brings down a curse on himself, and often on his descendants. In the Old Testament, the story of Cain suggests—albeit indirectly—that evil is mandated by Yahweh Himself, since He *protects* the murderer. Popular story, from fairy tale to Hollywood movie, continues to believe that evil is part of the human essence, perennial and indestructible like energy itself. Those who are possessed by it do not choose but *incarnate* it. There is no explanation or 'cause' for what they do, and therefore no permanent remedy. The villain could well say, as Yahweh does: *I am what I am.*

Since fairy tales often associate evil with an otherworldly figure—with the supernatural or unconscious—we understand it to be a threat to all, a potential in our own hearts. Perhaps it seems 'real' to us because we sense that the witches, trolls, and wicked stepmothers live *within* and not just among us. While evil in the movies today is perpetrated by human beings—mad-dog killers or murderous psychopaths—they too are atavistic figures possessed by the unconscious, and so continue to imply that there is evil in all of us.

Popular story permits us at once to believe in evil and to exorcise it by projecting it onto another—one who is *unlike* us: the outsider or stranger. Shakespeare plays a similar double game. Lear is a difficult, egocentric man capable of cruelty and injustice, but the villains in the play are so monstrous that he soon becomes "more sinn'd against than sinning." At first Goneril and Regan treat him as we might ourselves: his willfulness seems to justify their mistrust of him; they don't *usurp* his power; he surrenders it freely, or rather, compulsively. Even his plan to bestow the largest share of his kingdom on the daughter who loves him most may be an attempt to advantage Cordelia. Yet, almost from the start, Lear experiences everything her sisters do as evil, and inasmuch as the narrative and verse render *his* point of view more consistently than any other, we see things as he does. During the first two acts, the *facts* serve to counterbalance his feelings, but in Act Three the play becomes unmistakably biased in his favor and turns his older daughters into monsters. While revenge is the source of Edmund's malice, Goneril and Regan seem possessed by a motiveless malignancy that isn't accounted for within the narrative. Perhaps they must be understood as abandoned children. Like Edmund, Poor Tom, and the Fool, they are waifs. There are no *mothers* in *King Lear*, and if—as Bradley suggests—there is a question about the children of Lady Macbeth, we may surely wonder about Lear's wife: neither he nor his daughters mention her even once.[17]

The understanding that tragedy—unlike melodrama—brings to its villains, and the fact that its heroes are *not* simply virtuous and innocent, could be attributed to class differences. The 'elite,' in order to lead, must have access to its energy and so to its own evil; Oedipus assumes that evil is other only to discover it in himself. But since the audience of fairy tales and melodrama is expected to *accept* the status quo, evil can be projected onto a villain. Whereas Dostoevski makes an absolute connection between evil and suffering—we understand *why* Rogoshin and Raskolnicov do what they do—popular story has no sympathy for the devil. There is a hint of past suffering in the villain's physical deformity—he is ugly, limps, has a hunchback, or is missing an eye—but he is shown no mercy, just as in everyday language "bastard" and "son of a bitch" suggest the genesis of a man's nasty qualities without invoking our sympathy. Popular story is judgmental: it knows right from wrong and identifies wholeheartedly with the hero. If *he* does the forbidden, it is with good reason and the best of intentions. The 'antihero' of recent movies is simply a hero with dirty fingernails, who—unlike Hamlet and Othello—is never cruel to the innocent and defenseless. When Paul Newman initiated the sequel to *The Hustler*, he chose to play the villain, but unlike George Scott—who, in the original film, seduces the hero's girl and causes her suicide—Newman caters to what the audience expects of a "leading man" and ends up *protecting* the couple.

Popular story shows us as we are supposed to be and wish to see ourselves. Like the community itself, it represses what tragedy includes. By projecting evil onto the other, it purges us of our dark and dirty secrets, frees us of self-division, and fosters *communitas* by giving us someone to hate and fear. Yet *unlike* Positivism, it retains its belief in the power of evil. Indeed, without a destructive threat—whether it be divine or human—

there *is* no story. Most narratives begin when something goes wrong, and evil is often the energy that drives it forward. Moreover, we don't come to story—even popular story—just to see good people doing well but to make contact with the negative qualities in ourselves. We are often more interested in those who do wrong than in those who are virtuous. As Hitchcock says:

The more successful the villain, the more powerful the story.[18]

Hitchcock was himself an effective purveyor of melodrama. His heroes are often passive—or even immobilized, as in *Rear Window*—trapped in webs that were spun, in the films of the 1930s and early 1940s, by foreign conspirators and, after the war, by the pathology of 'psychos.' When he says that the "Macguffin"—the object the spies or villains are after—is irrelevant, he assures us that evil in his stories is formulaic and need not be taken seriously. In his later films, he keeps winking at us reassuringly, so that our fear can become an aesthetic *frisson*. His villains motivate the action and maintain our interest, but we need not believe in them. They can be enjoyed, much as the audience enjoys the villainous schemes of J. R. in *Dallas*.

Horror movies are truer to traditional melodrama, since they engender a sense of helplessness in the face of unspeakable and often pervasive evil. Here the terrifying is not smiled away, even if it elicits *shrieks* of laughter, and evil inheres in the very nature of things—an atavistic reassertion of a past from which no one is safe, a manifestation of the supernatural or sub-human. Death dominates scene after scene: when someone isn't dismembered, skewered, or decapitated, we sit in tense anticipation of the next horror. Though virginity is no longer sacred to us, the old morality reasserts itself: unwed young couples are often caught *in flagrante delicto* and brutally killed by a madman or monster. At story's end, the evil may be briefly put to rest but we know it will rise again—immortal, like energy itself.

PLOT IN POPULAR STORY

Though our movies are clearly formulaic, the audience believes in them, just as we once believed in myths, legends, and fairy tales. They tell us what we know and confirm the truths we live by. They are 'true' even when they are poorly written and badly performed. They are 'true' despite—or because of—the contradictions they engender. Just as most popular music has a strong melodic line, so popular stories are carried by their strong plot.

We want our Positivist assumptions confirmed, yet—since we refuse to sit through a story without narrative thrust—need to see them invalidated.

Postmodern and Marxist aesthetics suggest that the audience is naive and unaware of story's double message. But perhaps we recognize or sense in its contradictions an accurate rendering of our own situation, which demands that we be at once confident of our freedom and aware of its limitations. Most people are obliged, at an early age, to accept the insignificance of their existence as individuals and their dependence on circumstances they cannot control. Plot, which the aesthetic indicts for promoting the illusion of a just, predictable universe, clearly suggests that we cannot foretell the outcome of our actions—an implication that the educated and specialized, who are expected to establish *predictable* sequences and to enhance the control we exercise over our lives, must reject. The audience at large is surely aware that the movie is over before it begins, that John Wayne is at the mercy of scriptwriters, and that the power and skill of the Terminator depend on special effects and stuntmen. Moviegoers must *sense*—even if they do not 'know'—that our Positivism is only valid within limits, and that the gung-ho hero—Rambo no less than Oedipus—is undermined by the precluded plot.

PLOT AND MIDDLE-CLASS NARRATIVE

Significantly, plot is often the weakest element in stories addressed to the educated middle class. Here, instead of "the things from outside" that determine melodrama, the narrative originates in and is shaped by relationships and feelings. This is true not only of sentimental stories but of the novels of Virginia Woolf and the early work of E. M. Forster, which imply that within the charmed circle of the truly civilized, relationships and events are governed by ethical and aesthetic sensibilities—by choice rather than fate or circumstance. Necessity, both in its biological and economic form, is marginalized and evil is rendered mostly as selfishness, a disregard for the rights and feelings of others, a failure of the imagination; needs are so subdued or deenergized that they produce no outright conflict and seldom reveal any darkness in those who carry the story's point of view.

The more confined and intimate the setting, the easier it is for us to assume that the figures exercise a measure of control. Stories in *The New Yorker* often derive their appeal from their limited scope, their open-ended form, and lack of finality. Unlike the stories of Hemingway or Strindberg's short play *Miss Julie*, they tend to focus on an *aperçu*. They may not claim that we determine our own lives, but the absence of a foreclosed plot can leave us with the illusion of freedom. Virginia Woolf once said that though she could write *scenes* she couldn't write a plot—perhaps because she could not bear to believe in one.

DETECTIVE STORIES

In the detective story, with its middle-class readership, the Positivist tenor of the narrative is *not* undermined by the plot, which is clearly designed and manipulated for our entertainment. The author is in absolute control and the detective, who is both his puppet and alter ego, incarnates rationalist and Positivist principles. Not surprisingly, detective fiction enjoys the enthusiastic approval of contemporary aesthetics. And yet the *first* detective stories—Hoffmann's *Das Fräulein von Scuderi* and Poe's *The Murders in the Rue Morgue*—were composed by authors who were preoccupied with the supernatural and inexplicable. The figures in their tales are beset by forces—benign in Hoffmann and malign in Poe—they can neither escape nor understand:

> It was to (his own) powerful impulse toward the irrational that (Poe) opposed the . . . potent sense of reason which finds its highest expression in "The Murders in the Rue Morgue" and "The Purloined Letter." Against the metaphors for chaos, found in his other tales, he sets, in the Dupin stories the essential metaphor for order: the detective.[19]

> Dupin has a positivistic bent. He trusts the omnipotent ability of human reason to provide enlightenment. . . . (But) what his enlightenment is directed towards is the quintessence of horror and inhumanity. The murderer is an ape. In this extreme polarization of reason and inhumanity, "The Murders in the Rue Morgue" seems like a programmatic statement which was never again to be expressed so purely.[20]

> The value of a detective novel can be quite neatly defined by the affront to reason and experience contained in its point of departure, and the more or less complete and believable way that both reason and experience are satisfied at its conclusion. At bottom, the unmasking of the criminal is less important than the reduction of the impossible to the possible, of the inexplicable to the explained, of the supernatural to the natural. . . . What the reader demands is that a lone man with believable human motives pull off a crime that seems to defy reason but that reason can eventually discover.[21]

Detective fiction is a triumph of rational inquiry. Here, indeed, art creates order out of chaos:

The detective encounters effects without causes, events in a jumbled chronological order, significant clues hidden among the insignificant. . . . His role is to reestablish sequence and causality.[22]

The detective story exhibits a reality structured as a set of ambiguous signs which gain their meaning from a . . . history that must be uncovered so as to order the production of these signs as a chain of events, eventually with a clear origin, intention and solution, and with strong causal connections between each link.[23]

We are, at the end, left with perfect understanding: every contradiction turns out to be but the *appearance* of a contradiction; all ambiguity is removed and guilt and innocence are established unequivocally. Perhaps, as Richard Alewyn suggests, the genre has its origin in the Gothic novel, but it reduces the frightening, dark and unknown to the familiar and comprehensible.[24] Even Father Brown, Chesterton's priest-detective, can be counted on to demonstrate that the murderous Hammer of God was thrown by a man. Death itself has been brought under human control.[25]

Oedipus Rex is often called a detective story, but while the murder of Laius is solved, we are left with the far greater mystery of why it had to happen. Rational inquiry reveals an 'order' but not one we can understand. Oedipus fails precisely where his modern counterparts succeed. He thinks he is an objective investigator but discovers that he is himself the source of the problem; he not only committed the crime but violated fundamental laws. We cannot conceive of Sherlock Holmes murdering his father and marrying his mother. The hero of detective fiction is *above* the fray—free of guilt and of the need for vengeance. Since he is nonviolent, operates within the law, and turns the evildoer over to the authorities, his story renders approved forms of retribution and inhibits the very impulses that find expression in traditional narrative. Little remains of the demonic and horrifying that compelled Hoffmann and Poe. The physical dimension of life—and death—is largely ignored: there are no pits, no rats, and no visceral fear. As Holmes tells Watson: "I am a brain. The rest of me is mere appendix."[26]

When movies transformed the detective story into *film noir* and the thriller, they brought it closer to melodrama. The characters and settings are no longer genteel, and the action has shifted from the drawing room, the country house, and the Orient Express to urban streets, bars, and dingy hotels. Physical conflict, brutality, and fear take the place of intellectual inquiry. The private eye or rogue cop is no longer an objective observer but directly involved and often motivated by revenge or hate. His own life is at stake, his friends are killed, and his wife or child is in mortal danger.

285

While he is brave and persistent, he is not particularly smart. Unlike Holmes, he does not have the situation in hand and is at the mercy of events that we—who are familiar with the genre—can predict more accurately than he.

HAPPENINGS

During the 1960s, the limitations traditional plot imposes on the fictive figure were well understood by those who—in an interface between avant-garde aesthetics and their desire for social-political change—produced the Happening. They attempted to create a genuinely open, democratic fiction in which the action and participants were in no way precluded by an existing, 'authoritative' structure. Happenings were based on the assumption that since there is no author, the course of events is no longer predetermined. Ignorance of the outcome and the absence of a precluding text were taken to mean that the participants were free to act in accordance with their own needs and wishes.[27] Yet one kind of predetermination was simply replaced by another. The fact that the actors did not know what they would do until they did it in no way set them free, even if it gave them and their audience the illusion of freedom.[28]

ATHLETIC GAMES

A more persuasive Positivist spectacle—one that continues to hold large numbers of people captive day after day—is provided by athletic events. The players are bound by rigid rules, but there is no author or text. While betting on the outcome of *Oedipus Rex* would be pointless, the score of a hockey game is uncertain, even if the odds favor one team or the other. On the playing field, control over the body, the ball and, if possible, the opposite player is crucial. Teams and individuals plan and rehearse their strategies carefully, and their training, skill and will to win determine the outcome.

Athletics confirm our Positivist assumptions far more persuasively than any fiction, and many people find it easier to lend their feelings to a football game or track event than to a movie. The players appear truly in charge of their own 'fate' and are not victims even when they lose. No suspension of disbelief is required, for the participants are physically committed and not just *pretending* to act. Wrestling matches are the exception; they alone de-

286

pend on the *imitation* of an action. Given Barthes's postmodern aesthetic, it isn't surprising that he preferred them to boxing.[29]

During the past few decades, the athlete has become a national celebrity. He is the hero of a story or myth that he lives out and enacts for us, risking public failure or achieving glory and riches. A college football player told me that one Saturday afternoon in the stadium he realized he was performing in a 'movie' for the benefit of the crowd; he left the team soon after.

André Jolles points out that the athletic record is an equivalent of the miracle performed by the medieval saint, though it is of course a miracle achieved through the application of will power.[30] Some athletes, like the heroes of myth, are up against the gods as much as against other contestants. Like Icarus, they try to exceed the physical limitations imposed on mortal beings. Significantly, athletic contests in Greece coincided with and may have originated in religious ritual.[31]

There are fans who, when they watch a game taped during their absence, will make every effort to remain ignorant of the score. They wish to preserve the suspense so that they can suffer and rejoice in an event that is, in fact, long over. Ignorance of the outcome is clearly important to the spectator, since it enhances the identification and catharsis that make the athletic contest an equivalent of traditional fiction. Yet, when we watch a film of the 1936 Olympics, knowing who won and lost in no way lesssens our kinetic and emotional participation: the final score—however important—is not the most significant part of the experience. We respect and identify with athletes not simply because they win but because, like the heroes of story, they are utterly committed and persist even when they suffer. The Olympic Games end with the marathon, a test of endurance; and *to win*—which is rooted in the Anglo-Saxon *winnan*, "to strive, struggle, fight, labor"—is a cognate of the Gothic *winnan*, "to endure." Endurance may be the fundamental link among athletics, myth, tragedy, and contemporary narratives, including our Movies of the Week.

COMEDIANS

All stories performed for a live audience carry an element of uncertainty, even though they adhere to a preclusive text. The performer risks public failure and survives—like the athlete—by dint of arduously acquired skills. The safety net in the circus is a physical analogue of the hazard he or she must face.

Comedy often derives from and includes elements of improvisation. We expect the comedian to surprise us—and indeed, himself—without losing

287

his equilibrium or poise. We expect him to take chances. "To joke" and
"to juggle" both have the same root, and many great clowns have also
been jugglers, equilibrists, equestrians, and trapeze artists:

> The circus clown often plays the role of a clumsy buffoon who seems intent
> on killing himself as he strives to imitate his betters, delighting audiences with
> the comedy of near-misses and well-planned falls. His comic effects involve
> real danger and are a direct extension of his physical skills, which are in every
> way equal to those of his fellow performers.[32]

> (The French *grotesque* Auriol) could run along the tops of a row of bottles
> without knocking them over and then balance in a free headstand atop the last
> bottle while playing the trumpet. He could balance on an unsupported ladder
> or scale walls "like a fly." With the help of a *tremplin* (springboard), Auriol
> leaped over eight mounted horses or over twenty-four soldiers with mounted
> bayonets. He was one of the few acrobats who could safely somersault out of
> and back into his slippers. His ability to seemingly defy gravity earned him the
> nickname *L'Homme Oiseau* (The Birdman).[33]

Nijinsky, too, appeared to fly when he leaped and, indeed, to pause for a
moment in mid-air before landing on stage. Art often approximates the
miraculous or magical *without* resorting to tricks; it actualizes the impossible. W. C. Fields began to juggle when he was a child and practiced for
hours on end every day for years:

> I still carry scars on my legs from those early attempts at juggling. I'd balance
> a stick on my toe, toss it into the air, and try to catch it again on my toe. Hour
> after hour the damned thing would bang against my shinbones. I'd work until
> tears were streaming down my face. But I kept practicing, and bleeding, until
> I perfected the trick. I don't believe that Mozart, Liszt, Paderewski, or Kreisler
> ever worked harder than I did.[34]

His performances were no less 'impossible' than those of a great athlete or
concert artist.

In film comedy, success—or the perfect take—is assured and performers
are not at risk in front of a live audience. Yet Keaton, like many clowns in
the past, repeatedly risked his life for effects that pass so effortlessly and
quickly we are unaware of the danger. In the violent storm that ends *Steamboat Bill Jr.,* the entire facade of a building comes crashing down on him
"like a gigantic fly swatter";[35] he survives, upright and unperturbed, only
because a second-story window is open and its frame has passed around
him with just inches to spare. The gag would have killed him had there
been even the slightest miscalculation:

The clearance of that window was exactly three inches over my head and past each shoulder. And the front of the building . . . weighed two tons.[36]

Though chance, nature, and fate play a large role in the films of Keaton and Chaplin, their work has a stronger Positivist component than classical comedy. Both survived horrendous childhood experiences by developing and drawing on extraordinary talents and skills. Their comedies—like Houdini's brushes with death, Harold Lloyd's thrill pictures, and nineteenth-century melodrama—continually threaten them with extinction, either physical or psychological, and our laughter derives from their hair's-breadth escapes. Though their survival is assured from the start, their physical mastery and inventiveness suggest that they determine their own fate. They themselves, moreover, engineer the disasters that befall them—as if Oedipus were not only the protagonist but the author of his own myth. Perhaps, indeed, they were freer than many storytellers to assign a dominant role to chance and fate because they could counter its overwhelming effect with their genius.

'High' comedy, unlike the work of Chaplin and Keaton, favors a social perspective and is rarely focused on an extraordinary individual, who—like Charlie and Buster—can free himself of the constraints that limit the rest of us. Charlie is as undefined and limitless as a child: he is both brilliant and stupid, clumsy and graceful, greedy and generous, devious and innocent, cruel and tender-hearted. His access to a wide range of human responses separates him from the figures of Molière, Ben Jonson, Sheridan, and Wilde, who haven't his scope and are constrained by their situation as well as their fixed, often obsessive characters.

All comedy permits us to face our limitations, including those imposed on us by chance and circumstance. Jesters and clowns have always made the truth bearable by telling it playfully and within a safe arena. They effectively *use* our limitations to liberate us. By making us face and laugh at our own helplessness, they free the energy we must use in daily life to repress the truth.[37] In comedy, as in jokes, we can confront our worst fears: death, dismemberment, deformity, hunger, abject poverty, raw sexuality, aggression, violence, stupidity, and failure. We can even face the evil in ourselves and recognize that it is often critical to our survival.

While evil in melodrama is always 'other,' in 'low' or popular comedy the hero has easy access to his nasty qualities. Punch is a troublemaker who abuses everyone; the circus clown is often coarse and brutal; Fields and the Marx Brothers trust and respect no one and nothing; and Charlie in the early shorts is capable of cruelty, vindictiveness, and crude sexuality. The hero of 'low' comedy survives not only because the plot, or fate, is on his side but because he marshals the very energies society must inhibit, and uses them to defend himself and attack targets of opportunity. He seems to operate on the premise that attack is the best defense, and most of his activities are aggressive or destructive.

Bergson's definition of laughter as a corrective that reintegrates the misfit into society applies to 'high' comedy only.[38] In 'low' comedy, *society* is unfit and we identify with the rebellious outsider. Most comedy is reductive, but in 'low' comedy we are reduced to our instinctual core and reconnected with energies that are essential to us, even if—in their raw state—they destroy relationships and community. We should note, however, that in 'high' comedy, too, there is often a wily servant who plots successfully to restore the role of nature, which is critical to the social order: he engineers a match between young lovers or liberates youth from the tyranny and pretensions of old age. Here, too, natural forces, albeit in civilized form, emerge victorious. The attempt to thwart nature, rather than to accept and live in accord with it, is doomed to failure.

The link between instinct and comedy is ancient and deep. The satyr play served as a complement to the tragic stories of men and women who had separated from the community—or chorus—and come into open conflict with the gods. Punch, with his long nose, pointed cap, and cudgel, is clearly an instinct figure and the devil, who has horns, a tail, a goat's foot, and lives underground, not only roars with laughter but is in many legends a comic figure.[39] The instincts that nourish 'low' comedy constitute fate in its *biological* form. Like much of the truth, they must be hidden from view and can be safely encountered only in a context that claims, as comedy does, to be utterly untrue—a mere game.

CHAPTER

21
___

Four Storytellers and the Enlightened Tradition

GOETHE'S *FAUST*

Goethe was deeply suspicious of assumptions we would today call Positivist. Yet *Faust*—the work both he and the critical tradition deemed his greatest achievement—is a core fable of Positivism.

In the original legend—which was widely disseminated during the Renaissance by Faust books, popular ballads, puppet plays, and Marlowe's tragedy—the hero is damned because he arrogates to himself the powers of the sacred. As in *Genesis*, human knowledge is associated with the devil, and he who transgresses the limits set by divine law is punished with death and damnation. But Goethe stood the old story on its head, or—as Marx might say—right side up. Perhaps following a suggestion made by Lessing, a key figure in German Enlightenment, that the legend needed a new and positive ending, Goethe has Faust acquire the powers of a god without paying with his life and soul. Like Oedipus, he is a man of intellectual ambition, science, and reason, but *his* knowledge turns out to be an unmitigated blessing. The sorcerer's apprentice benefits from the spell he casts and it is his master, the devil, who ends up impotent.

Though Goethe calls his play a tragedy, it bears the same relationship to the tragic as *Apocalypse Now* does to *Heart of Darkness*. *Faust* carries to an extreme what Erich Heller calls Goethe's "avoidance of tragedy."[1] He ignores the dark dimension of consciousness—our need for control and our restless striving, which, as the word suggests, is directly connected with strife—and celebrates, instead, the advantages and satisfactions that accrue

291

to the striving individual. In *Faust*, our *Unruhe* becomes the source of our salvation.

The play deliberately constitutes itself a new and secular scripture. Faust is dissatisfied with the Gospel text, "In the beginning was the Word," and proclaims instead that "In the beginning was the deed." In this story, action is not an inevitable transgression a double-bound hero must commit whether he wants to or not. Unlike the tragic figures of old, this doer need not suffer, and *Faust* is surely the only tragedy on record in which the protagonist has one interesting and enjoyable experience after the other. Yet, for a man committed to deeds, Faust *does* surprisingly little. While most stage action, even in Shakespeare and Brecht, is talk, the words *constitute* an action. But Faust never really leaves his study. Like Sherlock Holmes, he is primarily a brain, and only some of the poetry and the lone figure of Margaret invoke a concrete, sensory relationship to life: as long as he is involved with her, there is a flurry of actions and of dramatic—rather than poetic—interactions.

Much of the narrative in Part One takes the familiar form of a *Bürgertragö-die*, albeit one within a larger, metaphysical framework, for Faust is no mere *Bürger*. Though briefly troubled by his love and pity for Gretchen, he emerges unscathed. His destiny is to move up and on, and the tragedy is hers alone.[2] *His* life is tragic much as Othello's would be if the play, after he murders Desdemona, were to take him on a series of exotic, edifying adventures. Margaret's death has no lasting effect on him. There is no mention of her in Part Two until she reappears as an incarnation of the eternal feminine to intercede on Faust's behalf with the heavenly powers. His past not only fails to haunt him but becomes the mechanism of his apotheosis.

Part Two abandons narrative altogether. It has neither plot nor action, though Faust briefly envisions using his powers to create a paradise on earth for "many millions." If, instead of composing a sequence of poetic interchanges with mythological and historical figures, Goethe had sought and found a *story*, the darker dimension of being human would have surely emerged. As it stands, the absence of plot leaves Faust free of all constraints. Damnation and salvation are his to choose not just at the beginning of the play but throughout. His compact with the devil is entirely conditional; he is doomed only if he ever says to the moment: "Linger, for you are so beautiful." Not his *actions* but a few jinxed words can damn him—words any clever child would know how to avoid. And indeed, when the prospect of a happy moment arises, Faust carefully shifts into the subjunctive: *Dann würde ich zum Augenblicke sagen*—"Then I *would* say to the moment—." He can't lose. Whereas in the original legend we *know* he is doomed, Goethe's version assures his survival from the start—in a prologue borrowed from that most unlikely source for a Positivist fable, *The Book of Job*. Goethe's Satan is no miltonic rebel. He operates entirely by divine license and stands no chance of winning his bet with God. God Himself is rendered as a kindly old gentleman with nothing of the numinous or terrifying about Him; He clearly has no intention of inflicting the kind of suffering on Faust that Yahweh inflicts on Job.

God in Goethe is less persuasive than the devil, but Mephisto, too, is without real power:

Faust:	Who are you then?
Mephisto:	Part of that power
	That ever wills evil and ever creates good.

A universe in which even Satan cannot help doing good is fortunate indeed. Goethe's devil appears to be the opposite of St. Paul, who *did* the evil he did not *want* to do. Since Mephisto has no destructive will and little pride, Faust's own *hubris*—his striving—does not derive from Satan and can be presented as an unmitigated virtue, the very source of his salvation.

Thomas Mann says:

Mephistopheles is the most vital figure of a devil in all literature; the clearest-cut, the most animated by creative genius.[3]

Hardly! And, indeed, hardly evil. He is just a smart talker, who confirms the humanist hope that evil has no visceral reality—that even the devil is reasonable. In *Faust*, evil is no threat, for as Mann says:

We see how the poet plays with his conception of the Evil One.[4]

If we can "play" with evil, we are in no danger. Yet Mann, like Goethe, wants to have it both ways:

Mephistopheles is the personification of the hatred of light and life; he is primal night and Chaos' son, the emissary of the void.[5]

A grand vision, but not one borne out by the text. Like almost everything else in the play, evil is cerebral. There is no energy, need or compulsion in it. Though Goethe often spoke of the demonic element in his own life, there is little of it in Mephisto, where we might expect to find it.[6] This devil is a court jester, good-natured and amusing. Like his creator, he is controlled and singularly unpossessed—an eighteenth-century figure, without the supernatural or unconscious powers with which both earlier and later storytellers endowed him.

Damnation and salvation are no more real to Goethe than the magic Mephisto puts at Faust's disposal. He has no faith whatever in the supernatural—a poor predicate for retelling the Faust legend, unless the agenda, intended or unintended, is to undermine it. Moreover, the natural forces that move the universe and creation are in Goethe entirely generative and not also destructive. Death and disasters are ignored. Staiger points out that Goethe himself avoided the subject of mortality and used euphemisms whenever he spoke of dying.[7]

Until recently, *Faust* cast a hypnotic spell over the German-speaking world. While critical attention has been largely directed at the play as poem and 'idea,' it is surely Goethe's revision of the old legend that turned Faust into the patron saint of nineteenth-century Positivism.[8] The play apotheosizes the human to the point where, when Faust dies, the devil himself says: *Es ist vollbracht*—"It is finished"—the last words spoken by Jesus in Luther's translation of *The Gospel According to St. John*. Of course Faust ascends to heaven without having to suffer the crucifixion.

Goethe said that Shakespeare was more of a poet than a dramatist—a deeply subjective statement by an author whose own gift was primarily lyric. Though *Faust* is ostensibly a dramatic work, it is largely governed by his feelings and thoughts, with no objective force to counter or limit them. Like a poem, it is harmonious from the start. In Part Two there can *be* no dissonance or narrative, since there is no human figure of consequence apart from Goethe/Faust himself. Nothing in the "tragedy" countermands the curse-blessing of an all-encompassing subjectivity—which may well be the source not only of German music and philosophy, and the basis of Heidegger's "We are the most metaphysical people," but also of its political disasters.

When Goethe claimed that nothing human was alien to him, "he might have included nature and the sacred. He felt he contained it all. Nature made him feel whole; it neither cast him out nor doomed him to violate it. As Heller puts it:

> He came to identify the inner order, inherent in his genius, with the spirit of nature itself. There is for Goethe in the last analysis no specifically *human* spirit. It is one with the spirit of nature.[9]

He was deeply respectful of Spinoza and deemed himself a pantheist. But, in an odd shift, he seems to have *identified* with God and become the all, rather than remaining part of it. He infused pantheism with Positivism in an intoxicating mix. Here indeed was a model for the new man: human, yet one with sacred. He managed to avert his gaze from everything that suggested doubt or self-division, and saw no reason to conclude, as Schopenhauer did, that an absolute pantheism must recognize God even in "the most terrible and abominable phenomena." Valéry says:

> He constantly turned, like one of the plants he loved, to what was warmest and most luminous in the passing moment.[10]

Nothing human was alien to him except the *"unnatural"*—which has, traditionally, been central to the human:

> "Unnatural," in the mouth of Goethe, was one of the strongest invectives. "Diese verdammte Unnatur!" he exclaimed, faced with the productions of Kleist, and Kleist was judged.[11]

Kleist, Hölderlin, and Beethoven, whom Goethe found repellent, carried the very burden of self-division and alienation that Faust is spared. They were outcasts—*verdammt* indeed, like Faust in the old legend, and like so many of us.

In 1771, Goethe observed:

> All of (Shakespeare's plays) revolve around the secret point—which no philosopher has yet seen or determined—in which the singularity of our ego, the claimed freedom of the will, collides with the necessary course of the whole.[12]

By the time he wrote *Faust*, this collision was no longer of interest to him. In a letter to Schiller, he said:

> The mere attempt to write tragedy might be my undoing.[13]

It was nothing of the kind. It left him unscathed and confident. He either failed to recognize that *Faust* is atragic, or perhaps thought he had evolved a new kind of tragedy—one that *denies* the tragic. In an essay that summarizes a widely held view, Valéry says approvingly:

> Goethe had to have everything.

> Poet and Proteus, (he) lived many lives in one. He assimilated everything, and out of it formed his substance.[14]

Why shouldn't an Olympian "assimilate" the tragic along with everything else? Nothing was too big or frightening, nothing so large as to overwhelm him. He became for his admirers a kind of god-man—one of the first supermen bestriding the new era. Yet he remained all of his life a strangely provincial figure, who preserved his confident calm by staying aloof from what his great contemporaries knew, felt, or sensed. Less fortunate and less adroit than he, they were unable to insulate themselves and had to suffer what he contemplated from a safe distance. They illuminated, at grave cost to themselves, the path many of us have had to travel.

Goethe has often been compared to Napoleon, with whom he formed a mutual admiration society. The Emperor—who had in early youth written the fragment of a novel—carried a copy of *Werther* on his campaigns and said, on their first face-to-face meeting: *Voilà un homme!*—perhaps *his* version of *ecce homo*. Goethe, in turn, saw "his Emperor" as the man who had overcome the French revolution to create a new order.[15] He called him "the ever illuminated, ever clear, ever decisive" and spoke of the "productivity of his deeds."[16] Perhaps his own identification with nature was an equivalent of Napoleon's with destiny. Both were—like Faust—without clearly defined objectives or principles, and Goethe's life bears out Napoleon's comment:

> I would have found it very difficult to assert with any degree of truth what was my whole and real intention.[17]

As Valéry observes:

> Nothing struck (Goethe) more forcibly than the ability of living things to adapt themselves and to assume the forms that are most appropriate to their environment.[18]

He would no doubt have concurred with Napoleon's:

> To absorb, to emit, to form new combinations—this is life.[19]

Many of us would agree. It is the dismissal of the tragic dimension—the cost to human relationships, to the fabric of the community, and to those less gifted and less adaptable—that might give us pause.

With evident approval, Goethe reports a conversation with the Emperor:

> (He) came back to the subject of drama and made very significant remarks, like a man who was observing the tragic stage with the intentness of a criminal judge and who had deeply felt the deviation of the French theater from nature and truth. Thus he was also led to criticize the tragedies of fate. "What do they want from fate in our age?" he said. "Politics is fate."[20]

Hermann Grimm, a literary historian and critic in the age of Bismarck, says admiringly that if Faust and Mephisto were to appear before the *Reichstag*,

> (They) would immediately size up the situation, choose the right moment and with a few penetrating ideas create for themselves an attentive audience.[21]

No doubt—but not, perhaps, what we once expected of poetry or narrative.

As a generalist who turned his gaze on everything under the sun and wrote in almost every literary form, Goethe is alien to the modernist—a specialist in an age of specialization. He may be closer in spirit to postmodernism: inclusive, witty, playful, unconsumed by passion, pursuing pleasure rather than essences, finding meaning at the surface and not in the depths. The striving that most interpreters see as the heart and meaning of *Faust* is more of a verbal thread, an *attempt* at a unifying motif, than a deep, structuring force in a play that effectively *has* no core. Faust meanders rather than strives. As Nietzsche, who admired both Goethe and the play, suggests:

> The world liberator Faust finally becomes just a world traveler.[22]

Valéry notes that

> Goethe is the great apologist of the world of appearances.[23]

He certainly was not, in any deeper sense, inward:

> What man observes and feels inside himself seems to me to constitute the least important part of his life. At such times he is much more aware of what he lacks than of what he possesses.[24]

To discover that he *lacked* anything, or fell short, was not part of his program. Yet despite his claimed lack of interest in the inner realm, he was not an exacting observer of the world without. His gift was 'romantic': he *inhabited* what he beheld, broke down the barriers between self and other, and became one with 'everything.' Whereas Shakespeare actually seems to have *become* the other, to the point where we can guess at almost nothing about him, Goethe inheres in—and limits—everything he wrote or said. We know *all* about him: he recorded himself continually. His genius, or *daimon*, is that of the personality that unfolds and actualizes every potentiality in its own being:

To be a personality implies the highest happiness on earth. Every destiny can be endured, if you do not miss yourself; one may lose everything, if one only remains what he is.[25]

His response to the doubt and anxiety that assailed his great contemporaries was a confident assertion of himself.

DICKENS AND *BLEAK HOUSE*

Unlike Goethe, Dickens was an *avowed* Positivist both in his conduct and his extensive nonfiction writing. He believed absolutely in the efficacy of the will, in our ability to get things done, and in progress. He worked ceaselessly to improve the lot of the exploited, and may, as Daniel Webster said, have done

> more to ameliorate the condition of the English poor than all the statesmen Britain has sent into Parliament.

During the ten years he published *Household Words*, there was "a continuous stream of articles on science and invention";[26] and though his fiction, like melodrama, often looked to a bygone day, he had no illusions about the past:

> He . . . derived considerable amusement from inventing titles for dummy volumes of books in his London home. Among them were "History of a Short Chancery Suit," 21 vols., and "The Wisdom of Our Ancestors," of which the successive volumes were labelled: "I. Ignorance. II. Superstition. III. The Block. IV. The Stake. V. The Rack. VI. Dirt. VII. Disease." Alongside this bulky work was "The Virtues of Our Ancestors," a single volume so narrow that the title had to be printed sideways.[27]

He worked like one possessed and clearly believed that he was in charge of his own fate. After a childhood of deprivation, his success, wealth, and influence seemed vivid proof that human beings can change their circumstances. Like many an artist, he exercised power not only over but *through* his work. His private and public readings were enthralling performances to which he himself became addicted. In the last twelve years of his life he gave nearly 450 public readings in Britain and the United States—surely because they allowed him to experience the effect he had on an audience even more directly than did the stage versions of his novels. Here he was totally in charge—both author and actor:

If you had seen Macready last night, undisguisedly sobbing, and crying on the sofa as I read, you would have felt, as I did, what a thing it is to have power.[28]

He particularly relished terrifying audiences with his rendition of Nancy's murder by Sikes:

There was a fixed expression of horror of me, all over the theatre, which could not have been surpassed if I had been going to be hanged. . . . It is quite a new sensation to be execrated with that unanimity; and I hope it will remain so![29]

But despite his Positivist orientation, Dickens predicated the structure of his fictions on circumstance and Providence—or its agent, coincidence— and assigned but the smallest role to the human will. The figures in his novels are usually helpless and appear to render the very aspect of his experience that his *life* strenuously denied—though his prodigious energy, discipline, and constant activity may have had their origin in a deep, pervasive sense of fatality.

In his stories, he returns again and again to a childhood that made him—as it makes many artists—kin to all who are threatened with extinction: the abandoned, exploited, and poor. As a comic writer, moreover, he worked in a tradition in which the notion of human freedom has ever had limited play. And as a popular storyteller with an affinity for melodrama he was never far from the fairy tale, with its passive hero or heroine.

At the center of a Dickens novel there is usually a young person who suffers a series of hardships for which he or she is in no way responsible. His stories often begin with an abandoned child:

As Oliver gave this first proof of the free and proper action of his lungs, the patchwork coverlet which was carelessly flung over the iron bedstead, rustled; the pale face of a young woman was raised feebly from the pillow, and a faint voice articulated the words, "Let me see the child, and die."[30]

David Copperfield's father died before he was born and though his mother lives until he is ten, her marriage to Murdstone effectively orphans him. In the first sentence of *Great Expectations*, the hero reports the facts of his abandonment with a startling absence of feeling:

As I never saw my father or my mother, and never saw any likeness of either of them . . . my first fancies regarding what they were like, were unreasonably derived from their tombstones.[31]

Since the events and happy endings in Dickens are brought about not by the figures themselves but by Providence—or by the author, assuming its mantle—perhaps his enormous appeal to the English and American middle class lay in his rendering of the *shadow* side of Positivism, which his readers could not acknowledge. But while the Positivism that sustained Dickens in daily life fails to assert itself *within* his narratives, it is clearly evident in his willingness to manipulate their plots: he enjoys playing fate and doesn't hesitate, in *Nicholas Nickleby* and *Little Dorrit*, to subject the action to his wishes.

Bleak House is the exception. Here fate is pervasive and all-powerful. One might have to go to Racine—or, indeed, Greek tragedy—for a narrative as nakedly determined by outside forces. In *Bleak House,* they take the form of the chancery suit, a web in which the figures are caught at birth or early in life and can neither escape nor understand. The law—like the Golem or Frankenstein's monster—may have begun as the creation of man but has long acquired an inexorable force of its own. Yet the novel is not really about chancery or the social system that produced it, for the action is entirely and explicitly determined by coincidence. Everyone in *Bleak House* is connected to everyone else by an invisible web, and even those who never meet turn out to be part of the same mysterious design.

John Forster, a close friend of Dickens and his first biographer, says:

> On the coincidences, resemblances, and surprises of life, Dickens liked especially to dwell, and few things moved his fancy so pleasantly. The world, he would say, was so much smaller than we thought it; we were all so connected by fate without knowing it; people supposed to be far apart were so constantly elbowing each other; and tomorrow bore so close a resemblance to nothing half so much as to yesterday.[32]

In *Nicholas Nickleby,* the profusion of coincidences is a mere convenience to the storyteller. Dickens *uses* them. Significantly, in this early work, he looks back not to the fairy tale but to eighteenth-century picaresque, which he infuses with elements of melodrama. The story begins with the attempted seduction of a poor, virtuous maiden by an uncouth aristocrat, and centers on a headstrong but noble-hearted young man who bests the scheming villain. In *Great Expectations* and *David Copperfield* coincidences are less important to the narrative, yet continue to be used rather than 'served.' Dickens says of *Little Dorrit*:

> It struck me that it would be a new thing to show people coming together in a chance way, as fellow-travelers, and being in the same place ignorant of one

another, as happens in life; and to connect them afterwards, and to make the waiting for that connection a part of the interest.[33]

But even in *Little Dorrit*, "chance" and "connection" are manipulated by the author, and not until *Bleak House* is coincidence free of his contriving will. Here the narrative seems to have been 'dictated' to him by his experience of childhood helplessness—to which he lends himself unreservedly and recreates in the beholden lives of his figures.

Bleak House is almost free of the melodramatic incidents that occur at critical points in the other novels. The author of melodrama often pays lip service to the role of fate or Providence even if he no longer believes in them: he purveys what his audience came to see, but fails to give it substance and credibility. In *Bleak House*, fate is a palpable presence. Though the novel has been called an indictment of industrial England, the figures at the apex of the economic system are as helpless as everyone else, and the lone captain of industry is rendered as upstanding and wholly sympathetic. Even the villain, Tulkinghorn, is curiously passive and incapable of achieving his ends. Unlike Blandois in *Little Dorrit*—whose death ends the threat and therewith the narrative—Tulkinghorn dies well before the conclusion, murdered by a woman who is not primarily concerned with killing him. The only effective action permitted the figures are small acts of kindness. They can do little more than light a candle against the dark. Their circumstances shift but their characters are fixed, and none undergo the rather predictable changes that mark the development, or *Bildung*, of David Copperfield and Pip.

In *Nicholas Nickleby*, Dickens says:

But now, when he thought how regularly things went on, from day to day, in the same unvarying round; how youth and beauty died, and ugly griping age lived tottering on; how crafty avarice grew rich, and manly honest hearts were poor and sad; how few they were who tenanted the stately houses, and how many those who lay in noisome pens, or rose each day and laid them down each night, and lived and died, father and son, mother and child, race upon race, generation upon generation, without a home to shelter them or the energies of one single man directed to their aid; how, in seeking not a luxurious and splendid life, but the bare means of a most wretched and inadequate subsistence, there were women and children in that one town, divided into classes, numbered and estimated as regularly as the noble families and folks of great degree and reared from infancy to drive most criminal and dreadful trades; how ignorance was punished and never taught; how jail-doors gaped and gallows loomed, for thousands urged towards them by circumstances darkly curtaining their very cradles' heads, and but for which they might have earned their honest bread and lived in peace; how many died in soul and had no chance of life; how many who could scarcely go astray, be they vicious as they would, turned haughtily from the crushed and stricken wretch who could scarce do otherwise, and who would have been a great wonder had he or she done well, than even they had they done ill; how much injustice, misery, and wrong there was, and yet how the world rolled on, from year to year, alike careless and indifferent, and no man seeking to remedy or redress it; when he thought of all this and selected from the mass the one slight case on which his thoughts were bent, he felt, indeed, that there was little ground for hope, and little reason why it should not form an atom in the huge aggregate of distress and sorrow, and one small and unimportant unit to swell the great amount.[34]

The vision conjured up here was not to be fully realized until *Bleak House,* for in *Nicholas Nickleby* Dickens was still preoccupied with the part that the individual might play in determining his or her life. Economic and social conditions are clearly secondary, with no persuasive link between them and the personal narrative.

Nicholas Nickleby ends happily, and in *Bleak House* too the *personal* story, Esther's, finds a happy resolution. The family—perhaps the oldest source of human consolation—is reconstituted, as it is in most fairy tales and comedies; indeed, even *Oedipus Rex* can be thought of as a family reunion: its plot, like many a comedy, depends on mistaken identities, and under the surface of discrepant appearances there is a secret link, an unexpected connection. In Dickens, happiness can be found *only* at the hearth—where he himself was unable to find it. Though we owe the happy ending of *Great Expectations* to a suggestion by Bulwer-Lytton, it seems perfectly in keeping with his own longings and convictions:

> I took her hand in mine, and we went out of the ruined place; and, as the morning mists had risen long ago when I first left the forge, so the evening mists were rising now, and in all the broad expanse of tranquil light they showed to me, I saw no shadow of another parting from her.[35]

At the end of *Nicholas Nickleby,* the circle of light around the central figures seems to dispel the darkness, but in *Bleak House* the resolution of Esther's story in no way redeems the vast majority of lives that have been cut short, or drag on without hope. The light enveloping Esther and her family is the one bright spot in a dark landscape. It does not, as in his sentimental work, transfigure reality—just as *Hansel and Gretel* reunites the children with their widowed father *without* letting us forget that their parents tried to kill them. The happy ending of Esther's story is not unrealistic, for there are always a few who escape—especially, as Dickens knew well, when there is enough money to shelter them.

Though all of his plots are informed by the past, *Bleak House* is entirely foreclosed by it. It conditions and preoccupies everyone. The illegitimate birth of Esther to Lady Dedlock is not only the foundation of the narrative and the secret that endows Tulkinghorn with his power, but it also ties most of the figures into the central story. The novel is presented in riddle form and many incidents can be understood only in retrospect; when we first read about them, they puzzle and confuse us. Like movies today, but unlike other nineteenth-century narratives, the story begins by cutting from scene to scene and from person to person without making connections, without explaining the jumps. We have to *assume* the coherence of the early chapters and must guess how the pieces fit together. Why is Esther removed from Greenleaf? Who are her parents and what is Lady Dedlock's secret? The questions multiply and the solution of one only gives rise to another.

A secretive, riddling plot is, of course, well-suited to serial publication with its need for suspense. But it also constitutes the point of view of a child—for whom everything is mysterious, confusing, and frightening—and renders the incomprehensibility of the law, guarded like a sacred rite by those who make their living from it. It approximates, moreover, the fragmented, 'meaningless' surfaces of urban life—through which we move confidently only because we are deaf and blind; we are spared anxiety and confusion by hand-me-down assumptions that, in fact, seldom apply. Like the Talmud student who ran out of the Yeshiva yelling: "I've got a most marvelous answer—will someone please tell me the question!", we are so prepared with answers that we don't actually *hear* the questions. We cannot *afford* to become aware of the uncertainties and ambiguities that present themselves wherever we turn. Only children and those who, like Dickens, have maintained their relationship to childhood, remain in the continuous state of surprise or shock that may be the most appropriate, if not the most comfortable, response to our situation.

As long as we knew our place in the scheme of things, the answer to the central narrative riddle or secret could be *known* to the audience, as in *Oedipus Rex*. But once the old explanations became invalid, the secret had to be hidden not only from the figures but from us; the *known* plot became a plot of discovery. Though the structure of *Bleak House* is as precluded as *Oedipus Rex*, the *reader* is often as puzzled by the events as the figures who are caught up in them.

A plot of discovery suits our Positivist orientation, for as we move through the narrative we keep changing our view of the events and are allowed to believe that the figures, too, are moving and changing. But of course they remained as fixed as the figures in a painting, and the 'action' is entirely in *us*.

We have noted that in *Bleak House* Dickens plays with an open hand. Except for the scene with Detective Bucket, he doesn't deliberately mislead us, and there are no figures whose perception of reality we are asked to share entirely: we always know and see a little more than they, for we see *them*. This is clearest, of course, when they are comic or absurd. But our detachment throughout is made *absolute* by the 'impersonal' narrative that alternates with Esther's account and gives us, quite literally, a double perspective on the events unique not only in Dickens but, in this particular form, without precedent in Western fiction.

Esther's story conforms to a journey of discovery but the 'impersonal' narration, despite its use of the present tense, hints from the start at a truth that the figures themselves have yet to discover. It effectively sets Esther's account, which unfolds in *time*, into a *spatial* context, and offers us the same perspective that the known myth granted to audiences of *Oedipus Rex*. While Esther's narrative engages us empathetically, the 'impersonal' account—by enlarging the context and conveying a sense of inevitability—stops us from losing ourselves in the feelings of individual figures, and abrogates the sentimentality that undermines the structures of other Dickens novels.

Whereas in *Oliver Twist* and *David Copperfield* Dickens assumes the point of view of his central character, in *Bleak House* he identifies with no one, yet is passionately, subjectively engaged. The 'impersonal' narrative is far from impersonal: it engenders a sense of urgency and immediacy that involves us more deeply than the calm, reflective voice of Esther. It is full of contradictions—at once pitying and scathing, brutal and tender, Christian and pagan. Its source is surely the very core of Dickens, where rage and violence burned under a layer of ice.[36]

His rage in *Bleak House* is directed not just at human cruelty or the injustice and indifference of society, but at the very scheme of things, at the ultimate, inaccessible powers. There is a note of despair in his voice. It is, like the narrative itself, haunted by death. As Carlyle says:

(Under his) sparkling, clear, and sunny utterance, (beneath his) bright and joyful sympathy with everything around him, (there were) deeper than all, if one has the eye to see deep enough, dark, fateful, silent elements, tragical to look upon, and hidden amid dazzling radiances as of the sun, the elements of death itself.[37]

Esther's voice is that of the trusting Christian. For her, God is still in his heaven:

> I opened my grateful heart to Heaven in thankfulness for its Providence to me and its care of me, and fell asleep.[38]

But Esther's faith is not imposed on us, for she is safely sheltered from the larger world of the novel, where a loving, just and personal God is notably absent. We can accept her passivity and forbearance more easily than Little Dorrit's—a girl who stands in the thick of a corrupt world but remains unblemished, and emerges rich and happy to boot. Esther's faith does not oblige the novel, while elsewhere Dickens blurs the sharp focus of his vision with unpersuasive professions of faith. We tend to admire his work *despite* the pious middle-class values that resolve them. But in *Bleak House*, as Hillis Miller says:

> The acceptance of the bourgeois Protestant ethical principles of duty, public service, domesticity, responsibility, frugality, thrift, cleanliness, orderliness, and self-discipline is qualified and in a way undermined by the juxtaposition of the two modes of narration.[39]

While much of the scope and power of the novel derive from the impersonal narrative, the *story* Dickens tells—the only story he or anyone *can* tell—is personal. It is Esther who holds together the entire book, though she, like the rest of us, is but a "small and unimportant unit"—of no consequence in "the large amount." The secret of Little Dorrit's fortune fails to cohere the marvelous sprawl of *Little Dorrit*—it is simply a device—and though Smike's abandonment is central to the plot of *Nicholas Nickleby*, the novel marginalizes him. But the hidden connection between Esther and Lady Dedlock underpins *Bleak House* from the start. Here the past is active and not just a storehouse of secrets the author can raid at his convenience. The double narration integrates the personal and the public—Esther and all of London. It permits Dickens to tell a tragic story without depending—as Melville and Dostoevski must—on figures who are larger than the rest of us. Esther's situation is close to our own: *she* is 'ordinary,' yet the *context* is tragic, whereas, traditionally, tragedy was focused on the life of an *extraordinary* individual.

In *Bleak House* perhaps more vividly than elsewhere, Dickens renders the discrepancies and contradictions that charge and vitalize his work. There is an unresolved tension between the often hilarious hyperactivity of the social scene and the helpless passivity and melancholy at the core of the novel.

Yet the figures themselves exhibit few contradictions; they are consistent and altogether predictable. Only Sir Leicester—callous and boring in his public aspect, yet suffering and forgiving in relationship to his wife—is an exception. Adults in Dickens usually have a comic or grotesque dimension—distortions that may originate in the perceptions of a child, who is apt to fasten on a few peculiarities: a way of speaking or walking that 'polite' adults pretend not to notice but that are, for the child, a person's identifying mark. In Dickens even cherished and admired figures are drawn with a few sharp, unambiguous lines that resemble, but never quite become, caricature. Tagging characters with their peculiarities seems altogether 'realistic' in a mercantile and industrial society, in which most people are marked by the one-dimensional roles they have been assigned, and perhaps one reason children in Dickens are *not* usually comical or absurd is that they haven't been twisted out of shape yet.

His figures appear to be drawn from without. Indeed, Dickens fails to render *inner* states, like the maturation of Pip or David Copperfield, with great success. However, the vivid, voluble exteriority of his characters may constitute a crystallization of inner states. No one *talks* like his figures, but we may well *think* and *feel* the way they speak—insistently, repetitiously, obsessively. If the characters seem slightly crazed, so, of course, are we—though we usually know enough to hide our aberrations and obsessions in public, whereas the figures in Dickens never fail to give themselves away. They speak their subtext, disguised as text, and their behavior is consistently animated by impulses the rest of us have learned to camouflage. 'Reality' in Dickens derives—as it does in most stories—from the inner world, which we recognize instantaneously as 'true,' even if we haven't the artist's involuntary and often uncomfortable access to it.

Though a Dickens novel contains a wide range of material information and observed detail, he never loses touch with the subjective component of 'reality.' His physical facts—perhaps because they are so intensively rendered: even the weather is extreme—seem but an exhalation of the inner world, and the descriptions and images are often hallucinatory and expressionist, closer to *Woyzeck* and Kafka than to *Madame Bovary*:

> His neck was so twisted that the knotted ends of his white cravat usually dangled under one ear; his natural acerbity and energy, always contending with a second nature of habitual repression, gave his features a swollen and suffused look; and altogether, he had a weird appearance of having hanged himself at one time or other, and of having gone about ever since, halter and all, exactly as some timely hand had cut him down.[40]

> "My time being rather precious," said Mr. Merdle, suddenly getting up, as if he had been waiting in the interval for his legs and they had just come.[41]

Like Dostoevski—who admired him above all other novelists—he was "a realist in the higher sense of the word." There were occasions when, speaking as a Positivist, he called the inner realm—all that which is not 'fact'— "Fancy." But while "Fancy" in most of his novels is allowed to suffuse the 'facts' with a roseate sentimentality, in *Bleak House* the subjective realm is rendered as objectively as the material world. The feelings are neither made irrelevant by the facts nor allowed to sentimentalize them. Surely all true 'objectivity' *includes* the subjective—just as all true rationality acknowledges and respects the irrational. Maintaining a balance between them is as crucial to traditional storytelling as it is to our existence.

IBSEN AND POSITIVISM

Despite Ibsen's reputation for skepticism and pessimism,[42] the Positivist aspect of his work has often been stressed. Shaw made him a reformer in his own image—"one of the major prophets of the modern Bible," whose "parable of the doll's house is more to our purpose than the parable of the prodigal son"—and proclaimed him the founder of "a frankly doctrinal theatre" of discussion and enlightenment, that "(penetrates) through ideals to the truth."[43] His work was called

> A new religion, under which every human being will obey his or her own laws without being daunted by a sense of guilt, and self-fulfillment shall be deemed as justifiable and meaningful as self-sacrifice.[44]

Though Ibsen deemphasized and often denied his role as a reformer and progressive, he was in fact determined to explore "the more important questions of our time," spoke of his "crusading joy," and said that, unlike Zola, he descended into the sewer not to "bathe" in it but to "cleanse" it.[45] Beginning with *A Doll's House*, his narrative structures are imbued with a scientist's faith in causal connections, and his plots are effectively investigations into the problem presented on stage. The focus of the action is not on *what* happens but *why*, and there is invariably a moment when the keystone is inserted into the arch to perfect our understanding.

Ibsen believed in knowledge: knowledge as mastery and power. His working method consisted of a relentless effort to gather all the facts and to place them in their proper sequence. He always knew far more than he used. Once, late in life, he referred to someone called Eleanora. When a member of his family asked who she was, he said it was Nora, but that neither her father nor Helmer ever used her full name.[46] Most writers would have been glad to include this fact in the play, but to Ibsen and his painstaking process of substantiation, it simply suggested the belittling diminutives that Helmer uses to address his wife.

While his method and the structures it engendered bear the marks of Positivism, the burden of his plays is entirely traditional. Ironically, in his consequential Positivist pursuit, he arrived at narratives in which the figures have no freedom whatever. He had their *dossier* all right; he knew not only what they had done but what they would—or must—do. Since his knowledge was absolute, they were entirely in his grasp and could not make a single unexpected move. While his certainty constituted power for *him,* it revealed his figures in a state of helpless immobilization. The pursuit of Positivism to its logical conclusion carried him to its complementary opposite: determinism.[47]

Perfect knowledge or understanding in the realm of human affairs can be achieved only after an action is completed, and Ibsen's process of teasing out causal sequences propelled his stories relentlessly into the past. In his work—no less than in the case histories of Freud, who held him in high esteem—everything of consequence has already happened. The plays move forward into the past, a past that both explains the present and advances it to its precluded end. His work bears out La Mettrie's *L'homme machine* (1747):

> Why then would it be absurd to think that there are physical causes by reason of which everything has been made, and to which the whole chain of this vast universe is so necessarily bound and held that nothing which happens, could have failed to happen?[48]

In Proust, the recovery of time past *reconstitutes* the self—in Ibsen it nullifies us.

Though *Ghosts* is as precluded as a Greek myth, it invokes no higher powers. Traditional story ultimately 'blames' the unknown—fate, chance, or the gods—but in Ibsen the problem is caused by human failing. Oswald's illness is the fault of his elders: when his mother fled her dissolute husband, Pastor Manders persuaded her to return home. If she had slammed the door on her marriage as Nora did, the disaster could presumably have been averted. We and society make our fate, though, by the time we realize it, it is too late.

Ibsen himself is the god of his plays. Unlike Stendhal, Flaubert, and Dostoevski, he did not find or discover his stories but *built* them. There are no accidents or uncertainties in his work. He believed in his own will, in his ability to *make* his stories, and put no credence or trust in anything beyond it. He defined his task in a short poem:

To live is to fight against
the spook of dark forces within oneself.
To be a poet means to sit
in judgement over one's own self.[49]

His need to maintain control was both deeply personal and characteristic of the society he rendered. The sacred had been reasoned out of existence, but continued to haunt the middle class as a destructive, inhibiting "spook," and his figures, despite their rational, often progressive outlook, are helplessly enthralled to the "dark forces" they no longer believe in.

Like Freud, Ibsen saw our relationship to instinct and the unconscious as a battleground. *Id* and *ego* cannot coexist tranquilly and the price of being human is our unhappiness, our *Unbehagen*. The two men shared a ruthless devotion to the truth and a disregard for the personal consequences of revealing it. One might say that Freud's work had its inception in the very conditions Ibsen describes. It lays bare the natural or sacred forces that haunt so many of Ibsen's figures, despite their attempt to deny them.

His realist plays were a reaction against the romantic theatre and its disregard for actuality. Nineteenth-century playwrights—with exceptions like Kleist and Büchner—followed the example of Schiller and used freely invented plots as vehicles for their feelings, ideas, and ideals.[50] The stage was a platform for declaiming poetry—much of it bombast—while economic, social, and historical facts were subordinated to the inner, subjective realm. What Lenz said, critically, of classical French drama is truer by far of Schiller: he rendered "not a portrait of nature but a likeness of the author's soul".[51] But whereas in Racine the soul is subject to compelling forces—which we, today, would call forces of nature or the unconscious—in Schiller the soul is free.

In response to the unimpeded flow of subjectivity on the romantic stage, feelings in Ibsen are given short shrift—not just by the figures, but by the playwright himself. He once said that three things meant nothing to him: flowers, music, and children. All are directly linked to our feelings and senses, which his plays repress, no doubt because they might give us access to the "dark forces" or passions that assert themselves in Racine with tragic consequences. Ibsen's realist plays present a tight, factual surface that inhibits the direct expression of subjective or inner reality. He said of his own process:

At the time of conception one must be on fire, but at the time of writing, cold.[52]

All passionate and sensory life is repressed. The men are so wholly identified with their social and vocational roles that they become predictable and even comic. The crucial event is often the strangling of a woman's passion, of her joy in life. Yet despite his open condemnation of what he calls "soul murder," we are not persuaded that Ibsen actually believed in the soul or put any stock in joy. His plays indict civilization and men for the crimes they commit against nature, woman, and feeling, yet are themselves guilty of the same violations. Their very form and texture embody the middle-class life they condemn *as* restrictive and stifling.

No doubt there is a control freak in most artists, but in Ibsen's middle and late period the spontaneous and unpredictable have been totally eliminated. Everything is functional and meaningful. There are no loose ends and, since there is little sensory impact, few surprises that are not derived from the narrative line. More successfully than society itself, his plays inhibit action, sudden moves, and raised voices. When Hedda Gabler shoots herself, Brack exclaims: "But one doesn't *do* things like that!" Though we may laugh and, like the playwright, think Brack absurd, the plays *embody* Brack's judgement: the forbidden is no longer admissable even in the safe arena of art.

The flow of time in Ibsen appears to be objective. His realist narratives are constrained into three, four, or at most five acts, each representing a half-hour of real time. This required heroic effort, a joiner's work of meticulous dovetailing—as against the ease with which Shakespeare could accommodate his stories in thirty or more scenes. Ibsen told William Archer:

> It is much easier to write a piece like *Brand* or *Peer Gynt*, in which you can bring a little of everything, than to carry through a severely logical scheme, like that of *John Gabriel Borkman*.[53]

The dialogue in the realist plays is restricted to the prose of ordinary speech, while verse affords Shakespeare not only the freedom to develop his figures and their relationships rapidly but admits the subjective. Strindberg says of *Richard III:*

> In the first act, the widow walks beside the body of the murdered Edward IV. Stop! Richard woos her and after eight pages the murderer has just about obtained a Yes. This is done so masterfully that it seems credible. . . . Yet today a French author would have used all five acts to get the widow to the point where she could give the murderer her consent. . . . Two different approaches—both equally valid![54]

The narrative of *Ghosts* is far less complex than *Bleak House*, but since its tight three-act structure permits only two breaks in the flow of 'real' time, human process is not always respected. At the end of the play, Oswald makes his mother promise to give him an overdose of morphine should his illness recur, and almost as soon as she agrees he has an ominous seizure. *Bleak House* seems lifelike because its plot—itself an analogue of process rather than a construct—is embedded in a profusion of textured incidents and involves a large cast of characters. But in Ibsen *everything* is plot. His realist plays are focused on a small group and confined not only in time but place. Despite their double-stranded storylines, they are entirely purposeful and devoid of digressions. As a consequential nineteenth-century material-ist, he could not allow chance or the unknown a role in his narratives and even the subjective life of his figures, which might have permitted the natural or sacred to assert itself, is under his rigid control.

His determination to get all the facts was at once a distinguishing mark of his plays and their limitation. For though, as Courbet says, art must strive to be "the most complete expression of an existing thing,"[55] any *absolute* rendering is unpersuasive. Courbet's own work displays an exacting respect for the 'reality' of the object, yet the known in his paintings always shades into the unknown, just as the world of *Bleak House* is both substan-tive *and* uncertain. Leonardo's *'sfumato* suggests all that which lies beyond our grasp—the image persuades in part *because* it is incomplete[56] —while Ibsen's very certainty limits him. We cannot say of his figures what Thi-baudet says of Proust's:

> A portrait by Proust, even Swann's, extending over hundreds of pages, never leaves the impression, in all its wealth of substance and diversity, that it has exhausted the character's capacity to take an unexpected turn and spring a surprise.[57]

Ibsen was deeply aware of the restrictions limiting his work. When, in 1891, the young Hamsun attacked him in a series of lectures—for among other things, "the inherent stiffness and poverty of his emotional life"— Ibsen sat prominently in the front row on at least one occasion.[58] In 1895, he bought a large portrait of Strindberg and hung it in his study, so that "that mad-man," staring down at him with his "demonic eyes," could help him work. "He is my mortal enemy, and shall hang there and watch while I write."[59]

Hamsun and Strindberg openly expressed what Ibsen sat in judgement over and repressed. In his last plays, he himself made an effort to reach what Kafka called "the frozen sea within."[60] But instead of actualizing his feelings on stage, all he could do was render them symbolically. Only the *absence* of feeling seems persuasive in *When We Dead Awaken*. He abandoned the material world of his realist plays for what Maeterlinck called "the atmosphere of the soul"—moving directly from 'object' to 'subject' without finding the balance between them that Flaubert achieved in *Madame Bovary*. The action is set entirely within; there is no conflict between self and other; and, as in the romantic theater, the sole reality is subjective.

Though Ibsen had no respect for Schiller's work with its disregard for fact,[61] the subjective realm asserts itself in his own plays and often determines their outcome. Figures like Rosmer and Rebecca West are not constrained by economic or social forces but by something *within* them. While Ibsen seems to suggest that we can exorcise the "spook" of "dark forces," it may have been his task to rediscover, in the context of late-nineteenth-century individualism, that we are anything but free. His figures are not in charge of their own actions or reactions. They are both isolated *and* bound. Their private lives are not private and their most intimate relationships are governed by external forces that have been introjected. It is almost as if he had set out to prove—by dint of his own fierce and relentless will—that the will is of no consequence. His work makes a hash of Schiller's Enlightenment faith in human freedom.

Like many of his contemporaries, Schiller believed that the human being "originates his own situation" and that our will is free.[62] This led to his basic misunderstanding of traditional narrative.[63] As he sees it, the purpose of tragedy is to move and elevate us through the suffering of the central figure.[64] He makes no mention of the situation that—in traditional story—*causes* the suffering and permits us to put ourselves in the hero's or heroine's place.[65] Significantly, even suffering in Schiller is subordinate to his ultimate agenda:

> The tragic poet is allowed to push . . . suffering to great length, as long as it does not lead to the suppression of *moral freedom*.[66]

His theater is a "moral institution" and serves an ideal vision of human life, which it at once depicts *and* helps us achieve—presumably by proving that it is within the realm of the possible. Unfortunately, his effort to raise the human being to a higher level—the *Veredlung* or ennobling of the species—often obliged him to shortchange facts.[67]

Though Schiller's ideals have, in Ibsen's work, turned into "spooks," they retain enough force to crush his figures. The high ethical standards of Rosmer "ennoble" Rebecca but rob her of energy, joy, sensuality, and finally of life. Like Schiller, Ibsen emphasized the will—albeit his own, rather than that of his characters—and he too was deeply suspicious of the senses.[68] Yet Shaw's statement that Ibsen's "prophetic belief in the spontaneous growth of the will made him a meliorist"[69] is wishful thinking. He reendowed the theatre with the sense of inevitability that is the basis of Greek tragedy. Nora's newly gained awareness may enable her to change her life, but in *Ghosts,* and in all of the plays after *An Enemy of the People,* the knowledge that comes to the figures comes too late. They end up like Oedipus, knowing what they have done, or failed to do, but are unable to act constructively in the present. The only action open to Rosmer, Rebecca, Hedda, Solness, Hedvig, Irene, and Rubek is suicide.

Their inability to act does not in any way reflect the middle-class society, which the plays purport to render. Unlike the enervated, backward-looking leisure class of prerevolutionary Russia on which Chekhov modeled his figures, the bourgeoisie of nineteenth-century Europe was neither despairing nor incapable of action. Ibsen may have overcome his own sense of impotence by subjecting his stories to his relentless will, but it leached back into the plays and robbed his figures of energy. He discovered *their* lack of freedom, but failed to turn his insight back on himself, or he might have been less insistent on his own control. He had nothing to oppose to Positivism but Positivism—and so effectively demolished it from within, undermining the structure of his own plays in the process.

One might well wonder why nineteenth-century audiences and readers were drawn to stories determined by circumstance—inner in Ibsen and *Madame Bovary* and external, or apparently external, in Zola—unless they gave expression to a sense of helplessness that could not be acknowledged.

Zola was an activist with a firm belief in change and progress, yet many of his figures are enthralled not just to their economic and social condition but to their biological past. He says of *L'Assommoir:*

> My novel is simple enough. It relates the downfall of a working-class family ruined by its environs; the husband drinks, the wife loses courage, shame and death are the result.[70]

But it is family heritage and not the "environs" that causes their downfall. The twenty novels chronicling the Rougon-Macquarts are linked by heredity, which functions like the family curse in myth. Jacques Lantier is *born* a psychopath who cannot help what he does, and Flaubert was right to say that "Nana turns into myth without ceasing to be real." She does not understand the role she plays in Paris society and the power she exerts is not her own:

> She became a force of nature, a ferment of destruction, without wishing to be, corrupting and disorganizing Paris within her snowy thighs.

313

Despite Zola's faith in progress, his commitment to materialism and his ceaseless, courageous activity on behalf of reform, his figures are doomed and his novels, like the late plays of Ibsen, are structured by a subjectivity that—perhaps because it *isn't* acknowledged—seems to be at cross purposes rather than to coexist with his carefully researched facts. He wanted *Thérèse Raquin* to be truly scientific—a story of human animals without souls:

> I chose to portray individuals existing under the sovereign dominion of their nerves and their blood, devoid of free will and drawn into every act of their lives by the inescapable promptings of their flesh. Thérèse and Laurent are human beasts, nothing more.[71]

Yet after they kill her husband, Thérèse and her lover are haunted and destroyed by something an earlier age would have called their conscience. The novel itself undermines Zola's stated intentions. In *Thérèse Raquin*, as in Ibsen, consciousness brings with it a sense of guilt that vitiates the very pleasure that drove the "beasts" to murder.

Ibsen's plays are not frequently performed or even read today, yet his influence is very much with us. In the classical and romantic theater we are privy to the thoughts and feelings of the figures. They keep secrets from each other and themselves but hardly ever from us. In Ibsen, however, surfaces *imply* rather than reveal, and we are asked to ferret out the sub-text—what the figures really want and feel, which is not often what they say. This continues to be true for much of the dialogue in film and television, no doubt because it mirrors our experience. When communities were small and stable we knew not only each other but each other's parents and grandparents, while today we interact with hundreds of people we barely know and must make our way by rapidly reading implications. The 'truth' is seldom spelled out for us; we have to deduce it from clues and watch for small hints and signs, intended or unintended. We note and interpret inflections, intonations and slight movements of the face and body, and must be expert in the very processes of perception that Ibsen pioneered on stage.

Though many films and most teleplays are extensions of Ibsen's theater, they go well beyond the *théâtre intime*. The camera moves us from the fixed vantage point of our seats into the midst of the action and penetrates the private space of the figures. Close-ups reveal what is going on within them, just as the microphone spares performers the need to project in order to be heard in the last row, and picks up nuances that undermine or complicate the manifest text. Film has both greater physical scope than the classical stage and greater intimacy than the chamber play. By vividly rendering movement and texture, it engages our senses as directly as the theater that employed verse rather than prose. It gives us access to the entire visible, audible world—to water and rocks, wetness and cragginess—and moves, like Shakespeare's poetry, from one setting and moment to another in a split second. But its freedom—the very ease with which it meets our need to be kept busy and entertained—often makes for shoddy work, and one finds oneself wishing that film makers would adopt not only Ibsen's use of symptomatic dialogue and subtext, but his rejection of cheap effects. A measure of his self-critical vigilance would give our movies greater substance and credibility.

BRECHT

The playwrights who succeeded Ibsen felt as restricted by realism as he did himself at the end of his life. But while Chekhov, Pirandello, and Strindberg's naturalistic plays opened up the stage to the inner, subjective world without violating the surfaces of everyday life, it was the Expressionists and Brecht who broke most decisively with Ibsen's "psychological theatre."[72]

Brecht abandoned the tight, confining plot of the realistic play and evolved a looser, "epic" narrative. He found his stories in mythology, history, and the classics, ranged the world for his settings, included music and song, ignored the traditional separation between drama and vaudeville, and turned the composition of his plays into a collaborative process that militated against a self-oriented, inward perspective. He was not interested in isolated figures—whose central problem *is* their isolation—but placed them explicitly in the social, economic, and historical context that Ibsen's middle class had internalized as psychology. His stage is open, the walls are down, and his characters are up against dire necessity: their lives are at stake, they are brutally oppressed and, in turn, often oppress those who are weaker.

Marxism helped Brecht survive a dark time and gave his work a theoretical foundation. He opposed to the "dramatic" or Aristotelian play—which depicts human beings as changeless, engages the spectator's feelings, and undermines our faith in action—an "epic" theater, which was to make the spectator an observer, render us capable of change, and urge us to act.[73] It has often been noted, however, that Brecht's "theatre for a scientific age"—in which our enhanced understanding is to replace the cathartic process—remains, for the most part, theory. Despite his attempt to depict Mother Courage as wrong and, indeed, villainous, she arouses the very empathy and identification he scorned as "laxatives of the soul."[74] His plays are graphically situational. Most are set in the past and subject the figures to forces that leave them no alternatives. We may recognize, intellectually, that they are 'wrong' and should do otherwise, but as fellow human beings we know we would do the same. They may seem freer to act than Ibsen's figures, yet what they do is of little avail. Like the poor everywhere, they have no personal past and are trapped by historical circumstance—just like Rosmer and Mrs. Alwing.

Brecht's approach is profoundly contradictory. His intention was to abstract but his motto reads: "The truth is concrete," and the incidents and language of his plays, as well as his own productions of them, stress the physical and particular—the very detail Marx scorns as catering to the bourgeoisie. In his later work, the music of Eisler and Dessau was to interrupt and comment on the action but adds, instead, a dimension of strong feeling—just as in *Die Dreigroschenoper* and *Mahagonny* Weill's melodic score both supports and counterpoints Brecht's cool, ironic text.

As a Marxist, Brecht no doubt believed that the duality of his figures[75]— from the Good Woman of Setzuan, who is both good and evil, to Mother Courage, of whom he said: "She renders the opposites in all their abruptness and irreconcilability"[76]—would be redeemed by the overthrow of the old order. But though his plays consistently blame our social and economic structures, they inspire no confidence that the contradictions can be resolved. His work is imbued with a powerful sense of human suffering and helplessness, and under the vivid, vital surface runs a current of deep melancholy. As Esslin says, "Play after play depicts the horrors of the world *before* the revolution."[77] His Marxism was the tragic socialism of the 1930s, and his aesthetic has little in common with the Positivist premise and promise of Socialist Realism. If he had really believed that the stage can move an audience to action, he might have made common cause with his friend Piscator, who wanted his theater "to intervene in life as a moving force."[78] At heart, perhaps, Brecht had no faith in power and action of *any* kind, and was too much of a realist to believe that what we plan and do will have the intended results. Even *The Measure Taken*, which deals with Communists in action, is dark and ambiguous in its implication.

Marxism gave him hope—*das Prinzip Hoffnung*, as Bloch called it—and the conviction that the playwright, like the philosopher, is no longer confined to merely describing the world. But since his figures are as fixed and unchanging as those of Molière, the only change he can hope to produce is in *us*. To this end he stressed the *Verfremdungseffekt*—even spelling out the 'meaning' of a scene above the stage to make sure we would leave the theater with our understanding enhanced. Bacon's "Knowledge is power" is transformed into the rather more modest hope that a shift in the awareness of a working-class audience will lead it to political action.

Yet, even in East Berlin, Brecht's audience was largely middle class and his influence was most deeply felt by those who responded to the ambiguity and contradictions in his work. Though the legend above the stage is unequivocal, the action *on* stage countermands it—transmitting exactly the either-*and*-or paradoxes Barthes abhors. The plays undermine all instructional, Positivist purposes. They may bring us closer to others and ourselves, but hardly prompt us to act.

The importance of *Verfremdung*—which informed every aspect of his *practice* long before it appeared in his theories—could be attributed to its central, potentiating impact on his life. It allowed him to believe he was liberating the audience and himself from the passivity to which traditional narrative condemns its figures. Yet, surprisingly, Marxism with its Positivist premise enabled him to tell *traditional* stories. Brecht's *Verfremdung* is a form of irony and combines with a strong empathetic thrust in his work to produce the double perspective of classical narrative—just as his insistence on the "fable," which he calls "the heartpiece of the theatrical occasion,"[79] is equivalent to Aristotle's emphasis on plot.

In practice, though not in theory, Brecht stands far closer to Kafka and Rilke—whose work he firmly rejected—than to the committed political theater. He succeeds as an artist precisely because he failed in his political objectives, and failed in his political objectives because he succeeds as an artist.

Kant refers to the "purposeless purposiveness" of art.[80] It has no ascertainable agenda and we can say of it only that, in a nonspecific way, it serves and preserves the species. It is certainly not functional and may be ultimately committed to pleasure—pleasure in the deepest sense: it relieves our fear and pain, consoles, reconciles, and makes us briefly whole. At the end of his life, Brecht called the theater the "realm of the pleasurable."

CHAPTER

22

Henry James, Postmodernist

When Henry James was on a tour of the Rockefeller Institute, he met a scientist many years his junior. "How magnificent!" he said. "To be young and have divine powers!" But though James was no Positivist, elements in his fiction depart as radically from traditional narrative as Positivist story.

Classical irony reveals the 'real' under the apparent, and derives from the discrepancy between what *we* know and what the figures believe. James, however, defines "operative irony" very differently:

> (It) implies and projects the possible other case, the case rich and edifying where the actuality is pretentious and vain.[1]

In traditional fiction what *is* ironizes what is *not*. But in the novels of James's "major phase," what is *not* ironizes what *is*. Milly Theale's purity— "the possible other case"—not only casts an 'ironic' light on the machination of the others but actually *redeems* them. Her story goes well beyond the fairy tale. In James, the innocence and generous spirit of Snow White— "the case rich and edifying"—changes the heart of the wicked stepmother.

His inversion of traditional irony may derive from his conviction that "art is nothing if not exemplary":[2]

> When it's not a campaign, of a sort, on behalf of something better (better than the obnoxious, the provoking object) that blessedly, as it is assumed, *might* be, it's not worth speaking of.

> How can one consent to make a picture of the preponderant futilities and vulgarities and miseries of life without the impulse to exhibit as well from time to time, in its place, some fine example of the reaction, the opposition or the escape?[3]

319

We are not far from Schiller's *Veredlung*—the "ennobling" of humankind. The artist's task is to render the world as it *might* be, and inadequate, short-lived fictions are those that fail to foster our belief in something better than "vain and pretentious actuality":

> The bad is swept away with all the daubed canvases and spoiled marble into some unvisited limbo, or infinite rubbish-yard beneath the back-windows of the world, and the good subsists and emits its light and stimulates our desire for perfection.[4]

Since the "object" is "obnoxious" and "provoking" until it is purified by art, James was critical of everything that undermines the artist's control. He thought the novels of Tolstoy and Dostoevski flawed—"large baggy monsters with . . . queer elements of the accidental and arbitrary"—whereas his own work resembles well-made plays. Lubbock speaks of his "well-made fictions" and opposes to them books like *War and Peace* which, despite its fine qualities, "has no centre" and lacks "comeliness of form."[5] Since the events in it are determined by the "accidental" and *force majeure*, it constitutes the antithesis of the *pièce bien faite*. Like the detective story, which evolved during the same period, the well-made play was crafted to manipulate an audience. "*A moi, Scribe; à moi, Sardou,*" James exclaimed in his notebook, even if it was the more refined theater of Jones, Pinero, and Ibsen that served as his immediate model.[6]

The influence of Ibsen is evident not only in James's own plays but in the novels of "the major phase." Though he found *Ghosts* "shocking" and *Rosmersholm* "dreary,"[7] he came to praise

> (Ibsen's) admirable talent for producing an intensity of interest by means incorruptibly quiet, by that almost demure preservation of the appearance of the usual in which we see him juggle with difficulty and danger. . . . His recurrent ugliness of surface as it were, is a sort of proof of his fidelity to the real, in a spare, strenuous, democratic community.[8]

Despite his own failed venture into the theater, James was deeply persuaded that the structure of a sound narrative, on the page no less than on stage, is the painstaking work of a master builder or joiner:

> The fine thing in a real drama, generally speaking, is that more than any other work of literary art, it needs a masterly structure. It needs to be shaped and fashioned and laid together, and this process makes a demand upon an artist's rarest gifts. He must combine and arrange, interpolate and eliminate, play the joiner with the most attentive skill. . . . The five-act drama—serious or hu-

morous, poetic or prosaic—is like a box of fixed dimensions and inelastic material, into which a mass of precious things are to be packed away. It is a problem in ingenuity and a problem of the most interesting kind.[9]

In his notebooks, he consoled himself for the five years he spent writing unsuccessful plays, for they taught him *"the singular value for a narrative plan . . . of the . . . divine principle of the scenario"*—an outline that pins down the action scene by scene.[10] Control was for him the heart of the exercise, and he subscribed wholeheartedly to the premise that art makes order out of chaos. "The high honor of the painter's life (is) always to *make* a sense," even when "the cluster of appearances can *have* no sense":

The last thing decently permitted him is to recognize incoherence—to recognize it, that is, as baffling.[11]

He described how Turgenev, whom he greatly admired, arrived at his narratives:

The first form in which a tale appeared to him was as the figure of an individual, or a combination of individuals, whom he wished to see in action, being sure that such people must do something very special and interesting. They stood before him definite, vivid, and he wished to know, and to show, as much as possible of their nature. The first thing was to make clear to himself what he did know . . . and to this end he wrote out a sort of biography of each of his characters, and everything they had done and that had happened to them up to the opening of the story. He had their *dossier*, as the French say. . . . With this material in hand he was able to proceed: the story all lay in the question, *What shall I make them do?*[12]

It seems unlikely that the author of *First Love* asked himself: "What shall I *make* them do?" A traditional storyteller like Turgenev observed and *followed* his figures. James himself, in the Preface to *The Portrait of a Lady*, remembers that Turgenev saw his figures as *disponibles*—"subject to the chances, the complications of existence"[13]—in other words, at the 'disposal' of forces not under the author's control. In the same text, he says that his own "primary question" regarding Isabel Archer was: "What *will* she do?"—a very different question from: "What shall I *make* her do?"

He sets forth his strong preference for well-made narratives in a frequently cited letter to Horace Walpole:

(Tolstoy and Dostoievsky) are fluid puddings, though not tasteless, because the amount of their own minds and souls in solution in the broth gives it savour and flavor, thanks to the strong, rank quality of their genius and their experience. But there are all sorts of things to be said of them, and in particular that we see how great a vice is their lack of composition, their defiance of economy and architecture, directly they are emulated and imitated; then, as subjects of emulation, models, they quite give themselves away. There is nothing so deplorable as a work of art with a *leak* in its interest; and there is no such leak of interest as through commonness of form. Its opposite, the *found* (because the sought-for) form is the absolute citadel and tabernacle of interest.[14]

The forms of Dostoevski and Tolstoy *are* of course "found"—though, unlike James's, they were often found in 'common' life and admitted a great deal that he deliberately excluded. James could not—as Dostoevski, Stendhal, Flaubert, and Zola did on occasion—derive his plots from newspaper accounts. While their stories are an interface between the world within and the world without, his are largely extrusions from the inner realm. Blackmur speaks of his "poetic plots," derived from "movements of the soul otherwise ineluctable," and refers to the action in them as "the action of the soul in its poetic drama."[15]

With the exception of Milly Theale and Ralph Touchett, whose lives are bounded by illness, the major figures of James are free of physical constraints. He says of Balzac:

> In reading him over, in opening him up almost anywhere today, what immediately strikes us is the part assigned by him, in any picture, to the *conditions* of the creatures with whom he is concerned.[16]

> (Characters) are interesting, in fact, as subjects of fate, the figures round whom the situation closes, in proportion as, sharing their existence, we feel where fate comes in and just how it gets at them. In the void they are not interesting—and Balzac, like nature herself, abhors a vacuum.[17]

But in his own fiction he largely avoids the press of fate and circumstance. His figures are subject to ethical constraints and good manners but seldom to their biological or economic condition—to the physical circumstances that limit most of us. They do not work, yet can say confidently with Strether: "I shan't starve." While money is a central motive in *The Portrait of a Lady* and *The Wings of the Dove*, it motivates only those of whom James disapproves; Kate Croy is a single exception. Unlike Balzac and Dickens, James has no sympathy for those compelled by need or greed. Evil in his stories often manifests in and through money, though not in those who have *inherited* it—who, in his own phrase, have been "immemorially protected."[18] Like Ralph Touchett, he seems to believe that by endowing his figures with wealth, he sets them free. Titles and large houses in James are unencumbered by family obligations or psychological burdens. His stories suggest that those with inherited wealth are freer than you and I, not only to enjoy themselves but to be "finely aware"—to make truly moral decisions.

Discussions of James stress his sense of the past, though the past plays almost no role in his novels. With few exceptions, the major figures are *newborn* into their stories, free of bonds and attachments, unfettered by what he himself called "the strange, inevitable tentacles" of family life.[19] The *dossier* Turgenev compiled on his characters—which informed him of "everything they had done or that had happened to them up to the opening of the story"—is oddly absent in his own work. The central figures have almost no history. Isabel arrives on the scene orphaned, a *tabula rasa*, free to make her own life, her own mistakes. One may, of course, draw conclusions about her past from the relationships she *does* make, but James himself—while analyzing her motives and responses in minute detail—tells us nothing of her prior history. The past Isabel encounters is not her own but Osmond's and Madame Merle's. In James's work, the discovery of Europe may well serve—as it did in his life—to obscure *American* antecedents. Though the past dominates *The Turn of the Screw*, it is a horror story he himself called hackwork: "A piece of ingenuity pure and simply, of cold artistic calculation."[20] The supernatural in it is a sham, perhaps because James, unlike Ibsen, was unwilling to meet up with *real* ghosts.[21]

In his novels, the absence of pressure from without is matched by a lack of pressure from within. His characters are largely free of compulsions, conflict, and contradictions. They are, indeed, rather simple figures, who gain their appearance of complexity from his own elaborations, not from anything *they* do. The heart of the narrative is often a love story, but one free of emotional need, sexuality, or jealousy. Even Kate and Densher are passionless; their feelings, hopes, and desires are set forth clearly but given no urgency, just as Kate's failed relationship to her father lacks the rancor and bitterness that would make it a compelling force in her story. Edel says that in *The Wings of the Dove* James writes "for the first time . . . believably of sexual passion."[22] One wonders. As Geismar points out, Kate seems to have no difficulty "lending" the man she loves to Milly, and the absence of a strong sexual bond between them makes Densher's willingness to participate in her scheme—her ascendancy over him—something of an abstraction. Their one sexual encounter leads to no other. It seems, in fact, to propel him into falling in love with a doomed girl.

James is most persuasive when feelings are indirect and relationships transpire in a social rather than intimate context. Drawing-room comedy, incisively observed, engenders some of his most effective scenes, while his attempts to render strong, direct emotion—the deathbed scene between Ralph and Isabel, for instance—are not always credible. The unmediated and unmitigated is precisely what his stories and method mean to evade. Proust's figures, too, are untouched by economic necessity, yet many of them are struck down by passion—by an inner necessity that leaves them as helpless and 'absurd' as Woyzeck and Phèdre.

Since there is seldom a compelling force, no one in his stories is obliged to act. Robert Caserio points out that

> In the young James there is a characteristic identification of virtuous behavior with a denial of action. Indeed, in his early work James insists that the creativity appropriate to Americans is located in their ability to keep free of deeds, in their aloofness from any temptation or provocation to enact plot.[23]

This holds true for the late novels as well. Maria Gostrey says of Little Bilham:

> "The others all wanted so dreadfully to do something, and they've gone and done it, in too many cases, indeed. It leaves them never the same afterwards; the charm is always somehow broken. Now *he*, I think, you know, really won't. He won't do the least dreadful little thing. We shall continue to enjoy him just as he is. No—he's quite beautiful. He sees everything."[24]

Action in James is a coarse commitment, whereas inaction seems to constitute freedom. Until a deed is done, nothing is fixed and everything seems possible. For him, the unwillingness or inability to *do*—which Ibsen and Chekhov deem tragic—is a mark of distinction. The only action he believes in is the 'doing' of the artist, even if the storyteller—as he reminds himself in his notebooks—is, in fact, charged with *finding* an action:

> The *march of an action* is the thing for me to, more and more, attach myself to: it is the only thing that really, for *me*, at least, will *produire l'oeuvre*, and *l'oeuvre* is, before God, what I'm going for.[25]

As is often the case, he recognizes the demands of narrative but is unable to meet them. In his own work, the "march" of the action frequently depends on *inhibiting* the action. His characters are allowed no want or need—which are, of course, the chief source of action in fiction and life.

For James, "story" is "just the spoiled child of art."[26] Caserio says that

> To designate the narrative modes by which he works, (he) repeatedly uses four terms in the prefaces to the New York edition: *picture, drama, story, plot*. He

appears to use these terms interchangeably, favoring each and all by turns, yet usually reserving his highest praise for *picture*.[27]

He likened the writer's work to the painter's and says of *The Scarlet Letter:*

(It) achieved the fortune of the small supreme group of novels: it has hung an ineffaceable image in the portrait gallery, the reserved inner cabinet, of literature.[28]

His own idealized "pictures" suspend movement, and his style excludes or hides far more than it reveals. Unlike Proust—whose sentences stop only for "negative reasons," because they cannot go on forever, though, in their urge to include and connect, they might well do so[29]—James erects an elaborate superstructure of analysis and speculation on a narrow base. He effectively substitutes his own refinement and subtlety for the coarse substance of reality. In a letter to his niece he says:

I hate the American simplicity. I glory in the piling up of complications of every sort. If I could pronounce the name James in any different and more elaborate way I should be in favor of doing it.[30]

His often cited statement that

The great thing is to be *saturated* with something—that is, in one way or another, with life[31]

remains a touching exhortation he did not, or could not, obey, for James did not much *like* life. While the aesthetic impulse may often derive from a deep dissatisfaction with our existence, it combines—in the work of most artists—with a strong "affluent of reality." James himself counseled the novelist "to try to be one of those on whom nothing is lost," yet consistently turned his back on "clumsy Life at her stupid work"[32] and felt, like Wilde, that

The more we study Art, the less we care for Nature. What Art really reveals to us is Nature's lack of design, her curious crudities, her extraordinary monotony, her absolutely unfinished condition.[33]

Though, unlike Scribe, James did not *cater* to his readers,[34] he ignored aspects of reality that preoccupied his great contemporaries. He criticized Baudelaire for trying "to make fine verses on ignoble subjects," and thought the story of Emma Bovary not altogether worthy of Flaubert's genius and "perfection."[35]

Proust says that our books are written by our better selves, but James insists they should be written *about* them as well. Because all art is severely limited in scope, it must purify and intensify by excluding what it deems unimportant, but it intensifies the dark and destructive, not just the bright and hopeful. For James, however, art constituted a refuge—a "luminous paradise," a "high chamber . . . and gardens divine,"[36] an "absolute citadel" and a "tabernacle." Whereas the need to escape motivates many artists, they also confront, at grave risk to themselves, the condition that *prompted* their flight. As Dickens says:

> I am the modern embodiment of the old Enchanters, whose Familiars tore them to pieces.[37]

James kept *his* familiars at bay by sealing his later fictions hermetically in form as well as subject. Though his early work is deeply committed to "specification,"[38] the late novels are devoid of concrete, sensory information. The external world becomes ever less substantial, and the sharp social observation that helps give life to *The Bostonians* and *The Portrait of a Lady* is largely absent.[39] He himself observes that

> The most fundamental and general sign of the novel, from one desperate experiment to another, is its being everywhere an effort at representation—this is the beginning and the end of it.[40]

But in practice he thought of narrative as an artifact—as *not* representing reality. In *The Ambassadors*, Strether/James speaks of the precious *"illusion of freedom"*—an illusion that the traditional storyteller grants only to his fictive figures.[41] In his late novels, James wants to preserve it for the reader—and himself—as well. Within the confines of his art he feels himself to be truly at liberty and endows his figures with a freedom and existence as individuals, for which he could find no evidence in life.

Freedom is the true concern and province of his fiction:

> There goes . . . for the heroine of *The Wings of the Dove*, a strong and special implication of liberty, liberty of action, of choice, of appreciation, of contact . . . and this would be in particular what we should feel ourselves deeply concerned with.[42]

His extravagant elaboration of the inner realm is surely an attempt to shore up the autonomous subject that materialism and naturalism had put in doubt, and which he himself could demonstrate only in an art that did *not* represent. The late novels seem trapped in a no-man's land between traditional narrative, with its preclusive plot, and Positivist fiction, with its apparent confidence in human freedom and will.

In *The Ambassadors*—his own favorite—the figures and their circumstances are entirely rendered through Strether. As Lubbock says, the novel is "the picture of *un état d'âme.*"[43] Since we are locked into Strether's point of view, which often excludes the actual situation, we may *think* that the figures are free, and since Strether's perceptions keep changing, it may seem as if nothing is irrevocably fixed. Strether himself is of course rendered largely through his own ruminations and not in 'objective' relationships, leaving us without the basis for an independent judgement.

James justifies his escape *from* reality by recourse *to* reality. In an early essay, he quotes de Maupassant:

> How childish . . . to believe in reality, since we each carry our own in our thoughts and in our organs. Our eyes, our ears, our sense of smell, of taste, differing from one person to another, create as many truths as there are men upon earth. And our minds, taking instruction from these organs, so diversely impressed, understand, analyze, judge, as if each of us belonged to a different race. Each one of us, therefore, forms for himself an illusion of the world. . . .[44]

As Blackmur says:

> James never put his reader in direct contact with his subjects; he believed it was impossible to do so, because his subject really was not what happened but what someone felt about what happened, and this could be directly known only through an intermediate intelligence.[45]

Yet that "intermediate intelligence" conveniently serves to *exclude* what James was not prepared to face. He says about one of his figures:

> The action of the drama is simply the girl's "subjective" adventure—that of her quite definitely winged intelligence; just as the catastrophe, just as the solution, depends on her winged wit.[46]

Alas, the catastrophes of our existence are largely independent of our "wit."

We all know that we are prisoners of our subjectivity and try to compensate for it—just as traditional story tries to enlarge its individual-centered perspective or point of view through the impersonal plot. But in *The Ambassadors*, Strether's point of view rules absolutely. The one 'objective' or verifiable element is the dialogue. Everything else is filtered through his limited perceptions. James says of Balzac:

> The place in which an event occurred was in (his) view of equal moment with the event itself; it was part of the action; it was not a thing to take or leave, or to be vaguely and gracefully indicated; it imposed itself; it had a part to play; it needed to be made as definite as anything else. There is accordingly a very much greater amount of description in Balzac than in any other writer, and the description is mainly of towns, houses and rooms.[47]

But the towns, houses, and rooms in *The Ambassadors* are vague at best, and when Strether makes his excursion into the countryside, our view is conditioned by a painting—

> (a) certain small Lambinet that had charmed him, long years before, at a Boston dealer's, and that he had, quite absurdly, never forgotten. . . . He really continued in the picture—that being for himself his situation—all the rest of this rambling day.[48]

Whereas the natural subjectivity of the artist, his preoccupation with himself, his own responses, and his work, are usually counterbalanced by the urgent need to render an object, in *The Ambassadors* James failed "to get out of (his) own box."[49] The novel suffers a surfeit of attachment. As L. C. Knights says, James is far too close to Strether, and traps us into a nearly total dependence on his sensibility.[50] Though the adventures of Huckleberry Finn, too, are reported entirely through the perceptions of its central figure, we are free to see beyond his limited perspective. Huck himself can't understand the events or their implications but *we* never lose sight of them, nor of the river that carries him whither it will.

In *The Ambassadors*, we must accept on faith—with little independent evidence—the "fineness" of Maria Gostrey and the "genius" of Mme. de Vionnet—"her exquisite amiability . . . her high rarity, her distinction of every sort." We are limited to Strether's account of Chad and the magical changes that Paris and Mme. de Vionnet have wrought in him:

> Chad was brown and thick and strong and, of old, Chad had been rough. Was all the difference therefore that he was actually smooth? Possibly; for that he *was* smooth was as marked as in the taste of a sauce or in the rub of a hand. The effect of it was general—it had retouched his features, drawn them with a cleaner line. It had cleared his eyes and settled his color and polished his fine square teeth—the main ornament of his face; and at the same time that it had given him a form and a surface, almost a design, it had toned his voice, estab-

lished his accent, encouraged his smile to more play and his other motions to less. He had formerly, with a great deal of action, expressed very little; and he now expressed whatever was necessary with almost none at all.[51]

We don't realize until late in the novel that Chad is as shallow as he is charming and may well abandon Mme. de Vionnet "for the money in it." But even this, as Yvor Winters points out, is not altogether clear.[52]

James uses Strether's point of view to preserve the illusion of *his* freedom, yet leaves *us* helplessly imprisoned. The great majority of scenes are conversations between two people—Strether and another—with no one else present as a witness. While on stage a scene between two figures permits us to draw our own conclusions, the encounters in *The Ambassadors* are reported by a deeply, often unconsciously engaged narrator.[53] The meeting of Strether, Sally Pocock, and Mme. de Vionnet is a telling exception—one of the few in the book involving three people. Here the dialogue permits us an independent vantage point, and though Strether remains unaware of it, *we* can see that Mme. de Vionnet is manipulating him. We notice not only his naiveté, but something distinctly *unfine* in her: she mentions his relationship to Maria Gostrey in a way that is bound to give Sally the wrong idea. An ironic gap opens up in the narrative, though it closes very quickly, leaving us blind and helpless once again.

It is often said that James changed the history of the novel by dispensing with the omniscient narrator, yet he dispensed with him only in *The Ambassadors*. Isabel Archer's awareness is "the center of the subject" but *in the telling* her story is not substantially different from Emma Bovary's or, indeed, Lear's and Hamlet's. Lear's consciousness engages us as deeply as Strether's, and Lubbock observes of *Crime and Punishment*—which Dostoevski began as a first-person narrative before shifting to an omniscient narrator—that "anyone who has been through the book has become truly Raskolnicov."[54]

Fitzgerald, in *The Great Gatsby*, wisely places his point-of-view figure at one remove from the hero. Nick Carraway engages us in an ongoing investigation like Strether's, but with the essential difference that the reader isn't blindsided. Our helpless immersion in *The Ambassadors* is a limitation, and the claim that the novel's perspective constitutes a radical innovation springs from a failure to understand the role of point of view, or its equivalent, in traditional story. To say, as Charles Marowitz does, that "*Hamlet* takes place *in* Hamlet" is an overstatement but it makes a point.[55]

Like most of us, Strether is slow to realize the truth about himself and those who engage his feelings. Action and confrontation would have accelerated the narrative by forcing him to recognize what is going on much sooner, *and* provided us with the basis for an independent perspective. As we have noted, James thought action and confrontation 'coarse'—the province of grubby people in industry and trade, like Sally Pocock. He clearly dislikes her, no doubt because she *is* direct and confrontational. Unlike Mme. de Vionnet, moreover, who "could be graceful with her elbows on the table," poor Sally has no style, though today, her descendants at Ivy League schools, are learning how to appreciate the subtleties of the Master.

In his concern with "winged intelligence" or awareness James can misread the work of others:

> The figures in any picture, the agents in any drama, are interesting only in proportion as they feel their respective situations. . . . Their being finely aware—as Hamlet and Lear, say, are finely aware—*makes* absolutely the intensity of their adventure, gives the maximum of sense to what befalls them. We care, our curiosity and our sympathy care, comparatively little for what happens to the stupid, the coarse and the blind; care for it, and for the effects of it, at the most as helping to precipitate what happens to the more deeply wondering, to the really sentient. Hamlet and Lear are surrounded, amid their complications, by the stupid and the blind, who minister in all sorts of ways to their recorded fate.[56]

Lear is "finely aware" of his *own* pain and, eventually, of the kinship of suffering that links him to others. But much of the time he and Hamlet are blind to themselves and their own situation, as well as crudely insensitive to the lives of others. The figures of fiction—from Achilles to Mother Courage—are "stupid," "coarse," and "blind" as often as they are "finely aware," and James's characters can be at their finest only because the forces that constrain and warp human existence are kept at a safe distance.

His novels are in the tradition of the *Bildungsroman*—accounts of an emerging sensibility which, in James, is primarily moral. While Proust's hero, like Oedipus, discovers necessity, Milly and Isabel discover that the world is an imperfect place and renounce their claim to it.

Peter Brooks has pointed to the relationship between James and melodrama,[57] which is, in turn, linked to the fairy tale. In James, too, the good are good and the wicked wicked. Kate Croy is the exception, for she is an alloy—a crux of opposites, as her name suggests. She wants something badly enough to scheme for it, while most of his central figures are truly innocent—a quality he treasures and protects. Virtue in his novels is often personified by a young woman not yet exposed to the world who, like Snow White, remains pure even after she comes face to face with corruption. Yet he insists on consciousness and choice. A knowing egotism is the unforgivable sin, and freely elected unselfishness the greatest virtue. The wicked in James, since their survival isn't at stake, are not constrained into wickedness and the virtuous can *choose* virtue. Compared to the ethical freedom enjoyed by Milly and Ralph Touchett, Prince Myshkin is utterly compelled. He is saintly but sick and his actions, unlike Milly's, do not redeem the others but doom them. At the end of *The Idiot*, the figures, like Kate and Densher, will never again be as they were—but with a significant difference: Nastasya is murdered, Rogoshin goes to prison, and Myshkin is taken back to the asylum without hope of recovery.

In traditional story, the central figure discovers what we already know, but in *The Ambassadors*—as in detective fiction—we and Strether learn the truth at the same time. On his excursion into the countryside he comes upon Chad and Mme. de Vionnet, and in the moment they take before acknowledging him, he understands their illicit relationship. Here, as elsewhere in his stories, a key discovery is derived from a "picture," not an action. Isabel Archer is made aware of the past intimacy between her husband and Mme. Merle because she sees him comfortably seated while Mme. Merle stands. Significantly, such moments are brought about by a confluence of the very "arbitrary" or "accidental" of which James disapproves in fiction: "*Comme cela se trouve!*" Mme. de Vionnet exclaims after Strether has discovered her with Chad. The plot—or fate—briefly takes over and threatens to deprive the figures of their carefully guarded freedom. Since, however, the moment is a "picture" and seen at some distance, no one is forced into action and conflict. Isabel need not confront her husband or 'make a scene.' Despite the import and impact of her discovery, she can remain poised and in command of herself.

Much has been made of James's sense of evil, perhaps because critics pay attention to what he says rather than does. Peter Brooks suggests that "the Jamesian 'theology' . . . gives a large part to the forces of blackness,"[58] and Graham Greene claims that James believed in "supernatural evil . . . not in supernatural good"; he speaks of a "sense of evil religious in its intensity," and calls Kate an "incomparable" figure of evil, one of "his great gallery of the damned."[59] Yet finding evil in James isn't easy. Osmond? Mme. Merle? Kate *might* have been evil if she were passionate or desperately needy. But James is too keen on preserving her freedom and fine qualities; there is nothing really ruthless or destructive about her. She isn't impatient for Milly to die, plans to deceive her without doing her any harm, and suffers just a few pangs of jealousy at the end. She is, moreover, unfailingly honest with herself and not the least bit blind. Like Milly, she "sees all"— often before the others.

Since James did not believe in the supernatural, he could hardly believe in "supernatural evil." Brooks says that his work points to "hidden forces and truths"—that he was unwilling to "exclude occulted meanings from the systems operative in human life and its fictions."[60] But while he may have *wished* for "occulted meanings" in life, he *believed* in them only in fiction. Milly and the touch of her wings are products of his imagination and skill, and don't claim to resemble the working of the spirit in actuality. His urgent need to safeguard the freedom and purity of his figures kept him from facing the depravity, cruelty, mean-spiritedness, jealousy, arrogance, vanity, and vindictiveness that Proust renders so vividly, and that create the dark reality within which the grandmother's goodness gleams like the light in a Rembrandt. There is, in *The Wings of the Dove*, no crude physical reality, no real sexual or financial corruption to set off Milly's spirituality—no Rogoshin, Ganya, or Lebedev to her Myshkin, no Old Karamazov to her Alyosha. Evil in James is desiccated and passionless, for when he transformed the processes of life into something "better," he robbed them of their energy.

Parallels as well as differences between *The Wings of the Dove* and Ibsen's *Rosmersholm* are revealing. We don't know how conscious James was of the impact Ibsen's play had on him, but its influence seems pervasive.[61] He first sketched out his novel in 1894, and though he did not see the London production of *Rosmersholm* in 1891, he read it that year, for he wrote to Gosse that he found it "of a grey mediocrity . . . *jusqu'à en être bête*," ("to the point of stupidity").[62] In both play and novel, a vibrant, strong-willed, and assertive woman loves a sensitive but essentially passive man; in both, she is waiting for the death of an invalid who also loves him; in both, the sick woman discovers the relationship between the lovers and acts to assure their future; and in both, the lovers find themselves unable to make a life together after her death because the man has scruples.

The differences are, however, no less revealing. In *Rosmersholm*, the figures are prisoners of the past. When the curtain rises, the essential action is over. As Freud suggests, Rebecca West's destiny is determined by her incestuous relationship to her father.[63] Rebecca herself tells the invalided wife that she has fallen in love with Rosmer, implies that he shares her feelings—which is not, at that moment, true—and suggests that Beata take herself out of the picture. Beata responds by writing a letter to the local paper, ostensibly to defend her husband against vicious rumors but effectively to arouse suspicion. Her suicide, which is intended to set him free, is clearly also an act of vengeance.

James, on the other hand, permits Kate to leave behind her "odious" father and her past in the first chapter. They motivate her desire for money and a gracious life, but in no way constrain her. She has *no* share in revealing to Milly that Densher is committed to her, and Milly's response, in turn, is free of all jealousy and vindictiveness—though by making Densher her heir she stops the lovers as effectively as Beata. Rebecca West is "ennobled" and kills herself, but Kate Croy is spared—touched by the wings of the dove and not the angel of death.

James thought the basic material of his novel "ugly and vulgar" and set about to refine and spiritualize it.[64] He not only ennobled the figures but protected them against the few harsh facts he admits into their story. We never find out for sure whether Milly *understands* that Densher was to marry her for her money. But while the indirect presentation shelters his "princess" from the truth, it also robs her of the anger that might have aroused her will to live. Her illness is mysterious and possibly psychosomatic. She may be doomed because she is at the mercy of *James's* needs and not of her own situation.

In his early work, James attends as carefully to social reality as he does to the inner life of his figures. In an 1884 essay on Turgenev he says:

> The world as it stands is no illusion, no phantasm, no evil dream of night; we wake up to it again for ever and ever; we can neither forget it nor deny it nor dispense with it.[65]

In *The Portrait of a Lady*, completed in 1881, the irony is traditional. The plot clearly moves in one direction while the figures try to move in another. Isabel sees herself as having boundless possibilities but is, in our view, distinctly limited. When she says: "I wish to choose my fate," she is as blind as Oedipus, and we see her enter marriage to Osmond almost as we see Little Red Riding Hood walk into her grandmother's house. She thinks she is marrying "to please herself" only to discover that she has been manipulated by others. Moreover, her attitude to Osmond—"she would be his providence"—smacks of *hubris*, albeit *hubris* in its most generous form.

Unlike most figures in the late novels, Isabel wants something badly enough to commit herself. She embarks on what she believes to be an "irresistible action," confident that what she wants will be hers. As James says in the Preface to the 1908 edition, she "affronts" her destiny. Moreover, she comes alive not just because of her attractive qualities but because she is headstrong, insensitive, self-involved, and egotistical. When she says to Ralph: "I wish I could be as interesting to myself as I am to you!" he answers: "You're extremely interesting to yourself," and we know he is right.[66]

In the early novels, a pervasive sense of irony keeps the affection with which James treats his central figures from cloying. When Ralph leaves half his estate to Isabel, he thinks he is freeing her to go her own way but is, in fact, setting her up for the schemes of Mme. Merle. Nor are we obliged to see him as a dying saint, for he may well be trying to bind her to him in spirit. There is the suggestion of a will to power—he will "*make*" her life—that is altogether absent in the portrait of Milly Theale. Our picture of Osmond, too, is free of the illusions that enveil Mme. de Vionnet. Instead of being entirely trapped in Isabel's feelings, as we are in Strether's, we are free to see him through Ralph's skeptical eyes.

When James looks back at *The Portrait of a Lady* in the 1908 Preface, he recalls that the story first came to him in "the character and aspect of a particularly engaging woman," and that he faced the task of "positively organizing an ado about her."[67] He reports that he said to himself:

> "Place the centre of the subject in the young woman's consciousness . . . and you get as interesting and as beautiful a difficulty as you could wish."[68]

In retrospect, he finds that the chapter in which Isabel turns inward after discovering the truth about her marriage is "obviously the best thing in the book." But as F. R. Leavis points out:

> The James of the Prefaces . . . is so much *not* the James of the early books that he shouldn't be taken as a critical authority upon them, at any rate where valuation is concerned.[69]

Isabel's fate is hardly an "ado," nor is it "organized positively." Her story seems 'found' rather than made, and develops far more organically than the highly structured late novels. Though we remain aware of her point of view throughout, we always see *her* as well. While the scene in which she sits by the fire, "motionlessly *seeing*," is fine indeed, it is clearly of special interest to James in 1908 because it sounds the concerns of his major phase.

For good reason, contemporary critical attention has focused on Isabel's deliberate return to her unhappy marriage—a development that breaks with the sequence of persuasively reported events. Throughout, there has been nothing of the martyr about her and yet, at the end, she willingly assumes a burden of lifelong suffering—ostensibly to keep her promise to Osmond's frightened daughter.

The difficulty begins with James's account of her marriage, in which he condenses three years—during which Isabel has lost her only child—into a few pages. When we meet her again, she is aware that her marriage is a house of "darkness" and "suffocation,"[70] and Osmond himself has become repugnant to her.[71] Given such strong, clear feelings, why live with him—or rather, permit him to live with her? Though divorce was frowned upon, it constituted no hardship for a woman of independent means. Her decision to stay is quite out of character with the Isabel we know, unless she has gone through a sea change during the three years she was out of our sight.[72]

We might, of course, conclude that self-denial and not self-assertion is Isabel's true nature and that, throughout the story, she has tried to countermand it with her energy and venturesomeness. Perhaps, when she married Osmond, she *did* know—unconsciously—what she was getting into, and "the house of suffocation" may be what she really 'wanted.' Since she is fully aware of her mistake yet makes it a *second* time—as deliberately and as sure of her "straight path" as she was when she first married him—we might infer that her past, unknown and unacknowledged, has finally caught up with her—that her marriage to Osmond was not a mistake but her destiny.

Poirier says of James what James himself says of Balzac—that in *The Portrait of a Lady* he showed "respect for the liberty of the subject."[73] And indeed, throughout the greater part of the novel, Isabel is free—free of the *author* and free to *feel* free—though she is in fact trapped. But at the end, at the very moment when James says without a trace of irony:

When darkness returned she was free[74]

she is free no longer. She has ceased to be an altogether credible woman and becomes a figure in an *allegory* of freedom. Ironically, though not surprisingly, she loses whatever freedom and independence she may have had when James *declares* her free—at the very moment when she is no longer fated.

It is one thing for a storyteller to start out believing that his figures are free; quite another for him to insist on their freedom at the end. When Isabel decides to return to Osmond, she is not free but has become one with the novelist: she must choose what *he* chooses *for* her. She is free only to resign herself and withdraw. Her moral decision is an equivalent of James's aesthetic one. But whereas he withdrew from the world of action and intimate relationships to "do" his stories, Isabel appears to withdraw into a vacuum.

Her decision to stay in her marriage may have drawn critical attention because it indicates the direction in which James was to move in his later work. Among his novels, *The Portrait of a Lady* occupies a place not unlike *L'Avventura*'s in the films of Antonioni. A major subjective theme is sounded, but without overwhelming every other reality. Isabel Archer and

Antonioni's Claudia are full of hope, energy, and strong feeling—not figures in an allegory of resignation or alienation. Their stories maintain the tension between an 'objective' reality and the author's subjectivity—denying neither—that approximates our own optimal experience.

Of course fictive figures are never truly free of the storyteller's unconscious. Nor do we want them to be, for only if they come from deep within—from common ground—can we connect with them. But the figures in late James, instead of springing from his unconscious like the Underground Man from Dostoevski's, are subject to and censored by his moralizing intelligence. If Harold Bloom is right to see the influence of Emerson,[75] it is a pernicious limitation, for their 'freedom' robs them of energy and makes them anemic.

The kinship between James and *The Scarlet Letter* has often been noted, but the differences are as noteworthy. Hawthorne's story begins in *medias res* and his figures are inextricably bound to their past. Hester and Dimmesdale cannot undo their adulterous love or the existence of their child, and Chillingworth is devoured by his need for revenge. All three are haunted and though we, like Hawthorne, stand at some distance from the Puritan sense of sin—from what James called "the pressing moral anxiety, the restless individual conscience"[76] —it seems familiar and relevant, for we recognize in it the claims that *all* societies make on the individual. In seventeenth-century New England, God's law was the law of society and to violate one was to violate the other. Hester may say to Dimmesdale: "What we did had a consecration of its own,"[77] but since it is forbidden by the community, it is burdened with shame or guilt—a guilt we can understand even if, today, we experience it as anxiety.

Hawthorne's figures are bound to each other by love or hate:

> It is a curious subject of observation and inquiry whether hatred and love be not the same thing at bottom. Each, in its utmost development, supposes a high degree of intimacy and heart-knowledge; each renders one individual dependent for the food of his affections and spiritual life upon another; each leaves the passionate lover, or the no less passionate hater, forlorn and desolate by the withdrawal of his object.[78]

The figures in *The Scarlet Letter* are utterly unfree, and their story is "the darkening close of a tale of human frailty and sorrow."[79] Yet there may be more strength in their frailty than in James's untested figures. Once Hester has sinned and is expelled from the sheltering community, she can become truly conscious. As in *Genesis*, sin is the beginning of her existence as a separate being and endows her with a complexity she could not have attained as the obedient, faithful wife of Chillingworth. "A" stands not only for Adultery but for "Able" and "Angel."[80] It is also the first letter of the alphabet and so of speech and writing. Whereas, in James, the "finely aware" are untouched women who discover evil in others, awareness in Hawthorne comes to those who discover it in themselves.

In its ambiguity, the "romance" of *The Scarlet Letter* seems more contemporary than the novels of James. The uncertain picture we have of Chad derives entirely from Strether's blurred vision, but Hawthorne's story is *itself* poised on the edge of darkness and uncertainty, just as the village of Boston is bordered by the primeval forest. The figures live in an uncharted world, beset by forces and passions they cannot understand or manage. The darkness around them extends within, and their actions—reported but not explained—are at once clear and contradictory. So Hester mounts the scaffold dressed in a rich gown to which she has fixed the scarlet letter, embroidered with "fantastic flourishes of gold-thread." She is shamed yet defiant, sinful but proud of her sin. When she refuses to incriminate Dimmesdale and promises Chillingworth not to reveal that she was his wife, she acts out of her love for the minister—yet condemns him to seven years of purgatory and affords Chillingworth his satanic revenge.

As James says, Hawthorne turns up

the under side of common aspects—the laws secretly broken, the impulses secretly felt, the hidden passions, the double lives, the dark corners, the closed rooms, the skeletons in the cupboard and at the feast.[81]

(His is) much more a terrible sense of human abysses than a desire rashly to sound them and rise to the surface with his report. On the surface—the surface of the soul and the edge of tragedy—he preferred to remain.[82]

Yet Hawthorne clearly *believed* in the abyss and the tragedy—the ceaseless, grinding, necessary conflict between nature and culture in which so many of us are maimed or destroyed. And he surely believed in the soul. He felt and rendered its presence, whereas we can't be sure that James thought of it as anything but a fiction—the product of art or, at most, the distinctive possession of a privileged few. When James noted that Hawthorne's "ingenuity"

made . . . and cherished for fancy's sake, a mystery and a glamour where there were otherwise none very ready to its hand[83]

he may have been describing his *own* process.[84] *The Scarlet Letter* was *not* composed or cherished "for fancy's sake." Hawthorne calls it a romance, but in his view romance "sins unforgivably" if it swerves "aside from the truth of the human heart."[85] His story renders its figures persuasively as both unfree *and* unpredictable, passionately committed *and* self-divided. They are mortgaged to their own fate—"it has all been a dark necessity"[86]—and not to Hawthorne's will. He makes the traditional claim of being a mere reporter or bystander, and says he *found* the book wrapped in a mysterious bundle at the Salem custom house. In his view, the storyteller may

> find that (the tale) shapes itself against his intentions; that the characters act otherwise than he thought; that unforeseen events occur; and a catastrophe occurs which he strives in vain to avert. It might foreshadow his own fate—he having made himself one of his personages.[87]

Conversely, James remained throughout his life persuaded of the artist's "boundless freedom."[88] As Poirier says:

> (His craft was) his best weapon in defence of a kind of freedom which, if defenceless in life, might, he fondly hoped, find an existence this side of death in the fictive world of his novels.[89]

Despite his lifelong emphasis on consciousness, James seems to have been unaware of his own compelling need to tell stories in which the figures are *un*compelled—a blind spot that accounts for some of his critical misjudgments.[90] Edith Wharton gives us a touching picture of him:

> One day I said to him: "What was your idea in suspending the four principal characters in *The Golden Bowl* in the void? What sort of life did they lead when they were not watching each other, and fencing with each other? Why have you stripped them of all the *human fringes* we necessarily trail after us through life?
>
> He looked at me in surprise, and I saw at once that the surprise was painful, and wished I had not spoken. I had assumed that his system was a deliberate one, carefully thought out, and had been genuinely anxious to hear his reasons. But after a pause of reflection he answered in a disturbed voice: "my dear—I didn't know I had!" and I saw that my question, instead of starting one of our absorbing literary discussions, had only turned his startled attention on a peculiarity of which he had been completely unconscious.[91]

There are occasions—in his reflections on art if not in his practice—when he acknowledges that the artist *isn't* free:

One never really chooses one's general range of vision—the experience from which ideas and themes and suggestions spring: this proves ever what it has *had* to be, this is one with the very turn one's life has taken; so whatever it "gives," whatever it makes us feel and think of, we regard very much as imposed and inevitable. The subject thus pressed upon the artist is the necessity of his case.[92]

Perhaps the "necessity" that was pressed upon James—one we must "regard very much as imposed and inevitable"—is the need to remain aloof from life, to escape it. Peter Brooks speaks of his "moral manicheanism," of the melodramatic split between good and evil in his work.[93] But there is, in the major phase, a parallel split between art and life—between the inner, spiritual and outer, material realm. He turned away from the sharply observed and often comic reality in the early stories, cast off what Zola called the "ballast" of reality, and privileged "the possible other case." He conjured up in his later fiction an alternative domain in which he could breathe freely, and obscured the fact that many of his figures have little substance by spinning a web of speculations and reflections around them. If we are to believe in an "unspotted princess" like Milly, she *must* be kept at a distance:

> I go but a little way with the direct—that is, with the the straight exhibition of Milly; it resorts to for relief, this process, whenever it can, to some kinder, more merciful indirection: all as if to approach her circuitously, deal with her at second hand, as an unspotted princess is ever dealt with.[94]

James says of Flaubert:

> He was born a novelist, grew up, lived, died a novelist, breathing, feeling, thinking, speaking, performing every operation of life, only as that votary.[95]

He himself was, of course, such a votary. He cites Flaubert's comment that he had been "from the first afraid of life"—a fear with which James, too, was familiar. It drove him into the sanctuary of his fiction.[96] He notes that Flaubert's "connection with Mme. Colet, such as it was, rears its head for us in something like a desert of immunity from such complications."[97] And he, too, was of course fearful of all binding relationships and cultivated his own "desert of immunity." In 1878, on the occasion of William James's engagement, he wrote to him:

> I had long wished to see you married; I believe in matrimony as much for other people as I believe in it little for myself—which is saying a good deal.[98]

James celebrates the detachment and renunciation of his figures without putting them through the purgatory of an intense attachment. Strether's wife and son, long dead, are mere abstractions; Isabel realizes that she loves Ralph when he is on his deathbed; and Densher falls in love with Milly after she has died. All are safe from the "complications" of an actual commitment. Perhaps James centers his stories on the innocent because they appear to be disconnected and free. He disregards—in his later work—what *The Portrait of a Lady* makes vividly clear: that innocence leaves us not free but bound unconsciously.

In James evil, like virtue, resides in an *absence* of life. Osmond is cold and withdrawn, without passion or energy. He hates Isabel because he cannot make her conform to his vision of aesthetic perfection. Mme. Merle seems to find satisfaction not in enriching the daughter she has abandoned but in manipulating the feelings and fate of Isabel. Like Chillingworth, she violates "in cold blood, the sanctity of a human heart."[99] The crimes she and Osmond commit are akin to the 'soul murder' both Ibsen and James excoriate—though they throttled the passionate life in themselves and their figures.

Suffering for James may be the *inability* to suffer, to feel deeply. The "formal feeling" that in Emily Dickinson comes *after* great pain[100] would appear, in James, to be an alternative to pain—a way of keeping pain at a distance. Life seems to him so ugly and intolerable that even within the refuge of his fiction he must seek a *more* recondite shelter: the softly lit interior of his figures, where their thoughts and feelings open up to his loving scrutiny. The inner world in James is not an interface between the conscious and the unconscious but a realm of uncontaminated consciousness. Indeed, freedom for him is freedom *from* the unconscious—a state of grace that need not be earned by facing the heart of darkness or the beast in the jungle.

His fear of sexuality has often been noted. In sexual relationships we are, of course, apt to be least conscious, least free, least 'ourselves,' and most profoundly enthralled to forces beyond our control. Isabel's fear of sex is made explicit in her final encounter with Goodwood:

> She believed just then that to let him take her in his arms would be the next best thing to dying.[101]

When Densher makes his participation in Kate's scheme contingent on her coming to his room, his approach is oddly cerebral and bloodless. As it turns out, the wings of the dove permit him to escape the touch of a living woman.

Critics have pointed out that James associates perfect freedom with death. After Minnie Temple died, he wrote to Howells:

> I can't talk about death without seeming to say too much—I think so kindly of it as compared to life. . . .[102]

On the same occasion, he said in a letter to William:

> She has gone to where there is neither marrying nor giving in marriage!—(a place of) freedom and eternal rest.[103]

He remarks of Isabel Archer:

> She envied Ralph his dying, for if one were thinking of rest that was the most perfect of all. To cease utterly, to give it all up and not know anything more— the idea was as sweet as the vision of a cool bath in a marble tank, in a darkened chamber, in a hot land.[104]

As Arnold Kettle says, James desired "not merely to be free *in* this world but to be free *of* this world."[105]

The renunciations that end *The Portrait of a Lady, The Ambassadors,* and *The Wings of the Dove* are, in every instance, rendered as an ethical decision. But since the figures are not in conflict with themselves, renunciation costs them little. It seems, rather, to crystallize their deepest inclination. Even Kate, who might be expected to put up a fight, resigns gracefully. Given the attention James lavishes on the subtlest shifts and changes, her transformation takes place with lightning speed in a single scene. She has, in fact, been programmed for resignation in a carefully controlled, well-made fiction. Strether's reason for renouncing Maria Gostrey is equally suspect:

> "Not, out of the whole affair, to have got anything for myself."[106]

There is no irony here. By claiming that his renunciation, like Isabel's and Densher's, is *ethically* motivated—by failing to acknowledge their fear and revulsion of life—James taints his stories with sentimentality.

In Chekhov, resignation is the mark of an enervated class that was—as Henry Adams said of its American counterpart—becoming as "defunct as the dodo."[107] But James had little interest in the social, political, and economic context of his later fictions. For him, as Edith Wharton says:

> Every great novel must first of all be based on a profound sense of moral values.[108]

In *Rosmersholm* and *The Scarlet Letter*, moral values produce conflict and suffering. They destroy life even as they make human existence possible. But James—though he said early in his career that "evil is insolent and strong" and "goodness very apt to be weak"[109]—chose to ignore the "weak" element in virtue and created in his fiction a "luminous paradise" where, in contrast to Eden, goodness can triumph.[110]

He claimed for himself "the imagination of disaster" and—in his notes and prefaces—speaks almost lovingly of catastrophes. But the disasters and catastrophes in his work are betrayed trusts and broken vows that shatter the feeling-life of privileged young women. The sexual secret that powers the narrative line of his fictions is—unlike the violation of children in Dostoevski—merely a relationship that breaks with the morality of the middle class, and Geismar is justified in calling him a "genteel middle class writer."[111] His fictions suppress conflict, strong feeling, and bad behavior, and render kindness, consideration, and sensitivity to the wishes of others as supreme virtues. While Dickens, too, treasured these qualities, he did not make the mistake of endowing the rich or the poor with them.

James's heroines are not subject to the coarsening degradation of Emma Bovary, the despair of Anna Karenina, or the anguished jealousy of Nastasya Filipovna—three women who are "vulgarly troubled" much of the time.[112] He prefers virgin princesses who, like Milly, suffer nobly and in silence. Nina Baym points out that in the New York edition of 1908—twenty-seven years after the first publication of *The Portrait of a Lady*—he subjected Isabel Archer to significant changes:

> Isabel Archer as redrawn is much more like Milly Theale than like the original Isabel Archer.[113]

He made her less lively, less spontaneous, less active, and more withdrawn. Yet even in the original version, Isabel's progress is toward passivity and suffering—which, for James, is a heightened state of awareness:

> Suffering was an active condition . . . it was not a chill, a stupor, a despair; it was a passion of thought, of speculation, of response to every pressure.[114]

We are far from the blind anguish of Lear or Woyzeck.

In James, the pure, suffering woman of popular nineteenth-century fiction and melodrama became the prism that refracts, refines, and ennobles the entire action. He says astutely of Hawthorne:

> Like almost all people who possess in a strong degree the story-telling faculty, (he) had a democratic strain in his composition, and a relish for the commoner stuff of human nature.[115]

He himself did not relish the commoner stuff. He began his sojourn in Europe in the hope of finding in its leisured and cultivated elite a community in which he could feel at home—a truly civilized society. When he found nothing of the kind, he proceeded to create an idealized upper class, combining the moral—indeed, Puritan—values of his own upbringing with the sensibilities of the artist and the refined manner of the aristocracy.

He must have been familiar with the circumstances that wedded American heiresses to English aristocrats. Yet he elected—like the film maker John Ford—to "print the legend." In his stories, the "international theme" constitutes a morality play that bears no resemblance to historical fact. In 1873, Jennie Jerome, the beautiful nineteen-year-old daughter of an American millionaire, fell passionately in love with Randolph Churchill, the second son of the Duke of Marlborough. Despite the Duke's initial objections, they were joined in "one of the great international marriages of the time."[116] Jennie was a spirited, independent, and highly intelligent girl who had a profound effect on her young husband. He said that until he met her he had lived "an idle and comparatively useless life," and counted on her to "encourage (him) to exertions and to do something for (himself)."[117] When he decided to stand for Parliament in the family borough of Woodstock, he wrote her:

Public life has no great charms. . . . Still it will all have greater attractions for me if I think it will please you and that you take an interest in it and will encourage me to keep up to the mark.[118]

After winning the election, he wrote:

Ever since I met you, everything goes well with me—too well. I'm afraid of a nemesis.[119]

A nemesis that, he knew, was sure to come. For though he loved Jennie, he had kept from her that as a student he had contracted syphilis,[120] an incurable and, in some stages, highly infectious disease.

Jennie apparently learned the truth soon after the birth of her first son, Winston. She was twenty-one when Randolph's illness, which had been in remission, reasserted itself—as it would with increasing frequency and ever more devastating symptoms throughout his short life. Her situation was not uncommon. Emperor Franz-Joseph had infected his wife and she, in turn, infected their only son. Though, at the time, an Englishman with syphilis was legally entitled to intercourse with his wife, Churchill withdrew from Jennie and threw himself into politics. During the 1880s, he was instrumental in transforming the moribund Tory party into a more progressive, democratic movement and was widely expected to become the Conservative leader. But soon after becoming Chancellor of the Exchequer and Leader of the House, he resigned. The reasons he gave were political but his deteriorating condition, known to very few, was surely a major factor.

The story of Jennie Jerome—whose father, on his deathbed, said to his daughters: "I have given you all I have. Pass it on."—might have served as the source of a James novel, were it not mottled with darkness and contradiction. The secret Randolph kept from his bride was far more devastating than Osmond's and Mme. Merle's. Like Isabel, Jennie stayed with her husband and, to remove him from the London scene when he lost control over body and mind, accompanied him on a trip around the world. In Singapore, his condition grew so critical that she had to add a lead-lined coffin to their luggage. But Jennie was no Jamesian virgin. She may well have been pregnant at her wedding[121] and she was seldom without lovers—among them the Prince of Wales and James's friend, the novelist Paul Bourget. After Randolph's death, she was courted by many and, though perpetually short of funds, turned down the proposal of William Waldorf Astor. She married twice more—men young enough to be her sons. Constantly in the public eye, she played an important role in Churchill's early career, was the leader of Anglo-American society in Britain and a member of the royal circle, raised funds for a hospital ship during the Boer War and sailed it to Capetown, associated with many artists and writers of her day, wrote two produced plays, published a literary review—to which James, who met her in 1895, contributed—and went into the purchase, redecoration, and resale of London houses to improve her finances. She had boundless energy, courage, and great personal warmth. As one of her many admirers said:

> Her desire to please, her delight in life and the genuine wish that all should share her joyous faith in it, made her the center of a devoted circle.[122]

Her nephew, Leslie Shane, said of her:

> She had a touch of Cleopatra in her and she never lost heart.[123]

Though Jennie had all the qualities with which James endowed Isabel Archer, the events of her life were clearly outside the domain of his fiction. They violated his moral system. Yet in her person and destiny she may have been more uniquely American than either Isabel or Milly.

Given the limited scope and elitist bias of James's work, one may wonder why he continues to fascinate readers in the academy. His critical reputation was firmly established after World War II, when young people from 'Woollett' came to East Coast universities both as students and teachers, eager to escape the restrictions of narrow ethnic backgrounds, confining family relationships, and the pressure of commerce and money. Perhaps the world of James's fiction offered a refuge where feelings and relationships were refined, sophisticated, and, above all, free of the past.

This, however, is just part of the picture. The problematic of James—the very qualities in his work that some find hard to accept—is surely the very reason it continues to hold our interest. His gift as an observer of the social scene, his psychological acuity, and his ability to capture shifting currents of feeling and thought make the early novels fine examples of *nineteenth-century* fiction. But it is the stories of the "major phase" that preoccupy critics—perhaps because they touch on our own doubts.

Already in *The Portrait of a Lady* we sense that James's concern with the freedom of his figures is, in fact, a concern with identity. Identity crises ran in the James family. As F. O. Mathiessen says of a critical time in the life of Henry James, Sr.:

> He had lost all confidence in his self-hood, indeed had come to believe that self-hood is "the curse of mankind." He was to find his way back to mental health slowly, through his conversion to Swedenborgianism. He never lost the belief which he acquired during that breakdown . . . that "the fall is self-sufficiency."[124]

William James says that during the gravest crisis in his life he was haunted by

> the image of an epileptic patient whom I had seen in the asylum, a black-haired youth with greenish hair, entirely idiotic. . . . *That shape am I,* I felt, potentially. Nothing that I possess can defend me against that fate, if the hour for it should strike for me as it struck for him. There was such a horror of him . . . that it was as if something hitherto solid within my breast gave way entirely and I became a mass of quivering fear. After this the universe was changed for me altogether.[125]

It would hardly be surprising if James himself was haunted by similar fears. As Peter Brooks says:

> "Abyss" is a word that recurs with insistent frequency in (his) writing.[126]

But while he often *invoked* the abyss, he never looked into it. We may guess that it represents the unconscious, which threatened him with the dissolution of human identity—the absolute horror of nothingness. He no doubt feared that if he were to confront it, he would learn with certainty that we have no freedom—that we barely exist. In James, "unconsciousness kills."[127] He could not see that it also gives us life. He would not look into the abyss, yet was transfixed by it—as he was by sexuality and death, which at once make human existence possible *and* annihilate our individuality.

His early and lifelong preoccupation with 'character' may spring from a concern with identity. In 1884 he wrote:

> What is character but the determination of incident? What is incident but the illustration of character? What is either a picture or a novel that is *not* of character?[128]

Yet character, in traditional story, is incidental to event and situation. His creation of an all-encompassing point of view in *The Ambassadors* is very likely an attempt to prove the continuity of the individual. His indirect rendering of the action and the filtering of everyone and everything through Strether's perception are surely an effort to establish the subject—a subject separate from and free of the object. The novel is proof of Strether's existence: the *world* exists only inasmuch as *he* does. We are close to post-modernism: reality is text.

Just as his brother William saved his sanity by pulling himself up by his own bootstraps—declaring pragmatically: "My first act of free will shall be to believe in free will"[129]—so Henry was determined to prove his existence by making the act of writing an act of free will. The emphasis he placed on control over the work was surely an effort to affirm his identity. As Harold Bloom says:

> Everything in the art of Henry James is sublimely deliberate.[130]

He was, Bloom notes, far more interested in what *he* could do than in what was going on around him:

> (He) is perfectly ruthless in his application of what has come to be the Formalist principle that subject matter in literary art is precisely what does not matter.[131]

Yet, in 1884, James warned explicitly against "intimating that the idea, the subject of a novel or a picture does not matter."[132] There is a sea change between the early and late work—with James progressively less interested in and respectful of 'reality.' Whereas his brother William saw "the gaping contrast between the richness of life and the poverty of all possible formulas,"[133] Henry experienced a gaping contrast between the poverty of *life* and the richness of all superior aesthetic creations.

James is indeed a precursor of postmodernism.[134] "Art," he wrote to H. G. Wells, "*makes* life, makes interest, makes importance"; there is no substitute for "the force and beauty of its process."[135] One thinks—by way of contrast—of Giacometti's comment that everyone walking the street was more complex and interesting than his sculptures. "In a burning building," he said, "I would save a cat before a Rembrandt."[136] He might not have acted on it, but it compensated for the artist's single-minded concern with art and kept him connected to life.

Since James felt compelled to assert the freedom of his figures over and against the facts, fiction became a game for him—"the game of literature."[137] He responded to his own grave doubts about the existence of the self by asserting that there is *only* self—or only text. The artist, as James perceived him, exemplifies Weber's "animal suspended in webs of significance that he himself has spun."[138]

Beneath the surface of his fiction there is a sense of despair, which—unlike Melville's and Dostoevski's—is not openly confronted and so pervades it.[139] Not until World War I destroyed the world in which he and the "immemorially protected" had been sheltered, did he make explicit what his stories had long implied. In a letter to an English friend, he says:

> Black and hideous to me is the tragedy that gathers and I'm sick beyond cure to have lived on to see it. You and I, the ornaments of our generation, should have been spared this wreck of our belief that through the long years we had seen civilization grow and the worst become impossible. . . . It seems to me to *undo* everything, everything that was ours, in the most horrible retroactive way—but I avert my face from the monstrous scene.[140]

He had sensed from the start that freedom is an illusion, albeit a necessary one:

> Really, universally, relations stop nowhere, and the exquisite problem of the artist is eternally to draw, by a geometry of his own, a circle in which they shall happily *appear* to do so.[141]

But in his late fiction, the word *appear* has become irrelevant. By drawing a magic circle around his figures and permitting as little as possible—from without *or* within—to constrain their freedom, he *denies* that "relations stop nowhere." Though he knew, as he wrote Edith Wharton, that "nothing happens as we forecast it," he refused to surrender his figures to the plot and assumed that in his work he—like the young scientist at the Rockefeller Institute—had "divine powers."

He asserts the liberty of his figures, yet has so little faith in it that he cannot expose them to a lived life. They can breathe only in the hothouse of his fiction. His novels are Christian allegories told by someone who believes neither in God nor in the reality of goodness. He is convinced that only in art would Kate and Densher be touched by the wings of the dove. In life, they would take the money and run.

His withdrawal into art—into the self—and his use of the text as a defense against reality, may have undermined the very *subject* James was trying to prove. As early as 1883 he enunciated his supreme faith in consciousness:

> Consciousness is an illimitable power, and though at times it may seem to be all consciousness of misery, yet in the way it propagates itself from wave to wave, so that we never cease to feel, and though at moments we appear to, try to, pray to, there is something that holds one in one's place, makes it a standpoint in the universe which it is probably good not to foresake.[142]

Traditionally, consciousness is more than a consciousness of self, even if the object of our awareness is limited *by* self. Consciousness is also an awareness of the other—both the human and nonhuman. But in late James, the affirmation of self seems increasingly to involve a *denial* of the other, just as his concern with the inner realm serves to keep reality at bay. If we are right to think that the self is an *interface* with the other, and that the *object*, in its interface with the subject, *proves* the subject, Strether's carefully preserved isolation, intended to guarantee his freedom, undermines his very existence.

We may find ourselves in agreement with Mme. Merle—of whom James is severely critical—when she says to Isabel:

> "When you've lived as long as I you'll see that every human being has his shell and that you must take the shell into account. By the shell I mean the whole envelope of circumstances. There's no such thing as an isolated man or woman; we're each of us made up of some cluster of appurtenances. What shall we call our 'self'? Where does it begin? Where does it end?"[143]

This restates—albeit in confining materialist terms—James's own comment that "relations stop nowhere." As we have noted, however, he often ignored his own critical observations. In the late novels, his figures lack an "envelope of circumstances" just as they lack a past. They are *not* like Mme. Merle, who "existed only in her relations, direct or indirect, with her fellow-mortals."[144] James wanted them to be at once free *and* have an identity, an identity without an obliging past, without attachments, without commitments—just as he tried to render the inner life without reference to the unconscious. It was a hopeless undertaking. He was caught in a classical American dilemma, one very much with us still. Since we insist on denying the past—or rather, are *obliged* to deny it by constant change—we find ourselves trapped in a permanent identity crisis.

Proust, as deeply committed to proving the subject as James, achieved his identity through the *recovery* of lost time. Marcel substantiates himself by *accruing* the world and responding to it—by remaining stubbornly in touch with the very realities that James, in his later work, dismisses. Proust's legendary insistence on precise physical detail renders the *world* as concretely as his own feelings, and Marcel emerges as a subject out of his interface with the object—with others. There *is* no freedom in *Remembrance of Things Past*. The novel discovers the connections that bind the figures and establishes the very links between past and present that James evades. In much the same way, *Bleak House*—with its web of relationships tying all to all and everyone to the past—substantiates the figures by *not* endowing them with freedom. The profusion of detail at which Dickens excels—James called him "the greatest of superficial novelists"[145] and was surprised that Turgenev "rated him so high"[146]—embeds his characters in life and so proves their existence.

James's despair, his lack of faith and confidence, made it almost impossible for him to expose his figures to the plot that governs traditional story. Yet by establishing them in an altogether separate realm, he is caught in contradictions that undermine rather than enhance his work. He fled the crude Positivism of the Pococks, their gung-ho belief in will and action, but was himself driven by the urgent need for freedom and control that is at the core of American Positivism.[147] The unselfishness and self-sacrifice that distinguish his favorite figures transform rather easily into the very self*less*ness against which his work was to serve as a bulwark. His stories often conclude with the figures in a state he himself dreaded: a surrender of self—albeit presented as an act of highest virtue. His evasion of life with its crudities, his emphasis on the interior realm and on "winged intelligence," and above all his unwillingness to render the role of necessity, wipe out the very margin in which we could be said to exist—the interface in which we attain such freedom as may be ours.

PART FOUR

And Now?

The Death of God

GOD IS DEAD, BUT THE GODS ARE ALIVE

Zarathustra was surely right: "God is dead." Many of us no longer believe in an all-knowing, just, and loving deity. But we also tend to think that *all* the gods are dead, though their names may have simply changed to biology, history, economics, culture, the unconscious, grammar, and chance.[1] They don't know we exist, but determine our lives as completely as the gods of old.

We used to believe that God was on our side and spoke to us. The metaphysical coincided with the social, and the sacred was embodied in the community. The laws of society were also the laws of God. It was *He* who told us not to steal. But today the gods no longer tell us anything. Perhaps they—or 'reality'—still 'speak,' but if they do, it is in a language we have yet to learn.

Though God is dead, Pan must be alive or our species would have ceased to be. But we find it hard to accept an unconscious, indifferent deity and tend to say, like children: if God can't take care of us or empower us, who needs Him? If He reflects an image of us as largely irrational and unfree, we'd *rather* he were dead. Indeed, the notion that all the gods are dead may recreate the world in accordance with our wishes, for if they are dead, perhaps *we* are in charge. But science and technology have greatly improved our lives, the promise of Positivism remains unfulfilled. We haven't mastered our destiny.

THE REAPPEARANCE OF THE INCOMPREHENSIBLE

For centuries we maintained our faith in a rational, predictable universe even when we ceased to believe in a rational deity. The death of God did not distress us as long as our world continued to function in a comprehensible way, obeyed the 'law' of cause and effect, and allowed us to think that we had a measure of control. Reason banished chance from the working of things. We felt confident that we could elicit causes and modify their effects. Our lives might be subject to unpredictable intrusions, but they would eventually yield to our understanding.

Chance first reappeared in Western thought in nineteenth-century science, the most Positivist of our endeavors, when Darwin established "the extreme chanciness and contingency of life's history":[2]

> (He) assumed that the changes that occur in generic characteristics have a mutational, accidental character, and that only subsequently do certain of these changes turn out to be useful, others harmful, to the existence of the genus.[3]

As Jacques Monod puts it:

> Chance *alone* is at the source of every innovation, of all creation in the biosphere. Pure chance, absolutely free but blind, at the very root of the stupendous edifice of evolution: this central concept of modern biology is no longer one among other possible or even conceivable hypotheses. It is today the *sole* conceivable hypothesis, the only one that squares with observed and tested fact. And nothing warrants the supposition—or the hope—that on this score our position is likely ever to be revised.[4]

Twentieth-century physics has discovered chance in the most fundamental of physical processes:

> An atom erupts whenever it likes to: and if it does, this is, quite literally, an *uncaused* event.[5]

Quantum mechanics is indeterministic and acausal. It is founded on the idea that "atomic physics is distinguished essentially from classical physics by the existence of discontinuities."[6]

The universe of Einstein, as Bertrand Russell points out, is governed not by cause and effect but by the "law of cosmic laziness":

> The sun exerts no force on the planets whatever[7]. . . . (It) acquires its apparent (gravitational) power through the fact that there are modifications of space-time all around the sun. . . . To say that the sun 'causes' these modifications of space-time is to add nothing to our knowledge. What we know is that the modifications proceed according to a certain rule, and that they are grouped symmetrically about the sun as centre. The language of cause and effect adds

only a number of quite irrelevant imaginings, connected with will, muscular tension, and such matters.[8]

In the universe—as in the plot of traditional story—events would seem to occur synchronically rather than sequentially.

As long as the 'law' of cause and effect was invalidated only in outer space, in our evolutionary past and within the atom, we were safe. But today unpredictability, indeterminacy, and discontinuity are an inescapable part of our daily experience. We used to live in a circumscribed realm in which surprise was minimized. We could feel reasonably secure and effective. The pace of life was slow and governed by repetition, so that the outcome of an action—our own or that of others—could be predicted with a degree of accuracy. But the realm we inhabit today is vast and the pace at which things happen has accelerated enormously. In 1913, the futurist Marinetti spoke of "the earth shrunk by speed";[9] more recently, Buckminster Fuller called our world a global village, and McLuhan claimed, optimistically, that "the electronic age returns us all to . . . a re-achieved intimacy."

One wonders. For though distant places have become instantly accessible to us, we can hardly call our relationship to them "intimate." Meanwhile, the realm we *actually* inhabit has become unfamiliar and subject to rapid change. Our interconnectedness and interdependence have robbed us of the confidence that we can understand and control our lives. In a world shrunk by speed, cause-and-effect relationships—which depend on a connection in time—become irrelevant or too complex to predict, even if the computer has greatly enhanced our capacity for lateral thinking.

We did not choose interdependence. Like change, it was thrust upon us and induces a sense of helplessness. What happens anywhere on earth can have an almost immediate effect on us, and our own actions, in turn, may have consequences in far-away places. Positivism held out the promise of greater freedom, but freedom and connectedness are mutually exclusive. To be "close"—from the Latin *clausus*, "closed, or shut"—also means "to be shut in."

The information explosion both enables us and leaves us prostrate. Knowledge no longer translates into power and control, and the profusion of available facts is as often confusing and paralyzing as it is empowering. Much of the time, social and economic problems no longer respond to expert intervention. Though *simple* cause-and-effect relationships continue to hold, once we move beyond them, our predictions are barely more accurate than prophesies based on reading the entrails of an animal. Our leaders, with access to all ascertainable facts, are often as baffled and at the mercy of events as the rest of us. Robert Kennedy said that though JFK had initiated the Cuba blockade, he had no way of controlling the consequences[10]—which comes as a surprise only in a context of our Positivist expectations. As Lincoln said:

> I claim not to have controlled events, but confess that events have controlled me.

Though our power as a species has increased exponentially, industrial processes and weapons of mass destruction have reduced the individual to a mere statistic. In hand-to-hand combat, men had a measure of control over their fate, but modern warfare turns them into "luck freaks."[11] Today, planning can seem pointless. It may leave us feeling like the man who tried to kill himself by jumping off an express train only to land in a haystack, from where he saw the train hurtle off an open bridge into a canyon. Often, we have no idea *why* what happens happens, or how it could have been avoided.[12] "Shit happens!" is our version of Tolstoy's "It had to occur because it had to." The hero of *Metamorphosis* wakes up one morning as a cockroach, and K in *The Trial* is found guilty and executed without ever understanding his crime. What happens to us may be deterministic or indeterministic—governed by cause or chance—but it is seldom governed by us.

When we don't understand the cause, events seem meaningless, for cause and meaning are deeply linked. The psychotic who shoots fifteen people in a mall doesn't 'mean' any of them: they just happen to be there. Perhaps their death is comprehensible or 'meaningful' in the context of our *society*, but in the lives of the individuals and their families it constitutes a meaningless intrusion of chance. They die for no 'reason.'

Like Captain Ahab, we resist the concept of fate as blind and indifferent to us, for it undermines our existence as individuals. As long as the community assigned us our place and acknowledged us, we could survive without a God who knows us. But once society, too, turned us into mere numbers, our situation became untenable. We have tried to find ways of reconstituting indifferent, unpredictable forces into caring gods. Even gambling can be seen as a form of "struggling with God or fate,"[13] an effort to determine whether they are for or against us. The story of Raskolnicov—who murders an old woman to prove he is a free being and not a louse—was conceived after Dostoevski suffered a disastrous losing streak at the roulette table, and he composed *The Gambler* between two chapters of *Crime and Punishment*.

Since chance is unaccountable, we mistrust and reject it, just as the Judeo-Christian tradition rejected the ancient gods.[14] Yet chance—like the gods—does 'good' as well as harm. In the evolutionary process, it may indeed be in the service of a blind, impersonal force—or 'god'—who 'wants' our species to survive and life to continue. But since our sense of personhood depends on our own accountability, this is hardly reassuring: we expect—or are expected—to play a critical part in shaping our destiny.

As Positivists, we experience helplessness more intensely than traditional cultures. It devastates us, and under the surface of our can-do society runs a strong current of doubt and despair. The either/or in our self-perception—we have either real power or *none*—can make our marginal, uncertain influence over events seem meaningless. Our Positivism veers easily into fatalism. If we are not in charge, we don't exist.

THE POWERLESS INDIVIDUAL

The price we have had to pay for the enhanced power of our species is the depotentiation of the individual, who may have the worst of both worlds—neither freedom nor a sense of community. Though we are caught in a situation of extreme interdependence, we have no sense of belonging to a larger whole. We are, moreover, interconnected in time as well as place. Even sexuality—a realm in which we seemed to have gained new freedom—is once again governed by the past. As Susan Sontag says:

> The fear of AIDS imposes on an act whose ideal is an experience of pure presentness (and a creation of the future) a relation to the past to be ignored at one's peril. Sex no longer withdraws its partners, if only for a moment, from the social. It cannot be considered just a coupling; it is a chain, a chain of transmission, from the past.[15]

Sex outside committed relationships is once again associated with death—as it was for women until Semmelweiss discovered the cause of puerperal fever, and for everyone while syphilis was fatal. Perhaps, as Sontag says, AIDS is no metaphor and 'means' nothing, but it confronts us—as all disasters do—with our marginality:

> If there is one lesson I have learned (from AIDS) . . . it is the lesson of powerlessness . . . . There is nothing I can do about it.[16]

Of course this is a "lesson" that those suffering from AIDS have every right to reject, since it stops them from doing what they *can* do—like fighting a blind, indifferent society.

Our industrial democracy tries to persuade each of us that we matter, though we are perfectly aware that we count only in statistics and elections. As long as we had a sense of our own value, the equality enjoined upon us by our institutions was not reductive, but once we became interchangeable and replaceable, equality devalued us and generated a scramble for status, importance, and difference. Our society must emphasize the rights and freedom of the individual because it comes so close to destroying them. It may attempt, in the economic realm—where we are urged to assert our will and do better and more than others—to make up for the lack of liberty we enjoy elsewhere. Among the few freedoms remaining to most of us is a choice between commercial brands and the ability to move from one place to another.[17]

Our pervasive sense of helplessness makes it impossible for us to *acknowledge* our helplessness.[18] We are so frightened of passivity that we no longer know how to be patient, and delude ourselves into believing that we are effective when we are merely hyperactive. Since our will and action appear irrelevant, we have lost confidence in the future, and see no point in sacrificing present gratification for future gain. Consciously, we may deny that we are beholden to circumstance but unconsciously we are close to the ancient conviction that "You are what each day makes you." Our sense of our existence is so frail that those who are different from us can constitute a grave threat, and many respond to it by insisting on the otherness or, indeed, inferiority of the other.

FASCISM AND THE DEATH OF GOD

A totalizing or totalitarian approach attracts those who feel invalidated by promising them a significant place or role. Though German fascism was rooted in economic, political, and historical circumstance, it clearly filled the vacuum left by the death of God and man. The source of Hitler's personal magnetism lay in his ability to repotentiate Germany and lead it out of despair. He was a 'religious' and, indeed, messianic figure who believed absolutely in his spiritual mission: the regeneration of a desperate, abused people. Though many Nazi leaders were nihilists with no faith in anything but power, Hitler himself was animated by more seductive convictions, and those close to him, while skillfully exploiting the religious aura he exuded, were themselves captive to it. When Goebbels briefly lost hope and confidence, he noted in his diary:

> I no longer believe completely in Hitler. That is the worst part of it; it's as though I've lost my inner support. I am cut in half.[19]

Hitler's public appearances were quasi-religious rituals, replete with symbols like the *Hakenkreuz*, which took the place of the Christian cross, and

Blutfahnen, blood-stained flags that served as sacred relics of the martyrs who had died in Nazi street battles. His appearances were orchestrated to turn him into the savior of his people and *Deutschland* into a sacred realm. His apotheosis could be viewed as an extreme distortion of the glorification of man inherent in humanism. In a deadly parody of the traditional relationship between the human and the sacred—in which we gain our identity and such freedom as may be ours by acknowledging our beholden status—the Germans regained their will and their 'freedom' by surrendering them to Hitler, the party, and the *Reich*.

Utter depotentiation converts all too easily into megalomania. A stateless would-be artist became an all-powerful *Führer* and a vanquished nation was transformed into the Master Race. Since the identity of Hitler's Germans derived from the delusion of their superiority, it had to be continually fed by war and conquest, at which they excelled. They could not stop—*Morgen die ganze Welt*—for unless all others were at their mercy they were nobodies once again. Objectively, the invasion of Russia made no sense but subjectively it was inevitable, since Hitler was convinced that the Soviet Union was run by Jews and bound to collapse as soon as he attacked. His extreme subjectivity was at once the wellspring of his power and the cause of his downfall.

The Germans urgently needed an inferior other—the Slav, the Black, and, closest at hand, the Jew—for their 'inferiors' empowered them and confirmed their own essential difference. *Without* them, their submission to Hitler, even unto death, might have been recognized as enslavement. They depended on the very *Unterrassen* they tried to wipe off the face of the earth. The concentration camps were not an excess or aberration of the system but its very essence: the guarantee of fascist existence. Just as virulent anti-Semitism was necessary to their rise, so the extermination of Jews had to continue until the very last hours of the *Reich*, long after everyone knew the war was lost. Killing Jews was more important than everything else. When the camps were about to be liberated by the Russian army, many prisoners were marched or trucked West, at once worthless and invaluable.[20] The Master Race could not survive without them. Hitler—who saw ridding the world of Jews as the heart of his mission and urged, in his political testament, that Germany continue "the merciless resistance against the world poisoner of every people, international Jewry"[21]—derived his *existence* from the Jew.

In 1851, Wagner wrote to Liszt:

> I harbored a long-contained resentment against (the) state of affairs corroded by the Jews, and this resentment is as necessary to me as gall is to blood.[22]

His anti-Semitism—like Hitler's—was essential to him, his life's blood. In *Das Judentum in der Musik*, he calls on Jews to undertake an *Erlösungsw-erk*—to 'redeem' themselves by wiping themselves off the face of the earth:

> Know that you can be released from your curse only through the solution of Ahasverus—your (own) annihilation.[23]

The Nazis, too, were familiar with the story of Purim and King Ahasverus, who hung a powerful minister for plotting the extermination of all the Jews in his kingdom. When Julius Streicher mounted the gallows after the Nuremberg trial, his last recorded words were: *"Purimfest, 1945."*

Within the camps, the SS were the fate of their prisoners—necessity itself, gods who understood that death is the most palpable aspect of the sacred. Celan, who had been at Auschwitz, says: *Der Tod ist ein Meister aus Deutschland*—"Death is a master from Germany." As de Sade implies, when we can no longer prove our existence in an interface with the sacred, we can try to prove it by subjecting others to our will. We potentiate ourselves and establish our own 'freedom' by enslaving, torturing and killing those who are weaker.

In the camps, the Nazis sought power not only over the life and death of their victims—which has always been within easy reach of those with the requisite brutality—but over their innermost being. Through systematic starvation, abuse, terror, and torture they tried to reduce those whom they did not kill immediately to an abject state that would confirm their own superior identity. The Polish prisoner at Buchenwald who refused the com-mand of an SS officer to bury alive two of his fellow inmates chose certain death.* But *in a defining moment,* the guard did *not* shoot him. He under-stood that if he killed the Pole, the man would have remained a hero, capable of self-sacrifice like the Germans. Instead—and on the spur of the moment—he conceived a scenario that reduced a heroic man to 'common' humanity, and so confirmed his own superiority. Only an evil genius or someone whose existence was at stake could have come up with a solution that exceeds the destructive brilliance of an Iago or Stavrogin. There isn't a moment in the entire Jacobean theater to equal it. Beside this apparently unexceptional SS man, the evildoers of Ford, Webster, Tourneur, and Shakespeare pale into stage villainy.

It is hard to account for the camps without recourse to the ancient con-cept of evil—evil as something other than a "product" like sugar and vit-riol. Within the bureaucratic system required to organize slave labor,

---

*See chapter two, page 15.

schedule the trains with their cattle cars, and arrange for the proper transfer of funds, evil was diffuse, workaday and "banal." But one may doubt that Dr. Mengele—standing inside the gates of Auschwitz with his elbow resting in the cup of one hand and indicating with a flick of his index finger who, in the endless procession of new victims, was to go to the left, or the gas chamber, and who to the right, or 'life' in the camp—was unaware he was playing God or, as the inmates called him, the Angel of Death. It is hard to think of the guard who pumped water into the intestines of prisoners through a hose and then jumped on their bloated bellies to explode them, as "banal." He seems, rather, to have proved his own abysmal existence by making others suffer in terror and pain. "You scream, therefore I am."

Just as Judaism and Christianity had done away with the evil in God, so humanism and Positivism did away with *human* evil. It took the Nazis to demonstrate that the death of individual man can, at least in the West, recreate him as a monster. There is little doubt that if Hitler had possessed atomic weapons, he would have, facing defeat, given orders to wipe out every being on earth. In his last days, he called down the *Götterdämmerung* on his own people. They had derived their identity and power from him and they owed him a death.

HIROSHIMA AND NAGASAKI

Der Tod ist ein Meister aus Deutschland. But not only *aus Deutschland.* The words that came to Oppenheimer when he witnessed the explosion of the first atomic bomb are from the *Baghavad Gita*:

> I am become death,
> The shatterer of Worlds.[24]

Though our reasons for using the bomb seemed legitimate at the time, at Hiroshima and Nagasaki *we* became "the pillar of fire" and the cloud that had once been Yahweh. However well-intentioned we are as a people, we, like the scientists who are our servants, are capable of sin.[25] We live under a constitution that severely limits the power of the individual, yet seem to entertain no doubt about the virtue of limitless power for the nation and the species. We know that as individuals we have little freedom and that our will is often ineffective, but we remain heirs to Positivism and continue to believe in our ability to better the lot of humankind at home and abroad. The dilemma of the can-do hero in the old stories confronts us as well. We feel impelled to act, though the final consequences of our actions are beyond our control and often turn out to be tragic not just for others but for ourselves.

24

Postmodernism and the Death of Man

Perhaps deconstructing the "unitary subject" connects the highly specialized humanist in the university with the community at large. But elsewhere in our society the individual needs to be revalidated rather than undermined. Even in the academy, critical thought seems first and foremost engaged in self-validation. We have noted that Derrida's emphasis on writing—a process involving individuals with other individuals, each of whom reads and writes alone—supports the very subject Postmodernism appears to undermine. Writing derives from individual continuity and affirms consciousness. As Walter Ong says:

> Though inspiration derives from unconscious sources, the writer can subject the unconscious inspiration to far greater conscious control than the oral narrator. The writer finds his written words accessible for reconsideration, revision, and other manipulation.[1]

The written word is open to the intervention of reason and encourages self-detachment:

> (It) introduces division and alienation, but a higher unity as well. It intensifies the sense of self and fosters more conscious interaction between persons. Writing is consciousness-raising.[2]

Whereas speech stresses communality and essence, the written text is at once more individuated and less immediately attached to the person who produced it. Since the writer is not in direct contact with his audience, he is freer than the speaker and leaves the reader freer, or more detached, than speech leaves the listener.

Postmodernism, though it pronounces "the death of man,"[3] may well be a *response* to it. *Il n'y a pas de hors-texte* could be read as the assertion of a radical humanism: we *are* the text and we *make* the world. Derrida says:

> The idea of the (traditional, i.e. Platonist) book . . . always refers to a natural totality.[4]

His own idea of a book appears to refer to a *non*-natural or human totality. Following his lead, American deconstructionists—like nineteenth-century Positivists—perceive God's death as an opportunity and a liberation.[5] In a comment on Victorian novelists, Hillis Miller defines his own perspective:

> The annihilation of God transforms everything for man, changing not only his experience of the world but also his experience of himself. It is associated with a situation in which human subjectivity seems to become the foundation of all things, the only source of meaning and value in the world. Nothing now exists unless I think it.[6]

Subjectivity, traditionally perceived as a limitation, now serves to confirm our existence. As Mark Taylor says:

> With the movement from Descartes, through the Enlightenment, to Idealism and Romanticism, attributes traditionally predicated of the divine subject are gradually transferred to the human subject. Through a dialectical reversal, the creator God dies and is resurrected as the creative subject. As God created the world through the Logos, so man creates a "world" through conscious and unconscious projection.[7]

Derrida is well aware that the subject remains "absolutely indispensable"— even if it does not exist:

> I believe that the center is a function, not a being—a reality, but a function. And this function is absolutely indispensable. I don't destroy the subject; I situate it. That is to say, I believe that at a certain level both of experience and of philosophical and scientific discourse one cannot get along without the notion of subject. It is a question of knowing where it comes from and how it functions. Therefore I keep the concept of center . . . as well as that of subject.[8]

TOWARD A 'SOCIOLOGY' OF THE AESTHETIC

Whereas modernism was defined by artists, the postmodern aesthetic has been largely defined by critics and academics, and most postmodern artists are university-trained. As a critical endeavor, it is, moreover, centered in universities that educate an elite. Not long ago, a president of Yale said that it was the mandate of his college to produce a thousand leaders a year.[9] Since leadership and excellence are generally predicated on a confident, 'positive' approach, Yale College—like other Ivy League schools—is a citadel of positive and, indeed, Positivist thinking. Whatever else students are taught, they are confirmed in the conviction that where there is a will there is a way.

Elite academies select students who will distinguish themselves as specialists. While public schools stress cooperation and good citizenship, prep schools expect their students to excel and, in this sense, to differentiate themselves from the rest of the community. Even as the economy obliges the workforce to become interchangeable, Ivy League colleges continue to emphasize individual development, on the legitimate assumption that society will benefit from the achievement of distinguished specialists.

Teachers of art and literature find themselves in the paradoxical situation of professing disciplines that emphasize the unitary subject, even though the subject has been undermined by doubt. A century after Ernst Mach declared that there is no saving the "I," they must try to communicate the relevance of work predicated on individual existence and experience. In a culture committed to action, they must, moreover, give students access to fictions that, by their very form, cast doubt on action, freedom, and the human will. Unlike their colleagues in science or law—who are focused on the acquisition of 'objective' knowledge and skills—they are concerned with inward continuity, though their own faith in it has eroded and though it no longer seems to serve the community at large. Understandably, they see themselves as "belated"—as having no legitimate role to play.

The anomalous place of an elitist academy in a democratic society may help account for the contradictory thrust of postmodern criticism. Though deconstruction is radically democratic in its ethos, it is inaccessible to most. By virtue of its own texts, it is a highly specialized discipline and endorses an art that is itself exclusive and inaccessible. Like the academies that promote it, postmodern theory is committed to human liberty, yet its own faith in our freedom is undermined by the suspicion that since nothing we think and feel is actually ours, we don't exist. Reestablishing the critic's faith in his own identity may, indeed, be a primary concern of contemporary criticism.[10]

To most of us, though we are vaguely aware of the role played by tradition and genre, the concept that art rather than 'reality' begets art seems a limitation. We want texts that reflect—or appear to reflect—our lives, not texts focused on other texts. Few paintings render a piece of sculpture—itself at one remove from life.[11] But while intertextuality is of little interest to the audience, it liberates and enables the critic. It validates his work, which is inevitably and almost exclusively an interaction with other texts. It spares him, as well, a confrontation with the sacred or Nothingness—the empty canvas that forced Edward Hopper to paint—for he remains safely in the reassuring presence of another text. If reality is *constituted* by texts, moreover, those who interpret them become figures of consequence in the community.

We have noted that the 'attack' on plot and story has come from an intellectual elite. Perhaps they see further than the rest of us, or have more to lose if their individuality and freedom are put in doubt. The threat to their self-determination may account, as well, for the dismissal of psychology by postmodern critics, who seem to suffer from what R. D. Laing calls "psychophobia." In the interpretation of texts, psychological factors are largely disregarded, though tenets of postmodern theory have long been familiar to depth psychology. Freud and Jung arrived at a radically reductive picture of the individual psyche well before postmodernism. As Jung says:

> (The layers of the psyche progressively) lose their individual uniqueness . . . that is to say as they approach the autonomous functional systems, they become increasingly collective until they are universalized and extinguished in the body's materiality, i.e. in chemical substances. The body's carbon is simply carbon. Hence "at bottom" the psyche is simply "world."[12]

Presumably the aesthetic dismisses psychology because it is no longer relevant—because man is dead. Yet depth psychology has made no great claim for human freedom—within or without. Both Freud and Jung believe that if we exist at all, it is as a narrow margin of consciousness wedged between compelling inner and outer determinants. They suggest that our best hope of gaining a voice in the 'deliberations' of unconscious forces lies in *acknowledging* their ascendant role. Perhaps contemporary criticism shows little interest in the unconscious because—like most of us—its practitioners need to believe we are masters in our own house.[13]

An aesthetic that affirms the individual and human liberty even as it insists on "the death of man" may assuage the isolation of those who are highly individuated *without* eradicating their difference. Perhaps it serves the same balancing function our structures and institutions perform for the rest of us. It claims to wipe out individuality yet confirms it, and permits the critic to feel that his work is useful to the community—that, indeed, he can use his position of secure privilege to invalidate privilege. Within the academy, moreover, the concept of intertextuality fosters democratic, nonhierarchic discourse among the living and with the illustrious dead.

LIMITATIONS OF THE AESTHETIC

While the artwork has traditionally incarnated the "invisible" or spiritual, the approach of contemporary criticism is materialist. It seems beguiled by the ancient dream of wholeness, which was given new life when Christianity—predicated on spirituality, human dividedness, and the relegation of wholeness to a life *after* death—lost its hold. Yet surprisingly, the materialist with his faith in a totality often thinks like a Manichean—albeit with reversed polarities. His world, too, is split into inimical forces. Since he believes that claims made on behalf of the spirit falsify and obscure the fundamental reality of matter—just as the Manichean deemed matter and the senses inimical to the spirit—he undermines them wherever they present themselves.

The dream of wholeness can beguile even the subtlest thinkers, perhaps because their work leaves them painfully fragmented and isolated. So Adorno writes to Benjamin:

The goal of the revolution is the elimination of anxiety.[14]

Even in Heidegger, after *Destruktion* and the presumed end of philosophy and metaphysics, there is a return to a genuine if archaic sense of wholeness, an "immersion" in *being* that removes us from the world of technology, and returns us to our oneness and our home.

As we have noted, postmodern theory dismisses human duality. "The death of man" and *Il n'y a pas de hors-texte* are totalizations. Though consciousness is central to deconstruction, it is not perceived as an inevitable source of our dividedness. Traditionally, human identity was *constituted by* our duality: it defined and distinguished us: we *were* our problematic. If, however, the text is the only reality, our self-division is an illusion. By dismissing it, postmodern thought wipes out the traditional source of our identity and so *constitutes* "the death of man." One might call it a self-fulfilling prophesy.

Seen positively, the invalidation of human duality challenges our assumptions, reveals the cause of needless conflicts and divisions, and opens up the possibility of new combinations and reconciliations. But in the realm of aesthetics, postmodern thought may be constricted and restrictive, for it cannot admit the existence of reality or necessity without returning us to the Platonist fold. If there *is* something beyond the text, art—and, indeed, philosophy—cease to be wholly intertextual, the sacred is reconstituted, and metaphysics is no longer at an end. *Il n'y a pas de hors-texte* is not a position Derrida takes simply to shake up our philosophical and aesthetic assumptions—one he "(preserves) as an instrument" though he criticizes its "truth value."[15] The rejection of all reality outside the text is indispensable to his approach. The beginning is the word or text—which is all we *know* and therefore all there *is*.

Though deconstruction celebrates doubt, in its relationship to the real or necessary it is committed to certainty. In this respect, deconstructionists fit Freud's description of "modern Messiahs, who proclaim the relativity of all knowledge except their own."[16] There can be nothing 'playful' in Derrida's rejection of the real or sacred. Engels points to the conflict between "the whole dogmatic context of Hegel's *system* which is declared to be absolute truth, in contradiction to his dialectical *method*, which dissolves all dogmatism."[17] Derrida dissolves all dogma, but despite attempts to qualify his position, his rejection of an anterior, transcendent 'objective' reality has been—and perhaps must be—dogmatic.[18]

POSTMODERNISM AND SCIENCE

In part, the realist position of science accounts for the antiscientific stance of modern thinkers, from Heidegger and Wittgenstein to Foucault.

The humanist's mistrust of science dates from the Renaissance, when science at once potentiated humankind *and* displaced us from the center of creation. At the very moment, moreover, when European culture assigned a central role to the individual, science set in motion developments that would in time undermine the individual and his creator. The "two worlds" of C. P. Snow appeared as soon as the humanities were called upon to defend the inner realm and metaphysics against science, with its commitment to objectivity and the physical world. Specialization forced the two disciplines ever further apart. But whereas the scientist could afford to ignore the humanist, nineteenth-century humanism could no longer ignore science, which—as the discipline with immediate, practical consequences—had become the dominant force in society. In order to maintain their authority, the humanities, too, had to become scientific, or *wissenschaftlich*. Yet contemporary humanists—while subscribing to positions, like the death of the individual, they rejected for centuries—remain stubbornly antiscience. As Richard Rorty says in his discussion of contemporary "textualists" and nineteenth-century idealists:

> Both movements adopt an antagonistic position to natural science. Both suggest that the natural scientist should not be the dominant cultural figure, that scientific knowledge is not what really matters. Both insist that there is a point of view other than, and somehow higher than, that of science. They warn us against the idea that human thought culminates in the application of "scientific method." Both offer to what C. P. Snow called "the literary culture" a self-image, and a set of rhetorical devices.
>
> From Hegel on, intellectuals who wished to transform the world or themselves, who wished for more than science could give, felt entitled simply to *forget* about science. Hegel had put the study of nature in its place—a relatively low one.[19]

For Derrida, science—like philosophy—is a form of writing, or literature. Since he defines literature as entirely intertextual, science can make no legitimate claim on a reality beyond the text. Here, as in the matter of our freedom, deconstruction positions itself as an antithesis to Lévi-Strauss, who places his work firmly within a scientific context.[20]

Yet given the rapid progress and highly specialized language of science, the humanist's grasp of it is almost inevitably out of date.[21] So we find Gadamer saying:

> (We must) once again . . . take up the Socratic legacy of a 'human wisdom' that is ignorance itself when measured against the divine infallibility of what is known by modern science.[22]

"Divine infallibility" hardly describes twentieth-century physics, which has discovered uncertainty, unpredictability, and chance in the most fundamental processes. Adorno is equally out of touch when he writes that

> In sharp contrast to the usual ideal of science, the objectivity of dialectical cognition needs not less subjectivity but more.[23]

What he ascribes to "the usual ideal of science" applies only to Kuhn's "normal science." As Schroedinger says:

> We have to admit that our conception of material reality today is more wavering and uncertain than it has been for a long time. We know a great many interesting details, learn new ones every week. But to construct a clear, easily

comprehensible picture on which all physicists would agree—that is simply impossible. Physics stands in a grave crisis of ideas. In the face of this crisis, many maintain that no objective picture of reality is possible.[24]

Science today accepts subjectivity as an inescapable element of reality and knows that, on the most fundamental level, the predictable and 'objective' model it had built of life and the universe is no longer valid.

Heidegger's critique of science[25] addresses its *hubris*—its confident, rationalist approach:

> The comedy—or rather the tragedy—of the present situation of science is that one thinks to overcome positivism through positivism.[26]

No doubt there are still 'mad' scientists, imbued with principles of pure Positivism and convinced—like Doctors Faustus and Frankenstein[27] —they can become gods. But most are well aware that scientific knowledge is limited, that they often have no way of predicting the consequences of their work, and that, indeed, they may do grave harm.[28]

Given the postmodern stress on uncertainty, one would expect contemporary humanists—some of whom do not, of course, *call* themselves humanists—to seek an alliance with science instead of remaining antagonistic to it. The inconsistency is resolved if we see postmodernism, despite all assertions to the contrary, as a *defense* of 'man.' Its most basic objection to science is that it remains committed to a reality beyond the text—a reality that is independent of us and casts grave doubt on our freedom and independence.

Science continues to believe in objective systems. Events in the atom are deemed to occur whether we are present to observe them or not. Most scientists remain 'realists' and posit forces and laws that determine our existence.[29] Whether they believe, like Einstein, that God did not "play dice," or that, at the core of matter, events are subject to chance, the universe of the scientist exists beyond the text. Schroedinger remains a Platonist. He says only that we may not be able to attain an "objective *picture*" of reality—not that there *is* no reality.[30]

Science effectively returns us to a perspective in which the forces that created and determine us are as unconscious as archaic gods. Humanists—who at one time mistrusted science because it undermines the sacred and man—now mistrust it for the opposite reason: it keeps necessity in full view. Though scientists are engaged in extending our reach, they are seldom given to the inflated view of themselves or our species that humanists have, on occasion, indulged.

Postmodernists pronounce the death of both God and man. But in science, the gods—whether perceived as order and law, or as chaos and chance—remain very much with us. Science, moreover, continues to believe that human beings can understand the 'gods'—at least up to a point. Its processes of discovery and understanding validate us and our awareness, and constitute an interface with the sacred that confirms both the gods, or their modern equivalents, and humankind.

Science maintains a psychological balance between freedom and necessity. It does not despair of our ability to 'act,' for—at least in pure science—discovery, which we might call an extension of consciousness, is valued for its own sake and constitutes an affirmation of the human. Conversely, scientists often preserve a sense of awe or reverence and a secure awareness that we are part of a larger whole. When Einstein was asked whether he was afraid of death, he replied:

> I feel myself to be so much a part of life that I am not in the least concerned with the beginning or end of the concrete existence of any particular person in this unending stream.[31]

In science, we continue to have a place in the scheme of things, albeit one so modest and insignificant that today's humanists—despite their insistence that man is dead—may be too frail to occupy it.

At one time defenders of the soul and spirit, humanists now find science appearing on their 'right,' in positions that could be called traditional—committed to necessity, essences, and objective reality. These absolutes have, of course, been the foundations of Western structures and institutions, and were long used—or misused—to justify the status quo. Rorty says that postmodernism—which he equates with his own brand of pragmatism—rejects science as a *metaphysic*:

> A post-Philosophical culture . . . would be one in which men and women felt themselves alone, merely finite, with no links to something Beyond. On the pragmatist's account, positivism was only a halfway stage in the development of such a culture—the progress toward, as Sartre puts it, doing without God. For positivism preserved a god in its notion of Science . . . the notion of a portion of culture where we touched something not ourselves, where we found Truth naked, relative to no description . . . .
>
> Pragmatism, by contrast . . . views science as one genre of literature.[32]

Those who feel themselves to be "alone . . . with no links to something Beyond," clearly hope to free themselves of the very connections that science continues to elicit and demonstrate.[33]

371

CHAPTER TWENTY-FOUR

WE ARE HAUNTED POSITIVISTS

Since postmodernism and our culture at large insist on human freedom, both must reject traditional story, which—like science—is predicated on a reality or truth outside the text. Yet, ironically, they may reject it not because they don't believe it, but because they *do*.

Stories depend on an awareness of necessity *and* on faith in human action. In periods of surging confidence—like the Renaissance and the nineteenth century—narratives were governed by strong plots, whereas we, who are not sure we exist, cannot face our helplessness even in fiction. By severing the link between art and reality, by insisting that texts are 'playful' or entertaining, the aesthetic—like the culture at large—may be trying to preserve an illusion of freedom that daily life no longer affords us.

Necessity is so threatening to our sense of ourselves that we face it—often without resources—only when it imposes itself inexorably. Yet as depth psychology suggests, what we banish from reality or consciousness is apt to reappear in the inner realm. Since we are no longer free to acknowledge the gods, we live in anxiety, for despite our faith in reason we sense that the irrational or nonhuman is ever-present within and around us, and may well determine us.

Our Positivism is haunted. We believe in things we *don't* believe. If religious feeling springs out of fear and an awareness of human helplessness, perhaps we are closer to its archaic origin than our lack of faith suggests.

Envoy

THE USES OF NECESSITY

An awareness of our helplessness may seem debilitating and pointless. But as William James says:

> Let us see . . . whether pity, pain, and fear, and the sentiment of human helplessness may not open a profounder view and put into our hands a more complicated key to the meaning of the situation.[1]

Perhaps the crisis of meaning that afflicts our culture springs from our inability to acknowledge necessity. For necessity *is* meaning. As Feuerbach says:

> Existence without needs is superfluous existence. . . . A being without distress is a being without ground.[2]

Those the world over who are engaged in a daily struggle for survival yearn to be free of physical need. *Their* gods are too much with them and may have to die as ours did, for they are often used to justify human misery and perpetuate the status quo. But we in the West suffer the opposite problem. Our distress is, in part, a product of our success at distancing ourselves from necessity. We have gone from being 'prisoners' of meaning to an existence that often seems meaningless.

For legitimate reasons, the Enlightenment tradition has conflated our rights vis-à-vis our institutions with our freedom in relation to the gods. But while we are entitled to equality vis-à-vis our fellow beings, we are not equal to the gods and can likely lead sane and balanced lives only if we respect rather than dismiss them.

Since we have cause to fear and mistrust the sacred, most religions separate good gods from bad—God from Devil. But we in the West, after two thousand years of believing that God is our loving father, have come to think of *all* gods as our enemies, and deem everything beyond our control inimical to us. We blame disasters on the stars but give them no credit for the good that befalls us,[3] and think of miracles as mere superstitions, relics of a naive faith. Yet one *could* make a case that evolution is more 'miraculous' than the creation of the world by an all-powerful deity.

Those not raised in the conviction that we are in charge of our fate take a different and perhaps more realistic view. The old saying "It's a gift" is an expression of gratitude—a folk version of Leibniz's and Heidegger's "astonishment at being." It acknowledges that the gods owe us nothing, that we are indebted to them. Even if we *lack* faith, we might say that life—unconscious though it be—'wants' us to live and, indeed, to 'stand out,' since our existence serves human survival and the community. But Positivists do not take easily to gratitude or reverence. To be grateful is akin to being graceful—the two words share the same root—and a state of grace is not one to which we aspire. It smacks of acceptance and resignation.

Individually, we recognize that we must reconcile ourselves to necessity. We fight the process of aging but are obliged, in the end, to accept it. Most of us *do* go gentle into that good night—aware that we are better off surrendering willingly, or gracefully, what will otherwise be taken from us brutally. As a Roman proverb has it, those who refuse to go hand in hand with their fate will be dragged along—mostly likely screaming. The difficulty, of course, lies in recognizing when we are actually up against fate or necessity, and when it is merely a mask for the will of another person, a calcified law, an outworn custom, or a manipulative, exploitative power structure that has donned the mantle of necessity.

Our culture at large is firmly committed to nonacceptance and rejects all resignation as abdication. Susan Sontag speaks for many when she says:

Resignation, resignation, it drives me wild.[4]

But though we believe in battling the inevitable and reject *amor fati*, as individuals we try to steer a middle course between resistance and resignation, rejection and acceptance, action and passivity. We distinguish, as best we can, between situations we can change and those about which we can do nothing. When in doubt, we legitimately act as though our actions will make a difference. Indeed, our doubt *enables* us to act—which is not to claim, as some do, that our heightened awareness of uncertainty and unpredictability allows us to consign necessity to the ash-heap of false assumptions. Significantly, though Nietzsche proclaimed the death of God, he did not dismiss necessity:

> Our total lack of responsibility for our actions and our being is the bitterest medicine the conscious person must swallow if he was used to seeing in our sense of responsibility and duty the distinguishing marks of our humanity. All his estimations, distinctions, aversions are thereby invalidated and proved false; his deepest feelings, which he reserved for the hero and the sufferer, sprang from a misapprehension; he is no longer entitled to praise or blame, for it makes no sense to praise or blame necessity.[5]

An affirmative relationship to necessity may actually constitute a positive relationship to life itself. Though we have ceased to believe in a God who loves us, learning to love necessity or the sacred may have pragmatic value, for it reconnects us to the rest of creation, to each other and ourselves.

Jung says:

> As far as we can discern, the sole purpose of human existence is to kindle a light in the darkness of mere being. It may even be assumed that just as the unconscious affects us, so the increase in our consciousness affects the unconscious.[6]

Many of us would agree with the first sentence. But the second presents a problem, for it suggests that by changing our relationship to the unconscious, we can actually change its relationship to *us*—an equivalent of the belief that prayer intercedes with the gods. If, however, instead of reading it in the context of individual existence and consciousness, we read it in the context of the species, it may be acceptable. For we have clearly learned to modify not only the 'gods' around us but those within. Nietzsche says:

> We are the figures in the dream of a god who understand how he dreams.[7]

But we have gone further still. We have actually *changed* his dream!

WOMEN AND MEN

Though human communities are no longer an integral part of nature, they cannot afford to block the raw energy of our instincts. We *adapt* them and adapt *to* them; we at once give them their due and channel what, in the animal kingdom, is often violent and destructive, into relationship and community. As social science has noted, we have transformed the ingestion of food—which, in the creature world, is often fiercely competitive—into a ritual sharing that sustains and enhances rather than threatens relationships. Energies that might fragment the community are, instead, used to strengthen it.

Among primates as in many species, the sexual instinct puts the male on a war footing with other males, while *oestrus* restricts his access to individual females. The human female, however, has learned to bond an individual male and to integrate him into the community by being sexually available to him at most times. Briffault and others have suggested that the bonded pair was the basis of human society, for it channeled the energy of the male into protecting his mate and their offspring, and allowed the nurturing, tender instinct of the female an extended development.[8] It is widely assumed that maternal feelings, and the prolonged immaturity of the infant they make possible, have fostered the emergence of human society and sensibility:

> Tender emotions and affections have . . . their origin not in sexual attraction but in maternal reactions. Apart from the relation between mother and off-spring there is in competitive animality no germ of that order of feelings. Just as the transferred affection of the female for the male is a direct derivative of maternal feelings, so all feelings of a sympathetic, altruistic character, which . . . in direct contrast to biological impulses are almost entirely absent in animals, and are specific characters of human psychology, are extensions of maternal reaction. They owe the mere possibility of their existence to the development of maternal feelings.[9]

Though more recent research may have established the presence of "altruistic" instincts in the animal kingdom, Briffault's observations remain of interest, for in most societies the socializing of male sexuality has been perpetuated—or institutionalized—by placing the young, during their most formative years, in the care of women. Perhaps the male has *had* to be raised by women in order to become sensitive and responsive to their needs, in order to become truly civilized[10]—which is not to suggest that this function cannot, today, be shared by men.

Traditionally, Eve has been rendered as a temptress and instinct figure. Yet she merely *used* instinct to tempt Adam into consciousness, difference, and the knowledge of good and evil. Perhaps Satan addressed himself to *her*—

"Your eyes shall be opened, and you shall be as gods, knowing good and evil"

—because woman is the primary socializing, civilizing force. *Her* instincts are not destructive of the community and it is the male who must be seduced into consciousness and society.

Though the socialization of sexuality is essential, it is fraught with complications and conflict. Instinctual energy cannot be permanently channeled and kept in place. As the needs and configurations of society shift, our instincts must accommodate to new channels and new relationships, creating a situation between the sexes that is subject to constant, often profound change.

In Western society, specialization and industrialization have turned men into absent, often remote figures, and children spend their early years in what is effectively a matriarchy.[11] They derive not only sustenance and care from women but are granted their very sense of existence by maternal recognition and approval. Though today the socialization of women into gentle, feeling beings engaged primarily in fostering and sustaining relationships, is under legitimate attack, it served communal needs for an extended period. In part, women have been denied access to their anger and aggression because, as primary caregivers, they could destroy their offspring physically and emotionally. The power they exercise over the young—and continue to exert psychologically over many adult men—is, of course, experienced *as* power only when it is negative and destructive, rather than loving and supportive. In defense of their families, they were always expected to be as fierce as men.

The psychological tutelage of the male to woman has been, and surely *needed* to be, so effective that men have long carried with them a residual fear of women.[12] In many societies, young males continue to be caught in a double bind, for while they must learn to become sensitive to women, they must establish their identity not—like girls—by *identifying* with their mothers but by differentiating themselves.[13] It is hardly surprising that their identity has often been more conflict-ridden and less secure than women's.

The repression of woman by the patriarchy to the great advantage of males may be rooted in the insecure identity of men. Superior intellectual and moral powers are claimed by the sex that feels not only beholden to the other but may well be persuaded, deep down, of its own marginal role in the business of life. Man comes out of woman, not woman out of Adam's rib. Our so-called higher functions and all the 'important' activities in the community ultimately serve to assure the continuity of human existence, in which woman and her offspring play the crucial role. Since men

377

believe, with good reason, that women are the bearers of life's central energies, they suffer an often unacknowledged sense of inadequacy.

Men and women are today engaged in a difficult, often painful effort to
evolve new connections both within themselves and to each other. The
couple as we know it constellates an interface not only between two individuals but between culture and nature and between past and present.
Many of us are virtually alone on unfamiliar ground. Gender relationships
in prior generations no longer serve as a viable model, and institutions that
have lost their validity can offer us little guidance. The surprising thing is
not that many couples fail to make it, but that any do.

Our sense of individual existence has been so thoroughly undermined
that we may actually *cling* to gender identity, though both economic circumstance and inner need urge us to surrender it. Moreover, the very differences that created the gulf between the sexes have, in the past, also
served to bond them, for our relationship to each other has long been based
on the incompleteness of each sex. When men and women ruled separate
realms, contact as well as conflict between them was minimized, while now
the boundaries defining the domain of each are blurred and exacerbate our
insecurity. The very process of opening ourselves to the other sex has added
to the tension and fear that keep us apart.

Today's couple may constitute the most demanding and complex relationship our society has evolved, and its survival seems assured only because
it has become, for many, the one lasting, dependable connection. All other
ties have attenuated or frayed. Yet its singular, central importance adds to
the difficulties, for the relationship between two people, in marriage and
out, is often expected to meet ontological needs—to give us our place, our
reason for being, our very hold on life and ourselves—that our structures
and institutions can no longer meet.

An equally heavy burden is placed—or misplaced—on the sexual act.
Sexuality, like the natural or sacred of which it is an aspect, carries a wide
range of meanings and is subject to extensive metaphorization. It changes
meaning not only from culture to culture, but from age to age, and—in
our society—from person to person. We *re*define it as we redefine ourselves, and the effort to strip it of all metaphysical, metaphoric meaning
has been but a necessary prelude to the emergence of new meanings and
metaphors. For whenever we encounter instinct, we are face to face with
the sacred, and since confronting it in its original, naked form would destroy us, we must veil it in metaphors and taboos.

Though the sexual act cannot meet our ontological needs, it remains an
interface between the human and the sacred, at once an acknowledgment
of the sacred and an affirmation of the human. It is an interaction between

the instinctual and the civilized, the impersonal and the personal—a transformation of nature into culture that violates neither. Like all encounters with the sacred, it is both frightening and exhilarating. It blurs boundaries, wipes out differences, and threatens to shatter our individuality. Therein lies its ontological force, for—like ritual—it holds out the promise of a union that will heal the wound of consciousness: the inner and outer realm can briefly come into harmony and the needs and will of another may coincide perfectly with our own. Here opposites are reconciled: 'violence' with tenderness, fear with trust, action with passivity. We call it an act, though it is done *through* as much as by us. It offers evidence that we are loved—though not for ourselves alone. It requires that we be in touch with each other *and* ourselves even while we are in the grip of an overriding, depersonalizing force. It is a confluence of the particular and the universal that allows us to affirm our relationship to each other *in—and in spite of—* the palpable presence of the sacred.

But though sexuality is a 'god,' it is no substitute for the God who died. It cannot, for longer than a moment, give us our place, keep us connected to the creation, or prove that we are wanted and necessary. The intense pleasure we feel and may give offer no lasting evidence for our existence, and if we expect it to meet our ontological needs—if our life isn't itself part of a larger whole—it will leave us desolate.

Our changing relationships have turned sexuality into a no-man's land in which many couples are alone—or free—and must find their way without help. But find it they will, for it constitutes the basis of a bond that has endured since Adam and Eve left the walled garden of unconsciousness— solitary but hand in hand. We owe human love in all of its permutations to our fall from grace or wholeness, and the force that binds us to each other derives, like the force that bonds the community, from our incompleteness—our need to be part of a whole.

THE OPEN SELF

The uncertainty facing us everywhere is but a prelude to our growth. Boundaries must rupture to expand, and the crisis we suffer individually and as a species is surely propelling us toward a more inclusive identity and more inclusive communities. To survive, we must become complex and, indeed, multiple personalities, who can shift rapidly from one facet of ourselves to another as we move through the day with its fragmented, fragmenting encounters. We can no longer afford to be consistent—to carry an 'attitude' from one situation to the next, where it is apt to be out of place.[14]

Instead, we need a fluid, 'uncertain' ego—a continuity that consists, in large part, of a willingness to become discontinuous. We must move well beyond the position Rieff ascribes to Freud:

> A tolerance of ambiguities is the key to what (he) considered the most difficult of all personal accomplishments: a genuinely stable character in an unstable time.[15]

We can no longer sustain "a genuinely stable character." Hegel speaks of and praises "the game of self-dissolution,"[16] and Jung said in 1922:

> It is, in particular, the phenomena of somnambulism, double consciousness, split personality, etc . . . that have enabled us to accept the possibility of a plurality of personalities in one and the same individual.[17]

The contemporary self with its collage structure is prefigured in the Cubist work of Braque and Picasso, in which the image—and therewith the perceiving, experiencing self—is composed of patches, including bits of the morning newspaper.[18]

An identity crisis, when Erikson first used the term, was a state we traverse in our youth.[19] It has become the foundation of our existence. The crisis *is* our identity. But just as the gods are not dead, neither are we. Our lives *had* to become meaningless before new meaning could emerge, and if we must 'die' it is only in order to live.[20] What we experience as an ending that violates us as individuals and appears to undermine all relationships that were derived from a stable identity is also a beginning.

Change and growth are seldom harmonious, and the ceaseless transformation that is required of us leaves us permanently anxious. Few can live with a constant threat of disintegration and many withdraw into an ethnic or religious shell. They respond to the new by circling their wagons around the old and continue to exclude the 'other'—who not only serves to confirm their own identity but becomes a scapegoat on which they can focus their fear and the violence it engenders.

To be in genuine harmony with our situation, we would have to live in a state of nonexclusive, nonhierarchic difference—at once truly ourselves and open to all others. But even the most inclusive self will inevitably exclude. With the wolf of necessity and mortality never far from the door, we are bound to hierarchies of importance, and individuals as well as communities are forever engaged in a process of triage—prioritizing those who contribute to their immediate survival and neglecting or dismissing others.

In an ideal society—one not bound upon the wheel of need—everything we do might have the same value, irrespective of its immediate importance and regardless of its success or failure. Inadequacies and imperfections could be disregarded, for there would be room and time to make up for them. We might thus become truly equal, not just before the law and in the voting booth but, more significantly, in each other's eyes. Even today, in our own, imperfect communities, we are well aware that the 'unimportant' things we do all day are, in their endless repetition, the most meaningful ones: the very stuff of life. We pay lip service to the 'importance' of those who are spot-lit—heroes and heroines in every field of human endeavor—but at the deepest level we value them because they sustain our common, ordinary existence. We may even sense—though we cannot live by it—that *all* human effort is ultimately equal and that all of us do what we can, however little or inadequate it may seem. This is, of course, the burden of traditional story, which—like James's "pity, pain, fear and . . . human helplessness"—*does* "open a profounder view" on our existence.

POSTMODERNISM AND THE OPEN SELF

Postmodern thought is committed to doing away with all exclusionary and hierarchic authority. The end of philosophy and metaphysics and the death of narrative are part of a relativization of all cultures and values—a necessary attempt to delimit us and prepare us for what may, some day, become one world.[21] Ideally, a "post-philosophical culture" would be "answerless"[22] —as *Sein und Zeit* is said to be—and therefore open to all possible answers. Perhaps the multiplicity and indeterminacy of deconstruction responds to our own need to become indeterminate, to gain access to our multiplicity, though thus to interpret it links the text to a reality beyond it. Indeed, postmodern thought cannot be deemed truly inclusive and "answerless" unless it makes room for essences, human duality, reality, and the sacred— for traditional philosophy and art.

Perhaps there can *be* no "answerless" thought—no thought without a position, without reference to a 'reality.' Though the work of Derrida is sometimes called nihilistic, it is far from a self-contained game. Even the philosophy of Heidegger, which inspired the anti-essentialist stance of post-modernism, finally proposes an 'answer,' or at least a direction. In his return to the archaic, exclusive, and singular, he moves to the 'right,' while Der-rida and his colleagues move to the 'left.' Neither offer us simple or 'vulgar' solutions, and both suggest a much-needed alternative to the rigidity that, in time, afflicts all human structures and systems. As Derrida says:

I strongly and repeatedly insist on the necessity of the phase of reversal, which people have perhaps too swiftly attempted to discredit. . . . To neglect this phase of reversal is to forget that the structure of the opposition is one of conflict and subordination and thus to pass too swiftly, without gaining any purchase against the former opposition, to a *neutralization* which in *practice* leaves things in their former state and deprives one of any way of *intervening* effectively.[23]

Surely the impact and influence of postmodern thought would be minimal if it were without practical consequences and irrelevant to our social and political condition. Its very rejection of 'reality' might be deemed a 'realistic' response to our situation. In the early 1970s, someone scrawled on a Boston fence: "Reality is the changing face of need." Contemporary reality, or need, changes its face so frequently that any 'fix' we have on it is apt to become a liability. Every defined position, or 'reality,' is indeed unrealistic.

Yeats pointed out that some of our greatest teachers did not write books. Perhaps Socrates spoke rather than wrote because he was engaged in an open, fluid process in which those with whom he spoke were as important as the speaker *and*, indeed, as the subject under discussion. Perhaps Derrida, in shifting continually, attempts on the printed page what Socrates did in his dialogues. His refusal to stay put could be seen, in part, as a response to the structuralist critique of writing as a form of domination, and his continuous reversals may be an effort to give the written text a truly open, democratic character.

If we approach deconstruction as a dialectical process that implies both polarities even when it affirms only one, it enables us to move beyond the violent oppositions and hierarchies that dominate our own culture as they do many others, and gives us access to a more inclusive perspective. It is, however, a perspective open only to a privileged minority—those who are not obliged to choose between 'either' and 'or' but can opt for both or move rapidly back and forth between them. It is a perspective, moreover, far more easily maintained by the intellect than in daily life.

There is of course nothing new or radical about 'either *and* or.' The ideal of reconciling or balancing opposites is as old as consciousness itself and central to most religions. If we were free of need, we would surely opt for the "mystery of reconciliation" that is "the secret of Hegelian dialectic."[24] We would choose both past *and* present, present *and* future, individual *and* community, subject *and* object, mind *and* matter, body *and* soul, trust *and* doubt, reason *and* feeling, sequential *and* synchronic modes of thought. Since, however, we are limited by need and mortality, all reconciliations are temporary. At best, being human is an oscillation between opposites, and all we can hope for from 'either *and* or' is an awareness of both—an avoidance of rigid polarizations and of violent swings between extremes. Today, the safest, sanest and most realistic response to our situation is surely found in a continually shifting, uncertain, ambiguous, insecure, and anxiety-ridden middle ground.

THE USES OF UNCERTAINTY

Though uncertainty seems emblematic of our time, it has always been central to human experience. We find it so threatening that we have often banished or killed those who hold to a different certainty. In the past, our structures and institutions sheltered us. They minimized uncertainty by setting before us a menu of our options and their price. The consequences of our actions were clearly laid out for us: the wages of sin were death, and a compact with the devil led to eternal damnation. But today, society can offer us few assurances. We no longer know the consequences of our actions. We may not even *want* to know, for certainty would inhibit our presumed freedom and mobility. The price we pay for our 'liberty' is anxiety. Even two hundred years ago, as de Tocqueville noted, Americans were surprisingly anxious.

The constant, leveling flux in our industrial democracy keeps us from holding on to anything, and as members of an open society we are bound to be placeless and insecure. But though we want freedom, we must have security. Since few can survive in a state of permanent uncertainty, some cling fiercely to certainties that no longer apply, while others patch together—like Lévi-Strauss's *bricoleurs*—a 'system' of private and public beliefs they hope will see them through.

Our uncertainty and loss of control are at once an ordeal and an opportunity. Bertrand Russell says of the young Wittgenstein:

He is the only man I have ever met with a real bias for philosophical skepticism; he is glad when it is *proved* that something can't be known.[25]

Perhaps he was "glad" because uncertainty and unpredictability are manifestations of the sacred. For until rationalism possessed us entirely, God *was* the unknown—at once an expression of our fears and their resolution.[26]

If we can learn to live with uncertainty, it may engender a new and different relationship to the sacred—a sacred that, unlike the God who died, includes all and contradicts itself. As long as we lived in stable communities, we could afford a deity who was clearly defined and excluded those who were different. But today the gods are no longer '*ours*.' They are everybody's and nobody's, or, as Borges puts it, "many and no one," "everything and nothing." There is, of course, a precedent for this in the pantheism of antiquity, among Christian mystics, the Kabbalists, and the founders of Hassidism, who saw God everywhere and to whom everything was sacred.

Perhaps our uncertainty can 'remystify' the world and make us, as a species, more respectful and less rash. Though the sacred is unconscious and issues no instructions, we can surely learn from it, for if we know how to look and listen, everything speaks to us, teaches us, informs us. Just as servants know more about their masters than their masters do about them, so we may understand more when we stand *under* things and are beholden to them. If the knowledge that we are not in charge doesn't panic us into frantic activity, it can make us modest, democratic, and kind—kin to all others and, indeed, to everything in creation.

Uncertainty may even prompt us to accept the possibility of a nonmaterial reality. We reject the spiritual not only because it cannot be proven—for nor can our will and our freedom—but because it has been used to justify exploitation and has often led to a disdain for the body. Today even devout Christians believe that if the body is neglected, the spirit will sicken and die. We are pragmatists who put first things first and attend to the physical and economic before we concern ourselves with the spirit or soul. Yet the spirit, too, clearly serves and preserves life, even if it is apt to become a significant force only when our physical and mental powers begin to fail. As consequential pragmatists, it behooves us to suspend our materialism, for the spirit too has survival value. It 'works.'

Significantly, our materialist culture is disrespectful of matter, which we waste, while we worship an abstraction: money. Like the supernatural of old, money can assume an infinite variety of shapes. It is the *sine qua non* of our physical existence; our key or solution to most problems; the guarantee of our freedom, well-being, and security; and, for many, a way of establishing identity or difference. Yet it is a mere symbol, with no more substance than the God who died. Unlike gold, it cannot even be used decoratively, and in most instances it no longer actually passes through our hands. Like the sacred in the life of the believer, it seems real and immediate but is, in fact, absent and abstract. When an old woman I knew felt the approach of death, she abstracted herself into cash by selling everything she owned. A confirmed nonbeliever, she nonetheless transformed herself into an equivalent of the spirit, became 'liquid,' and prepared to let her possessions, like her body, assume a new and different form.

Some think that since the 'certainty' or 'truth' we live by isn't the only truth, there *is* no truth. But *one* truth has simply fragmented into many, all of them valid in their time and place. Perhaps the challenge to our assumptions and the loss of our confidence and 'meaning' have merely returned us to the situation before rationalism and Positivism claimed that certainty was within our grasp. Our 'crisis' may be nothing more than the realization that the expectations of Positivism cannot be met, and that the "religion of humanity" is not, after all, an abiding faith.

Traditionally, it was assumed that our 'truth' or 'reality' is relative to a truth beyond it. A contemporary interpretation might suggest that we can move toward it by making our lives and experience a process of continuous qualification. Uncertainty, which was at one time identical with the sacred, may once again become the one dependable, 'stable' base on which our unstable human enterprise must rest—the central, fundamental and incontrovertible foundation of our existence.

Of course communities must continue to depend on certainty. We cannot live with unpredictable laws and ambiguous traffic signals, or entrust our lives to waffling engineers and physicians. But while traditional societies, too, were predicated on certainties, they created a space for uncertainty in the safe or 'privileged' arena of ritual and art. Story rendered the sacred in its archaic form—*as* uncertainty—and its preclusive structure undermined our will and our faith in cause and effect. Traditional story 'knew' that we cannot count on anything, and the plot constituted an analog of the unpredictable—a structure that invalidated *our* structures. Traditional story gives no instructions and permits no clear conclusions. We may *derive* a morality from it, as we do from necessity and mortality. But since it denies our freedom, it cannot itself be moral and exemplary. Unlike thought, it is truly "answerless."

In narratives that deal directly with the sacred—parables, for instance—uncertainty is not only implicit in the structure but often explicit in the action:

> It was said of a Hassidic master that he would wander from town to town searching for the Elijah, who is the harbinger of the Messiah. One day he came upon a stranger in the market place and called out in great excitement: "There he is!" The stranger looked at him and said: "Jew—if you know, why do you speak?" and disappeared.[27]

Storytellers are closer than most of us to the time in our lives when we were ignorant of reason and cause and effect—when everything seemed mysterious, magical, and incomprehensible. In childhood, though we are unaware of it, we live in close proximity to the sacred and the unconscious—to all that which, as adults, we must ignore and forget, so that our lives may make sense, bend to our will, and qualify us for membership in the community.

The storyteller tells his story in large part out of anxiety—to ascertain the fate of his figures and perhaps his own. But by the time he knows the outcome, the story is over and what he has discovered is necessity. He cannot change the fate of his figures, and if he has been true to his task nothing he does will make any difference. He cannot even refuse to report it, for the tale compels him to tell it. Like Oedipus, he is *forced* to know. His mastery lies in serving, and his will finds expression in his willingness.

Yet his effort is far from pointless. For in discovering necessity he himself becomes necessary. Like Celan's poem, the story establishes its validity by acknowledging its own marginality. It proves the storyteller's existence— and ours—by proving the sacred. It demonstrates that we exist because we *know* that we don't. Like consciousness, which was 'granted' to us by unconscious powers, traditional story permits us to acknowledge and even to know the forces which cannot know us, though they created us.

Today, most stories help us to live and die by *distracting* us from the sacred. But if we can face our situation, they may once again help us by serving as an encounter between the human and the sacred. If we can accept our uncertainty, even though we cannot trust it as we once trusted God, story may regain its credibility, and, by affirming rather than distracting us from necessity, recover its ancient, persuasive and telling role. For what we call 'fiction' embodies a reality we cannot afford to face in life, and what we call 'reality' is, in fact, a fiction that allows us a measure of consciousness without casting us into despair. It may well be the reality and contradictions we can face only in fiction that give our lives meaning and shape.

Notes

CHAPTER 1

1. "Story" is a phonological variant of *historia*, a Latin borrowing from Greek *historia*, "inquiry." The etymological source of Greek *historia* is a root, *wid-tor*, whose first element appears also in the Latin cognate *videre*, "to see"; Sanskrit *vid*, "to perceive"; Gothic *witz*, "to know"; and in the English *wit*, "to know." The element *wid* is the root from which Greek *idein*, "to see," and *oida*, "to know," are formed. An Indo-European root, *gnâ*, "to know," gives us "narrative."

2. My work on four half-hour films with Bernard Knox obliged me to read *Oedipus Rex* carefully, and my view of the play is indebted to his.

3. "Tragedy as a Dramatic Art," in *The Philosophy of Fine Art*, in *Hegel on Tragedy*, ed. Anne and Henry Paolucci (New York: Harper Torchbooks, 1962), 85–86.

4. Though Hamlet is the prototype of the self-divided modern hero, Hegel explicitly exempts the Shakespearean figure from being vacillating and self-divided. (*Hegel on Tragedy*, 88, 208.)

5. "Modest," from *modestus*, is related to the noun *modus*, "limit." "Arrogant" derives from *ad* and *rogans*, present participle of *rogo*, "to ask, or desire."

6. "I have often said that the sole cause of man's unhappiness is that he does not know how to sit quietly in his room." Pascal, Pensée 136, in *Pensées* (New York: Penguin, 1976), 67. Of course this may be true only in Western culture.

7. John Locke, "Essay Concerning Human Understanding," II, XXI, cited by Peter Gay, *The Enlightenment: An Interpretation*, vol. 2: *The Science of Freedom* (New York: Alfred A. Knopf, 1969), 179.

8. G. W. F. Hegel, *Vorrede, Die Phänomenologie des Geistes*, identifies *Unruhe* with the self. In vol. 2 of *Sämtliche Werke*, ed. Hermann Glockner (Stuttgart: Friedrich Frommann Verlag, 1964), 26.*

*Note: Throughout, when no translator is given for a German text, the translation is mine.

CHAPTER 2

1. Our need to make connections may be one reason why storytelling and mathematics share so many words. "Tell" derives from the Anglo-Saxon *tellan*, "to tell, announce, count"; "tale" is rooted in *talu*, meaning both "speech" and "number"; and "account" and "figure" are shared terms.

2. *Wit*—from Anglo-Saxon *witan*, "to know"—is related to Latin *videre*, "to see"; the Sanskrit *vid*, "to know or perceive"; the Greek *idein*, "to see"; and the Greek *oida*, "to know."

Megill points out that both Nietzsche and Derrida associate the act of seeing with our logocentric culture. Allan Megill, *Prophets of Extremity: Nietzsche, Heidegger, Foucault, Derrida* (Berkeley: University of California, 1985), 215.

3. Richard Leacock, *Happy Mother's Day*, 1963.

4. Henry James, "The Lesson of Balzac" (1905), in Henry James, *The Future of the Novel*, ed. Leon Edel (New York: Vintage Books, 1956), 119.

5. Chaplin, in *Focus on Chaplin*, ed. Donald W. McCaffrey (Englewood Cliffs, N.J.: Prentice-Hall, 1971), 49.

6. Sigmund Freud, "The Uncanny," in vol. 17 of *The Standard Edition of the Complete Psychological Works of Sigmund Freud*, ed. James Strachey (London: The Hogarth Press and the Institute of Psycho-Analysis, 1975), 241, 249.

7. "Heraclitus," in G. S. Kirk, J. E. Raven, M. Schofield, *The Pre-Socratic Philosophers*, 2nd ed. (Cambridge: Cambridge University Press, 1983), 210–11.

8. We prefer to attribute our condition to nurture rather than nature, no doubt on the assumption that this gives us greater control. Perhaps it does, but whatever freedom we gain hardly extends to those *being* nurtured, who may find it no easier to free themselves of nurture than of nature. Both operate in us, for the most part, unconsciously.

9. Aristotle, *Poetics*, 6, 1450a24.

10. Roland Barthes, *On Racine*, trans. Richard Howard (New York: Octagon Books, 1977), 13.

11. This is Max Scheler's paraphrase of Schopenhauer, in "On the Tragic," in *Moderns on Tragedy*, ed. Lionel Abel (New York: Fawcett Publications, 1967), 260. The reference is to Arthur Schopenhauer, *Die Welt als Wille und Vorstellung* (Leipzig: Inselverlag, n.d.), 2: 1194 ff.

12. Hebbel, *Tagebücher I*, in *Friedrich Hebbels Werke*, (Berlin: Deutsches Verlaghaus Bong, n.d.), Neunter Teil, 7 Oktober 1942, entry 2114.

13. Eugen Kogon, *The Theory and Practice of Hell: The German Concentration Camps and the System Behind Them*, trans. Heinz Norden (New York: Farrar, Straus, 1949), 91–92.

CHAPTER 3

1. René Girard, *Violence and the Sacred* (Baltimore: Johns Hopkins University Press, 1977).

2. Aeschylus, *Choephoroe* 313.

3. E. F. Dolin, "Prometheus Psellistes," *California Studies in Classical Antiquity*, vol. 2, 1968.

4. Friedrich Nietzsche, *Die Geburt der Tragödie, Werke in drei Bänden*, ed. Karl Schlechta (München: Carl Hanser Verlag, 1976), 1: 48.

5. W. B. Yeats, *The Autobiography of William Butler Yeats* (New York: Macmillan, 1965), 326.

6. We should note that fictive figures, despite their high station, generally represent 'ordinary' human beings rather than those heroes and heroines in life, who *knowingly* undertake tasks that are likely to end in their own destruction. Antigone in Sophocles is one of the few fictive figures who is fully aware of the consequences of her actions. Significantly, the last quarter of the play shifts *away* from her to Creon, who commits himself to a course of action *without* seeing where it will lead: he sets out to free Antigone but arrives too late: she has hanged herself; his son, who was betrothed to her, kills himself in front of his father; and when Creon returns to the palace, his wife, too, has committed suicide.

7. Charles Baudelaire, "On the Essence of Laughter and, in General, On the Comic in the Plastic Arts," in *The Painter of Modern Life and Other Essays*, trans. and ed. Jonathan Mayne (London: Phaidon Press, 1964), 164.

8. Henri Bergson, "Laughter," in *Comedy*, ed. Wylie Sypher (New York: Doubleday, 1956), 71.

9. Baudelaire, "On the Essence of Laughter," 152–53.

10. Wilhelm Worringer, *Abstraction and Empathy*, trans. Michael Bullock (New York: International University Presses, 1967), 3–26.

11. Tomashevsky makes the point that in some stories "the 'hero' himself is . . . a kind of narrative thread"; he becomes "a covert [potential] narrator." Boris Tomashevsky, "Thematics," in Lee T. Lemon and Marion J. Reis, eds., *Russian Formalist Criticism* (Lincoln: University of Nebraska Press, 1965), 75, 77.

Though *The Idiot* is what Bakhtin calls a polyphonic novel, it is rendered from Myshkin's perspective. He is the feeling center of the story and the keystone of the action. We would say this is true of most though not all stories. *As I Lay Dying* and *The Sound and the Fury* clearly render multiple points of view. Yet the very title *As I Lay Dying* suggests that Addie is the novel's point of view figure.

12. E. F. Dolin, Introduction, *Anthology of Greek Tragedy*, ed. Albert Cook and Edwin Dolin (New York: Bobbs-Merrill, 1972), xxx; see also 62.

Since, in the case of the Oedipus story, there appears to have been just one version of the myth, we can say that Sophocles preserved the "basic facts." But many myths appeared in variants and the playwright was free to choose among them. Aeschylus, in the *Oresteia*, uses a version of the myth in which Iphigenia dies. Agamemnon's own situation, however, is basic to all variants of the myth.

13. Gilbert Murray, *Aeschylus: The Creator of Tragedy* (Oxford: Clarendon Press, 1940–1964), 160. Murray cites Aeschylus in Atheneus, *The Deipnosophists*, trans. Charles Burton Gulick (New York: G. P. Putnam's, 1930), 4: 75 (*Deipnosophistae*, viii.347).

14. Hegel emphasizes the importance of subjectivity in "modern" drama, but assigns it no role in classical tragedy. *Hegel on Tragedy*, ed. Anne and Henry Paolucci (New York: Harper Torchbooks, 1962), 79–80, 84.

15. Joseph Conrad, *Nostromo: A Tale of the Seaboard* (New York: Penguin Books, 1977), 409.

16. *Hegel on Tragedy*, 67.

17. W. H. Auden, "The Christian Tragic Hero," *New York Times Book Review*, 16 December 1945.

18. *The Journal of Eugène Delacroix*, trans. Walter Pach (New York: Crown Publishers, 1948), 224.

19. Bertolt Brecht, "Against Georg Lukács." I was unable to locate the magazine in which I read this essay in a translation by Stuart Hood. Compare Heidegger: "The oldest of the old follows behind us in our thinking, and yet it comes to meet us." Epigraph to Modern Science, Metaphysics, and Mathematics, in *Basic Writings*, ed. David Farrell Krell (New York: Harper and Row, 1977), 243.

20. The 'conservative' element in Delacroix's thinking is evident in a journal entry of September 5, 1847: "Leroux has most assuredly found the great word, if not the thing itself, to save humanity and to pull it out of the mire: 'Man is born free,' he says, following Rousseau. Never has a heavier piece of foolishness been uttered, no matter how great the philosopher who spoke it." *Journal of Eugène Delacroix*, 172.

21. The phrase is Leonard Meyer's, in *Music, the Arts and Ideas* (Chicago: University of Chicago, 1967), cited by Frank Kermode, *The Genesis of Secrecy* (Cambridge, Mass.: Harvard University, 1979), 162.

22. Kermode, *Genesis of Secrecy*, 163.

23. Thomas S. Kuhn, *The Structure of Scientific Revolutions* (Chicago: University of Chicago Press, 1962), 64–65. Compare Derrida: "The simple practice of language ceaselessly reinstates the new terrain on the oldest ground." "The Ends of Man," in *Writing and Difference*, trans. Alan Bass (Chicago: University of Chicago Press, 1978), 135.

24. Stravinsky quotes an unidentified source: "A tradition is carried forward in order to produce something new"; it clearly represents his own view. *Poetics of Music in the Form of Six Lessons*, trans. Arthur Knodel and Ingolf Dahl (New York: Random House, 1947), 59.

Compare D. W. Winnicott: ". . . in any cultural field *it is not possible to be original except on a basis of tradition.* Conversely, no one in the line of cultural contributors repeats except as a deliberate quotation, and the unforgivable sin in the cultural field is plagiarism. The interplay between originality and the acceptance of tradition as the basis for inventiveness seems to me to be just one more example, and a very exciting one, of the interplay between separateness and union." D. W. Winnicott, *Playing and Reality* (New York: Basic Books, 1971), 99.

25. Karl Reinhardt in "Oedipus Tyrannus," says: "For Sophocles, as for the Greeks of more ancient times, fate, even when foretold, even when recurring with the strictness of law, never had the meaning of determinism, and was seen as a

spontaneous unfolding of the demonic. There is no fatal determinism before the time of the Stoics and the triumph of astrology." In *Moderns on Tragedy*, ed. Leon Abel (New York: Fawcett, 1967), 191. Given the preclusive nature of all narrative and the Oedipus myth in particular, one wonders how Sophocles could altogether avoid "fatal determinism."

26. Letter to Louise Colet, 16 January 1852, in *The Selected Letters of Gustave Flaubert*, trans. and ed. Francis Steegmuller (New York: Farrar, Straus, and Young, 1953), 127–28. The letter continues: "It is for this reason that there are no noble subjects or ignoble subjects; from the standpoint of pure Art one might almost establish the axiom that there is no such thing as subject, style in itself being an absolute manner of seeing things."

27. Letter to Louise Colet, 15 January 1853, ibid., 146.

28. Victor Brombert, *The Novels of Flaubert: A Study of Themes and Techniques* (Princeton: Princeton University Press, 1966), 67.

29. Ibid.

30. The naturalist Buffon spoke of "l'enchaînement des êtres"; in William Cecil Dampier, *A History of Science and Its Relations with Philosophy and Religion* (New York: Macmillan, 1938), 294.

31. Friedrich Nietzsche, *Nachgelassene Schriften*, in vol. 1 of *Werke in zwei Bänden*, ed. Gerhardt Stenzel (Salzburg: Verlag "Das Bergland-Buch," 1953), 803.

32. Trotsky may have had in mind Spinoza's comment that our faith in free will is the equivalent of a rock hurtling downhill, convinced that it can determine where to stop.

33. Blackmore speaks of Mach's "positivistic belief that all problems were either solvable or 'meaningless.' " John T. Blackmore, *Ernst Mach: His Work, Life and Influence* (Berkeley: University of California Press, 1972), 316–17.

The Logical Positivists take the same position. Moritz Schlick says: "Wherever there is a meaningful problem one can in theory always give the path that leads to its solution." Schlick, "The Turning Point in Philosophy," in *Logical Positivism*, ed. A. J. Ayer (Glencoe, Ill.: Free Press, 1959), 56.

In *The Analysis of Sensations* (Chicago, 1914), Mach says "I should like the scientists to realize that my view eliminates all metaphysical questions indifferently, whether they be only regarded as insoluble at the present moment, or whether they be regarded as meaningless for all time. . . . Everything that we can want to know is given by the solution of a problem in mathematical form, by the ascertainment of the functional dependency of the sensational elements on one another. This knowledge exhausts the knowledge of 'reality.' " (p. 369), cited in Blackmore, *Ernst Mach: His Work, Life and Influence*, 167–68.

34. Walter Benjamin, "The Storyteller," in Walter Benjamin, *Illuminations*, ed. Hannah Arendt (New York: Schocken Books, 1969), 94.

35. Friedrich Nietzsche, *Aus dem Nachlass der Achtziger Jahre*, *Werke in drei Bänden*, 3: 832.

36. Hegel says that with reference to classical tragedy the notion of guilt or innocence is "false": "We must . . . place on one side the false notion of *guilt* or

innocence. The Heroes of tragedy are quite as much under one category as under the other. If we accept the idea as valid that a man is guilty only in the case that a choice lay open to him, and he deliberately decided on the course of action which he carried out, then these plastic figures of ancient drama are guiltless." Hegel, *The Philosophy of Fine Art* (1920), trans. F. P. B. Ostmaston, in *Moderns on Tragedy*, ed. Lionel Abel (Greenwich, Conn.: Fawcett Publications, 1967), 474. However, compare Hegel: "The strength of great characters consists precisely in this that they do not choose, but are entirely and absolutely just that which they will and achieve. . . . One can in fact urge no thing more intolerable against a hero of this type than by saying that he has acted innocently. It is a point of honor with such great characters that they are guilty." In *Hegel on Tragedy*, 70. We should note that Hegel is deeply concerned with the "masculine integrity" of the Greek tragic figure (ibid., 74), which even Antigone, his favorite figure, could be said to exemplify.

37. Otto Rank, *The Trauma of Birth* (New York: Harper and Row, 1973), note on pp. 123–24. It originally appeared in "Buch von der Schöpfung des Kindes," in *Kleine Midraschim.*

CHAPTER 4

1. Viktor Shklovsky, "Sterne's *Tristram Shandy*: Stylistic Commentary," in Lee T. Lemon and Marion J. Reis, eds., *Russian Formalist Criticism: Four Essays* (Lincoln: University of Nebraska, 1965).

2. Aristotle, *Poetics*, 6I, 1450a4. Other translations use the word "combination" instead of "arrangement," suggesting the hand of the author less strongly.

3. Paul Ricoeur (*Time and Narrative*, trans. Kathleen McLaughlin and David Pellauer [Chicago: University of Chicago Press, 1984], vol. 1, chap. 2) gives Aristotle's "plot" (*mythos*) a formalist interpretation. He calls the tragic poet a "maker of plots" (p. 42) and the plot "emplotment." This reading of Aristotle may be justified, since certain formulations in the *Poetics* have a 'positivist' tinge.

4. Dostoevski, in conversation with Varvara Timofeeva, a young woman who read the proofs of *The Diary of a Writer*, cited in Leonid Grossmann, *Dostoevsky, A Biography*, trans. Mary Mackler (New York: Bobbs-Merrill, 1975), 491.

5. Dostoevski's respect for newspaper stories is apparent in an often cited passage from his letters: "I have my own idea about art, and it is this: What most people regard as fantastic and lacking in universality, I hold to be the inmost essence of truth. Arid observation of everyday trivialities I have long ceased to regard as realism—it is quite the reverse. In any newspaper one takes up, one comes across reports of wholly authentic facts, which nevertheless strike one as extraordinary. Our writers regard them as fantastic, and take no account of them; and yet they are the truth, for they are facts. But who troubles to observe, record, describe, them? They happen every day and every moment, therefore they are not exceptional." *Letters of Fyodor Michailovitch Dostoevsky to His Family and Friends,* trans. Ethel Colburn Mayne (London: Chatto and Windus, 1914), 166–67.

When Bakhtin says "To the all-devouring consciousness of the hero (Dostoevsky) can juxtapose only a single objective world—a world of other consciousnesses with equal rights to those of the hero," he is not altogether true to Dostoevsky, who juxtaposes the *plot* to the hero's consciousness. Mikhail Bakhtin, *Problems of Dostoevsky's Poetics*, ed. and trans. Caryl Emerson (Minneapolis: University of Minnesota Press, 1984), 49–50.

6. This is the view expressed by Pierre Simon, Marquis de Laplace, *A Philosophical Essay on Probabilities* (1814), trans. Frederick Wilson Truscott and Frederick Lincoln Emory (New York: Dover, 1951), 4: "Given an intelligence which could comprehend all the forces by which nature is animated and the respective situation of the beings who compose it—an intelligence sufficiently vast to submit these data to analysis—it would embrace in the same formula the movements of the greatest bodies of the universe and those of the lightest atom; for it, nothing would be uncertain and the future, as the past, would be present to its eyes."

7. Victor Hugo, *Notre Dame de Paris*, in vol. 12 of *Oeuvres Complètes* (Paris: Le Club Français du Livre, 1967–70), 356, cited in Victor Brombert, *Victor Hugo and the Visionary Novel* (Cambridge, Mass.: Harvard University Press, 1984), 85.

8. Cited by Georges Poulet in *Studies in Human Time*, trans. Elliott Colemen (New York: Harper Torchbooks, 1959), 320.

9. Aristotle, *Poetics*, 6II, 1450a22.

10. E. M. Forster, *Aspects of the Novel* (New York: Harcourt, Brace, 1954), 155–56.

11. Ibid., 156.

12. Aristotle, *Poetics*, 1453b33.

13. Tolstoy, *War and Peace* (New York: Macmillan, 1943), 665–66.

14. Henry James, Preface to *Roderick Hudson* (New York: Augustus M. Kelley, 1971), vii.

15. Though this view of art did not originate in the Enlightenment aesthetics of Kant, it was clearly given authority and impetus by it.

16. Peter Brooks, *Reading for the Plot: Design and Intention in Narrative* (New York: Vintage Books, 1985), 12.

17. Paul Ricoeur, "Narrative Time," in *On Narrative*, ed. W. J. T. Mitchell (Chicago: University of Chicago Press, 1981), 167.

18. Paul Ricoeur, *Time and Narrative*, 1: 56.

19. Ibid., 31. For a very different view, see Artaud: "Stage language, if it exists and if it is to be found, will be by nature destructive, threatening, anarchic, it will evoke chaos." Cited in Tzvetan Todorov, *The Poetics of Prose* (Ithaca, N.Y.: Cornell University Press, 1977), 208–9.

20. Ibid., 178.

21. Ibid., 148.

22. In *Kierkegaard*, (Frankfurt am Main: Suhrkamp Verlag, 1966), 129, Adorno points out that for Kierkegaard uncertainty of meaning *is* the meaning. Cited by Susan Buck-Morss, *The Origin of Negative Dialectics* (New York: Free Press, 1977), 269.

23. Claude Lévi-Strauss, *Myth and Meaning* (New York: Schocken Books, 1979), 17.

24. Werner Heisenberg, *Physics and Philosophy: The Revolution in Modern Science* (New York: Harper, 1958), 189–90.

25. G. W. Leibniz, "On the Radical Originality of Things," in *Philosophical Papers and Letters: A Selection,* trans. and ed. Leroy E. Loemker (Boston: J. Reidel, 1969), 487. See also Wittgenstein: "It is not *how* things are in the world that is mystical, but *that* it exists." *Tractatus,* cited in Allan Megill, *Prophets of Extremity: Nietzsche, Heidegger, Foucault, Derrida* (Berkeley: University of California Press, 1985), 170.

26. See Albert S. Cook's discussion of proverbs in *Myth and Language* (Bloomington: Indiana University Press, 1980), 211–24.

27. I believe this point is made by Marie-Louise von Franz but could not locate it in her several studies of fairy tales.

28. Perhaps it was the absence of fate in the tales of Hans Christian Andersen that prompted Kierkegaard to remark: "Andersen has no idea what fairy tales are." Cited in Josiah Thompson, *The Lonely Labyrinth: Kierkegaard's Pseudonymous Works* (London: Feffer and Simons, 1967), 222, note 42.

Also see Kafka: "Es gibt keine unblutigen Märchen. Jedes Märchen kommt aus der Tiefe des Blutes und der Angst. Das ist die Verwandtschaft aller Märchen. Die Oberfläche ist verschieden. Nördliche Märchen sind nicht von so einer üppigen Fauna der Phantasie erfüllt wie afrikanische Negermärchen, aber der Kern, die Tiefe der Sehnsucht ist die gleiche." Cited in Gustav Janouch, *Gespräche mit Kafka* (Frankfurt am Main: Fischer Bucherei, 1961), 61.

29. Hegel takes a different view. He speaks of the "rationality of destiny" (p. 71) and of tragedy's "vision of eternal justice" (p. 51). *Hegel on Tragedy,* ed. Anne and Henry Paolucci (New York: Harper Torchbooks, 1962).

30. Thomas Rymer coined the term "poetic justice," which suggests that what we meet up with in story is *not* what happens in 'nonpoetic' reality. Thomas Rymer, *The Tragedies of the Last Age: Consider'd and Exam'd by the Practice of the Ancients, and by the Commonsense of All Ages* (London: Printed for Richard Tonson, 1678), 25–26, in facsimile edition by Arthur Freeman (New York: Garland, 1974).

31. *Heraclitus: The Cosmic Fragments,* ed. G. S. Kirk (Cambridge: Cambridge University Press, 1978), 180 (fragment 102). (emphasis added)

32. As Lévi-Strauss says: "The prime role of culture is to ensure the group's existence as a group, and consequently, in this domain as in all others, to replace chance by organization." Lévi-Strauss, *Tristes Tropiques,* trans. John and Doreen Wrightman (New York: Atheneum, 1974), 32.

Compare Freud: "Order is a kind of compulsion to repeat which . . . decides when, where and how a thing shall be done, so that in every similar circumstance one is spared hesitation and indecision." "Civilization and Its Discontents," in vol. 21 of *The Standard Edition of the Complete Psychological Works of Freud,* 93.

33. See Charles Segal, *Tragedy and Civilization: An Interpretation of Sophocles* (Cambridge, Mass.: Harvard University, 1981), 42.

34. Honoré de Balzac, cited without attribution by Frank O'Connor, *The Mirror in the Roadway: A Study of the Modern Novel* (New York: Alfred A. Knopf, 1956), 87.

35. As Herbert Feigl observes, the Logical Positivists "were adamant in excluding as nonsensical any question that, in the light of logical analysis, revealed itself to be absolutely unanswerable." In our view, it is of course precisely this kind of "nonsense" that is the province of narrative. Feigl, "The Origin and Spirit of Logical Positivism," in *The Legacy of Logical Positivism,* ed. Peter Achinstein and Stephen F. Barker (Baltimore: Johns Hopkins University Press, 1969), 5.

Since story offers no *solutions,* it differs from philosophy, which, to borrow Hume's phrasing, offers us an "ought" that follows from an "is."

36. In their *Introduction to Secular Ritual,* Moore and Myerhoff say: ". . . ritual is a declaration of form *against* indeterminacy, therefore indeterminacy is always present in the background of any analysis of ritual." (Amsterdam, 1977), 17, cited by Victor Turner, "Social Drama and Stories about Them," in *On Narrative,* ed. W. J. T. Mitchell (Chicago: University of Chicago, 1981), 154.

CHAPTER 5

1. Alexander Marshack suggests that Story is an "equation of process": " 'Story' refers to the nature of the communication of meaning and, even more, to a certain sort of meaning which is time-factored, relational, and concerns process." Alexander Marshack, *The Roots of Civilization: The Cognitive Beginnings of Man's First Art, Symbol and Notation* (New York: McGraw-Hill, 1972), 119.

2. Werner Heisenberg, *Physics and Philosophy: The Revolution in Modern Science* (New York: Harper and Row, 1958), 189–90.

In *Myth and Meaning* (New York: Schocken Books, 1979), 43, Lévi-Strauss points out that we, in our culture, want the future to be different from the past, whereas people in earlier cultures wanted it to be the same. Perhaps we *want* change simply because it has become inevitable; we "*choose*" what has been imposed on us, because it gives us a sense of control.

3. Marshack, *Roots of Civilization,* chap. 9.

4. Ibid., 131. ". . . the capacity to understand and communicate a 'story' was perhaps the basic, humanizing intellectual and social skill, the primary tool and technique of developing human culture. . . ."

5. Marcel Proust, "À propos du style de Flaubert," *Nouvelle Revue Française,* 1 January 1920, cited in George Painter, *Marcel Proust: A Biography* (New York: Random House, 1978), 2: 299.

6. Sigmund Freud, "The Ego and the Id" (1923) in vol. 19 of *The Standard Edition of the Complete Psychological Works of Sigmund Freud,* ed. James Strachey (London: The Hogarth Press and the Institute of Psycho-Analysis, 1961), 23.

7. C. G. Jung, "Commentary on 'The Secret of the Golden Flower,' "*Alchemical Studies,* in vol. 13 of *The Collected Works of C. G. Jung,* (Princeton: Princeton University Press, 1967), 37.

8. Jung uses the term "constellate" to describe the process by which unconscious complexes present themselves to our awareness.

9. Hegel says: "Die Hexen im Makbeth . . . erscheinen als äussere Gewalten,

welche dem Makbeth sein Schiksal vorausbestimmen. Was sie jedoch verkünden ist sein geheimster eigenster Wunsch, der in dieser nur scheinbar äusseren Weise an ihn kommt. . . ." G. W. F. Hegel, *Vorlesungen über die Ästhetik*, Erster Band, *Sämtliche Werke*, ed. Hermann Glockner (Stuttgart: Friedrich Frommann Verlag, 1964), 312.

10. Sigmund Freud, *Jokes and Their Relation to the Unconscious*, trans. and ed. James Strachey (New York: Norton, 1963).

CHAPTER 6

1. Rudolf Otto, *The Idea of the Holy: An Inquiry into the Non-rational Factor in the Idea of the Divine and Its Relation to the Rational*, trans. John W. Harvey (London: Oxford University Press, 1946), 28.

2. In the *Phenomenology*, Hegel says: "The 'beyond' has already escaped. . . . The 'other' cannot be found where it is sought; for it is meant to be just a 'beyond,' that which can *not* be found." G. W. F. Hegel, *The Phenomenology of Mind*, trans. J. B. Baillie (London, 1909), 258.

Also see Frazer: "The advance of knowledge is an infinite progression toward a goal that for ever recedes." James George Frazer, *The Golden Bough: A Study in Magic and Religion* (New York: Macmillan, 1940), 712–13.

3. David Bevington, *Medieval Drama* (Boston: Houghton Mifflin, 1975), 4. The parallel to the origin of Greek drama, in which first one and then a second actor separated from the Chorus, seems evident.

4. C. G. Jung, "Symbols and the Interpretation of Dreams," *The Symbolic Life*, in vol. 18 of *The Collected Works of C. G. Jung* (Princeton: Princeton University Press, 1976), 244–52. Also see Jung, "Psychology and Religion," in vol. 11 of *The Collected Works* (Princeton: Princeton University Press, 1969), 64.

5. C. G. Jung, "Psychic Energy," *The Structure and Dynamics of the Psyche*, in vol. 8 of *The Collected Works*, (Princeton: Princeton University Press, 1969), 59. Also: Jung, *Symbols of Transformation*, in vol. 5 of *The Collected Works* (Princeton: Princeton University Press, 1970), 228.

6. Antonin Artaud, "No More Masterpieces," in *The Theatre and Its Double*, trans. Mary Caroline Richards (New York: Grove Press, 1958), 79.

Compare Kafka: "Wir brauchen aber Bücher, die auf uns wirken wie ein Unglück." Letter to Oscar Pollack, 27 January 1904, in Franz Kafka, *Briefe, 1902–1924* (New York: Schocken Books, 1958), 27.

7. Arthur Schopenhauer, *Die Welt als Wille und Vorstellung* (Leipzig: Inselverlag, n.d.), 2: 1210.

8. Honoré de Balzac, cited without attribution by Frank O'Connor, *The Mirror in the Roadway: A Study of the Modern Novel* (New York: Alfred A. Knopf, 1956), 87.

9. Henri Bergson, "Laughter," in *Comedy*, ed. Wylie Sypher (New York: Doubleday, 1956), 61–190.

10. Ibid., 147.

11. Charles Baudelaire, "On the Essence of Laughter and, in General, on the Comic and Plastic Arts," in *The Painter of Modern Life and Other Essays*, trans. and ed. Jonathan Mayne (London: Phaidon Press, 1964), 153.

12. Eric Bentley, "Farce," in Robert W. Corrigan, ed., *Comedy: Meaning and Form* (San Francisco: Chandler, 1965), 196.

13. In *Einfache Formen*, (Tübingen: Max Niemeyer Verlag, 1958), André Jolles says: "Myth is an answer that comprises a question." (p. 129) It is a question we *cannot* answer—a question, moreover, we are likely to miss or ignore. We prefer to be comforted by the answer that myth and story *appear* to give.

A reference to Jolles in Albert S. Cook, *Myth and Language* (Bloomington: Indiana University Press, 1980) prompted me to read *Einfache Formen*.

14. G. W. F. Hegel, *Hegel's Logic: Being Part One of the Encyclopedia of the Philosophical Sciences*, trans. William Wallace (Oxford: Clarendon Press, 1975), 124–27.

15. *Hegel on Tragedy*, ed. Anne and Henry Paolucci (New York: Harper Torchbooks, 1962), 90. Hegel does not recognize accident as an element in classical tragedy (*Hegel on Tragedy*, p. 80) even though—as A. C. Bradley points out in "Hegel's Theory of Tragedy"—the death of Antigone is accidental. Bradley calls Hegel's theory of tragedy an attempt to rationalize fate. In *Hegel on Tragedy*, 378.

16. Feuerbach says: "Chance—especially favorable chance—is therefore the principal object of religion. It seems contradictory that, as Pliny the Elder puts it, the very thing which makes man doubt the existence of a God, should itself be taken as a god. But chance has this essential and original characteristic of divinity: it is something unintended and unwilled, independent of human knowledge and will, and yet man's fate depends on it." Ludwig Feuerbach, *Lectures on the Essence of Religion*, trans. Ralph Manheim (New York: Harper and Row, 1967), 309.

17. Robert Oppenheimer, Lecture to UNESCO, Paris, 13 December 1965, in Ronald Clark, *Einstein: The Life and Times* (London: Hodder and Stoughton, 1973), 501–2. Wolfgang Pauli believed that Einstein's difficulty with quantum theory lay in its denial of classical realism. The realist position in physics is not necessarily deterministic even if—in the world at large—realism and determinism are related. Today the physicist can be a realist *and* accept chance (or indeterminism) as real.

During the nineteenth century, realism and determinism were associated. We thought we could observe the system accurately from an objective position, and that the system itself was entirely predictable. Today, however, we can be realists— that is, believe in the system 'out there'— accept that we cannot observe it objectively or accurately, *and* that chance is real. Chaos theory suggests that the system would not be entirely predictable even if we *could* observe it accurately.

18. A version of this often quoted statement appears in a letter from Einstein to Born; in David C. Cassidy, *Uncertainty: The Life and Science of Werner Heisenberg* (New York: W. H. Freeman, 1992), 252. See also *The Born-Einstein Letters* (New York: Walker, 1971), 90.

19. Roger Caillois, *Man, Play, and Games*, trans. Meyer Barash (New York: Free Press of Glencoe, 1961), 109.

20. Jacques Monod says: "A mutation is in itself a microscopic event, a quan-

tum event, to which the principle of uncertainty consequently applies. An event which is hence and by its very nature *essentially* unpredictable." Monod, *Chance and Necessity: An Essay on the Natural Philosophy of Modern Biology*, trans. Austryn Wainhouse (New York: Alfred A. Knopf, 1971), 114–15.

21. Frederick Waismann, "The Decline and Fall of Causality," in *Turning Points in Physics: A Series of Lectures Given at Oxford University in Trinity Term, 1958* (Amsterdam: North-Holland, 1959), 141.

22. Ibid., 137. See also Niels Bohr: "Those who are not shocked when they first come across quantum theory cannot possibly have understood it." Cited by Werner Heisenberg, *Physics and Beyond: Encounters and Conversations*, trans. Arnold J. Pomerans (New York: Harper and Row, 1972), 206.

Bronowski makes the point that though the uncertainty principle refers to "very small particles and events . . . these small events are not by any means unimportant. They are just the sorts of events which go on in the nerves and the brain and in the great molecules which determine the qualities we inherit. And sometimes the odd small events add up to a fantastic large one." In J. Bronowski, *The Common Sense of Science* (Cambridge, Mass.: Harvard University, 1979), 68.

23. Fritz Rohrlich, "Facing Quantum Mechanical Reality," *Science*, vol. 221, no. 4617 (23 September 1983): 1254.

24. Konrad Lorenz, *On Aggression* (New York: Bantam, 1967), 218. "The fact that birds evolved from reptiles or man from apes is a historically unique achievement of evolution. By laws that govern every living being, evolution has a general trend to the higher but, in all its details, is determined by *so-called* chance, that is by innumerable collateral chains of causation which in principle can never be completely apprehended."

25. See John Earman, "Determinism in the Physical Sciences," in *Introduction to the Philosophy of Science* (Englewood Cliffs, N.J.: Prentice-Hall, 1992), 241.

26. E. M. Forster, *Aspects of the Novel* (New York: Harcourt Brace, 1954), 164. This seems to me a more perceptive comment on *Tristram Shandy* than Shklovsky's: "The action is continually interrupted. . . . Whole ten-page passages are filled with whimsical digressions about fortifications or about the influence of a person's nose or name on his character. Such digressions are unrelated to the basic narrative." "Sterne's *Tristram Shandy*," Lee T. Lemon and Marion J. Reis, eds, *Russian Formalist Criticism: Four Essays* (Lincoln: University of Nebraska Press, 1965), 27. Shklovsky recognizes the relevance of Sterne's digressions, yet fails to see that a person's nose or name can, in fact, have an effect on his character or fate. The "unimportant" is as "important" as the "important." Sterne's digressions don't play with the conventions of narrative; they challenge our assumptions about time progressions and cause-and-effect sequences. They are not unrelated to but, rather, *constitute* "the basic narrative."

27. Persi Diaconis and Frederick Mosteller.

28. Friedrich Hebbel, *Tagebücher II,* in vol. 9 of *Friedrich Hebbels Werke* (Berlin: Deutsches Verlaghaus Bong, n.d.), 93 (20 May 1847, entry 3537).

29. Letter to Collins, *Letters of Dickens*, 3: 125, cited in Hillis Miller, "Bleak

House," in Miller, *Charles Dickens: The World of His Novels* (Cambridge, Mass.: Harvard University Press, 1965), 205.

30. Charles Dickens, *Little Dorrit* (Baltimore: Penguin, 1967), 63.

31. C. G. Jung, in an interview in *Good Housekeeping*, December 1961, cited by E. F. Edinger, *Ego and Archetype: Individuation and the Religious Function of the Psyche* (New York: G. P. Putnam's, 1972), 101.

32. "Wir sind die Figuren im Traum des Gottes, die erraten, wie er träumt." Epigraph, *Nachgelassene Schriften*, 1871–84, Nietzsche, in vol. 1 of *Werke in zwei Bänden*, 779.

33. Rohrlich, "Facing Quantum Mechanical Reality," 1253.

CHAPTER 7

1. Compare Feuerbach: "The ancient atheists, and even a great many theists both ancient and modern, have called fear the ground of religion; but fear is merely the most widespread and obvious expression of the feeling of dependency. As the Roman poet said: *Primus in orbe Deos fecit Timor*—Fear first made the gods in the world." Ludwig Feuerbach, *Lectures on the Essence of Religion*, trans. Ralph Manheim (New York: Harper and Row, 1967), 25–26.

See also: "All mythology masters and shapes the forces of nature in and through the imagination; hence it disappears as soon as man gains mastery over the forces of nature." Karl Marx, *Grundrisse*, in Karl Marx, *Selected Writings*, ed. David McLellan (Oxford: Oxford University Press, 1978), 359.

"Belief" is etymologically related to "leave," in the sense of "permission," and implies a subservient relationship.

2. The formalists were a response to the Symbolists, much as the Vienna Circle responded to nineteenth century metaphysics and idealism. See Boris Eichenbaum: "What brought together the initial group of the Formalists was the desire to liberate the poetic word from the fetters of philosophical and religious tendencies, which had achieved considerable prominence in Symbolism." Boris Eichenbaum, *Literatura*, 90–91, cited in Viktor Erlich, *Russian Formalism: History-Doctrine* ('S-Gravenhage: Mouton, 1955), 52. At the time, this was of course a necessary dialectical or balancing move, just as the Symbolists, in *their* time, had been a necessary reaction to nineteenth century materialism and positivism.

3. Boris Eichenbaum, "The Theory of the 'Formal Method,' " in Lee T. Lemon and Marion J. Reis, eds., *Russian Formalist Criticism: Four Essays* (Lincoln: University of Nebraska, 1965), 116.

4. Boris Tomashevsky, "Thematics," in Lemon and Reis, *Russian Formalist Criticism*, 68. Tomashevsky uses the terms plot and story as Shklovsky does. "Plot is distinct from story. Both include the same events, but in the plot the events *are arranged. . . .*" (p. 67).

5. Shklovsky uses defamiliarization in two distinct ways. In "Art as Technique" he says: "Habitualization devours works, clothes, furniture, one's wife, and the fear of war. . . . Art exists that one may recover the sensation of life; it exists to

make one feel things, to make the stone, stony. The purpose of art is to impart the sensation of the things as they are perceived, and not as they are known." Viktor Shklovsky, "Art as Technique," in Lemon and Reis, *Russian Formalist Criticism*, 12. Inasmuch as art returns to us the sensory, particularized experience of which life in society has *necessarily* robbed us, this definition of defamiliarization maintains the traditional relationship between art and reality, or "things." Only when he begins to insist that defamiliarization is focused on aesthetic convention—when the convention itself becomes the center of the artist's endeavor—does formalism break with traditional aesthetics.

6. Viktor Shklovsky, "Sterne's *Tristram Shandy*: Stylistic Commentary," in Lemon and Reis, *Russian Formalist Criticism*, 54.

7. Arthur Schopenhauer, *Die Welt als Wille und Vorstellung* (Leipzig: Inselverlag, n.d.), 1: 237 ff. He uses *Objekt*, which could be translated as "object" but is, I believe, rendered more accurately as "objective."

8. The formalists see every component of the artwork as a device or convention. So Tomashevsky says: "The audience of ancient comedy or the comedy of Molière overlooks the fact that in the last act all the characters turn out to be close relatives." Tomashevsky, "Thematics," 81. Though for him, such recognition scenes are a dead device, we see them as predicated on psychic reality: we respond to an aesthetic convention in large part because it corresponds to something we sense to be true to our 'experience.' A dead convention will, in our view, wither away; it cannot be resuscitated, though there is a time lag between its death in life and its demise in art.

9. Shklovsky, "Art as Technique," 12, and "Sterne's *Tristram Shandy*: Stylistic Commentary," 57.

Tzvetan Todorov has contributed the most explicit formalist analysis of narrative in the postwar period. In *The Poetics of Prose* (Ithaca, N.Y.: Cornell University Press, 1977), he makes the point that the *Odyssey*, like *The Arabian Nights*, is "a narrative of narratives." (p. 61) "The theme of the *Odyssey* is not Odysseus' return to Ithaca; this return is, on the contrary, the death of the *Odyssey*, its end. The theme of the *Odyssey* is the narrative forming the *Odyssey*, it is the *Odyssey* itself. This is why, returning home, Odysseus does not think about it, does not rejoice over it; he thinks only of 'robbers' tales and lies'—he thinks the *Odyssey*." (p. 63) Todorov calls the narrative process in both the *Odyssey* and *The Arabian Nights* "embedding," which is in his view "the most essential property of all narrative." ". . . the embedding narrative is the *narrative of a narrative*. By telling the story of another narrative, the first narrative achieves its fundamental theme and at the same time is reflected in this image of itself." (p. 72) "The act of narrating is never, in the *Arabian Nights*, a transparent act; on the contrary, it is the mainspring of the action." (p. 73) Since everyone in *The Arabian Nights* tells stories and since the stories, like Chinese boxes, contain more stories, Todorov concludes that storytelling is more important than the events they tell. He does, however, say that "Narrative equals life; absence of narrative, death. If Scheherezade finds no more tales to tell, she will be beheaded." (p. 74) Once we say that "narrative equals life," we reestablish a direct relationship between story and life, though Todorov himself returns us to the realm of intertextuality: ". . . literature remains its own essential object. By speaking of desire it continues to speak . . . itself. Hence we can now advance a hypothesis as to the nature of the semantic universals of literature: they will never be anything but transformations of literature itself." (p. 107)

10. Robert Scholes, *Semiotics and Interpretation* (New Haven: Yale University Press, 1982), 24. "Saussure, as amplified by Roland Barthes and others, has taught us to recognize an unbridgeable gap between works and things, signs and referents."

11. Derrida's formulation *Il n'y a pas de hors-texte* and his qualification of it will be discussed at a later point.

12. Roland Barthes, "Myth Today" (1956), in *A Barthes Reader*, ed. Susan Sontag (New York: Hill and Wang, 1982), 145–46.

13. Ibid., 138, 141. Barthes's early work on Racine may have served as the basis for his later critique of myth and traditional narrative. *On Racine*, trans. Richard Howard (New York: Octagon Books, 1977). ". . . in Racine, there is only one relation, that between God and His creature." (p. 47) "The world [of tragedy] consists of pure contraries that are never mediated. God raises up or casts down—that is the monotonous movement of creation. Examples of these inversions are countless. It is as if Racine constructed his entire theatre on this model, which is, etymologically speaking, the peripeteia, and only afterwards invested it with what is called psychology." (pp. 41–42) "The [Racinean] hero always feels driven by a force external to himself, by a remote and terrible otherness, of which he feels himself to be the plaything." (pp. 36–37)

14. Mary Gentile, *Film Feminisms: Theory and Practice* (Westport, Conn.: Greenwood Press, 1985), 144.

15. Laura Mulvey, "Visual Pleasure and Narrative Cinema" (1973), in Mulvey, *Visual and Other Pleasures* (London: Macmillan, 1989), 22.

16. Roland Barthes, "Gide and His Journal" (1942), in *A Barthes Reader*, 15.

17. Vladimir Nabokov, *Lectures on Russian Literature* (New York: Harcourt Brace Jovanovich, 1981), 381.

18. Northrop Frye, "Myth, Fiction, and Displacement" (1961), in *Fables of Identity: Studies in Poetic Mythology* (New York: Harcourt, Brace and World, 1963), 31.

19. Roland Barthes, *Mythologies,* selected and translated from the French by Annette Lavers (New York: Hill and Wang, 1982), 128.

20. Roland Barthes, Inaugural Lecture, Collège de France, 1977, in *A Barthes Reader*, 475.

21. Jean-Pierre Vernant and Pierre Vidal-Naquet, *Tragedy and Myth in Ancient Greece* (Atlantic Highlands, N.J.: Humanities Press, 1981), 57. "We know that the Greeks did not consider the artist or artisan producing their works through their *poiesis* to be their true authors. *They* create nothing. Their role is simply to embody in matter some pre-existent form that is independent *from* and superior to their *techne*. The work itself is more perfect than the worker; the man is less than his task."

22. Roland Barthes, *S/Z*, trans. Richard Miller (New York: Hill and Wang, 1974), 151. One recalls Duchamp's "The spectator makes the image."

23. Ibid, 4.

24. Barthes, "Myth Today," 97.

25. Barthes, Inaugural Lecture, 465.

Matisse formulates the relationship of the artist to reality as follows: "An artist must recognize, when he is reasoning, that his picture is an artifice; but when he is painting, he should feel that he has copied nature. And even when he departs from nature, he must do it with the conviction that it is only to interpret her more fully." Henri Matisse, "Notes of a Painter," in Jack D. Flan, *Matisse on Art* (Oxford: Phaidon Press, 1990), 39.

26. Scholes, *Semiotics and Interpretation*, 145.

27. Heinrich Wölfflin, *Kunstgeschichtliche Grundbegriffe* (1929), 243, cited by Arnold Hauser, *Mannerism: the Crisis of the Renaissance and the Origin of Modern Art*, trans. Eric Mosbacher (New York: Alfred A. Knopf, 1965), 29–30.

28. Harold Bloom, *The Anxiety of Influence* (Oxford: Oxford University Press, 1975).

29. In a slightly different version this is reported in *Toulouse-Lautrec* (London: South Bank Centre, Réunion des musées nationaux, 1991), 28.

30. W. B. Yeats, "To a Young Beauty," in *The Collected Poems* (London: Macmillan, 1972), 138.

31. Maurice de Vlaminck. A slightly different version of this anecdote appears in Klaus G. Perls, *Vlaminck* (New York: Hyperion Press, 1941), 56. Compare Cézanne: "The people who preceded you are guarantors. In all walks of life. The path they took is a pointer to the way forward and not a barrier against you. They have lived, and that in itself means that they have experience. To recognize what that is doesn't mean diminishing yourself." *Joachim Gasquet's Cézanne: A Memoir with Conversations*, trans. Christopher Pemberton (London: Thames & Hudson, 1991), 209. See also: "[Cézanne] said that [Pissarro] was 'like the Good God,' and he once signed himself a 'pupil of Pissarro.' He said, 'He was a father to me.' " Cited in Jack Lindsay, *Cézanne: His Life and Art* (Greenwich, Conn.: New York Graphic Society, 1969), 150.

Compare Picasso: "Cézanne! It was the same with all of us—he was like our father. It was he who protected us. . . ." Cited in *Cézanne in Perspective*, ed. Judith Wechsler (Englewood Cliffs: Prentice-Hall, 1975), 78.

32. Thomas S. Kuhn, *The Structure of Scientific Revolutions* (Chicago: University of Chicago Press, 1962), 523.

33. Though Derrida says little about narrative, his questioning comment: "How could a narrative account for a phenomenon in progress?" suggests how limited and limiting the preclusive structure of narrative appears to him. Jacques Derrida, *Memoires: For Paul de Man* (New York: Columbia University Press, 1986), 13.

34. Jorge Luis Borges, "A New Refutation of Time," in *Labyrinths: Selected Stories and Other Writings* (New York: New Directions, 1964), 234. Although the

standard translation of the phrase is: "The world, unfortunately, is real; I, unfortunately, am Borges," I cite the one in Robert Scholes, *Semiotics and Interpretation*, 24.

35. Sigmund Freud, in Philip Rieff, *The Triumph of the Therapeutic: Uses of Faith after Freud* (New York: Harper and Row, 1966), 83.

36. Sigmund Freud, *Jokes and Their Relation to the Unconscious*, trans. and ed. James Strachey (New York: Norton, 1963).

37. Sigmund Freud, *The Interpretation of Dreams* (1900), in vol. 5 of *The Standard Edition of the Complete Psychological Works of Sigmund Freud,* ed. James Strachey (London: The Hogarth Press and the Institute of Psycho-Analysis, 1975), 613. For Freud, "original instinctual impulses" are the predicate of human nature, human behavior and social relationships. See Freud, *New Introductory Lectures on Psychoanalysis,* trans. W. J. H. Sprott (New York: W. W. Norton, 1933), 244. See also: "The instincts are mythic beings, superb in their indefiniteness. . . . We are never certain of seeing them clearly." Freud, *New Introductory Lectures,* 131. Compare: "We have always had the feeling that behind these multitudinous little instincts, something grave and powerful is buried, something that we wish to approach cautiously. The theory of instincts is, as it were, our mythology; the instincts are wonderfully vague mythical beings. In our work we cannot take our eyes off them for a moment, yet at the same time we never see them clearly." Sigmund Freud, *Gesammelte Schriften* (no publisher or date given), 10: 345 ff., cited in Ludwig Binswanger, *Being-in-the-World: Selected Papers of Ludwig Binswanger,* trans. Jacob Needleman (New York: Harper and Row, 1967), 151.

38. "Historical processes, according to Marx, are characterized by change. But for Freud, the more things change the more they remain the same." Philip Rieff, *Freud: The Mind of the Moralist* (Chicago: University of Chicago Press, 1979), 213.

"In Freudian 'doctrine' . . . the main stress is placed not upon existence as change but upon that which persists and remains amid change, the instinct." Ludwig Binswanger, *Freud's Conception of Man in the Light of Anthropology,* 168.

39. Letter from Friedrich Engels to J. Bloch, 21 (-22) September 1890, in Karl Marx and Fredrich Engels, *Selected Works in Three Volumes* (Moscow: Progress Publishers, 1973), 3: 488.

40. Ibid. The passage reads: ". . . history is made in such a way that the final result always arises from conflicts between many individual wills, of which each in turn has been made what it is by a host of particular conditions of life. Thus there are innumerable intersecting forces, an infinite series of parallelograms of forces which give rise to one resultant—the historical event. This may again itself be viewed as the product of a power which works as a whole *unconsciously* and without volition. For what each individual wills is obstructed by everyone else, and what emerges is something that no one willed. Thus history has proceeded hitherto in the manner of a natural process and is essentially subject to the same laws of motion. But from the fact that the wills of individuals—each of whom desires what he is impelled to by his physical constitution and external, in the last resort economic, circumstances (either his own personal circumstances or those of society in general)—do not attain what they want, but are merged into an aggregate mean, a

common resultant, it must not be concluded that they are equal to zero. On the contrary, each contributes to the resultant and is to this extent included in it." For further discussion of this issue, see chapter 9.

41. A. S. Cook, *The Meaning of Fiction* (Detroit: Wayne State University, 1960), 76.

42. Claude Lévi-Strauss, "Overture," *The Raw and the Cooked* (New York: Harper and Row, 1969), 10.

43. Compare Marx: "It is not the consciousness of men that determine their being, but on the contrary, their social being that determines their consciousness." Marx, Author's Preface to a Contribution to the Critique of Political Economy (1859), trans. N. I. Stone (Chicago: Charles H. Kerr, 1904), 11.

44. Claude Lévi-Strauss, "Structuralism and Myth," *Kenyon Review*, v. 3, no. 2 (Spring 1981): 65. Sartre agrees that existentialism is a humanism: "It took two centuries of crisis . . . for man to regain the creative freedom that Descartes placed in God, and for anyone finally to suspect the following truth, which is an essential basis of humanism: man is the being as a result of whose appearance a world exists." Cited in Shalvey, *Lévi-Strauss*, 122–23.

45. Rudolf Otto, *The Idea of the Holy: An Inquiry into the Non-rational Factor in the Idea of the Divine and Its Relation to the Rational*, trans. John W. Harvey (London: Oxford University Press, 1946).

Lévi-Strauss does not totally disregard human fear. In *The Raw and the Cooked*, he describes the passage from nature to culture, which displaced our species and cut us off from the gods and the animal kingdom. To ward off the anxiety that threatened us as a result, 'primitive' peoples—in their rites and stories—called on animals to reestablish the place of humankind in the universal order.

46. Claude Lévi-Strauss, *The Savage Mind* (Chicago: University of Chicago, 1966), 46.

47. Compare Lévi-Strauss: ". . . The effort to find a deeper and truer reality behind the multiplicity of apparent realities . . . seems to me to be the condition of survival for the human sciences, whatever the undertaking is called."

48. Friedrich Nietzsche, *Morgenröte*, in vol. 1 of *Werke in drei Bänden*, 1095. Though this passage can be read to question the existence of reality itself, it may only put in doubt our experience (*Erleben*) of that reality.

49. Hegel, *Philosophy of Right*, trans. T. M. Knox (Oxford: Clarendon Press, 1942), 178.

50. Cited in "Some Considerations Touching the Usefulness of Experimental Philosophy" (1663), cited in Martha Ornstein, *The Role of Scientific Societies in the Seventeenth Century*, 3rd ed. (1938), 58–59.

51. Werner Heisenberg, *Physics and Philosophy: The Revolution in Modern Science* (New York: Harper and Row, 1958), 82.

52. Einstein, in conversation with Rabindranath Tagore, cited in Ronald W. Clark, *Einstein: The Life and Times* (New York: World Publishing, 1971), 415.

53. Arthur W. Burks, *Chance, Cause, Reason: An Inquiry into the Nature of Scientific Evidence* (Chicago: University of Chicago Press, 1977), 589. "In its fullest for-

mulation, quantum theory describes a probabilistic system. On the basis of a foundational analysis of quantum mechanics, John von Neumann argued that quantum mechanical systems are inherently probabilistic and cannot be embedded in deterministic systems. As he expressed it, there are no "hidden parameters" in quantum mechanics. If this view is correct, quantum theory is incompatible with determinism. Note that in any case, quantum theory is compatible with near-determinism and hence with our presuppositions of induction." Ibid., 589.

54. "Einstein's views on quantum mechanics are not widely accepted. Instead, the 'Copenhagen interpretation' of quantum mechanics, devised by Niels Bohr, is accepted by most physicists. But though they have used this interpretation for decades, it is open to objections like the Einstein-Rosen-Podolsky paradox." Ibid., 590.

55. Fritz Rohrlich, "Facing Quantum Mechanical Reality," *Science*, 221, no. 4617 (23 September 1983): 1254–55.

56. Heisenberg, *Physics and Philosophy*, 160.

57. Rohrlich, "Facing Quantum Mechanical Reality," 1254.

58. Burks, *Chance, Cause, Reason*, 590. See also John Earman, "Determinism in the Physical Sciences" in *Introduction to the Philosophy of Science* (Englewood Cliffs, N.J.: Prentice-Hall, 1992), 236–37: "The theory of probability arose in part as an attempt to quantify the risks associated with games of chance. It is therefore a testimony to the power of the vision of determinism that one of the most eloquent expressions of the vision occurs in Laplace's pioneering work on probability, *A Philosophical Essay of Probabilities* ([1814], 1951), 3: 'All events, even those which on account of their insignificance do not seem to follow the great laws of nature, are a result of it just as necessarily as the revolutions of the sun. In ignorance of the ties which unite such events to the entire system of the universe, they have been made to depend upon final causes or upon hazard, according as they occur and are repeated with regularity, or appear without regard to order; but these imaginary causes have gradually receded with the widening bounds of knowledge and disappear entirely before sound philosophy, which sees in them only the expression of our ignorance of the true causes.' "

59. The physicist J. A. Wheeler appears to take a position on reality that is akin to deconstruction's: "No elementary phenonomenon is a phenomenon until it is an observed phenomenon." "Frontiers of Time," in Italian Physical Society, *Proceedings of the International School of Physics, "Enrico Fermi," Course LXXII, Problems in the Foundation of Physics*, ed. G. Toraldo di Francia (New York: North-Holland Publishing, 1979), 398. I was referred to this quotation by Jeffrey Bub.

60. Arthur Schopenhauer, *Die Welt als Wille und Vorstellung*, 1: 378–79. "What we fear in death is . . . the destruction of the individual . . . and since the will to life manifests in the individual, our entire being strains against it."

61. Edward F. Edinger, *Psychotherapy and Alchemy IV, Mortificatio Quandrant* (Spring 1981), 35. Compare Malinowski: "Of all the sources of religion . . . death is of the greatest importance." Bronislaw Malinowski, *Magic, Science and Religion* (Boston: Beacon Press, 1948), 29.

62. Marie-Louise von Franz, *On Dreams and Death* (Boston: Shambhala, 1986), 72.

63. "The Four Ages of Man," *The Collected Poems of W. B. Yeats* (New York: Macmillan, 1972), 286.

64. Walter Benjamin, "The Storyteller," in *Illuminations*, ed. Hannah Arendt (New York: Schocken Books, 1969), 94.

65. Max Horkheimer and Theodor W. Adorno, *Dialectic of Enlightenment*, trans. John Cumming (New York: Herder and Herder, 1972), 19.

66. "The very ritual that gives expression to the realm of the extraordinary also painstakingly controls it." Walter Burkert, *Homo Nekans* (Berkeley: University of California Press, 1983), 60. Jung refers to the *temenos*—"the precincts of a [Greek] temple or any isolated sacred space . . . [which] protects or isolates an inner content or process that should not get mixed up with things outside." C. G. Jung, *Psychology and Religion: West and East*, vol. 11 in *The Collected Works of C. G. Jung*, trans. R. F. C. Hull (Princeton: Princeton University Press, 1969), 95.

67. Theme-park designers speak of "immersive experiences." On most amusement park rides we are not in control; perhaps that is the heart of the thrill. "Virtual reality" is billed as "the ultimate immersion experience"; like fiction, it is safe.

68. The loss of control is less voluntary on the part of the artist.

69. Freud, *Jokes and Their Relation to the Unconscious*, 127, 137, 154, 170, elsewhere.

70. René Girard, "In Perilous Balance: A Comic Hypothesis," in *"To Double Business Bound": Essays on Literature, Mimesis, and Anthropology* (Baltimore: Johns Hopkins University Press, 1978), 134.

71. In *Grundrisse*, Marx says: ". . . the difficulty is not in grasping the idea that Greek art and epos are bound up with certain forms of social development. It lies rather in understanding why they still constitute for us a source of aesthetic enjoyment and in certain respects prevail as the standard and model beyond attainment. A man cannot become a child again unless he becomes childish. But does he not enjoy the artless ways of the child, and must he not strive to reproduce its truth on a higher plane? Is not the character of every epoch revived, perfectly true to nature, in the childs's nature? Why should the childhood of human society, where it had obtained its most beautiful development, not exert an eternal charm as an age that will never return?" (p. 360)

72. "It is a fearful thing to fall into the hands of the living God." Hebrews 10: 31.

73. Schopenhauer, *Welt als Wille*, 1: 341.

74. Napoleon, in conversation on the eve of the battle of Austerlitz. Compare Freud: "The coercive power of the oracle should have acquitted (Oedipus) of guilt in our judgement and in his own . . ." *An Outline of Psychoanalysis,* in vol. 23 of *The Standard Edition of the Complete Psychological Works of Sigmund Freud* (London: The Hogarth Press and the Institute of Psycho-Analysis, 1973), 205. Perhaps the most pertinent discussion of the guilt/innocence of Oedipus is in G. W. F. Hegel, *Vorlesungen über die Ästhetik*, 545.

75. *Hegel on Tragedy*, ed. Anne and Henry Paolucci (New York: Harper Torch-books, 1962), 70–71.

76. René Girard, *Violence and the Sacred* (Baltimore: Johns Hopkins University Press, 1977).

77. Not surprisingly, Lévi-Strauss separates myth—which he deems a rational, symbolic and theoretical account—from ritual, which is not, in his view, rational. He explicitly rejects Malinovsky's theory that myth and rite have the same structure and takes issue with Hubert and Mauss, who said that the "ultimate end" of their research into myth was "the study of the sacred." (Cited in Ivan Strenski, *Four Theories of Myth in Twentieth-Century History* (Iowa City: University of Iowa Press, 1987), 147.

Those anthropologists who, like Lévi-Strauss, are resolutely unsympathetic to religion, are of course likely to reject the precedence of ritual over myth, since it suggests that there is an emotional-mystical rather than rational foundation to human existence—in other words, that *fear* precedes *reason*. Lévi-Strauss has said of himself that he never "felt the slightest twinge of religious anxiety." Lévi-Strauss, *The Naked Man* (New York: Harper and Row, 1981). Like the entire discussion of myth and ritual in our time, his view of myth as a logical structure may be partly contingent upon the emergence of fascism. In this sense, it bears directly on our study of the shifting perception of narrative, which is deeply influenced by political events and considerations.

These writers who are sympathetic to the religious impulse are apt to give ritual precedence over myth. So Walter Otto suggests in *Dionysus* that *cultus* came first: "[Before myth] . . . God had, as yet, no history which could be related and imitated. His myth lived in cult activity, and the actions of *cultus* expressed in plastic form what He was and what He did. Before the faithful visualized the image of their God, and gave verbal expression to His life and works, He was so close to them that their spirit, touched by His breath, was aroused to holy activity. With their own bodies they created His image. His living reality was mirrored in the solemnity of their actions long before this mute or inarticulate myth was made eloquent and poetic.

The great era of this myth, strictly speaking, dawned only after *cultus* began to lose its original freshness and creative vitality and (became) fixed. At that time great sculptors drew anew from the same divine abundance out of which practises of *cultus* had arisen." Otto, *Dionysus: Myth and Cult,* trans. Robert B. Palmer (Bloomington: Indiana University Press, 1965), 22.

Among recent anthropologists, Victor Turner argues that "ritual in its performative plenitude in tribal and many post-tribal cultures is a matrix from which several other genres of cultural performance, including most of those we tend to think of as 'aesthetic,' have been derived." Victor Turner, "Social Dramas and Stories about Them," in *On Narrative*, ed. W. J. T. Mitchell (Chicago: University of Chicago Press, 1981), 157.

A narrative of the process by which ritual becomes story is told by Gershom G. Scholem, who, in turn, heard it from S. J. Agnon: "When the Baal Shem had a difficult task before him, he would go to a certain place in the woods, light a fire and meditate in prayer—and what he had set out to perform was done. When a generation later the Maggid of Meseritz was faced with the same task he would go to the same place in the woods and say: We can no longer light the fire, but we can still speak the prayers—and what he wanted done became reality. Again a generation later Rabbi Moshe Leib of Sassov had to perform this task. And he too went into the woods and said: We can no longer light a fire, nor do we know the secret meditations belonging to the prayer, but we do know the place in the woods to which it all belongs—and that must be sufficient; and sufficient it was. But when another generation had passed and Rabbi Israel of Rishin was called upon to perform the task, he sat down on his golden chair in his castle and said: We cannot light the fire, we cannot speak the prayers, we do not know the place, but we can tell the story of how it was done. And, the story-teller adds, the story which he told had the same effect as the actions of the other three." *Major Trends in Jewish Mysticism* ((New York: Schocken Books, 1961), 349–50.

78. "Ritual is always conservative." Also see Jane Ellen Harrison, *Themis: A Study of the Social Origin of Greek Religion* (Cambridge: Cambridge University Press, 1912), 492.

79. Walter Benjamin, "The Work of Art in the Age of Mechanical Reproduction," in *Illuminations*, 224. It might be legitimate to associate Benjamin's determination to free the work of art from ritual with Lévi-Strauss's insistence that myth and ritual are separate. Both may well be antifascist in origin.

Susan Buck-Morss points out that in his essay on Baudelaire, Benjamin saw the loss of aura in the artwork negatively. Buck-Morss, *The Origin of Negative Dialectics* (New York: Free Press, 1977), 161.

80. Barthes, Inaugural Lecture, 475.

81. The invalidation of dualism and of human duality is discussed in chapter 9.

82. Heisenberg, *Physics and Philosophy*, 181.

CHAPTER 8

1. Wilhelm Worringer, *Abstraction and Empathy: A Contribution to the Psychology of Style* (New York: International Universities Press, 1963), 14–25.

2. In Sanskrit and Indian drama, tragic resolutions are prohibited, surely because they assert the preeminence of an individual figure.

3. Karl Reinhardt, "Oedipus Tyrannus" in *Moderns on Tragedy*, ed. Lionel Abel (New York: Fawcett Publications, 1967), 222.

4. Ibid., 191.

5. Arthur Schopenhauer, *Die Welt als Wille und Vorstellung,* (Leipzig: Inselverlag, n.d.), 1: 341. He quotes Calderon's "The gravest sin of the human being/ Is to have been born."

6. Ibid., 425.

7. See Friedrich Nietzsche, *Die Geburt der Tragödie,* in *Werke in drei Bänden,* ed. Karl Schlechta (München: Carl Hanser Verlag, 1976), 1: 44ff.

8. Charles Segal, *Tragedy and Civilization: An Interpretation of Sophocles* (Cambridge, Mass.: Published for Oberlin College by Harvard University Press, 1981). "The hero stands at the point where the the divine and human sphere intersect, where the separation between them becomes difficult and mysterious, where the intelligible order of life meets with darker levels of existence." (p. 8) "The king's (and hero's) special power, whether of body or of spirit, places him in a position to violate the taboos which ordinary men must respect. . . . Performing the dangerous function of interceding between the sacred and the profane for his people, he is, as the priest says of Oedipus in the *Tyrannus*, "the first of men . . . in the encounter with the gods." (p. 44)

9. Émile Durkheim, "The Division of Labor in Society," in *Selected Writings*, ed. and trans. Anthony Giddens (New York: Cambridge University Press, 1972), 127.

10. Durkheim says: "We now see the real reason why the gods cannot do without their worshippers any more than these can do without their gods; it is because society, of which the gods are only a symbolic expression, cannot do without individuals any more than these can do without society. Here we touch the solid rock upon which all the cults are built and which has caused their persistence ever since human societies have existed." In Robert Nisbet, *The Sociology of Émile Durkheim* (New York: Oxford University Press, 1974), 181.

11. Hyppolite says Hegel liked quoting Meister Eckhart's "If God did not exist, I would not exist; if I did not exist, He would not exist." Jean Hippolyte, *Genesis and Structure of Hegel's Phenomenology of the Spirit*, trans. Samuel Cherniak and John Heckman (Evanston, Ill.: Northwestern University Press, 1974), 542. In the *Phenomenology*, Hegel says that without "the calvary of history, spirit would be lifeless solitude." Ibid., 528.

12. C. G. Jung, *Aion: Research into the Phenomenolgy of the Self*, in vol. 9, part 2 of *The Collected Works of C. G. Jung* (Princeton: Princeton University Press, 1970), 109. Perhaps the views of Hegel and Jung are equivalent to saying that when the object ceases to be, so does the subject.

13. G. W. F. Hegel, *Phenomenology of the Mind*, trans. J. Baillie (London, 1909), 135.

14. Karl Marx, "Critique of the Hegelian Dialectic and Philosophy as a Whole," in *Economic and Philosophical Manuscripts of 1844*, ed. Dirk J. Struik, trans. Martin Milligan (New York: International Publishers, 1964), 189.

15. Sigmund Freud, *An Outline of Psychoanalysis*, in *The Standard Edition of the Complete Psychological Works of Sigmund Freud*, ed. James Strachey (London: The Hogarth Press and the Institute of Psycho-Analysis, 1973), 23: 157.

16. Erich Neumann, *The Origins and History of Consciousness*, trans. R. F. C. Hull (Princeton: Princeton University Press, 1970), 16.

17. Compare: "Der Teufel . . . als der älteste Freund der Erkenntnis." Nietzsche, *Jenseits von Gut und Böse, Werke in drei Bänden*, 2: 634.

18. Neumann, 121. Compare Jung: "So far as we know, consciousness is always ego-consciousness. In order to be conscious of myself, I must be able to distinguish

myself from others." C. G. Jung, *The Development of Personality: Marriage As a Psychological Relationship,* in *The Collected Works of C. G. Jung,* trans. R. F. C. Hull (Princeton: Princeton University, 1970), 190.

19. "Margaret Mead claims that from the time of birth, girls can begin to take on feminine identity through identification with their mothers, while for boys, masculine identification comes through a process of differentiation, because what would be their natural identification—identification with the person they are closest to and most dependent upon—is according to cultural values unnatural; this works against their attainment of stable masculine identity. The boy's earliest experience of self is one in which he is forced, in the relationship to his mother, to realize himself as different, as a creature unlike the mother, as a creature unlike the human beings who make babies in a direct, intelligible way by using their own bodies to make them." Nancy Chodorow, "Being and Doing," in *Woman in a Sexist Society: Studies in Power and Powerlessness,* ed. Vivian Gornick and Barbara K. Moran (New York: Basic Books, 1971), 182. Margaret Mead, *Male and Female: A Study of Sexes in a Changing World* (New York: William Morrow, 1975), and Dorothy Dinnerstein, *The Mermaid and the Minotaur: Sexual Arrangements and Human Malaise* (New York: Harper, 1977).

20. Nancy Chodorow, "Family Structure and Feminine Personality," in *Woman, Culture and Society,* ed. Michelle Zimbalist Rosaldo and Louise Lamphere (Stanford: Stanford University Press, 1974), 50. In most societies, women are: "defined relationally (as someone's wife, mother, daughter, daughter-in-law; even a nun becomes the Bride of Christ). Men's association (although it too may be kin-based and inter-generational) is much more likely than women's to cut across kinship units, to be restricted to a single generation, and to be recruited according to universalistic criteria and involve relationships and responsibilities defined by their specificity." (pp. 57–58)

21. "Girls are . . . pressured to be involved with and connected to others, boys to deny this involvement and connection." Ibid., 55.

22. Sherry Ortner, "Is Female to Male as Nature is to Culture?" in *Woman, Culture and Society,* ed. Rosaldo and Lamphere, 67–87.

23. Ferdinand de Saussure, *Course in General Linguistics,* ed. Charles Bally and Albert Sechehaye, trans. Wade Baskin (New York: Philosophical Library, 1959), 120.

24. Ibid. Saussure says that the terms *a* and *b* are "radically incapable of reaching the level of consciousness—one is always conscious of only the a/b difference." *Course of Linguistics,* 113. See also: "A segment of language can never in the final analysis be based on anything except its noncoincidence with the rest." Ibid., 118.

25. Albert Camus, *The Rebel: An Essay on Man in Revolt,* trans. Anthony Bower (New York: Alfred A. Knopf, 1961), 8. Nothing reaches us in 'unevaluated' form. All perception, as Gestalt psychology demonstrates, depends on evaluation, on 'judging'; we cannot perceive unless we instantaneously order perception. "The operations of the senses," Lévi-Strauss says, "have from the start an intellectual aspect." "Structuralism and Myth," *Kenyon Review,* v. 3, no. 2 (Spring 1981): 78.

26. Perhaps this is one implication of Spinoza's *Omnis determinatio est negatio*—a sentence Hegel deemed to be "von unendlicher Wichtigkeit." G. W. F. Hegel, *Wissenschaft der Logik* I, in vol. 5 of *Werke in zwanzig Bänden* (Frankfurt am Main: Suhrkamp Verlag, 1969), 121. Compare C. G. Jung: "Exclusion, selection, and discrimination are the root and essence of everything that lays claim to the name 'consciousness.' " *The Archetypes of the Collective Unconscious*, in vol. 9, part 1 of *Collected Works*, 288.

27. Edward F. Edinger, *Ego and Archetype* (New York: G. P. Putnam's Sons, 1972), 18. The words "whole" and "holy" are, of course, etymologically linked.

28. Ibid.

29. Lévi-Strauss says consciousness—by which he means individual consciousness or Descartes's *cogito*—is the "enemy" of the human and social sciences. Thomas Shalvey, *Claude Lévi-Strauss: Social Psychotherapy and the Collective Unconscious* (Amherst: University of Massachusetts Press, 1979), 164. But it is also the "enemy" of life itself, and the source of the exacerbated state we call alienation. In a later comment, Lévi-Strauss says: "I've never had any other intention than to further knowledge, that is, *to achieve consciousness*. However, for too long now philosophy has succeeded in locking the social sciences inside a closed circle by not allowing them to envisage any other object of study for . . . consciousness than consciousness itself." Lévi-Strauss, "Structuralism and Myth," 65.

30. Gershom G. Scholem, *Major Trends in Jewish Mysticism* (New York: Schocken, 1961), 261.

31. Friedrich Nietzsche, *Die Geburt der Tragödie*, in vol. 1 of *Werke in drei Bänden*, 99.

32. Theodor W. Adorno, "The George-Hoffmannsthal Correspondence, 1891–1906," in *Prisms*, trans. Samuel and Shierry Weber (London: Neville Spearman, 1967), 224. Hyppolite says: "Unhappy consciousness is the fundamental theme of (Hegel's) *Phenomenology*. Consciousness, as such, is in principle always unhappy consciousness, for it has not yet reached the concrete identity of certainty and truth and therefore it aims at something beyond itself." Jean Hyppolite, *Genesis and Structure of Hegel's Phenomenology of the Spirit*, 190.

33. Martin Heidegger, *Sein und Zeit/Being and Time*, trans. John Macquarrie and Edward Robinson (New York: Harper and Row, 1962), 277.

34. Hegel's philosophy stresses the positive in negativity, and Schopenhauer says that wanting, willing and striving are the essence of being human and predicated on need or lack. *Die Welt als Wille*, 1: 414.

35. René Girard, *Violence and the Sacred* (Baltimore: Johns Hopkins University Press, 1977), 76.

36. In Hegel, *Unruhe* or disquiet is existential. In the "Vorrede" to *Die Phänomenologie des Geistes*, Hegel identifies it with the self. (In vol. 2 of *Sämtliche Werke*, ed. Hermann Glockner [Stuttgart: Friedrich Frommann Verlag, 1964], 26.)

37. Marshack says: "[Agriculture] is a 'time-factored' activity, extending over the whole year, and therefore completely unlike the assumed primitive hunt which might begin and end in a day." Alexander Marshack, *The Roots of Civilization: The*

Cognitive Beginnings of Man's First Art Symbol and Notation (New York: McGraw-Hill, 1972), 14. Herding, too, is less dependent on 'time-factoring' than agriculture.

Perhaps Cain, and we, learned to 'reject' life as it was given from Yahweh himself, who rejected *us* as we were in Eden and made our existence conditional—much as our parents make our relationship to them in part conditional.

38. Ludwig Binswanger, in *Being-in-the-World: Selected Papers of Ludwig Binswanger*, trans. Jacob Needleman (New York: Harper and Row, 1967), 163–64.

39. See G. W. F. Hegel, "Vergleichung des Schellingschen Prinzips der Philosophie mit dem Fichteschen," in vol. 2 of *Hegels Werke* (Frankfurt am Main: Suhrkamp Verlag, 1970), 107.

40. Perhaps we can interpret Derrida's statement "I'm obsessed with death. I am at every minute attentive to the possibility that in the following hour I will be dead. . . . All my writing is on death," as a preoccupation with personal identity. Mitchell Stephens, "Jacques Derrida," *The New York Times Magazine*, 23 January 1994: 25.

41. It is nonetheless true that in art, as in science, the "end" is often intuited early in the process of discovery. The mathematician Gauss said: "I have the result, only I do not yet know how to get to it."

42. Niels Bohr, quoted in D. Ter Haar, "The Quantum Nature of Matter and Radiation," in *Turning Points in Physics: A Series of Lectures Given at Oxford University in Trinity Term, 1958* (Amsterdam: North-Holland Publishing, 1959), 44.

43. This appears in Gustave Flaubert, *Notes de Voyage*. I was unable to locate the English text in which it is cited.

44. "The most we can do is to *dream the myth onwards* and give it a modern dress." "The Psychology of the Child Archetype," in *C. G. Jung: Psychological Reflections: A New Anthology of His Writings, 1905–1961*, ed. Jolande Jacobi and R. F. C. Hull (Princeton: Princeton University Press, 1953), 45.

45. Elizabeth Bowen, "Notes on Writing a Novel," in *Pictures and Conversations* (New York: Alfred A. Knopf, 1975), 169.

46. The focus of the contemporary aesthetic on human freedom and potentiation is discussed at several later points.

47. Matthew Arnold, "The Strayed Reveller," in *The Poems of Matthew Arnold*, ed. Kenneth Allott (New York: Barnes and Noble, 1965), 73.

48. Jacques Derrida, "Freud and the Scene of Writing," in *Writing and Difference*, trans. Alan Bass (Chicago: University of Chicago Press, 1978), 211. Conversely, see Trotsky: "The Formalists . . . are followers of St. John. They believe that 'In the beginning was the Word.' But we believe that in the beginning was the deed. The word followed as its phonetic shadow." Leon Trotsky, *Literature and Revolution* (New York: Russell & Russell, 1957), 183.

49. Compare Freud: ". . . Do not let us depise the *word*. After all it is a powerful instrument; it is the means by which we convey our feelings to one another, our method of influencing other people. Words can do unspeakable good and cause terrible wounds. No doubt 'in the beginning was the deed' ('Im Anfang war die Tat,' Goethe, *Faust*, I, scene 3) and the word came later; in some circumstances it

meant an advance in civilization when deeds were softened into words. But originally the word was magic—a magical act; and it has retained much of its ancient power." Sigmund Freud, *The Question of Lay Analysis*, in vol. 20 of *The Standard Edition of the Complete Psychological Works of Sigmund Freud*, ed. James Strachey (London: The Hogarth Press and the Institute of Psycho-Analysis, 1978), 188.

50. In his introduction to Ernst Cassirer's "The Question of Jean-Jacques Rousseau," Gay points out that "Rousseau directed his energy toward discovering not a state of nature without culture but a culture that would realize man's true nature." Peter Gay, *The Enlightenment: An Interpretation*, vol. 2: *The Science of Freedom* (New York: Alfred A. Knopf, 1969), 170–71.

51. See Erich Neumann: "The consciousness of the individual originally develops with the aid of the collective and its institutions, and receives the 'current values' from it. The ego, therefore, as the centre of this consciousness, normally becomes the bearer and representative of the collective values current at any given time. . . ." Erich Neumann, *Depth Psychology and a New Ethic* (New York: Harper and Row, 1973), 36–37.

52. Hegel says: "One more word about giving instruction to what the world ought to be. Philosophy in any case always comes on the scene too late to give it." G. W. F. Hegel, "The Philosophy of Right," trans. T. M. Knox, cited by Jean Hippolyte in *Genesis and Structure of Hegel's Phenomenology of the Spirit*, 43.

53. In "French Sociology," Lévi-Strauss says that "every moral, social and intellectual progress" was made "as a revolt against the group"—a revolt by "individual thought and spontaneity." In *Twentieth Century Sociology*, ed. Georges Gurvitch and William E. Moore (New York: Philosophical Library, 1945), 520.

CHAPTER 9

1. G. W. F. Hegel, *Wissenschaft der Logik*, II, in vol. 6 of *Hegels Werke* (Frankfurt am Main, Suhrkamp Verlag, 1971), 75. The German text reads: "Er (der Widerspruch) aber ist die Wurzel aller Bewegung und Lebendigkeit; nur insofern etwas in sich selbst einen Widerspruch hat, bewegt es sich, hat Trieb und Tätigkeit." In our text, "contradiction" refers only to the human and to that made by the human.

2. Karl Marx, *Economic and Philosophic Manuscripts of 1844*, ed. Dirk Struik, trans. Martin Milligan (New York: International Publishers, 1964), 135.

3. Georg Lukács, *History and Class Consciousness: Studies in Marxist Dialectics*, trans. Robert Livingstone (Cambridge, Mass.: MIT Press, 1971), 54. The argument is lucidly summarized by Susan Buck-Morss in *The Origin of Negative Dialectics* (New York: Free Press, 1977), 26–27: "Lukács analyzed the tradition of bourgeois philosophy, demonstrating that the antinomies which continuously appeared within it had the same structure as the contradictions of bourgeois economic production. He argued that the fundamental problem of idealism, the dualistic separation of subject and object, had its prototype in the problem of commodities, in which products appeared as objects divorced from the workers who had produced them. The concept of reification provided the key to both. The significance of Lukács's analysis

was that instead of seeing bourgeois theory as a mere epiphenomenon, a thin veil for naked class interests, he argued and attempted to demonstrate that even the best bourgeois thinkers, in their most honest intellectual efforts, were not able to resolve contradictions in their theories, because the latter were based on a reality which was itself contradictory. Once these thinkers accepted given social reality as the reality, they had to come upon a barrier of irrationality which could not be overcome (and which had led Kant to posit the thing-in-itself), because that barrier could not be removed from theory without being removed from society. Conversely, if theorists could see through the reified appearances, they would recognize that the antinomies of philosophy were due not to the inadequacies of reason, but to those of the reality in which reason tried to find itself."

4. Henri Wallon, "The Origins of Thought in the Child," in *The World of Henri Wallon,* ed. Gilbert Voyat (New York: Jason Aronson, 1984), 72. The same point is made by R. Jakobson and M. Halle, "Phonology and Phonemes," in Roman Jakobson, *Selected Writings*, vol. 1: *Phonological Studies* ('S-Gravenhage: Mouton, 1962), 499–500: "The binary opposition is a child's first logical operation. Both opposites arise simultaneously and force the infant to choose one and suppress the other of the two alternative terms."

5. He criticizes structuralism for placing structures out of play. Jacques Derrida, *Writing and Difference*, trans. Alan Bass (Chicago: University of Chicago Press, 1978), 279.

6. ". . . The opposites are the ineradicable and indispensible preconditions of all psychic life, so much so that life itself is guilt." C. G. Jung, *Mysterium Coniunctionis*, par. 206, cited in Edward F. Edinger, *The Living Psyche* (Wilmette, Ill.: Chiron Publications, 1990), 189.

7. Erich Neumann, *The Origins and History of Consciousness*, trans. R. F. C. Hull (Princeton: Princeton University Press, 1970), 121, 290–301, 315, 317–18. See also Edinger: "Duality, dissociation and repression have been born into the human psyche simultaneously with the birth of consciousness." Edward F. Edinger, *Ego and Archetype* (New York: G. P. Putnam's Sons, 1972), 20.

8. Otto Rank, *The Trauma of Birth* (New York: Robert Brunner, 1952). Rank calls the birth trauma "the most powerful of all 'memories,' " and proposes that "the primal repression of the birth trauma may be considered as the cause . . . of the partial capacity for remembering." (p. 8) "Every infantile pleasure has as its final aim the reestablishment of the intrauterine primal pleasure" (p. 17)—in other words, the reestablishment of the sense of wholeness, unconsciousness and belonging that consciousness has damaged.

9. See Neumann: "The importance of family relationships lies precisely in the fact that the personal figures of the environment who are the first form of society must be able, as soon as the ego emerges from the primary security of the uroboric state, to offer it the secondary security of the human world." Neumann, *Origins and History of Consciousness*, 402.

10. William James called consciousness "an organ, superadded to the other organs which maintain the animal in the struggle for existence." William James, *The*

Principles of Psychology (New York: Henry Holt, 1890), 1: 183, in David W. Marcell, *Progress and Pragmatism: James, Dewey, Beard, and the American Idea of Progress* (Westport, Conn.: Greenwood Press, 1974), 161.

11. See Nietzsche: "Das Leben, welches des Ja nicht vom Nein zu trennen weiss." *Aus dem Nachlass der Achtziger Jahre, Werke in drei Bänden*, ed. Karl Schlechta (München: Carl Hanser Verlag, 1976), 3: 798.

12. C. G. Jung, "The Psychology of the Transference," in *The Practice of Psychotherapy,* in vol. 16 of *Collected Works* (New York: Bollingen Foundation, 1966), 167–73.

13. Friedrich Nietzsche, "Sils-Maria," in *Werke in drei Bänden,* ed. Karl Schlechta (München: Carl Hanser Verlag, 1976), 2: 271.

14. See Durkheim: ". . . since society cannot exist except in and through individual consciousness, this force must also penetrate us and organise itself within us. It thus becomes an integral part of our being and by that very fact this is elevated and magnified." Emile Durkheim, "The Elementary Forms of Religious Life," in Emile Durkheim, *Selected Writings,* ed. and trans. Anthony Giddens (Cambridge: Cambridge University Press, 1972), 229–30. See also: "A verbal similarity has made possible the belief that individualism necessarily resulted from individual, and thus egoistic, sentiments. In reality, the religion of the individual is a social institution like all known religions. It is society which provides us with this ideal as the only common end which is today able to offer a focus for men's wills. To remove this ideal, without replacing it with any other, is therefore to plunge us into that very moral anarchy which it sought to avoid." Ibid., 149.

15. G. W. F. Hegel, in Alexandre Kojève, *Introduction to the Reading of Hegel: Lectures on the Phenomenology of Spirit,* trans. Knut Tarnowski and Frederic Will (Evanston, Ill.: Northwestern University Press, 1973), 163–64.

16. Erich Fromm, *The Sane Society* (New York: Rinehart, 1955), 77. Compare Hebbel: "Der Mensch hat freien Willen—d.h. er kann einwilligen ins Notwendige." Friedrich Hebbel, *Tagebücher I,* in *Friedrich Hebbels Werke* (Berlin: Deutsches Verlaghaus Bong, n.d.), Neunter Teil, 2 März 1842, entry 2028.

17. "In its reality (the essence of man) is the totality of social relations." Karl Marx, Thesis VI, "Theses on Feuerbach," in *The German Ideology,* by Karl Marx and Friedrich Engels, parts 1 and 3, ed. R. Pascal (New York: International Publishers, 1947), 198.

18. Émile Durkheim, in Robert Nisbet, *The Sociology of Émile Durkheim* (London: Heinemann, 1975), 181.

19. Ibid., 62.

20. Ernst Bloch, *Geist der Utopie* (Frankfurt am Main: Suhrkamp Verlag, 1964), 322. Ernst Cassirer points out that Rousseau rejected "the Aristotelian doctrine that man is 'by nature' a social being. . . . He does not believe in that 'social instinct' on which the theorists of the seventeenth and eighteenth century hoped to found society. . . . It is not man's physical nature or any sort of originally implanted need which drives him to his fellows. By nature man has but a single instinct—the instinct of self-preservation. This basic demand *suum esse conservare* man must re-

nounce as soon as he enters society. . . . Never again can he find 'himself'; he is entangled in a thousand claims and demands addressed to him from without." Ernst Cassirer, *Rousseau, Kant, Goethe: Two Essays* (Princeton: Princeton University Press, 1970), 27–28.

21. Arthur Schopenhauer, *Die Welt als Wille und Vorstellung* (Leipzig: Inselverlag, n.d.), 2: 1332. A friend of mine said: "As I get older I realize that the stronger my will is, the less it is 'mine.' "

22. See Voltaire: "It seems that nature has given us *l'amour propre* for our preservation and *la bien veillance* for the preservation of others, and, perhaps . . . without these two principles (of which the first should be the stronger) there could have been no society." Voltaire, *Notebooks*, 219, in Peter Gay, *The Enlightenment: An Interpretation*, vol. 2: *The Science of Freedom* (New York: Alfred A. Knopf, 1969), 170.

23. As individuals we owe allegiance to more than one entity and are often divided by conflicting loyalties. On occasion, society fails to make the determination for us and we must decide ourselves to which entity we owe greater allegiance. In most states the law recognizes the conflict when it spares us from testifying against our spouses. We *are,* however, obliged to testify against our own parents and children, and are not allowed to betray our country for the good of our family or the world community.

24. ". . . in the early stages of the emotional development of the human infant a vital part is played by the environment which is in fact not yet separated off from the infant by the infant. Gradually the separating-off of the *not-me* from the *me* takes place, and the pace varies according to the infant and according to the environment. The major changes take place in the separating-out of the mother as an objectively perceived environmental feature. If no one person is there to be mother the infant's developmental task is infinitely complicated." D. W. Winnicott, *Playing and Reality* (New York: Basic Books, 1971), 111. See also: "What does the baby see when he or she looks at the mother's face? I am suggesting that, ordinarily, what the baby sees is himself or herself." Ibid., 112.

25. Seen 'objectively' from a distance, the earth is whole: it is *we* who introduce the polarities: we fragment everything, including time and space; we divide and conquer. Perhaps the polarities are in large part attributable to our severely limited awareness, which cannot hold more than binary multiples at any one time. In order to avoid being overwhelmed, we may have to reduce the infinite multiplicities that face us *everywhere* to simple binary differences, or opposites.

26. The criticism leveled at Descartes by both Lévi–Strauss and deconstruction is focused on the support his philosophy has provided for subjectivity and consciousness, as well as on his dualism. As Descartes himself makes clear, *cogito* means more than "I think": "By the word thought I understand all that of which we are conscious as operating in us. And that is why not only understanding, willing, imagining, but also feeling are here the same thing as thought."

27. Max Horkheimer and Theodor W. Adorno, *Dialectic of Enlightenment*, trans. John Cumming (New York: Herder and Herder, 1972), 247–48. See also Adorno in

a letter to Ernst Krenek (1936): "In reified society, all progress occurs via continued specialization." *Theodor W. Adorno und Ernst Krenek: Briefwechsel* (Frankfurt am Main, 1974), 220, cited in Susan Buck-Morss, *The Origin of Negative Dialectics* (New York: The Free Press, 1977), 31.

28. John Dewey traces all Western polarities—"mind and matter, body and spirit, man and nature . . . subject and object, the changeless and the changing," as well as the division of labor and the hierarchies and elites it produced—to the dualistic perspective of Greece. See David Marcell, *Progress and Pragmatism: James, Dewey, Beard, and the American Idea of Progress* (Westport, Conn.: Greenwood Press, 1974), 208–9. Heidegger, too, points to the dualistic divisions that appear in Greek philosophy, most clearly in Plato and Aristotle. ("The Age of the World Picture," in *The Question Concerning Technology and Other Essays,* trans. Albert Hofstadter (New York: Harper and Row, 1971). Yet surely the same divisions, albeit in far less emphatic form, appeared along with early awareness. The subject may well have separated from the object at the moment Yahweh suggested the *possibility* of eating the apple *and* prohibited it.

In Hegel's view, while pagan consciousness was not dualistic and alienated, "the element of duality, of otherness is precisely the *Dasein* of life": "Die (menschliche) Entwicklung ist . . . nicht das harm-und kampflose blosse Hervorgehen, wie das des organischen Lebens, sondern die harte, unwillige Arbeit gegen sich selbst." *Vorlesungen über die Philosophie der Geschichte,* in vol. 12 of *Hegels Werke* (Frankfurt am Main: Suhrkamp Verlag, 1971), 76. Hegel's view of classical tragedy as a conflict between 'good' and 'good' may be predicated on the inevitability of human self-division. *Hegel on Tragedy,* ed. Anne and Henry Paolucci (New York: Harper Torchbooks, 1962), 79–80, 84. In an early essay (1802), Hegel himself foresees a philosophical "ferment" in which—"under the ashes"—new life emerges, along with a philosophy that counters Cartesian dualism. G. W. F. Hegel, *Über das Wesen der philosophischen Kritik uberhaupt und ihr Verhältniss zum gegenwärtigen Zustand der Philosophie insbesondere,* in vol. 1 of *Sämtliche Werke,* ed. Herman Glockner (Stuttgart: Friedrich Frommann Verlag, 1964), 187.

See also Heidegger's comment that dualism "permeates all thought." "What is Metaphysics?" in *Basic Writings,* ed. David Farrell Krell (New York: Harper and Row, 1977), 107.

It is worth noting that individuals—the heroes and heroines of myth, for example—in whom raw energy isn't channeled and curtailed by communal constraints and who have (involuntary) access to it, must use some of that energy to keep it from becoming destructive. If they are not self-divided, they may turn into monsters.

29. Friedrich Nietzsche, *Fünf Reden zu fünf ungeschriebenen Büchern,* in vol. 3 of *Werke in drei Bänden,* 278.

30. Philip Rieff, *Freud: The Mind of the Moralist* (New York: Viking Press, 1959), 377–78. Compare: "Perhaps we shall accustom ourselves to the idea that there are certain difficulties inherent in the very nature of culture which will not yield to any effort at reform." Sigmund Freud, *Civilization and Its Discontents,* in

The Standard Edition of the Complete Psychological Works of Sigmund Freud, ed. James Strachey (London: The Hogarth Press and the Institute of Psycho-Analysis, 1961).

31. Theodor W. Adorno, "The George-Hoffmannsthal Correspondence, 1891–1906," in *Prisms,* trans. Samuel and Shierry Weber (London: Neville Spearman, 1967), 224.

32. Theodor W. Adorno, "Subject-Object," in *The Essential Frankfurt School Reader,* ed. Andrew Arato and Eike Gebhardt (New York, 1978), 499, cited in Martin Jay, *Adorno* (Cambridge, Mass.: Harvard University Press, 1984), 63. Rousseau says: "Human nature cannot turn back. Once man has left the time of innocence and equality he can never return to it." *Rousseau juge de Jean-Jacques,* in *Oeuvres Complètes,* 1: 935, cited in Gay, *The Enlightenment,* 2: 95.

33. Werner Heisenberg, *The Physicist's Conception of Nature,* trans. Arnold J. Pomerans (New York: Harcourt, Brace, 1958), 124. See also Bohr: "It is often said that quantum theory is unsatisfactory because, thanks to its complementary concepts of 'wave' and 'particle' it prohibits all but dualistic descriptions of nature. Yet all who have truly understood quantum theory would never even dream of calling it dualistic. They look upon it as a unified description of atomic phenomena, even though it has to wear different faces when it is applied to experiment . . ." In Werner Heisenberg, *Physics and Beyond: Encounter and Conversations,* trans. Arnold J. Pomerans (New York: Harper and Row, 1972), 209–10.

34. C. G. Jung, *The Structure and Dynamics of the Psyche,* in vol. 8 of *The Collected Works of C. G. Jung,* trans. R. F. C. Hull (Princeton: Princeton University Press, 1969). See also endnote xxv, 12.

35. Allan Megill, *Prophets of Extremity: Nietzsche, Heidegger, Foucault, Derrida* (Berkeley: University of California Press, 1985), 318.

36. The phrase is Philip Rieff's, *Freud: The Mind of the Moralist* (Chicago: University of Chicago Press, 1979), 378.

37. Toril Moy, *Sexual/Textual Politics: Feminist Literary Theory* (New York: Methuen, 1985), 104–5.

38. Jacques Derrida, *Positions,* trans. Alan Bass (Chicago: University of Chicago Press, 1981), 41.

39. Marx and Engels call the division of labor "one of the chief forces of history." They assume it is based on "the natural division of labor in the family and the separation of society into individual families." *The German Ideology,* ed. R. Pascal (New York: International, 1947), 39, 21.

40. Victor Turner, *Dramas, Fields, and Metaphors* (Ithaca, New York: Cornell University Press, 1974), 200.

41. Rieff, *Freud: The Mind of the Moralist,* 255.

42. Adam Smith appears to have been the first to discuss the division of labor extensively. He established that though it is clearly the basis of economic growth and wealth, it creates a vast system of mutual dependence and limits the development of those who are obliged to repeat the same task over and over—who "generally (become) as stupid and ignorant as it is possible for a human being to become." *An Enquiry into the Causes and Nature of the Wealth of Nations* (Oxford: Clarendon

Press, 1976), 782. Of course even those who do not have to repeat the same task end up as partial, limited human beings—highly developed in one direction and underdeveloped in most others. See also: "The subdivision of labor is the assassination of a people." D. Urquhart, cited by Karl Marx in *Capital: A Critique of Political Economy*, ed. Friedrich Engels (New York: Modern Library, n.d.), 399. The Urquhart quote appeared in *Familiar Words* (London, 1855), 119.

43. Vilfredo Pareto defines an elite as the best in a given field. Experts are clearly an elite, though there are also elites derived from power and wealth, which can be inherited rather than earned. Pareto, "The Manual of Political Economy," section 102, in Pareto, *Sociological Writings*, trans. Derick Mirfin (London: Pall Mall Press, 1966), 105.

44. G. W. F. Hegel, *Philosophy of Right*, trans. T. M. Knox (Oxford: Clarendon Press, 1942), 160–61.

45. Ernst Cassirer, *Rousseau, Kant, Goethe*, 9.

46. G. W. F. Hegel, *Phänomenologie des Geistes*, ed. Georg Lasson und Johannes Hoffmeister (Leipzig, 1905), 140.

47. Martin Luther, "Treatise on Christian Liberty," in *Martin Luther, Selections from His Writings*, ed. John Dillenberger (Garden City, New York: Doubleday, 1961), 53.

48. Foucault is not, of course, a utopian, though denying the split between subject and object has utopian connotations.

49. Michel Foucault, *The Foucault Reader*, ed. Paul Rabinow (New York: Pantheon Books, 1984), 14.

50. C. G. Jung, Foreword to Erich Neumann, *Depth Psychology and a New Ethic*, trans. Eugene Rolfe (New York: Harper and Row, 1973), 16.

51. See Rousseau: "Whoever refuses to obey the general will shall be constrained to do so by the whole body; which means nothing less than that he shall be forced to be free. . . ." Jean-Jacques Rousseau, *The Social Contract*, ed. Lester G. Crocker (New York: Washington Square Press, 1971), 22, cited in Thomas Shalvey, *Claude Lévi-Strauss: Social Psychotherapy and the Collective Unconscious* (Amherst: University of Massachusetts Press, 1979), 61.

52. Changes in the community and its structures may, of course, themselves be an attempt to maintain balance.

53. Martin Buber, *Die Erzählungen der Chassidim*, in *Werke* (München: Kösel Verlag; Heidelberg: Verlag Lambert Schneider, 1963), 3: 484.

54. Claude Lévi-Strauss, *The Savage Mind* (Chicago: University of Chicago Press, 1977), 73–74.

55. Mario Vargas Llosa, "In Nicaragua," *New York Times Magazine*, 28 April 1985.

56. Erik Erikson, *Childhood and Society* (New York: Norton, 1950), 244, cited by Kai T. Erikson, *Wayward Puritans: A Study in the Sociology of Deviance* (New York: John Wiley and Sons, 1967), 53–54.

57. Rabbi Bunam, in Buber, *Erzählungen der Chassidim*, 633.

58. Justice Potter Stewart in a Yale Law School lecture on the First Amendment and freedom of the press.

59. Kai Erikson, *Wayward Puritans*, 189–191. As Erikson says, "The Puritan approach to life was a fabric woven almost entirely out of paradoxes"—as is our own. Ibid., 50.

60. Though I recollect that this is Pareto's formulation, I have not been able to find the phrase in his work. Erwin Schuler says that "for (Pareto) Marxism becomes a kind of 'alchemy' of political economy, and . . . *Capital* develops the characteristics of 'uncertainty and darkness' that, as (Pareto) puts it, one finds in all sacred books." Erwin Schuler, *Pareto's Marx-Kritik* (Tübingen: Albert Becht, 1935), 23–24.

61. Karl Marx, *The Eighteenth Brumaire of Louis Bonaparte* (New York: International Publishers, 1963), 15.

62. Friedrich Nietzsche, *Also Sprach Zarathustra, Werke in drei Bänden*, ed. Karl Schlechta (München: Carl Hanser Verlag, 1976), 2: 455.

63. Karl Marx in a letter to Ludwig Kugelmann, 17 April 1871, in *Karl Marx, Frederick Engels: Collected Works* (New York: International Publishers, 1989), 44: 137.

64. Karl Marx, Introduction to *A Contribution to the Critique of Hegel's Philosophy of Right*, trans. Annette Jolin and Joseph O'Malley (Cambridge: Cambridge University Press, 1970), 137. In the same text Marx says confidently that Germany's "status quo will be shattered by philosophy." (p. 138)

65. Herbert Marcuse, *Studies in Critical Philosophy*, trans. Joris de Bres (London: NLB, 1972), 183. (emphasis added)

66. Karl Marx, Letter to J. B. Schweitzer, London, 14 January 1865, in Marx, *The Poverty of Philosophy*, Introduction by Friedrich Engels (New York: International Publishers, 1963), 202. Marx is deeply committed to rationalism and believes absolutely in the eventual resolutions of all contradictions in society—contradictions which, as he saw clearly, Hegel had failed to resolve. (See Marx, *A Contribution to the Critique of Hegel's Philosophy of Right*.) He never abandoned his belief in the human being as a potentially rational animal, who would eventually find his private interest totally at one with the interests of the community.

67. Tony Bennett says: "The reasons for this are many and complex. In part, it reflects the ambiguity of Marx's own writings on literary and artistic matters. Although he did not attempt to develop a systematic theory of art and literature, Marx did comment frequently and often at length on these matters. Unfortunately, it is not always easy to reconcile what he has to say in these passages with the concerns and procedures embodied in the approach he took to the questions of economic and political analysis with which he was more centrally concerned. The question of the value that is to be placed on these writings is thus a vexed one. . . .

"It is quite clear, however, that the greater part of Marx's writings on art and literature, although penned by Marx, are in no sense indicative of the position of 'Marxism' on these matters." Tony Bennett, *Formalism and Marxism* (London: Methuen, 1979), 100–101.

Marcuse, in *The Aesthetic Dimension* (Boston: Beacon Press, 1977), cites—not without reservations—Hans-Dietrich Sander's *Marxistische Ideologie und allgemeine*

Kunsttheorie, which concludes, in Marcuse's words, that "most of Marxist aesthetics is not only a gross vulgarization—Marx's and Engels' views are also turned into their opposite!" (Marcuse, p. 76, note 8)

68. Ernst Bloch, "Erinnerung," in Theodor Adorno et al., *Über Walter Benjamin* (Frankfurt am Main: Suhrkamp Verlag, 1968), 17.

69. Theodor Adorno, "Notizen zur neuen Anthropologie" (1942), *Gesammelte Schriften* (Frankfurt am Main, 1972), 8: 376, cited in Buck-Morss, 189.

70. Compare Derrida: "Writing structurally carries within itself (counts-discounts) the process of its own erasure and annulation, all the while marking what remains of this erasure. . . ." Derrida, *Positions,* 68.

Derrida recognized the kinship between his view of 'reality' and Goedel's Incompleteness Theorem. Perhaps there is a connection as well to Bohr's complementarity principle. Pascual Jordan says that according to Bohr there exists "a complementarity between the clarity (*Deutlichkeit*) and the rightness (*Richtigkeit*) of a statement, so much so that a statement which is too clear always contains something 'false.' " Pascual Jordan, *Die Naturwissenschaftler vor der religiösen Frage* (Hamburg, 1963), 341, cited by Gerhardt Adler, "Depth Psychology and the Principle of Complementarity," in *Dynamics of the Self* (London: Coventure, 1979), 109. Heisenberg says that Bohr's "wave-corpuscle dualism" describes: "A situation in which it is possible to grasp one and the same event by two distinct modes of interpretation. These two modes are mutually exclusive, but they also complement each other, and it is only through their juxtaposition that the perceptual content of a phenomenon is fully brought out." Werner Heisenberg, *Physics and Philosophy,* trans. Arnold J. Pomerans (New York: Harper and Row, 1971), 79.

71. Wilhelm Worringer, *Abstraction and Empathy: A Contribution to the Psychology of Style,* trans. Michael Bullock (New York: International University Presses, 1967), 45.

72. We can see a parallel to the effect of the plot in Foucault's description of the impact of "effective" historical writing. It is written by us, yet "introduces discontinuity into our being, and deprives the self of the reassuring stability of life and nature." Michel Foucault, *Language, Counter-memory, Practice: Selected Essays and Interviews,* ed. Donald F. Bouchard (Ithaca, New York: Cornell University Press, 1977), 154, cited in Allan Megill, *Prophets of Extremity: Nietzsche, Heidegger, Foucault, Derrida* (Berkeley: University of California Press, 1985), 235–36.

73. Letter to A. S. Suvorin, 27 October 1888, in *Letters of Anton Chekhov,* selected and ed. Avraham Yarmolinsky (New York: Viking Press, 1973), 88. The passage continues: "The court is obliged to pose the questions correctly, but it is up to the jurors to answer them, each according to his own taste." Compare Kafka: "Wirklich schwer und unlösbar sind nur die Probleme, die man nicht formulieren kann, weil sie die Problematik des ganzen Lebens zum Inhalt haben." Cited in Gustav Janouch, *Gespräche mit Kafka* (Frankfurt am Main: Fischer Bucherei, 1961), 87.

Since story is structured by contradiction, it cannot finally be prescriptive. But nothing can or should prevent us from drawing prescriptive conclusions from the stories we hear, just as we cannot help drawing conclusions—often contradictory ones—from our mortality.

74. Charles Baudelaire, *Oeuvres II* (Paris: La Pléiade, n.d.), cited in Georges Poulet, *Studies in Human Time,* trans. Elliott Coleman (New York: Harper & Brothers, 1956), 276.

75. Baudelaire says of Constantin Guys—an artist he admired—that he "is an 'I' with a passionate appetite for the 'non-I.' " Charles Baudelaire, "The Painter of Modern Life," in *The Painter of Modern Life and Other Essays,* trans. Jonathan Mayne (London: Phaidon Press, 1964), 9.

Gasquet quotes Cézanne: "The nature that is there . . . (he points towards the green and blue plane) and the nature that is here (he tapped his forehead) both of which have to fuse in order to endure. . . ." *Joachim Gasquet's Cézanne,* 150.

Adorno speaks of the artwork as a "force-field" between subject and object. A parallel in the sciences is suggested by Heisenberg: "Natural science does not simply describe and explain nature; it is a part in the interplay between nature and ourselves: it describes nature as exposed to our method of questioning." Werner Heisenberg, *Physics and Philosophy: The Revolution in Modern Science* (New York: Harper and Row, 1958), 81. Compare Bronowski: "Relativity derives essentially from the philosophic analysis which insists that there is not a fact and an observer, but the joining of the two in an observation." J. Bronowski, *The Common Sense of Science* (Cambridge, Mass.: Harvard University Press, 1979), 77.

Intellectual theories can clearly function in a similar way: "Anthropology affords me an intellectual satisfaction: it rejoins at one extreme the history of the world and at the other the history of myself, and it unveils the shared motivation of one and the other at the same moment." Lévi-Strauss, *Tristes Tropiques,* trans. John and Doreen Wightman (London: Jonathan Cape, 1973), 62. Conversely and significantly, de Man calls the subject-object polarity "the binary polarity of classical banality." Paul de Man, *Allegories of Reading: Ritual Language in Rousseau, Rilke, and Proust* (New Haven: Yale University Press, 1979), 107.

76. Baudelaire, "On the Essence of Laughter and, in General, On the Comic in the Plastic Arts," in *"The Painter of Modern Life" and Other Essays,* 165.

77. Ibid., 154–55, 156.

78. Jean-Pierre Vernant and Pierre Vidal-Naquet, *Tragedy and Myth in Ancient Greece* (Atlantic Highlands, N.J.: Humanities Press, 1981), 13–14. "Yet, even in Aeschylus, tragedy never provides a solution which could eliminate the conflicts either by reconciling them or by stepping beyond the oppositions. And this tension which is never totally accepted nor entirely obliterated makes tragedy into a questioning to which there can be no answers. In a tragic perspective man and human action are seen, not as things that can be defined or described, but as problems. They are presented as riddles whose double meanings can never be pinned down or exhausted." Also see Barthes: "The myth starts from the contradictions and tends progressively toward their mediation; tragedy, on the contrary, refuses the mediation, keeps the conflict open." Roland Barthes, *On Racine,* trans. Richard Howard (New York: Octagon Books, 1977), 13. In our view, of course, there is no basic difference between the structure of myth and tragedy.

79. Bradley says: "In almost all (of Shakespeare's tragic heroes) we observe a marked one-sidedness, a predisposition in some particular direction; a total incapacity, in certain circumstances, of resisting the force which draws in this direction a fatal tendency to identify the whole being with one interest, object, passion, or habit of mind." A. C. Bradley, *The Substance of Shakespearean Tragedy* (New York: Macmillan, 1956), 20.

80. Turner, *Dramas, Fields, and Metaphors*, 88–89.

81. Letter to his brother Jérome, 1805, in *The Mind of Napoleon*, ed. J. Christopher Herold (New York: Columbia University Press, 1955), 43.

82. Letter to Josephine, 1806, ibid., 43.

83. Napoleon (1806).

CHAPTER 10

1. See Nietzsche: "Das 'Subjekt' ist nur eine Fiktion." Nietzsche, *Nachgelassene Schriften*, in vol. 1 of *Werke in zwei Bänden*, ed. Gerhardt Stenzel (Salzburg: Verlag "Das Bergland-Buch," 1952), 837. See also Ernst Mach: "The I cannot be saved." This often cited statement was apparently first made in a lecture at Vienna University in 1895. John T. Blackmore, *Ernst Mach: His Work, Life and Influence* (Berkeley: University of California, 1972), 35, 155.

2. Claude Lévi-Strauss, *Tristes Tropiques,* trans. John and Doreen Wrightman (London: Jonathan Cape, 1973). It is striking that this sentence appears on the last page of a book that often resembles Proust's novel in its concern with sense impressions and sense memories.

3. Fredric Jameson, "Imaginary and Symbolic in Lacan: Marxism, Psychoanalytic Criticism, and the Problem of the Subject," in Jameson, *The Ideologies of Theory: Essays, 1971–86* (Minneapolis: University of Minnesota, 1988), 1: 75–115.

4. G. V. Plekhanov takes a different position: "Bonaparte was a man of iron energy and was remorseless in the pursuit of his goal. But there were not a few energetic, talented and ambitious egoists in those days, besides him. The place Bonaparte succeeded in occupying would, probably, not have remained vacant. Let us assume that the other general who had secured this place would have been more peaceful than Napoleon, that he would not have roused the whole of Europe against himself, and therefore, would have died in the Tuileries and not on the Island of St. Helena. In that case the Bourbons would not have returned to France at all; for them, such a result would certainly have been the 'opposite' of what it was. In its relation to the internal life of France as a whole, however, this result would have differed little from the actual result." G. V. Plekhanov, *The Role of the Individual in History*, trans. J. Fineberg (Moscow: Foreign Language Publishing House, 1944), 40. As Plekanov himself suggests, Napoleon's effect on the rest of Europe was unique and unmistakable.

5. See Horkheimer and Adorno: "In the psychology of the modern masses, the *Führer* is not so much a father-figure as a collective and overexaggerated projection of the powerless ego of each individual—to which the so-called "leaders" in

fact correspond." Max Horkheimer and Theodor W. Adorno, *Dialectic of Enlightenment*, trans. John Cumming (New York: Herder and Herder, 1972), 236.

6. Alexandre Kojève, *Introduction to the Reading of Hegel: Lectures on the Phenomenology of Spirit*, assembled by Raymond Queneau (New York: Basic Books, 1969), 41. Though Kojève's interpretation is influenced by his Marxist orientation and does not always reflect Hegel accurately, his comment seems pertinent to our discussion.

7. Ibid., 236.

8. Louis Althusser, *Lenin and Philosophy, and Other Essays*, trans. Ben Brewster (New York: Monthly Review Press, 1971), 172–73.

9. "Letter on Humanism," trans. Frank A. Capuzzi in collaboration with J. Glenn Gray, in Martin Heidegger, *Basic Writings*, ed. David Farrell Krell (New York: Harper and Row, 1977), 219.

10. Herbert Marcuse, *The Aesthetic Dimension: Toward a Critique of Marxist Aesthetics* (Boston: Beacon Press, 1978), 38–39. The group is "the order of orders" but it can be murderous, as those who have lived under fascist rule or confronted a mob know. There are situations when the only hope lies with those individuals who are in some measure independent of the group.

11. Theodor W. Adorno, *The Jargon of Authenticity*, trans. Knut Tarnowski and Frederick Will (Evanston, Ill.: Northwestern University Press, 1973), 163–64.

12. De Sade says: "I am alone here, I am at the world's end. Withheld from every gaze, here no one can reach me, there is no creature that can come nigh where I am; no limits, hence no barriers. I am free." The Marquis de Sade, *The 120 Days of Sodom*, in *The 120 Days of Sodom and Other Writings* (New York: Grove Press, 1966). Perhaps because he is "free" and alone he must hurt others, forcing them to acknowledge his existence.

13. Ernst Bloch, *Geist der Utopie*, (Berlin: Paul Cassirer, 1923), 226, cited by Susan Buck-Morss, *The Origin of Negative Dialectics* (New York: Free Press, 1977), 82–83. Hyppolite says that Hegel's concept of spirit "presupposes both the transcendence of individual consciousnesses and the maintenance of their diversity within substance." However, he also says: "Spirit is a 'we': we must begin not with the *cogito* but with the *cogitamus*." Jean Hyppolite, *Genesis and Structure of Hegel's Phenomenology of the Spirit*, trans. Samuel Cherniak and John Heckman (Evanston, Ill.: Northwestern University Press, 1974), 321, 322.

14. C. G. Jung, "The Realities of Practical Psychotherapy," *Appendix to the Practice of Psychotherapy*, in vol. 16 of *Collected Works*, trans. R. F. C. Hull (Princeton: Princeton University Press, 1973), 329.

15. The Second City comedy troupe performed a skit in which two actors, one on each side of the stage, mimed steering the wheels of two great ships. The first calls to the second: "What ship be you?" "The Pequod." "Have you seen anything of a white whale?" "Yes. Two days ago. We killed it." "Oh shit!" In *Something Wonderful Right Away: An Oral History of the Second City and the Campus Players,* ed. Jeffrey Sweet (New York: Avon Books, 1978), 193.

16. Rainer Maria Rilke, *Duineser Elegien*, "Die Neunte Elegie," in vol. 1 of

Sämtliche Werke, Herausgegeben vom Rilke-Archiv in Verbindung mit Ruth Sieber-Rilke, besorgt durch Ernst Zinn (Frankfurt am Main: Im Insel Verlag, 1962), 717.

17. Georges Poulet, *Studies in Human Time,* trans. Elliott Coleman (New York: Harper and Brothers, 1956). The title of Northrop Frye's *Fables of Identity* (New York: Harcourt Brace and World, 1963) clearly expresses his approach to literature as a narrative of identity.

18. Benjamin Constant, Letter to Mme. de Nassau, in *Lettres*, ed. Mélégeri (Paris: Albin Michel, n.d.), 288, cited in Poulet, 206.

19. Gustave Flaubert, *Novembre*, 178, cited in Poulet, 256.

20. Gustave Flaubert, *Correspondance*, in *Oeuvres*, 3: 332, cited in Poulet, 257.

21. Marcel Proust, *Remembrance of Things Past*, trans. C. K. Scott Moncrieff (New York: Random House, 192–93), 1: 776, cited in Poulet, 297.

22. Compare Descartes: "From the fact that *I had been* a little while ago, it does not follow that I ought to be *now.* . ."; "From the fact that *I am now*, it does not follow that *I must be hereafter* . . ." A.T. IX, 38, ibid., VIII, 13, cited by Georges Poulet, *Studies in Human Time*, 58.

23. De Man, in his essay on Poulet, interprets Proust's relationship to the past very differently: "The power of memory does not reside in its capacity to resurrect a situation or a feeling that actually existed, but is a constitutive act of the mind bound to its own present and oriented toward the future of its own elaboration. *The past intervenes only as a purely formal element.*" (emphasis added) Paul de Man, "The Work of Georges Poulet," in *Blindness and Insight* (Minneapolis: University of Minnesota Press, 1983), 92, cited in Jacques Derrida, *Memoires: For Paul De Man* (New York: Columbia University Press, 1986), 59.

24. Marcel Proust, *Remembrance of Things Past*, vol. 2: *The Past Recaptured*, trans. Frederick A. Blossom, 1123. The stress on "desire" in *Remembrance* is effectively also a way of assuring continuity: "Perhaps the great austerity of my life, without journeys, without walks, without company, without sunlight, is a contingency which renews in me the *perenniality* of desire." *Cahiers.* (emphasis added)

25. Sören Kierkegaard, *The Concept of Dread*, trans. Walter Lowrie (Princeton: Princeton University Press, 1946), 116. See also: "I can imagine nothing more excruciating than an intriguing mind that has lost the thread of its own continuity." Sören Kierkegaard, *Either/Or I*, trans. David and Lillian Marvin (Garden City, N.Y.: Anchor Books, 1959), 304.

26. Arthur Rimbaud, "Lettre du Voyant" (1871), in *Oeuvres Complètes* (Paris: Gallimard, Pleiade, 1963), 270.

27. James Lord, *Giacometti: A Biography* (New York: Farrar, Strauss, Giroux, 1985), 437.

28. "Hört mich! denn ich bin der und der. Verwechselt mich vor allem nicht!" Friedrich Nietzsche, Vorwort, *Ecce Homo, Werke in drei Bänden*, ed. Karl Schlechta (München: Carl Hanser Verlag, 1976), 2: 1098.

29. Compare Lacan: "The ego, every ego, is paranoid," and Alfred Adler: "To be human is to feel inferior."

Presumably the artist experiences the condition of being an individual more painfully than the rest of us, since he was abandoned more explicitly and hasn't closed himself off to his own experience and feelings. He suffers more intensively and voices the isolation and "freedom" we all suffer.

The word "abandon" comes from an old French word that meant "to leave free," "to free from control."

30. *The Autobiography of William Butler Yeats* (New York: Macmillan, 1965), 358.

31. Among other texts, in "The World of Art in the Age of Mechanical Reproduction," in Walter Benjamin, *Illuminations*, ed. Hannah Arendt, trans. Harry Zohn (New York: Schocken Books, 1969), 358.

32. Walter Benjamin, "On Some Motifs in Baudelaire," in Benjamin, *Illuminations*, 159.

33. Viktor Shklovsky, "Art As Technique," in Lee T. Lemon and Marion J. Reis, eds. *Russian Formalist Criticism: Four Essays*, (Lincoln: University of Nebraska Press, 1965), 12.

34. Benjamin, "On Some Motifs in Baudelaire," 159.

35. For a critical perspective, see Sartre: "Proust chose himself to be a bourgeois. He made himself into an accomplice of bourgeois propaganda . . ." Jean-Paul Sartre, *What Is Literature and Other Essays* (Cambridge, Mass.: Harvard University Press, 1988), 259.

36. Andy Warhol, *The Philosophy of Andy Warhol* (New York: Harcourt, Brace, Jovanovich, 1975), 7. His studio is "the factory"—an original and, in this sense, "individual" departure from the accepted role of the artist.

37. Hartman's "To be conscious is already to be writing" points to the link between writing and self. Geoffrey Hartman, "The Interpreter: A Self-Analysis," in *"The Fate of Reading" and Other Essays* (Chicago: University of Chicago, 1975), 18.

38. Perhaps walking down the street with a Walkman is a way of preserving one's inner continuity by excluding the rest of the world.

39. Gerhardt Adler, "On the Question of Meaning in Psychotherapy," in *Dynamics of the Self* (London: Coventure, 1979), 77.

40. Konrad Lorenz, in *On Aggression*, calls the family a "moveable territory." (New York: Bantam, 1967), 181. The rugs of nomadic Bedouins serve a similar function.

41. Lévi-Strauss says: "A native thinker makes the penetrating comment that 'all sacred things must have their place.' It could even be said that being in their place is what makes them sacred for if they were taken out of their place, even in thought, the entire order of the universe would be destroyed. Sacred objects therefore contribute to the maintenance of order in the universe by occupying the places allocated to them." *The Savage Mind* (Chicago: University of Chicago Press, 1970), 10.

42. Friedrich Hebbel, *Zweites Tagebuch, Hebbels Werke in zehn Teilen*, ed. Theodor Poppe (Berlin: Deutsches Verlaghaus, n.d.), 9: 383 (21 November 1843).

43. Igor Stravinsky, in a letter to Lincoln Kirstein. He expresses the same idea in *Stravinsky: The Poetics of Music in the Form of Six Lessons* (New York: Vintage Books, 1947), 66–68. See also Arnold Schoenberg: "I believe art is born of 'I must,' not of 'I can.' "

44. Friedrich Hebbel, *Neues Tagebuch*, in *Friedrich Hebbels Werke* (Berlin: Deutsches Verlaghaus Bong, n.d.), 9: 154, 5 Dezember 1838, entry 1016.

45. Roland Barthes, *S/Z*, trans. Richard Miller (New York: Hill and Wang, 1974). Barthes includes both *jouissance* and intellectual pleasure.

46. "We live in an age when unnecessary things are the only necessities." *The Portrait of Mr. W H*, cited in *The Wit of Oscar Wilde*, comp. Sean McCann (London: Leslie Frewin, Publishers, 1969), 118. Significantly, the modernist Degas says: "What if it bores me to distract myself?"

47. According to Gide's autobiographical *Si le grain ne meurt. . . ,* Wilde said to him: "I have a duty to amuse myself frightfully." In Richard Ellmann, *Oscar Wilde* (New York: Alfred A. Knopf, 1988), 429.

48. Herman Melville, *Moby Dick* (New York: Random House, 1926), 526.

49. Ibid., 563–64.

50. Sören Kierkegaard, *The Concept of Dread*, trans. Walter Lowrie (Princeton: Princeton University Press, 1946), 139. In Kierkegaard's view, "He . . . who has learned rightly to be in dread has learned the most important thing." Ibid., 139–40.

51. Arthur Schopenhauer, *Die Welt als Wille und Vorstellung* (Leipzig: Inselverlag, n.d.), 1: 340. Compare Friedrich Hebbel: "Das Leben ist der grosse Strom, die Individualitäten sind Tropfen, die tragischen aber Eisstücke, die wieder zerschmolzen werden müssen und sich, damit dies möglich sey, an einander abreissen und zerstossen." *Hebbels Werke in zehn Teilen*, 9: 348 (Journal entry 2175, 6 March 1843).

52. Victor Turner, *The Ritual Process: Structure and Anti-structure* (Chicago: Aldine, 1969), 96 ff.

53. Victor Turner, *Dramas, Fields, and Metaphors* (Ithaca, New York: Cornell University Press, 1974), 243. Compare Durkheim: "There can be no society which does not feel the need of upholding and reaffirming at regular intervals the collective ideas which make its unity and its personality." In Robert Nisbet, *The Sociology of Émile Durkheim* (London: Heinemann, 1975), 174.

54. Turner, *Ritual Process*, 179–80.

55. Bakhtin's concept of "carnivalization" (in the novels of Cervantes, Balzac et al.) is perhaps a way of saying that within the plot, or at carnival, we are all equal. In the Soviet Union it was not possible to speak of the gods, fate or chance, and carnivalization may have served as an alternate, socially grounded term. Carnival creates *communitas*. Mikhail Bakhtin, *Problems of Dostoevsky's Poetics*, ed. and trans. Caryl Emerson (Minneapolis: University of Minnesota Press, 1984), 122.

56. Claude Lévi-Strauss, *Myth and Meaning* (New York: Schocken Books, 1979), 20. We may find, in Lévi-Strauss's comment, an explanation for the startling and violent reassertion of nationalism and tribalism in "the global village."

57. Turner, *Dramas, Fields, and Metaphors*, 129.

58. G. W. F. Hegel, *Die Phänomenologie des Geistes*, ed. Georg Lasson und Johannes Hoffmeister (Leipzig: Meiner Verlag, 1905), 140.

59. G. W. F. Hegel, "Fragment of a System" (1800), in *Early Theological Writings*, trans. Richard Kroner (Philadelphia: University of Pennsylvania Press, 1971), 312.

60. G. W. F. Hegel, cited by Mark C. Taylor, Introduction to *Deconstruction in Context: Literature and Philosophy* (Chicago: University of Chicago, 1986), 8.

61. Vladimir Propp, *Morphology of the Folktale*, trans. Laurence Scott (Austin: University of Texas Press, 1968), 64–65.

62. E. M. Forster, *Aspects of the Novel* (New York: Harcourt, Brace, 1927), 240.

63. Sigmund Freud, *Civilization and Its Discontents,* in vol. 21 of *The Standard Edition of the Complete Psychological Works of Sigmund Freud,* 118ff.

64. This may be an equivalent of the words Pascal ascribes to Jesus: "Take comfort, you would not be seeking me, had you not already found me." "The Mystery (of the Agony of Jesus)," in *The Essential Pascal*, ed. Robert W. Gleason, S. J. (New York: New American Library, 1966), 209.

65. Martin Heidegger, "Modern Science, Metaphysics, and Mechanics," in *Basic Writings*, 252. Hegel cites Plato's assertion in the *Meno* that "one can actually learn nothing, but that rather learning is a recollection of what we already possess, know." Hegel goes on to say that "Erinnerung" has not only the meaning of recollection but also "Sichinnerlich machen, Insichgehen," a point Heidegger might well make himself. G. W. F. Hegel, *Vorlesungen über der Philosophie, II,* in vol. 18 of *Sämtliche Werke*, ed. Hermann Glockner (Stuttgart: Friedrich Frommann Verlag, 1965), 203–4.

66. Sigmund Freud, "The Case of Miss Lucy R.," *Studies on Hysteria,* in vol. 2 of *The Standard Edition of the Complete Psychological Works of Freud,* ed. James Strachey (London: The Hogarth Press and the Institute of Psycho-Analysis, 1973), 117.

67. Samuel Taylor Coleridge, *Biographia Literaria, or, Biographical Sketches of My Literary Life and Opinions*, ed. James Engalls and Walter Jackson Bate (Princeton: Princeton University Press, 1983), 2: 15.

68. Friedrich Wilhelm Joseph von Schelling, "System des Transzendentalen Idealismus," in *Werke*, ed. Manfred Schroeter (Munich: Beck, 1956–60), 2: 617, cited by Allan Megill, *Prophets of Extremity* (Berkeley: University of California Press, 1985), 16, note 31.

69. Claude Lévi-Strauss, *Structural Anthropology* (New York: Basic Books, 1976), 229.

70. Jacques Derrida, "Dissemination," in Megill, *Prophets of Extremity*, 292.

71. Paul de Man, *Allegories of Reading: Ritual Language in Rousseau, Rilke, and Proust* (New Haven: Yale University Press, 1979), 12. Though I have linked deconstructive views of narrative to the Russian formalists, with respect to poetry criticism has moved a long way from the positivist approach of the formalists. See Paul de Man, "The Dead-end of Formalist Criticism," in *Blindness and Insight* (Minneapolis: University of Minnesota Press, 1983) 229–45.

72. I believe the term is Roman Ingarden's.

73. René Girard, *Violence and the Sacred* (Baltimore: Johns Hopkins University Press, 1977), 293.

74. Roland Barthes, "Myth Today," in *Mythologies*, selected and trans. from the French by Annette Lavers (New York: Hill and Wang, 1972), 148.

75. Because Adorno, like Benjamin, was unwilling to force the artwork into a political framework and often contradicted his own effort to do so, his aesthetic judgements remain of greater interest than those of many politically motivated critics.

76. Theodor W. Adorno, "The George-Hofmannsthal Correspondence, 1891–1906," *Prisms* (London, 1967), 32, in Martin Jay, *The Dialectical Imagination: A History of the Frankfurt School and the Institute of Social Research, 1923–1950* (Boston: Little, Brown, 1973), 179.

77. Adorno, *Zur Metakritik der Erkenntnistheorie* (Frankfurt, 1971), 47, cited in ibid., 69.

78. Herbert Marcuse, *One-dimensional Man: Studies in the Ideology of Advanced Industrial Society* (Boston: Beacon Press, 1964), 62.

79. Beckett says this with reference to an incident in "Waiting for Godot," cited in *Casebook on "Waiting for Godot,"* ed. Ruby Cohn (New York: Grove, 1967), 51.

80. Milan Kundera, *The Art of the Novel*, trans. Linda Asher (New York: Grove Press, 1986), 134.

81. Werner Heisenberg, *Physics and Philosophy: The Revolution in Modern Science* (New York: Harper, 1958), 160.

82. Ibid., 49. The physicist Freeman Dyson writes that Bohr "liked to apply (the principle of complementarity) to . . . situations in ethics and philosophy as well as in physics. Complementarity says that nature is too subtle to be described from any single point of view. To obtain an adequate description, you have to look at things from several points of view, even though the different viewpoints are incompatible and cannot be viewed simultaneously. Statements that are true when seen from one point of view may be false when seen from another. There is no logical contradiction here, because the behavior of the object you are observing changes as you change your point of view. Here is a quotation from Niels Bohr:

'In the Institute in Copenhagen, we used often to comfort ourselves with jokes, among them the old saying of the two kinds of truth. To the one kind belong statements so simple and clear that the opposite assertion obviously could not be defended. The other kind, the so-called "deep truths," are statements in which the opposite also contains deep truth.' " Freeman Dyson, *From Eros to Gaia* (New York: Pantheon Books, 1992), 188.

In story as in physics, the opposites may only *appear* to be opposites. Behind the "pictures" we have of reality—which seem mutually exclusive—there may be a "reality" we can never apprehend with certainty—one which reconciles what appear to us as opposites.

83. Robert Frost, "The Figure a Poem Makes," Introduction to *The Complete Poems of Robert Frost* (New York: Henry Holt, 1959), viii.

84. Paul Celan, *Rede anlässlich des Georg-Büchner-Preises*: in *Ausgewählte Gedichte, Zwei Reden* (Frankfurt am Main: Suhrkamp Verlag, 1968), 133–48.

85. Cited in Peter Cotes and Thelma Niklaus, *The Little Fellow: The Life and Work of Charles Chaplin*, (New York: Citadel Press, 1965), 100.

86. Friedrich Nietzsche, in Megill, *Prophets of Extremity*, 49.

87. Yet, in a very different, nonreductive sense, art makes the other the same. Not only Flaubert but the *reader* "becomes" Mme. Bovary.

88. Frank Kermode suggests rightly that Heidegger reads the poetry of Hölderlin as a sacred text. Frank Kermode, *The Genesis of Secrecy* (Cambridge, Mass.: Harvard University Press, 1979), 40. See also: "Hölderlin is the only one whom Heidegger cites as a believer cites holy writ." Paul de Man, "Heidegger's Exegesis of Hölderlin," *Blindness and Insight*, 250, cited in Derrida, *Memoires: For Paul De Man*, 7.

89. "Wer an allem zweifeln wollte, der würde auch nicht bis zum Zweifel kommen. Das Spiel des Zweifelns selbst setzt schon die Gewissheit voraus." Ludwig Wittgenstein, *Über Gewissheit*, Herausgegeben von G. E. M. Hanscombe und G. H. von Wright (New York: J. and J. Harper Editions, 1969), 18. Doubt is effectively an attempt to arrive at certainty.

90. See Goffman: "Self . . . is not an entity half-concealed behind events, but a changeable formula for managing oneself during them." Erving Goffman, cited by E. O. Wilson, *On Human Nature* (Cambridge, Mass.: Harvard University Press, 1978), 93.

91. Hegel equates consciousness with freedom: "Wer sich nicht gedacht hat, ist nicht frei—wer nicht frei ist, hat sich nicht gedacht. . . ." *Grundlinien der Philosophie des Rechts*, in vol. 7 of *Werke in zwanzig Bänden* (Frankfurt am Main: Suhrkamp Verlag, 1969), 51.

92. Emily Dickinson, letter, cited without attribution by Richard Chase, *Emily Dickinson* (Westport, Conn.: Greenwood Press, 1977), 182.

93. See Hegel: "Knowledge brought about the Fall, but it also contains the principle of Redemption." G. W. F. Hegel, in *Vorlesungen über die Geschichte der Philosophie*, Redaktion Eva Moldenhauer und Karl Markus Michel, in vol. 18 of *Werke in zwanzig Bänden* (Frankfurt am Main: Suhrkamp Verlag, 1971). Compare: "Consciousness . . . *distinguishes* from itself something, to which at the same time it relates itself." Introduction, *Phenomenology of Mind*, trans. J. M. Baillie (New York: Humanities Press, 1966), 139.

94. Gustav Janouch, *Gespräche mit Kafka* (Frankfurt am Main: Fischer Bücherei, 1961), 68.

95. The concept that we can be free only in necessity is fundamental to Hegel: "Diese Einäusserung der Einzelheit als Selbst ist das Moment, wodurch das Selbstbewusstsein den Übergang dazu macht, allgemeiner Wille zu sein, den Übergang zur positiven Freiheit." *Texte zur Philosophischen Propädeutik, Nürnberger Schriften*, "Bewusstseinslehre für die Mittelklasse" (1809), *Werke in zwanzig Bänden*, 4: 121.

96. Friedrich Nietzsche, *Ecce Homo*, in *Werke in drei Bänden*, 2: 1098. In a letter to Overbeck, he refers to *amor fati* as "(eine fatalistische) Gottergebenheit." *Werke,*

3: 118. Compare Hegel: "The Greek who has within him the feeling of necessity calms his soul with that. *It is so;* there is nothing to be done against it; with this I must content myself; just in this feeling that I must be content with it, that this even pleases me, we have the freedom which is implied in the fact that it is mine." G. W. F. Hegel, *Lectures on the Philosophy of Religion,* trans. E. B. Speirs and J. Burton Sanderson (London: K. Paul, Trench, Trübner, 1895), 2: 239–43. Of course *amor fati* may simply be a way of making a virtue of necessity.

97. Rilke, "Die Erste Elegie," *Duineser Elegien,* in vol. 1 of *Sämtliche Werke,* 685.

CHAPTER 11

1. J. W. von Goethe, *Maximen und Reflexionen,* 35, in Ernst Cassirer, *Rousseau, Kant and Goethe* (New York: Harper Torchbooks, 1962). Even the approach of C. G. Jung—who, as a depth psychologist, is associated with essentialist positions—has a pragmatic dimension, perhaps because he was a practicing psychotherapist. "One should not be deterred by the objection that nobody knows whether these old universal ideas—God, immortality, freedom of the will, and so on—are "true" or not. Truth is the wrong criterion here. One can only ask whether they are helpful or not, whether man is better off and feels his life more complete, more meaningful and more satisfactory with or without them." In *C. G. Jung: Psychological Reflections: A New Anthology of His Writings, 1905–1961* (Princeton: Princeton University Press, 1953).

2. "The nervous system is an apparatus which has the function of getting rid of the stimuli that reach it, or of reducing them to the barest possible level; which, if it were feasible, would maintain itself in an altogether unstimulated condition." Sigmund Freud, *Instincts and Their Vicissitudes,* in vol. 14 of *The Standard Edition of the Complete Psychological Works of Sigmund Freud,* ed. James Strachey (London: The Hogarth Press and the Institute of Psycho-Analysis, 1978), 120.

3. Karl Marx, Author's Preface to *A Contribution to the Critique of Political Economy* (1859), trans. N. I. Stone (Chicago: Charles H. Kerr, 1904), 12.

4. Horkheimer says: "[The] mentality of man as the master [which was the essence of the Enlightenment view] can be traced back to the first chapters of Genesis." Cited by Martin Jay, *The Dialectical Imagination: A History of the Frankfurt School and the Institute of Social Research, 1923–1950* (Boston: Little, Brown, 1973), 258.

5. Friedrich Nietzsche, *Die Fröhliche Wissenschaft, Werke in drei Bänden,* ed. Karl Schlechta (München: Carl Hanser Verlag, 1976) 2: 222.

6. Leucippus, in William Cecil Dampier, *A History of Science and Its Relations with Philosophy and Religion* (New York: Macmillan, 1938), 26.

7. G. W. Leibniz, in John Earman, "Determinism in the Physical Sciences," in *Introduction to the Philosophy of Science* (Englewood Cliffs, N.J.: Prentice-Hall, 1992), 233.

8. In his "Essay on the Calculus of Probabilities," Laplace says: "We may

regard the present state of the universe as the effect of its past and the cause of its future. An intelligence which at a given moment knew all the forces that animate nature, and the respective positions of the beings that compose it, and further possessing the scope to analyse these data, could condense into a single formula the movement of the greatest bodies of the universe and that of the least atom: for such an intelligence nothing could be uncertain, and past and future alike would be before its eyes." Cited by Frederick Waisman, "The Decline and Fall of Causality," in *Turning Points in Physics: A Series of Lectures Given at Oxford University in Trinity Term, 1958* (Amsterdam: North-Holland, 1959), 93.

9. Friedrich Nietzsche, *Nachgelassene Schriften*, in vol. 1 of *Werke in zwei Bänden*, ed. Gerhardt Stenzel (Salzburg: Verlag "Das Bergland-Buch," 1952), 803.

10. Friedrich Nietzsche, *Die Geburt der Tragödie*, in vol. 1 of *Werke in drei Bänden*, 84.

11. Aeschylus, *Prometheus Bound*, trans. Edwin Dolin and Alfred Sugg, in *An Anthology of Greek Tragedy*, ed. Albert Cook and Edwin Dolin (New York: Bobbs-Merrill, 1972), lines 250–52, p. 74.

12. Marie-Louise von Franz, *The Interpretation of Fairytales* (Dallas: Spring Publications, 1978), 93. Critics committed to Enlightenment skepticism and mistrustful of all spiritual endeavors hold a negative view of the early Christians. Gilbert Murray ascribes a "failure of nerve" to them, and associates the rise of Christianity with "a rise of asceticism, of mysticism, in a sense, of pessimism; a loss of self-confidence, of hope in this life, a cry for infallible revelation; an indifference to the welfare of the state, a conversion of the soul to God." Gilbert Murray, *Five Stages of Greek Religion* (1935), 123, cited by Peter Gay, *The Enlightenment: An Interpretation*, vol. 2: *The Science of Freedom* (New York: Alfred A. Knopf, 1969), 5.

13. G. V. Plekhanov points out that Islam was energized by its fatalism: ". . . history shows that even fatalism was not always a hindrance to energetic, practical action; on the contrary, in certain epochs it was a *psychologically necessary basis for such action*. In proof of this we will point to the Puritans, who in energy excelled all the other parties in England in the Seventeenth Century; and to the followers of Mahomet, who in a short space of time subjugated an enormous part of the globe from India to Spain." Plekhanov, *The Role of the Individual in History*, trans. J. Fineberg (Moscow: Foreign Language Publishing House, 1944), 7.

14. In some versions of the myths, Zeus *is* the ultimate authority. Burkert says that fate (*moira*) "is not a person, not a god or a power, but a fact: the word means portion, and proclaims that the world is apportioned, that boundaries are drawn in space and true. . . . Zeus would have the power to act differently, but the other gods do not applaud this, and therefore he does not do so, just as a good and wise ruler does not use his real power to encroach on the limits set by custom." Walter Burkert, *Greek Religion*, trans. John Raffan (Cambridge, Mass.: Harvard University Press, 1985), 129–30. This could, of course, be read as an equivocation, one that hides our uncertainty about the ultimate authority in the universe.

15. Cited by Schopenhauer as the epigraph for *Die Welt als Wille und Vorstellung*.

16. In our culture, Christianity itself has often become Positivist and lost contact with the fearful, uncertain element that was, for millennia, at the core of religious feeling. The sacred need no longer fills the Christian with awe, but serves to support and endorse his endeavors. "God gave me the money," said John D. Rockefeller—who saw himself as the Lord's trustee and his wealth as a trust: "I am a trustee only and cannot shake off the weighty responsibility resting upon me; nor would I if I could." Allan Nevins, *John D. Rockefeller*, abridgement by William Greenleaf of *A Study in Power* (New York: Charles Scribner's, 1959), 228.

17. Nietzsche blames Socrates for our attempt "to correct existence" ("das Dasein zu korrigieren"). *Die Geburt der Tragödie*, vol. 1 of *Werke in drei Bänden*, 76. It surely antedated the Greeks, even if they gave it impetus.

18. Marx says: "For a popular revolution and the emancipation of a particular class to coincide, for one class to stand for the whole of society, another class must . . . concentrate in itself all the defects of society, must be the class of universal offense and the embodiment of universal limits. A particular social sphere must stand for the notorious crime of the whole society, so that liberation from this sphere appears to be universal liberation. For one class to be the class *par excellence* of liberation, another class must . . . be openly the subjugating class." Karl Marx, *Critique of Hegel's Philosophy of Right*, trans. Annette Jolin and Joseph O'Malley, ed. Joseph O'Malley (Cambridge: Cambridge University Press, 1970), 140.

19. Émile Durkheim, "The Division of Labor," *Selected Writings* (Cambridge: Cambridge University Press, 1972), 127. See also Konrad Lorenz: "Discriminative aggression toward strangers and the bond between the members of a group enhance each other." Konrad Lorenz, *On Aggression* (New York: Bantam, 1967), 182. René Girard says: "The various 'scapegoat' phenomena are not the reflection of some ill-articulated guilt complex, but rather the very basis of cultural unification, the source of all rituals and religion." Girard, *Violence and the Sacred* (Baltimore: Johns Hopkins University Press, 1977), 302.

20. Erich Neumann, *Depth Psychology and a New Ethic*, trans. Eugene Rolfe (New York: Published by G. P. Putnam's Sons for The C. G. Jung Foundation for Analytical Psychology, 1969), 54.

21. William Blake, "Marriage of Heaven and Hell," in *The Marriage of Heaven and Hell*, intro. by Clark Emery (Coral Gables, Fla.: University of Miami Press, 1970), plates 4 and 3.

22. This is Martin Buber's paraphrase of Rabbi Nachman's statement, which reads: "One can serve God with one's evil drive if one directs its flames and its glow of desire toward God. Without evil our religous service is incomplete." Martin Buber, Rabbi Nachman von Bratzlaw, *Schriften zum Chassidismus*, in *Werke*, Dritter Band (München: Kösel Verlag; Heidelberg: Verlag Lambert Schneider, 1963), 908.

23. Friedrich Nietzsche, *Nachgelassene Schriften, 1881–1885*, in vol. 1 of *Werke in zwei Bänden*, 965.

24. Ludwig Binswanger, "Freud's Conception of Man in the Light of Anthropology," in *Being-in-the-World: Selected Papers of Ludwig Binswanger*, trans. Jacob

Needleman (New York: Harper Torchbooks, 1963), 152. This is, of course, close to Hegel's positive view of the negative.

25. When Roosevelt told the American people they had a rendezvous with destiny, he and they saw it as a grand opportunity. They assumed either that destiny was on their side or that they could battle it successfully. Earlier cultures would have been less confident.

26. Hegel writes: "I saw the Emperor—this world-soul—ride out of town on reconnaissance; it is an altogether extraordinary experience to see an individual who, concentrated into a point and seated on a horse, reaches across the world and rules it. . . . It is impossible not to admire him." Hegel in a letter to F. J. Niethammer, 13 October 1806, in *Briefe von und an Hegel* (Hamburg, Felix Meiner Verlag, 1969), 1: 120. (elision Hegel's)

27. Friedrich Nietzsche, *Aus dem Nachlass der Achtzigerjahre, Werke in drei Bänden*, ed. Karl Schlechta (München: Carl Hanser Verlag, 1976), 3: 784. The complete passage reads: "Was bedeutet eine pessimistische Kunst? Ist das nicht ein Contradictio?—Ja.—Schopenhauer irrt, wenn er gewisse Werke der Kunst in den Dienst des Pessimismus stellt. Die Tragödie lehrt nicht 'Resignation.' . . . Die furchtbaren und fragwürdigen Dinge darstellen ist schon selbst ein Instinkt der Macht und Herrlichkeit am Künstler: er fürchtet sie nicht. . . . Es gibt keine pessimistische Kunst. . . . Die Kunst bejaht. Hiob bejaht. . . . Wie erlösend ist Dostoievsky." (elision Nietzsche's) See also: *"Was teilt der tragische Künstler von sich mit? Ist es nicht gerade der Zustand ohne Furcht vor dem Furchtbaren und Fragwürdigen, das er zeigt?—Dieser Zustand selbst ist eine hohe Wünschbarkeit; wer ihn kennt, ehrt ihn mit den grössten Ehren." Götzendämmerung, Werke in drei Bänden*, 2: 1005.

28. Sigmund Freud, *Beyond the Pleasure Principle*, in vol. 18 of *The Standard Edition of the Complete Psychological Works of Sigmund Freud,* ed. James Strachey (London: The Hogarth Press and the Institute of Psycho-Analysis, 1968), 10–11.

29. Bernard C. Meyer, *Houdini: A Mind in Chains; A Psychoanalytical Portrait* (New York: Dutton, 1976), 119.

30. In Edgar Johnson, *Charles Dickens: His Tragedy and Triumph* (New York: Viking, 1977), 277.

31. See note 28.

32. Jean-Paul Sartre, *L'existentialisme est un humanisme* (Paris, 1946), 95, cited by Herbert Marcuse, *Studies in Critical Philosophy* (Boston: Beacon Press, 1972), 171.

33. Jean-Paul Sartre, *Being and Nothingness: An Essay on Phenomenological Ontology*, trans. Hazel E. Barnes (New York: Philosophical Library, 1956), 476.

34. Joseph Conrad, *Nostromo: A Tale of the Seaboard* (New York: Penguin, 1977), 409, cited in Meyer, *Houdini*, 94.

35. Richard Rorty, Introduction, *Consequences of Pragmatism (Essays: 1972–1980)* (Minneapolis: University of Minnesota Press, 1982), xv–xviii, xxxviii–xxxix.

36. See Leszek Kolakowski: "The term 'pragmatism' was coined by Charles Sanders Peirce . . . who used it to characterize a scientific method for distinguishing properly formulated questions from fictitious ones, valuable answers from unre-

warding ones, real matters of controversy from purely verbal ones. In connection with this program Peirce formulated rules closely allied to the best traditions of positivism." Kolakowski, *The Alienation of Reason: A History of Positivist Thought*, trans. Norbert Guterman (Garden City, N.Y.: Doubleday, 1968).

Rorty's distinctions between positivism and pragmatism are nonetheless useful, as is his insistence that positivists—unlike pragmatists but like Platonists—see humankind "guided, constrained, not left to its own devices," with Platonists ascribing the guidance to "something eternal" and positivists to "something temporal." Rorty, *Consequences of Pragmatism*, xxxix.

37. David W. Marcell, *Progress and Pragmatism: James, Dewey, Beard, and the American Idea of Progress* (Westport, Conn.: Greenwood Press, 1974), xii.

38. Stanley Aronowitz, Introduction to Max Horkheimer, *Critical Theory: Selected Essays*, trans. Matthew J. O'Connell et al. (New York: Herder and Herder, 1972), xv.

39. Napoleon, 1817. Like all 'numinous' figures, Napoleon was a man of glaring contradictions. Alistair Horne says: "[He] once claimed 'I never had a plan of operations.' It was quite untrue. He was, recalls Baron Jomini, '. . . in reality his own Chief of Staff; holding in his hand a pair of compasses . . . bent, nay, often lying over his map, on which positions of his army corps and the supposed positions of the enemy were marked by pins of different colors, he arranged his own movements with a certainty of which we can scarcely form a just idea. . . .' " Alistair Horne, *Napoleon: Master of Europe, 1805–1807* (New York: Morrow, 1979), 82.

40. Despite contrary findings in atomic physics, Einstein never changed his mind on this point. Ronald Clark, *Einstein: A Life and Times* (London: Hodder and Stoughton, 1973), 120. See also: "Einstein believed that the universe had been designed so that its working could be comprehensible; therefore these workings must conform to discoverable laws; thus there was no room for chance and indeterminacy—God, after all, did not play the game that way. At a different level he stressed these beliefs in an interview in October, 1929, when the argument about quantum mechanics was at its height. 'I claim credit for nothing,' he said, at a mention of his modesty. 'Everything is determined, the beginning as well as the end, by forces over which we have no control. It is determined for the insect as well as for the star. Human beings, vegetables or cosmic dust, we all dance to a mysterious tune, intoned in the distance by an invisible piper.' " Ibid., 333. See also: ". . . The Laws of Nature, the processes of Nature, exhibit a much higher degree of uniformity or connexion than is contained in our time-causality!" Einstein, in Alexander Moszowski, *Conversations with Einstein*, trans. Henry L. Brose (New York: Horizon Press, 1970), 165.

41. Leszek Kolakowski, *The Alienation of Reason: A History of Positivist Thought*, trans. Norbert Guterman (Garden City, N.Y.: Doubleday, 1968), 23.

42. Werner Heisenberg, *Physics and Philosophy: The Revolution in Modern Science* (New York: Harper, 1958), 80–81.

43. Descartes, *Discourse on Method*, part vi, cited in Herbert Marcuse, *Reason and Revolution: Hegel and the Rise of Social Theory* (New York: Humanities Press, 1954), 16–17.

44. Claude Bernard, in Kolakowski, *Alienation of Reason,* 75–76.

45. Helmholtz, in F. Waismann, "The Decline and Fall of Causality," in *Turning Points in Physics: A Series of Lectures Given at Oxford University in Trinity Term, 1958* (Amsterdam: North-Holland Publishing, 1959), 90.

46. Heisenberg, *Physics and Philosophy,* 196–97.

47. Planck, cited in John Earman, "Determinism in the Physical Sciences," 234.

48. J. Bronowski, *The Common Sense of Science* (Cambridge, Mass.: Harvard University Press, 1979), 95.

49. Victor Weisskopf, "The Privilege of Being a Physicist."

50. Robert Sinsheimer, 1983 conference at MIT.

51. Megill, *Prophets of Extremity,* 10.

52. Kolakowski, *Alienation of Reason,* 45.

53. Hume, *Enquiry Concerning Human Understanding,* cited in Editor's Introduction in A. J. Ayer, *Logical Positivism* (New York: Macmillan, 1959), 10.

54. Marcuse, *Reason and Revolution,* 7.

55. Peter Gay, *The Enlightenment: An Interpretation,* vol. 2: *The Science of Freedom* (New York: Alfred A. Knopf, 1969), 188.

56. Marcuse, *Reason and Revolution,* 331–32, 343–44. Marcuse stresses the politically conservative aspect of Comte's positions, his emphasis on "resignation" and the "apologetic and justificatory" character of his thinking. He quotes and analyzes Comte's statement that ". . . True resignation, that is, a disposition to endure necessary evils steadfastly and without any hope of compensation therefore, can result only from a profound feeling for the invariable laws that govern the variety of natural phenomena. The 'positive' politics that Comte advocates would tend, he declares, 'of its very nature to consolidate public order,' even as far as incurable political evils are concerned, by developing a 'wise resignation.' " Ibid., 345.

57. G. W. F. Hegel, in Marcuse, *Reason and Revolution,* 238, note 29. Compare Comte, who describes the "chief object" of his book *Positive Philosophy* as an effort "to discover and demonstrate the laws of progress, and to exhibit in one unbroken sequence the collective destinies of mankind, till then invariably regarded as a series of events wholly beyond the reach of explanation, and . . . depending on arbitrary will."

58. G. W. F. Hegel, *Vorlesungen über die Philosophie der Geschichte,* in *Werke* (Frankfurt am Main: Suhrkamp Verlag, 1970), 12: 32. Hegel is positive that history moves inevitably toward human freedom, since history is ultimately governed by *Vernunft.* Ibid., 20. In his view, the innermost reality of things is positive: "Gott regiert die Welt, der Inhalt seiner Regierung, die Vollführung seines Plans ist die Weltgeschichte. Diesen will die Philosophie erfassen. . . ." Ibid., 53; see also 74.

59. Marx continues: "The call to abandon illusions about their condition is the call to abandon a condition which requires illusions. Thus, the critique of religion is the critique in embryo of the vale of tears of which religion is the halo." Karl Marx, *Introduction to the Critique of Hegel's Philosophy of Right* (1884), trans. Annette Jolin and Joseph O'Malley, ed. Joseph O'Malley (Cambridge: Cambridge Univer-

sity Press, 1970), 131. See also, "Theses on Feuerbach," in Karl Marx and Friedrich Engels, *The German Ideology, parts I and III*, ed. R. Pascal (New York: International Publishers, 1947), 198.

60. G. W. F. Hegel, Letter to Schelling, April 1795, in *Briefe von und an Hegel*, ed. Karl Hegel (Leipzig, 1887), in Marcuse, *Reason and Revolution*, 12.

61. How close we are to Comte emerges from the contrast he draws up between his own program and traditional philosophy. In Marcuse's summary: ". . . positive sociology is to concern itself with the investigation of facts instead of . . . transcendental illusions, with useful knowledge instead of leisured contemplation, certainty instead of doubt and indecision, organization instead of negation and destruction." *Reason and Revolution*, 341. There are few points on which our own *conscious* positions are very different from Comte's. We too are basically meliorists and our system is predicated on the wisdom of gradual rather than radical change. See Thomas Jefferson, who wrote to John Adams that "we are destined to be a barrier against the returns of ignorance and barbarism. Old Europe will have to lean on our shoulders, and to hobble along by our side, under the monkish trammels of priests and kings, as she can. What a colossus shall we be, when the southern continent comes up to our mark! What a stand will it secure as a ralliance for the reason and freedom of the globe!" in Marcell, *Progress and Pragmatism*, 69, quoted from Arthur A. Ekirch, *The Idea of Progress in America, 1815–1860* (New York: 1951), 32. Also see Thomas Paine: "We [Americans] have it in our power to begin the world over again. A situation, similar to the present, hath not happened since the days of Noah until now. The birthday of a new world is at hand." *The Writings of Thomas Paine*, ed. Moncure Daniel Conway (New York, 1894), 1: 114, cited in Marcell, *Progress and Pragmatism*, 68.

62. V. I. Lenin, *What Is To Be Done?* ed. Victor J. Jerome, trans. Joe Fineberg and George Hana (New York: International Publishers, [1902], 1969). I am taking the liberty of stressing the principle of actualization shared by Marxism and pragmatism. Lenin, of course, stood for revolution rather than reform, and *What Is To Be Done?* was written to win adherents to the cause of a revolutionary Marxist party.

63. "The philosophers have only *interpreted* the world in various ways; the point is to *change* it." Marx, Thesis XI, in "Theses on Feuerbach," 199.

64. John Dewey, *Essays in Experimental Logic* (Chicago: University of Chicago Press, 1916), 312, in David W. Marcell, *Progress and Pragmatism*, 215.

65. Gay, *The Enlightenment*, 2: 551. (emphasis added).

66. Ibid., 563.

67. Marcuse, *Reason and Revolution*, 355.

68. Bertrand Russell, cited without attribution, by Kolakowski, *Alienation of Reason*, 204.

CHAPTER 12

1. Cited in Terence Martin, *The Instructed Vision: Scottish Common Sense Philosophy and the Origin of American Fiction* (New York: Kraus Reprint, 1969), 158. Jeffer-

son's view of novels was akin to Diderot's. Excepting the work of Samuel Richardson, Diderot called novels "a tissue of frivolous and fantastic events which it was dangerous to read for (their effect on) both your taste and your behavior." Éloge de Richardson, 1761, in John Hope Mason, *The Irresistible Diderot* (New York: Quartet Books, 1982), 151–57. For Diderot, *conte* was a pejorative term.

2. Tony Tanner, *City of Words: American Fiction, 1950–1970* (New York: Harper and Row, 1971).

3. The complete sentence reads: "I am not far from believing that, in our own societies, history has replaced mythology and fulfills the same function, that for societies without writing and without archives the aim of mythology is to ensure that as closely as possible—complete closeness is obviously impossible—the future will remain faithful to the present and to the past." Claude Lévi-Strauss, *Myth and Meaning* (New York: Schocken Books, 1979), 42–43. Given the fact that history—like myth and tragedy—is full of cruelty, death and disasters, the "closeness" of the future to the present and past is not simply reassuring.

4. Reuven Frank, Executive Producer of NBC Evening News, in a 1963 staff memorandum; cited in Edward Jay Epstein, *News from Nowhere* (New York: Vintage Books, 1974), 4.

5. Alain Robbe-Grillet, "On Several Obsolete Notions," in John Hersey, *The Writer's Craft* (New York: Alfred A. Knopf, 1974), 97. Rilke said in 1910: "Telling stories, really telling stories, must have happened well before my time." *Die Aufzeichnungen des Malte Laurids Brigge* (Leipzig: Insel Verlag, 1927), part 2: 23. See also Derrida: "I have never known how to tell a story." *Memoires, for Paul de Man* (New York: Columbia University Press, 1986), 3, 10.

6. Donald Barthelme, cited without attribution in Tony Tanner, *City of Words* (New York: Harper and Row, 1971), 400.

7. Ronald Tavel, in *Edie: An American Biography*, Jean Stein with George Plimpton (New York: Alfred A. Knopf, 1982), 234. "Andy had said, 'Get rid of Plot'. . . . So I thought what I could introduce was to get rid of characters. That's why the character's [sic] names in KITCHEN are interchangeable. Everybody has the same name, so nobody knows who anybody is."

8. E. M. Forster, *Aspects of the Novel* (New York: Harcourt, Brace, 1954), 45.

9. Northrop Frye, "*Myth, Fiction and Replacement,*" in *Fables of Identity: Studies in Poetic Mythology* (New York: Harcourt, Brace and World, 1963), 29.

10. Samuel Taylor Coleridge, *1818 Lectures on European Literature II*, Lecture 5, *The Collected Works of Samuel Taylor Coleridge* (Princeton: Princeton University Press, 1987), 5: 130.

11. Walter Kerr, "Around the Globe, Shakespeare Remains a Mirror for Mankind," *New York Times*, 12 September 1976, sec. 2.

12. Peter Brooks, *Reading for the Plot: Design and Intention in Narrative* (New York: Alfred A. Knopf, 1984), 314.

13. Umberto Eco, *New York Times*, 15 January 1984.

14. Steve Tesich in "Steve Tesich Turns Memories into Movies," by Barney Cohen, *New York Times,* 7 January 1982.

15. Frank Pierson, in an address to a screenwriting seminar at Sundance, Utah. It is worth noting that Pierson is the author of *Dog Day Afternoon*—an unusual film in which the fate of a central figure is clearly foreclosed.

16. Claude Lévi-Strauss, *The Savage Mind* (Chicago: University of Chicago Press, 1966), 25–26.

17. Irving Howe, *Thomas Hardy* (New York: Macmillan, 1967), 144.

18. Lewis Thomas, "On the Uncertainty of Science."

19. Tavel, in *Edie*, 234.

CHAPTER 13

1. Friedrich Schlegel, *Kritische Schriften* (München: Carl Hauser Verlag, 1964), 6.

2. "Die eigentlichen Philosophen . . . sind Befehlende und Gesetzgeber: sie sagen, 'so soll es sein!' " Friedrich Nietzsche, *Jenseits von Gut und Böse*, in vol. 2 of *Werke in drei Bänden*, ed. Karl Schlechta (München: Carl Hanser Verlag, 1973), 676.

3. There are, of course, many stories that conclude an "ought" from their "is." They date rapidly and may be of little aesthetic interest, yet have a far more immediate and 'positive' effect on society than most great works of literature. *Uncle Tom's Cabin* is an obvious example and so, more recently, is *Schindler's List*. Shaw has a point when he says that *A Doll's House* did more good in the world than *Romeo and Juliet*.

4. The phrase is Hermann Cohen's. Also see Hegel: "Der einzige Gedanke, den die Philosophie mitbringt ist . . . der einfache Gedanke der Vernunft." G. W. F. Hegel, *Vorlesungen über die Philosophie der Geschichte, Sämtliche Werke* (Frankfurt am Main: Suhrkamp Verlag, 1970), 12: 20.

5. Paul Valéry, Avant-propos, *Encyclopédie française*, v. 16: *Arts et littératures dans la société contemporaine* (Paris, 1935), cited in Walter Benjamin, "On Some Motifs in Baudelaire," in *Charles Baudelaire: A Lyric Poet in the Era of High Capitalism*, trans. Harry Zohn (London: Verso, 1983), 146.

6. J. Hillis Miller, "Deconstructing the Deconstructors," *Diacritics* (Summer 1975): 24–31.

7. Postmodernism has been defined as *post*-Enlightenment. Allan Megill argues persuasively that Derrida and Foucault, like Nietzsche and Heidegger, stand *against* the Enlightenment. (Megill, *Prophets of Extremity: Nietzsche, Heidegger, Foucault, Derrida* (Berkeley: University of California Press, 1985), 340. Inasmuch as the Enlightenment was essentialist, the postmodern position can indeed be called *post*-Enlightenment. See Peter Gay: " 'It is universally acknowledged,' David Hume wrote in a famous passage, 'that there is a great uniformity among the actions of men, in all nations and ages, and that human nature remains still the same, in its principles and operations. The same motives always produce the same actions.' The passions of 'ambition, avarice, self-love, vanity, friendship, generosity, public spirit,' mixed 'in various degrees, and distributed through society, have been, from the beginning of the world, and still are, the source of all the actions and enterprizes,

which have ever been observed among mankind.' Indeed, 'Mankind are so much the same, in all times and places, that history informs us of nothing new or strange in this particular.' " Hume, *An Enquiry Concerning Human Understanding*, in *Works*, vol. 4, cited in Peter Gay, *The Enlightenment: An Interpretation*, vol. 2: *The Science of Freedom* (New York: Alfred A. Knopf, 1969), 168–69. Horkheimer and Adorno trace totalitarian components in the Enlightenment and conclude that "Enlightenment is totalitarian." Max Horkheimer and Theodor W. Adorno, *Dialectic of Enlightenment*, trans. John Cumming (New York: Herder and Herder, 1972).

But even though postmodern philosophy stands against central aspects of eighteenth-century Enlightenment, *all* philosophical endeavors—unlike ritual and art—are ultimately engaged in enlightening us. Clearly the postmodern aesthetic shares with the Enlightenment and Positivism a determination to liberate and potentiate us; they see ritual and traditional art as being "on the right."

8. In a critical area, postmodern thought is diametrically opposed to Positivism. Indeed, one might see in the uncertainty that is central to deconstruction a parallel to the idealist conviction that, as Marcuse puts it: "a decisive portion of the human world . . . (can) not be verified by observation." (Herbert Marcuse, *Reason and Revolution: Hegel and the Rise of Social Theory* [New York: Humanities Press, 1954], 343.) Deconstruction gets around the difficulty this poses by denying the existence of an *actual* uncertainty, an *actual* area that cannot be "verified by observation." There is only text.

9. Gustav Janouch, *Gespräche mit Kafka: Aufzeichnungen und Erinnerungen* (Frankfurt am Main: Fischer Bücherei, 1961), 66–67.

10. Wallace Stevens, "Adagia," in *Opus Posthumus, The Collected Poems of Wallace Stevens* (New York: Alfred A. Knopf, 1966), 160, 166. The contradictory statements about the 'real' in "Adagia" are striking and artful: "It is life that we are trying to get in poetry." (p. 158) "Poetry has to be something more than a conception of the mind. It has to be a revelation of nature. Conceptions are artificial. Perceptions are essential." (p. 164) "Poetry increases the feeling for reality." (p. 162) "There is nothing in the world greater than reality. In this predicament we have to accept reality itself as the only genius." (p. 177) "Eventually an imaginary world is entirely without interest." (p. 175) "In the long run the truth does not matter." (p. 180) "Reality is a vacuum." (p. 168) "Life is the reflection of literature." (p. 159)

11. Alain Robbe-Grillet, *Pour un nouveau roman* (Paris: Editions de Minuit, 1963), 135. See Nietzsche: "Jede gute Kunst hat gewähnt realistisch zu sein." Nietzsche, *Nachgelassene Schriften*, in vol. 1 of *Werke in zwei Bänden*, ed. Gerhardt Stenzel (Salzburg: Verlag "Das Bergland-Buch," 1953), 821.

12. *Biography, Letters and Notes from the Notebooks of F. M. Dostoevsky* (St. Petersburg, 1883), 373, cited by Mikhail Bakhtin, *Problems of Dostoevsky's Poetics*, ed. and trans. Caryl Emerson (Minneapolis: University of Minnesota Press, 1984), 6.

13. Edith Wharton, *The Writing of Fiction* (New York: Charles Scribner's Sons, 1925), 3.

14. Arthur Schopenhauer, *Die Welt als Wille und Vorstellung* (Leipzig: Inselverlag, n.d.), 2: 1174.

15. Carl Th. Dreyer, *Jesus* (New York: Dial Press, 1972), 290.

16. Charles Baudelaire, "The Painter of Modern Life," in *The Painter of Modern Life and Other Essays*, trans. and ed. Jonathan Mayne (London: Phaidon Press, 1964), 8. One wonders whether it is "at will." The artist's "recovery" of childhood often seems more like a helpless repetition, reinforced—today—by the rewards of fame and wealth. See Sigmund Freud, *The Future of An Illusion*, in vol. 21 of *The Standard Edition of the Complete Psychological Works of Sigmund Freud*, 17–18.

17. See Hegel: "Die Kunst durch ihre Darstellungen befreit innerhalb der Sinnlichen Sphäre zugleich von der Macht der Sinnlichkeit. Zwar kann man vielfach die beliebte Redensart vernehmen, der Mensch habe mit der Natur in unmittelbarer Einheit zu bleiben, aber solche Einheit in ihrer Abstraktion ist gerade nur Rohheit und Wildheit, und die Kunst eben, insoweit sie diese Einheit für den Menschen auflöst, hebt ihn mit milden Händen über die Naturbefangenheit hinweg." G. W. F. Hegel, *Vorlesungen über die Ästhetik*, Erster Band, *Sämtliche Werke*, ed. Hermann Glockner (Stuttgart: Friedrich Frommann Verlag, 1964), 81–82.

18. Paul Klee, *Das bildnerische Denken* (Basel: Schwabe, 1964), 76.

19. Friedrich Nietzsche in a letter to Georges Brandes, Turin, 23 May 1888, in *Werke in drei Bänden*, ed. Karl Schlechta (München: Carl Hanser Verlag, 1976), 3: 1295.

20. Compare Hegel: "What is 'familiar' is not properly known, precisely because it is 'familiar.' " G. W. F. Hegel, Preface, *Phenomenology of Mind*, 92.

21. Henri Matisse, "Exactitude is not Truth" (1947), in Jack D. Flan, *Matisse on Art* (Oxford: Phaidon Press, 1990), 117.

22. Matisse, "Notes of a Painter," in ibid., 37.

23. Aristotle, as Freud himself points out, ascribes aesthetic pleasure to recognition. Sigmund Freud, *Jokes and Their Relation to the Unconscious*, trans. and ed. James Strachey (New York: W. W. Norton, 1963), 121. Perhaps we suspend our disbelief not simply because art fulfils our wishes but because we recognize, or connect with, something in it—something 'known,' which could, of course, be skeptically reduced to our familiar, reassuring assumptions.

24. Picasso to Françoise Gilot, Françoise Gilot and Carlton Lake, *Life with Picasso* (New York: McGraw-Hill, 1964), 266.

25. Sigmund Freud, "The Relation of the Poet to Day-Dreaming" (1908), in *On Creativity and the Unconscious: Papers on the Psychology of Art, Literature, Love, Religion*, selected by Benjamin Nelson (New York: Harper and Row, 1958), 45.

26. Freud, *Jokes and Their Relation to the Unconscious*, 114. Freud speaks of the faulty thinking that equates "phantasy and reality"—the kind of thinking he repeatedly found in his neurotic patients.

27. Sigmund Freud, "Formulierungen über die zwei Prinzipien des psychischen Geschehens," in *Jahrbuch für psychoanalytische und psychopathologische Forschungen*, 3, cited in Henri C. Ellenberger, *The Discovery of the Unconscious*, 529.

28. Huizinga summarizes the opinion of most ethnologists and anthropologists in this matter: "There is an underlying consciousness of things 'not being real.' " Johan Huizinga, *Homo Ludens* (Boston: Beacon Press, 1955), 22–23.

29. Sigmund Freud, *Beyond the Pleasure Principle,* in vol. 18 of *The Standard Edition of the Complete Psychological Works of Sigmund Freud,* ed. James Strachey (London: The Hogarth Press and the Institute of Psycho-Analysis, 1968), 10–11.

30. Antoinette Baker, "A Time to Laugh; A Study in Laughter: Its Psychology and Its Role in Analysis" (Ph.D. diss. in Kristin Mann Library at the C. G. Jung Foundation, New York, 1980), 42.

31. Keaton's stunts involved grave risk in the productions of *Paleface, Our Hospitality, Sherlock Jr., and Steamboat Bill Jr.* See Rudi Blesh, *Keaton* (New York: Collier, 1971), 127, 197, 233, 249.

32. Perhaps for the same reason, the Catholic church insists that the wafer and wine of the Mass are not symbols but transsubstantiate into the body and blood of Christ.

CHAPTER 14

1. Georg Lukács, "Franz Kafka or Thomas Mann?" in *Realism in Our Time: Literature and the Class Struggle* (New York: Harper Torchbooks, 1964), 78.

2. "Far from referring back to an object that would be its cause, the poetic sign sets in motion an imaging activity that refers to no object in particular. The 'meaning' of the metaphor is that it does not 'mean' in any definitive manner." Paul de Man, "The Dead-end of Formalist Criticism," in *Blindness and Insight* (Minneapolis: Univerity of Minnesota Press, 1983), 235. We agree that the "poetic sign" refers to an object that doesn't " 'mean' in any definitive manner," but believe there *is* such an "object."

3. Richard Kearney, ed., *Dialogues with Contemporary Continental Thinkers* (Manchester: Manchester University Press, 1984), 124. The Kearney interview postdates Derrida's original formulation, which has been widely quoted and applied—no doubt because it coincides perfectly with the interlocking mirrors of intertextuality.

However valid Derrida's insistence on his freedom to *shift* may be in the pragmatic sense, at times his refusal to be held to any position brings to mind the Gingerbread man, who makes escape after escape, crying: "Run, run, run as fast as you can! You can't catch me, I'm the Gingerbread Man!"

4. For Derrida, the 'objective reality' to which both art and science have traditionally subscribed is an "ultimate referent" and constitutes idealism. See Richard Rorty, "Nineteenth Century Idealism and Twentieth Century Textualism," in *Consequences of Pragmatism* (Minneapolis: University of Minnesota Press, 1982). In Derrida's definition, idealism extends back far beyond the nineteenth century. Derrida, *Positions,* 65.

In a discussion following his seminal presentation at Johns Hopkins (Derrida, "Structure, Sign and Play in the Discourse of the Human Sciences," in *The Language of Criticism and the Sciences of Man,* ed. Richard Mackay and Eugenio Donato [Baltimore: Johns Hopkins University Press, 1970], 267), Derrida says of the "Einsteinian constant" that "[it] is not a constant." In Einstein's view, however, the speed of light *is* a constant, even though it isn't a "center starting from which an observer could master the field." (Ibid.) Relativity theory posits the constancy of the speed of light even if, to an observer traveling at the same speed, light would appear to be standing still. In 1911, Joseph Petzoldt, a friend and follower of Ernst Mach, wrote enthusiastically to Mach that, as a consequence of relativity, in theoretical physics "all absolutism and a priorism are finished. Old Protagoras is rising from his grave, a rebirth, now that the gushing current of the holy spirit of relativism is once again being followed." Berlin-Spandau, 1 June 1911, in John T. Blackmore, *Ernst Mach: His Work, Life and Influence* (Berkeley: University of California Press, 1972), 274. But as Petzoldt wrote to Einstein regretfully 16 years later: "Your insistence on the constancy of natural laws is really an absolute theory." Berlin-Spandau, 3 March 1927, in Blackmore, *Mach*, 282.

5. Roland Barthes, "Structural Analysis of Narratives," in *A Barthes Reader*, ed. Susan Sontag (New York: Hill and Wang, 1982), 287.

6. Friedrich Nietzsche, *Nachgelassene Schriften*, in vol. 1 of *Werke in Zwei Bänden*, ed. Gerhardt Stenzel (Salzburg: Verlag "Das Bergland-Buch," 1952), 821. Nietzsche's comments about art are often and legitimately cited in support of the postmodern "aestheticist" position that there is no reality outside the text. There are, however, statements by Nietzsche that point the other way. If, as he says, "we have art so that we need not perish of the truth," there is clearly something beyond the text. See also: "Die Kunst ist die grosse Stimulans zum Leben: wie könnte man sie als zwecklos, als ziellos, als art pour l'art verstehn?" Nietzsche, *Götzendämmerung*, vol. 2 of *Werke in drei Bänden*, ed. Karl Schlechta (München: Carl Hanser Verlag, 1976), 1004.

7. All art has highly stylized or mannerist components. But the traditional work encourages us to overlook them, whereas mannerism seems to urge them on our attention. Even so, the great mannerist painters—among whom art historians often include not only El Greco but Michelangelo—could also be called 'realists,' at least in Dostoevski's "higher" sense of the word.

Maniera originally meant "fashioned by the hand"—a hand to which the mannerist appears to draw attention. He purposefully includes and stresses himself—or rather, his inner, subjective reality. The 'mannerist' work of El Greco may effectively return us to the spiritual 'reality' of the Middle Ages. The sacred and inner realms are not—as in most high Renaissance work—contained and constrained by matter but, instead, *determine* the shapes and colors on the canvas. Perhaps we call El Greco a mannerist because *his* reality is not 'real' to *us*.

Though mannerism appears to prefigure the postmodern, only the later, lesser mannerists were explicitly intertextual and played with conventions. In their work, what had once been animated by conviction and strong feeling became sophisticated and rhetorical, ironic or sentimental. The great mannerist figures seem closer to modernism. They were, says Arnold Hauser, extreme individualists, preoccupied with paradox, contradiction, and uncertainty. Their work rendered the conflict-ridden world of the sixteenth century: "It would . . . be superficial to regard the conflicting elements that make up a work of mannerist art as mere play with form.

The conflict expresses the conflict of life itself and the ambivalence of all human attitudes; in short, it expresses the dialectical principle that underlies the whole of the mannerist outlook. This is based . . . on the permanent ambiguity of all things, great and small, and on the impossibility of attaining certainty about anything."

Arnold Hauser, *Mannerism: The Crisis of the Renaissance and the Origin of Modern Art*, trans. Eric Mosbacher (New York: Alfred A. Knopf, 1965), 1: 13. See also: "Mannerist art—and this is probably its most unique and characteristic feature— never confronts the spiritual as something that can be completely expressed in material form. Instead it considers it so irreducible to material form that it can be only hinted at (it is never anything but hinted at) by the distortion of form and the disruption of boundaries." Ibid, 10. "The feeling that mannerism always awakens is that there is no firm ground anywhere beneath one's feet." Ibid., 50.

8. Derrida says: "If one wished to schematize . . . what I have attempted can *also* be inscribed under the rubric of the 'critique of idealism.' Therefore it goes without saying that to the extent that dialectical materialism also operates this critique, it in no way incurs my reticence. . . ." Derrida, *Positions*, trans. Alan Bass (Chicago: University of Chicago Press, 1981), 62. But he differs with Marx, among other reasons, because: "It is not only idealism in the narrow sense that falls back upon the transcendental signified. It can always come to reassure a metaphysical materialism. It then becomes an ultimate referent, or it becomes an 'objective reality' absolutely 'anterior' to any work of the mark, the semantic content of a form of presence which guarantees the movement of the text in general from the outside." Ibid., 65.

9. One is tempted to suggest that Derrida is political by *not* being political, by not taking 'sides' and preserving an ambiguous and in this sense open position. Marx would of course label him a typical bourgeois—committed to noncommitment.

10. Jacques Derrida, "The Ends of Man," in *Margins of Philosophy*, trans. Alan Bass (Chicago: University of Chicago Press, 1982), 134–35.

11. Jacques Derrida, "The Conflict of Faculties," in Jonathan Culler, *On Deconstruction: Theory and Criticism after Structuralism* (Ithaca, N.Y.: Cornell University Press, 1982), 156.

12. Theodor W. Adorno, "Culture Criticism and Society," in *Prisms: Cultural Criticism and Society*, trans. Samuel and Shierry Weber (London: Neville Spearmans, 1967), 26.

13. Though there is the suggestion that, within the context of intertextuality, writing constitutes a measure of freedom, Derrida goes nowhere as far as Sartre's: ". . . since the one who writes recognizes, by the very fact that he takes the trouble to write, the freedom of his readers, and since the one who reads, by the mere fact of his opening the book, recognizes the freedom of the writer, the work of art, from whichever side you approach it, is an act of confidence in the freedom of men." Jean-Paul Sartre, *What Is Literature?*, trans. Bernard Frechtman (New York: Philosophical Library, n.d.), 63. Structuralism *criticizes* the concept of freedom in Sartre's existentialism; one would expect deconstruction to be sympathetic to it.

Postmodern thought is as firmly opposed to E. O. Wilson's sociobiology as it is to structuralism. Both are essentialist and, ultimately, determinist even if the biologist assigns a major role to chance. Neither, of course, allow any importance to the self: "In a Darwinist sense the organism does not live for itself. Its primary function is not even to reproduce other organisms; it reproduces genes, and it serves as their temporary carrier." E. O. Wilson, *Sociobiology: A New Synthesis* (Cambridge, Mass.: The Belknap Press of Harvard University Press, 1975), 3. As we have noted, many deconstructionists seem to be engaged in trying to save the self.

14. The Wiener Kreis "proclaimed its outlook as a philosophy to end all philosophies," albeit—unlike Derrida—its members saw their approach "as a decisive turn toward a new form of enlightenment." Herbert Feigl, "The Origin and Spirit of Logical Positivism," in *The Legacy of Logical Positivism,* ed. Peter Achinstein and Stephen F. Barker (Baltimore: Johns Hopkins University Press, 1969), 1.

15. Jacques Derrida, *Of Grammatology* (Baltimore: Johns Hopkins University Press, 1976).

16. Derrida says: "Logocentrism is . . . fundamentally an idealism. It is the matrix of idealism. Idealism is its most direct representation, the most constantly dominant force. And the dismantling of idealism is simultaneously . . . a deconstitution of idealism, or spiritualism in all their variants." *Positions,* trans. Alan Bass (Chicago: University of Chicago, 1981), 51. See also: "The motif of homogeneity, the theological motif *par excellence,* is decidedly the one to be destroyed." Ibid., 63–64. We would add that whereas theology attempts to be homogenous or consistent, the sacred is *in*consistent—at least as far as *we* are concerned.

17. Megill, *Prophets of Extremity,* 325.

18. Ibid., 326.

19. Jacques Derrida, "Freud and the Scene of Writing," in *Writing and Difference,* trans. Alan Bass (Chicago: University of Chicago Press, 1978), 211.

20. Michel Foucault, *Language, Counter-Memory, Practice: Selected Essays and Interviews,* ed. Donald F. Bouchard, trans. Donald F. Bouchard and Sherry Simon (Ithaca, N.Y.: Cornell University Press, 1977), 208, cited in Megill, *Prophets of Extremity,* 195.

21. Judith Fetterly, *The Resisting Reader: A Feminist Approach to American Fiction* (Bloomington: Indiana University Press, 1977), cited in Jonathan Culler, *On Deconstruction: Theory and Criticism after Structuralism* (Ithaca, N.Y.: Cornell University Press, 1982), 52–53.

22. Compare: "The relationship between author and critic does not designate a difference in the type of activity involved, since no fundamental discontinuity exists between two acts that both aim at full understanding." "Form and Intent in the American New Criticism," in *Blindness and Insight* (Minneapolis: University of Minnesota Press, 1983), 31. Very few artists would agree that their aim is "full understanding." See also: ". . . Critics can be granted the full authority of literary authorship." "The Work of Georges Poulet," in ibid., 80.

23. *Roland Barthes,* by Roland Barthes, cited in Introduction, *A Barthes Reader,* ed. Susan Sontag (New York: Hill and Wang, 1982), xv.

24. Geoffrey H. Hartman,"The Interpreter: A Self-Analysis," in *"The Fate of Reading" and Other Essays* (Chicago: University of Chicago Press, 1975), 3. See also: "We have entered an era that can challenge even the priority of literary to literary-critical texts." Hartman, "The Interpreter," 17. In the same collection, however, he says: "Even the best (critical) essays are secondary products, stimulated by the literature on which they comment. We read them to remain in the shadow of something that is greater and that we don't wish to face all the time." "Signs of the Times," 303. In "The Interpreter," Hartman says that as a young man he thought the artist "suffered . . . fragmentation in the flesh, with primary rather than secondary materials." Ibid., 4–5; he may have been correct.

25. "Structure, Sign, and Play in the Discourse of the Human Sciences," in Derrida, *Writing and Difference,* trans. Alan Bass (Chicago: University of Chicago Press, 1978), 292.

26. "The absence of the transcendental signified extends the domain of the play of signification infinitely." Derrida, "Structure, Sign, and Play in the Discourse of the Human Sciences," 280.

27. Theodor Adorno, *Gesammelte Schriften,* vol. 6, cited by Gillian Rose, *The Melancholy Science: An Introduction to the Thought of Theodor W. Adorno* (New York: Macmillan, 1978), 23. Compare: Nietzsche, "Erkenntnis ist Fälschung des Vielartigen und Unzählbaren zum Gleichen, Ähnlichen," *Nachgelassene Schriften,* in vol. 1 of *Werke in zwei Bänden, ed.* Gerhardt Stenzel (Salzburg: Verlag "Das Bergland-Buch," 1952), 848.

28. Derrida, *Positions,* 56–57.

29. Bringing low what was high is to lead to "the irruptive emergence of a new concept, a concept that can no longer be, and never could be, included in the previous regime." Ibid., 42.

30. Theodor Adorno, "Subject-Object," 499–500, cited in Martin Jay, *Adorno* (Cambridge, Mass.: Harvard University Press, 1984).

31. Megill, in *Prophets of Extremity,* 284, speaks of Derrida's attempt to escape the "dialectical maw." See also Richard Rorty, "Philosophy As a Kind of Writing," in *Consequences of Pragmatism* (Minneapolis: University of Minnesota Press, 1982), 93, 107–9.

32. Roland Barthes, "The Death of the Author," in *Image, Music, Text,* trans. Stephen Heath (New York: Hill and Wang, 1977), 147.

33. I first ran across mention of *le divin imprévu* in Robert M. Adams, *Stendhal: Notes on a Novelist* (New York: The Noonday Press, 1959), 110.

34. Significantly, Julien's act not only surprises *him* but presents something of a problem to contemporary critics. Since they are engaged in teasing out cause and effect relationships, they find it difficult to account for an intrusion from the unknown or unconscious. See Frank O'Connor, *The Mirror in the Roadway: A Study of the Modern Novel* (New York: Alfred A. Knopf, 1956), 54.

CHAPTER 15

1. The complete sentence reads: "Our imagination is stretched to the utmost not, as in fiction, to imagine things which are not really there, but just to compre-

hend those things which *are* there." Cited by James Gleick, *New York Times Magazine*, 20 September 1992.

2. Maurice Merleau-Ponty, "Cézanne's Doubt," trans. Hubert L. Dreyfus and Patricia Allen Dreyfus, in *Cézanne in Perspective* (Englewood Cliffs, N.J.: Prentice-Hall, 1975), 123. In a somewhat different version, the quotation appears in *Joachim Gasquet's Cézanne: A Memoir with Conversations*, trans. Christopher Pemberton (London: Thames and Hudson, 1991), 150: "The landscape is reflected, humanized, rationalized in me. I objectivize, project it, fix it on my canvas. . . . It may sound like nonsense, but I would see myself as the subjective consciousness of that landscape, and my canvas as its objective consciousness."

3. Friedrich Nietzsche, *Epigraph Nachgelassene Schriften*, in vol. 1 in *Werke in zwei Bänden*, ed. Gerhardt Stenzel (Salzburg: Verlag "Das Bergland-Buch," 1952), 779.

4. Vladimir Nabokov, *Lectures on Russian Literature* (New York: Harcourt Brace Jovanovich, 1981), 11. Both here and in his *Lectures on Literature* Nabokov suggests that—as a reader—he himself sometimes identified with the 'boy' or 'girl' in the book rather than with its author. Cf. his lecture on Anna Karenin(a).

5. The traditional artist sees life as more complex and, indeed, more interesting than the artwork. He does not think of his work as endowing life with interest, but tries to endow his work with life. As Kafka says, "Aus dem Leben kann man verhältnissmässig leicht so viel Bücher herausheben, doch aus Büchern so wenig, ganz wenig Leben." Gustav Janouch, *Gespräche mit Kafka* (Frankfurt am Main: Fischer Bücherei, 1961), 30.

6. John Cage, in "A Musical (a) Anarchist or (b) Liberator Is Turning 80," by Allan Kozinn, *New York Times*, 2 July 1992. Susan Sontag makes a similar comment when she says of her novel *The Volcano Lover* that she wanted "to do something that takes into account all the options you have in fiction." *The New York Times Magazine*, 2 August 1992.

7. Louis-Sebastien Mercier, "Nouvel essai sur l'art dramatique," 1773, cited in Peter Gay, *The Enlightenment: An Interpretation*, vol. 2: *The Science of Freedom* (New York: Alfred A. Knopf, 1969), 318.

8. Immanuel Kant, *Kritik der Urteilskraft*, in vol. 5 of *Immanuel Kants Werke*, ed. Otto Buek (Berlin: Bruno Cassirer, 1922), 393, cited in Gay, *The Enlightenment*, 2: 314.

9. Roman Jakobson and Pëtr Bogatyrëv, cited by Victor Erlich, *Russian Formalism: History-Doctrine* ('S-Gravenhage: Mouton, 1955), 37. Jakobson's view of science is emphatically Positivist.

10. Vladimir Propp, among others, refers to plot as a device for retarding the ending.

11. Paul de Man, "Form and Intent in the New American Criticism," *Blindness and Insight: Essays in the Rhetoric of Contemporary Criticism* (Minneapolis: University of Minnesota Press, 1983), 27.

12. Ibid., 26–27.

13. Cleanth Brooks, *The Well Wrought Urn* (New York: Reynal and Hitchcock, 1947), 159.

14. De Man, "Form and Intent in the New American Criticism," 26. De Man's inclusion of Kant might be somewhat qualified by the following passage: "Dass aber in allen freien Künsten dennoch etwas Zwangsmässiges, oder, wie man es nennt, ein Mechanismus erforderlich sei, ohne welchen der Geist, der in der Kunst frei sein muss und allein das Werk belebt, gar keinen Körper haben und gänzlich verdunsten würde: ist nicht unratsam zu erinnern (z. B. in der Dichtkunst, die Sprachrichtigkeit und der Sprachreichtum, imgleichen die Prosodie und das Silbenmass), da manche neuere Erzieher eine freie Kunst am besten zu befördern glauben, wenn sie allen Zwang von ihr wegnehmen und sie aus Arbeit in blosses Spiel verwandeln." *Kritik der Urteilskraft*, 379.

15. Jean-Paul Sartre, *Being and Nothingness: An Essay on Phenomenological Ontology* (Philadelphia: Philosophical Library, 1956), 433.

16. Rodin said to Rilke: "Artists are no longer workers in the proper sense: in the whole of Paris there are perhaps five or six who truly work, the rest are just amusing themselves. . . . And no one has any patience. But that is everything: patience and work. To do this I devoted my youth, and to this I devote every one of my days." Rainer Maria Rilke, *Briefe an Ernst Hardt* (Marbach a. N., 1975), 18, cited by Donald Prater, *A Singing Glass: The Life of Rainer Maria Rilke* (Oxford: Clarendon Press, 1986), 90.

17. Igor Stravinsky in the documentary film "A Stravinsky Portrait" by Richard Leacock and Rolf Lieberman (New York: Pennebaker Associates, 1965).

18. T. S. Eliot, "Wilkie Collins and Dickens," in *T. S. Eliot: Selected Essays* (New York: Harcourt, Brace, 1950), 411.

19. I was alerted to the relationship between the postmodern aesthetic and commercial work by A. S. Cook in a personal communication.

20. This may be a reformulation of a passage in Boris Tomashevsky's "Thematics": "The reader knows, the main characters do not; some of the characters know, some do not; the reader and some of the characters do not know; no one knows (The truth is discovered by accident); the characters know, but the reader does not." Lemon and Reis, *Russian Formalist Criticism*, 73–74.

21. Alan Friedman, *The Turn of the Novel* (New York: Oxford University Press, 1966), 182.

22. Ibid., 182.

23. Perhaps it is the gradual and gentle rather than sudden, brutal confrontation with the sacred that made the novel the preferrred fictive form of the middle class.

24. Friedrich Nietzsche, *Menschliches, Allzumenschliches, Werke in drei Bänden*, 1: 547.

25. G. W. F. Hegel, *Aesthetics: Lectures on Fine Art*, trans. T. M. Knox (Oxford: Clarendon Press, 1975), 1: 11, cited by Martin Heidegger in *The Origin of the Work of Art*, in Heidegger, *Poetry, Language, Thought*, trans. Albert Hofstadter (New York: Harper and Row, 1971), 80. From a postmodern perspective, once traditional art is "past," the sacred, too, is safely in the past.

26. Though Hollywood subordinates chance and accident to its Positivist world view, "disaster movies" were for some years a very successful genre.

27. A. C. Bradley, *The Substance of Shakespearean Tragedy* (New York: Macmillan, 1956), 15.

28. Ibid. See also: "What we do feel strongly, as a tragedy advances to its close, is that the calamities and catastrophe follow inevitably from the deeds of man, and that the main source of these deeds is character." A. C. Bradley, *The Substance of Shakespearean Tragedy: Lectures on Hamlet, Othello, King Lear, Macbeth* (London: Macmillan, 1956), 13.

29. Ibid., 13n.

30. Aristotle, *Poetics*, XXIV, 10.

31. E. M. Forster, *Aspects of the Novel* (New York: Harcourt, Brace, 1954), 150.

32. E. M. Forster, *A Passage to India* (New York: Harcourt, Brace, 1952), 322.

33. Peter Brooks, *The Melodramatic Imagination* (New York: Columbia University Press, 1985), 198.

34. Mikhail Bakhtin, *Problems of Dostoevsky's Poetics*, ed. and trans. Caryl Emerson (Minneapolis: University of Minnesota Press, 1984), 176–77.

35. Jean Pierre Vernant and Pierre Vidal-Naquet, *Tragedy and Myth in Ancient Greece* (Atlantic Heights, N.J.: Humanities Press, 1981), 81.

36. Ibid., 81.

37. Albin Lesky, *Greek Tragedy*, trans. H. A. Frankfort (New York: Barnes and Noble, 1967), 117.

38. Bradley, *The Substance of Shakespearean Tragedy*, 14.

39. John Updike, in "Books," *The New Yorker*, 59 (1 August 1983), 90.

40. J. Hillis Miller, "Bleak House," in *Charles Dickens: The World of His Novels* (Cambridge, Mass.: Harvard University Press, 1965), 207.

41. Ibid., 209.

42. Ibid., 210.

43. Ibid., 218. Compare: Monroe Engel, "*Bleak House*: Death and Reality," in *Dickens: Bleak House; A Casebook*, ed. A. E. Dyson (London: Macmillan, 1969), 196: "The fog and mire of *Bleak House* are the fog and mire of ignorance." "The attack on Chancery, and on the law and legal process, is an attack on irresponsibility." "Chancery is the set theme of this novel, death is the reality against which the foggy irresponsibility of legal process is assessed, and epidemic—moving by terrible indirection—symbolizes all too realistically the disaster that continued irresponsibility will bring." (p. 199)

44. Bruno Bettelheim, *The Uses of Enchantment: The Meaning and Importance of Fairy Tales* (New York: Vintage Books, 1977).

45. Franz Kafka, *Tagebücher, 1910–1923* (New York: Schocken Books, 1949), 370.

46. Arthur Schopenhauer, *Die Welt als Wille und Vorstellung* (Leipzig: Inselverlag, n.d.), 1: 269–75. Bergson takes this approach to an unwarranted extreme: "The object of art is to put to sleep the active or rather resistant powers of our personality, and thus to bring us into a state of perfect responsiveness, in which we realize the idea that is suggested to us and sympathize with the feeling that is expressed. In the processes of art we shall find, in a weakened form, a refined and in some measure

spiritualized version of the processes commonly used to induce the state of hypnosis." Henri Bergson, "Essai sur les données immédiates de la conscience," trans. R. L. Pogson, *Time and Free Will* (London: Macmillan, 1912), 14 ff., cited by Ernst Cassirer, *An Essay on Man* (New Haven: Yale University Press, 1944), 161. This is of course precisely why Adorno and Brecht opposed identification, and why the formalists insisted on art as "device."

47. Letter to George and Thomas Keats, 21 December or 27 December 1818, in *The Letters of John Keats*, ed. H. E. Rollins (Cambridge, Mass.: Harvard University Press, 1958), 191.

48. Leon Trotsky, *Literature and Revolution* (New York: Russell & Russell, 1957), 145; see also 141–44.

49. Theodor W. Adorno, "George und Hoffmannsthal," in *Zur Dialektik des Engagements*, 79–80.

50. Ibid.

51. Roland Barthes, "Structural Analysis of Narrative," in *A Barthes Reader*, ed. Susan Sontag (New York: Hill and Wang, 1982), 294–95.

52. Compare Hegel: "Die Veränderungen in der Natur zeigen nur einen Kreislauf, der sich immer wiederholt; in der Natur geschieht nichts Neues unter der Sonne." *Vorlesungen über die Philosophie der Geschichte,* in vol. 12 of *Sämtliche Werke* (Frankfurt am Main: Suhrkamp Verlag, 1970), 74.

53. Sören Kierkegaard, *Die Wiederholung*, in *Gesammelte Werke* (Jena: Eugen Diederichs, 1923), 3: 119–20. (The passage was translated from a translation into German.) Freud associates repetition with instinct and speaks of it as "*an urge inherent in organic life to restore an earlier state of things. . . .*" For him, it is a manifestation of Thanatos, the "death instinct," though we could surely associate it with Eros as well. Compare: "It would be counter to the conservative nature of instinct if the goal of life were a state never hitherto reached. It must rather be an ancient starting point which the living being left long ago, and to which it harks back again by all the circuitous paths of development. If we may assume as an experience admitting of no exception that everything living dies from causes within itself, and returns to the inorganic, we can only say, 'the aim of all life is death,' and, casting back, 'inanimate things existed before living ones.' " *Beyond the Pleasure Principle*, in vol. 18 of *The Standard Edition of the Complete Psychological Works of Sigmund Freud* (London: The Hogarth Press and the Institute of Psycho-Analysis, 1968), 36. See also *New Introductory Lectures on Psycho-Analysis*: "(The instincts) reveal an effort to restore an earlier state of things. . . . (They) bring about a phenomena (sic) which we can only describe as a 'compulsion to repeat.' He speaks of "the *conservative* nature of instincts." In vol. 22 of *The Standard Edition of the Complete Psychological Works of Sigmund Freud*, 106.

54. Laura Mulvey, "Visual Pleasure and Narrative Cinema," in Mulvey, *Visual and Other Pleasures* (London: Macmillan, 1989), 26.

55. Most narratives resemble riddles, which involve us by making us guess. There are even stories—movies, in particular—in which we have to decide what, in a scene, is significant, and where to focus our attention. In complex films, the

frame is often as open as possible. We are not "taken" by the hand or eyes and told what to watch.

CHAPTER 16

1. Herbert Marcuse, in "Karl Popper and the Problem of Historical Laws," in *Studies in Critical Philosophy* (Boston: Beacon Press, 1972), 199.

2. Joseph Marie de Maistre, Étude sur la souverainte, in vol. 1 of *Oeuvres Completes* (Lyon, 1891–92), 354, cited in Herbert Marcuse, *Studies in Critical Philosophy*, trans. Joris de Bres (London: NLB, 1972), 118.

3. In a somewhat different translation, this appears in Jean-Paul Sartre, *Existentialism and Humanism*, trans. Philip Mairet (Brooklyn, N.Y.: Haskell House Publishers, Ltd., 1948), 28.

4. Cited in Marcuse, *Studies in Critical Philosophy*, 8.

5. Paraphrasing Marx's position in "Economic and Philosophical Manuscripts of 1844," Marcuse says: "It is precisely the unerring contemplation of the essence of man that becomes the inexorable impulse for the initiation of radical revolution." Ibid., 29.

6. Richard Rorty cites James's "The true is what is good in the way of belief" in "Philosophy As a Kind of Writing," in *Consequences of Pragmatism*, 97. He adds that James was "simply trying to debunk epistomology; he was not offering a 'theory of truth.' " Isaac Levi pointed out to me that "better"—in James's context—has a 'moral' dimension; it is not simply to our own advantage.

7. William James, *Pragmatism and Four Essays from the Meaning of Truth* (Cleveland: World Publishing, 1968), 196.

8. Leszek Kolakowski, *The Alienation of Reason: A History of Positivist Thought*, trans. Norbert Guterman (New York: Doubleday, 1968), 159.

9. Theodor Adorno, "Reaktion und Fortschritt (1930), in *Moments Musicaux* (Frankfurt am Main, 1964), 160, cited in Susan Buck-Morss, *The Origin of Negative Dialectics* (New York: The Free Press, 1977), 49.

10. Michel Foucault, "Two Lectures," in *Power/Knowledge: Selected Interviews and Other Writings, 1972–1977*, ed. Colin Gordon, trans. Colin Gordon, Leo Marshall, John Mepham, and Kate Soper (New York: Random House, 1980), 85, cited in Allan Megill, *Prophets of Extremity: Nietzsche, Heidegger, Foucault, Derrida* (Berkeley: University of California Press, 1985). The term "antiscience" is used by Foucault, "Two Lectures," in *Power/Knowledge*, 83, cited in Megill, 250.

11. Foucault, *Power/Knowledge*, 133, cited in Megill, *Prophets of Extremity*.

12. Megill, *Prophets of Extremity*, 223–24. Compare Kolakowski's comment on C. S. Peirce: "Reality is not the 'manifestation' of any other, 'deeper,' more enigmatic and so more authentic reality. The world contains no mystery, merely problems to be solved. Differences between phenomenon and essence, between empirical qualities and the nature of things are purely verbal. The criterion of practice serves only to unmask the cognitive futility, the fictitious character of such

differences that, when taken for granted, are destructive of human thinking, of life itself, of the whole universe of values." Kolakowski, *Alienation of Reason*, 159–60.

13. Susan Sontag, Introduction to *A Barthes Reader* (New York: Hill and Wang, 1982), xxviii.

14. Thomas Wertenbaker, *The Puritan Oligarchy*, cited by Kai Erikson, *Wayward Puritans: A Study in the Sociology of Deviance* (New York: Grosset and Dunlap, 1947), 189–91.

15. Anne Fausto-Sterling, *Myths of Gender: Biological Theories about Women and Men* (New York: Basic Books, 1985). She criticizes E. O. Wilson, *Sociobiology: A New Synthesis* (Cambridge, Mass.: The Belknap Press of Harvard University Press, 1975).

16. Ibid., 195. See also: "The notion of a naked human essence is meaningless because human behavior acquires significance only in a particular social context." Ibid., 199.

17. E. O. Wilson, *On Human Nature* (Cambridge, Mass.: Harvard University Press, 1978), 19.

18. E. O. Wilson, *Biophilia* (Cambridge, Mass.: Harvard University Press, 1984), 106: "I am not suggesting the existence of an instinct. There is no evidence of a hereditary program hard-wired into the brain. We learn most of what we know, but some things are learned much more quickly and easily than others."

19. Wilson, *Sociobiology*, cited by Fausto-Sterling, *Myths of Gender*, 195.

20. Fausto-Sterling, *Myths of Gender*, 221.

21. Ibid., 256.

22. Mikhail Bakhtin, *Problems of Dostoevsky's Poetics*, ed. and trans. Caryl Emerson (Minneapolis: University of Minnesota Press, 1984), 87.

23. Boris Tomashevsky, like his fellow formalists, emphasizes genre, yet recognizes that there is a "unique logic" in "plot construction" which is "significantly similar" in stories wherever and whenever they were told. Boris Tomashevsky, "Thematics," in Lee T. Lemon and Marion J. Reis, eds., *Russian Formalist Criticism* (Lincoln: University of Nebraska Press, 1965), 92.

24. Gay, *The Enlightenment*, 2: 92; The Locke quotation is from John Locke, *Second Treatise of Civil Government*, par. 103.

25. Karl Marx, *The Eighteenth Brumaire of Louis Napoleon* (1852) (New York: International Publishers, 1963), 15.

26. Kolakowski, *The Alienation of Reason*, 119.

27. Eugène Delacroix, *The Journal of Eugène Delacroix*, trans. Walter Pach (New York: Crown, 1948), 224.

28. Diderot says: "But what is the voice of the present? Nothing. The present is only a point, and the voice we hear is always that of the future or that of the past." Diderot, *Oeuvres*, ed. Assézat, II, XVIII: 97, cited in Georges Poulet, *Studies in Human Time*, trans. Elliott Coleman (New York: Harper Torchbooks, 1959), 186.

29. Descartes says "The power of judging aright . . . what is called good sense or reason, is by nature equal in all men." René Descartes, *A Discourse on Method*,

trans. John Veitch (New York: Dutton, 1969), 3. Of course the concept of human-kind as instinct-impelled also makes us 'essentially' alike.

30. Herbert Marcuse, *Reason and Revolution: Hegel and the Rise of Social Theory* (New York: Humanities Press, 1968), 359.

31. Marx, Author's Preface to *A Contribution to the Critique of Political Economy* (1859), trans. N. I. Stone (Chicago: Charles H. Kerr, 1904), 11. See also: "By individual (we) mean no other person than the bourgeois, than the middle class owner of property. This person must, indeed, be swept out of the way, and made impossible." *The Communist Manifesto*, in Karl Marx, *Selected Writings*, ed. David W. McLellan (Oxford: Oxford University Press, 1978), 233.

32. Horkheimer and Adorno, *Dialectic of Enlightenment*, cited in Susan Buck-Morss, *The Origin of Negative Dialectics: Theodor Adorno, Walter Benjamin and the Frankfurt Institute* (New York: Free Press, 1977), 61.

33. Émile Durkheim, "Rules of the Sociological Method," in *Selected Writings*, ed. and trans. Anthony Giddens (Cambridge: Cambridge University Press, 1972), 127.

34. Claude Lévi-Strauss, "Geneva Lecture on Rousseau," in Thomas Shalvey, *Claude Lévi-Strauss: Social Psychotherapy and the Collective Unconscious* (Amherst: University of Massachusetts Press, 1979), 67. Yet Rousseau also insists he is unique: "I am not made like any of those I have seen; I dare believe that I am not made like anyone in existence . . . Nature . . . has broken the mold in which she cast me." Rousseau, *Confessions*, Livre I (Hachette ed., 8: 1), cited in Ernst Cassirer, *The Question of Jean-Jacques Rousseau*, trans. and ed. Peter Gay (New York: Columbia University Press, 1954), 128. His simultaneous focus on and dismissal of the self are but opposite sides of the same coin: one complements and is necessary to the other.

35. "Private property has its source in the *personality*—in the *freedom* of the single individual." G. W. F. Hegel, *Vorlesungen über die Philosophie der Religion II*, in *Werke* (Frankfurt am Main: Suhrkamp Verlag, 1969), 17: 88. See also: "Der freie Wille muss sich zunächst, um nicht abstrakt zu bleiben, ein Dasein geben, und das erste sinnliche Material dieses Daseins sind die Sachen, das heisst die äusserlichen Dinge. Diese erste Weise der Freiheit ist die, welche wir als Eigentum kennen sollen. . . ." Hegel, *Grundlinien der Philosophie des Rechts*, in vol. 7 of *Werke in zwanzig Bänden* (Frankfurt am Main: Suhrkamp Verlag, 1969), 91. Also see Hegel, *Early Theological Writings*, trans. Richard Kroner (Philadelphia: University of Pennsylvania Press, 1971), 156.

36. "Luther, without question, defeated servitude through devotion, but only by substituting servitude through conviction. He shattered the faith in authority, by restoring the authority of faith. . . . He freed man from external religiosity by making religiosity the innermost essence of man." Marx, "Introduction to a Contribution of the Critique of Hegel's Philosophy of Right," 138.

37. Jean-Paul Sartre, "Matérialisme et révolution," *Les Temps Modernes* 10 (Paris, July 1946): 14, cited by Marcuse in *Studies in Critical Philosophy*, 182.

38. W. R. D. Fairbairn, "A Revised Psychopathology of the Psychoses and Psychoneuroses." in *Psychoanalytic Studies of the Personality* (London: Routledge & Kegan Paul, 1976), 34.

39. Karl Marx, *The German Ideology* (Moscow, 1968), 195, cited in Marcuse, *Studies in Critical Philosophy*, 142.

40. Karl Marx, in Marx-Engels, *Gesamtausgabe*, part I, vol. 6, 519, cited in Marcuse, *Studies in Critical Philosophy*, 143. See also: "The bourgeois family will vanish as a matter of course when its complement vanishes, and both will vanish with the vanishing of capital." *The Communist Manifesto*, in Karl Marx, *Selected Writings,* ed. David McLellan (Oxford: Oxford University Press, 1978), 234.

CHAPTER 17

1. Arthur Schopenhauer, *Die Welt als Wille und Vorstellung*, (Leipzig: Inselverlag, n.d.), l: 269–72.

2. Diane Arbus says: "I have this funny thing which is that I'm never afraid when I'm looking in the ground glass. This person could be approaching with a gun or something like that and I'd close my eyes glued to the finder and it wasn't like I was really vulnerable. It just seemed terrific what was happening." When Stan Brakhage shot *The Act of Seeing With One's Own Eyes* in the autopsy room of a Pittsburgh hospital, he always raised the camera to his eye before pushing the swinging door open with his foot.

3. H. W. Frink, *Morbid Fears and Compulsions: Their Psychology and Psychoanalytic Treatment* (London: William Heineman, 1918), 254: "An emotion . . . is an undischarged action, a deed yet retained in the organism. Thus anger is an unfought combat; fear an unfled flight."

4. Of course only a complex and fundamentally contradictory artwork will permit such a process.

5. Robert Bechold Heilman, *Tragedy and Melodrama* (Seattle: University of Washington Press, 1968), 85: "By monopathy I mean the singleness of feeling that gives one the sense of wholeness. The unifying feeling may be found almost anywhere in the spectrum of emotional possibilities. A sense of oneness may come from a monopathy of hope, but also from a monopathy of hopelessness; from a monopathy of contempt for the petty, discontent with destiny, indignation at evildoing or apparent evildoing, or castigation of the guilt of others."

6. Roland Barthes, "Inaugural Lecture, Collège de France," in *A Barthes Reader,* ed. Susan Sontag (New York: Hill and Wang, 1982), 475.

7. In the view of some, even Logical Positivism was in large part a response to the rise of fascism: "The august membership of the [Vienna] Circle—philosophers, physicists, mathematicians, and logicians—loathed and feared the German idealistic philosophies which appeared to be legitimating the rise of irrationalism in continental politics. The goal of the Vienna Circle was to destroy philosophy except for the philosophic analysis necessary to establish an absolute certain foundation for the sciences. The goal of logical positivism was to establish, in place of metaphysical speculation, a tough, empirical 'scientific mentality.' " Thelma Zeno Lavine, *From Socrates to Sartre: The Philosophic Quest* (New York: Bantam Books, 1984), 398.

8. After the 1934 *Parteitag* at Nuremberg, Riefenstahl's *Triumph of the Will* was

shown in theaters all over Germany; it was produced explicitly to engage the entire nation in a ritual occasion.

9. René Girard, *"To Double Business Bound"*: *Essays on Literature, Mimesis, and Anthropology* (Baltimore: Johns Hopkins University Press, 1978), 168.

10. Martin Heidegger, *Holzwege*, 271, cited in James Demske, *Being, Man and Death: a Key to Heidegger* (Lexington: University Press of Kentucky, 1970), 135.

11. Heidegger, *Holzwege*, 248, in ibid., 127.

12. Heidegger, *Holzwege*, 272, in ibid., 127.

13. Heidegger, "Letter on Humanism," in Martin Heidegger, *Basic Writings* (New York: Harper and Row, 1976), 193. A related statement—"Language, by naming beings for the first time, first brings beings to word and to appearance"— occurs in "The Origin of the Work of Art," in Heidegger, *Basic Writings*, 185. See also: "Man acts as though he were the shaper and master of language, while in fact language remains the master of man. . . . For strictly, it is language that speaks. Man first speaks when, and only when, he responds to language by listening to its appeal . . . Language beckons us, at first and then again at the end, towards a thing's nature." ". . . Poetically Man Dwells . . . ," in Martin Heidegger, *Poetry, Language, Thought*, trans. Albert Hofstadter (New York: Harper and Row, 1971), 215–16.

14. Heidegger, *Holzwege*, 25–28, in Demske, *Being, Man and Death*, 120–21; Heidegger, *Nietzsche*, 1: 364, in ibid., 122–23. In "The Origin of the Work of Art," Heidegger italicizes "Beauty is one way in which truth essentially occurs as unconcealedness (of Being)." Art, he says, "is the creative preserving of truth in the work. Art then is the becoming and happening of truth." (pp. 178, 183)

15. Heidegger, "Brief über den Humanismus," 76, in ibid., 126; Heidegger, Erläuterungen zu Hölderlins Dichtung, 57, in ibid., 124; Heidegger, Erläuterungen zu Hölderlins Dichtung, 71, 71, 71, and 68, in ibid., 125.

16. Heidegger, "Letter on Humanism," 210.

17. Hans-Georg Gadamer, in "Martin Heidegger: An Essay in Philosophical Apprenticeships," trans. Robert R. Sullivan (Cambridge, Mass.: MIT Press, 1985), 52. Heidegger's longing for fusion with the whole is, of course, the predicate of his critique of the modern, technological world. If Marx mythologizes the end of history, Heidegger mythologizes its beginning.

18. Friedrich Nietzsche, *Aus dem Nachlass der Achtzigerjahre, Werke in drei Bänden*, ed. Karl Schlechta (München: Carl Hanser Verlag, 1976), 3, 464. A saying attributed to Novalis has it that: "Philosophy is properly nostalgic—the aspiration to be at home everywhere." See also Nietzsche: "Die Philosophie will was die Kunst will." *Menschliches, Allzumenschliches*, in *Werke in drei Bänden*, 1: 451.

19. See: "Das dichtend Gesagte und das denkend Gesagte sind niemals das Gleiche. Aber das eine und das andere kann in verschiedenen Weisen dasselbe sagen." Martin Heidegger, "Was heisst Denken?" in *Vorträge und Aufsätze* (Pfüllingen: Neske, 1954), 138, cited in Albert Cook, *Canons and Wisdoms* (Philadelphia: University of Pennsylvania Press, 1993), 56. See also: "Only poetry stands in the same order as philosophy." Heidegger, *Introduction to Metaphysics*, 26, in Richard Rorty, "Overcoming the Tradition," in *Consequences of Pragmatism* (Minneapolis:

University of Minnesota Press, 1982), 45. Schelling says that philosophy will return to "the universal ocean of poetry from which it started out." F. W. J. von Schelling, *System des Transzendentalen Idealismus,* in *Schellings Werke,* ed. Manfred Schroeter (Munich: Beck, 1927–28), 2: 629, cited in Allan Megill, *Prophets of Extremity: Nietzsche, Heidegger, Foucault, Derrida* (Berkeley: University of California Press, 1985), 170. Conversely, Plato insists on the radical difference between poetry and philosophy. *Republic,* 10.607b.

20. It is almost as if Heidegger briefly suffered from a crude form of Hegelianism, in which the state becomes an actualization (*Verwirklichung*) of the "union of union with non-union."

21. Maurice Merleau-Ponty, "Metaphysics and the Novel," in *Sense and Nonsense,* trans. Hubert L. Dreyfus and Patricia Allen Dreyfus (Chicago: Northwestern University Press, 1964), 28.

22. Jacques Derrida, *Of Grammatology,* trans. Gayatri Spivak (Baltimore: Johns Hopkins University Press, 1976), 112.

23. Derrida, *Of Grammatology,* 140. Derrida speaks of "the improbability . . . of pure presence." (p. 24) The "supplement" is present at the very beginning. If we call the "supplement" consciousness, it becomes apparent why it is present—or why *we* are absent—from the start. In "Freud and the Scene of Writing" (*Writing and Difference,* 226), Derrida says: "We must be several in order to write." We must also be "several" to be conscious.

24. Christopher Norris, *Derrida* (Cambridge, Mass.: Harvard University Press, 1987), 14.

25. Lévi-Strauss sees the incest taboo differently: "The prohibition of incest is less a rule prohibiting marriage with the mother, sister or daughter, than a rule obliging the mother, sister or daughter to be given to others." Claude Lévi-Strauss, *Elementary Structures of Kinship,* trans. James Bell, John von Sturmer, Rodney Needham (Boston: Beacon Press, 1969), 481, cited in Thomas Shalvey, *Claude Lévi-Strauss: Social Psychotherapy and the Collective Unconscious* (Amherst: University of Massachusetts, 1979), 31. In the view of Lévi-Strauss, "Exogamy is the archetype of all other manifestations based upon reciprocity, and . . . provides the fundamental and immutable rule ensuring the existence of the group as a group." Ibid., cited by Shalvey, *Claude Lévi-Strauss,* 74. Though this removes the incest taboo from the realm of psychology, the psychological and the social can be seen as directly related. By detaching the boy from the mother and the girl from the father, the young become psychologically available to outsiders. Of course biologists assume that the incest taboo is biological in origin: it fosters genetic variety and inhibits genetic disease.

26. Douglas R. Hofstadter, *Gödel, Escher, Bach: An Eternal Golden Braid* (New York: Basic Books, 1979), 67. Hofstadter calls that drawn or painted figure "recursive" whose "ground can be seen as a figure in its own right. The 're' in 'recursive' represents the fact that both foreground *and* background are cursively drawable—the figure is 'twice cursive.' Each figure-ground boundary in a cursive figure is a double-edged sword."

27. W. B. Yeats, "Among Schoolchildren," in *Collected Poems* (New York: Macmillan, 1972), 212.

CHAPTER 18

1. A survivor of the Holocaust, in *Jewish Responses to Nazi Persecution*, ed. Isaiah Trunk (New York: Stein and Day, 1979), 149.

2. Charles Baudelaire, "On the Essence of Laughter, and, in General, on the Comic in the Plastic Arts," in *"The Painter of Modern Life" and Other Essays*, trans. and ed. Jonathan Mayne (London: Phaidon Press Ltd., 1964), 153.

3. Pierre Schneider, *Matisse*, trans. Michael Taylor and Bridget Strevens Romer (New York: Rizzoli, 1984), 558, 582.

4. Nabokov objects strenuously to the concept of empathy. In his view, when a reader "identifies himself with a character," that "is the worst thing (he) can do." *Lectures on Literature*, 4. "We are not disgusted or horrified by the bloody ending of the three greatest plays ever written: the hanging of Cordelia, the death of Hamlet, the suicide of Othello give us a shudder, but a shudder with a strong element of delight in it. This delight does not derive from the fact that we are glad to see those people perish, but merely from our enjoyment of Shakespeare's overwhelming genius." Nabokov, *Lectures on Russian Literature* (New York: Harcourt Brace Jovanovich, 1981), 106. Control is clearly of the greatest importance to Nabokov. He thinks of the fictive figures as "puppets" to which he has given "the power to live." Ibid., 162. This clearly connects with the emphasis on "intentionality" in contemporary criticism.

5. Leszek Kolakowski, *The Alienation of Reason: A History of Positivist Thought*, trans. Norbert Guterman (Garden City, N.Y.: Doubleday, 1968), 85.

6. Gorky, in Edmund Wilson, *To the Finland Station: A Study in the Writing and Acting of History* (New York: Farrar, Straus and Giroux, 1977), 524.

7. Theodor Adorno, *The Jargon of Authenticity*, trans. Knut Tarnowski and Frederic Will (Evanston, Ill.: Northwestern University Press, 1973), 65.

8. Friedrich Nietzsche in a letter to Overbeck, Nice, February 1888. On 25 July 1882, he wrote to Peter Gast that after 1876 he was in many ways more of a battlefield than a human being. Nietzsche, *Werke in drei Bänden*, ed. Karl Schlechta (München: Carl Hanser Verlag, 1976) 3: 1185.

9. Friedrich Nietzsche, *Aus dem Nachlass der Achtzigerjahre,* in vol. 3 of *Werke in drei Bänden*, ed. Karl Schlechta (München: Carl Hanser Verlag, 1976), 832.

10. Pavese says: "The man who cannot live with charity sharing other men's pain, is punished by feeling his own with intolerable anguish. Pain is rendered acceptable only by raising it to the level of our common destiny and sympathizing with other sufferers." Cesare Pavese, *The Burning Brand: Diaries, 1935–1950*, trans. A. E. Murch with Jeanne Moli (New York: Walker, 1961), entry of 30 January 1945, p. 277.

11. Bertolt Brecht, "Die Dialektik auf dem Theater," *Versuche 15* (Berlin: Suhrkamp Verlag, 1957), 104.

12. See Peter Gay: "To men of the eighteenth century nothing could be of greater interest than a contest in which, perhaps for the first time in history, reason might triumph over necessity." *The Enlightenment: An Interpretation*, vol. 2: *The Science of Freedom* (New York: Alfred A. Knopf, 1969), 564. Marcuse points out that Robespierre's *être suprême* is "the counterpart to the glorification of reason in Hegel's system." Marcuse, *Reason and Revolution: Hegel and the Rise of Social Theory* (Atlantic Highlands, N.J.: Humanities Press, 1983), 5. Robespierre was convinced that "all fictions disappear before truth and all follies fall before reason," while Hegel believed that "the French Revolution enunciated reason's ultimate power over reality." Ibid., 6.

13. See Martin Jay, *The Dialectical Imagination: A History of the Frankfurt School and the Institute of Social Research, 1923–1950* (Boston: Little, Brown, 1973), 60. Marcell says: "Dewey believed that logic had always been a 'progressive discipline.'" David Marcell, *Progress and Pragmatism: James, Dewey, Beard, and the American Idea of Progress* (Westport, Conn.: Greenwood Press, 1974), 223. The Dewey quote is from John Dewey, *Logic: The Theory of Inquiry* (New York: Henry Holt, 1938), 14.

14. "Cogito and the History of Madness," in Derrida, *Writing and Difference*, trans. Alan Bass (Chicago: University of Chicago Press, 1978), cited by Allan Megill, *Prophets of Extremity: Nietzsche, Heidegger, Foucault, Derrida* (Berkeley: University of California Press, 1985), 218. "Order is . . . denounced within order."

CHAPTER 19

1. Cited in E. A. Burtt, *The Metaphysical Foundations of Modern Physical Science* (Garden City, N.Y.: Doubleday, 1954), 116.

2. He says that "perception is interdependent with the concept of origin and center and consequently whatever strikes at the metaphysic . . . also strikes at the very concept of perception." Derrida, "Structure, Sign and Play in the Discourse of the Human Sciences," in *The Language of Criticism and the Sciences of Man*, ed. Richard Macksey and Eugenio Donato (Baltimore: Johns Hopkins University Press, 1970), 272. This statement appears in the discussion section and is not included in the version of the essay in *Writing and Difference*.

Postmodern philosophy is persuaded that all experience is so deeply bound to language that there *is* no experience apart from language. As a dialectical response to the traditional view that sensory experience is primary, this is useful and indeed necessary; as an absolute it seems questionable. In "Freud and the Scene of Writing," Derrida says: "Pure perception does not exist"—a statement with which most would agree. In *Writing and Difference*, trans. Alan Bass (Chicago: University of Chicago Press, 1978), 226.

3. Thomas S. Kuhn, *The Structure of Scientific Revolutions* (Chicago: University of Chicago Press, 1962), 65.

4. Theodor Adorno, *Minima Moralia,* cited in Susan Buck-Morss, *The Origin*

of Negative Dialectics: Theodor W. Adorno, Walter Benjamin, and the Frankfurt Institut (London: Free Press, 1977), 260.

5. G. W. F. Hegel, Vorrede, *Phänomenologie des Geistes,* in vol. 2 of *Sämtliche Werke,* ed. Hermann Glockner (Stuttgart: Friedrich Frommann Verlag, 1964), 24.

6. Jung says: "All understanding in general, which is conformity with a general point of view, has the diabolical in it and kills. It is the wrenching of another life out of its own course, forcing it into a strange one in which it cannot live." Letter to Hans Schmid, in Laurens van der Post, *Jung and the Story of Our Time* (New York: Pantheon Books, 1975), 122. Yet Jung, like Lacan, also conjugates the particular to the universal. He was convinced, as was Marx, that our separation from the whole is at the root of our distress and endeavored to reconnect the conscious to the unconscious and the human to the sacred, just as Marx tried to repair the broken link between the alienated individual and the community. Though the differences between them seem irreconcilable, they—like the artwork—refuse to sacrifice either the particular or the whole, the human *or* the natural, the individual or the community.

7. Fredric Jameson, "Imaginary and Symbolic in Lacan: Marxism, Psychoanalytic Criticism, and the Problem of the Subject," in Jameson, *The Ideologies of Theory: Essays, 1971–86* (Minneapolis: University of Minnesota Press, 1988).

8. Walter Benjamin, "The Storyteller," in Walter Benjamin, *Illuminations,* ed. Hannah Arendt, trans. Harry Zohn (New York: Schocken Books, 1969), 83.

9. See Walter Benjamin, "Charles Baudelaire," *Walter Benjamin Gesammelte Schriften,* 1: 2, 509–604. "Chockerlebnis" appears in the same essay.

10. Theodor Adorno, et al, in *Über Walter Benjamin* (Frankfurt am Main: Suhrkamp Verlag, 1970), 26.

11. Viktor Shklovsky, "Art as Technique," in Lee T. Lemon and Marion J. Reis, eds., *Russian Formalist Criticism: Four Essays,* (Lincoln: University of Nebraska Press, 1965), 12.

12. Kuhn, *Structure of Scientific Revolutions,* 64.

13. Ibid., 62–63.

14. Todorov suggests the opposite. He reads the "fantastic" in narrative as a form of "pandeterminism" that permits us to subordinate even chance to a cause— "even if this cause can only be of a supernatural order." Tzvetan Todorov, *The Fantastic: A Structural Approach to a Literary Genre,* trans. Richard Howard (Cleveland: The Press of Case Western Reserve University, 1973), 110; see also 161.

15. There are several interpretations of Hegel's comment that art is something of the past. Some read it as announcing "the end of art" and its displacement by philosophy; Hegel clearly ranks philosophy above art, even as he ranks religion above both. See Stephen Bungay, *Beauty and Truth: A Study of Hegel's Aesthetics* (Oxford: Oxford University Press, 1984), 71–75. Annemarie Gethmann-Siefert says that Hegel, like Schiller, values art as an "invaluable means of educating (us) into reason." *Die Funktion der Kunst in der Geschichte,* Hegel Studien Beiheft 25 (Bonn: Bouvier Verlag Herbert Grundmann, 1984), 45.

16. G. W. F. Hegel, *System der Philosophie,* Dritter Teil, in vol. 10 of *Sämtliche*

Werke, ed. Hermann Glockner (Stuttgart: Friedrich Frommann Verlag, 1964), 371. See also: Hegel, *Vorlesungen über die Ästhetik:* "Zufriedenheit ist das Gefühl der Übereinstimmung unserer einzelnen Subjektivität mit dem Zustande unseres bestimmten, uns gegeben oder durch uns hervorgebrachten Zustandes." In vol. 14 of *Werke in zwanzig Bänden* (Frankfurt-am-Main: Suhrkamp Verlag, 1970), 85–86.

17. Theodore Taylor, a nuclear physicist, cited in John McPhee in "Theodore B. Taylor: The Curve of Binding Energy," *The New Yorker*, 49 (10 December 1973), 108.

18. "Once when (Lessing) was attempting to explain to himself the source of 'tragic pleasure,' he said that 'all passions, even the most unpleasant, are as passions pleasant' because 'they make us . . . more conscious of our existence, they make us feel more real.' " "On Humanity in Dark Times: Thoughts about Lessing," in Hannah Arendt, *Men in Dark Times* (New York: Harcourt Brace Jovanovich, 1968), 6.

19. There is, as the words suggest, a direct connection between "tension" and "intensity." Huizinga locates tension in the realm of play: "To dare, to take risks, to bear uncertainty, to endure tension—these are the essence of the play spirit. Tension adds to the importance of the game and, as it increases, enables the player to forget that he is only playing." Johan Huizinga, *Homo Ludens: A Study of the Play Element in Culture*, trans. R. F. C. Hull (London: Routledge & Kegan Paul, 1949), 51. Tension, like fear, is of course very much part of our lives—often an unpleasant part—and its appearance in art is not simply a product of the "play spirit." But Huizinga's point that it enhances the *reality* of the game may help to explain why it is of no interest to postmodernist theory and practice. The crisis structure of most traditional narratives—which escalates intensity and fosters catharsis—is highly suspect to the postmodern aesthetic, though it raises no objections to the crisis structure of comedy and farce.

20. Kuhn, *Structure of Scientific Revolutions*, 24, 35, and 38.

21. Ibid., 80.

22. Ibid., 24.

23. David Sylvester, *Francis Bacon* (New York: Pantheon Books, 1975), 56. Bacon said to Lawrence Gowing: "The moment you know what to do, you're just making another form of illustration."

24. In a letter to Douglas Cooper in 1955, Nicolas de Staël says: "I lose contact with the canvas at each instant, find it again, lose it again . . . This is necessary because I believe in the accidental—As soon as I sense a logic, too much logic, I become unnerved, and naturally tend towards the illogical." Douglas Cooper, *Nicolas de Staël* (New York: Norton, 1961), 76. (elision is de Staël's or Cooper's)

25. No doubt this is one reason they speak to us still, though their landscapes, unmarked by industry, evoke a world that was gone or vanishing even when they were painted. With rare exceptions—like Monet's "Gare St. Lazare" and Van Gogh's "Factories at Clichy" (1887, The City Museum of St. Louis)—industry is relegated to a few distant factory chimneys.

26. W. B. Yeats, *The Autobiography of William Butler Yeats, Consisting of Reveries*

over Childhood and Youth, The Trembling of the Veil, and Dramatis Personae (New York: Collier Books, 965), 358.

27. Some years ago, in a piece for the *New York Times*, Walter Kerr said that many successful playwrights write the audience rather than the play. Compare Oscar Wilde: "It is the spectator, and not life, that art really mirrors." Preface to *The Picture of Dorian Gray,* in *The Picture of Dorian Gray and Other Writings by Oscar Wilde,* ed. Richard Ellmann (New York: Bantam Books, 1982), 3.

28. Rilke speaks of "Dinge machen aus Angst," to make objects out of fear. He surely meant that the artist makes them both *because* he is afraid, and *out* of his fear.

29. Ricoeur emphasizes Aristotle's definition of the poet as a *maker* of plots; he sees mimesis as the art of composition and action as "the 'construct' of (the) construction that the mimetic activity consists of." Paul Ricoeur, *Time and Narrative,* trans. Kathleen McLaughlin and David Pellauer (Chicago: University of Chicago Press, 1984), 1: 34–36. For Ricoeur, mimesis as poesis is located in what he calls "mimesis."[2] (pp. 64–70) In his view, "the Aristotelian mimesis is the emblem of the shift (*décrochage*) that, to use our vocabulary today, produces the 'literariness' of the work of literature." (p. 45) The link to the Russian formalists seems clear.

30. Aristotle, *Poetics,* 1448 B4-11.

31. Pierre Schneider, *Matisse,* trans. Michael Taylor and Bridget Strevens Romer (New York: Rizzoli, 1984), 523.

32. Theodor W. Adorno and Max Horkheimer, *Dialectic of Enlightenment,* trans. John Cumming (New York: Herder and Herder, 1972), 227. (emphasis added)

33. Maurice Denis, *Théories: 1890–1910* (Paris: L'Occident, 1919), 1, in *From the Classicists to the Impressionists: Art and Architecture in the Nineteenth Century,* ed. Elizabeth Holt, vol. 3 of *A Documentary History of Art* (New York: Anchor Books, 1966), 509.

34. Stendhal says: "Praise is a certificate of resemblance." Of course strong *dis*like or hate can also be based on likeness—an unacknowledged one.

35. Letter to Émile Bernard, Arles, April 1888, in Herschel B. Chipp, *Theories of Modern Art: A Source Book by Artists and Critics* (Berkeley: University of California Press, 1968), 32.

36. Cited by Matisse, Letter to Henry Clifford, 1948, in Jack D. Flan, *Matisse on Art* (Oxford: Phaidon Press, 1990), 121.

37. Schneider, *Matisse,* 41, note 42.

38. Freud used the word *Imago*—related to *imitari*—for the childhood conception of the parent retained in the unconscious. *On the Universal Tendency to Debasement in the Sphere of Love* (1910), in vol. 11 of *The Standard Edition of the Complete Psychological Works of Sigmund Freud,* ed. James Strachey (London: The Hogarth Press and the Institute of Psycho-Analysis, 1973), 181.

39. Sigmund Freud, *Jokes and Their Relation to the Unconscious,* trans. and ed. James Strachey (New York: Norton, 1963), 208.

40. Barbara Johnson, *The Critical Difference* (Baltimore: Johns Hopkins University Press, 1980), 5, cited in Jonathan Culler, *On Deconstruction: Theory and Criticism after Structuralism* (Ithaca, N.Y.: Cornell University Press, 1982), 213.

41. Adorno found himself constrained to reject film because it "forces its victims to equate it directly with reality." Theodor Adorno, "Arnold Schoenberg," in *Prisms*, trans. Samuel and Shierry Weber (Cambridge, Mass.: MIT Press, 1990), 154.

CHAPTER 20

1. James L. Smith, *Melodrama* (London: Methuen, 1973), 16.

2. Peter Brooks, *The Melodramatic Imagination: Balzac, Henry James, Melodrama, and the Mode of Excess* (New Haven: Yale University Press, 1976), 86.

3. Smith, *Melodrama*, 36.

4. Brooks, *Melodramatic Imagination*, 205.

5. Substitutes for the sacred came in many forms. For the Romantics, nature was clearly numinous, and romantic love—which de Rougemont traces back to the Middle Ages—had a 'sacred' dimension: it took those who were enthralled to it out of the social and economic sphere. In aesthetics, the eighteenth-century concept of the *sublime* reconstituted the sacred in the work of art.

6. Once the audience of popular story learned to read, it turned to the serialized novels of authors like Dickens, who himself moved effortlessly between page and stage. In print, as in the theater, popular narrative continued to proclaim that human life is watched over by a just and kindly fate.

7. A summary of Gilbert B. Cross, *Next Week—East Lynne: Domestic Drama in Performance, 1820–1874* (London: Associated University Presses, 1977), in *Melodrama*, ed. Daniel Gerould (New York: New York Literary Forum, 1980), 260.

8. Daniel Gerould and Julia Przybos, "Melodrama in the Soviet Theatre, 1917–28," in *Melodrama*, ed. Daniel Gerould, 76.

9. Ibid., 79.

10. John Steinbeck, *Speech Accepting the Nobel Prize for Literature, Stockholm, 10 December 1962* (New York: Viking Press, n.d.), 9.

11. Werner Heisenberg, *Physics and Philosophy: The Revolution in Modern Science* (New York: Harper, 1958), 27.

12. Anatoli Lunacharsky, "What Kind of Melodrama Do We Need?" cited in Gerould and Pryzbos, 78–79.

13. John Markoff, "A Celebration of Isaac Asimov," *New York Times*, 2 April 1992, sec. 3.

14. Hippolyte Taine, *History of English Literature*, trans. H. Van Laun (New York, 1872), 1: 6. Though Taine was no Positivist and objected to the use to which his statement was often put, it concisely summarizes the Positivist view of evil.

15. At the turn of the century, Hermann Cohen's influential 'rational Judaism' negated the reality of evil: "Evil is non-existent. It is nothing but a concept derived from the concept of freedom. A power of evil exists only in myth." Hermann Cohen, *Ethik des reinen Willens* (1907), 452, in Gershom G. Scholem, *Major Trends in Jewish Mysticism* (New York: Schocken Books, 1978), 36. The assertion that there is no evil because our will is unfree is humanist through and through. In the tradi-

tional view, evil exists irrespective of our will, as a part of our condition. Though the community has always had to insist that we can choose or reject it, evil was perceived as intrinsic or 'original': humankind was stuck with it.

16. Ibid., 35–36.

17. Strindberg says of *King Lear*: "There is no mother, and no one mentions her by name. So she is dead! But people generally in family get-togethers recall a dead mother. . . . Here there is complete silence!" August Strindberg, *Open Letters to the Intimate Theatre*, trans. Walter Johnson (Seattle: University of Washington Press, 1967), 96.

18. François Truffaut, *Hitchcock* (New York: Simon and Schuster, 1967), 141.

19. Michael Holquist, "Whodunit and Other Questions: Metaphysical Detective Stories in Post-War Fiction," in *The Poetics of Murder: Detective Fiction and Literary Theory*, ed. Glenn W. Most and William W. Stowe (New York: Harcourt Brace Jovanovich, 1983), 156.

20. Helmut Heissenbüttel, "Rules of the Game of the Crime Novel," in *The Poetics of Murder*, 80.

21. Roger Caillois, "The Detective Novel as Game," in *The Poetics of Murder*, 3, 9.

22. Dennis Porter, *The Pursuit of Crime: Art and Ideology in Detective Fiction* (New Haven: Yale University Press, 1981), 29–30.

23. Peter Brooks, *Reading for the Plot: Design and Intention in Narrative* (New York: Vintage Books, 1985), 270.

24. Richard Alewyn, "The Origin of the Detective Novel," in *The Poetics of Murder*, 74–77.

25. G. K. Chesterton, "The Hammer of God," in *The Father Brown Stories* (London: Cassel, 1951), 118–43.

26. A. Conan Doyle, "The Adventure of the Mazarin Stone," in vol. 2 of *The Complete Sherlock Holmes* (Garden City, N.Y.: Doubleday, 1953), 1014.

27. It is interesting to note that the American biologist E. O. Wilson assumes that because we cannot know the future, we are free: "The mind is too complicated a structure, and human social relations affect its decisions in too intricate and variable a manner, for the detailed histories of individual human beings to be predicted in advance by the individuals affected or by other human beings. You and I are consequently free and responsible persons in this fundamental sense." Edward O. Wilson, *On Human Nature* (Cambridge, Mass.: Harvard University Press, 1978), 77. See also: "Thus because of mathematical indeterminacy and the uncertainty principle, it may be a law of nature that no nervous system is capable of acquiring enough knowledge to significantly predict the future of any other intelligent system in detail. Nor can intelligent minds gain enough self-knowledge to know their own future, capture fate, and in this sense eliminate free will." Ibid., 73–74.

28. In 1965, Charles Marowitz said of Hamlet that "the play is imprisoned in its own narrative," and wondered whether it was "possible to express one's own view of (it) without the crutch of a narrative." Charles Marowitz, *The Marowitz "Hamlet"* (Harmondsworth, England: Penguin, 1970), 10. In *his* production, he

proceded to 'liberate' the text from its narrative by jumbling the scenes into a collage that brought it closer to a happening.

29. Roland Barthes, "The World of Wrestling," in *A Barthes Reader*, ed. Susan Sontag (New York: Hill and Wang, 1982), 19.

30. André Jolles, *Einfache Formen* (Halle: Max Niemeyer Verlag, 1930), 60–61.

31. Like the heroes of myth and tragedy, athletes in Greek footraces sometimes collapsed and died—like the heroes of myth and tragedy—in the course of completing their task.

32. John H. Towsen, *Clowns* (New York: Hawthorn Books, 1976), 83.

33. Ibid., 164.

34. Ibid., 289.

35. Rudi Blesh, *Keaton* (New York: Macmillan, 1966), 290.

36. Buster Keaton, ibid., 290.

37. The liberation, or economy, of energy in joking is a major theme in Freud, *Jokes and Their Relation to the Unconscious*, trans. and ed. James Strachey (New York: Norton, 1963), 118 and many others.

38. Henri Bergson, "Laughter," in *Comedy*, ed. Wylie Sypher (Garden City, N.Y.: Doubleday, 1956), 61–190.

39. God, at least in Judeo-Christian tradition, never laughs or makes us laugh.

CHAPTER 21

1. Erich Heller, "Goethe and the Avoidance of Tragedy," in *The Disinherited Mind* (New York: World Publishing, 1957), 37–63.

2. It has often been noted that Faust, like Goethe, does not look back; the past is of little interest to him. See Georg Simmel, "Bemerkung über Goethe," in *Georg Simmel Gesamtausgabe*, ed. Otthein Rammstedt (Frankfurt am Main: Suhrkamp, 1993), 195. Emil Staiger points out that Goethe often said of women he loved: "Sie blieb sich immer gleich."

3. Thomas Mann, in "Goethe's 'Faust,' " in *Goethe's "Faust," Part One: Essays in Criticism*, ed. John B. Vickers and J'nan Sellery (Belmont, Calif.: Wadsworth Publishing, 1969), 11.

4. Ibid., 13.

5. Ibid., 14.

6. Though Georg Simmel, 296, stresses that Goethe was well aware of the ghosts and demons within himself, he kept them largely out of his work.

7. Emil Staiger, *Goethe* (Zürich: Atlantis Verlag, 1958), 2: 481.

8. Gadamer says: "[Goethe] can justly be called the symbol of the bourgeois society of the nineteenth century." Hans-Georg Gadamer, *Reason in the Age of Science*, trans. Frederick G. Lawrence (Cambridge, Mass.: MIT Press, 1981), 22.

9. Heller, "Goethe and the Avoidance of Tragedy," 51.

10. Paul Valéry, "Address in Honor of Goethe," in *Masters and Friends*, trans. Martin Turnell, in vol. 9 of *Collected Works of Paul Valéry* (Princeton: Princeton University Press, 1968), 167.

11. Heller, "Goethe and the Avoidance of Tragedy," 51. Hegel's aesthetic takes a similar position and Hegel, like Goethe, disapproves of works in which the "Krankheit des Geistes" becomes visible: "Aus dem Bereiche der Kunst . . . sind die dunkeln Mächte gerade zu verbannen, denn in ihr ist nichts dunkel, sondern alles klar und durchsichtig. . . ." G. W. F. Hegel, *Vorlesungen über die Ästhetik I*, in vol. 13 of *Werke in zwanzig Bänden* (Frankfurt am Main: Suhrkamp Verlag, 1970), 314–15.

12. In Emil Staiger, *Goethe*, 1: 93.

13. Heller, "Goethe and the Avoidance of Tragedy," 40.

14. Valéry, "Address in Honor of Goethe," 158, 156.

15. Staiger, *Goethe*, 1: 528.

16. Ibid., 3: 257; Ibid., 2: 428.

17. See also: "I had few really definite ideas, and the reason for that was that, instead of obstinately trying to obey circumstances, I obeyed them, and they forced me to change my mind all the time. Thus it happened that most of the time, to tell the truth, I had no definite plans but only projects." *The Mind of Napoleon: A Selection from His Written and Spoken Words*, ed. and trans. J. Christopher Herold (New York: Columbia University Press: 1955), 43.

18. Valéry, "Address in Honor of Goethe," 155.

19. Napoleon, in conversation, 1819, in *The Mind of Napoleon*, 30.

20. Napoleon, in conversation with Goethe, 1808, in *The Mind of Napoleon*, 149.

21. Cited in Ronald Gray, "Faust's Divided Nature," in *Goethe's Faust, Part One: Essays in Criticism*, 107.

22. Friedrich Nietzsche, *Unzeitmässige Betrachtungen, Werke in drei Bänden*, ed. Karl Schlechta (München: Carl Hanser Verlag, 1976), 1: 316.
The word "gleichsam," which I translate as "finally," means, among other things, "as it were." See also: "Der Goethesche Mensch ist eine erhaltende und verträgliche Kraft—aber unter der Gefahr . . . dass er zum Philister entarten kann." Ibid.

23. Valéry, "Address in Honor of Goethe," 161.

24. Ibid., 161.

25. Cited without attribution by Richard Kroner, "The Tragedy of Titanism in Goethe's 'Faust,' " in *Goethe's "Faust": Part One*, 49.

26. Edgar Johnson, *Charles Dickens: His Tragedy and Triumph* (New York: Viking, 1977), 361.

27. Ibid., 389.

28. Ibid., 277.

29. Ibid., 556.

30. Charles Dickens, *Oliver Twist* (Oxford: Clarendon Press, 1966), 2.

31. Charles Dickens, *Great Expectations* (Oxford: Oxford University, 1953), 1.

32. John Forster, *Life of Dickens* (Philadelphia, 1873), 112, cited in J. Hillis Miller, "Bleak House," in *Charles Dickens: The World of His Novels* (Cambridge, Mass.: Harvard University Press, 1965), 206.

33. Charles Dickens in a letter to John Forster, 19 August 1855, in *The Letters of Charles Dickens*, ed. Graham Storey, Kathleen Tillotson, and Angus Easson (Oxford: Clarendon Press, 1993), 7: 692–93.

34. Charles Dickens, *The Life and Adventures of Nicholas Nickleby* (Oxford: Oxford University Press, 1950), 693–94.

35. Dickens, *Great Expectations*, 460.

36. He used to joke about his "murderous instincts." While writing *David Copperfield*, he said: "I have been hard at work these days, and still have Dora to kill. But with good luck, I may do it tomorrow." In Johnson, *Charles Dickens*, 354.

37. Ibid., 581.

38. Charles Dickens, *Bleak House,* ed. George Ford and Sylvere Monod (New York: Norton, 1977), 214.

39. Miller, "Bleak House," 222.

40. Charles Dickens, *Little Dorrit,* ed. John Holloway (Harmondsworth, England: Penguin Books, 1980), 77.

41. Ibid., 676.

42. Strindberg called him a "fanatical sceptic." Michael Meyer, *Ibsen: A Biography,* (Harmondsworth, England: Penguin Books, 1985), 449.

43. Bernard Shaw, *The Quintessence of Ibsenism* (New York: Hill and Wang, 1958), 187, 186, 187, 184.

44. Ellen Key in a speech at a dinner honoring Ibsen in Stockholm, in Meyer, *Ibsen*, 815.

45. Meyer, *Ibsen*, 422, 258, 515.

46. Ibid., 855.

47. In his influential *Hamburgische Dramaturgie* (1768), Lessing says: "Only occurrences which are grounded one in another, only linkages of causes and effects can occupy the genius. Tracing effects to their causes, balancing causes against effects, *eliminating everywhere the fortuitous,* causing everything that happens to happen in such a way that it cannot happen otherwise, that is the business of the genius working in the realm of history, in order to transform the useless items of memory into nourishment for the spirit." In Francis Andrew Brown, *Gotthold Ephraim Lessing* (New York: Twayne, 1971), 109. Yet, ironically, by "tracing effects to their causes" and "causing everything to happen in such a way that it cannot happen otherwise," Ibsen arrived at narratives that flatly contradict Lessing's own article of Enlightenment faith: *Kein Mensch muss müssen*—"No human being need obey a 'must.'"

48. La Mettrie, "Man a Machine," in *The Age of Enlightenment*, ed. Lester C. Crocker (New York: Walker, 1969), 102.

49. Translated from the German in Henrik Ibsen, "Vers," in vol. 1 of *Sämtliche Werke,* (Berlin: S. Fischer Verlag, 1916), 1: 117. In another translation it appears in *Ibsen's Poems in Versions by John Northam* (Oslo: Norwegian University Press, 1986), 135.

50. John Prudhoe points out that the nineteenth-century theater was deeply influenced by Schiller's "stress on *choice* and free will." Prudhoe, *The Theatre of Goethe and Schiller* (Totowa: N.J.: Rowman and Littlefield, 1973), 118.

51. J. M. R. Lenz, *Anmerkungen übers Theater, Gesammelte Schriften,* Herausgegeben von Ludwig Tieck (Berlin: G. Reiner, 1828), 220. Significantly, though Lenz's theoretical writing makes a clear distinction between *Sturm und Drang* playwrights and the religious theater of the Greeks, in at least two of his own plays, *Der Hofmeister* and *Die Soldaten,* social and economic conditions are as preclusive as the myth-structured plots of Aeschylus, Sophocles, and Euripides.

52. Meyer, *Ibsen,* 425.

53. Ibid., 312–13.

54. In a somewhat different translation, this appears in August Strindberg, "Hamlet: A Memorial, Second Letter to the Intimate Theater," in *Open Letters to the Intimate Theater,* trans. Walter Johnson (Seattle: University of Washington Press, 1967), 59.

55. "Imagination in art consists in knowing how to find the most complete expression of an existing object, but never in imagining or creating the object itself." Gustave Courbet, in "To a Group of Students," trans. from *Courbet, Raconté par lui-même et par ses amis* (Genève: P. Cailler, 1950), 2: 204–7, in *From the Classicists to the Impressionists: Art and Architecture in the Nineteenth Century,* ed. Elizabeth Holt, vol. 3 of *A Documentary History of Art* (New York: Anchor Books, 1966), 352.

56. Gombrich takes a more reductive view: "The sfumato or veiled form . . . cuts down the information on the canvas and thereby stimulates the mechanism of projection." E. H. Gombrich, *Art and Illusion* (Princeton: Princeton University Press, 1961), 221.

57. Albert Thibaudet, "Faces of Proust," in *Proust: A Collection of Critical Essays,* ed. René Girard (Englewood Cliffs, N.J.: Prentice-Hall, 1962), 50. (original title: "Marcel Proust and the French Tradition," trans. Angelo Bertocci, in *From the NRF,* ed. Justin O'Brien [Meriden Books, 1958].)

In *Aspects of the Novel,* E. M. Forster says that "in the novel we can know people perfectly." It may be true for comedy, but as Freud says: "The poet [does] not . . . permit his hero to give complete expression to all his secret springs of action. By this means he obliges us to supplement, he engages our intellectual activity, diverts it from critical reflections and keeps us closely identified with his hero. A bungler in his place would deliberately express all that he wishes to reveal to us, and would then find himself confronted by our cool, untrammeled intelligence, which would preclude any great degree of illusion." Freud, "Some Character-Types Met with in Psycho-Analytic Work," in vol. 4 of *Collected Papers* (London: Hogarth, 1948), 323. Though this seems to confirm the formalist assumption that art is a deliberate device, elsewhere—in his reading of *Hamlet,* for instance—Freud makes clear that the artist's own control is far from complete and that the power of his work often resides in what he does *not know*—in the unconscious.

58. Meyer, *Ibsen,* 707–10.

59. Ibid., 770.

60. Letter to Felix Pollack, 27 January 1904, in Franz Kafka, *Briefe, 1902–1924* (New York: Schocken Books, 1958), 28.

61. In *Die Jungfrau von Orleans,* Joan breaks her prison chains, leads the French

to victory, and dies gloriously on the battlefield; two men are in love with her, and she herself is transfixed by instantaneous passion for an English officer she is about to run through with her sword. When she stands [sic] dying, a vision of the Virgin appears to her:

"She holds the sacred child against her breast
And, smiling, stretches out her arms toward me."

One wonders just how safe Jesus was in her care. Friedrich Schiller, *Die Jungfrau von Orleans*, in vol. 3 of *Werke in sechs Bänden,* auf Grund der von Arthur Kutscher besorgten Ausgabe neu bearbeitet von Prof. Alfred Brandstetter (Zürich: Stauffacher Verlag, 1967), 494.

62. Friedrich Schiller, in vol. 5 of "Über Anmut und Würde," *Werke in sechs Bänden,* 300: "Der Mensch aber ist zugleich eine *Person,* ein Wesen also, welches *selbst* Ursache, und zwar absolut letzte Ursache seiner Zustände sein, welches sich nach Gründen, die es aus sich selbst nimmt, verändern kann. Die Art seines Erscheinens ist abhängig von der Art seines Empfindens und Wollens, also von Zuständen, die er selbst in seiner Freiheit und nicht die Natur nach ihrer Notwendigkeit bestimmt.

"Wäre der Mensch bloss ein Sinnenwesen, so würde die Natur zugleich die *Gesetze* geben und die *Fälle* der Anwendung bestimmen; jetzt teilt sie das Regiment mit der Freiheit, und obgleich ihre Gesetze Bestand haben, so ist es nunmehr doch der Geist, der über die Fälle entscheidet."

In "Über das Pathetische," vol. 5 of *Werke in sechs Bänden,* 441, he defines human beings as those who, unlike the creature, live under the sign of freedom. See also ibid., 448.

In "Über das Erhabene," vol. 6 of *Werke,* 439.

63. In his "Über naive und sentimentalische Dichtung" (*Werke,* 6: 360–438), he differentiates between poets like Homer and Shakespeare—whom he calls "naive" because they feel themselves to be one with nature and render it realistically—and "sentimental" poets like himself, who feel that they are separate from nature and seek a return to it in their work. "The poet . . . either *is* nature, or seeks it." Ibid., 6: 379. In his view, the Greek authors—with exceptions like Euripides—were "naive," since they recognized no conflict between humankind and nature: "Their mythology was the inspiration of naive feeling, the off-spring of a happy imagination, not that of introverted reason like the religion of later nations." Yet the conflict between hero and god at the core of many Greek myths constitutes the same absence of harmony between man and nature that Schiller observed in himself. Perhaps myth and tragedy had to remain inaccessible to a dramatist whose plays largely ignore the role of necessity.

64. The emphasis in Schiller's view of tragedy is on *Rührung*—on touching or moving us. "Über die tragische Kunst," ibid., 288. He ignores that we are most deeply "moved" by the situation of the hero, by the impact of necessity on him. In Schiller *Rührung* is produced by suffering. "Über das Pathetische," 433.

65. Schiller's plays are heavily plotted, in the sense of intrigue, but with exceptions like the *Wallenstein* trilogy, show little evidence of nonhuman forces at work.

Of course the liberties he takes with historical facts make Schiller himself the 'outside' force that determines his narratives.

66. "Über das Pathetische," 433; compare ibid., 442. (emphasis added)

67. In "Über naive und sentimentalische Dichtung," Schiller recognizes that whereas the naive *Dichter* "limits himself to imitating reality," his own concern with the "ennobling" (*Veredlung*) of the species led him to disregard facts.

68. Schiller, "Über das Pathetische," 434, 436. He praises the Greek dramatists, who don't deny the claim of nature and sensuality yet are never enslaved by them. All "melting feelings" and "Rührung" are excluded by the "noble and masculine tone (*Geschmack*) of art, for they please only the senses, to which art is to have no relationship. . . ." In *Über Anmut und Würde*, he stresses the human struggle with and victory over sensuality.

69. Shaw, *Quintessence of Ibsenism*, 71.

70. Emile Zola in a letter to Albert Millaud, 9 September 1876, cited by Allan Schom, *Emile Zola* (London: Macdonald, 1987), 65. The letter appears in Zola, *Correspondance II*, *Oeuvres Complètes*, ed. Gilbert Sigaux, 68.

71. Émile Zola, *Thérèse Raquin*, trans. Andrew Rothwell (New York: Oxford University Press, 1992), 1–2.

72. Bertolt Brecht: "The psychological theatre is dead."

73. Bertolt Brecht, "Anmerkungen zur Oper *Aufstieg und Fall der Stadt Mahagonny*." Brecht, *Versuche* 1–4 (Berlin: Suhrkamp Verlag, 1959), 103.

74. Oscar Büdel says: "(Brecht) rewrote parts of "Mother Courage" after the Zürich production because the audience had 'identified' . . . with the heroine, in spite of the usual precautions he had taken in this respect." Oscar Büdel, "Contemporary Theatre and Aesthetic Distance," in *Brecht: A Collection of Critical Essays*, ed. Peter Demetz (Englewood Cliffs, N.J.: Prentice-Hall, 1962), 75. In the final version of *Galileo Galilei*, he tried "to bring out the criminal element in the character of the hero." Martin Esslin, *Brecht: A Choice of Evils* (London: Eyre Methuen, 1980), 234. The phrase "laxatives of the soul" is cited in James K. Lyon, *Bertolt Brecht in America* (Princeton: Princeton University Press, 1980), 56.

75. Sokel and Esslin have explored "the duality of the Brechtian character," which—in my view—is an attribute of his/her double-bound situation. During the last years of his life, he called his theatre "dialectical" rather than "epic." As Esslin points out, "the Hegelian dialectic gave an aura of rationality to (Brecht's) most glaringly ambivalent attitudes and emotions." See Esslin, *Brecht: A Choice of Evils*, 235ff., 230, and Walter H. Sokel, "Brecht's Split Characters and His Sense of the Tragic," in Demetz, *Brecht*, 127–37.

76. Bertolt Brecht, *Die Dialektik auf dem Theater*, *Versuche* 29/39 (Berlin: Suhrkamp Verlag, 1957), 101.

The evidence accumulated by John Fuegi, while largely focused on the (unacknowledged) contributions to Brecht's work made by Elizabeth Hauptmann, Grete Steffin, Ruth Berlau and others, suggests that Brecht's mentality bordered on the criminal. His life and work were fueled by extreme, irreconcilable opposites. However, as Fuegi himself says with reference to *Mother Courage*, Brecht's unacknowledged use of the labor and point of view of others is a source of his scope and power. John Fuegi, *Brecht & Co.* (New York: Grove Press, 1994), 381. Since Brecht was clearly the unifying force, the work is, in that sense, his.

77. Esslin, *Brecht*, 239.

78. Ernst Schumacher, "Piscator's Political Theater," in Demetz, *Brecht*, 90.

79. Brecht, "Kleines Organon für das Theater," *Versuche* 27/32, 135. Even in Brecht's theater songs there is a strong narrative line, an unfolding story.

80. Immanuel Kant, *Kritik der Urteilskraft*, vol. 5 of *Immanuel Kants Werke*, ed. Otto Buek (Berlin: Bruno Cassirer, 1922). The German is "Zweckmässigkeit ohne Zweck."

CHAPTER 22

1. Henry James, Preface to *The Lesson of the Master*, in *The Art of the Novel: Critical Prefaces by Henry James.* (Boston: Northeastern University Press, 1984), 222. It seems significant that James's view of irony somewhat resembles de Man's: ". . . All true irony at once . . . asserts and maintains its fictional character by stating the continued impossibility of reconciling the world of fiction with the actual world." Paul de Man, "The Rhetoric of Temporality," in *Blindness and Insight* (Minneapolis: University of Minnesota Press, 1983), 218.

2. Cited without attribution by A. S. Cook, *The Meaning of Fiction* (Detroit: Wayne State University Press, 1960), 162. On this point, the aesthetic of James does not seem substantially different from Schiller's.

3. James, Preface to *The Lesson of the Master*, 222, 223. Schiller, too, emphasizes the ennobling 'function' of art—a rendering of the possibilities, in which he believes, whereas James doubted them: "Die ästhetische Kraft beruht . . . keineswegs auf dem Interesse der Vernunft, dass gerecht gehandelt *werde, sondern auf dem Interesse der Einbildungskraft, dass recht handeln möglich sei. . . .*" "Über das Pathetische," vol. 5 of *Werke in sechs Bänden,* auf Grund der von Arthur Kutscher besorgten Ausgabe neu bearbeitet von Prof. Alfred Brandstetter (Zürich: Stauffacher Verlag, 1967), 5: 453.

4. Henry James, "The Art of Fiction," 28, in *The House of Fiction: Essays on the Novel by Henry James*, ed. Leon Edel (London: Rupert Hart-Davis, 1957).

5. Percy Lubbock, *The Craft of Fiction* (New York: Viking Press, 1957), 39–40.

6. *The Complete Notebooks of Henry James*, ed. Leon Edel and Lyall H. Powers (New York: Oxford University Press, 1987), entry for 12 May 1889, 53. In a Notebook entry on 26 December 1881, he says: "The French stage I have mastered . . . I have it in my pocket, and it seems to me that this is the light by which I must work today." Ibid., 226–27. On 2 August 1882, he noted: "The dramatic form seems to me the most beautiful thing possible." (Ibid., 232) The dramatic form he was thinking of was clearly the well-made play.

7. Leon Edel, *Henry James: A Life* (New York: Harper and Row, 1985), 404.

8. James, cited without attribution in Michael Meyer, *Ibsen: A Biography* (Harmondsworth, England: Penguin Books, 1985), 694.

9. "Mr. Tennyson's Drama," *Galaxy,* 20 (September 1875): 396–97, cited in part in Sarah B. Dougherty, *The Literary Criticism: Henry James* (Athens: Ohio University Press, 1981), 129.

10. Entry for 14 February 1895, in *The Complete Notebooks of Henry James,* 115.

11. James, cited without attribution in Robert Caserio, "The Story In It: *The Wings of the Dove,"* in *Plot, Story, and the Novel: From Dickens and Poe to the Modern Period* (Princeton: Princeton University Press, 1979), 229.

12. Henry James, "Ivan Turgénieff," in *The Art of Fiction and Other Essays* (New York: Oxford University Press, 1948), 111. (emphasis added)

13. Preface to *The Portrait of a Lady,* in *Art of the Novel,* 43.

14. Letter to Hugh Walpole, 19 May 1912, *The Letters of Henry James,* ed. Percy Lubbock (New York: Charles Scribner's Sons, 1920), 2: 237.

15. R. P. Blackmur, "The Golden Bowl," in *Studies in Henry James,* ed. Veronica Makowsky (New York: New Directions, 1983), 148–49.

16. Henry James, *The Lesson of Balzac* (1905), in *The House of Fiction,* 80.

17. Ibid.

18. Frank O'Connor says: "He portraits innocence as rolling in money and corruption as seedy and hard-up." Frank O' Connor, *The Mirror in the Roadway: A Study of the Modern Novel* (New York: Alfred A. Knopf, 1956), 229.

19. Letter to his sister-in-law, in Edel, *Henry James: A Life,* 692.

20. Cited without attribution in Maxwell Geismar, *Henry James and the Jacobites* (Boston: Houghton Mifflin, 1963), 161. In a letter to Dr. Louis Waldstein, 21 October 1898, James referred to *The Turn of the Screw* as "that wanton little Tale," and seems clearly embarrassed by Waldheim's high regard for it. *The Letters of Henry James,* 1: 297. In a letter to F. W. H. Myers, 19 December 1898, he calls it "rather a shameless pot-boiler." Ibid., 300. For a very high estimation of "The Turn of the Screw" see Tzvetan Todorov, *The Poetics of Prose* (Ithaca, N.Y.: Cornell University Press, 1977), 157–59.

21. James's many ghost stories suggest that he continued throughout life to be 'interested' in the supernatural while believing it to be a purely subjective manifestation. See Todorov, *The Poetics of Prose,* 179–89.

22. Leon Edel, *Henry James: A Life* (New York: Harper and Row, 1985), 551.

23. James, in Caserio, "The Story in It," 204–5. In "The Lesson of Balzac," (p. 82) James says: "The presence of the conditions, when really presented, when made vivid, provide for the action—which is, from step to step, constantly implied in them." Since he keeps most of his own figures *free* of "conditions," they have no compelling need to act.

24. Henry James, *The Ambassadors* (New York: Harper and Brothers, 1930), 90.

25. Henry James, *Notebooks,* cited without attribution in Michael Egan, *Henry James: The Ibsen Years* (New York: Barnes and Noble, 1972), 38.

26. James, Preface to *The Ambassadors, Art of the Novel,* 315.

27. James, in Caserio, "The Story In It," 200. In the Preface to *The Ambassadors*—the novel in which story and action are most clearly suppressed—James says: "There is always, of course, for the story-teller, the irresistible determinant and

the incalculable advantage of his interest in the story *as such*; it is ever, obviously, overwhelmingly, the prime and precious thing (as other than this I have never been able to see it) as to which what makes for it, with whatever headlong energy, may be said to pale before the energy with which it simply makes for itself." Henry James, Preface to *The Ambassadors*, in *The Art of the Novel*, 314–15. James clearly *isn't* interested in "the story as such." In the novels of the major phase, he may well have sensed that "the story as such" inevitably imprisons the characters.

28. Henry James, "Nathaniel Hawthorne" (1897), in *The House of Fiction*, 179. In "The Art of Fiction" (*The House of Fiction*, 25) James says: "The analogy between the art of the painter and the art of the novelist is, as far as I am able to see, complete."

29. See Albert Thibaudet, "Faces of Proust," in *Proust: A Collection of Critical Essays*, ed. René Girard (Englewood Cliffs, N.J.: Prentice-Hall, 1962), 51. (original title: "Marcel Proust and the French Tradition," trans. Angelo Bertocci, in *From the NRF*, ed. Justin O'Brien [Meridian Books, 1958].)

30. Letter to Peggy James, cited in *Henry James: A Life*, 687.

31. Cited without attribution by Leon Edel, ibid., 115.

32. Cited in Richard P. Blackmur, Introduction in James, *Art of the Novel*, xxiv.

33. Oscar Wilde, *The Decay of Lying: An Observation* (New York: The Sunflower Company, 1902), 2.

34. In an address to the French Academy (1836), Scribe said that the truth depressed his audiences, whereas artifice and falsehood entertained them. Cited by Michael Egan, *Henry James: The Ibsen Years*, 27.

35. Henry James, "Charles Baudelaire," in *French Poets and Novelists* (Freeport, New York: Books for Libraries Press, 1972), 82. Henry James, "Gustave Flaubert," ibid., 198–201.

36. The passage reads: "As soon as I really re-enter [the luminous paradise of art]—cross the loved threshold—stand in the high chamber, and the gardens divine—the whole realm widens out again before me and around me—the air of life fills my lungs—the light of achievement flushes over all the place, and I believe, I see, I *do*." *The Complete Notebooks*, 22 October 1891, 61.

37. Charles Dickens, letter to Mrs. Watson, in Edgar Johnson, *Charles Dickens: His Tragedy and Triumph* (New York: Viking, 1977), 454.

38. Henry James, "The Lesson of Balzac," 76.

39. Frank O'Connor says: "As James's work develops, it tends to become more and more disembodied." O'Connor, *Mirror in the Roadway*, 230.

40. Ibid.

41. Henry James, *The Ambassadors*, 150.

42. Henry James, Preface to *The Wings of the Dove* (New York: Modern Library, 1946), x–ix.

43. Lubbock, *Craft of Fiction*, 167. The phrase is Paul Bourget's.

44. Guy de Maupassant, cited in Henry James, "Guy de Maupassant" (1888), in *House of Fiction*, 141.

45. Blackmur, Introduction to James, in *Art of the Novel*, xxvi.

46. Henry James, Preface to *What Maisie Knew*, in *Art of the Novel*, 157. The reference is to the girl in "In the Cage"; he likens her to Maisie. (p. 156)

47. Henry James, "Honoré de Balzac" (1878), in *French Poets and Novelists*, 118.

48. James, *The Ambassadors*, 374.

49. Henry James, "The Lesson of Balzac," 73.

50. L. C. Knights, "Henry James and the Trapped Spectator," *Southern Review*, 4 (Winter 1939).

51. James, *The Ambassadors*, 104.

52. Yvor Winters, "Maule's Well, or Henry James and the Relation of Morals to Manners," (1937), in *Maule's Curse: Seven Studies in the History of American Obscurantism* (Norfolk, Conn.: New Directions, 1938), 183–84. Winters is not critical of the ambiguity in James's rendering of Chad.

53. Lubbock's claim that "everything in the novel is . . . dramatically rendered" (p. 170) is undone by his own observation that "the book is . . . an indirect impression received through Strether's intervening consciousness beyond which the story never strays" (p. 170). Though Lubbock says that "when Strether talks it is almost as though we were outside him" (p. 166), we tend to remain captives of his limited perception. Lubbock, *Craft of Fiction*.

54. Ibid., 144.

55. Charles Marowitz, *The Marowitz "Hamlet"* (Harmondsworth, England: Penguin, 1970), 37.

56. Henry James, Preface to *The Princess Casamassima*, in *Art of the Novel*, 62.

57. Peter Brooks, *Melodramatic Imagination*, chap. 6.

58. Brooks, *Melodramatic Imagination*, 168.

59. Graham Greene, "Henry James: The Religious Aspect," in *Graham Greene: Collected Essays* (New York: Viking Press, 1969), 52; Greene, "Henry James: The Private Universe," in ibid., 23, 25, and 35. I was alerted to Greene's comments by Brooks, *Melodramatic Imagination*. R. P. Blackmur says that James, like his father and brother, "suffered in youth a central damage from an experience of the immanence of overwhelming evil and its menace to the self." His self was certainly damaged—but why by "overwhelming evil"? Blackmur, *Studies in Henry James*, 98.

60. Brooks, *Melodramatic Imagination*, 199.

61. Perhaps because Michael Egan, like James himself, focuses on character and "theme" in his discussion of *The Wings of the Dove*, he traces Ibsen's influence on the novel to *Hedda Gabler* and *John Gabriel Borkman*, not to *Rosmersholm*. Egan, *Henry James: The Ibsen Years*, 116–38.

62. Letter to Edmund Gosse, 28 April 1891, in *Letters of Henry James*, ed. Leon Edel, 339–40.

63. Sigmund Freud, "Some Character-Types Met with in Psycho-Analytic Work," in vol. 14 of *The Standard Edition of the Complete Psychological Works of Freud* (London: Hogarth Press and the Institute of Psycho-Analysis, 1957), 324–31.

64. Edel, *Henry James: A Life*, 550.

65. An article about Turgenev written by James in 1874, cited in Leon Edel, *Henry James: The Conquest of London* (Philadelphia: J. B. Lippincott, 1972), 168.

66. Henry James, *The Portrait of a Lady* (New York: Modern Library, 1936), 1: 211.

67. Henry James, Preface to *The Portrait of a Lady*, in *Art of the Novel*, 48.

68. Ibid., 51.

69. F. R. Leavis, *The Great Tradition: George Eliot, Henry James, Joseph Conrad* (New York: New York University Press, 1969), 154. Though *The Ambassadors* was James's own favorite, Leavis says it is "not only not one of his great books but . . . a bad one." Ibid., 126.

70. James, *Portrait of a Lady*, 2: 196.

71. Ibid., 2: 200.

72. Harold Bloom accounts for her decision by proposing that it leads her to the "renewed Emersonian realization that she is her own alternative." Introduction to *Henry James's The Portrait of a Lady*, Harold Bloom, ed., *Modern Critical Interpretations* (New York: Chelsea House, 1987), 14. Maria Ramalho Santos suggests that by staying with Osmond, Isabel "sanctions" her original commitment. She now knows that though she did not marry him of her own accord: "In sanctioning her first act, in turning it, retroactively, into a free act, Isabel finally *creates* (or invents?) her real freedom, the liberty of fully expanded consciousness, backwards and forwards, in complete, calculating control of itself.

"Isabel's return . . . is a choice of freedom *in the past*: her gesture ratifies her first decision to marry Osmond, which now becomes truly a free decision." Maria Irene Ramalho de Sousa Santos, "Isabel's Freedom: Henry James's *The Portrait of a Lady*," in ibid., 125, 127. The unusual concept of a retroactive "freedom in the past" makes sense only if *The Portrait of a Lady* is, as Poirier suggests, "A novel of ideas more than of psychology, an imitation of a moral action more than a drama of motive." Richard Poirier, *The Comic Sense of Henry James: A Study of the Early Novels* (New York: Oxford University Press, 1960), 245. But it *isn't* a novel of ideas. It becomes one only at the end.

73. James, "The Lesson of Balzac," 78.

74. James, *Portrait of a Lady*, 2: 436. In a Notebook entry of 1881, he says of *The Portrait*: "The obvious criticism of course will be that it is not finished—that I have not seen the heroine to the end of her situation—that I have left her *en l'air*—this is both true and false. The whole of anything is never told." Far from having left the story unfinished and Isabel *en l'air*, he brought her to a very definite stop. She goes back into the "house of darkness," from which there appears to be no exit until she or Osmond dies. *The Complete Notebooks of Henry James*, ed. Leon Edel and Lyall Powers (New York: Oxford University Press, 1987), 15.

75. See note 72. With respect to the later novels, Geismar seems justified in saying: "The Jamesian manipulation of these Jamesian characters (or embodied fantasies) is at the core of the novel; it is the real secret, and perhaps the real fascination, of *The Wings of the Dove*." Geismar, *Henry James and the Jacobites*, 231. His manipulations may fascinate us because they coincide with our own "Emersonian" need for freedom.

76. James, "Nathaniel Hawthorne," in *House of Fiction*, 177.

77. Nathaniel Hawthorne, *The Scarlet Letter* (New York: Modern Library, 1926), 224.

78. Ibid., 299.

79. Ibid., 53.

80. Ibid., 184, 180. See: "The scarlet letter was her passport into regions where other women dared not tread." Ibid., 229.

81. James, "Nathaniel Hawthorne," 178.

82. Ibid., 186. Richard Brodhead says: "Over and over again James denies that Hawthorne's works have substantial vision behind them, the merits of which might be discussed in their own right as a statement about life. What they have instead (the word becomes a kind of traitor's kiss in this volume) is "charm"—that exquisite, impalpable grace to be found in perfection in works that have no other claim to importance." Richard H. Brodhead, *The School of Hawthorne* (New York: Oxford University Press, 1986), 135.

83. Ibid., 178.

84. In his *Notebooks*, James not infrequently refers to ideas for stories as "fantasies" or "fantaisies." He generally starts with an incident that has been reported to him—not one in which he was a participant—and then lets his imagination elaborate it. The facts are seldom pursued; they were of little interest to him. In a Notebook entry for 5 February 1892, James begins with an incident from life in which an American shot the French lover of his wife in a Cannes hotel. He then proceeds to develop it into a narrative that *omits* the shooting and has the lover marry the woman. *The Complete Notebooks of Henry James*, ed. Leon Edel and Lyall H. Powers (New York: Oxford University Press, 1987), 65.

85. Nathaniel Hawthorne, Preface to *The House of the Seven Gables* (Harmondsworth, England: Penguin Books, 1982), 1.

86. Hawthorne, *Scarlet Letter*, 199.

87. Nathaniel Hawthorne, *The American Notebooks*, ed. Claude M. Simpson, in vol. 8 of *Works* (Columbus: Ohio State University Press, 1972), 16.

88. James, in Preface to *The Portrait of a Lady*, in *Art of the Novel*, 47. In an 1899 address to the Deerfield Summer School, he said that with regard to the art of the novel, he had only two words that remotely approach rules: "One is life and the other freedom." "The Great Form," in *The House of Fiction*, 47. In "The Art of Fiction," he says: "It appears to me that no one can ever have made a seriously artistic attempt without becoming conscious of an immense increase—a kind of revelation—of freedom." (p. 38) Given his preoccupation with the freedom of the artist, his insistence on "form" is striking. But as we have noted, the form of his late novels is essentially derived from the well-made play, which depends on a plot tightly structured by the dramatist. James's form—unlike the 'leaky' structures he criticized in the Russian novelists—was a rigidly bounded space within which he felt in control and therefore "free." James stresses "organic" form, but few narrative structures are less organic than "well-made fiction."

89. Poirier, *Comic Sense of Henry James*, 255.

90. "The good little Thomas Hardy has scored a great success with *Tess of the*

D'Urbervilles, which is chock-full of faults and falsity, and yet has a singular charm." Cited in Leavis, *The Great Tradition*, 22. No doubt the central role of fate and circumstance in Hardy's novel struck James as false and faulty. Yet he could recognize in Balzac's work, that "Nothing appealed to him more than to show how we all are, and how we are placed and built-in for being so. What befalls us is but another name for the way our circumstances press upon us—so that an account of what befalls us is an account of our circumstances." James, "The Lesson of Balzac," 81.

91. Edith Wharton, *A Backward Glance* (New York: D. Appleton-Century, 1934), 191, cited in Leavis, *Great Tradition*, 166. In *The Writing of Fiction*, Edith Wharton says that James's "last books are magnificent projects for future masterpieces rather than living creations." (New York: Charles Scribner's Sons, 1925), 117.

92. "One never really chooses one's range of vision . . ." Cited, in part and without attribution, by Cook, *The Meaning of Fiction*, 55.

93. Brooks, *Melodramatic Imagination*, 5, 167.

94. James, Preface to *The Wings of the Dove*, in *Art of the Novel*, 306.

95. James, "Gustave Flaubert," 188.

96. Ibid., 190.

97. Ibid., 191.

98. Letter from Henry James to William James, 1878, in Edel, *Henry James: A Life*, 244.

99. Hawthorne, *Scarlet Letter*, 224.

100. Emily Dickinson, Poem 341, in *The Complete Poems of Emily Dickinson*, ed. Thomas H. Johnson (Boston: Little, Brown, 1960), 162.

101. James, *Portrait of a Lady*, 435.

102. F. O. Matthiessen, *Henry James: The Major Phase* (New York: Oxford University Press, 1944), 50.

103. F. O. Matthiessen, *The James Family: Including Selections from the Writings of Henry James, Senior, William, Henry and Alice James* (New York: Alfred A. Knopf, 1947), 261; Ibid., 26.

104. James, *Portrait of a Lady*, 2: 391.

105. Arnold Kettle, *An Introduction to the English Novel*, vol. 2, *Henry James to the Present Day* (New York: Hutchinson's University Library, 1953), 34.

106. James, *The Ambassadors*, 432.

107. "Society is ready for collectivism; it has no fight left in it; and our class is as defunct as the dodo." Henry Adams in a letter to Charles Milnes Gaskell, 1910, cited in David W. Marcell, *Progress and Pragmatism: James, Dewey, Beard, and the American Idea of Progress* (Westport, Conn.: Greenwood Press, 1974), 335.

108. Cited in R. M. Lovett, *Edith Wharton* (1925), 55, cited in Matthiessen, *The James Family*, 678.

109. Cited in Leon Edel, *Henry James: The Conquest of London*, 168.

110. Entry for 22 October 1891, in *The Complete Notebooks of Henry James*, 61.

111. Geismar, *Henry James and the Jacobites*, 237. Compare Blackmur: "To James

the height of intelligence was choice; intelligence was taste in action. . . . It was by taste that James got hold of, valued and judged the life to which his intelligence reacted." Blackmur, *Studies in Henry James,* 116.

112. James, *The Ambassadors,* 404.

113. Nina Baym, "Revision and Thematic Change in *The Portrait of a Lady,"* in *Henry James's The Portrait of a Lady,* ed. Harold Bloom (New York: Chelsea House, 1987), 73: "Making her live intensively in her mind rather than her feelings, he deprives her of some of the appealing spontaneity, vivacity, and activity of the 1881 character." Ibid., 73. Ms. Baym points to James's flattening and coarsening of many of the other figures, in order to heighten our sense of Isabel's special qualities.

114. James, *Portrait of a Lady,* 2: 189.

115. James, *Nathaniel Hawthorne* (Ithaca, N.Y.: Cornell University Press, 1967), 37.

116. Ralph G. Martin, *Jennie: The Life of Lady Randolph Churchill* (Englewood Cliffs, N.J.: Prentice-Hall, 1969), 1: 91.

117. Letter from Randolph Churchill to Jennie, ibid., 60.

118. Letter from Randolph Churchill to Jennie, ibid., 74.

119. Letter from Randolph Churchill to Jennie, ibid., 83.

120. Ibid., 56–57. Martin's account is based on the account given in Frank Harris, *My Life and Loves* (New York: Grove Press, 1963).

121. Winston was born "prematurely," seven months after the wedding. Ibid., 108.

122. Viscount d'Abernon, in ibid., 126.

123. Ibid., 2: 322. Asquith said, "She lived every inch of her life up to the edge." Ibid., 2: 401. Jennie and a friend "agreed that if they could begin again from the age of seventeen, they would do the same as they had done, only more so. 'Then we decided that we could not have done more so if we had tried.' " Ibid.

124. Matthiessen, *Henry James: The Major Phase,* 140–41.

125. William James, *The Varieties of Religious Experience* (New York: Collier, 1961), cited in part by Matthiessen, *Henry James,* 140–41.

126. Brooks, *Melodramatic Imagination,* 173.

127. Brooks speaks of James's "melodrama of consciousness." But it is a "melodrama" in which the central figure is assumed to be free and no such freedom exists in melodrama. Ibid., 189.

128. James, "The Art of Fiction," 34.

129. *The Letters of William James* (Boston: Atlantic Monthly Press, 1920), 147–48, cited in Marcell, *Progress and Pragmatism,* 153–54. The passage reads: "I think that yesterday was a crisis in my life. I finished the first part of Renouvier's second 'Essais' and see no reason why his definition of free will—'the sustaining of a thought *because I choose to* when I might have other thoughts'—need be the definition of an illusion. At any rate, I will assume for the present—until next year—that it is no illusion. My first act of free will shall be to believe in free will. . . . I will . . . voluntarily cultivate the feeling of moral freedom, by reading books favorable to it as well as by acting.

". . . I will posit life (the real, the good) in the self-governing *resistance* of the ego to the world."
130. Harold Bloom, Introduction to *Henry James's "The Ambassadors,"* ed. Harold Bloom, *Modern Critical Interpretations* (New York: Chelsea House, 1988), 9.
131. Ibid.
132. James, "Art of Fiction," 37.
133. William James in Matthiessen, *The James Family*, 210.
134. Todorov's analysis of James's tales and ghost stories supports this position. (*The Poetics of Prose*, 143–89.) Everything I have found troubling in James's work commends itself to Todorov and 'proves' *his* view of narrative: "Art, then, is not the reproduction of a 'reality,' art does not follow after reality by imitating it. Art requires quite different qualities, so that being 'real' can even be disastrous. In the realm of art, there is nothing which is antecedent to the work, nothing which is its origin. The work of art itself is original; the secondary is the sole primary. This accounts for a tendency of James's comparisons to explain 'nature' by 'art,' for example: 'a pale smile that was like a moist sponge passed over a dimmed painting,' or 'she bore a singular resemblance to a bad illustration.' Or again: 'That was the way many things struck me at that time in England—as reproductions of something that existed primarily in art or literature. It was not the picture, the poem, the fictive page, that seemed to me a copy; these things were the originals and the life of happy and distinguished people was fashioned in their image.' " (p. 168–69)
135. Letter to H. G. Wells, in Edel, *Henry James: A Life*, 702.
136. James Lord, *Giacometti* (New York: Farrar, Straus, and Giroux, 1985). Perhaps in the same spirit the painter Frank Auerbach says: "I think that [Ingres'] "Le bain Turc" is really much better than anything in one's memory but it isn't quite as good as a lot of people in a Turkish bath . . ." "A Conversation with Frank Auerbach" (London: Arts Council of Great Britain, 1978), 20.
137. In the Preface to *The American*, James says: "The art of the romancer is 'for the fun of it,' insidiously to cut the cable (between romance and experience), to cut it without our detecting it." *Art of the Novel*, 34.
138. Max Weber, in Martin Jay, *The Dialectical Imagination: A History of the Frankfurt School and the Institute of Social Research, 1923–1950* (Boston: Little, Brown, 1973), 78.
139. In "Gustave Flaubert" (1902), (*House of Fiction*, 198–201), James expresses his amazement at the "doom" that had been laid upon his fellow novelist. James's own work was, as he says, "conceived in joy," whereas Flaubert was engaged in work that confronted his existence: his sense of "doom" generated *Madame Bovary*. Perhaps James would have found it less pleasurable to write if he had faced the same task as Flaubert—if his fiction had constituted a confrontation, not an escape.
140. Letter to Rhoda Broughton, in Edel, *Henry James: A Life*, 694.
141. James, Preface to *Roderick Hudson*, in *Art of the Novel*, 5. (emphasis added) The passage continues: "He is in the perpetual predicament that the continuity of things is the whole matter for him, of comedy and tragedy; that this continuity is never broken, and that to do anything at all, he has at once intensely to consult and intensely to ignore it."

142. Letter to Grace Norton, 1883, cited without attribution by Cook, *The Meaning of Fiction*, 164.

143. James, *Portrait of a Lady*, 287.

144. Ibid., 1: 274.

145. James, "Our Mutual Friend," in *House of Fiction*, 256.

146. James, "Ivan Turgénieff," in *Art of Fiction*, 113. In 1865, James calls *Bleak House* "forced." (*House of Fiction*, 253). His own need for freedom wins out over his critical judgement. If the author is in charge, as James fervently believed, the "forced" quality of *Bleak House* is attributable to Dickens, not to the circumstances in which the characters find themselves, and which—in our view—correspond to circumstances outside the text of this or any fiction.

147. James's meticulous, detailed analyses of motives could be called positivist in spirit; they constitute a form of mastery or control. Actions without visible causes are open to multiple interpretations and uncertainty, whereas James spells out the motives of his figures in great detail.

CHAPTER 23

1. Friedrich Nietzsche, *Also Sprach Zarathustra*, in vol. 2 of *Werke in drei Bänden*, ed. Karl Schlechta (München: Carl Hanser Verlag, 1976), 340. See also ibid., 431: "Das eben ist Göttlichkeit, dass es Götter aber keinen Gott gibt!" The old joke: " 'God is dead,' says Nietzsche; 'Nietzsche is dead,' says God," is based on the misconception that Nietzsche dismissed all gods.

2. The phrase is Stephen Jay Gould's.

3. Leszek Kolakowski, *The Alienation of Reason: A History of Positivist Thought*, trans. Norbert Guterman (Garden City, N.Y.: Doubleday, 1968), 90.

4. Jacques Monod, *Chance and Necessity: An Essay on the Natural Philosophy of Modern Biology*, trans. Austryn Wainhouse (New York: Alfred A. Knopf, 1971), 112–13.

5. F. Waismann, "The Decline and Fall of Causality," in *Turning Points in Physics: A Series of Lectures Given at Oxford University in Trinity Term, 1958* (Amsterdam: North-Holland Publishing, 1959), 142.

6. Max Born and Werner Heisenberg, "La mécanique des quanta," in *Electrons et photons: Rapports et discussions du S. Conseil de Physique . . . Institut International de Physique Solvay* (Paris, 1928), 143, cited in David C. Cassidy, *Uncertainty: The Life and Science of Werner Heisenberg* (New York: W. H. Freeman, 1992), 250.

7. Bertrand Russell, *The ABC of Relativity* (London: George Allen and Unwin, 1971), 120.

8. Ibid., 124.

9. F. T. Marinetti, "Technical Manifesto of Futurist Literature," in "Destruction of Syntax—Imagination without Strings—Words-in-Freedom," in *Futurist Manifestos*, ed. Umbro Apollonio (New York: Viking Press, 1973), 97.

10. "President Kennedy had initiated the course of events, but no longer had

control over them." Robert Kennedy, *Thirteen Days: A Memoir of the Cuban Missile Crisis* (New York: Norton, 1969), 71.

11. The phrase "luck freak" is reported in connection with the Vietnam War in Michael Herr, *Dispatches* (New York: Alfred A. Knopf, 1977), 91.

12. The false nuclear alert of 3 June 1980, when Strategic Air Command received a message that Soviet submarine missiles had been launched, was attributed by some investigators to a malfunctioning computer chip that was purchased in Taiwan at a cost of $.46.

13. D. W. Winnicott, *Playing and Reality* (New York: Basic Books, 1971). In response to a patient who asked for help in understanding the "quagmire" in which she found herself playing solitaire endlessly, Winnicott told her: "You are struggling with God or fate, sometimes winning, sometimes losing . . ." Ibid., 36.

14. René Girard says: "Modern man flatly rejects the notion that Chance is the reflection of divine will. Primitive man views things differently. For him, Chance embodies all the obvious characteristics of the sacred. Now it deals violently with man, now it showers him with gifts. Indeed, what is more capricious in its favors than Chance, more susceptible to those rapid reversals of temper that are invariably associated with the gods?" Girard, *Violence and the Sacred,* trans. Patrick Gregory (Baltimore: Johns Hopkins University Press, 1977), 314.

15. Susan Sontag, *AIDS and Its Metaphors* (New York: Farrar, Straus, Giroux, 1988), 72–73.

16. Larry Josephs, "The Harrowing Plunge," *The New York Times Magazine,* 11 November 1990, 46.

17. The gasoline shortage of 1979 constituted a veritable crisis in the national psyche. The constraints on our freedom of movement seemed catastrophic to many, and not only because it was hard to get to work.

18. We are haunted by contradictions our society can no longer reconcile. Girard says: "As we discover the unknown forces that shape our destinies, they are supposed to come at least partly under our control. Every new discovery gives us new manipulative powers over our environment and our fellow men. We are constantly told . . . on the one hand that we are absolute nonentities, and on the other that a world is being created that will be entirely dominated by human will." René Girard, "Perilous Balance: A Comic Hypothesis," in *To Double Business Bound: Essays on Literature, Mimesis, and Anthropology* (Baltimore: Johns Hopkins University Press, 1978), 134.

19. Eugene Davidson, *The Making of Adolf Hitler* (New York: Macmillan, 1977), 262.

20. Of course in part their motivation for moving the prisoners was to stop evidence of the extermination process from falling into Allied hands.

21. Davidson, *Making of Adolph Hitler,* 211.

22. Martin Gregor-Dellin, *Richard Wagner: His Life, His Work, His Century* (San Diego: Harcourt Brace Jovanovich, 1983), 311.

23. Ibid., 311, 314.

24. William Laurence, of *The New York Times,* in Lansing Lamont, *Day of Trin-*

ity (New York: Atheneum, 1965), 235. Laurence himself, the only journalist who was permitted to attend the test, filed a more optimistic report: "On that moment hung eternity. Time stood still. Space contracted to a pinpoint. It was as though the earth had opened and the skies split. One felt as though he had been privileged to witness the birth of the world—to be present at the moment of Creation when the Lord said: "Let there be light." In Stephane Groueff, *Manhattan Project: The Untold Story of the Making of the Atomic Bomb* (Boston: Little, Brown, 1967), 355.

25. The phrase "capable of sin" is Robert Oppenheimer's. Lamont, *Day of Trinity*, 297.

CHAPTER 24

1. Walter Ong, *Orality and Literacy: The Technologizing of the Word* (New York: Methuen, 1982), 148.

2. Ibid., 178–79.

3. Foucault predicts that man will disappear "like a face drawn in the sand at the edge of the sea." Michel Foucault, *The Order of Things: The Archeology of the Human Sciences* (New York: Random House, 1970), 387.

4. Jacques Derrida, *Of Grammatology* (Baltimore: Johns Hopkins University Press, 1976), 18.

5. Hegel and Jung have a different perspective. See chapter 8, notes 10 and 11.

6. J. Hillis Miller, *The Form of Victorian Fiction: Thackeray, Dickens, Trollope, George Eliot, Meredith, and Hardy* (Cleveland: Arete Press, 1979), 31–32.

7. Mark C. Taylor, *Deconstruction in Context: Literature and Philosophy* (Chicago: University of Chicago Press, 1986), 3.

8. Derrida, "Structure, Sign, and Play in the Discourse of the Human Sciences" in *The Language of Criticism and the Science of Man,* ed. Richard Macksey and Eugenio Donato (Baltimore: Johns Hopkins University Press, 1970), 271. His approach is similar to one he ascribes to Lévi-Strauss: "[He] will always remain faithful to this double intention: to preserve as an instrument that whose truth-value he criticizes." Ibid., 284.

See Lévi-Strauss: "And yet I exist. Not in any way, admittedly, as an individual: for what am I, in that respect, but a constantly renewed stake in the struggle between the society, formed by the several million nerve-cells which take shelter in the anthill of the brain, and my body, which serves society as a robot?" Claude Lévi-Strauss, *Tristes Tropiques*, trans. John Russell (New York: Atheneum, 1970), 397.

9. Kingman Brewster.

10. Committed to intertextuality, deconstructionists recognize no significant difference between creative and critical writing. Derrida and Hartman conceive of their criticism as an artform, suggesting that self-validation is a primary concern. Hartman and de Man began their work in Romantic literature, which is preoccu-

pied with salvaging the subject; Miller's and de Man's interest in Poulet points to a concern with personal continuity.

11. Cézanne, like others before him, made numerous sketches of statues. There is a small *putto* in at least one still life, painted in 1895.

12. See also: "Since psyche and matter are contained in one and the same world, and moreover are in continuous contact with one another and ultimately rest on irrepresentable, transcendental factors, it is not only possible but fairly probable, even, that psyche and matter are two different aspects of one and the same thing." C. G. Jung, *The Structure and Dynamics of the Psyche*, in vol. 8 of *The Collected Works of C. G. Jung*, trans. R. F. C. Hull (Princeton: Princeton University Press, 1972), 215.

13. Freud said that opposition to his work was based in large part on our extreme reluctance to accept that we are not masters in our own house. Sigmund Freud, in vol. 4 of *Collected Papers*, ed. J. Riviere and J. Strachey (London: The International Psycho-Analytical Press, 1924–50), 350 ff. Compare Feuerbach: "[Man] is conscious, yet he achieves consciousness unconsciously. . . . He is a stranger in his own house." Ludwig Feuerbach, *Lectures on the Essence of Religion*, trans. Ralph Manheim (New York: Harper and Row, 1967), 311.

14. Cited in Susan Buck-Morss, *The Origin of Negative Dialectics: Theodor Adorno, Walter Benjamin, and the Frankfurt Institute* (London: Free Press, 1977), 240. Marx was, of course, certain our duality would be redeemed: "Communism [is] the positive transcendence of *private property* as *human self-estrangement* and therefore . . . the real *appropriation of the human* essence by and for man; communism therefore [is] the complete return of man to himself as a *social* [i.e. human] being—a return become conscious, and accomplished within the entire wealth of previous development. . . . [Communism] is the genuine resolution of the conflict between man and nature and between man and man—the true resolution of the strife between existence and essence, between objectification and self-confirmation, between freedom and necessity, between the individual and the species. Communism is the riddle of history solved, and . . . knows itself to be this solution." Karl Marx, *Economic and Philosophic Manuscripts of 1844*, ed. Dirk J. Struik, trans. Martin Milligan (New York: International Publishers, 1964), 135.

Rieff points out that in our positivist society even Freud's tragic vision of human self-division has been reinterpreted to hold out the hope of a cure—an achievable sense of wholeness. *The Function of the Therapeutic* is a critique of those—Jung, Adler, Reich—who have, in Rieff's view, tried to subvert the meaning of Freud's work into a message of 'salvation,' one that redeems the split between the part, or individual, and the whole. Philip Rieff, *The Triumph of the Therapeutic: Uses of Faith After Freud* (New York: Harper and Row, 1966), see especially 79–98. Compare Norman O. Brown: "The aim of psychoanalysis—still unfulfilled, and still only half-conscious—is to return our souls to our bodies, to return ourselves to ourselves, and thus to overcome the human state of self-alienation." Brown, *Life against Death, The Psychoanalytic Meaning of History* (Middletown, Conn.: Wesleyan University Press, 1959), 159. Brown believes Freud was misled "by his metaphysical bias toward dualism" (p. 53) and is confident that "our modification of Freud's ontology restores the possibility of salvation." (p. 84) He suggests that he has found "a way out of history." (p. 19) His utopian approach—and his kinship with certain tenets of postmodernism—is implicit in the following: "Psychoanalysis suggests the eschatological proposition that mankind will not put aside its sickness and its discontent until it is able to abolish every dualism." (p. 52)

Today the dismissal of our duality, and of the dualisms that derive from it, coincides with the holistic and New Age thinking prevalent in many quarters.

15. Jacques Derrida, "Structure, Sign and Play," 284.

16. Sigmund Freud, in Rieff, *The Triumph of the Therapeutic*, 96.

17. Friedrich Engels, *Ludwig Feuerbach and the Outcome of German Classical Philosophy* (Moscow: Foreign Languages Publishing House, 1946). Marx, in his *Contribution to Hegel's Philosophy of Right*, says substantially the same thing.

18. One could, of course, say that Derrida himself always knew his positions were provisional and dialectical, whereas others, less able to tolerate uncertainty, saw his statements as rocks to which they could anchor their work. Derrida's influence on American deconstruction would, I believe, have been diminished if statements like *Il n'y a pas de hors-texte* had been immediately undermined by him. In the Kearney interview (Richard Kearney, ed., *Dialogues with Contemporary Thinkers* [Manchester: Manchester University Press, 1984]), Derrida says he is simply trying to "challenge or complicate our common assumptions about [reality, which] does not amount to saying that there is *nothing* beyond language." Yet his determination to dispense with all "ultimate referents"—rather than simply to endow them with uncertainty—surely took him in the direction of *Il n'y a pas de hors-texte*.

19. Richard Rorty, "Nineteenth-Century Idealism and Twentieth-Century Textualism," in *Consequences of Pragmatism* (Minneapolis: University of Minnesota Press, 1982), 139, 149.

20. "What we call structuralism in the field of linguistics, or anthropology, or the like, is nothing other than a very pale and faint imitation of what the 'hard sciences' . . . have been doing all the time." Claude Lévi-Strauss, *Myth and Meaning* (New York: Schocken Books, 1979), 9. "Science will never give us all the answers. What we can try to do is increase very slowly the number and the quality of the answers we are able to give, and this, I think, we can do only through science." Ibid., 14.

21. See Jacob Bronowski, *The Common Sense of Science* (London: Heinemann, 1951), 124–25. "As so often happens when philosophers take up arms for science, the science that is being defended is long out of date." This is no less true when philosophers take up arms *against* science.

22. Hans-Georg Gadamer, "On the Origins of Philosophical Hermeneutics," in *Philosophical Apprenticeships*, trans. Robert R. Sullivan (Cambridge, Mass.: MIT Press, 1985), 183.

23. Cited in Buck-Morss, *Origin of Negative Dialectics*, 40.

24. Erwin Schroedinger, *What Is Matter. Condensed from a Lecture Entitled, "Our Conception of Matter,"* Geneva, 1952; reprinted from *Scientific American*, September 1953 (San Francisco: W. H. Freeman, n.d.), 2.

25. See Allan Megill, *Prophets of Extremity: Nietzsche, Heidegger, Foucault, Derrida* (Berkeley: University of California Press, 1985), 108.

26. Martin Heidegger, "Modern Science, Metaphysics, and Mathematics," in *Basic Writings* (New York: Harper and Row, 1977), 248.

27. In some stage and movie versions, reflecting "the more moralistic and simplified world of melodrama, Victor Frankenstein was assimilated to the myth of the godless and 'presumptive' scientist, tampering with nature's secrets." Albert J. Lavalley, "The Stage and Film Children of Frankenstein," in *The Endurance of Frankenstein* (Berkeley: University of California Press, 1979), 249.

28. Recently it has been suggested that AIDS could have been transmitted to our species as a result of malaria experiments in which blood was transfused into human subjects from monkeys that carry the virus.

29. Whitehead says: "The essence of dramatic tragedy is not unhappiness. It resides in the remorseless working of things. . . . This remorseless inevitableness is what pervades scientific thought. The laws of physics are the decrees of fate." Alfred North Whitehead, cited without attribution in Phillip Frank, *Einstein: His Life and Times* (New York: Alfred A. Knopf, 1947), 141.

30. Schroedinger, *What Is Matter*, 2.

31. Einstein to Frau Born, in Ronald Clark, *Einstein: The Life and Times* (London: Hodder and Stoughton, 1973), 191. See also Einstein: "In every true searcher of Nature there is a kind of religious reverence; for he finds it impossible to imagine that he is the first to have thought out the exceedingly delicate threads that connect his perceptions. The aspect of knowledge which has not yet been laid bare gives the investigator a feeling akin to that experienced by a child who seeks to grasp the masterly way in which elders manipulate things." Alexander Moszowski, *Conversations with Einstein*, trans. Henry L. Brose (New York: Horizon Press, 1970), 46.

32. Richard Rorty, *Consequences of Pragmatism (Essays: 1972–1980)* (Minneapolis: University of Minesota Press, 1982), xlii–xliii.

33. With respect to science, postmodernism is post-Enlightenment, since Enlightenment thinkers thought they could adopt Newton's system without his God. Voltaire, as Peter Gay notes, was engaged in a "dogged" study of Newton. Gay, *The Enlightenment: An Interpretation*, vol. 2: *The Science of Freedom* (New York: Alfred A. Knopf, 1969), 137.

CHAPTER 25

1. William James, *Varieties of Religious Experience* (Cambridge, Mass.: Harvard University Press, 1985), 115–16.

2. Feuerbach, cited in Herbert Marcuse, *Studies in Critical Philosophy*, trans. Joris de Bres (London: NLB, 1972), 20.

3. *Fatal* has come to mean "deadly"; *hazard,* which once meant "chance" or "luck," now means "risk" or "danger"; *omen* has devolved into "ominous"; and *demonic*—from the Greek *daimon,* a good *or* evil spirit—connotes only the devilish.

4. "Susan Sontag Finds Romance," by Leslie Garis, *The New York Times Magazine*, 2 August 1992, 43.

5. Friedrich Nietzsche, *Menschliches, Allzumenschliches*, vol. 1 of *Werke in drei Bänden*, ed. Karl Schlechta (München: Carl Hanser Verlag, 1976), 1: 513.

6. C. G. Jung, *Memories, Dreams, Reflections*, ed. Aniela Jaffe, trans. Richard and Clara Winston (New York: Random House, 1965), 326.

7. Friedrich Nietzsche, Epigraph, *Nachgelassene Schriften*, in vol. 1 of *Werke in zwei Bänden*, ed. Gerhard Stenzel (Salzburg: Verlag "Das Bergland" Buch, 1952), 779.

8. The division of functions between the sexes once clearly had survival value, and may be a source of the wide range of specialized tasks found in every human community. Since this division of labor, which obliged the male to differentiate himself emphatically from the female, served the community, the individual male had little choice in the matter. His social role as combatant or problem-solver required his separation from her; the male peer group that shaped him with its code of honor, courage, and rationality acted on behalf of the community. Unless we subscribe to a devil theory, we must assume that what society obliges us to be and do at one time served the common weal. There is, of course, a pernicious time lag: our institutions perpetuate themselves—to the advantage of those who hold power in them—far longer than their usefulness warrants.

9. Robert Briffault, *The Mothers: The Matriarchal Theory of Social Origins* (New York: Macmillan, 1931), 51.

10. In Europe, in the class that expected its males to become gentlemen, boys were often dressed like girls in early childhood. The governess in the middle-class home in which I was raised dressed me like a girl and kept my hair shoulder-length until I was six.

11. Though the father was not actually absent from home until the Industrial Revolution, he is rendered as a marginal figure in the foundation myth of Christianity, which has—at least since the Middle Ages—focused on the relationship between Mary and her ideally sensitive and conscious son. Mother and Son intercede for us with the *heavenly* Father, whose remote but absolute authority seems intended to make up for the marginal role of Joseph. Of course the importance of mother and child in the spiritual realm may also be an attempt to compensate for the material power *denied* to women and children by the patriarchy.

12. Karen Horney attributes the male "dread of women" to the fact that they are the "primary socializers" of boys. Nancy Chodorow, "Being and Doing: A Cross-Cultural Examination of the Socialization of Males and Females," in *Woman in Sexist Society: Studies in Power and Powerlessness*, ed. Vivian Gornick and Barbara K. Moran (New York: Basic Books, 1971), 184.

13. Margaret Mead, *Male and Female* (New York: William Morrow, 1949), cited by Chodorow, "Being and Doing," 182.

14. Colloquially, an "attitude" has come to mean something close to prejudice: an inability to meet everyone and everything with an open mind.

15. Philip Rieff, *The Triumph of the Therapeutic: Uses of Faith after Freud* (New York: Harper and Row, 1966), 57.

16. G. W. F. Hegel, *Phänomenologie des Geistes,* vol. 2 of *Sämtliche Werke,* ed. Hermann Glockner (Stuttgart: Friedrich Frommann Verlag, 1964), 372.

17. C. G. Jung, *Psychological Types,* in vol. 6 of *The Collected Works of C. G. Jung,* a revision by R. F. C. Hull of the translation by H. G. Baynes (Princeton: Princeton University Press, 1971), 464.

18. As Philip Rahv has shown, the same fragmentation is already evident in Raskolnicov. It may be true, as well, of Julien Sorel and, indeed, of Hamlet. Philip Rahv, "Dostoevsky in *Crime and Punishment,*" *Partisan Review,* 27 (1960), reprinted in *Dostoevsky,* ed. René Wellek (Englewood Cliffs, N.J.: Prentice-Hall, 1962).

19. Erikson notes that in creative individuals identity crises can last far longer than adolescence.

20. Adorno called the individual a "Durchgangsinstrument" which had to be preserved in a higher synthesis. In Martin Jay, *The Dialectical Imagination: A History of the Frankfurt School and the Institute of Social Research, 1923–1950* (Boston: Little, Brown, 1973), 276.

21. Invalidating the academic canon is clearly part of the effort to expand the limited self, as well as to open up the community.

22. The term is Max Mueller's, who says: "Thinking is only thinking in the Heideggerrian sense when it persists in its answerlessness." Mueller, "Martin Heidegger: Philosopher and Politics; A Conversation," in *Martin Heidegger and National Socialism,* ed. Günther Neske and Emil Kettering, trans. Lisa Harries (New York: Paragon House, 1990), 195. Significantly, in a comment on Heidegger's "Why is there anything at all, and not rather nothing?" A. J. Ayer says: "This is indeed the kind of question that people expect philosophers to put: it has an air of profundity about it. The trouble is that it does not admit of any answer." A. J. Ayer, Editor's Introduction, *Logical Positivism,* ed. A. J. Ayer (New York: Macmillan, 1959), 16.

23. Jacques Derrida, *Positions* (Paris: Minuit, 1972), 56–57, cited in Jonathan Culler, *On Deconstruction: Theory and Criticism after Structuralism* (Ithaca, N.Y.: Cornell University Press, 1982), 165–66. (emphasis Derrida's) In the English edition of *Positions,* Derrida defines his "general strategy of deconstruction" as an effort "to avoid both simply neutralizing the binary oppositions of metaphysics and simply residing within the closed field of these oppositions, thereby confirming it." *Positions,* trans. Alan Bass (Chicago: University of Chicago Press, 1978), 41.

24. Hans-Georg Gadamer, *Reason in the Age of Science,* trans. Frederick G. Lawrence (Cambridge, Mass.: MIT Press, 1981), 35. Not either/or but either *and* or is a central element of Gadamer's dialogical philosophy—of his "return to the primordial dialogic of the human experience of the world," his intention to stop nowhere, to take Hegel to its furthest extreme, to "[get] over every fixation through the further development of conversation." Hans-Georg Gadamer, "On the Origins of Philosophical Hermeneutics," in *Philosophical Apprenticeships,* trans. Robert R. Sullivan (Cambridge, Mass.: MIT Press, 1985), 185.

25. Cited in Brian McGuinness, *Wittgenstein: A Life: Young Ludwig, 1889–1921* (London: Gerald Duckworth, 1988), 106. As a young man, Wittgenstein was haunted by uncertainty. Russell says: "My German was very argumentative and

tiresome. He wouldn't admit that it was certain that there was not a rhinoceros in the room." Ibid., 89. One of Wittgenstein's favorite quotations was Gottfried Keller's: "Always remember, when things are going well, that they don't have to." Ibid., 203. Significantly, Carnap says of Wittgenstein that "his point of view and his attitude toward people and problems, even theoretical problems, were much more similar to those of a creative artist than to that [sic] of a scientist . . . [He] tolerated no critical examination by others, once the insight had been gained by an act of inspiration. . . ." Rudolf Carnap, *Intellectual Autobiography*, 29, in John T. Blackmore, *Ernst Mach: His Work, Life, and Influence* (Berkeley: University of California Press, 1972), 308.

26. The word "prayer" derives from *precaria*, which also gives us "precarious."

27. This is a paraphrase of a story told about Rebbe Yaacov Yizchak of Psysha in Martin Buber, *Die Erzählungen der Chassidim, Schriften zum Chassidismus*, in *Werke,* Dritter Band (München: Kösel Verlag; Heidelberg: Verlag Lambert Schneider, 1963), 613.

Even riddles and jokes, which keep us in suspense until they are resolved by an unexpected turn in the action or language, sometimes leave us uncertain: "One day, when the Rebbe and his disciples were out walking, a chained dog barked at them ferociously. The disciples were frightened until the Rebbe assured them that barking dogs don't bite. Just then the beast tore its chain and charged toward them. The disciples panicked and fled over a fence—where, much to their surprise, they found the Rebbe. "How come you ran away," they asked him, "if barking dogs don't bite?" "Ah!" said the Rebbe, "*I* know it, and *you* know it, but maybe the dog doesn't!" We cannot be sure whether the Rebbe is clever or stupid.

Index

489

493